left handed

left handed

a navajo autobiography

walter and ruth dyk

Columbia University Press
New York   1980

The author and publisher gratefully acknowledge
the generous support given them by the National
Endowment for the Humanities.

Library of Congress Cataloging in Publication Data

Left Handed, Navaho Indian, 1868–
  Left Handed, a Navajo autobiography.

  Translated from Navaho.
  Continues Son of Old Man Hat.
  Includes index.
  1. Left Handed, Navaho Indian, 1868–   2. Navaho
Indians—Biography.   3. Navaho Indians—Social life
and customs.   4. Indians of North America—Southwest,
New—Social life and customs.   I. Dyk, Walter.
II. Dyk, Ruth.   III. Title.
E99.N3L5454   970.004'97   80-11954
ISBN 0-231-04946-3

Columbia University Press
    New York   Guildford, Surrey

contents

moves beside him . . . They quarrel and she moves away with all her daughter's things . . . Slim Man talks about her and about how to treat a husband and wife . . . They put up a hogan for Old Man Hat's sister . . . A marriage is arranged for his mother, Woman Who Walks Alone.

foreword

SON OF OLD MAN HAT is still the classic autobiography of a Navajo Indian from childhood to maturity and has been hailed as "the most detailed and accurate story ever written of an American Indian." But when that volume was published in 1938 it represented only part of the massive account recorded by Walter Dyk in the early 1930s. This second part, in which Left Handed recounts the trials and tribulations of three years of his life as a newly married and young adult, is even more impressive. Here the central themes of making a marriage work and establishing a place in Navajo society in the late 1880s are presented with a frankness and intensity that is rarely found.

Walter and Ruth Dyk were in the field much of the period between 1933 and 1935. Walter had taken his doctorate at Yale in linguistics and cultural anthropology under Edward Sapir in 1933, and Sapir had arranged for a postdoctoral fellowship from the National Research Council to study the functioning of the clan system and kinship on the Navajo reservation. To put the data in context Walter began to take down life histories, first from Old Mexican, which he later published as *A Navaho Autobiography* (1947) and then from Left Handed in the following year. He notes that Left Handed, like Old Mexican, passed rapidly over the first twenty years of his life, and only seriously began his account with his marriage. The narration is chronological and vivid, recording in great detail the protagonist's relations with women, in and out of marriage; the accumulation of property in sheep, cattle, and horses; the role of kinsmen and clansmen in daily life; deer hunting and its rituals; illness and curing; and the role of witchcraft in Navajo life. Both Old Mexican and Left Handed relived their lives with an intensity that was painful, and Left Handed at times became so disturbed and worn out that he would take several days off to visit relatives and regain his composure.

According to Walter Dyk the Navajo at that time were able to remember conversations directly, word for word, and their accounts had a quality of immediacy and veracity generally lacking in our own reports. The speakers do not intrude but let the original words speak for themselves. Even in translation—the work of the Navajo interpreter, Philip Davis—the narration has an impartial and objective quality which is very close to the Navajo original.

Son of Old Man Hat was published by Harcourt, Brace and Company in 1938 as a commercial venture, and was a critical success, with laudatory reviews and a distinguished Foreword by Edward Sapir. Walter Dyk then turned to the preparation of the briefer autobiography that he had recorded from Old Mexican in 1933, covering the period from 1871 to 1919, a period when acculturation was acute in the Four Corners region of the Navajo reservation. In the Preface to *A Navaho Autobiography*, which was not published until 1947 in the Viking Fund series, Dyk provides an account of his procedures, both in the field and in the editing process, and he appends a detailed series of notes which contain his analyses and interpretations of Navajo life and culture, as derived from the biographical accounts.

Walter and Ruth Dyk, in the meantime, had begun the preparation of the second part of *Son of Old Man Hat*, beginning with his marriage about the age of twenty. The onset of Parkinson's disease had greatly restricted Walter's activities, but they were able to spend the period of 1947–1948 in the Southwest, Walter utilizing a wire recorder to get a final record from Left Handed and additional data for editing the manuscript. Growing ill health forced Walter into early retirement and he was not able to continue the editing, but after his death his wife took up the task and has carried it through in exemplary fashion.

The present volume covers only three years in the life of Left Handed, but these three years, at the end of the 1880s, are presented in an almost day-by-day account and carry the reader along irresistibly. As Walter Dyk says in the Preface to the first volume, he was initially interested in collecting material for a study of the functioning of clan and kinship in Navajo society, but these interests, with the passing of time, have become secondary to the broader account of Navajo life in all its dimensions—social, cultural, and philosophical. To avoid any chance of error he left the Navajo names of people, places, clans, and kinship terms untranslated, and later enlisted the assistance of Father Berard Haile in putting them into English. But Father Berard was later incapacitated by a series of strokes, and we have had to call on a series of specialists on Navajo language and culture to provide for their translation.

Today we have a much better understanding of the Navajo kinship system and we have relied on Mary Shepardson's and Blodwen Hammond's *The Navajo Mountain Community* (1970), which provides a detailed account of the social organization and kinship terminology of the Navajo mountain region to the north of Black Mesa—Kayenta in northeastern Arizona, over which Left Handed moved. And more recently Gary Witherspoon has provided a more theoretically oriented account in *Navajo Kinship and Marriage* (1975), based in part on data from the Rough Rock region just to the east of Black Mesa. What the *Son of Old Man Hat* uniquely provides is a sense of the importance and pervasiveness of kinship and clan organization in these newly settled regions and examples of kinship behavior and usage in a relatively unacculturated context.

In the 1930s the names of Navajo clans were still largely untranslated. But while the development of the Navajo clan system is not yet clear, except in broad outline, most of the clan names mentioned by Left Handed can now be translated, and we have utilized the list found in the account by Shepardson and Hammond. Left Handed's own clan, the Bit'ahnii, can now be translated, but "The Within-His-Cover People" is not very informative and we have left the Anglicised version, Bitahni, in the text. Names for Navajo clans are frequently derived from places and Navajo geography abounds in place names which are descriptive. Once these are systematically mapped it should be possible to trace the movements of Navajo families and test traditions of clan movement and clan linkages.

Personal names among the Navajo are still a difficult problem. "Navajo names have a quality of magic about them," and are usually known only to relatives and close friends, and should not be used in the presence of the owner. This may be the reason why Left Handed never refers to his wife by name. Most Navajo acquire nicknames based on behavior or appearance, and these might change in later life. English names are now provided by school teachers or traders and are used on birth certificates and census records. Picturesque examples of naming abound in Left Handed's and Old Mexican's accounts but names are an uncertain aid in unravelling relationships. Unlike the Western Pueblos, there is no stock of clan names, which are utilized to provide an identification of the father's clan. Here there is a patrilineal emphasis in naming, as in the *son* of "Old Man Hat," but it is on an individual basis, and Left Handed's "father," Old Man Hat, was his real father's older clan brother.

The vividness and richness with which these autobiographies recreate Navajo life and culture would seem to make their recording an obvious solution for securing the kinds of information that anthropologists wish to obtain. It is puzzling, therefore, that since the initial efforts of Walter and Ruth Dyk in the 1930s there have been few other attempts to duplicate their results among the Navajo. There are some exceptions. Clyde Kluckhohn collected and later published some brief autobiographical accounts from Navajo in the Ramah region, and encouraged Alexander and Dorothea Leighton to collect others in connection with the Ramah Project, including the life history of a Navajo diagnostician, which they presented under the title of *Gregorio, the Hand Trembler: A Psychobiological Personality Study of a Navaho Indian* (1949).

What would be particularly welcome would be autobiographical accounts which surveyed Navajo life from the standpoint of women participants. Gladys Reichard, of course, has provided some approximations in her *Spider Woman, A Story of Navajo Weavers and Chanters* (1934) and in *Dezba, Woman of the Desert* (1939), but these accounts do not have the same impact that a straight autobiographical account might have. One reason for the relative lack of such accounts is of course the sheer amount of time involved. A.L. Kroeber somewhere estimates that the recording of *Son of Old Man Hat* required a thousand hours or more, and the preparation of the text for publication took an equivalent amount of time. But the modern tape recorder can facilitate the process in many ways.

Ruth Dyk shared in her husband's work in the field and in the preparation of the first volume, and has been largely responsible for the style and editing of the second volume. It is to be regretted that tape recorders were not available in the 1930s to preserve the Navajo text and it is probably impractical to translate the *Son of Old Man Hat* back into Navajo. But it may be a model for younger Navajos to carry on. With the examples of the Rough Rock school and the Navajo Community College in utilizing materials relative to Navajo language and culture, it should be possible to record the life of ordinary Navajo of different ages in their own words for the benefit of future generations. As the work of Walter and Ruth Dyk has demonstrated, a pedestrian account of ordinary daily life can result in the highest drama. There must be many such unrecorded lives among the present Navajo population.

My own role in this enterprise stems from the fact that Walter and I were fellow graduate students at Chicago before he went to Yale with Sapir, and he asked Ruth to get in touch with me with regard to some of the technical problems of editing. To all who helped with special information, or who provided the necessary resources, I add my thanks. But the most credit should go to Ruth Dyk.

Fred Eggan

acknowledgments

DURING THE PERIOD my husband collected and edited the material in this volume he was greatly indebted to the National Research Council, to Yale University, with which he was affiliated, and to the Wenner-Gren Foundation for Anthropological Research for their generous support. Professor Edward Sapir of Yale University, under whose auspices the research was begun, and Dr. Henry A. Murray of the Harvard Psychological Clinic stood out as being most helpful in their continuing critical interest. Father Berard Haile was of great assistance in contributing translations. In his preface to the first volume my husband expressed praise and thanks to Philip Davis for his patient and skillful interpreting. And to Left Handed, the son of Old Man Hat, he paid the greatest tribute.

To many friends on the reservation—Navajo and traders and, in particular, the Franciscan Fathers of Lukachukai—I wish to express my gratitude for their many kindnesses and for the hospitality shown to me and to my husband, whom I accompanied in the field.

I am especially indebted to Professor David Aberle for his help in providing translations and in elucidating some of the Navajo terms. Professors Oswald Werner, Gary Witherspoon, Ivvy Goosen with the help of his students Lemuel and Marie Littleman, and Professor Robert Young and his colleague William Morgan were most generous in helping with translations. David Murray provided additional information. Christopher Day of the University of Rochester was of great help in transferring material from wire to plastic tapes. I also wish to thank the "anonymous" readers who made valuable suggestions about the manuscript. My son, Timothy B. Dyk, my daughter, Penelope Dyk Carter, and my son-in-law, Anthony Carter of the University of Rochester were interested and supportive. Most of all I am grateful to Professor Fred Eggan of the University of Chicago. Without his encouragement and knowledge the editing of this volume would not have been attempted and could not have been completed. The Wenner-Gren Foundation for Anthropological Research most generously gave me a grant to complete the editing.

introduction

THE PRESENT NARRATIVE is the sequel to a first volume, *Son Of Old Man Hat*. The two volumes present the life story of Left Handed, a Navajo indian, as told to my husband, Walter Dyk, during the years 1934–35 and, in the case of the last chapter 1947–1948.

In 1934 Walter Dyk, as a fellow of the National Research Council, went to the Navajo reservation to collect material for a study of clan and kinship functions in Navajo society. He began by inquiring about ideals and theories and by asking his informants for illustrative anecdotes.

It soon became clear, however, that what was needed were accounts of day to day behavior rather than descriptions of highly dramatic situations such as death, birth, incest, murder, and witchcraft, which the anecdotes centered on. He therefore asked one informant, Left Handed, to relate whatever he could remember of his life, leaving out nothing, however trivial. And so Left Handed's narrative of his memories began.

Since Left Handed did not know English he told his story in Navajo, and it was translated bit by bit by Philip Davis, a Navajo. Left Handed would speak for a minute or two, Philip would then translate, and my husband would write down the translation. During the telling, the names of people, places, clans, and ceremonies were written down in Navajo.

In recalling his life Left Handed, according to my husband, was often profoundly affected. "At times he became so disturbed and so worn out that he would have to take four or five days off, going away to his home or to visit relatives." In contrasting Old Mexican (the author of *A Navaho Autobiography*) and Left Handed, Walter Dyk also mentions as characteristic of Left Handed his "humor and tolerance toward himself, toward others, and toward society."[1]

In the preface of *Son of Old Man Hat* my husband described Philip Davis as "skillful and patient." In addition to the word-by-word translation into English Walter Dyk often requested clarifications, explanations, or elaborations from Left Handed. The fact that these queries, translated into Navajo by Philip, were for the most part met with pertinent responses suggests that Philip, in passing on the questions, must have been tactful and perceptive in his phrasing. (Walter Dyk has mentioned somewhere that informants hate to be interrupted.)

Except for the last chapter, which was narrated and taped in our house in Santa Fe, the story was told in the house of Philip Davis. This was a log house just across the wash from where my husband and I were tenting in Lukachukai, Arizona. During the narration only Left Handed, Philip, and my husband were present.

The editing of the present volume was begun by Walter Dyk. Because of a long illness he was not able to complete the work and, after his death in 1972, I continued the editing using the guidelines he had stated: add nothing and leave out only minor experiences, repetitious episodes, and recurring passages, such as the details of moving from day to day, so that the edited version differs in no essential way from the first telling. An exception to this occurs in chapter 19, where the story of the hunt, which was originally related at some length, has been summarized. Since the rituals performed and many of the day-to-day events (except for the encounter with the whites and the kissing of the crows), were so similar to those described in chapter 2, where they were told in more detail, I thought that including the complete narrative in the later chapter would only burden the reader and add nothing to his knowledge. However, in order to preserve the continuity of the narrative, some indication of the events of that period seemed essential.

1. See *A Navaho Autobiography*, recorded in 1933 (Viking Publications in Anthropology, 1947), pp. 6 and 7.

The earlier volume begins with Left Handed's birth, a month before his time, in the spring of 1868 when the Navajo were journeying home after a four-year stay at Fort Sumner. His own mother, of the Bitahni clan, was very sick at his birth and had no milk, so her older sister Abaa found milk for him and raised him.[2] Throughout the narrative Left Handed calls Abaa "mother" and her husband, Old Man Hat, "father." Old Man Hat, in turn, was Left Handed's own father's older "clan brother," that is, both belonged to the Many Goats clan.

The first volume is Left Handed's story of growing up from infancy to manhood. In it he tells of the death of Old Man Hat. The volume ends with Left Handed's discovery of women, proposals of marriage at an Nda (referred to in English as a Squaw Dance), and his marriage to a woman of the Red Clay clan when he was about twenty years old.

In order to help the reader identify and follow the numerous characters and their relations, I have attached a list of characters. These are divided into two groups. In the first I have included those who appear frequently and in significant roles throughout the narrative. In the second group I have listed those who appear infrequently or indeed only once, but are nonetheless important persons in Left Handed's life story. I have identified the episodes with which they are concerned. Characters who appear only incidentally, such as persons Left Handed meets at ceremonies or who visit him in the course of their travels, are not listed.

For those readers who may be confused by the kinship terminology used, some explanation may be in order. No kinship term in Navajo is used in exactly the same manner as in English. It will be noted, for instance, that Left Handed calls many persons "mother" besides his real mother or his adoptive mother, Abaa. The same is true of other kinship terms, such as father, brother, sister, uncle, and aunt, etc. The relation is sometimes made clearer by stating explicitly "my real mother" or "clan uncle." Moreover, usage of a term

2. The death of his real mother is recorded in *Son Of Old Man Hat*. I have no information about his real father.

such as "uncle" does not correspond to usage in English. For example, the terms translated "my uncle" and "my nephew" refer to men who are respectively older or younger than the speaker, regardless of whether they belong to the generation above or below him. Further, in an affectionate greeting a man may simultaneously call another man "my father," and "my baby." Reference to the list of major characters will help the reader to understand Left Handed's connection to them. His use of kinship terms, though it may seem strange at first, is something to which the reader will quickly become accustomed.

In concluding the preface to *Son Of Old Man Hat* my husband expressed the hope that these memoirs of Left Handed might "help allay once and for all that strange and monstrous apparition, the 'primitive mind.' " It is with this thought in mind that I have completed his work.

main characters

Left Handed:

The narrator, born in the spring of 1868 while the Navajo were incarcerated at Fort Sumner. His mother was ill at the time and her older sister took care of him and brought him to Chinle when they were allowed to return to the reservation. Here her former husband found her. His name was Old Man Hat and he was an older clan brother of Left Handed's real father. His clan was Many Goats. Left Handed's clan was Bitahni, sometimes translated as Within His Cover People.

Abaa:

Wife of Old Man Hat and older sister of Left Handed's real mother. She brought him up and he refers to her as "mother" and to Old Man Hat as "father."

Left Handed's Wife:

Never given a name. She belonged to the Red Clay clan. Her father was a member of Bitter Water clan. Left Handed's wife's mother, her Mother's mother, and her brothers and sisters, were all of the Red Clay clan.

Slim Man:

A clan nephew of Old Man Hat. He belonged to Many Goats clan and Left Handed calls him "father."

Slim Man's Wife:	Called "mother." She and her mother and children were all of the Red From The Waist Down clan.
Slim Man's Sons:	Called "younger brothers" by Left Handed.
Slim Man's Niece:	Called Who Went After The Enemies. His real sister's daughter.
Choclays Kinsman:	Real younger brother of Old Man Hat. Referred to as "father" or "old father." His slave is called Choclay. A girl slave is not named, nor is Choclays Kinsman's wife.
Who Has Mules:	Old Man Hat's clan nephew. Left Handed calls him "father." Who Has Mules has two sons. The older son had an affair with Left Handed's wife.
Woman Who Walks Alone:	Old Man Hat's clan sister. Left Handed calls her "mother" or "older sister." Her deceased son was called Who Caught Madness.
Son Of Late Grey Hat:	Husband of Woman Who Walks Alone. Bitahni clan.
Lost His Moccasins:	Son-in-law of Old Man Hat's real sister. Left Handed's wife calls him "uncle." He was the first medicine man when Abaa was ill. Member of Red Clay clan.
Lost His Moccasins' Wife:	Belongs to Many Goats clan. Left Handed calls her "mother."
Walks Up In Anger:	Clan uncle (Bitahni clan) to Left Handed. He was married to the daughter of Lost His Moccasins.
G-string:	Married into Left Handed's father's clan (Many Goats). Calls Left Handed's wife "granddaughter." Both of Red clay clan.

G-string's Son:	Belonged to Many Goats clan.
His Horse Is Slow:	His mother was Old Man Hat's real younger sister. She belonged to Many Goats clan.
Giving Out Anger:	Left Handed's wife's clan (Red Clay) grandfather. One of the wealthy men on the reservation.
Horse's Ass's Wife:	Woman with whom Left Handed earlier had an affair.
Hosteen Black's Wife:	Member of Salt clan with whom Left Handed has an affair. Her mother is Woman With No Teeth.
Nephew Of Who Has Land:	A member of the Deer Spring clan, a branch of Bitter Water. Calls Left Handed "younger brother" because their fathers were both Many Goats.
Wife of Nephew Of Who Has Land:	A member of the Bitahni clan.

other characters

Mexican Blanket:	Left Handed's wife's clan grandfather. His wife is from Left Handed's clan (Bitahni).
Lots Of Boys:	A clan (Bitahni) uncle of Left Handed. Helps Left Handed with cattle and is quoted by Left Handed as a source of advice.
Yellow Singer's Wife:	Woman (Many Goats clan) who died and left her husband, son, and daughter. Left Handed called her "older sister."

Old Man Hat's real sister:	Woman (Many Goats clan) not named, who died.
Walk Up:	A clan uncle of Left Handed who helps him with cattle and in whom Left Handed confides about his affair.
Son Of Dead Belcher:	The Man (Red Clay clan) who was responsible for Abaa's remaining at Carriso mountain. It is not clear whether this is an unnamed man she married earlier.
Unnamed old man:	Married Abaa but left her.
Rough Woman:	Left Handed's sheep got mixed with hers but she ignored this "marriage proposal."
Unnamed woman of Red Clay clan:	The woman with whom Left Handed played after he separated from his wife.
Gray Hair and his wife:	Left Handed and his wife (Red Clay clan) stayed with them during the Xatal. Gray Hair belonged to Dectcini clan (relative clan of Red Clay). His wife belonged to the Bitahni clan.
Unnamed girl with swollen glands:	Left Handed treated her successfully. Because he had treated her he refrained from an affair with her mother.

Traders:

Round: Ran store at Aneth.

Hosteen Bahi: Ran store at Blue Canyon.

Worn Out Hat: Son of Hosteen Bahi who dug in the ruins and sold what he found.

Old Mexican: Ran store at Ganado.

A Mexican: Ran store at Chinle wash.

Medicine men:

Slow: At ceremony for Abaa.

Hosteen Liar: At One Day Sing for Slim Man. It was his grandchildren of Red House clan who killed each other.

Hosteen Wind Chant Singer: Treated Slim Man's wife.

Little Deer Spring: Treated girl with swollen glands.

Leather Leggings: Treated Slim Man's clan mother who died.

Medicine man not named: Treated Old Man Hat's real sister who died. He also treated Left Handed.

Woman With Gummy Mouth: Treated Left Handed's wife. She is referred to as sort of a medicine woman.

Men on first hunt:

Tunes To His Voice (leader, Many Goats clan), Ruins (Many Goats), Blind Mexican (Many Goats), Many Goats (Many Goats), Many Goats' brother-in-law (clan unknown), Ugly Man (clan unknown), Left Handed, Slim Man, Choclays Kinsman, and two unnamed men.

Connected with gambling:

Who Has a Hat, Has Done It, Turkey, White Horse, Yellow Thief, Badger For A Pet, Moves Her Hands Behind Her Back, Who Has Children.

left handed

1

Left Handed's wife comes to live
with him and his mother, Abaa . . .
They hide from his wife's husband . . .
Rounding up the cattle . . . Preparations
for winter and the move to their winter camp . . .
He takes his wife to visit her family and her
grandmother demands more gifts . . . His
mother accuses him of being stingy . . .
They sell their wool.

The first volume ends with Left Handed's marriage to a woman of the Red Clay clan, a "niece" of Lost His Moccasins. She already has a husband. She seduces Left Handed—perhaps in collaboration with Abaa—and prevents his marrying a daughter of Old Man Gentle, a marriage for which Slim Man (Left Handed's "clan father") had completed arrangements. Left Handed's marriage to a woman of the Red Clay clan is opposed by Slim Man, who is ashamed that he cannot keep his promise to Old Man Gentle. He also believes the woman's husband will kill her and Left Handed. Mexican Blanket, the woman's clan grandfather, also objects to the marriage. "It's not right for her to do that because she's got a husband and her husband is at home." He comes to Left Handed's place and whips his granddaughter. But when he finds that she is accepted by Left Handed and Abaa he returns to his home. The narrative ends with "the woman stayed with us there that night and never did go back."

We never did find out anything about her husband, nor what this man, her grandfather, Mexican Blanket, had done or said when he got home. So from there on this woman stayed with us.

1

About two days after that my father (clan father, not real father), Slim Man, came to our place. He said, "I heard that fellow is around here." He meant my wife's husband. He was an Along The Water (clan name). "He is around here now. Some fellows saw him. He is carrying a rifle and revolver. That's why I came here, to tell you about it. I told you what that man would do. And now that I know he is after you I think you both better be gone. He will be around here this evening, so you had better watch out for yourselves. He may be looking at us from someplace right now." Then he said, "Now, my son, you just watch out for yourself. I am going home now. Have your rifle ready, because you might get a chance. When he wants to kill you, if he misses you, then you might have a chance to kill him. So have your rifle already loaded." I said, "I have a rifle and a revolver but the revolver isn't working. It works all right sometimes, but, I don't know why, sometimes it won't work." He wanted to see it, so I got it out and gave it to him. He worked it a few times and then said, "This revolver isn't any good at all. You will sure be killed if you have this revolver along." He threw the revolver down and picked up the rifle. "This rifle is in good shape. Oil it and clean it out well. I have a revolver at home you can have." After I had oiled and cleaned it and loaded it I went over to his place and got that revolver from him. Then I was set all right. As I started back to my home he said to me again, "Now watch out pretty closely. I know very well that he is after you. Maybe he is only after you, or maybe he is after his wife. Maybe he is after you both, so now you just watch out closely for yourselves." We stayed way out in the hills that night, and came home the next morning.

My father came over to our place again that day. He said, "I want all of you to help me on the corn. In that way we will soon have all the corn in. I will send one of my boys over here and he will herd the sheep for you. Take your guns with you, and while we are working on the corn you can keep your revolver by you all the time." We said, "All right," and he went back home. Soon after that one of his boys came. He went out with the sheep and we went over to his place to help him. Everything was ready, all ready to be eaten. After

2

we ate we all went out and started to work on the corn. While we were working more people came, four women, three men, and one boy. They all started to work on the corn. About evening we all came back and we ate some more lunch. He said to us, "I want you to help me again tomorrow morning. We'll get the corn all in; we'll pack it on our backs. If we all do that we'll get it all in by tomorrow noon, or maybe a little after noon." Everybody said all right. Then we all went home and we stayed there. About evening we went out to the hills and stayed out there all night again. Nobody was around. We came back that morning and the boy was there again for herding and we all went over to help on the corn. My father was sure thankful and when we were through he gave us all thanks. So that's two days we'd been helping him on the corn.

In the daytime we stayed at home. At night we always went out and stayed around the hills. Then my father came to our place again. He told me not to go on the other side of the wash. He said, "The man is always around over there on the other side. You stay on this side all the time and do not leave your wife. When she goes out with the sheep go after her and, while you tend to the horses, you look after her too, so that man won't get after her. And you should have your rifle with you all the time so you'll be kind of safe. Look for him and if you see somebody riding a horse you just lay for him, because you don't know who it might be. If you don't watch for him, when he comes close to you, when he recognizes you, he'll sure get you." Then the next day my father told us to go and round up all the horses for him, and we went out that morning and we went all around the flat and the valley and way on the other side of Lots Of Wool and we just chased the horses toward the water. We did that all day. Next day we got another horse and we turned all the horses out and we drove them toward home. From there we got some more horses. So that's what we were doing for two days, gathering up the horses.

When I came home that evening my wife was out herding. My mother said, "She went back to her home today and brought all her things from there, all the sheep pelts that she

3

had, blankets, robes, buffalo skins, buckskins, one silver belt and one red belt. There are her things piled there." There was a big pile of things. My mother said, "When she came back with her things, she said 'My folks told me to go and take all my things back to your husband's place, because if I stay around here we know you will get killed. The man was around here for several days looking for you. He was carrying guns around saying that he was after you and that he was going to kill you. That's why I brought all my things back with me,' " she said.

The next day my two younger brothers, Slim Man's sons, and my wife and I went up on the mountain to round up the cattle. I wasn't thinking of taking her with me, but my mother said, "Take her with you. You know what your father said to you, 'You must keep her safely with you,' and he told you to go around with her all the time." Then I said, "All right," and we started off.

We were on the mountain five days, rounding up the cattle, but we didn't get them all. We only brought down eighteen head. Ten were mine, and eight belonged to Slim Man. We let the others go. We said, "We'll let those go, and anytime we want beef we can come up here and kill them." When we got out in the flat we separated my cattle from his. I told the boys, "I am going to put my cattle in the canyon called Another Canyon. In that canyon they'll be safe. They will be just as though they were fenced in. Nothing will get out of that canyon." So there we separated the cattle, and the boys went home with theirs, and my wife and I went on with ours toward Another Canyon.

When we got to Lost His Moccasins' place (his wife was Many Goats, so she was my "mother"), I said to my wife, "We will stop here. I'm sure we'll get something to eat, and we'll get some water." As soon as we went inside the hogan I said, "My mother, we are hungry and thirsty. We haven't had anything to eat since yesterday morning. Last night we camped up on the mountain; we had a little beef there, but we didn't eat much because there was nothing besides." She said, "There is some water there," and she had some food al-

4

ready cooked. We had plenty to eat and I told her, "We have had enough to last us all day." So we thanked her and then started off again. When we were about to get on our horses, she came out after us and said, as she looked at the sun, "You will be at that place about sundown, where your father is living." She meant His Horse Is Slow. "He lives there, and you can stay there at his place tonight. I know he is there now, because he was here the other day and said he was living there."

Then we went on, driving the cattle across the flat, passing Water Under Rocks and on to Another Canyon. And my mother was right. She guessed it pretty close. We got there when the sun was pretty well down. I went over to the hogan where my father was living and told him, "I have some cattle that I want to drive in this canyon." Right away he said, "All right, that's fine. I'll have some cattle. There is a little canyon right close by. Drive them in there for tonight. There's quite a space way back, but out here it's narrow so that you can put a rope across. After you put the rope across hang some blankets and saddle-blankets on it, so that they can't get out. They'll stay in there tonight, and tomorrow you can put them in the other canyon." So I went back over to where my wife was and we started driving the cattle in the canyon. In the meantime my father had got on his horse and caught up with us. He said to my wife, "Go back. I'll help drive the cattle in the canyon." So she went back to the hogan and we two drove them in the canyon and fixed up a fence. When we got back everything was ready to be eaten, and after we ate we began to talk. He started asking me about a whole lot of things, and I started telling him about the thing that had happened. All at once he gave a little laugh and said, "We heard over here that you were going to marry another woman, but I see now you have got a different one." I laughed and said, "Yes, that is right." We talked for a long time that night.

In the morning we drove the cattle into another canyon. I rode way up in the canyon, and there was lots of feed for the cattle, and no tracks of anything. When I got back out to where my wife was I said, "There is plenty of feed for the cattle and lots of water. I know they won't starve or thirst to

5

death. Anyway my father will watch them for me all the time, so I think they will be all right. I don't think they will get away." We stayed at his place all that day and overnight again. He had a great many black sheep and lots of horses, some great big white man's horses. He had bought one mare from the white man and raised all those big horses from her. He said to me, "You can go now, and I'll tend to your cattle. You don't need to worry about them, because I'm here. And you don't need to come every once in a while. Just go ahead and tend to your work." He asked me, "How many did you leave up on the mountain?" I said, "It's about fifteen head that I left up there, because I just can't get them. They are too wild. I had twelve, but two of them got away from me, and so there are only those ten that I brought here." He said, "Well, the others that you left up on the mountain, they are not any longer yours, because that fellow Who Has Mules will get them and take them away from you. That's what he does to the people. Whenever he sees a head of cattle that doesn't belong to him in his bunch, he sure gets it. Maybe he will kill them, butcher them, and sell the beef to the Hopi. Or he may drive them away and trade them off for something, so those fifteen head that you left up on the mountain are not yours."

That morning we started back. I was outside ready to get on the horse when my father came out. He came up to me and asked me about the horses. "How many horses did you give to that woman (my wife)?" I said, "I gave her six, but I haven't told her about that yet. That's the way I'm thinking about it. I thought I would give her six horses." Then he said, "Five will be enough, and I will let her have one. She can send one of her brothers over here for that horse. It will be a two-year-old, and you can have one too, just the same size." Then I said, "Thanks, my father, I am glad that you have helped me out." He said, "Yes, that's what we have horses for, to help one another with. And tell Slim Man he can put up two, because he has got lots of horses. He doesn't know what to do with them. He doesn't know how many horses he has got, so he ought to put up two." On our way I told my wife about the horses. I said, "You have a horse here, at my father's place. You can give that to one of your brothers or nephews or uncles, or to your grandfather. And there are four horses at home. You can have those four also." Then she said, "I'll give the horse your father gave me to my uncle," meaning Old Man Gentle. He was Red Clay; the man whose daughter I had been going to marry. I said, "No, I think they all hate you, because you took me away from them, so give that horse to somebody else." She said, "All right, I'll give it to my younger brother, the tall one." I said, "It's all right if you give it to him."

We got back to our place at Anything Falls In that afternoon. Nobody was home. My wife started cooking, and when things were about ready, my mother came back with the herd. After we had eaten we began talking, telling my mother about the trips we had made. I was telling her about it when my wife started talking to her about it too, so I just told her to go ahead and tell it. So I got pushed out. I lay there while she was telling her how we had started from home, up to the foot of the mountain and on top, about getting the cattle, rounding them up, and starting back, and where we had camped up on the mountain, and how the two cows got away from us. Then she told me, "You go ahead now. From here on you tell the rest of our trip." After I was through telling her about it my wife started talking to her. They were talking for quite a while, and when they were through we went to bed.

In the morning, after we had eaten, I went over to my father's place and told him about our trip again. Then I told him, "I may have left fifteen or more head up on the mountain, and His Horse Is Slow said, 'Who Has Mules will get those. They belong to him now.' " Slim Man said, "You have taken your cattle a long way. You ought to have kept them right close by you. Those eight that you got down for me are right down here. You ought to get them all together and keep them where you can look at them every once in a while." I said, "I didn't think of that. If I had I would have them right here close by me." He said, "The four horses that you talked about, I'll put up two, and you will have to put up two, and we will give them to your wife. Don't give her a colt or an old horse. Give her a nice young mare, or give her a tame one, so she can use it." Then he said, "I got word from Tunes To His Voice; he wants us to go with him to hunt deer. He said, 'If some of you want to go along you can, because it's a good chance to get some buckskins.' So I am going, and your father, your old father, Choclays Kinsman, is going too. So if you want to go you can. This man Tunes To His Voice knows how to hunt. That's all he has been doing, hunting, so he wants us to go with him."

I thought immediately, "I will go along." I asked my father, "How does a fellow hunt? What should a fellow do?" He said, "I will tell you later on, when we camp." "About how many days from now are we going?" I asked him. "Some time this fall," he said, "you just go ahead and tend to your work. When the corn is all in, when all the crops are put away, and when everybody has moved to their winter camp and we have hauled some wood for our families, then the fellow who wants us to go hunting will put up a date. He might say in five days, or maybe he will say in seven days or nine days. That's the way they put up a date, when they want to go out hunting, so you go ahead and do your work."

It was late in the evening when I got home, so I went right to bed. The next morning I told my mother about what my father had said about the hunt. My mother said, "That's good. That's what the men used to do a long time ago. They used to set a date, and when the date was up they would go out hunting. Even though we have lots of sheep now, you go along with those men. You might get some meat, or you might get a buckskin. Some of your fathers and brothers and nephews and uncles, and some of your grandfathers, on both sides, used to go hunting around in the fall and get deer meat. In that way we will save sheep."

That day I dug a hole for the corn. It was about seven feet deep, and about six feet all around the bottom, and real narrow at the top. The day after I shelled all the corn my mother said, "Make a fire in the hole, so it will be good and dry. If the hole is not dry, if it's damp down at the bottom, the corn will get mouldy. And you should bury the corn early in the morning while it's still cool. If you put the corn in the ground in the evening, when it's warm, it will get mouldy too." So I built a fire, and the next day I put the corn into the hole. I was doing that all day. I left about a foot of space at the top and then put poles across and covered them with cedar-bark and then dirt. The sun was still up when I finished and went over to my father's place. There everybody was working on the corn too, some of them digging holes, some shelling corn, some had the poles ready, and some of them were gathering cedar-bark. My father asked me, "Did you get through with your corn?" I said, "Yes, I just got through with it." He said, "We are not through yet. We have got so much to do. After we put all our corn away, we will move to our winter camp. There we will make some hogans and sheep corrals, so it's quite a while yet before we go hunting. Help us on the corn and other things around here. We have got so much to do." I said, "I will." I went home that evening, but the next day I went over again and started helping them. We were working on the corn for three days. When we were through we put away the things that were around the hogan. We were doing that all that day, burying things in the ground and hiding them in the rocks and in the trees. For the next couple of days we were rounding up my father's horses. We drove home some of the tame ones that he wanted to move with and some that he wanted to use for hunting.

The next morning, while my mother took out the sheep herd, my wife and I started to haul some of our things to our winter camp. On our way back we went around by my father's place. He asked me, "Did you move already?" I said, "Yes, we have taken some of our stuff over to our winter camp." "We want you to help us," he said. "Take some of our things too." I said, "All right, I will be here tomorrow." He said, "Be sure and bring over some horses, and have everyone saddled up. We haven't got enough saddles over here, and bring some ropes with you too, to tie the packs with." I said, "I will." In the morning I went out and got some horses, and saddled up two, one for myself and one for my wife. I was going to take two or three pack-horses over, but my mother said, "Let them use their own horses, just take one over there with you." So we took only one extra horse with us.

Things were ready to be packed when we got there. They were piling them outside. My father said to us, "Take the corn over first for me." We took the corn over; it was close to our own winter camp where he was moving, and then we went back for another load of stuff. We made four trips in all that day. The next morning I didn't go over to his place again. I stayed home and started chopping down some trees, cutting poles for a hogan. Toward evening I got tired and quit. I could hear them chopping wood at my father's place, so I went over. They had a lot of poles cut already, because there were his boys and some others helping him. I just looked around and came back to my camp. I was by myself cutting poles. I cut a few more the next morning, and then started dragging them to the place where I wanted to put up a hogan. Before noon my father and one of his boys came over to help me. Later on my father's wife and family came over too and started gathering cedar-bark. When we got the hogan up we put the cedar-bark over it and dirt on top. We had the hogan done in one day. It was just a small one, because there were only three of us to live in it. "Now you have got the hogan up for yourselves," he said. "We want to put one up tomorrow, or maybe the next day." Early in the morning while everybody was still sleeping, I picked up my ax and went over to his camp. Nobody was around. I thought perhaps they were still sleeping, so I went ahead and started cutting down some trees. I had some poles cut before breakfast. That day and the next we put up two more hogans, and the day after that we made a great big corral for him, because he had lots of sheep. I told them that evening, "Help me tomorrow on the sheep corral." They said, "All right. Be sure and kill a fat mutton. The last time we helped you over there we never got any mutton, so this time you must kill one that is fat." I said, "All right. Maybe I'll find one someplace tonight or tomorrow."

Early in the morning I went out and roped a great big wether. I tied it up for my wife and she started butchering

10

and I started working on the corral. While I was working on it, my father and one of his boys came over. He walked up to me and said, "It's a long way over here, and it's hard to get fat mutton, but here we have nice, fat mutton. We have got to work hard for it before we get some." I said, "Yes, there is lots of mutton there for you to eat." Then my mother said, "He has got a few of those wethers, all belonging to him, and he won't kill one for us. He is too stingy for them. I don't know when he will use them. Some of them are too old now." My father said, "Who is going to kill all those wethers right on top of you when you are dead? No use being stingy with them. While you are living you must use anything that is good." "Oh," my mother said, "my son won't kill one for us at all. This is the first time that he has killed one." They joshed me about it, but I just laughed. "About how big do you want this corral?" he asked me. I pointed to some trees, "Around those trees over there, about that size." He said, "That's too small. We will make a large corral, so there will be plenty of room in it. You don't want your sheep to be crowded. They have to have plenty of air between them. When they are too crowded they are likely to get any kind of disease." I said, "All right," and we started making a great big corral. We were working on it all day, but there was still quite a space that we hadn't closed in. I finished it by myself the next day and did some other things besides.

Then I thought, "I'll go over to my father's place again." When I got there, he said, "Now you are fixed for the winter." Then he said, "You got a woman some time ago, but she has never gone back to her home yet. She went back once, but only for her stuff, and she hasn't gone back to her home since, so I think her folks must be looking for her, and worrying about her. And you haven't showed up over there at her place. Now you think about that. You ought to take her back to her home, just for a visit; or you might help her people for a few days. They might need help. If at any time you go over, take some food with you, so that they will be thankful." I said, "All right, my father, I'll think about it." When I told my mother what my father had said to me, she said, "That's right, everybody needs help. Not only we, but everybody, so

11

you had better do that. Go over and take those horses that you promised her. And, when you go, kill another sheep and take that with you. When you get there they may need help very badly. If they are that way, you stay over there and help those people, so they will be thankful to you and to all of us. Or maybe they will want to move. If they want to move over here close to us, it will be all right. We will have lots of help. We can help them, and they can help us too. So you stay over there if they want help. We are all fixed up now for the winter. You don't have to worry about anything at all. There are only the sheep to worry about, but I'll tend to them."

Two days after that I got the horses and we started for her home. When we passed by the place we had moved from we looked where we had buried our corn, and everything was all right. Then we went to my father's place, and looked all around, and everything was all right over there too. From there we went to where her people lived.

We got there about evening. I went into a hogan where she used to live. There was nobody in it, only tracks that you could hardly see. I thought that must have been her husband. My wife went over to her mother's home. She led a horse over there, and had lots of food with her. Soon I heard all the women crying. When they stopped my wife came over where I was and said, "I told my mother and my grandmother, 'I got a horse for you both. I got only one horse for the two of you. Half belongs to my mother, and half belongs to you, my grandmother.' My grandmother said, 'Only one horse? Why don't you ask for another one? You ought to ask for another.' Afterwards I told them, 'I have got another one over there at our place.' 'Well,' she said, 'That's two. You ought to ask for another.' I said, 'Over at Another Canyon there is a horse over there. And there are two more over at Slim Man's place, so there are five all together that I got.' Then my grandmother said, 'Why don't you ask for a head of cattle?' I told her, 'That is plenty for me. That one head of cattle won't do me any good, and it won't do any good to any of us. I have lots of help, that's what I want.' " I said, "If they want cattle why don't they let me have another daughter of theirs? If they give

12

me another daughter of theirs I will give them a head of cattle." My wife laughed. She pointed to her little sister, a girl about three years old. "Well, there is one over there," she said. "You can have her. She is my sister." I said, "Well, if your grandmother isn't satisfied with those five horses I will give them one head of cattle, but it has got to be butchered upon Black Mountain. If they want one I can go and get them one." So there I promised them one head of cattle. She went over to her mother's again, and then came back, saying, "There isn't any water at home. Go and get some water." I told her to get the jugs, and when she brought them I went after some water, brought it back and they all started cooking. My wife said, "Why don't you build a fire here? There is no wood chopped over there at my mother's place. Go over and chop some wood for that place and bring some back with you." I chopped some wood and brought some back with me, and she built a fire and swept out the hogan. My wife said, "My grandmother wanted that horse which we brought over, but my mother has got it already. My mother told her, 'There are more horses that have been given to us. If they are not tame they can easily tame them for you.' My grandmother said, 'I don't want wild horses. I want one already tamed.' "

The next morning I didn't have anything to do, so I went over on the other side of the wash and dragged in a big pile of wood. In the evening I asked my wife, "What kind of plan have they got?" She said, "They don't know what to do yet. My mother said, 'I was figuring on moving over to Hill Across, but we didn't move over there, because you were away. I don't know what we'll do. Maybe we will move over where you are now.' She wanted me to let you know. She said you might know where it was best for them to go. It was up to you, she said." I said to my wife, "We had better go back home. There are lots of things to do before I go hunting. It's up to them. If I told them to move over where we live now, perhaps they won't like it. They may like it all right, but I don't care to say anything at all. So you go over and tell your mother it's up to her. She can move wherever she wants to." When she came back from there she said, "My mother said, 'We will take the sheep over there where you live. Only the herder will take the sheep over there to you, and there you will watch the sheep and take good care of them. Tomorrow two of the boys are going over for those horses. We want to gather them up right now.' " We had the horses all ready, and I held them while she went over to her mother's once more. She was gone quite a while. When she returned she said, "My mother wants you to chop some wood for her first, before we go away." I said, "All right. Where is your mother?" She said, "Oh, she went out with the herd. So you don't have to be afraid."[1] Then we went over and I chopped all the wood which I had piled up the evening before. After I had chopped it we had lunch and started home.

The next morning, early, I went out and rounded up the horses and took them to the water. There were some trees close by and under these some people were camping. I went over to see who they were, and there was a man sitting with a robe around him and about five children of all different sizes. I went up to this man and shook hands with him. He had only one eye. He said, "We are going over to a man who is an uncle of my wife's. He is over at the foot of Black Mountain someplace. We are moving over there to him, to stay with him all winter. But on our way we will stop at a woman's place. This woman's name is Abaa. She is my mother, so we want to stay at her place for a couple of days." And that was my mother that he meant. I told him, "That's where I am from, so if you want to go over you can. She is home now." He asked me, "Where is she living?" I mentioned the place and then I told him, "She is my mother." He said, "That's your mother, hm? So then you are my younger brother." He got up and came up to me and shook hands with me again. I showed him where I lived and said, "You can go over." He asked me about the water. Then he said to his children, "Go and take the horses and sheep down to the water. The rest of us will go over to my younger brother's place. After you water the horses and the sheep bring them over to his home."

1. A son-in-law can't talk to or look at his wife's mother. Among the Navajo this is a relationship of extreme respect.

I went on after the horses, drove them down to the water and from there on home. My wife had gone out with the herd already. I ate some lunch, and not long after those people came to our place. They unpacked their horses and camped out. As soon as they had turned their horses loose they all came over to my mother and shook hands with her. My mother had known this man. He said, "I have been asking for you ever since we started moving from our place, and here we have found you. Now that we have found you we will stay right here at Abaa's place for a day or two. We are all hungry for meat. We have some sheep, but they are not good. We are all poor. We haven't got anything at all." But they had about thirty head of sheep and ten horses. My mother cooked for them, and they all ate some lunch and then began to talk. While they were still talking I went out and gathered some wood. I was doing that all day. By evening I had enough piled there for a few days. The other people had built a little brush shelter for themselves to camp in.

The next day I said to my mother, "I am going to separate all the lambs from their mothers and shear them." I went over to my father's place and borrowed some extra shears and those people, Narrow Eyes and his children, all helped us. That morning two of my wife's brothers came after the horses I had promised them. I said to them, "Help us shear." They were quick on shearing. About noon we quit and ate some lunch. Then I took the boys over to the horses and we rounded them up and took them to the water. There I pointed to a two-year-old colt and told them to rope it. They roped him and put a halter on him and took him back to their home. The next morning I separated some more lambs and, after the rest of the herd had gone out, we started shearing, and those people who were camping there at our place helped us again. My mother gave them a sheep. It was quite a good-sized wether. The man took the wether over to their camp and I said to my mother, "What do you want to give up a great big wether to that old man for? You ought to have given him one of the smallest ones." My mother turned around and looked at me, stared at me for a while and then said, "You are always trying to hold back on everything, on anything I want

15

to do. I did it because it was mine. Nobody will say anything to me about it. Why is it that you are so stingy? You must help the poor. I know they are poor, so that's why I want to help them out. You ought to help the poor, but you don't know anything about it yet, even though you are a man now." It wasn't only that time that she said that to me. She said that to me every once in a while. Whenever she wanted to give something away, I would tell her not to give anything away for nothing, and when I would say that to her she would name herself, she would say, "Your name goes by my name. Everybody knows me, and everybody knows you through me. Everybody calls you Son of Abaa. I think you have got such a nice name. When you have such a nice name why do you want to be stingy? You mustn't be stingy. They will call you Stingy after a while, instead of calling you by my name. You will make yourself a name if you don't look out." But when she died, as soon as she died, everybody began calling me Left Handed. She was just like a man. When she was still young she was tall and stout. Whenever she saw fellows fighting, if she knew one of them pretty well, she would pitch right in and go after the other fellow. Lots of times she did that. She used to be a strong woman.

The people had killed and butchered the wether. It was good and fat. After they had had lunch they all came and helped us shear, even the little children. In the afternoon when we were through, we turned the lambs out to get some feed, and these small children went out with the herd. They were lively, because they all had enough fat mutton. They were happy, running around helping us. Their hands and faces were greasy, because the wether had been so fat. The next morning I separated some more lambs. This time I got them all, and we started shearing again. In the afternoon when we got through we turned them out and the children all went out again herding these lambs until about dark.

I said to my wife and my mother in the morning, "Have the wool all ready for me. Have it packed in the blanket while I go after the horses. I want to start early this morning." While I was saying this to my mother and my wife, the children who were camping at our place must have heard me and

16

gone back to their camp to tell their father about it. My mother had let them shear some wool for themselves. This man came over then and said, "My son would like to go to the store with you, and I would like to borrow one of your horses. Mine are all tired out." I said, "All right, I am going after the horses right now."

That morning when I brought the horses back I loaned one to this man and his son and I started off for the store. We went across the flat, past Black Rocks Standing Up, past Thumbs Water, and got to Winds Cover The Water that evening. We stayed there that night. The next morning we started on again, down the red mesa, past Reeds Sitting Up High, and then past Many Young Cottonwoods And Houses In A Row and Black Water.

Then we crossed Chinle wash to where a Mexican had put up a store. It was noontime. After we sold our wool we started trading. We were both trading together. Some people were in the store, among them two women, holding each other by the hand and walking around. This boy that I was with had a blanket wrapped around himself. It was tied around his waist, and every time he bought something he put it in this blanket. Pretty soon he had a whole lot of things packed all around himself. As soon as the trader handed him the flour he went right out. I was still trading in the store. I bought a lot of stuff, grub and some dry goods.

When I was through trading I went outside. I looked for the boy. He wasn't around, and his horse was gone too. At last I saw him riding over a hill. He was almost over the top, and he was about to fall off his horse. I guess when he got on his horse the things he had put away in his blanket had all shifted to one side. I thought, "There is something wrong with that boy. He must be crazy." Then I went back in the store and took all my stuff out, and there were the two women, running around as if they had missed something. They were after him, because one of them was his wife. And he was only a boy too. Then I packed up my things and put them on the horse and went after him. I went over the hill where he had gone, but there was nobody on the other side.

17

When I was almost to the foot of the hill I looked toward the south and there he was, just packing his stuff. That night we stopped to rest, and the next morning while it was still dark we started on again, and way late that night we got home.

Preparation for the hunt . . .
He learns about proper behavior
on a hunt . . . They kill many deer . . .
They divide the meat and skins . . . And perform
the proper sacrifices . . . They return home.

my father, Slim Man, came the next morning. He said, "I was here after you left for the store two days ago. They put up a date three days ago. They said, 'We will go hunting in seven days,' so there are four more days from today on. So get ready." Some other people had moved near our place. The man's name was Blind Mexican. He was of the Many Goats clan, my father's younger clan brother. My father said, "I want to get that man. We will take him just to watch the camp when we go hunting. Get ready. Get your grub ready, and you should have two pair of moccasins to take along, because you wear them out pretty quickly. So make yourself another pair." I said to him, "I don't know anything about hunting. What shall I take for food?" He said, "Anything that will last long. Don't take too much meat. And when we start from here you should be quiet and don't say anything funny. But when we start I will tell you more about it."

Then I went over where my horses were and rounded them up close by the water, deciding which one to ride. The next day I went over to my father's place, and there was my old father, Choclays Kinsman. I called him my father and my grandfather too. Slim Man was his nephew. We called him by another name too; we called him Brother Of Old Man Hat. He was Old Man Hat's real younger brother. He said to me, "Are you going out hunting too, my grandson?" I said, "Yes, I am going. Are you going too?" He said, "Yes, I am going. I want you to go, to take care of me and my horses. So I want you to go along with me." (This was just joshing.)

When the date was up I went over to Slim Man's place again. My old father was still there, and I asked him, "When shall we start?" Slim Man said, "We will start in the afternoon. You go back and be ready. Those other fellows (who were joining them for the hunt) may have started this morning. But I think they have gone on the upper trail, I don't think they will come through here, for that other trail is a shortcut across the flat for them. We will take a shortcut too. We will start this afternoon and pass Green Slope Up straight over to Green Along The Foot Of The Cliff. Right there lives a man whose clan is Many Goats, and that's what we name him after. We call him Many Goats. We will stop at his place and stay over night there. He must be all ready too by now, and I suspect he is looking for us. He wants us to pass by his place, and we will go with him tomorrow morning from there on."

While I was still at my father's place Blind Mexican came. He was Slim Man's younger clan brother. They knew each other very well, but I didn't know him. I had never met him before. Slim Man said to him, "Well, my younger brother, we are starting out now for hunting. Are you going along with us?" He said, "Yes, I would like to go, for I like to hunt. It is lots of fun, so I would like to go with you fellows." Then he said to my father, "Well, my older brother, I am very glad to see you again. I haven't seen you for a long time." My father said to me, "You had better go home and get ready. Get your horse all ready. I will go out and get mine too." Blind Mexican said, "I have only one horse. That's the only one that is fat. I have others, but they are too poor; they are not fat. I ought to lead one horse." My father told him, "Come again when I bring my horses back, and you can take one with you." He said, "All right, I will go back home too and get ready." Again my father said to me, "Get ready. We will go right after lunch." At noon I had my horses all ready, saddles on them, my grub and bedding; I had everything all fixed up. As soon as I had eaten I started, leading a horse, to my father's place.

When I got there they were all ready too. They had everything on their horses and were just beginning to eat. They told me to eat again. I said, "I just ate a while ago." My grandfather, Choclays Kinsman, said, "Eat anyhow, for we have a long way to go." After lunch we said our prayers, saying, "We will have good luck. Our horses will be lively and fast. They won't give up. They won't go hungry. And so will we, too. We will be lively and quick on anything. We will get all kinds of things. We will be on the good journey today."

Then we started. There were four of us, each one leading a pack-horse. When we got out of the woods, out on the flat, we turned our pack-horses loose and drove them on ahead of us, down to Many Streams, down in the valley toward the north-west. I thought they wanted to go to Green Slope Up, over the shortcut, but instead they went way around the hills and then back. But I didn't say anything. I just went right behind them. When we got to Green Slope Up the sun was down. My father said, "We will go over to that hogan and stay there for tonight." "No," said my grandfather, "We shouldn't stay at a hogan when we are out hunting. We are supposed to camp outside, so we will just pass the hogan and camp on the other side." So we did. We watered the horses and hobbled them, and I built a fire and got some water, while my father went over to the hogan. While we were cooking, my grandfather said to me, "You have got to behave. You should go easy with things. You mustn't throw things around, and you mustn't walk over the wood-pile, and you must not laugh. You mustn't say anything that's funny. Be careful about everything and about yourself." I had been running around there, laughing about things. It was then that he said that to me.

When my father returned from that hogan he said, "Those fellows were waiting for us all day. They had everything ready, their horses packed, ready to start, but when we never showed up they turned their horses loose when the sun was pretty well down. Three fellows are going. A fellow named Sorcerer's Son. He has another name; they call him Ugly Man, too. He is going and Many Goats is going, and

21

Many Goats' brother-in-law. They were waiting for us ever since noon. They thought we would start from our place early this morning and pass here about noon, or a little after."

Early the next morning, while it was still dark, we all got up. My father and I went out and got the horses, while the other fellows were cooking. After we ate we saddled up our horses, and my father said, "We will go early this morning and take our time. You fellows go ahead, just walk your horses, don't trot them. I am going over to my brother's hogan again. I will start with them, and we will catch up with you some place." We went on until we came to the canyon called Small Canyon Meadow. There was a whole lot of grass in this canyon, but a lot of poison weeds were with it. It doesn't hurt the horses, but they will poison a person. My grandfather said, "We will let our horses eat some grass here. Here is good grass. How about it, are you afraid of these poison weeds?" I said, "Yes, I am afraid of it. I don't like to get near them." He said, "All right, then we will go on."

On top, quite a way from this little canyon, there was a trail. My grandfather said, "This is the trail that everyone wants to take." But there were no tracks at all over this trail. Only one horse had gone over it, but that had been perhaps the day before. He said, "We will stop here and wait for the fellows." We stopped and let out horses rest and eat some grass, and we just lay around there ourselves, until after a while they caught up with us, my father, Many Goats, and the others. Slim Man asked us, "Have the other fellows who are coming with us gone on yet?" My grandfather said, "No, there are no tracks over this trail. I think they are coming about by Big Oak now. Or maybe they are coming from Where A Mexican Dug Out A Spring. They may be coming from there; or they may be coming close, so we will unsaddle our horses and let them rest and roll around, so that they will be lively. So we did, and we just lay around there talking and cooked a little food. We didn't have much water. After lunch we waited a little while longer for those other fellows, but they didn't show up, so we started on again. My father said, "We will take our time, so they can catch up with us." We started from there when the sun was pretty well down and

22

got to the river after dark. We camped there by the river, but there was no feed for the horses.

Then, after we watered them, the other boy and I took them way back up on a hill and hobbled them where there was some feed. It was moonlight then. As we started to go back to camp this boy stopped and looked back and said, "I hear somebody talking." I said, "There is nobody around here. I don't think anybody lives around here. Maybe it was the fellows at camp." "No," he said, "that's too far. The sound was behind us." Then I said, "We will stop here and wait a while. Maybe it's the other bunch." Sure enough it was they, driving some pack-horses. We asked them, "Where are you fellows from? Are you from Black Mountain?" They said, "Yes, we are from there. We are from the foot of the mountain too." They asked us, "Where did you camp?" I said, "We camped by the river." "Well, what are you doing up here if you camped by the river?" I said, "We brought the horses here and hobbled them." They said, "Isn't there any feed over there, any grass around the river?" I said, "No, there is no feed for the horses at all." "Well, then, we will go on. We'll get down there quickly and bring the horses back up here too."

They went on and the two of us went along behind them. When we got to the camp they unpacked and unsaddled their horses, and then I and another fellow took them up on the hill and hobbled them. When we got back the other fellows had made a little brush corral.

The leader of the hunt, Tunes To His Voice, was sitting way back in the middle of this little brush hogan. The others were sitting along on both sides of him, with all us young fellows on the east side toward the doorway. They were just ready to eat when we returned from hobbling the horses. Tunes To His Voice said to us, "All of you must behave now, from here on. You mustn't throw things around in the hogan; you mustn't whistle and you mustn't sing; you mustn't talk about funny things, and you must not laugh. You can laugh, but you mustn't laugh out loud. And you should stay where you are. You know where you places are now; so from here

23

on wherever we camp again you will all know where to go, because now every one of you knows his place." After we ate and had put everything away, he started talking to us again about the same things. He was the leader. He was just like a headman. We should all obey him. Everything that he said we must do. We must pay attention to him, and that's what he said to us. "Do the things right, and take good care of your horses. Say a little prayer all the time for yourselves. And you have got to have your gun ready. Have it already loaded. Be ready for the deer, then we will get some soon, and we will get them easily too, if you all say the prayers."

Then he said, "If you want to take a leak you should go out and around toward the south and take a leak over there. Turn around toward the south all the time. And when you come back inside the hogan you must go around the fire, that is, you on the north side. When you want to go out, go out on that side, but when you come in, go around the fire. And you, who are staying on the south side, when you go out, go around the fire and out on the north side. You go out on that side, but coming in you should come in on the south side. You mustn't touch the top of your head, and you must not blow the ashes. When you want to start up the fire, don't blow it. And you mustn't push the charcoal back into the fire. When you lie down, don't lie on your back. Lie down on your side. And you mustn't stretch your legs. When you want to roll over, don't roll over while you are lying down. If you want to lie the other way, you must get up, sit up first and then lie down on the other side. When you want to talk about something, don't tell about your life, don't talk about the women. Only talk about the things you have received. Perhaps at some time you have received horses or cattle or sheep; you can tell about that, because that is something that you got, something you received from another fellow and you have it now. Things like that you can tell about, because we are going to get deer. We are doing after the deer and we will sure get them too. We will get them from Somebody and we will have them too." That's what he said to us. It was way late in the night.

24

Then he said, "We'll go to bed now. I think some of you want to sleep. Get all your guns and cartridges and lay them out. Let them all point toward the north." Then everybody got his gun out and cartridges right beside it; he started singing, and all of us helped him. First he sang the hogan-song, then the fire-song, then next the arrow-song, and last the sleeping-songs. After we were through singing, we took some corn pollen, and then he sang one more song. He told us, "Pick up your guns and hold them while I am singing." So we did, and everyone of us sang the last sleeping song. Then we put our guns away and went right to bed.

The next morning, early, some of the fellows started cooking and some of us went after the horses. That morning we crossed the river and stopped at the store at Bluff City. Some of the fellows had skins and a little wool. They sold that, and we all bought some grub and cartridges. Everyone of us had a .44 rifle, except one fellow, Ugly Man, who had a great big gun. I don't know what size that gun was. From the store we went on along the north side of the river until we got to another wash that comes out from Timber Mountain. We followed that wash for a long way and then went on top through woods and sagebrush, crossing arroyos and going over hills. We didn't stop at noon. We wanted to get up on the mountain as soon as we could. When we got into the woods, from there on were a lot of little canyons that we went through for a long way. The sun was down, but we still kept on going, until we got to a little stream of water, and then it was dark, so we stopped and camped there that night.

After we had unpacked our horses and hobbled them we put up a little brush hogan again and then started cooking. After we ate we began talking. We talked for a long time, and then the leader said, "We will go to sleep now." We got out all our rifles and started singing the same songs, but this time there were more. First we sang the hogan-song, then the fire-song, then the arrow-song; then we sang one song that is called the mountain lion-song, and one more called the wolf-song, and another called the menstrual-song, then the day-song, and after that the sleeping-songs. Then after we sang all

25

these songs we took corn pollen again, and did the same thing, picked up our guns, and, while we were holding them, we sang the fourth sleeping song.

The next morning, early, some of them started cooking and some of us went after the horses. When we brought them back, everything was cooked. After we ate we packed our horses again and were all ready to go. Then the leader said to us, "Now, from here on, on our way we will kill one deer, or maybe more. Be sure and get one. As soon as you see one don't let him go, kill him right there." He said to Many Goats from Green Slope Up, "You know all the country around here. Where shall we camp today?" Many Goats said, "There is a canyon way up in there where there is lots of water and lots of feed for the horses. That's where we will camp. It will be right between two deer trails. There is a deer trail on the other side of that canyon, and another on this side, right along Greasewood Springs. Se we will camp right in the middle of the trails."

Then we started off. We went quite a way and got to another wash that comes out from Timber Mountain. There was water in this wash, and in this wash were a lot of tracks. I thought it was a herd of sheep. One of the fellows said, "There are some deer tracks. They are all new. They must have been around here last night." It was still early in the morning. I had never seen a deer track before, and I was wondering what kind of tracks they were. The leader said, "Now all of you fellows look closely for these deer. It is early in the morning yet. I know they are still around here, so you all look for them. As soon as you see one, kill him right there." We watered our horses and went on. Quite a way from there some of the fellows saw some deer, but they were quite a distance away from us. They said, "There they go. A lot of them went in those oak trees." There was a grove of oak trees way up in the valley, but I never saw them. The leader said, "Some of you fellows go way around the hill, and some of us will wait here until you get over the hill and then we'll go around on the north side of this little valley." They told me, "Go up in the valley where the deer went." So I went after them. Everybody had his gun out. I had mine out, al-

26

ready loaded. I got to this place where the oak trees were, and there they came, out of the trees, about twenty of them. They kind of scared me, for they came out of the trees so swiftly. They were right close to me; I was kind of scared and just watched them go way up in the valley where the other fellows were. They started shooting, and there I found myself, sitting on the horse, holding the rifle. I never had taken a shot at them.

When they started shooting they kind of woke me up. I turned around and went back and caught up with the others just as they were crossing a wash. We went on through the woods and got to where there were a whole lot of springs right close to one another. There we stopped. They said, "We will camp right here. This is a nice place. It's a good hiding place." About then the other fellows who had gone after the deer came along. They hadn't shot a one. They said they had been shooting right into the brush but never hit one. Then we unsaddled our horses, it was still morning, and hobbled them. We chopped down some trees, put up a brush hogan and took all our stuff inside. The leader said to us, "After we eat our lunch we will say some prayers. I will take those who want to go over with me; we will go to some place, maybe upon the hill, maybe to a spring, maybe we will go to a young tree, and there we will put some pieces of turquoise or white beads, and we will put some corn pollen there; we will give that to the spring or tree or hill, so then we will have good luck. Then we will kill some deer."

When we were all through with everything he said, "Now we will go out. If any of you want to go with me we will go now." Then seven of them went out, the leader, Tunes To His Voice, Choclays Kinsmen, Ruins, Slim Man, both Many Goats, and Ugly Man. Those seven went out. The leader said, "We will put these turquoise right on a deer track, if we find one coming toward us. They went out and we four young fellows stayed at camp. We had the horses already saddled up, and as soon as they returned they got on the horses and left. Blind Mexican stayed and watched the camp, while I and the other two young fellows went out and took care of the horses and gathered some wood for the night.

27

In the evening five of them came riding back to camp, but they didn't have anything with them. Two others, Slim Man and Many Goats, hadn't showed up yet. At last, when it was real dark, we heard them coming, their horses trotting along. They both had a deer.

Some of the fellows broke off piñon branches and laid them on the ground on the east side of the wood pile. Then the leader went out and said, "Put the meat right down on these branches." While they were doing that he started singing out there. That song is called the branch-song. Then they brought some branches inside and laid them on the ground way back in this brush hogan. When he was through singing out there they brought the meat inside and laid it on the branches. Then we started cooking, roasting some of the meat on the charcoal and some we started boiling. The leader told us, "Hang the heart and lungs over the pole way back in the hogan, and you should leave them alone, and you shouldn't touch the right side of the ribs. That belongs to the man who shot the deer, and the kidneys belong to him too. So those three things you must leave alone. The rest of the meat you can have all you want. Now we have luck. We can kill as many as we want to. When a fellow kills a deer on the first day he has luck. If he doesn't shoot any deer on the first day then he will have a hard time getting them. So now we can get deer easily, from tomorrow on." Then we all ate, and, when we were through, we talked for a while. The leader said, "We will go to sleep now, because we have all got to get up early tomorrow morning." We got our guns out and started singing, sang all the songs that we had been singing, and when we were through we put our guns away and went right to bed.

Next morning, while it was still dark, we got up and made a quick breakfast. After breakfast those seven fellows got up, and with the leader at their head they sat down on the north side of the fire facing the doorway, and the leader started singing, and they all helped him. As soon as they stopped singing they all got up and went out. They were

28

gone all that day. We four young fellows stayed at camp, getting in more wood and looking after the horses.

About evening they started coming in. Some returned late in the evening. They had killed five deer and laid the meat up in the trees. My father, Slim Man, and Many Goats had been together again that day, and in the morning he told me, "We killed two deer yesterday and laid the meat up on the trees. You go over and bring it back." It was a hard place to find anything, too many arroyos and canyons and washes and lots of trees and brush and everything. He said to me, pointing to a hill sticking out from the middle of some trees— you could hardly see that hill, it was so far from camp—"You just start from here and track us back to that hill. When you get to that hill on top you will see a stump lying there. The top side is lying toward the foot of the mountain. When you get to where the stump is, you stand behind it and look down to the foot of that hill and you will see a little canyon, way down at the foot of the hill, and there you will see a little bare spot. There are a lot of willows and other trees around there, but only one piñon tree, right in the middle of all these others. We put the meat on this tree. I think your horse will be afraid to go near the meat, because horses are not used to deer meat. They haven't been used for hunting. When a horse smells the meat he will shy with you. He won't go near the place. So before you go close to it tie up your horse and go there on foot. You will find the meat piled up on the tree. Rub your hands over the meat where it is bloody, have your hands good and bloody and then go back to your horse and touch him with the blood all over his body, and rub some on his nose. Then he won't be smelling the meat, and won't be afraid of it."

Then I got on my horse and went over to the hill and there was the stump with the top part pointing down to the foot of the hill. I rode down the hill to where the meat was, but when I got close to it my horse wouldn't go any further. He shied and tried to run backward with me. So then I got off and started leading him, kind of dragging him toward the meat, until I got right up to it. The rope was just long enough. It just reached from the horse to where the meat was. I put my hand in the blood, rubbed the blood all over my hand and then touched the horse with it. When I put some on his nose he shied away and started running. He almost got away from me. He dragged me quite a way. It was a rough place where they had put this meat. I almost let the rope go. I was just going to let go, but then he turned right around. If he had gone a little further with me I would have let him run away. Then I held the bridle and the rope and started rubbing the blood over his nose. He was so scared, running around, jumping back and forth, standing up on his hind legs, but I kept rubbing the blood over his nose and face, and pretty soon he quieted down. I guess he got used to it. Then I led him over to where the meat was. When he saw it he started jumping around, but I got all the meat on him and then got on and went back. Sometimes he jumped around trying to buck me off, but I held him in, and after a while he quieted down. I got back to the camp in the afternoon. Blind Mexican, who was staying at the camp, said, "Thanks." That was all he said. Every time a fellow came back with meat he said, "Thanks."

The next day they said they were tired hunting on foot, so they went out on horseback, while we four fellows stayed at the camp and started cutting up the meat. We cut it into thin strips to dry. There was a whole lot of meat all over on the trees. The trees were decorated with meat. By evening only two fellows had come back. That was the little man, Ugly Man, and the fellow who was deaf, Many Goats. They were the only ones to come back that evening. The other five didn't come in. We waited for them a long time that night, but they didn't show up, so we went to bed. We didn't do anything, no singing, that night.

The next morning after breakfast Ugly Man said to me, "We'll go out hunting." I said, "We'll go and look at the horses. When we see all the horses, then, from there, we'll go hunting." We started over to where the horses were, but before we got there he said to me, "You go over and see if they are there together. I'll go around that hill." I went over, and there, right in the middle of the horses I saw a deer, a great big one. It was down in a little canyon. I went around to a point and looked down, and there was the deer, right beneath me, but I could barely see it. It was in the oak trees, right close by me. I thought, "I'll take a shot at it anyhow." So I took a shot at him. Maybe I shot the trees. Some leaves fell. The deer jumped and started running. I took another shot while he was running, and then another. Just as he was going over the hill I shot again. I didn't know whether I had hit him or not. I went down where I had shot at him first. There was no blood or anything around there. I went over to where I had taken the second and third shots, nothing there. But way on top of the hill there was blood splashed against the rocks, Then I turned around and went back to camp and got a horse and went after the deer, started tracking him. There was blood still on the tracks, but after I had tracked him a long way there was no more blood. From there on it had just walked along and been eating the grass, so I thought it was no use going after it. When I got back where the horses were I watered them and then hobbled them again and went on to the camp. The sun was pretty well down.

A little while after those five fellows came back. They all had meat. They looked around and said to us, "There are six of you staying at the camp, but we don't see any fresh meat around. What have been doing?" They were just joshing us. We brought all the meat inside the hogan. There was a big pile there, and a whole lot of lungs and hearts hanging up. I said, "I shot at a deer four times." They all started laughing at me, asking me, "How close were you to the deer?" I said, "It was standing close by me when I took a shot." They said, "So you missed it." I said, "Yes, I missed it." They said, "That deer must have holes." I said, "When it ran away from me I took three more shots, and from there on I saw blood splashed against the rocks." They said, "I don't think you shot that deer. Maybe the deer ran against a rock or something and scratched itself. Maybe that's what made it bleed. You must not like the meat; you let the deer go." They laughed about me and then we had our lunch that evening and they talked about their trips. They said, "There are lots of deer where we were. Tomorrow we will go over there again

31

on horseback. It's too far to go on foot. And we will kill some more. If two of you kill a deer, that's a whole lot. If three or four fellows kill deer, that's still more, so you all try to get a deer."

After we ate the next morning we sang some more and got the horses for them and when we were through singing they went out. But this little man, Ugly Man, didn't go. He said, "I'll stay and hunt around here." He went out with one of the other fellows while the rest of us tended to the horses and the meat. That was all we had to do all day, cut the meat into thin pieces and let it dry. That evening old Ruins came back. He said, "I lost the other fellows. I couldn't find them, so I just turned around and started back. Then I wasn't feeling well either. I was that way this morning, but I went ahead. I wanted to stay at camp, but I thought, 'I will get to feeling all right when I am out riding,' but I was still the same, and now I am still the same. I am not feeling well." He lay around there at camp that evening. We didn't sing at all that night, and those other fellows didn't show up. Way late in the evening the little man came back and we went to bed. Early in the morning, as the other fellows started cooking, Ruins picked up a gun and went out. And I picked up my gun and went over to the horses and rounded them up and drove them close to camp again. Ruins came back before noon, and he said to me, "I killed a small deer, a kid. I put the meat on a tree, and I want you to go over and get it. It's a little bit of a one, so you run over and get it." After lunch I went over. He showed me where he had put the meat, and it was a great big one. I got the skin down off the trees and spread it out and put all the meat on it and started carrying it on my back. When I was not far from camp it got too heavy for me, and there I stopped and sat down and took a rest. I had a hard time getting up with it again. When I was real close to the camp I couldn't go any further. I thought I would sit down and rest again. When I tried to get up I couldn't. I tried and tried. At last I managed to get up again but I almost fell over with it when I got back to camp.

The next morning the little man, Ugly Man, said to me, "We'll go after those fellows. We'll see where they are. They have been gone for two days. They ought to be back by now. Get two horses. We'll go over on horseback." Ruins said, "Get me a horse too. I'll go out hunting on horseback too, but I'll just hunt around here close by." I brought three horses back to camp that morning, and the little man and I went off, across the valley, through the woods and into a wash. Way on the other side were a bunch of trees, and around there were lots of tracks, like a herd of sheep. The little man said, "We'll unsaddle our horses and hobble them and start hunting on foot." We went into the woods, and there we found lots of deer. We started shooting at them, but we missed them every time. This little man had his great big gun, and every time he shot it sounded like a fellow putting dynamite under the rocks. It went off so loud. Pretty soon it kind of made me deaf. And the deer were right close to us. It seemed as though they were coming closer every time. They weren't afraid of us at all. When we took a shot at them they just jumped around; they didn't bother to run away. We made them so tame that toward evening they were around us like burros. We tried our best to shoot one. We would stand, and shoot while standing, then we would lean against a tree, but we missed them anyhow. We started laying our guns over dead logs; pretty soon we sat down and tried to shoot them. Late in the afternoon they started going out of the woods to an open place and began eating grass. I had shot all my cartridges away; not one was left in my belt. At last toward evening this little man killed a young one. We were both dizzy and deaf by then, and didn't know a thing for quite a while. When we talked we couldn't hear each other.

That's the way it is when you don't know how to hunt. This little man didn't know a song, not one song about hunting, and I didn't either, and we didn't know how to pray. That was why we had been missing them all day. And besides we had kept on shooting at the deer without cleaning our guns. When we stopped, when we had run out of cartridges, after we had butchered this deer, we looked at our guns, and they were so dirty you could hardly see through the barrel. When we shot we had no notion where the bullet went. We stayed there that night, and the next morning we

33

just started back. We got back to camp when the sun was pretty well down, and there they were. They all had a whole lot of meat.

The fellows who had been staying at the camp said, "Ruins killed three deer yesterday, and he went out early this morning again." I thought to myself, "I ought to have gone with Ruins. If I had gone with him I would have had three skins." I wasn't so sure about it. I was only thinking that way, thinking that perhaps he would have let me have all the skins, because when a man kills a deer, the fellow who kills the deer shouldn't have the skin, unless he is all alone; then everything is his. So if I had gone along with him that day, maybe he would have let me have all those three skins, because he was my cross-cousin. I called him cross-cousin because he was the son of my uncle; and he was also a clan brother of my father, so I called him my father's brother too.

In the evening Ruins came back, bringing a great big one. They all started telling about their trips. Two fellows said, "We found a lion that had killed a deer. We took it away from him, so there we got a skin that had never been shot." Another said, "I found one too, a lion that had killed a deer, and I took the deer away from him. So that's two skins that haven't been shot. Those kinds of skins are scarce and hard to find. They are worth more than the other skins." Then we all sang again that night; we sang the same songs, and in the morning we sang again.

They said, "There are a whole lot of deer way back in the mountain, so we will go over there again. Eight fellows went that time, and only three of us stayed at the camp. They wanted me to go along, but I said, "No, I'll stay at the camp." On the fourth day in the evening they came back. They unpacked the meat outside on the branches. That's what they always do. They put the meat outside on the branches first and from there we carried it inside. There was a whole lot of meat piled up again, and a whole lot of heads way back in the hogan, with the horns piled one on top of another. They were all good and fat. The fellows were all covered with blood, all their clothes and guns and gun-bags, everything was covered with blood. They had put blood all over themselves, because that's what they should do all the time.

Before we went to bed the leader said, "Now we'll start hunting around here on foot. I know there are a whole lot of deer around the camp now." Ruins said, "There are a whole lot around close to the camp. A lot of them are around here on the north side of us. And these two fellows said they saw a whole lot of deer the other day." He meant me and the little man. Every once in a while they would make fun of us about what we had done that day. They would say to us, "Why didn't you put a corral around them? If you can't shoot them you ought to throw your guns away and start making a corral. After you put up a corral around them you should make a club and hit them over the head. You might have killed some of them that way. Or why didn't you drive them all back to camp? If you knew you couldn't shoot any of them you ought to have done something else. You ought to have gotten some soap-weed stalks and made a rope out of them, and roped and tied them. Or you ought to have hobbled them. There are lots of ways to handle the deer." That's what they said to us every once in a while. That was why, when they asked me to go along, I said, "No, I'll stay at the camp."

But this little man always went out. That evening, after everybody had come back to camp, Many Goats said to me, "I killed one deer and put the meat in a tree. Tomorrow, early in the morning, you go over and get it." He told me just where it was, so the next morning I went over and brought the meat back. For two or three days more they hunted there around the camp. Every day they went out and killed some. When they came back in the evening they would say they had some meat piled up on some tree or other. At last the leader said, "Well, how are you fellows? Are you getting tired? If you are tired we will quit." They said, "Yes, we are tired." "Well, then," he said, "we will stop hunting now. We will go home in two days. How many did we kill?" he asked. Many Goats said, "I counted them last evening. We killed seventy-one." The leader said, "Well, then, we will quit now. We have got a whole lot. Tomorrow we will all fix our packs,

35

fix up the meat. We will do this tomorrow morning until noon, and in the afternoon we will make a sweat-house. We will have a sweat-bath all afternoon. And the next day we will pack up and go back to our homes."

Then everybody said, "We will do that. We will start fixing our stuff now and have some of it ready. We are all glad that we have a lot of meat." They all gave thanks to the leader. "We give thanks to you for all the meat and skins. We will have meat for some time, and we will have new moccasins out of these skins. Our moccasins were all worn out, so that's why we are very glad that you took us here for hunting." Then he said the same thing over again, "That's what we will do tomorrow all day, and the next day we will have a little ceremonial before we start back for our homes." That evening, before we went to bed, he said, "From now on you can go any place. Go wherever you want to go and say whatever you want to say and laugh all you want to."

Early in the morning we all got up and started cooking and brought the horses back. After we ate he said to us, "Spread out some robes." We spread some out on the ground, and he told us, "Get the meat down from the trees and pile it on those robes." We all started to work on the meat, taking it down off the trees and putting it on the robes. It was good and dry, except what they had killed the day before. When we got it all down there was a big pile on the blankets. Then he said, "Now all of you spread out your robes all around this meat." So everyone of us spread our robes around the meat, and he said to Many Goats, "Now, you get in there, and take a piece of meat at a time and put it on the robes. Pick up one piece each time and go around that way. Put it on the robes." He started doing that. When he had all the meat divided among us everybody had about the same. Then the leader said to us, "Now, everyone of you has got some meat. I don't want any of you to go back without meat. I don't want you fellows to be stingy about the meat, and you mustn't get mad about it. Don't think that one of you will get most of the meat. I want you all to get about the same. That's the way I like to see it."

36

Then he said to the fellows who had skins, "Those of you who have skins, some of you have eight or nine skins, I want you to give one skin to the man who has been taking care of the camp. It's all up to you," he said. Then everybody started fixing up the meat, and those who had skins got them and piled them beside their meat. Three of them each laid aside a skin for Blind Mexican, who had been taking care of the camp. He gave thanks to them, and after that they came inside the hogan again. There they took down the hearts and lungs and divided all that up again. I got three of them, and Many Goats gave me one side of the ribs, so I had a whole lot of meat, and two skins. One I got from Ruins the time I went after that great big deer he killed. When I brought the meat back for him he gave me the skin. And the other I got from the little man the time we went out hunting together. I gave thanks to the fellows who gave me the lungs and hearts, and everybody was happy. They had enjoyed hunting. Every one of the fellows who had skins gave one to the leader, and they all gave him one side of the rib. After we had divided up all the meat we started packing it up, and, when we were through, we put up a sweat-house and gathered some rocks and built a fire on them. We were at the sweat-house all that afternoon. Some of them stayed at the camp and had everything cooking when we came back. The leader said to us, "Now, every one of you has enough meat to last you a long time, and some of you have skins. I think every one of you is satisfied with the meat and skins." We all said, "Yes, we have plenty of meat and skins." And we all gave him thanks again. Everything was ready to be put on the pack-horses, and we were just lying around there that evening talking and telling about our trips until it got real dark, and then we went to bed.

Early in the morning the leader told us to get up, "We will go now. Be quick. Get the horses back and have them ready, and some of you start cooking. Cook lots, so that we will all have enough. We will all eat lots, because we are going back, and it's a long way to go." Some went after the horses; some started cooking.

When we brought the horses back everything was cooked, and after we ate he said, "Now, every one of you pick up all these horns. We will take them away now." He took the horns of the first deer that they had killed. He picked that up and put three more on top; that was four horns that he took, and the rest of us each took three or four, and he started out ahead of us toward the north. Then we turned around and toward the west. Quite a way from camp there was a nice young piñon tree, and there we piled all the horns on the east side of the tree. He got out a pouch of mixed-beads; he opened it, took out some and put them on the bone between the horns of the first deer killed, right between the horns, then some other stuff, then some blue-corn pollen, then corn pollen. After that we all of us put some there too. When we were through with that he started saying a prayer. He said a long prayer there and then he said to us, "Now, you can all say your own prayers. Just say you will get more deer some time, you will have more things all the time, and say we will get back to our home quickly, that our horses won't notice that they have a big pack on them, and that we all won't notice our trip, won't be tired. Say something like that for yourselves, and anything else that you want to say, say it in your prayers." We all said our prayers then, every one of us, and when we were through we turned around and went back to camp. That was what he meant when he said we would have a little ceremonial.

When we came back all the heads were in the hogan, just the bones, because we had eaten off all the meat. We left those right in the hogan. We took out our corn pollen again and sprinkled some on every one of them, and we all said our prayers there again. We said, "We will have some deer meat every time we go out hunting. We will live long. We will enjoy life. We will be happy all the time and have good things and good times always. We will be on the good path all the time and on the happy path, and we will have everything as long as we live." After that the leader said, "Now, you all bridle up your horses and saddle them up and put on all your things, tie them to the saddles. Put all your stuff on your pack-horses, and tie them down so they won't come un-

38

done. Have it good and solid, so you won't have any trouble with it."

We did what he said, and then, when we were all ready, we started off, leading the pack-horses, in and through the woods and across canyons and sagebrush. We were traveling all day. About evening we got to a wash where there was some water, close to the river. There we camped for the night. After we ate the leader said to us, "I am singing for all of you while we are going back to our home. These songs are called trip songs, so I am singing those songs for all of you. And before we leave one another I will say something to you fellows. Tomorrow maybe when some of you who live closer start to take the trail to your home, there I want to say something to you. However, I'll just mention it to you now. When we all get back to our homes, and when I get back to my home, I will set a date for Blessing Way.[1] I will get a Singer who knows about Blessing Way, so we can use some of his corn pollen. I want you all to be there."

After we ate in the morning we packed up our horses again and started on. We crossed the wash and went on to the river, to the store where some of the fellows sold their skins. While we were crossing the river the leader said, "Everybody watch yourself. Take care of one another and help the others while we are crossing the river." But we got across without any trouble, and went on. We didn't stop for lunch. That was the way to do. When returning home, on the way back at noon you shouldn't stop to eat lunch, or wait for anything. When we got to the trail that branches off, some of the fellows stopped there, and Tunes To His Voice set a date. He said, "We will have Blessing Way in 5 days." They were there for quite a while. I don't know what else they said to one another. Then the leader and his crowd branched off on to their trail and the others started coming after us. At Green Slope Up the little man and Many Goats and his brother-in-law branched off from us; we four went on, past Green Slope

1. Blessing Way is a ceremony frequently given to ensure health, prosperity, and general well-being. It is preventive and is not a cure.

Up and on past Cottonwood Row. A little beyond there was water. The sun was still up, but we stopped and camped there because there was no water from there on.

Early in the morning, after we ate, we packed up again and went on. Way late in the night we got back to our home. My father, Slim Man, and my grandfather, Choclays Kinsman, went to Slim Man's home, and Blind Mexican went to where his camp was. Before we left one another my grandfather said to us, "Now, when we get back to our homes tonight we mustn't touch our wives. That's the way to do when you have been out hunting."

In the morning I went out and got the horses, those used for herding, and I got one for myself. There was no water at home, so I said, "I'll go and get some water." While I was putting the jugs on the horse my father came and said to me, "Go over to the sweat-house. Your younger brother will be there too. Gather up some rocks and build a fire on them." I said, "There is no water at home, so I am going after some now. After I bring back the water then I'll go over and help my younger brother on the sweat-house." He said, "All right. Your old father, Choclays Kinsman, wants to go in the sweat-house this morning. And he said he is going to leave this afternoon. He wants to go home after he has washed all his clothes. We should all do that too. We should all go to the sweat-house and wash our clothes."

I put the jugs in the blanket, put the blanket over the saddle and went after the water. After I brought some back I went over to the sweat-house. My younger brother was already there. He had gathered some rocks and some wood and we built a fire on the rocks; we threw out the roacks which were in the sweat-house and the cedar bark too, and got some new cedar bark and put that inside to lie on. Then I went back with my younger brother to his home. The two fathers of mine were sitting there. There was a nice fresh mutton. We were all hungry for mutton, even though we had had lots of deer meat. After we ate we took some blankets over to the sweat-house. The rocks were good and hot. We put them inside and put the blankets over the door and then undressed and went in.

40

My old father said, "I don't think I will go back home today. I want to rest up some more. I'll stay around here all day again today, and tomorrow morning I'll start and go back to my home." He said to me, "Come up to my place when the first snow falls. If you want to come with somebody, you can get someone to go with you. Or if you can't get anybody you can come up by yourself. I want you to bring all my horses down here for me. I would like to move down here, and we will live right here together all winter through. So be sure and come up when the first snow falls. Of if you want to come before that, it's all right too, because it might snow deep at first." I said, "All right, I will." He said, "Be sure and do that. When you bring the horses down here for me we will start to move down right after you with the sheep. And your mother wants to come down, too (the woman we call Woman Who Walks Alone; we used to call her Cattle Woman, too). She wants to move down here for the winter. She is all alone, so you bring her down. After you bring my horses down for me you go back up there and bring her down, because she needs much help. And I haven't got many tame horses. When we move down here I want you to break some horses for me, because I can't do that myself. I'm getting too old now." I said, "All right. I like to tend to the horses." He said, "I will be very glad if you break some horses for me. A lot of them are good-sized now, that ought to be used, but they are not broken, so I want you to break them for me. I want you to do that, my son. Help me out, and help your mother too. And you are helping your father here too; just keep that up. Help us all, and we will try and do the same to you, because you are our only child. We will live right close together so if any of us needs help we will help one another."

I said, "All right, my father, I'll do that. I'll go on Black Mountain to your place, maybe before the snow falls, or maybe when the first snow falls, and help you on the horses; and we will all be glad to have you living with us here this winter. There is a whole lot of feed for the stock all along here at the foot of the mountain and out in the flat. And after you move down here I'll go up again for my mother. I'll get her down here too to live with us this winter. You told me I

41

should help her and I will, when she moves down here. And there are no big herds of sheep around here, only my father's and mine. Some people moved here from back of the mountain. They are living with us also, but they have got only a few sheep with them. So when you move down here, and my mother moves down here, even though you both have a big herd of sheep and horses, there is enough feed for them. So we will be glad to have you live with us." He said, "I will stay here again tonight and tomorrow I will go back, and when I get home I'll stay there one night and then we will have that ceremony.[2] It will be on the day after that." My father, Slim Man, said, "We'll go up there when they have started this ceremony." The next day, I guess, he left and went home. When the date was up for Blessing Way my father, Slim Man, went up there by himself. I didn't go, and Blind Mexican didn't go either. We just saw Slim Man passing our place on his way.

2. Blessing Way.

42

3

His folks and Slim Man's folks
move to the foot of the mountain
and he helps build the hogans . . .
His old father and his old mother are happy
to see him . . . He helps them and receives
gifts . . . And rounds up the horses and cattle.

After he came back from Blessing Way, Slim Man said, "You round up your horses tomorrow. We'll use them to move with. We'll move way up to the foot of the mountain, to the place called Where The Little Arroyos Stop. Close by there is The Upper Wash; we'll move there, where that big grove of trees is. There is a whole lot of wood that we can use this winter." I said, "All right, I'll gather up the horses. I'll move way on the other side, further than that, where there is more wood and more feed for the stock." Then I went back home and told my mother, "We'll move. Have everything ready around the hogan." Two or three days after that, during the night, it snowed a little. When we got up in the morning there were about two inches of snow on the ground. That night it snowed a little again. I went over to my father's place and said, "What do you think, my father, shall I go up on the mountain now or shall we move first?" He said, "Well, I guess we will move first. We'll move to The Upper Wash. We'll move over there and get fixed, and after that you can go up to Choclays Kinsman's place. If you go now the snow might be deep before we moved. And you won't be coming back from that place right away, because when you get there you have to hunt his horses and round them up. You can't tell much about the horses up there on Black Mountain. It's hard to gather them, because the woods are so thick."

The next morning I went after the horses. I rode up to The Upper Wash. There was snow on the ground. From the point called Tree Holding Up A Load, I looked for the horses and they were way out in the valley. I rode over there and rounded them up and started driving them back home. On my way I met my mother driving the sheep. She said, "I am taking the herd up to where we are going to move. You go on and hurry with the things. Bring as much as you can on the horses. Be sure and come before sundown, because there may be no wood around there." But I told her, "You just go ahead and take the herd up there. There is a whole lot of wood there. I'm going back, and I'll tend to the things there." When I got back I put ropes on four horses. Everything was ready to be put on the horses. There were bundles of things all around. The food was ready for me too, and my wife told me to eat. After I ate, my wife had the horses all saddled up and we started packing two of them. We put a lot of stuff on those two, and some on the two we were going to ride. There were some little things that we were going to leave there, some corn and deer meat, but I changed my mind. I thought, "We might as well take it all at once." I was thinking we would make two trips, but we took it all and started off through the woods and along the edge. Pretty soon we passed Where The Little Arroyos Stop. The sun was down then. On the other side of Tree Holding Up A Load we caught up with my mother. A big sheep corral used to be there and she had the herd in that corral. That's where we located.

The next day I started work on the sheep corral. My mother was out with the herd and about that time the other people moved. The next day I started on the hogan; I was working on the hogan two days and had everything fixed. The corral and the hogan were up and I had piled up a lot of wood for the two women so they would be all right when I went up the mountain. Then I went over to see if Slim Man's folks had moved yet. They had said they were going to locate on the other side of Where The Little Arroyos Stop. When I got there, there they were. Lots of trees had been chopped down and a lot of poles were lying around. They said, "We

44

moved here yesterday evening, but the horses went back. If they hadn't gone back we would have dragged in all the poles." I asked Slim Man, "When shall I go up on the mountain?" He said, "You wait a while. You stay around here and help us drag in these poles, and help us on the hogan. In that way we will put up a hogan soon."

I stayed around there then, because he told me to, and helped them on the hogan. He asked me, "Have you put up a hogan already?" I said, "Yes, I have got the hogan ready, and the sheep corral is ready." "Well, then, you are fixed up all right now. When we get through with the hogan then you can go up on the mountain with your two younger brothers. In that way you might get to round up the horses quickly. After that you start back right away. Let them (Choclays Kinsman and Woman Who Walks Alone) move with their sheep. If you stay around there then they will say, 'We want help when we move!' Don't let them keep you there, because they have got lots of help. They can get somebody to help them."

I stayed there that night and in the morning we started carrying the poles to one place where he wanted to put up a hogan. When we had them all piled there at one place, we started putting up the hogan. We put it up in one day. There were four of us working so it didn't take us long. Then we built a fire inside and went in and sat down. Slim Man got out his tobacco. While we were smoking he said, "Well, we got the hogan up. That's the one thing we wanted badly, and now we have got it up. I think you will start to go up on the mountain tomorrow. You can go with your younger brothers. We haven't got our horses around here right now, so let them use yours. You will only ride them going up there. You won't ride them around up there. When you get there you will use Choclays Kinsman's horses. You round up his horses for him with his own horses. The horses that you are going to use to ride up there with you just let them rest. And when you start back, use them coming back. So I want you fellows to go up on Black Mountain tomorrow." He said to me, "Tomorrow, early in the morning, you get the horses and bring them up here. Your mother and your wife will be all right. You don't

45

need to worry about them, because you already have wood for them." When I started back home he said, "When you get home tell your women about it and your mother, so that they will both know that you will be gone for several days. Tell them you are going with your younger brothers. In that way they won't worry about you, because you are going with them."

When I got back I told my wife and my mother about that and that I was letting them use my horses. My mother looked at me; she was staring at me for a long time. Then she said, "So you lent your horses to them?" I said, "Yes, I lent my horses to them, because they haven't got any with them." She didn't like that. "They always want to use the horses from here. They have got into the habit. We loaned them horses once; now they are beginning to use them all the time. Why don't they use their own horses? They have got horses. They don't want to use their horses for anything that far, that's why they said they hadn't any horses with them. They just want to use the horses from here." I said, "Don't bother about that. That's none of your business. You tend to your herd. This is my affair, so there is no use your talking about it. I want to help out my father. I want to help them, every one of them, because they are all my fathers. You have got nothing to do with it, so don't bother me about it. You just tend to your herd, that's all." I said that to her, because she always spoke to me like that, too. Whenever I tried to turn her down, she always said to me, "Don't bother me. You keep your mouth shut, because I am doing this myself."

While it was still dark I got up and dressed myself, got my bridle and saddle blankets and tied them up with my saddle and started off after the horses. They were right there close by. I got some that were good for riding and chased them over to my father's place. I didn't go back to my home. I thought, "I'll have something to eat at my father's place." The sun was just a little way up when I got there. They had made a small corral already that morning with the branches of the trees that had been cut down, and that's where I put my horses. After we ate we roped some of the horses and saddled them up. My father said to us, "Now, my children, you go up to your grandfather and help him up there on the horses. When you get there see about your mother (Woman Who Walks Alone). Maybe she would like to come down here, too. I think she will say she will come down, because she always goes around moving with your old father. If she wants to come she will need help too, so you help her, too." Before we left he said to us again, "When you pass our summer camp, you stop and look around, see if everything is all right. Look around where we buried our corn and stuff, see if they are all right."

Then we went on to our summer camp. Everything was all right, so we went on, passed Water Washed Our Rock then Water Flowing Out Of Canyon to the foot of the mountain and up to the place called Valley Coming To The Edge. Quite a way from there we saw sheep tracks. The snow was about six inches deep up there. We went on through the woods and there we found their place.

They had moved there not long before, my mother, Woman Who Walks Alone, and my old father, Choclays Kinsman. They were living right close by each other. When we got inside the hogan we started shaking hands. My old father's wife, she was my older sister, put her arm around me and started crying. "I am glad you came, my children. We were looking for you every day. When your father came back up here he said you were coming, so he went outside and looked for you every day. He was outside a while ago, looking for you, and when he saw you coming he started to run around here, he was so happy. He said, 'Our children are coming. Now we will move down to the foot of the mountain.' That's what he was saying a while ago."

After that she started cooking. She put one whole rib on the charcoals and had it roasting there for us and some other food. When we were through eating the sun was almost down. I said, "I'll go down to my mother's place. I'll stay down there with her tonight, because it has been a long time since I have seen her. I am eager to see her, so I will go down now and stay there over night. These boys can stay here tonight." I told the boys to get the horses the next morning. My older sister said to me, "Yes, that will be nice for you to go down there to your mother. She will be eager to see you too. It's not far. It's just a little way down here to where she lives."

I went over to Woman Who Walks Alone's place, but she wasn't staying in a hogan. It was just a little bit of a brush shelter, just as though you were staying outside. Her things were piled up on this brush shelter and she was sitting inside. When I got to the doorway she heard me coming; she turned around and looked at me. As soon as she recognized me she got up and pulled down a sheep pelt and laid it right by her side, and the tears were running down her cheeks. As soon as I sat down beside her she grabbed me, put her arm around me and held me as tight as she could against her breast. She started crying, trying to say something, but she couldn't, because she was crying so hard.

Then when she had quieted down a little she started talking about her son, saying, "My dear son and you used to go around together a lot, and he is gone, and now you are alone." She had been saying that while she was crying. She cried for a long time. After she had quieted down she let me go. Then she said, "I didn't gather any wood this evening, because I came back late with my herd. I usually gather some wood before it gets too dark. I only had a little and it's about all burned now," and she started cooking again. I told her not to, "I just ate a while ago," but she said, "No, I want to cook something for you anyhow. I don't want you to go to sleep without anything to eat from me." So, then, I just let her go; I didn't want to turn her down. I went out and started gathering some wood for her. I had a pile in a little while, because there was a lot of it around there close by.

She had prepared all kinds of things to eat. She said, "I had run out of food, but Who Has Mules' son came here the other day and said, 'I am going to Keams Canyon. I'll get you some food from there.' So he did. He went to Keams Canyon and on the way back he went around by the Hopi village, and there is where he got some food. So now I have got enough to last me a long time." I stayed there with her that night. Until way late in the night she was telling me all about herself, the

48

way she lived, the way she was going around, the way she ate and slept. She said, "I started to go around, to move around to different places, and when I moved around like that it seemed to me my son would be there at that place. I sure have missed my son. I have suffered a lot since he drowned. I have got a whole lot of things which I hid away piled up on the trees. Some of them will go to waste and rot on me, because I can't gather them all up by myself. I heard you were coming up here to help your father. He said to me, 'If you need help, if you want to go down to the foot of the mountain, your son will help you to move down there.' So I said to him, 'I'll go too. Whenever you move I'll move too.'" That was all she talked about, just herself.

I said, "Even though you are suffering all the time it's all right. You are living. We all know you are living, and we all come to see you and have a talk with you. A whole lot of your relatives come to visit you. That's what I like. If you had committed suicide the time your son was drowned, you would be there where you had committed suicide, and nobody would visit you there. I wouldn't visit you. We would all know that you had committed suicide and were buried there, and none of us would go there to your grave and visit you. It's a good thing you didn't do that. Today, whether it is summer or winter, we visit you." I wanted to go back to my father's place early the next morning, but she wanted me to stay until I had had something to eat. She cooked some food and we ate. Before I started back she said, "Be sure and send a boy over here to me. I want to know when they are going to move. Maybe they want to move today or tomorrow, so, please, be sure to send a boy over to me before I go out with the herd, so I'll know when they are going to move."

When I got back to my old father's place soon it would have been daylight. The boys had brought some horses back, but they hadn't found the others. My old father said to me, "Now, four of us will go and round up the horses. I said to my wife that you would round up the horses today, and, maybe the next day, after you had rounded up the horses, we would move down together. But my wife said she wanted to move right now. She wants to start moving today, so the rest of us will go and round up the horses, and one of you boys will help my wife and children to herd the sheep down. We will be around here, looking for the horses, maybe two or three days, rounding them up, because they are scattered around. They are not so far apart, but anyway it is just as though they were way apart from one another, because the timber is too thick. You can hardly find anything in the woods. They are right close together, but we will be looking for them two or three days."

Then he gave me a bunch of red beads. It was a good set. He said, when he handed them to me, "Here are some red beads for you. Those beads belonged to the man who got drowned. You can have them, because I have got no use for them, for I am getting too old and my wife is getting old too, and we have got a whole lot of beads already, so we both don't like to use those beads. You can have them, because you are young." So that's where I got the beads. They were nice beads. They were worth ten dollars a string, and there were three strings, so it was thirty dollars worth of beads that I had gotten from my father. I took them and put them around my neck. When I had them around my neck, the old man's wife joshed me about them. She knew I had them around my neck, but she made believe she didn't. She turned around, saw that I had the beads around my neck, and looked as if she were excited. While she was looking that way she said, "Oh, that's those red beads on you. I thought somebody had cut your throat. I thought that was blood around your neck." I said, "Yes, I have the beads around my neck, but I want more, so I'll get some more from you. You are my older sister, so you ought to give me some." She said, "I haven't got any beads with me, but you can have one of my horses, when they get down to the foot of the mountain." Then I thanked her for the horse. We all laughed about that.

My father said to us, "When you are looking for the horses, look for the cattle too, until you have gathered all. There was one good and fat that I saw the other day." He told me its colors and spots. "When you get them bring them along too, down to the foot of the mountain, and we will kill that cow, because it is good and fat, and we will use it for some time. I have changed my mind about staying up here with you to round up the horses. Instead of doing that I will go down with my family. I'll know where to move to, when I get down. I'll find a good place to locate for this winter right at once, so that we won't be moving around again."

He said to his grandchildren, Lost His Moccasins' children, who were visiting him from the foot of the mountain, "You have all got some cattle, and while you are rounding up the horses look for those, too, and kind of round them up. Sometime we will take those cattle down too. I don't want you to let your cattle go. I don't want you to have your cattle up here, because I don't want you to give them to Who Has Mules. That fellow takes the cattle away from the people, but I won't let him do that to me. When I die they will be all yours, my grandchildren. So he won't get any of them." Then he asked me about my cattle, "How many cattle did you leave up here?" I said, "I don't know just how many, but I think about thirteen,[1] or it might be more than that." He said, "Those that you knew very well are all yours. It doesn't make any difference whether Who Has Mules took them away from you. If you know them very well you just go and get them. He has got too many cattle right now. He doesn't know what to do with them. He has never paid for one yet. Those are all cattle that he took away from the other people, so be sure, now, that you look for them while you are rounding up the horses. Look for mine and look for your mother's and look for your own too, and when you see them, round them up with the horses and we will take them down to the foot of the mountain."

Then we started off after the horses. We rode down where my mother (Woman Who Walks Alone) lived. My father had told us to let her know when we passed her place. When I let her know what my father had said, she said, "All right, I'll be ready then." He had told us to go right straight to Green Around The Canyon. "Right in that canyon, I think, you can find almost all the horses, and, I think, over in Wil-

1. See chapter 1, where the number given is fifteen.

lows Coming Out canyon there are a lot in there too, so go up in all the canyons. Look closely and try and get everyone of them, and the cattle too."

We went over to this place called Green Around The Canyon and found lots of horses in there, and in Willows Coming Out canyon were many more. There was everything in this canyon. It was just like on the mountain. It was a nice place. We were there rounding up the horses all day. There were about eighty or ninety horses all together and fifteen mules. We had all good horses and good mules. One mare had three young mules. The others had only one each. When we were through looking at the horses and counting them we roped some and saddled them and then started driving them toward the west. In the evening we got to Yellow Water. A pasture was there, a fence across the canyon. I took the gate away and we drove the horses in there, and we stayed for the night. We fixed the gate, and built a fire there, right by the gate, where we always built a fire, and then cooked our lunch. After we ate we fixed our beds by the gate, and there we stayed over night. In the morning we drove the horses out of the canyon to the place called Two Valleys Running Together. We drove the horses into a big corral that was there and then went to look for the cattle. But there were no cattle. We only saw the tracks. There was another little canyon there. In this canyon were a whole lot of grass and great big greasewood and salt weeds, and it was in those greasewood bushes that the cattle were. They were all looking fine, but we didn't find the one my old father had wanted to kill, this one great big female. Some of Slim Man's cattle were in this bunch, and some of my old father's. I had three in this bunch.

Then, after we had separated our cattle from the others, we drove them over to where the horses were. We only brought down five. I told the other fellows, "You can drive the horses, and I will take these cattle alone. When we got to the place where they had been living there was nobody around, only the crows were jumping around there. Everybody had moved. We passed that place and got to the edge of the mountain, to the place called Valley Coming To The Edge. First we drove the horses down on the trail. One of the fellows went ahead, and right after him we chased the horses, and right behind them I drove the cattle. They went down nicely. About sundown we got to the foot of the mountain and went on, past our summer camp, and down to Where The Gray Hills Come Out. Right there we stopped. One steer had given up, because he was so fat, so I told the fellows, "We had better stay here tonight." There were a great many washes there right close together, and in the middle of these washes was quite an open space. We put the cattle in there and unsaddled our horses and hobbled them and made a fire right in the middle of the path. We stayed there, out in an open place. It was very cold. We almost froze that night.

We started off again early in the morning while it was still dark. When we got to Where The Little Arroyos Stop, Slim Man's son said, "I want to go home from here." So I told him, "Tell your father, if he is home, to come over to see what he will think and say about these horses and cattle. I want to know where he wants to put them." I said, "We'll stay here, because there is lots of grazing. The horse and cattle are hungry." We almost went to sleep there. Then we heard Slim Man coming. As soon as he rode up to us he said, "Thanks. We will have lots of meat for the winter. You fellows better go to my place and have something to eat there. I'll stay around here with the stocks." He looked at the horses and cattle; and was thanking us for getting some of his cattle down for him. The steer that had given up was his. He said, "I'll kill that steer. Go on and get something to eat at my place. Hurry and come back. I'll stay here, I'll go around for you and watch them for you, so you can both go ahead."

Both of us got on his horse and rode back to his home. There the food was all ready for us, and we started eating. After we ate we went right back, bridled our horses (they had had enough grass), and started driving them past Tree Holding Up A Load, past The Upper Wash. A little way from there my father said, "Choclays Kinsman is located way up in there, at Cottonwood Standing, and Woman Who Walks Alone too." We went there. My father said, "We will drive the horses and cattle way back on the other side of where Choclays Kinsman is living." We did that and then went back from there to his place. He had just got home. He had been out herding the sheep. He said, "I was out with the sheep, because I had sent only the little children after the herd. Well, my grandson," he said to me, "you have got the horses out here now, haven't you?" I said, "Yes, they are out here now." "That's all right. Now I don't think any of them will try and return, because there is a whole lot of feed for the stocks around here, more than up on the mountain, so I don't think they will get away. They will surely get acquainted with the country around here. Did you get all the horses out for me?" I said, "I don't know. It's up to those other fellows." He asked them then, and they said, "The horses that you say you have missed for a long time are still missing. We didn't find them." Then he asked about the cattle. They said, "The cattle are all there." He said, "Oh, well, just let those horses go. We have got enough horses anyway, so we will just let them go. Perhaps sometime we will go up there and look for those that I missed. But when we see a horse we will just kill it and bring down the meat."

Slim Man said, "I have got some cattle up on the mountain but I can't get them down, because it's too hard. I'll just let them go to Who Has Mules. He wants to have a lot of cattle. Even though he has got a whole lot and doesn't know what to do with them still he wants more, so I'll just let them go and give them to him. I am not sorry for them because I have got some now. That's the way with this Who Has Mules. When he sees a head or two in with his bunch, right away he will change the ear-mark, change it to his ear-mark. By such means he takes the cattle away from other people. So I'll let all mine go to him. Now, from today on, I will never go up on Black Mountain for my cattle."

My old father asked me, "How about you? What do you think about those others that you left up on Black Mountain? Do you want to let them go too and give them to that man up there?" I said, "No. Those that I have known, that I still know today, those are all mine. I won't let them go, because I know them. They are mine. Those that I don't know he can have.

54

One that turned around and went back had no horns on her. I won't let that one go." The old man said, "Yes, I know that one very well. She has a calf now. Her calf has black ears, on both sides. You could tell it easily by that." He said, "That's right. Don't let him have the cattle which you know are yours."

Slim Man said, "Well, I guess we will go home now." I said, "All right." Then the old man said, "Well, my children, come back in two days. I want you to kill that steer for me, butcher it for me and cut it up. Then I'll have beef for some time, and we will all have beef. Thank you very much for bringing beef back with you. Thank you for helping me to bring the horses down. Thanks in every way. I will help you some time too, maybe bigger than that."

4

He is surprised and sorry when
he shoots a ram by mistake . . .
He gives thanks to his old father for steer
meat . . . His mother-in-law moves beside
him . . . They quarrel and she moves away with all
her daughter's things . . . Slim Man talks about
her and about how to treat a husband and wife . . .
They put up a hogan for Old Man Hat's sister . . .
A marriage is arranged for his mother, Woman Who
Walks Alone.

It was evening when we got back home. My wife was there, and my mother was cooking some food. Everything was about ready. After we ate, I told them about my trip. Then I asked, "What were you two doing?" My mother said, "We haven't been doing anything, except what we always do. In the morning, as soon as we ate, one of us would go out with the herd. Sometimes I went out, and another morning she would go out," she said, pointing to my wife. "One morning she wanted to go over and round up the horses. She stayed out all day until the sun was down. When she came back she said, 'I didn't know all the horses. I don't know which is which, but anyway I rounded up all the horses that were around the place called Wooded Hill.' That's what she said when she came back." My wife said, "Yes, I was out that day trying to round up the horses. I rounded up all the horses anyhow." I asked her, "What kind of horses were they? How many were there in the bunch?" But she said, "I just don't know. There were a whole lot of horses all over there." Then I told her about the stallions, their color, one stallion was white and another was a bay, and the other was a sorrel. Those stallions each had a bunch of horses with them, a little over twenty in a bunch. "Yes, there was one bunch that way. I noticed the white stallion in this bunch, and another bunch, that was the sorrel stallion, and the bay had a bunch, and there were seven of them at one place. These were horses that we use all the time. And there was another place where there were three together, and at another place there were three more. That was all I saw. I rounded all those up." I said, "Well, that's all. They were all there, then. Not one of them lost. I thought I would go over and round up the horses tomorrow morning, but you have gathered them up and I know they are all there, so now I'll let it go until some other time."

My mother said, "Oh, we were out herding all the time and are tired of herding, so you go out with the sheep tomorrow morning." I said, "All right." Then I said to my wife, "I used one of my old father's horses. That's the one I rode back over here last night, so I want you to take that horse back to him." She said, "All right." My mother said, "We will both go over. I would like to go out and visit. I would like to see my daughter (she meant my old father's wife), because I haven't seen her for a long time, so we will both go over there. You go out with the sheep." I said, "All right, you two go then. I'll go out with the sheep in the morning and take my gun along and bring back some jackrabbits."

The next morning I took the herd out and took my gun along. I killed one. Then later on I killed another. I had four in all, when I spied another. That one ran into the herd. The sheep scattered out; they were afraid of the rabbit. There was the rabbit sitting up, with the sheep looking at him. I took a shot at him; the sheep all got scared and went away from there, quite a way away, and there I had shot a ram. I don't know how that happened. The ram was standing there; he tried to walk, but he only took a step or two and then fell down. I had shot it through the heart. I was so surprised and sorry about it, thinking, "What did I take a shot at the rabbit for? I ought to have let him go. I already had four rabbits. How many more did I want, anyhow? And what did I want that one for?" There I was, so sorry, standing right by the ram, looking at it. Then I rode over to the sheep; they had gone quite a way from there, and faced them toward home. Right away they knew which direction they were going. It was afternoon when I had killed this ram with my .44. While the sheep were on their way toward home, I got off my horse, tied him up and started butchering. I butchered the ram and cut it all up and put it over the saddle along with the rabbits. There were four rabbits and one ram, so that made five, and two different kinds of meat that I started back home with. I caught up with the sheep and just passed them. They knew I wanted them to go home. They all knew where they were going. My mother and my wife were home. It was well toward sundown. I stopped close to the hogan on the south side of the door and my wife came out. She said, "Oh, you have got all kinds of meat with you, jackrabbit and sheep." Then she saw the head, "Oh, this was a ram." I said, "Yes, it was my ram that I killed."

Then my mother came out too. "Why did you kill that ram? That was the best ram in the bunch. What did you want to kill that for?" I said, "Well, I wanted a lot of meat, that's why. This morning I noticed that we were running short of meat, so that's why I took the gun and I killed four jackrabbits. I thought, 'That isn't enough,' so I took a shot at my ram. Then I thought, 'Now we have enough meat, that will last us a few days.' " My mother was staring at me for a while; I don't know what she was going to say; she was just getting ready to say something; I could tell it by her mouth. I said, "I was going to kill another jackrabbit. The jackrabbit stopped right in the middle of the sheep. I took a shot at that jackrabbit and missed him. I just don't know how I shot the ram. The sheep were all out of there; there was only my ram standing there. He tried to walk, but he fell. So that's how I killed my ram. It was my ram. It didn't belong to anybody else." They took the rabbits and the meat inside, and we all went in.

I looked at my mother, but she looked all right. She didn't look as if she felt bad about it or sorry. Inside the hogan I said, "I killed one of my best rams. I am very sorry about it." She said, and she was kind of smiling when she said this, "Why are you sorry about it? We are not going to throw it to the dogs. We are going to eat it, so you don't have to be sorry for it. I am glad that we have got some meat now. Four jackrabbits and one ram." When she said that she kind of hit my heart. That's the way I felt about it. I thought she would be sorry for it too, but she didn't care. If it had belonged to her I don't know what she would have said. I didn't say anymore. I was just sitting there, feeling sorry for my ram. My mother said, "We brought some meat too. You are not the only one bringing meat home with you. We got over to the old man's place before the herd went out this morning and they killed a great big sheep. They gave us one whole side and they gave us all the insides too. So we got lots of meat also." Then she said to her daughter-in-law, "I'll cut off the ribs and cook them." She got out a sack, and it was real fat mutton that they had brought, but I didn't say anything.

A little while after that, before we started eating, she said, "You ought to have better sense than that, shooting in the middle of the sheep. If you had happened to kill more than one you would have been in a bad fix. A man like you not having sense enough. You shouldn't shoot anything against something else. If there is a good shot at something you should look all around first to see if anything is on the other side, horses, cattle, sheep, or the hogan. Somebody might be walking on the other side, or standing or sitting. You must watch around the thing you are going to shoot first. If there isn't anything on the other side then you can take a shot at it. So you must think. Use your head. That is what your head is for." Maybe she said that to me because I was sorry for it. I hadn't said a word when she had spoken to me before, and I didn't say anything again. I just let her talk.

The next morning my mother said to my wife, "You stay home and cut up the meat so as to dry it, and I'll go out with the sheep." I said, "I'll go over to the old man's place today. My father may be up there now waiting for me."

I went over. My father, Slim Man, was there already. He had come with his son and he had gone after the cattle. About noon he came back and drove them in the corral. We ate at noon, and after we ate we went outside and my father, Slim Man, took the gun and shot the steer in the forehead. They took the others back where they had been before. As they were taking them out of the corral my father said to his son, "Take the cattle back where they were before, so that they will be right there all the time, until after the snow is all gone. Then we will do something with them." So that left only four of those five we had brought down from Black Mountain. Woman Who Walks Alone came up and said, "I just let my sheep go. When I saw the cattle being driven toward the hogan I thought right away that you would kill one." In the meantime Slim Man's son had come back. Slim Man said to him, "You go over to your mother's herd. She said she just let her sheep go and started over here, so you go over and herd for her until noon." Right away the boy rode over there.

Then we all started butchering. We chopped down some piñon trees and put the branches on the ground, and there we laid the meat. That was the fattest calf I have ever seen. I never saw a calf like that before or since. Inside the ribs were great big chunks of fat, nothing but fat with just a little strip of meat. The old man told Slim Man to cut off one side of the rib and lay it aside. So he did. One side was given to him, the other side the old man took himself, and he gave me a front quarter and a chunk of meat. My mother, Woman Who Walks Alone, got a hind quarter and some pieces of meat from the inside. We enjoyed ourselves, eating nice fat beef, and we all gave him thanks. We were around there all day. We cut up the meat and put it in a sack, and toward evening we went home.

When I got home I saw a bunch of sheep right close by and, where the sheep were, smoke was coming up out of a hogan. There was a hogan close to ours that nobody had been using. That was my mother-in-law who had come with her son. I took the meat inside our hogan and laid it on a sheep pelt. "Here is nice, fat beef that I have brought," I said, as I laid it on the sheep pelt. "A front quarter, a chunk of meat and a piece of the backbone and some fat were all given to

60

me." My mother started crying; I didn't know what she was crying for. After a while she said, "When I had a husband he used to have a whole lot of cattle. He used to kill cattle all the time, and I used to have all the beef I wanted, and here today I got a little piece of my husband's cattle that was given to Choclays Kinsman. If my husband were still living I wouldn't have a piece like this. He would kill one for me and let me have the whole thing. That's the way he used to be, and I was treated by him that way." That was Old Man Hat, her husband.

I thought I had brought a whole lot of meat back with me, but she said it was only a little piece. I said, "Well, my mother, that's all right. We have got some meat, anyhow. And this isn't the first time that we have had beef. We have been getting beef right along that once belonged to my father. Whenever they kill a steer they always give us some, so you don't have to feel badly about it, my mother. We have got plenty of beef. It's not just a little piece. It's one whole front quarter and a chunk of meat and part of the backbone." Then she quit crying.

I just said a few words to her, and then asked, "Who are those people out there?" My mother said, "That's your mother-in-law. She moved here this afternoon. They have moved over here, so they are staying in that hogan." There were a whole lot of red goats. She had a lot of goats and just a few sheep. I asked my wife, "Have they got some meat?" She said, "No." Then I told her, "Take some over to them. There is a whole lot of mutton here and beef. Take both mutton and beef."

In the morning I picked up my ax and started chopping down some trees. I was making a corral for my mother-in-law all that day. She was awfully thankful for it. This hogan they were living in had no dirt on it. There were only the poles standing up. So the next morning I gathered up some cedar bark and put it all over the hogan and right on top I put the dirt. After I had finished covering it I got the dirt out from the inside, and that made it like a new hogan. When I was through I chopped up a whole lot of wood for her and put some inside the hogan. In the morning my wife went over to her mother's. When she came back she said, "My mother is lying there in bed. She ran a splinter into her foot, and she blames you, because you had piled some wood inside the hogan. She said, 'Who is going to say he is a man? If he hadn't put some wood in here I wouldn't have this splinter. I wouldn't be suffering like this from pain.' That's what my mother said." I said, "I thought I did good for her by chopping some wood and bringing it inside, so that she wouldn't have to go out and chop wood and bring it in, but that was wrong. I have done wrong. I won't do that any more from here on. I won't chop any wood, and I won't put it inside for her any more."

I went out that morning with the herd, and my wife went over and told her mother what I had said. When I came back that evening there was nobody around and no sheep. I thought perhaps the sheep were in the corral, but there was nothing in it, and the hogan was open too, nobody there. Then I went back to our own hogan. My mother and my wife were sitting there. My wife had only one sheep pelt spread out and she was sitting on that. She said, "I told my mother what you said this morning. I didn't think she would get mad that quickly, but she got mad as soon as I told her that. She said to me, 'Well, let's go then. We'll go home now. If he doesn't want to help me anymore why do you want to stay here? So we'll all go home now.'" My mother said, "They started packing their stuff this morning. She told her son to go with the sheep, and she packed her horse. While her son went on with the herd she rode up here to us. She tried her best to take her daughter, but she didn't want to go, so she gave up telling her to go back with her and just took all her things, all the pelts, all the bedding, blankets, and her belt and beads, and her moccasins. She took everything away from her. She has only the clothes she has on."

When I had come inside the hogan there had been nothing on our side, just one sheep pelt lying there. My mother put one of her sheep pelts down for me and I sat on that. On my mother's side were lots of pelts and things. I had my things on that side too. On our side there was nothing left.

Her mother had taken everything away from her. However, she had left the moccasins outside on the tree. I asked her, "What do you think about it?" She said, "I felt badly about it. I was so ashamed for my mother. I didn't think she would act that way. She told me to go back with her. She wanted me to go back very badly, but I told her I wouldn't go; that I would stay right here, and that's the way I am thinking about it. I am going to stay right here. That's what I came for. I came here myself. I took you away from the other people because I liked you. That's why I didn't go with her. I want to stay right here with you."

I said to her, "Well, then, if you think that way, if you like me and if you don't want to let me go, if you mean it, tell me right now." She said, "Sure I mean it. If I hadn't liked you I would have gone back with my mother. I didn't want to go with her, because I like you." "Well, then, let her have all the stuff that she took away. The sheep pelts that she took away, in my life I won't lie on one of them any more. And the buffalo skins that she took away, that were used for blankets at night. I won't use them either. And about your belt and your beads, I know you are sorry for them, but I don't want you to go after them; let her have them. We will do something for ourselves later on." Then we borrowed some sheep pelts from my mother. I had a robe, and we took another out of my sack and we went to bed.

While we were still sleeping my mother got up. She took the ashes out of the hogan, swept a little and made a fire. When she had made a fire she said, "Get up, wake up, both of you. Get up my daughter-in-law and you, too, my son. Wake up and get up. We were put here without anything yesterday, and we are that way. Everything was taken away from us. We haven't got anything with us, so we ought to do something about it." My wife got up. I just lay in bed. Then she began to talk. "I never thought about my son that way. I never treated my son that way, and I didn't want my son to be treated that way. I didn't want to throw my son on the ground in the dirt and I didn't want anybody to throw my son on the ground in the dirt, and now yesterday it happened. And old pelts like those I don't care for them, and an

63

old buckskin like that I don't care for that. I don't call that something that's worthwhile. She thinks the buffalo skin was worth a whole lot, but I think that's nothing, nothing to it. I don't care for it. If I had put my son some other place he wouldn't be treated like that. A lot of people wanted him from different places. These people that wanted him were all good people. If he went to one of them I don't think he would be treated that way. And here today he is on the ground in the dirt. That old thing acts like a mad dog, and she is a mad dog, the way she acted yesterday, so I call her a dog."

After we ate my mother began talking again, "Well, yesterday we were put in a poor spot, but I don't think we are put there. What she took was just nothing. It is nothing to me. It seems like something you threw away that was old and you couldn't use. That's the way I feel about it, so first it's up to me. That woman thinks that I am not a woman. She thinks that I am a poor woman, but I am not. She was a poor woman. So that's the way I am thinking about her."

While she was saying this she went and, way in back of her things, she got out a saddle blanket, bridle, a red belt, a blanket, and two more sheep pelts. She laid them out and said to me, "Now it's up to you. That old tramp thinks that you are poor. She thinks that you haven't got anything, so it's up to you now, and those are my things piled there. Now it's your turn." Then I got up, I got out my sack, got out the best and biggest buckskin and laid that on my wife's lap. I told her, "That is for your moccasins," and I took out some calico and velveteen and gave her that, and I told her that I gave her a horse. She knew the horse. It was a bay and tame. I told her, "You can have that horse." The beads that I brought back from Black Mountain, which my old father gave me, I gave those to her, and my mother put up two more sheep pelts. That made five great big sheep pelts. That is about how much we gave my wife. That morning I went out with the herd.

When I got back toward evening my father was sitting there. Everybody had seen this woman moving back. He had seen her too. He said he saw all the pelts that he knew and the buffalo skin. All this was what the woman had had on her horse, and he was wondering why she was taking all the stuff. That was what he wanted to know, and that was what he had come here for.

When I came in he was talking to my wife; he was saying, "Your mother isn't a woman. She doesn't think ahead. She is just like a dog. She only thinks when she is getting something to eat, and, after she eats, then she won't think. She is just like one deaf and dumb. If she thought ahead she would stay right here with you, where she knows she would live well. But she didn't think ahead. If she had lived right here she would have had everything that she wanted to eat and have. She wouldn't have had to work for her grub. She would just be staying inside her hogan where it's warm, and she would get what she wanted out of you and out of your husband. But she didn't think about this, so now she has left and is way off some place. That's the way with all Red Clay people. They don't know anything, they don't know what's good and what is not. They always want trouble. That's the way with all Red Clays. I say this because I know it and the old people used to say years ago that all the Red Clay people have a quick temper. They want trouble all the time and they start trouble. They are that way, every one of them. It's a good thing you stayed here. If your mother had chased you back, if you had gone back with your mother, we would have gotten another woman right now, today. So it's a good thing that you didn't go. If you really mean that you don't like to go with your mother, if you really mean that you want to stay here, later on you will be fixed well. One of these days you will be having everything you want. If you tend to things, and behave yourself, if you don't do anything wrong, soon you will be having everything that you want. You will have properties if you work for them. If you stay around here just for love, that's no use. Love is all right, but there is nothing to it. If you just love a man, you can't get anything out of it. If you love a man then you should work, work for something, work for your home, so that you will have a home, work for your properties, so that you will have properties, work for the sheep, horses, and cattle. If you work for them you will have

65

them, and pretty soon you will have everything. So it's up to you."

Then he said to me, "Now even if you are a man you don't know anything about women. You don't know how to take care of a woman, you don't know how to treat a woman, you don't know how to talk to a woman, and you don't know just how a woman is. You don't know all of these things. So now you've got a wife and you know you've got a wife and that's all you know about it. You just think that you got a wife, that's all. Now from here on you think for her and think for yourself. She's got nothing right now. She is left to you by her mother without anything so now you look at her and think for her. Now you've got to get her something, you've got to make her moccasins. You've got to fix her, you've got to get her everything that she wears, everything that she'll use and everything that she'll work with, and you've got to get her sheep and horses. Don't think that she is a poor woman and don't say to her, 'You are a poor woman.' You must not say that. You must just take good care of her and don't treat her bad and don't say anything that will make her feel bad. You just take good care of her so she'll be living good with you and she'll be happy with you all the time. If you treat a woman bad you'll make her crazy after a while so you must not say anything that makes her feel bad." That's all he said to us and he said, "It's getting late for me now; I want to go back home." He went back very late in the night.

One day I came back with my herd again and there was a woman there. This woman was Lost His Moccasins' wife; she was Many Goats. I shook hands with her and she told me, "I came here for help. I want you to help me out with a hogan. Would you put up a hogan for your grandmother (that was Choclays Kinsman's older sister; his real sister) because she is sick. We want to bring her over here. The hogan is what I came here for, my son, because I haven't got any help. I know some of the people but I always think this is the best place to go for help." Then I said, "About when will you move over here? I'd like to know just how long it will take you to get over here because I have much to do around here and I'm the only one doing all the work. I'm just like you, I need help. But even though I've got so much to do I'll help you anyway. Now I'm herding because I don't like to let my mother and my wife herd all the time but if you want to come I'll help you out a little."

Then I told her, "You can go back home and I'll try to work on the hogan. I'm all alone so I have to do the work all by myself. From tomorrow on it'll take me about five or six days to make a hogan so you can start to move five days from tomorrow. I'm sure that I'll have the hogan ready and so you go back now. She said, "Yes, my son, I thought you would help me out. I'm glad that you are going to help me out and I'll be very glad when you put up a nice hogan for us and I'll be very thankful to you my son. Now I guess I'll go back."
The next morning I said to my mother and my wife, "Now this morning I'll start chopping some trees down and you two can take turns and herd the sheep while I'm working on the hogan. After we ate I took the ax and a little lunch and water and I started cutting down the trees. I had a lot of them cut. There were lots of poles lying around and in the evening I got back home. The next morning early I went over where I was cutting the poles. I thought I'd cut some poles before they cooked. But I stayed over there, I didn't come back. I just kept cutting poles and about noon my wife came over and brought me some lunch. I had some water there already and, while we were eating lunch, a bunch of sheep scattered around us and there was my mother, Woman Who Walks Alone. She rode her horse up to us and said, "Is anybody helping you, my son?" I said, "No, nobody is helping me. I'm alone yesterday all day and today," and she said, "I thought some fellows were going to help you." I said, "I don't know. There isn't anybody around." Then she said, "Kill one of these sheep so you'll have something to eat while you are working." She got off of her horse and she said, "Get on this horse and round up all the sheep. Get them together right here."

I caught a great big black sheep and she said to me, "Don't kill it if it's a poor one. I want you to kill a fat one." I said, "This is all right." So then I carried it over where my wife was and, after we butchered it, my wife started cooking

67

some meat. The rest I put up on the trees. After we ate my wife said, "I'm going now. I'll fix up these things and I'll stretch this skin out to dry and I'll use it for the bed pelt." She was awfully thankful about it, and I was, too, so we gave thanks to my mother and she left some meat right there on the trees and she took some back with her. I cut some more poles. I worked there till night and then I took the meat home. Next morning I got up again early and I said to my wife, "I'm going over to gather up all the poles and you can bring me some lunch." I went over and started to gather up poles and about noon my wife came over with the lunch. After lunch I worked till night again but I didn't gather up all the poles so I went back home.

Next morning I went out again without anything to eat. It was close to noon time when I got all the poles gathered up and, just around that time, my wife came over with the lunch again. We both ate lunch there. After lunch I said to my wife, "Now I want you to help me. If you want to gather up some cedar bark I'll put it over the hogan, that is if you want to." She said, "I will. I'd like to gather up some cedar bark." Then I put the poles up about as high as the shoulder all around for a wall, but it got too dark so I stopped. My wife had the cedar bark all around the hogan. I started to work on the hogan again the next morning.

That morning Choclays Kinsman had come there. He brought an ax and a shovel, and then Blind Mexican came and then Slim Man came. He said, "We heard that you were going to work on the hogan and we were going to help you but we were away. We've been rounding up the horses for two days so that's why we didn't help you on cutting the poles and gathering them up. But you've got the hogan built already so now we will finish with it today. Before we start in we'll eat something." Then we started cooking and, after we ate, we started working on the hogan. Some of us were up on the hogan and some others down below handing us poles up there. When we were almost finished one of Slim Man's boys came again and Slim Man told the boys to put cedar bark all over the hogan, to put it on closely and kind of thick so when we put the dirt on it wouldn't go through the hogan. We got

68

finished with the poles, and the cedar bark was all over on top and we started to put the dirt on, and towards evening we got it finished. We took all the dirt out of the hogan. Then we built a fire in there and it was a good-sized hogan that we put up.

When I came back with the herd the next evening there was a horse tied outside. I went inside the hogan and a man was sitting there. His name was Son Of Late Grey Hat and he was my mother's maternal grandchild and he was also my uncle.[1] We began to talk while the others were cooking. He was talking while we were eating and I told him about my work on the hogan for five days. "They might have moved here last night," he said. "I saw them moving yesterday. There was a herd of sheep and horses, and there was a bunch of people moving from there, so I guess they moved over there last night." Then he said, "I came here because I heard you were here. I was living over at Rough Worthless Canyon and finally we got down here to Tree Holding Up A Load. There is where we are camping. I just gathered up some wood and I had a lot of it piled up. Then I came over here and my children are going over to visit their people. I won't go over there. This is as far as I'm going. I don't know just how long they'll stay over there, maybe all winter. When they go I'll stay around here."

He stayed over night with us and the next morning after we were through eating he said, "I'll go back home and I'll put up a brush hogan. My children were out in the open place so I better go now and I'll put up a brush hogan for them and I'll gather up some more wood for them." Then he went back and I went and got the herd out. I was going after them and I saw my mother there, Woman Who Walks Alone. She had come on horseback. I turned around and went over to her and she said, "I came over to ask for help but I see you are going out with the herd." I said, "Yes, mother, I'm going out with the herd. What did you want me to do for you?" She said, "I'm out in the open place and it's just too cold for me

1. Both Left Handed and Son Of Late Grey Hat were members of the Bitahni clan.

69

out in the open place so I want you to make me a brush hogan. That's what I came over here for, my son." I told her, "I'll do that but I'm going out with the herd this morning. Tomorrow I'll be over there." She said, "All right, fine and then I'll be in a warm place." Then she started to go in the hogan and I went after the herd.

When I came back with the herd again that evening there was Son Of Late Grey Hat again sitting in the hogan. After we ate we started talking and he began to talk about his wife. He said, "I've been working a whole lot for my wife and children but my wife doesn't like me to stay with her even though I help her a whole lot. She doesn't see that so now I've made up my mind. I'll let them go." The first time he came to our place he said his children were going to visit their relatives and this time he said he was going to let his children go. He said, "I'll let them go back to their relatives and I won't get to see them again because they are unkind to me." That was the way he was telling us about his family. He said, "I got back home from here and she told me, 'You ought to stay over there. Why did you come back over here?' I didn't say anything to her. I just thought about my children. They are out in open places and they are awfully cold so I just put them up a small brush hogan. I had it finished yesterday and I thought, 'I'll come over here and stay here again.' I don't like to stay with my wife because she always talks to me that way. Now I just can't stand what she is saying to me." Then I said, "I don't know. It's up to you. I can't say anything because I don't know how you are. I don't know just what kind of man you are so I can't say anything about it. It's all up to you because you know all about her and about yourself."

The next day I said to him, "I am going over to my mother's place (Woman Who Walks Alone). She wanted me to put up a brush hogan for her and I promised her that I would." Then he said to me, "How far is that and who is that mother of yours?" "It's my father's clan sister." Then he said, "Could I go over with you and help you and can you let me have your mother, my nephew?" "Well, I like a man that's a good hunter and I know you don't know anything about hunting." That's the way we joshed each other for awhile and

70

then I said, "If you want to go and help me we can go over now." We went over to my mother's place and we got there close to noon and she was just coming in with the herd. That's the way she did every morning. She turned her herd out when it was still dark. When the sheep got enough she brought them back and that's what she had done that morning. She said, "I was out with the herd since early this morning and I didn't have anything to eat yet. I just came in with the herd." There was lots of dry meat on the trees but she told me to catch one of the sheep. So I got out a three-year-old wether and we butchered it. She said, "We'll have some fresh meat."

After we ate she went out with the herd and we started to work on the brush hogan. Then we took a rest and this fellow said to me, "Well, my nephew, I kind of like this woman. I wonder what she'll say if I tell her that I'll stay with her? She is all alone now. She hasn't got a man with her. When she comes back with the herd tell her what I said about her. I like her so I'd like to stay with her." Then I said to him, "I don't know. I don't think she cares for a man. She talks that way and that's why she is all alone. If she cared for a man she could have a man right now. So I think she'll say 'no' and I don't like to talk to her about it." We finished the brush hogan and started home. While we were going back he was talking about it all the way. I never said anything to him and we got back home.

There he talked about it again to my mother, "My grandmother, I'd like to stay with that woman because I liked that woman. The first time I saw her I liked her and I'd like to stay right close to you too." My mother told him, "It's just up to you. We can't say anything about it, because we know that she doesn't care for a man and we know you've got a family and children to take care of. They are out in the open place right now. They are cold. You ought to get them back to their home, to their relatives. You ought to do that first and after that you can do something for yourself." He said, "No, you may think that my wife is all right. She is not a good woman. As soon as I get home from some place she always goes after me just like a dog and a dog is that way you know. When you come to a hogan and that dog sees you coming he'll go right after you and he'll try to bite you, try to fight you. If you want him to get away from you, he won't get away from you; he'll want to fight you and he'll want to get the best of you. That's the way with this woman so I just can't stand her treatment of me. Right now is as far as I can take it. She knows that too, and she thinks she is the only woman in the world and she thinks she can do everything. So now she can do for herself. She can take her children back to her place in the cold weather, because she doesn't care for anything."

The next morning after we ate breakfast he told me to put up a sweat-house. "Now I'm going back home and I'll be right back." So then I said, "All right." Then he turned around and he said to my mother, "My grandmother, will you please go over to that woman for me and tell her that I would like to stay with her. I like her so much." My mother said, "Oh, no. You are just going back to your family. You've got a wife and children and you are going back to your children. That's not right for me to do and I won't go over. I don't want to start up trouble. If I do that, I'll put myself in trouble. You'd better forget about it and go back to your children. If you were alone I'd be very glad to get you a woman. If you can't get that out of your mind you can take your family back to their relatives. After that we can talk about it and do something for you."

Then I went over to the sweat-house and I gathered up some rocks and I built a fire on them. There were some rocks inside the sweat-house. I threw them out when I put new cedar bark inside to lie on. While I was doing this he came back. He said, "I was back over where I was camping. There wasn't anybody around. They had moved already. They must have left there early this morning. I followed the tracks over to Where The Little Arroyos Stop and there wasn't anybody around there. I looked across the valley. There was nothing in sight so I just turned around and started back. They must have left early this morning." That's what he said when he came back, but he wasn't away long and his camp was three or four miles away, and, from there on over to Where The Little Arroyos Stop is quite a way. So I kind of didn't believe him. I thought he must be telling me a story because that is a long distance. He wouldn't get over there and back this quick. He began to talk about the woman and we went back home. We left the fire going on the rocks. He said to my mother again, "There wasn't anybody around. I got left, my grandmother. Everything was gone, even my horse and my saddle and my robes. I went after them but I didn't catch up with them. They had gone already. I wanted you to go and get me that woman this morning. If you had gone you would be back by now."

My wife was out with the herd and my mother said, "I'll see about it after a while. You fellows better eat something first before you go in the sweat-house because I won't be here all day. I'll leave some lunch here for you and when you come back from the sweat-house you can eat lunch." When we got through eating my mother said to him, "Now I'll go over to this woman. I'll try to get her for you. I don't know what she'll say. When she wants to talk she talks a whole lot and, if I tell her that you would like to stay with her, she won't say all right right away. When she starts talking then I won't bother with her. If she says all right right away then I'll have a talk with her. So I'll go over now and I'll talk to her about it. From there on I'll go over to the other place."

Then we went over to the sweat-house, we'd been lying there for a long while, and he just talked about his wife; I was tired of hearing him talk. When we got back home I began to talk to him. I knew that he was a gambler and I knew he lied a whole lot and I knew that he was a great cheater and a whole lot of other things that's not right. That's why his wife didn't like him. She tried her best to get him to quit gambling. That's why he had nothing at all. I said to him, "The people around here don't like gambling, they don't like a man that lies and cheats. They like a man who knows all about work, different kinds of work from a little thing like putting up a hogan and putting up a sheep corral, and they like a man who knows all about the stock. That's the kind of man they are looking for around here so I don't know how you are. There is no gambling business around here. Everybody tends to their work taking care of themselves, taking care of their families and taking care of their stock. That's all they do, around about this time of year, and from the spring on they tend to their farms and all summer long they work on their farms. Now I know that you are that way. If you want to live with this woman you've got to put all that away, you've got to promise first that you won't do all those things anymore from here on. If you put all those things away and she likes to have you, because she is alone now and just tends to her stock—she has got a lot of property and lots of stock, sheep, horses, and cattle—she'll be glad to have you. If you make up your mind to tend to all of her work, if you go right ahead and tend to all of the work, pretty soon you'll have property, sheep, horses, and cattle. So it's up to you if you take my word. As I said you'll have property and stock and then you'll have everything."

My mother didn't come back that day and we had been talking all that evening. I talked to him some more about how to live, and he began to tell about himself and he said he'd been treating his wife lots of good ways. "But even if I treated her that way she didn't like me. I've been with her for a long time and now I just can't stand her talk." That's what he had been telling us all that evening till we went to bed. While he was still talking I went to sleep. I don't know how long he talked after that.

Next morning my mother came back and then he said, "It was a long ways you had to go for a woman for me, my grandmother." She said, "Yes, it was a long way. I was over there last evening and I started to talk with her and pretty soon I told her, 'I have got a grandson. I would like you to stay with him for me. He had a wife and children with him but they moved away from him. His wife left him and so now he hasn't got a wife and this is as far as he went after his wife and children. He said he is going to turn around and go back but I told him to stay around here for a while so now he is staying at my place and I want you to take him. I want you to marry him and I think he'll help you a whole lot.' Woman Who Walks Alone said, 'I don't know anything about him. The first time I saw him was when he was here with my son so I don't know what kind of man he is. I don't think he is a

74

good man the way you talk about him. If he was a good man he wouldn't let his family go. That's why I don't think he's a good man. I don't like a gambling man because you can't get a gambling man to do anything. If he is that way he'll put me way back. He'll gamble for my stuff and pretty soon I won't have anything. If he is that way I won't want him. I like a man that knows all about the work. If he knows all about the work I'll be glad to have him because I'm all alone to do all the work myself.'

"That evening we just went to bed. We quit talking about it and early in the morning the first thing I said to her was, 'Before I go home, I want to know if you want my grandson. I don't want to go home until you promise me that you'll marry my grandson. Promise me now, my daughter.' She didn't say anything; she just laughed about it and she said, 'Wait until I think about it. I am thinking about it right now. When I decide either way, I'll let you know what I think.' When we ate breakfast she said, 'Well, I think it will be all right, I'll find him out right quick. I'll know just how he is if he comes and stays with me for a day or two. You can tell him now that I want six horses. I don't want you to put up one of your horses. Tell my son he mustn't put up one of his horses, I don't like to get one of his horses because they are all mine (because long ago they belonged to her brother, Old Man Hat). Let him get some horses. I guess he's got horses himself so you go now and tell him to get me six horses. I'll take him and have him as long as he wants to stay with me. If he runs away from me it's all right. I say this because he is on foot.' Then I said thankyou to her, 'Now I am happy. I'll go right back and tell my grandson about it.' "

When she came back, I said to Son Of Late Grey Hat, "Now we'll go over there again and we'll cut some more poles and we'll make a hogan for her." Right away he said, "All right," and then my mother said, "You'd better do that because she is out in the open place. Make her a hogan so she'll be in a warm place and she'll like it, too." Then I asked him again, "Are you willing to go over?" and he said, "Yes, I want to go over very badly." When we got there lunch was ready. She had gone out with the herd. After lunch we started to cut

75

poles till noon and then we ate lunch again. When we were through we gathered up the poles and then we found a tree. We fixed that thing up and we put it right at the door for the door frame and we began laying poles around and we started building the hogan. We finished with the poles and we put cedar bark over it. We finished with that and we started to put dirt over it. When we got half way with the dirt she came back with the herd. She started cooking lunch again. After we ate we put more dirt on it. We finished with the dirt that evening and then we cleaned it out from the inside and we cleaned around the hogan.

My mother came over and she went inside and looked around. "Thank you very much. This is a nice hogan, my son." She didn't say "my husband" to the other fellow. She just gave me the thanks and she didn't say anything to the other fellow. Then she went outside and brought in some wood and she built up a fire and she went out and got some cornmeal and she made a white spot with the cornmeal in all four directions. Then she sprinkled some inside all around and again she gave me thanks. This other fellow was standing outside the door. My mother was still inside. I went out to him and I said, "You wanted one of my father's clan sisters or nieces. Now here is a good chance for you. Now you can go right in. There is my mother. You can stay with her." I pushed him inside where my mother was. I just heard my mother laugh inside and then I left and went home.

5

Sickness and death of Old Man Hat's
real sister . . . His uncle has a bad
dream about him and he is treated . . .
The ways and thoughts of a medicine man.

next morning I said, "Mother, you go out with the
herd again this morning because I want to go over
where I made a hogan for those people. I haven't gone over
since they moved over. I want to see the woman that is sick,
to see how she is now, and maybe they need help too. Then
she said, "I'd like to go over to my daughter-in-law's place.
She meant Woman Who Walks Alone. I'll go over and get
some wedding grub (joshing). She said to my wife, "You go
out with the herd, my daughter-in-law."

I went out and got her a horse and I put the saddle on for
her, and my wife went out with the herd, and I went over to
the other place, to the hogan I had put up for Old Man Hat's
real sister. There was a man sitting there, a medicine man,
and he said to me, "my grandson" he calls me, "I'm here
treating her, and I don't know just what is wrong with her.
She is about the same. When I came here she was that way.
We used one man for 'shaking hands.' The hand-shaker
(diagnostician) said it was Ghost Sickness that was bothering
her. As soon as she was treated for that she would be all
right. We don't know if it's true or not. So we started to treat
her with Evil Way." [1] They were making a small sand painting inside around the fire and I started in to make some of the
sand painting. They were putting rainbow gods around the
fire, and I made one sand painting and there wasn't anybody
around, only Who Has Mules was there and three boys, Lost
His Moccasins' sons. Lost His Moccasins was in another

1. Evil Way chants are used in curing "ghost sickness" caused by native ghosts.

77

hogan where they were cooking. His wife was over there and her three daughters. They were cooking meals and the sick woman was coughing so I thought she must have something wrong with her lungs.

We finished with the sand painting and we built a big fire and then they called for her. She was in another hogan outside. Then they brought her over here and she was very sick. She was so weak that she could hardly walk herself so they were holding her while she was walking and they sat her down in the back of the hogan. I went up to her and shook hands with her and called her my grandmother. She said to me, "Is this you, my grandson?" I said, "Yes" to her and she said, "Are you the one that put up this hogan?" and I said "Yes" again and she said, "That was nice of you, putting up a hogan for me. This is a nice hogan that you put up."

Then I thought she wouldn't live long because she was very sick and she could not walk herself. After this treatment was over they helped her up and took her outside, and then they brought her back inside and she was treated by water again. This Singer sprinkled some water over her, and then we scraped up the sand painting, took all the ashes and stuff outside, and built a fire again. They brought us some food inside and there everybody ate some lunch. After that I went up to her and I sat down before her and I asked her, "How are you feeling, my grandmother? Are you feeling better or getting worse?" She said, "I think I'm getting worse all the time because I'm getting weaker all the time. Now when I want to get up they have to raise me up. I can't get up myself and I can't walk without someone holding me, and my mind, my thoughts, and my sight are all getting weaker and weaker all the time. Everything is going short on me so I don't think I'll live. That's the way I'm thinking about myself. They have been treating me for a long time but I'm just getting worse all the time and now they start treating me with another kind of a treatment but I don't think it will do any good. I don't think anybody will ever cure me. I think I'll die soon, because everything is going short on me."

Then she said, "They've been looking for you every day since we moved here and they've been wanting to know where you are." I said, "I was at home all the time and we've been trying to get a woman for one fellow. He was a Bitahni clansman." Then she asked me, "What Bitahni group does he belong to? There are several outfits of Bitahni, three or four of them." I told her the one he belongs to and then she said, "Maybe I know him. There used to be a boy that I knew before we went to Fort Sumner, as we started from here to go to Fort Sumner. He was a little boy then, maybe it's him and this boy was named Son Of Late Grey Hat." I said, "That's the one." "He must be getting old now," she said, and I said, "No, he's just a young man," and she said, "Oh, yes, I know him, but I don't think I'd know him now when I see him."

Then she said to me, "Well, that was nice, my grandson, I'm glad to hear that. I like to hear something like that. It kind of makes me feel well when a man or a woman sits by me and tells me something like that. I enjoy hearing what happens and what's going on. I'm glad you told me that now Woman Who Walks Alone has a partner; she's got a friend; she's got help and she's got a husband. She was alone for a long time and now you got her a husband. That was nice of you to help your mother that way. Now she can take a rest; she won't have to do as much work as she used to do. Her husband will do all the work for her and I hope she is very glad that she has a husband and her work is lessened for her. I know you are a kind man. You've been helping everybody around here. That's the way to be, just keep that up all your life, my grandson. I'm getting weaker all the time and I know I won't live long and it's all right with me because I'm not the only one that's going to die. I'm not the first one who is going to die. From years ago, I just don't know how many years ago, death started. There is a whole lot of different tribes of the people and they are all dying off every day and night, and I know all my grandfathers and mothers, uncles and nephews, brothers and sisters and everybody that was in my clan are all dead. I'm glad I'm going, too, and I know I'll meet them so I'm not afraid to die. I'm willing and I'd like to die. So it's all right with me. I don't worry about anything because I've done lots of things, I've seen lots of things; I've heard lots of things, I went around to lots of places. I've tasted all kinds of different

79

foods and I've tasted all kinds of different meat. I have enjoyed life and I'm thankful for all those things. I don't know who made me but I thank him. So I'm glad that I'm going to die. That's the way I'm feeling about myself, my grandson," she said to me again.

After that she just lay over. She was tired talking and then Who Has Mules said to me, "You go out and get some weeds the medicine man is going to use tonight. He is going to use those for an arrow to drive the bad spirit away from here. He said two arrows have to be used tonight and I want you to go out and get some. There are some boys around here but they are not sensible about these things so I want you to go out and find good weeds." I said, "I'll go." Then I brought these weeds back and some soap weed stalks which they were going to tie up with these weeds, and that evening this medicine man started to treat her with these arrows that he made. After he was through treating her with the arrows he untied them and we took them away, and after this he said some prayers for her. That was all and we went to bed.

Next morning we went out and gathered some wood that should be separated from the other wood. We had to break it off the trees there, dead branches, that was what the medicine man used for the fire. We gathered some and we brought some home and then they raised the patient up but she couldn't stand, she was so weak. She tried to stand up but she couldn't and then they just put her on a robe and carried her out. So we made the sand painting again all around the fire and after that they carried her in again. We just made a little fire. It should have been a big fire but we all knew that she couldn't stand the heat so we just had to build a little fire.

After the medicine man treated her we took all the sand paintings and the ashes out again. Then we got lunch and then they all talked about it. The medicine man said, "I don't think she'll get better. She is just getting worse and worse all the time. I don't think I'll cure her so I think I'll quit now. It's no use for me to treat her. I tried my best to cure her with my treatment, with my singing, and with my medicines, but she is getting worse all the time." After the medicine man had said that and the others had said the same he told us to take all the things and put them away some place, and then we all started taking all the things out which this medicine man had been using. He said, "It's no use for me to do any more treatment on her and I don't think any medicine man would cure her because I think it's her lungs and I know nobody will cure a person when a person gets like that so we might as well quit. I don't know. It's up to you people now. Maybe you would like to try another medicine man but I know no medicine man will cure her. I'll take my medicine outfit, I'll take it out now and I'll go home today."

When he said this Who Has Mules said to the medicine man, "We would like you to stay here with us and leave one rattle and your eagle feathers here. You can take the rest outside and you can help us with your singing and with your treatment still." Then he said, "All right," and they gave the patient some corn meal but she couldn't swallow it and when she tried to talk her voice was way low. You could hardly hear her. We did nothing all that day. We were just sitting by her just looking at her all day, and, in the evening, I went home. I told my mother and my wife all about these things and I said, "She is just going down all the time and the medicine man said there's no hope for her but he is still there. My mother said, "I hate to hear those kinds of things. It makes me feel very bad when I hear about a person like that but nobody can help when a person gets like that. A person won't get better so it's just too bad now that she is going to die. But when she dies she'll meet her brother (Old Man Hat)." When she said this my mother started crying. She said, "When her brother was alive she used to come and visit her brother and they used to josh each other and her brother died and she is going to die now too and when she dies she'll meet her brother for sure."

Then I asked my mother, "Where did you go yesterday morning? Did you go over to Woman Who Walks Alone's place?" She said, "Yes, I went over yesterday morning and she was at home and my son was out with the herd early in the morning and I said, 'I came here to eat some wedding food so you better be quick about it and cook me some wedding food.' When I said that to her she just laughed about it and she began to cook some food for me and that's the way I joshed her and we were talking while she was cooking some food for me. Then she said, 'He said the horses that he promised are all over at the foot of Carriso Mountain and he said he'd go for them this spring when the grass gets green. But I kind of don't believe him.' I said, 'Oh well, he might have horses but we'll see what he'll do about it. When he goes back to his home we'll find out just how he is.' Then she said 'If he doesn't get those horses for me it's all right because I don't care for the horses anyway. I just need help, that's all. I can keep him around here to help me right along. Those horses cannot help me out and they won't do me any good. What I need is help so he can stay with me and help me as long as he wants to. Maybe he won't stand all these tasks. If he can stand all the work then I'll be very glad to have him.' "

Then we talked about different things all day and then I said, "That was nice, I'm glad to hear that and that was nice for him to go out with the herd and I hope he'll keep that up all the time. I don't think he'll get tired doing that. I'm very glad that he is going to help my mother and I'm very glad I heard that my mother was at home taking a rest." Then my mother said to me, "Woman Who Walks Alone wants you to come over some time and she wants you to talk to him right before her so that he'll know what to do and she'll know just what you'll say. She said, 'He's got a whole lot of claims and he promised me that he'll do all the work for me, and he said he knows all about different kinds of work with the stock but I don't know just how good he is so I cannot believe him. So I'd like my son to come over and I'd like him to talk to him right before me and from there on I'll know just what he'll say.' " I said to my mother, "Why don't you go over and talk to him. You talk a whole lot. When I want to say something you always get the best of me. I don't know how to talk." She said, "Don't talk that way. Your mother wants you over there and I want you to go over too." I didn't say any more words and after that we went right to bed.

Next morning Lost His Moccasins came. The sick woman was his mother-in-law. After we ate he said, "Last night towards midnight, or maybe it was after midnight, my mother-

82

in-law died and we fixed her up. Who Has Mules and Blind Mexican, those two, are going to bury her, so they just want you to help them. He said 'We can dig a hole for her. We want to put her away as soon as we can. Three of us will fix her up.' So they want you over there to help them." Then my mother said, "You better go over, my son, and help your father."

Then I said, "All right, I'll go over but before I start helping them I'll say something to Who Has Mules, because he was the one who wanted me over there and he thinks I'll be right there to help him. He thinks I'll be over there just because he said it. But now I think it's a good chance for me to talk to him about my cattle. He is holding all my cattle up on the Black Mountain and I heard that he said he'll hold all that I left up there. I heard he won't let them go so I want to know about my cattle first before I start helping him on this burying business. I'm willing to bury my mother so I'll speak to him about it when I get over there." Then my mother said, "That will be fine. It's a good chance to talk to him right now so you better go over, my son, and talk to him about it." Lost His Moccasins said, "Yes, just talk to him about it and see if he means it. We'll find out right now this morning and don't be afraid to talk to him about your cattle. I'll say something first before you and then you just go ahead and talk to him."

Then we went over to that place again. My mother had died in the hogan that I built. They were all in the other hogan. Lost His Moccasins said to Who Has Mules, "I had a hard time to get him to come over on account of one thing. He had heard that you don't want him to get any more of his cattle down. That was why he didn't want to come but I begged him to come over and help us to bury the woman. Is it true that you won't let him have any more of his cattle? He wants to know about that first so tell him about it and let him know right now." Who Has Mules said, "I don't want to hear about those things. I don't hold any of those cattle in my herd. The cattle that I don't care for are all up on the Black Mountain and I don't care for those old cattle. That wasn't the thing that I wanted you over here for. I sent for you to help me in burying my mother. I didn't think you were that kind of man believing lies and I never said anything to you about the cattle and you never came up to me and you never talked to me about the cattle. Some liars have been telling you something about me and you believe those liars. The cattle that belong to you I know are still up there. Those that are still up there are all yours and they do not belong to me so get those cattle down whenever you want to. Bring them down because they are all yours and don't believe the liars. There are lots of fellows and I know all those fellows that talk about me that way. So you get all your cattle down, every one, any time when you want to." Then I said to him, "I don't want to start trouble with you. I said this because that's the way I heard the people talk about you and I'd like to know if it's true." He said, "I don't care about the cattle. You can just go ahead and take yours and you and your brother both know all about cattle so you and your brother can tend to it. Your brother knows all the cattle. Any time when you want yours just go to your brother and tell him that you want your cattle." He meant his son.

That's what he said to me again. That was all he said about those cattle and then he said, "Now we'll put that away. We'll drop it right now. Now we will undress and we'll put ashes all over ourselves. As soon as you touch the ashes from there on you shouldn't talk. We'll go only by a gesture. We'll be that way until we come back from the grave, we'll go by gesture till we wash ourselves." Then we undressed and put ashes all over ourselves and brought the horses right by the door. She had some things right by her and we took all her things out and put them back of the saddle. Then we got her out. We didn't take her out through the door. We took some poles out and took her out towards the south. We put her over the saddle. Then we led the horse with her away from that place. We buried her in a cave in the rocks. We buried her on the south side because on the north side there was no place to bury the body. While we were burying her Blind Mexican wanted to take a leak and he did so. When he took a leak he had his hand under it and he just put it all over himself and washed with it. That's the way to do, they say, when you bury the body. If you want to take a leak you

84

shouldn't take a leak on the ground, and you shouldn't spit on the ground. When you want to spit just swallow it or spit on your hand and rub on yourself. That's what they used to say during those years and they used to do it that way. When we came back to the hogan we took some more poles out and we let the hogan stand. We didn't set fire to it. From there on we went over where they had built a fire for us and where they had mixed medicines for us to wash with.

After the body was buried nobody went near this place because in our way and in our belief we shouldn't go near where the body is buried. We are afraid of it. We went back to the hogan where the people were and there we dressed ourselves. After lunch we all kept quiet. That's the way we always do, too, when we bury the body. From there on everybody should keep quiet till the four days are up. When the four days were up we all took a bath early in the morning. Then when we were dressed up we three went out a little ways from the hogan towards where we buried the body and we just looked over there. Then we came back inside the hogan and took some corn pollen. From there on we could do anything or we could go any place again. Then everybody started cooking and I went back to my home.

There was my uncle, that's Gray Hat, and he said to me, "I heard you were over where this woman died and I heard that you had been helping the people over there." I said, "Yes, I was over there for four days." Then he said, "I had a very bad dream about you, my nephew, last night. I thought we were around together and we were going along and you got in a quick sand, and as soon as you disappeared I cried out and I felt very bad about you and I said, 'Now I've lost my poor nephew; this is the last that I'll see him and now he is gone under the mud.' That's the way I dreamed about you last night and I thought I was crying as hard as I could and that scared me so badly in my sleep. I jumped up and I found myself sitting up and my tears were running down. After that I went back to bed but I never went back to sleep. I was awake all night long because it scared me so badly and early this morning I dressed myself to come over here. That's the way I dreamed last night. I thought it was true so I'm feeling very bad about it right now. So you both think about it, my nephew, my mother, my mother's mother. We don't want to let that go because it's a very bad dream. So think about a medicine man that knows about that. You know all the medicine men around here and you'd better get one. He'll do something for us so nothing will happen to us. You know I haven't got anything with me right now. I've got nothing to give to the medicine man so you both better think about it now." Right away my mother was kind of excited. She said, "I'm afraid to let that go so we'd better get a medicine man pretty soon. But there isn't any medicine man around here that knows about those things." She said to me, "You go back to that same medicine man (the one who had just treated the woman who died), and tell him about it. Tell him that your uncle had a bad dream about you and see what he'll say about it. Maybe he'll know something about it. If he does we'll get him to do something for us."

I went over to the man's place and there he was sitting right by his wife and her daughter and there was another man. This man was uncle to this woman and there were four of them living together. The man was there to take care of them. He always gathered up the horses for them. I said, "I was back early this morning and my uncle told us that he had a bad dream last night. He had dreamed about me in the quick sand. My mother didn't want to let this go. She wanted me to come over and tell you about it." After I told him about this he sat up. He had a pouch over his shoulder hanging down on his hip. He pulled that around onto his lap. He opened this pouch and got out a cigarette paper made from corn husks. He had it cut already to be used and it was about six inches long. He got that out and he put some tobacco in it; he rolled it and he used his cigarette for a poker to get out a charcoal from the fire. He lighted it and he puffed it three times and then he said, "Well, we always have dreams like that and anybody has dreams like that every night but I don't think it's dangerous. All you have to do is take some of your mixed beads and powdered rock and blue corn pollen and any kind of corn pollen. That's all you have to use."

86

Then I said to him, "I want you to do something about it for me, grandfather, because I don't like to let it go myself. I haven't got help right now so I have to come over here to you myself." He said, "We moved here after that woman died. Four days after that we moved here. I'd been using my medicine outfit on her but I have had my medicine outfit on this tree, the tree that was struck by lightning, for four days and I gathered up all the weeds that have stickers on them and set fire to them and I 'smoked' all my medicine outfit. My medicine outfit is all right. It's ready to be used again. It's up to you if you want me to straighten that up for you. You've got to fix everything at your place; clean up inside the hogan. You have to sweep away from the hogan and have it all clean around the hogan. We'll have to do something for that dream so that nothing will happen. I think I know a little about it so that I can help you out with it. Those things, like dreams, hearing things, cracking noises, and seeing things, these things are just little things. They are easy to be straightened. By putting out mixed turquoise and other beads and the corn pollen which we use on those things, by songs and prayers we could straighten these things out. So don't worry about yourself. It's just a little thing and it doesn't amount to anything so don't worry so much about yourself. I'll straighten the bad dream for you and nothing will happen to you and you'll live a long life. You'll get to see a grey hair."

Then he told me a little story. He said, "Some years ago a woman was digging out some kind of rocks that she used for black dyes. One day she was digging some of this stuff out of a hole in a bank. She was taking out these rocks and putting them right by her side. She reached in this hole for another piece of rock. When she got that rock out and when she had just put that rock on her side again she heard somebody singing 'what are you walking around here for, etc?.' That's the way the song was and it was right close to her. She looked around. She thought it was a man coming up to her. She looked around and there was nobody around and she looked toward where she heard the song and there was a coyote standing. It was a coyote that was singing. So then they came for me and I did something for her. I used my corn pollen and the other stuff that goes with it and I said prayers two nights for her and I gave her One Day Sing. So that woman lived for a long time. Nothing happened to her." Then he told me to go back now and tell my mother about it.

When I got home I told my mother all about what he had said to me. After I told this to my mother she said, "Well you'd better go over to your father, and tell him about this. You'd better go over right now, my son." I said, "I'll go over on horseback." She said, "You go over on foot. You don't have to use a horse to go over. It's not far to his place so you just run over and tell him about this. See what he'll say and think about it and maybe he'll want this to be done at his place or right here at our place. But right here we have such a small hogan. So you go over and tell him about it."

Then I went over to my father's place and I told everything just the same way that I had told it to this medicine man. Then he said to me, "Well I think all that you heard from your grandfather is all right because he knows all about those things. What he told you is the truth. He knows just what to do about it and I am glad that fellow told you about his dream. If he didn't tell, if he just hid it away, it would be wrong for him to do that. But he told you about it so I think it's all right to have that thing straightened for you. It's all right with me and I won't tell you to let that go. If we let that go something will happen sure." Then I said to him again that "my grandfather said some fellows want just one night prayers and one night singing but that's not much, and some of them say they want two nights of prayers and one night singing, and that's a little better, and some of them say they want four nights of prayers and one night singing, and that's the strongest treatment that way. He said, too, that if you want to go out and say prayers upon the hill you could do that; if you want to have this done for you we have to put mixed beads right on top of of the hill. If you want to put mixed beads to a young piñon tree it could be done. Some of these medicine men who know about ceremonies say you could just put mixed beads right on to a coyote track, the coyote track that goes towards the north. He also said that's a poor way to do. Nobody would say a prayer to a coyote; a coyote is just a coyote."

Then my father said, "We'll have this done as soon as we can. I'm glad you came and told me about it." I said, "Where will we have this doing? We've got such a small hogan. We'd like to have it in a hogan that has plenty of room." He said, "I've got a hogan and it has plenty of room but I've got so much stuff in it. There is a hogan sitting up and nobody is using it over at that hill, right upon that hill. We'll go over tomorrow and we'll renew the hogan and we'll use that because it's a good sized hogan." Then I said, "All right, we'll do that." Then he said, "Tomorrow, the first thing in the morning, we'll go over where this hogan is. We have got to take some poles off the hogan on the south side, the poles that weren't put up right. So we'll fix that up tomorrow and then we'll put the cedar bark over it and after that we'll put some dirt on top. So be sure and take a shovel and an ax with you and I'll take my ax and my shovel over there. We can fix the hogan in a day, easy. As soon as you get home go over and tell your grandfather about this and tell him that we want him over there in two days. We'll use him because he knows a whole lot about it and because he says all these little things do not amount to anything."

Then I said, "What shall I give to him?" He said, "What do you think you should give him?" I said, "I think I'll give him a horse." Then he said to me, "A horse! What do you want to give him a horse for? Why don't you give him that steer of yours so that he can use it. He can kill it and he'll have the meat for a long time and he'll use the hide for something and his children will have the meat for a long time and he'll be thankful about that. He won't care much about the horse so what do you want to give him a horse for? When you give him this steer you'll make him so happy and he'll say more prayers for you, too, and he'll sing more songs for you." I didn't say anything for a while and then I made up my mind I'd do that. I felt like he had cut a chunk of meat off of me. That's the way I felt about it. I said, "I'll go over now and tell him that I'll give him a steer." He said to me, "No

89

you shouldn't say that you'll give him a steer. You shouldn't say that to a medicine man who knows about the ceremonies. When you go over to him now today you just tell him that we are going over to fix up the hogan tomorrow and we'll have it all fixed by some time in the afternoon and tell him that I said I want him to be over there in two days. Tell him 'that's what my father said' and just tell him that we want to take some of his corn pollen. That's all you want to say to him. You mustn't say that I give you such a thing. And tell him that I said we want four nights prayer and one night singing and when he comes over there in two days to bring his medicine outfit. He will have it all out in the basket and, when he starts with his ceremony, then, right there, you'll say to him that you'll give him a steer for his corn pollen. That's all you've got to say to him."

Then I went over to that medicine man's place. There I told him what my father had said. Then he said, "All right. I know him very well. I've known Slim Man for a long time. If he wants me over there I'll go over because I don't like to turn him down. I don't like to say no to him because he is my brother's daughter's son. So if my maternal grandson wants me I'll go over. I'd like to see him very much, and there I'll see him, and I'll be glad to see him, too."

Then, when I got home, I told my mother about this and I said to my mother, "I wanted to give him a horse for this doing but my father turned me down. He told me to give that man a steer." My mother said, "I'm glad to hear that. I'm glad your father is going to help us. He is my only son. He never turns me down and I'm the same way to him." The next morning early I went over to the hogan. I took my ax and my shovel over there and Slim Man was over there too. He had his ax and his shovel with him and then we just tore half of this hogan down and started to build it again. Then we made this hogan a little larger than it was before.

While we were working on this somebody was coming towards us on horseback. That was my wife. She had come over with some things and she brought us grub too. She had some wool and jugs and dishes and a lot of other things. Then we said, "That's right; that's the way to do." This was

90

around midday. She said, "I brought these things because my mother told me to take these things over and she went out with the herd." Then we had all the poles up again and we put the cedar bark over it, and then we quit working on the hogan and we built a fire and melted some snow for water. When we got water my wife started cooking and we all ate lunch.

After we ate we put dirt on top of the cedar bark and when we had finished with the dirt the hogan was brand new again. We got out all the dirt from the inside. My wife was helping us and we cleaned around the hogan. We had the ground all levelled all around the hogan and then when we were through cleaning around we built a fire inside the hogan. We made a big fire and there wasn't any smoke at all. The smoke was all going up the smoke hole. We sat down in there and started to smoke. My wife smoked too. She used to smoke a whole lot and later on I used to hate her because she smoked too much. I said, "We didn't gather up wood but it's getting too late." It was almost sundown. Then he said, "Oh, well let it go. I can tend to the wood from tomorrow on and it's not far to get wood. It's getting late, we'd better be going home right now."

We started back to our home and Slim Man was there too for five days and five nights. He never went back to his home until this doing was over even though he was living close to the place. My mother was home with the herd. The next morning we packed up two horses and we put some things on the horse which my wife rode. My mother said, "I'll go out with the herd again this morning and I'll be over there with the herd this evening. You two now take all the things over there." We took everything all at once and then, before my mother started out with the herd, I said to her, "Bring the herd over to that place before noon because we've got only dry meat. We'll have some fresh meat for the old man."

We got to this place and we unpacked the horses and turned two horses loose and I kept one there and used that one for wood. I dragged a whole lot of wood and I had a pile by noon. At noon my mother came with the herd and then, while I was working on the wood, that medicine man was

91

coming with his whole outfit. They had moved there to that place. They drove four horses and they had been riding three horses and had stopped about two hundred yards from our place. There they camped under the trees and I told my mother and my wife to butcher one of the steers. I roped one and they cut its throat and they started butchering, and I began to work on the wood again. I started chopping wood. I had a pile of chopped wood and about that time Slim Man came again. The things were still piled around outside. He said, "Take all those things inside. First have the sheep pelts all laid out and fix a place for that old man. Before you take all those things inside get cornmeal and make white spots in all four directions inside of the hogan and sprinkle some all around and after that you can take all these things inside. Then I'll go over to that man and I'll tell him that I came for him and for his corn pollen and I'll come right inside with him." So then we did what he told us to do.

Then Slim Man said, "I'll bring him inside with his corn pollen. I won't tell him that we'll give him a steer until tonight when he starts with his doings. Then we'll let him know about that." He went over to this man and he was gone for quite a while and I went out and looked for him. About that time they were starting to come. Slim Man was going along ahead of this man and the man was walking behind him. He was carrying something big on his back and I was wondering what that could be. I stood outside and looked at them for a long time but I didn't find out what that was. I went back inside and I thought to myself, "I wonder what that could be that man is carrying" and I spread out a big sheep pelt and right over the sheep pelt I spread out calico. That's where he was going to put his medicine kit. Slim Man came in. He had this corn pollen and the other stuff. He laid that on this calico and then the old man came in and that was his whole medicine outfit that he was carrying. It was a great big sack and he had a whole lot of things in this sack. He laid it against the wall right by his side and he said, "I brought this over here because this whole thing is my body. I don't like to leave my body away from this place so that's why I brought this whole thing inside with me."

Then he started to tell about his different kinds of treatment, different kinds of singing and prayers and about the various ceremonies. He said, "I have used a lot of these things, the little things and the big things. I helped lots of people with my singing, prayers, and my treatment. So this isn't the first time I came for this thing. I have done these things lots of times. I have been doing right all the time so that's why I am getting grey now. If I had been doing wrong with these things I would have been dead a long time ago. I have done all in the right way; that's why I'm still living and I'm getting old. There are lots of different ways to do different things. When a man or a woman pisses on his bed when he's sleeping we put corn pollen where there is a damp place outside somewhere. When a man or a woman, or anybody, hears something we put the corn pollen where there is a wall of rocks, or in a cliff where there are a whole lot of echoes. That's where we put the corn pollen for this man who is hearing things."

Then Slim Man said to this man, "When shall we start? Shall we start right now with the prayers? It's kind of late in the night so I guess we'll start right now with the prayers. I don't know just how long the prayers and the songs are and how many of them will be used tonight." The old man said, "Some of them are small prayers; some of them are long prayers. The first one is for Monster Slayer and the next is for Bear, and the next is Big Snake prayer and the next is Lightning prayer. Then he took all his things out and he said, "We'll start with the prayers now." I said to him, "I'll give you a small billy goat that I have. Two boys went after it and they'll have it over tomorrow sometime. I'll give that to you for your prayers. It's two years old." He said, "All right," and then he looked up and he looked around in the hogan and he said, "You had the hogan spotted white inside all around. You folks have done that and it will be made all over again by me, because I'm here for this ceremony and I'll be known by that. So you have to put the white spots again on the same place where you have these white spots with the cornmeal and then we'll start in with the prayers. The last day when we have One Day Sing, that evening we'll make the spots with the corn pollen."

Then he started with the prayers but before he started he

handed me some medicines. There were two bunches. He gave them to me and told me to hold them with both hands and keep them separate. He said, "That which you hold with your left hand, one is what (live pollen) has been shaken off Bear, another is off Big Snake, next is what has been shaken off Lightening, next is from Big Wind, and the next is from Blue Lizard. Those are five different things that have been shaken off that you are holding with your left hand. This other bunch that you are holding with your right hand represents those six mountains that are called in Mountain Way, and that's earth medicine (in both hands), that's what that is." Then he started saying prayers for me and he told me to say them right after him. He started and I just followed after him and that was Monster Slayer, that's what he prayed for me. That was a long prayer. He repeated the same things over a long time. That was the prayer he said for me, just the same thing over for a long time.

After he was through saying prayers for me he said, "Now you put all around you close that one you are holding with your left hand, put it around you four times." I did that. "The other one you hold to your mouth and breathe it in and, if you are tired and stiff from sitting down so long, stretch yourself with that which you are holding with your right hand. Press it against yourself where you are stiff and sore." I did that and all the rest had been holding the arrow heads. The fellow who was sitting way in front by the door had hold of a great big arrow head. After that we all took the corn pollen and before we went to bed he said, "We'll do the same way tomorrow night. That's the way we'll start tomorrow night. We'll just say a short prayer now but tomorrow night it will be a little longer and the next night it will be a little longer again and the fourth night there will be long prayers, but all the prayers are just about the same."

We didn't say any prayers the next morning when we got up and ate breakfast. After we ate, my mother went out with the herd and these two men, Slim Man and the medicine man, started telling stories about all kinds of different things, about different kinds of singings and prayers and treatments. They told the stories all day long that day. At noon Slim

Man's sons brought the cattle back. They killed the steer over where they had camped and this steer was fat. That evening my mother came back with the herd and she put them in the corral and that night the medicine man prayed for me again. He gave me those things and I held them in both my hands and this time he said the prayer for Bear, and next he said prayers with me for Big Snake, and next was Lightning, and next Wind. It was a long prayer this time. That's as far as he said the prayers for me that night. Then we went right to bed. Next morning we got up and they had cooked some food. We all ate again and my mother went out with the herd and these two men told stories again. This medicine man was telling stories to Slim Man all that day.

In the evening my mother came back with the herd and, when my mother put the herd in the corral, she came back inside the hogan. She started to tell about her trip. She said, "I went out with the herd this morning and I was herding out on the flat. About noon I was riding a horse around the sheep and I happened to look up and I saw something pass over my head. It was pretty far up. I thought it was a bird or something flying over me. The sheep saw the thing too and they all scattered out and right in the middle of the sheep something fell. As soon as it fell on the ground the thing rolled over and I wondered what that was. I rode over there and there was a sunflower stalk lying there and on the roots there was mud and it was about a foot and a half long. I looked all around. I thought maybe someone had thrown this thing over to the sheep. But it was too far above me where I saw this thing. There wasn't anybody around. It was out in the flat and you could see a long ways. I kind of felt bad about it. I was wondering what that could be." Then she said to the medicine man, "What do you think about it?"

He said, "I don't think that's dangerous but we'll do something about it. That's just a little thing. You don't have to worry about it. There are two nights of prayer yet and three days with the last day." My mother said, "Can you treat two patients?" He said, "Yes, you can treat two, three, or four patients even; so we'll do something for that yet. We won't let that pass. A man or a woman can join in these

95

prayers at any time so think about it now." That night my mother started to be treated by this man. Before she joined me that day we all washed ourselves again and after we washed ourselves the medicine man told my mother, "Now you sit beside your son." That night my mother sat right beside me and the medicine man said prayers for us both. This prayer was called Straight Lightning. That was a long prayer, a little longer than the second night prayers. That night we went to sleep again and the next morning we all got up. My wife cooked some food and we all ate again. There was nobody to go out with the herd except my wife but she had to cook for us. Then Yellow Ears said, "Why don't you ask that man over there at my camp? I don't think he is doing anything. He just tends to the horses, that's all he does." My mother said, "I don't think he'll do it." The man said, "Yes, he'll do it. He'll do anything that you want him to do." Slim Man went over to this man and he came back from there and he said, "As soon as I asked him to help us on herding, before I stopped talking to him, he jumped up and said, 'All right you hurry and get the herd out for me and I'll go out with the herd.'" Then the man came over and he went out with the herd.

Slim Man and the medicine man were still telling stories about the sky, about the clouds, about the water, about the rain, about the fog, about the earth, about the mountains, about the different kinds of wild animals, about the sheep and horses, about the properties, about different color beads and about everything like that. They sat down there all day and smoked all day. They were that way all day long every day. They were telling about a whole lot of things, some little things and some big things, about different kinds of gods, about these prayers, about the sun and stars and moon, about the sunlight, about the lightning, rainbow, about different kinds of winds, about different kinds of waters, things like that. Some of them were short stories; some of them were long stories. I just knew a little about those things. I didn't know all of them.

That evening the man came back with the herd and we fed him a lot and he liked it very much and that evening the medicine man said prayers for us again. This time he said the prayer that is called Yaiya Nizin. There were long prayers this time. He said, "This is the strongest prayer and now nobody and nothing will bother you. If anybody tries to do something to you he can't do anything to you. If he tries to kill you he won't kill you. If anybody tries to witch you he can't witch you. He can't kill you with his witching. You won't get hurt by anything. Lots of things strike but you won't get struck by anything. In my say you'll live long and you'll get to see a grey hair and maybe you'll die in old age." That's what he said to us after he said this prayer, and after that we all went to bed.

Next morning everybody started cooking. The medicine man said, "After we eat we will start the doings. Everybody hurry with the things around here and straightening up and, if you want to kill a sheep, you can do it right now because after the doing starts then you shouldn't kill a sheep again until five days are up. So if you want to kill one butcher it now. I want to start early this morning so you'd better hurry and cook a little lunch and we'll just eat a little this morning."

After we ate they went out and got two sheep and they killed and butchered them. The man that herded for us yesterday helped butcher these sheep. After they butchered them they put the meat away on the trees and the medicine man told those who had butchered to wash their hands. They washed their hands and we started to pick out mixed beads and the other things that go with it. Then he asked for a tree that had been struck by lightning. It was right outside close by. Then we went out there. I went first, next my mother, and behind us, the medicine man. We went to this tree and we stood from the east side of the tree. I stood in the middle and my mother on my right side and the medicine man on the left side. We put the mixed beads and other stuff under this tree and then he said to us, "Hold the tree with your left hand; hold it, don't let it go until we are through saying prayers." We held the tree with our left hands and he started saying prayers for us and then when we had finished saying prayers from the east side—the prayers were for Black Lightning—we walked a little ways from the tree and we went towards the south and we turned around and we walked up to the tree from the south side, faced south, went a little ways from the tree, turned and faced north and went up to the tree. He told us to hold it again just the same way. So we held it again with our left hand and we started just the same way again. My mother stood on the right side of me and the medicine man on the left side and then he said, "We'll say a prayer that's called Blue Lightning." We said prayers again from the south side of the tree and then he backed out again and we passed in front of him again. We went towards the west and we turned towards the south and we walked up to the tree from the west side and we held the tree and we stood there just the same again, my mother on the right side and the medicine man on the left side. From there the prayers were called Yellow Lightning. We said prayers and then after we were through saying prayers we did just the same way again. The medicine man backed out and we passed him again and went towards the north a little ways from the tree. Then we turned around towards the south and we went up to the tree from the north side and we held it again with our left hands and we stood just the same way again. Then we stood from the north side of the tree and he started with White Lightning and we began to say prayers again.

After we said all the prayers we stood there for a long time. He was just saying prayers by himself. I don't know what kind of prayer; he didn't mention that prayer and it was a long prayer. When he was through he prayed to the different things again, praying to the earth, to the sky, to the sun and moon, to the mountains and to the waters and we repeated the prayers after him. He said, "From the east side everybody will know me and take care of me and from the south side everybody will know me and take care of me and from the west side everybody will know me and take care of me and from the north side everybody will know me and take care of me. I'll live long right in the middle of them. I'll have a long life and I'll enjoy life and I'll be happy all the time. I'll have lots of properties, sheep, horses, and other stocks. I'll have lots of grub of different kinds and so that I'll live long and I'll be strong, I'll be lively." That's the way he ended it and when we started back to the hogan. While we were going back he sang from behind us and when we got inside the hogan he was still singing for quite a while. When he stopped singing he said, "Now one of you better go and get the soap weed roots. Get two roots and after that you bring some dirt inside and put the roots right close to each other and right on top. Those two who are being treated will take a bath and when they are through taking a bath you take the dirt out and put it away some place in the shade. Now one of you go and get some soap weed."

Then Slim Man went out and, when the soap weed was brought back and the dirt was brought in and the water was brought in right there, I don't remember whether we used two baskets or one basket to bathe in. Anyway I took a bath first. I undressed but I left my g-string on, and bathed right before everyone. Then my mother undressed and bathed and the women stood around, holding blankets around her. After that the medicine man started to dry me with the white corn meal and he dried my mother with yellow cornmeal. Then he took the corn pollen out and he touched us with that. He touched us on the bottom of the feet, both sides, and on our knees and on both palms, and on our breasts and back on both shoulders and he gave us some. He put it on our tongue and he put some on top of our heads. This is what he did while he was singing and they took the dirt and the soap weed out and put them away someplace. Afterwards we dressed up again and we all ate.

After we ate he started saying some prayers again. He said a long prayer for us again, but this time he put all the arrow heads away and he took the bundle held with the left hand and put that away. He just gave me medicine and he gave my mother a prayer stick. We held it in our right hand and over our left hand. We held it with our left hand and we held it with both hands, and corn pollen also. Then we ate a lot. After we were through with these doings the medicine man said, "There are no more doings from here on all day. This is what you call One Day Sing right now. All you have to do is to talk, smoke, tell stories about different things to each other and eat all you want."

Then the medicine man and Slim Man told stories and they talked all day till evening again. That's the way they were in these four days. Slim Man never went back to his home. He stayed right there for four days. In the evening the man brought back the herd again and as soon as he put the herd in the corral he started to gather some wood and he chopped it. We had enough wood to last all night. When it got real dark Slim Man said, "We'll start right now, we'll start early this evening to sing and I'd like to hear some of my grandfather's songs. We want all the big songs, not small songs."

Then we started with the doings again. I spread out a robe and right on top I spread out some calico and on top of the calico I spread out a buckskin and on top he put the basket full of his medicine, and he said, "Put everything right here in front of this medicine. You can put ropes or bridles or whips right in front of the basket. The women, too, put your weaving outfits right in front of this basket and put your offerings right here with mine too." But we didn't have any corn pollen at all. Then he said, "Take this corn pollen, spot it over the white spots and after you finish spotting with this corn pollen in all four directions sprinkle some around in the hogan." Then Slim Man did those things.

After that the medicine man started singing and he kept on with his singing all night long. He had such long songs. The two fellows were singing after him. After midnight we all had lunch and he started singing again, and he sang all night till morning. He stopped singing while it was still dark in the morning and he told us to go out and look around and stand facing toward the east and spread out our hands and inhale the morning four times. We did. We went out and we inhaled the morning four times and then we turned around towards the south and went back inside the hogan. After we came back inside he gathered up his medicines, fixed them up and put them away in his sack. Then he said, "Now this is all about the Blessing Way and from here on don't be afraid of anything and don't worry about yourself and nothing will happen to you and you'll live long and your mother and you both will live long. As I said to you before, your mother will

100

die with old age and you'll be just the same too. I sang all the songs and all these songs are strong and the prayers are just the same. All the prayers that I said are all strong prayers so don't think that something will happen to you. I know we never missed any prayers or any songs."

He patted Slim Man on his lap and he said, "I know very well that we didn't miss anything and you know that very well too, my grandson." Then Slim Man said to this man, "Well, I'm glad you did all these doings for us and I know you did all of them in the right way and I'm very thankful to you. Thank you very much for helping us with your ceremony and with your treatment and I'm glad you came here. We stayed here for five days and we never went back to our home. I live close here and you live still closer. But we both never went back to our homes." Then the old man said, "Yes, grandson, that's right. I guess we ought to go back to our wives. I guess maybe they missed us and maybe they think that we left them. Maybe they think we are not coming back to them." Then he laughed about it and he said, "You are a great man, grandson. You came here just the same as I did, the same day, and you started to ask me about different things. Now I know you know a whole lot. I know you know it all." He said, "Take my medicine outfit out for me and take it back to my place. From there you can go home."

Then before he went he said to me, "You shouldn't go anyplace from here on. You should stay right here for four or five days and after that you can go any place you want again. After the four days are up some say you can take a bath again but in my way of thinking you shouldn't take a bath because I put the corn pollen all over you. You shouldn't wash that away. Leave it on you for a long time and then you can take a bath from there on." Then they both went out and they went back to their homes.

I kind of believed this old man after he treated us with his ceremony. He had said to us that we will live long and both will die in old age and he told us nothing will bother us. There are all different kinds of sicknesses around. They never bothered us. When a whole lot of people died off here with some kind of big sickness (influenza) it never bothered us.

There were lots of people dying off but I just didn't get that sickness and my mother lived a long time and she died with old age. Now I am getting to be an old man right now. So that's why I kind of believed that old man.

I was thinking that I would go out with the sheep that morning but the man that herded for us came in again and he said, "I want to herd again this morning. I'll let them go, I'll stay with you and help for a few days and then I'll go and catch up with them." I said, "All right, I'm glad that you want to help me. So he went out with the herd again that morning, and when the five days were up he was still herding. He said, "I like to herd the sheep very much and I get enough to eat, too, so that's why I like to herd for you, my father's brother. I'll stay around here with you." He stayed around there herding every day. It was just because he liked my mother. That was why he stayed around there.

6

Ceremonies, singing, prayers for
Slim Man's clan mother . . . His mother
"marries" the man who was herding for her.

Slim Man came to our place and he said, "I heard that
my mother (clan mother) up on the Black Mountain
is very sick. I'd like to know what you think about it. I'd like
you to go over there with me. We'll see our mother, see how
she is. So we'll go over. I'm figuring on going over tomorrow
morning and you get ready early tomorrow morning and
come over to my place and we'll start from there as soon as
we can." I said to him, "I'm willing to go over." Then he said
to this man that was herding for us, "How long are you going
to stay around here my younger brother?" This man said, "I
guess I'll stay around here and help until he comes back."
Then Slim Man said to him, "Well, that will be fine if you stay
around here. I'm glad you are staying here and helping these
people. You stay, my younger brother, he said to him again."
My father went back home and the next day I went out and
got the two horses which we used for the herding. I put
saddles on both of them and I said to my wife, "We'll go over
and if I can borrow a horse from there I want you to bring
this horse back." We went over to my father's place. My wife
started back home.

Slim Man and I started after we ate some lunch. We
passed many places and crossed the valley. Way on the other
side there was a hogan and we got to that place. We tied our
horses outside to the wood pile. We went inside and there we
found the woman was very sick. We went up to her and we
shook hands and Slim Man started to talk to her. When we
came up to her she started to cry. She tried to but she just
couldn't cry. She just hung her head for quite a while. She
asked Slim Man when we came and Slim Man said, "We just

103

came a little while ago." Then Slim Man got up and sat back. I went up to her again and I started to talk to her but she just didn't notice it. I told her, "You poor sister, you are very sick again. I've been around lots of these places where some of the patients died off and I've been helping them. I heard yesterday that you were very sick and now I am here and I find that you are very sick." But when I talked to her it seemed to me that she just didn't notice it and I looked up and there was Choclays Kinsman sitting there. I don't know when he got there and I guess he knew that she was sick and had heard it from somebody, but he never let us know. There was a medicine man there. His name was Leather Leggings. He was there treating her and Yellow Singer was there. That was his wife that was sick. A boy was there, Many Goats, and a girl, this woman's daughter. Yellow Singer was their stepfather. They said, "We've been treating her for a long time but she is getting worse all the time. We just don't know what's wrong with her. We did a lot of things for her, all kinds of ceremonies, singing, and prayers but she is just getting worse all the time. Choclays Kinsman said, "I was here and treated her too. We got this medicine man here again and he treated her but she is still the same way. He'll get through with his treatment tormorrow and then he is going home and I don't know what we'll do after that."

Slim Man said, "I'll find out myself what's wrong with her. I'll see what's bothering her. I'll see if she'll live or not. I'll find out myself right now so give me the water. I'll wash my hands." We gave him water and he washed his hands and he got his corn pollen out. He sprinkled it all over on his hand and on his arm and then he said prayers. He said, "My hand is moving and by that I'll find what is bothering my mother. My hand will tell me just what's wrong with her." After he said this little prayer he told the others to sing for him and then he started to shake his hand. He shook his hand for quite a while and then he stopped and sat back and said, "I just couldn't find anything. I don't know what's wrong with her but I know she is very sick and nobody in the world will cure her and she won't get well. There is just no hope for her. She'll live for three days. That's as far as we will

104

see our mother. From there on we cannot see her anymore. That's the way my hand told me."

It was around evening then and they told the medicine man to stay. "Don't try to go home. We want you to sing over her the songs that drive death and bad spirits away, and keep your eagle feathers here with you and try to drive the bad spirits away from her with your eagle feathers." The medicine man said, "It's no use for me to stay around here. I've been around here for several days." But Choclays Kinsman told him to stay to help anyway. Then this medicine man started to sing and wave his eagle feathers over this woman. When he was doing this I was so tired and sleepy I just went to sleep. I never did wake up until next morning. Everybody was still sitting up. Nobody had slept that night, only me.

Next day this medicine man cut up little sticks that are called Thunder God sticks. The medicine man treated the patient with those sticks and then Slim Man took these sticks away. He came back and he said, "It's just no use for us to do things. When I was out there with those sticks, when I put them away, a whole lot of great big blue flies scattered all around me so that means she won't live. We can't cure her." Then Choclays Kinsman kind of didn't believe that. He said, "Flies around! I never heard about flies being around in this time of year. I never saw a fly. I wonder what kind of flies there are at this time of year when the snow is on the ground. When it's cold like now there aren't any flies around." Yellow Singer said, "I believe it. That's not a regular fly. I don't think they are the flies that we see from spring on and all summer long, and that means bad luck when you see a fly this time of year." After that the medicine man said, "Well, it's no use for me to stay around here. When things happen like that I know that means bad luck. It means a patient won't live. When you see things like that, that's bad. I'll go home right now." Then he gathered up his medicine and he took it outside. Then Choclays Kinsman said to him, "Well all right, my nephew (they were not related at all; they just called each other that), you can go. You helped me a whole lot with your singing, with your treatment of all kinds, and I'm thankful about it, so you can go now." Then he went.

After he left they began to talk about him. They said, "That fellow is no medicine man if he is afraid of the patient. Even though the patient is still alive he gathered up all his stuff and he went home so he is not a medicine man." Choclays Kinsman said, "I don't do that. When I do something for the patient, even if the patient is very sick, I stay right with him till I cure the patient or till the patient dies. I don't leave the patient until I know the patient is really dead. That's the way I do." Then Choclays Kinsman said, "That is the right way to do but I know that fellow is afraid. It's no use for him to be afraid of the patient."

Then we just did nothing all that day; we just sat around there watching her and that evening Yellow Singer took his rattle and eagle feathers inside. He just waved around with his eagle feathers over his wife. He was doing that all night every once in a while. Everybody was awake again all that night. She couldn't swallow anything; she didn't know anything; she had no feeling at all. The next day, all day, we sat around in the hogan just watching her. That evening Slim Man said, "The days are coming to where my hand told me my mother will be dead in three days. The three days are coming closer." We just sat there and watched her. She was going down all the time and pretty soon her feet and hands started to get cold even though they had kept them warm. Pretty soon it was getting cold up to the knee and it was that way during the night. Pretty soon her legs were all cold just like when you are out and get cold all over. It was just like that. Pretty soon there was a little warm spot right at her breast. The rest was all cold. About midnight she died so that was the last of her and the work was over.

Then her children and her husband started to cry and the three of them were holding her while they were crying. Yellow Singer and I took the things over to another hogan and the others were all holding her while they were crying for quite a while. There we were all in sadness, and after a while they let her go and we all began to take things out. We took everything over to another hogan and we stayed around there. Then Choclays Kinsman came out and said to us, "Did you take all the things over to the hogan?" We told him we did and he told us not to go away until we fixed her up. He said to the others, "Now I guess you have got through crying. You all let her go now and you all know that she has died so it's no use for you to hold her. You can't get her back to life. You can't cure her so it's no use for you to hold her. You'd better let her go and we'll all fix her up." Then the two children were moved away from their mother and Yellow Singer was still holding his wife.

Then Choclays Kinsman went up to him and he took hold of him around his wrists and he told him, "Let the dead body go. She is dead. What do you want to hold on to the dead body for? Let that dead body go, my younger brother (he called him). You know she is dead. She cannot come back to life and it's not only you that's lost a wife. There are lots of others losing each other, like me. I lost my mother the other day too. She wasn't a real mother of mine but she had raised me and so when she died the other day, from then on I'm all alone." That's what he said to Yellow Singer and then he took him away from his wife and raised him up with both hands by holding his wrists, and he stood him up and walked him away from his wife. We all started to wash her and we put a rug skirt on her and then we put the red belt around her and a silver belt on top of this red belt and a bunch of beads around her neck. But those beads didnt have any string of turquoise on it.

After we dressed her we just lay her there and covered her up. We all started out and we picked up a coal and took it along with us to the next hogan. We just sat around there and everybody was crying and we were up all that night. Nobody went to sleep and we were just talking to each other all that night. We talked to each other about death. They thought that I was a good man because I was there with them all that time and I helped them with everything so they were kind of thankful about me. They gave me thanks for helping them all this while. Early that morning Yellow Singer said, "What will we do now? Talk about it?"

Then Slim Man said to him, "Well this morning we'll do some work before we eat anything, so you'd better bury your wife and you, too, my younger brother (referring to Many

Goats) better help. You are, both of you, my younger brothers so you both better go and bury the body. Fix it up yourself the way you want to and then, when you go over, get a horse and put a saddle on it and lead it to the door. That's to put her on and lead the horse away with her." Then they both undressed. Both untied their hair and they put ashes on themselves. Then they went over to the hogan where the body was and they took her out and put her on the horse, and they led the horse away with her. When they took her away a boy (Yellow Singer's nephew) made a fire for those two and he got the water over there for them where the fire was, and he put the medicine in the water for them. He had it all ready over there for them. I tended to the sheep, rounding them up right there at the hogan. Quite a while after they took her away we heard a shot and they had buried her and killed the horse. They came back from where they buried the body and they got to where this fire was and they washed themselves with this mixed medicine. After they washed themselves they came back to the other hogan, where they dressed themselves again. The others had food all ready and we all ate; after we ate they went out with the herd.

Afterwards I said to Choclays Kinsman, "I guess I'll go home now, my grandfather. I'd like to go back home now." He said, "No, you stay here with us. You know we are all alone. Stay with us. We'd like to have your help until after the four days are up. Then we can all go home. So don't go, my grandson." My father Slim Man was in sorrow. He didn't say anything to me. He was just keeping quiet and then we all kept quiet. These two that had buried the body stayed together like they always do. The girl who had dressed her mother just sat around. That's what they told her—they told her she mustn't do anything all day. From tomorrow on she could start cooking things, start to do things. I just helped around with water and wood and, in the evening, I took care of the horses. The man was in the hogan on the northwest side, and the boy on the northeast side. (When they go out the man gets up and goes out first and then the boy follows; when they come in the man goes first and the boy behind.)

Choclays Kinsman was the only one who talked to us.

That evening he said to us, "Now we all watch the fire and help it go all the time. You mustn't have darkness in the hogan and we have to sit up until way late in the evening. Then we'll go to bed and, when you lie down, cover yourself all up. You mustn't roll over while you're lying down. If you're tired lying one way you must get up and sit up and then if you want to lie another way you can. We should all get up early in the morning while it is still dark and we must keep this up all the time. There are only two ways to lie, only on your sides, sideways; not on your back and not on your belly. This evening while it's still kind of light make a line with the ashes on the north side of the hogan and nobody should go on that side and they shouldn't go over this line."

Next morning early I built a fire and I melted some snow for the water. When I had enough water two of us started cooking, myself and the boy, and, after we ate, we all just sat around there doing nothing. The herd was out again. There was only one person herding. Quite a while after we ate I went out and looked for the horses. I missed one horse, the one that I rode over, and I started to track it. I tracked the horse for a long ways. It was noon when I caught up with him. Then I rode the horse back and I got back to that place in the afternoon.

Choclays Kinsman was the only one who talked all the time. He said, "You must just keep quiet and you must not break things," and he said to the two who buried the body, "You shouldn't bother anything. You must leave everything alone. You mustn't touch your saddles, bridles, ropes, or whips and you mustn't talk about them. You mustn't talk about the sheep or the horses. You two just keep still and keep quiet. Let the things lie around till the days are up. From there on you can do all the work that you have been doing." I was the only one that went around for them all the time and then that evening we all stayed up until way late in the night again.

Next morning while it was still dark we all got up again and I started to do the same things again. I built a fire, I got the snow and melted it for the water. This time the girl cooked the meal and we all ate. After we ate the herd was out and I went after the horses again. This time the horses were all together so I just looked at them and I let them stay there. Then we were just sitting around there all that day again; and, in the evening, we went to bed again. We always went to bed way late in the night. Next morning I did just the same thing again. We all ate and after we ate the other fellow went out with the herd again. We ate in the morning, and in the evening we ate again, and sometimes at noon.

That was the third morning and Choclays Kinsman said to me, "Now, my grandson, you gather up some more wood and have enough chopped because tonight we have to sit up till midnight. We'll have a fire going all this time and, when you gather enough wood and chop enough, you gather up some snow and melt the snow for water and make enough water for all of us to use tomorrow. Early in the morning we'll wash ourselves with it. When you have enough water get some soap weed and have that ready for tomorrow too. We should get up a little earlier than we have been doing before because we have to wash ourselves and we have to be done before daylight. So you must get everything ready for tomorrow, my grandson."

Next morning early Choclays Kinsman woke us up. He told me to build a big fire and I went out and brought some wood in and I built a big fire. I had the water all warmed up and they made soap for those other two. First they both washed their hair and they washed themselves all over. After that we washed our hair and washed ourselves all over and then, when we were through washing, these two fellows went out and they went towards where they buried the body. They just looked over there and just gave one look over where they buried the body and then came back inside. This time they came inside the hogan on the south side and they both sat on the south side of the hogan. Then they took the corn pollen out and we all took some corn pollen. Then the old man said to us again, "Now from here on you can tend to your work, the work you have been doing, and you must take care of yourselves. Take care of each other, take care of your things and your herd and all your stock and you must pray for yourself all the time that you'll live a good and a long life."

110

Slim Man said, "Now I was here when my mother was still alive and I called her 'mother' and I had been saying 'my mother' all the time when I was here with her. It's four days ago now since I used to say 'my mother.' From here on I have no mother; I cannot say 'my mother' to anybody. All of my mothers are now dead. One died a few days ago and this one was the only remaining mother I had. She died four days ago. This is as far as I said 'mother.' From four days on I stopped saying 'mother' and I will be that way in all my life because I haven't got any mothers. I can say younger brother, younger sister, mother's brother, or sister's son—that's all I can say from here on. We haven't got any more mother, my younger brother. Now you've got nobody to talk to, nobody to go around with. You are all alone now. But it's up to you. You can go anywhere you want to go and you can get another wife for yourself. You are still a young man yet and I won't say anything about you because you've been taking good care of my mother for me so you can go and get you another wife."

Yellow Singer said, "That's right and I'm very thankful to you for what you have said to me and I'm glad that you think that way about me. I'm very sorry for my wife because I liked her very much and she was the same way to me, too, but I didn't live long with her. I just lived with her for a few days it seems to me. She was a kind woman and I was the same way to her and now she is gone away from me. I look around. It seems like she was just away to some place. It looks like she will be back some time so I'm glad that you talked to me that way. Now I'll be all alone and I'll sure miss my wife. I'll be in sorrow from here on. I don't know how long." And he hung his head down and he started to cry.

Then Slim Man talked to this boy and the girl. "Now you both are alone and there isn't anybody living around here close to you. You'll be lonesome and you sure will miss your mother. I can't say that I want you to go to some place be- cause if I said to go to some place maybe you won't like the place, so now it's up to you both. You can move anywhere you want to move. I live down here at the foot of the moun- tain and we both are living down there, I and my father (he meant me). I'm living right close to him because we help each

111

other right along and we are getting along nicely. There are other people down there and they are the same clan as your mother, so there are five families down there right close to each other, five with us two. So it's up to you both, if you want to move down there it will be fine." That was all about that.

They didn't say anything about the property and about the sheep and the horses. Nobody said anything about it so I don't know just how much property she had and I don't know how many sheep and horses she had. They didn't talk about those things but they just told the boy and the the girl they should take care of all their things, sheep and horses and everything they had. The boy, Yellow Singer's nephew said, "I'll stay around here for a while. When I want to I'll leave here. I've got relatives, many relatives and friends, all the way up in the canyon. I've got lots of relatives all around there so we two (Yellow Singer and his nephew) will go over there with some of them."

This was just after the four days were up; after we took a bath and after they were through talking. We brought the horses back; we put saddles on the horses and the others put their saddles on their horses and packed their stuff on their horses and turned the sheep out. "We'll help you drive the sheep for quite a ways and then from there on we'll all go back to our homes and when we are all moved one of you make a line across our track again." So they made a line across our track with the ashes and we moved away from there towards the southeast. We went a long ways from that place and then we told them, "You can move and camp some place tonight and from tomorrow on you can move any place you want to move." Then we went a long ways with them and there we let them go, and started back to our homes.

When I got home that afternoon there was that man[1] who herded gathering up the wood; he had a big pile of wood stacked. I thought he had run away from there. He and my mother were married and they were staying together. That's what I found when I got back home. I looked around

1. No name is given to this man.

112

there and I saw everything was all right and then I said, "I see that man is still around here. I thought he had left and gone some time ago but I see he's still around here." My mother said, "Yes, my son, he is still around here. He doesn't want to go away. He was begging me to stay with him and he was begging me that way for a long time. He said, 'I'd liked to stay around here and I'd like to stay with you and I will help you out, I will help you along with all these works you have. I see you've got lots of work to do and you are all alone so that's why I like to stay here and help you. I'd like to marry you.' When he said this to me I told him, 'No, I'm too old. I don't think about those kinds of things. I don't think about marriage anymore.' I told him to go and find a young woman but he said, 'No, even though you are old I want to stay with you.' Then my daughter-in-law said to me, 'Take him grandmother. Let him stay with you. I think he's a good man. He was around here for a few days now and I know now that he's a good man and he's a good worker and he can do anything without your telling him. He just goes ahead with all the works so take him grandmother.' That's what she said to me. So I didn't say any more words and I just went ahead and took him. So now he's staying with me. We are married."

I said to my mother and to my wife, "Well, I guess you think that he is a good man and a good worker but I don't think so. If he was a good worker and if he knew all about different kinds of works he would have a wife and family; he would have property and stock but he hasn't got anything. He just goes around to the different hogans and I think that he is a gambler. He is a liar and he is a cheater. I think that's the kind of man he is so you wait and see whether he is a good man or not. That's the way I'm thinking about him." That's all I said.

After a while he came back inside and he came up to me and he shook hands with me. He called me father's brother, brother's son, and I called him by the same term. "You've been away for a few days and we all kind of missed you." he said. I said, "Yes, I was away for all this while. That's what I always do. When I go someplace I always stay

113

away from home for quite awhile." He said, "I was out with the herd yesterday, way out in the flat. There one old wether played out on me and I left it there and yesterday evening when I came back with the herd I told about that and they told me to butcher it and bring the hide back tomorrow if the coyote hadn't bothered it. So this morning I went over there with the herd again. He was just the same. I couldn't get him to go any further and I opened his mouth. He had no teeth so I just cut his throat and I butchered him and I brought the skin back." I said, "Yes there are a lot of them that way. They are old now." Then he said, "I'd like to stay around here with you. I like you people so well so that's why I stayed here. I started to beg your mother to stay with her. She said it would be all right. So we are married now and that's why I'm still staying here." I just said, "Well I think it will be all right. It's all right with me." Then I said to my wife, "Did you go and see to the horses?" and she said, "Yes, I was out and I rounded up the horses two days ago and they are all right. They are all there." I said, "That's all right. I'm glad to hear that. I was worrying about my horses but now I know they are all right and they are all there." Then my mother said, "We ran out of corn, my son. We haven't got any corn so think about that. I think you'd better go and get some corn." I said, "All right, I'll go over tomorrow."

7

He and his wife go to where their
corn is buried . . . The old wethers
die off . . . Rounding up horses . . .
Visit to his wife's relatives . . . His mother's
husband leaves . . . They move to Gray Hills
and he never shows up again.

early next morning I brought some horses back. I took
two and I turned the rest out, and I saddled those
up and my wife and I started to go where we had buried the
corn. I said, "We'll just bring a little because we have to move
again pretty soon, as soon as the snow melts away." It was
quite a long ways and we just took our time and we got to
where we buried our corn when the sun was pretty well
down. It was too late to open the hole so we just went on to
where Slim Man had a hogan. We made a fire and my wife
started cleaning out the hogan and I took the horses where
there was some feed. I hobbled them over there and I gathered up some wood. We stayed in that hogan that night. Next
morning I went after the horses. They had gone a long way
from that place. I got the horses and we started back to where
we had our corn buried. We got some corn out there, two
sacks, both of them half full.

Next morning after we ate I said, "I want to put up a
fence across the canyon. I'll use that for pasture after the
snow melts." So I picked up my ax and I rode the horse all
around to see how the place looked. There was lots of food for
the stock and there were lots of different kinds of grass, all
kinds of weeds, different kinds of brush and different kinds
of trees. There were lots of different kinds of salt weeds. Then
I thought, "I will put up a fence across the narrow place and
I'll use this place for all my stock. There is plenty of food for

all of them." I went back to where the narrow place was and I chopped the trees down and I started to put up a fence across the canyon. I was doing this all day that day till night; then I went back home. Everything was all ready to be eaten. Then we just talked about things there. "That place is a big place and there is lots of feed for all the stock and we'll use that place when the snow melts away and maybe we'll move over to that place."

Then the man that stayed with my mother said, "Since I began herding sheep three wethers played out on me. I don't know why they are doing that and now I'm kind of scared of it." I said to him, "I told you to have a knife with you. There are lots of them that are old there. Lots of them will get that way and any time when they play out you just kill them and skin them." He said, "Oh I don't like to do that. I don't like to kill your sheep and I don't like to carry a knife around after the herd. They might think I am crazy carrying a knife after the herd." I said, "Don't be afraid. Just any time they play out you kill them and skin them and bring the skin back with you."

Next morning after we ate I told my wife and my mother, "You two better butcher those two old wethers and have the meat put up on the trees for the dogs. Those shepherd dogs are kind of hungry. I'll go and get the horses back and go over where I've been making the fence. I want you to help me on the fence, my father's brother." I told him and he said, "All right. While you go after the horses I'll butcher those two old wethers. Maybe by the time I'm through you'll be back with the horses." I brought back the horses I wanted to use and the horses that they use for herding, and when I got home the man was finished with the butchering. He put the meat in the trees and he washed his hands and he said, "It seems funny to me. I never saw or knew something to happen like this before." I said, "What is it?" He said, "Well, this is the first time in my life I got to see the old wethers dying off. They ought to have been used a long time ago and now they are wasted; only the dogs will eat the meat. They ought to have been used for something a long time ago. I was

116

around to different hogans but I never saw such a thing as this."

I said to him, "You are right. They ought to have been used a long time ago but we didn't have anything to use them for. We were only two at the time, only my mother and I, so that's why we didn't use them. We just used little lambs for meat to eat and that was enough for us. When we sometimes killed a big sheep it got rotten on us so that's why we let them get old. They are dying off now but I'm glad of that." While we ate we were talking that way and we heard the dogs barking outside. My wife went out to look and she came in and said, "There is Slim Man riding horseback. He is coming close here." Then he came in and he said, "You've got some sheep butchered. I see you've got a whole lot of mutton on the trees. It's going to knock that tree down. What did you kill so many sheep for? Are you going to Mopi's place?" I said, "No, that's the old wethers that are played out. They couldn't walk. They couldn't stand anything so we just killed them."

He said, "Where is your knife? You should use your knife on the throat when they are still young so they won't die on you. While they are still young you should kill them and eat them and then you won't waste them." Then he said, "If you had married long ago you wouldn't waste the meat because if you had married a long time ago you would have children. You would have five or six children by now and if you had children you wouldn't let the old wethers get too old on you because you'd use the wethers for mutton and for your children. But you didn't care for a wife and now you have nobody to help you." I just laughed about it and I said, "Yes, I didn't care for a woman because I thought they were not good for anything. I thought I can't use them for anything and my sheep, horses, and cattle were all that I thought about all the time. Those I can use and the woman I can't use for anything. I was single for a long time until now so now maybe I might have children." I laughed about it again and then the man that was there at our place said what he had said before. "Since I started herding sheep it seems funny that three old wethers played out on me. It looks like I am

117

killing them so I am kind of afraid of it, and every time I go out with the herd I'm always afraid." Slim Man told him, "You don't have to be afraid or worry about it. We don't worry about those things and we are not afraid of those things. We use them right along. We kill them any time when we want to. When they die they just die. We don't worry about them. Even if a good horse dies we shouldn't worry or be sorry for it because when the date is up they'll sure die off. We are all just the same, too. When our date is up we all die."

Then Slim Man said, "Where are you going? I see the horses standing out here. It looks like you are going off some place." I said, "No, I'm not going off any place. I'm just going over to that canyon. I was over there yesterday all day and I'm putting up a fence across the canyon where that narrow place is. That's where we are going this morning. We want to put up a fence across the canyon so that we'll use it for a pasture." He said, "I don't think that's a good place for the stock because the ground over there when it gets wet will sure catch something. All that place is gummy. That blue clay when it gets wet sure sticks and when it gets real wet it'll sure hold something tight. Maybe sheep, horses, or cattle will get caught in it. You ought to have your stock out in the flat and there is no water up there for the stock. You'll have too much work if you put your stock up there at that canyon. If you've got your stock out in the flat you don't have to bother with them all the time. When they want to get water they'll go and get water themselves." I said, "I want to put up a fence anyhow. I know there is no water up there but there is lots of feed. That's all I want." Then we put the saddles on our horses and we took the ax and we went along with Slim Man as far as where he lived, and then we went on. We got to that place and we started to put up a fence. We worked on the fence all day again and in the evening when we got home I told the man, "I want you to help me round up the horses. We'll take them up there." My mother had the herd back in the corral. The food was about ready and we started eating. After we ate we just sat around talking for a while and we went to bed.

118

Next morning I went out and got the horses again. I got one for myself and I got another one for the old man who had married my mother (I don't know just how old he was but I know he had some grey hairs). They had cooked the food again and, when we all ate, I told this man, "I want you to help me on the horses today. First we'll take the wild ones up there where we had the fence up. We'll go now. I'll go way around the hills. You go around here and round up the horses which are out here in the flats." Then he said, "I don't know about the horses. How about that? I don't know any of your horses. Maybe I'll get the horses that don't belong to you. Maybe I'll leave some of the horses that belong to you. I don't know anything about your horses. Your wife knows all the horses and you both ought to go and I will go out with the herd again." I said, "It's all right with me. You can go out with the herd and I'll go out with my wife." Then right away my wife said, "I'm willing to go. I like to ride," and we went out. She went around the flat and I went around the hills and we gathered up all the horses. We took them where we had put the fence up and put them in there. We had the gate fixed so they wouldn't get out.

We got home and the old man was back with the herd again. I asked him how many of the sheep were played out again. "None this time; only one sheep had a lamb." I said, "Yes, they'll start lambing from here on so I guess I'd better fix a corral for them. After that we'll move back over there. The next morning I went out for the horses again and I was thinking, "I'll take the man over with me to help me on the corral or maybe I'll take my wife over. I'll see after I bring the horses back."

When I got back with the horses my mother said, "My son, your wife would like to go and visit her folks. She said she is kind of lonesome for her grandmother. She would like to go and see her. She hasn't seen her grandmother for a long time. She said, 'Even though my mother left me I'm lonesome for them all.' " Then I thought, "That's right. She's been away from her home for a long time, over a year (even though

119

it's not a year, as soon as the winter passes they say a year, or from spring to fall). I'll take her back and let her visit her people again." Then I said to this man, "I was figuring on fixing up the corral for the sheep. They are starting to lamb and it will be a whole lot of work when they start lambing. I thought before they start we'll have the corral fixed up and ready for them. It's got to be two corrals and I was figuring on going over today but my mother told me that my wife wants to visit her people so I guess I'll let the corral go. I'll take her back to her home and I don't know in just how many days we'll be back. I don't know just where her people are living."

I asked him, "When are you thinking that you are going back to your home my father's brother?" He said, "That's what I'm thinking about, too. I am that way, too. I am kind of lonesome for my people because it's a long time now since I left my folks. So I'd like to go back home soon. It was since fall that I left my place and we've been out here all winter. But I'll stay around here until you both come back again," he said to me. I said to him, "That will be fine, my father's brother. Stay here and help us till we come back and then you can go home and visit your people. I just don't know how long we will be gone. That's what I like to hear from you and I'm glad that you want to stay around here until we come back. Any time when you want to go back home you let me know so then I can help you out on something. I know that you've been away from your place for a long time now and I know you want to go back and visit your people. That's the way with me when I go out some place, even just for a few days, I always want to go back home. When we come back then you can visit your folks. I think we're going to start today but before we go I'd like to gather up some wood so you won't have to bother with the wood. Then you can just tend to the sheep and other things. My wife can gather up some snow. I don't think we'll stay away long. Maybe when we get to her place we'll stay for two or three days. I'm sure we'll be back in three days."

Then he turned the sheep out and I told him, "Take an old blanket with you. Maybe they'll start lambing from here on. Maybe two or three of them will have little ones today.

120

Then you put them in the blanket and bring them back. Then they won't freeze on you. You should take care of them. Some sheep when they want to lamb kind of hide themselves. So you have to watch them close. If two or three of them lamb put the little ones right at one place and you just herd around them and watch them close so nothing will get them." Then he went out with the herd. I dragged in some wood and I started to chop it. My wife brought some snow on horseback. She had a lot of it piled, too. By that time it was noon and we got lunch and started off. Before we started I said to my mother, "I guess we'll start now and we are out of meat. To-morrow you can get another mutton so the old man can have some mutton all the time so he won't get hungry while he is herding. You kill a sheep tomorrow." She said, "I will. I'll do that."

Then we started off. We passed many places. There was somebody riding on horseback and we met him right where the trail crosses. I said to him, "We don't know just where we are going. We are going to my wife's mother's place; I wonder where she lives. Then he said, "I think she lives not far from here." So then we started on again and this fellow went on again, too. Then we got to where there was a little canyon. We went up the canyon and there was a rock point just a little ways from the hogan. There is where we stopped. We took the saddles off the horses and I said, "We'll stay here tonight. I'll take the horses up on the canyon and I'll hobble the horses up on top. You can go over to your home."[1]

The sun was down then and there were no dogs around. The dogs didn't see us or hear us and I took the horses on top of the canyon. I looked down from the canyon and I saw my wife go in the hogan. The dogs never did see her. As soon as she got inside the hogan I heard everybody crying as hard as they could and they were talking while they were crying. But I don't know just what they were saying. It was in a canyon and the wall of rocks was all around. So when they were cry-ing and talking the echoes went around the canyons, all around the walls. I kind of laughed about it. I hobbled the

1. Taboo prohibits a Navajo man from talking to or looking at his mother-in-law.

horses and I could still hear them crying even though I was quite a ways from there. I could hear the echoes go all around the canyon. I thought to myself, "What are they crying for? Maybe they thought about their old dead grandfathers and grandmothers." I went back down in the canyon. Then I gathered up some wood. I carried it down on my back and built a fire. She wasn't back yet. Then I went up again. It was getting dark and I gathered up some more wood and brought that down.

She had come back and I had lots of wood piled there. She said, "My folks were anxious to see me again. They almost tore me to pieces. They got on me and started crying and they all sure were anxious to see me again. They missed me very badly." I said, "That's good that your folks are anxious to see you. That's what I like to hear." She said, "They want me back over there again." So I told her, "Go ahead." She went over again and then she was gone for a while and I was staying there walking around the fire getting warmed up. Then she came back with some food. She came with her young sister. Her sister was about ten years of age. There was one whole rib cooked on the charcoal and there were some fried tortillas, some coffee, and some corn mush and water. Then her sister went back home and we started to eat. After we ate my wife had the bedding fixed up and she said, "They told me to come back again. 'When you are ready to go to bed, take your bed pelt and your buffalo skin and use it.' But I thought you had said you weren't going to use any of those sheep pelts or buffalo skins the rest of your life because they were taken away from us. So I said, 'We've got enough pelts for our bedding and enough blankets.' " "That's right," I said, "when they took away those things from us, I said of those pelts and buffalo skin, I won't use them again in my life so I'm thinking that way yet." But I told her, "You can go over again and talk with your folks for a while." Then she took all the dishes back and I just lay there.

While I was waiting for her four of her brothers came over and they shook hands with me and they said, "We came over to see you and we want to play the moccasin game." Older brother, they called me. I said, "All right." We started

122

playing; we bet each other with matches and silver buttons and we played for a long time. It would go one way and then another way. We kept on doing this all night and my wife had come back. At last we won. We got tired of playing and they went back home and we went to bed.

Next morning I dressed up and I just looked at the horses. It was almost daylight then and my wife came with some more food, some mutton and some fried tortillas and some coffee. When we ate my wife said, "My folks want to know when we are going back." I said, "We'll stay here again all day today and I'll go and take the horses to the water and then I'll bring them back and take them up and hobble them again on top of the canyon. I'll get some more wood for today and for tonight. So you can go over to your home and stay with your folks." Then she went over to her home. She took the dishes back and I stayed around there and after a while she came back and she brought over a piece of fresh meat. She said, "They wanted to kill one of my sheep so they killed one. She gave me that piece of meat and I put it on the charcoal and it was nice and fat. She went back again and then she brought one whole side of mutton and it was sure fat. I told her to cut it and have it laid out and let it dry. So she cut up the mutton thin and she spread the pieces all over the grease wood to have them dry.

Then I got the horses down and I took them to the water. After that I took them back up on top of the canyon, where I hobbled them again and then I gathered up some more wood. This time I had an ax with me; I threw a lot of it down to the foot of the wall and I cut some branches off of the trees. It was windy and I got down off of the canyon and dragged the branches over and laid them where the wind came from so then it was better. I brought wood over and piled it there. I was doing the little things all afternoon till evening and my wife came over again. She said, "My brother said he lost his silver button last night on the moccasin game so he said tonight I'm going to try to get it back." That evening when she came back she had a big bunch of beads around her neck, the beads her mother took away from her. She said, "I got my beads back. They told me, 'Take your beads. They are yours

123

from now on.' I didn't want to take them but they wanted me to. So I got my beads back." I said, "That's all right. Maybe some time they'll take them away from you again."

That evening the boys came again. The one that was on my side was on my side again and the oldest brother had brought one bow and some arrows. There were three arrows with the bow and my wife said to me, "Take it. You've got a bow and arrows at home, too." So then I said all right and he said, "If I win I'll go over to your place for the bow and arrows and then he said to his sister, "I'll bet you a goat, a year old goat." She said, "Which one? I know all your goats." He said, "That black goat's young one that's a yearling and it's a red goat." She said, "Oh, yes, I know that one" and then she said, "I've got a yearling about the same age." So they bet each other with goats and there were three on that other side and we were three, too, and then we started to play again. We played for a long time and at last we got all the sticks again and we won. Then they bet us again, they bet against their things. Pretty soon we got tired and we got hungry and I told my wife to make some lunch and when she had the lunch ready we quit playing. After we ate we played for a long time again. They got their things all back. We didn't win anything and they didn't win anything. They just got all their things back. It was around morning and we quit playing and then we went right to bed.

All at once I woke up and the sun was up and my wife was sleeping. I woke her up and we built a fire and while she cooked I brought the horses back and I said to her, "We'll go home this afternoon. Have the things all ready and you can stay with your folks till noon. I'd like to get back home as soon as I can because the sheep are starting to lamb. We'll go around where the corral is and maybe I can do something over there." We went to where our hogan was in the place where we were going to move and when we got there there wasn't any snow around nearby. There wasn't any water there and I said to my wife, "We ought to have borrowed a jug. If we'd done that we'd have water with us." Then I told my wife to ride over where the snow was and bring some snow back. She went over where the snow was and I cut

124

some branches down for the sheep corral. There was a sheep corral already made there but I wanted to put more brush around it to make it thicker so it would be warm for the sheep. While I was doing this my wife brought over some snow on the horse's back, and melted it. When she got water she started to cook and while she was cooking I had enough branches cut down and I dragged them in with the horse. She called me to eat so I went back to where she was cooking. After we ate I dragged the branches in again. I was doing that all day till evening and then I took the saddles off the horses, and I led them to where there was some feed for them. I hobbled them over there. We stayed there over night.

That evening my wife got out half a sack of corn meal. She said, 'This is what I got at my home. They wanted me to make some corn bread over there to take back to your mother but you wanted to go back home so I just put it in the sack.'' But she didn't tell me that when we were over at her place. If she had told me about it we might have stayed over there another day. Then we just went to bed and the next morning we got up and I went over where the horses were. They were close around there. She had the things ready to be eaten. After we ate I told her to take the saddle over to where the horses were and saddle up one and take the horses to the water. While she was gone I worked on the corral. I put some branches all around it. I started to make another one right against it. This was just a small corral for the lambs. She was away for a long time. When she brought the horses back I started to drag some more branches in with the horses and when I had enough dragged in I put some more over on the corral. I didn't have enough branches so I cut some more and then when I had put this one up against the other one I started with another smaller one. I had it half finished and I said to my wife, "I guess we'll go back home now. I'll finish the small one after we move here." She said, "We ought to stay here again tonight. You ought to finish with that one first. We've got enough food. We have some meat and some flour." But I told her, "I'll let it go. I'll fix that up when we move here so we'd better go home now."

Then she said, "All right," and then we saddled up our

125

horses, put our things on the horses and we started back home. We got back home when the sun was almost down. The man hadn't brought the herd back yet. I took the horses away and I turned them loose. My wife gave my mother that corn meal. My mother was so anxious to get the ·corn flour and she said, "Good for them and thank you all. I thank you all my children. I'm glad that they remembered me with the corn flour." She was awfully glad to get it. Then the man got back with the herd and there was lots of meat around and then my mother said, "There are three more old ewes that have played out. They were too old so he had to kill them and he brought the skins back with him. They all had little ones and one of the old wethers was played out too so I told him to take the knife and skin it and bring the skin back." Then I went out and I brought enough wood to last us tonight and tomorrow. I went back in the hogan and the old man was sitting there eating and my wife had some food cooked for me and we started to eat and my mother and the old man ate, too. While we were eating the old man said, "There are a whole lot of old ewes and wethers that are giving up and now I'm kind of scared of it. I hate to see them playing out. They were all right when I came here. As soon as I started to herd they started to play out on me so now I'm afraid. It worries me so much. It looks like I'm killing them." I said to him, "You don't have to be afraid of it and you don't have to worry about it. We all know lots of them got too old and we all know they all are going to die now. So we are not afraid of it and we are not worrying about it. Just let them die off. Every time they play out kill them and butcher them and just bring the skin back. That's all we care for. We don't care if the old ones die off. We'll have new lambs pretty soon, and we'll live on those lambs."

Then I said to him, "You wanted to go back home and to visit your people and you can go any time you want." Then he said, "I'll go in two days. I'd like to go back home and visit my relatives and I'm kind of lonesome for them. I don't think I'll be gone long. When I visit them all I'll come back again and help you on the lambing. I know you've got so much to do and I know you have to do all the work by your-

126

self so I'll be back and I'll help you." Then I said to him, "I will be glad when you come back and help me and I'll be thankful to you right now because you have helped me a lot. I think we'll be moving soon. I had the corral fixed so we'll be moving over there soon." After that he said, "Tell me about your trip, where have you been and how far is that place you went to." And so I did.

Next morning my wife and my mother had the food ready and, while we were eating, I said, "Today I'll go over where we took the horses and I'll see how they are. By now maybe they are staying at the gate and starving. One of you can go out with the herd." I told my wife, "I guess you have to go out with the herd this morning and let him take a rest. He's been herding for us all this time since he joined us so let him rest today and tomorrow. We know that he is going home to visit his relatives." I said to my mother, "Mother, you should make some lunch and kill one of those fat goats for him and cut it up in pieces. Let them dry today so he'll take that along with him and have some lunch for him so that when he is on his way he'll have something to eat. Fix every-thing nice for him because he's been helping us for a long time. Now be sure you do that, mother. Now you go and get one of your goats and kill it for him before the herd goes out." I told the old man, "You can take a rest today and get ready for tomorrow and my mother will have something fixed for you and she'll have something ready for you to take back to your home."

My wife was getting ready to take the herd out when my mother said to me, "You go and rope one for him. I haven't got any goats. Rope one of your goats. You've got lots of old ewes and wethers and the goats are just the same. I haven't got any so you go and rope one of yours. You are stingy for your sheep and goats and a lot of them got too old on you and are starting to die on you because you are stingy for them." I didn't say any more words. I picked up the rope and I roped a great big wether goat and I knew it was good and fat too. It was a yellow goat that I roped for him and I said to him, "Come over and get the goat, father's brother." He came over

127

and I gave him the rope and he tried to pull it but he couldn't. The goat just made one step or sometimes two steps. He tried his best to drag it over to the hogan. He got behind the goat and he took hold of both the hind legs. He tried to walk the goat with his front legs but the goat wouldn't go. He just looked back and looked at him and then he said, "Somebody come and help me." Then my wife went over and helped him. They both had a hard time pulling the goat. The goat was so big they couldn't carry it so they dragged it over to the hogan. They had lots of fun dragging it. Then they knocked the goat down and they had a hard time to tie its legs. I just stood around and laughed at them.

At last they had tied its legs and they cut the throat and they started to butcher it. The goat was sure fat. The whole meat was white with the fat. We had a hard time hanging it up. "Thank you very much, my son," he said to me. "You are so very kind. There is not a man in the world would let this kind of meat go. When I get back home my relatives will all be glad and they'll be anxious to have good and nice fat meat. I know they are wishing for meat like this." The old man was happy and was running around there giving us thanks every once in a while. Then my mother said, "Put a saddle on the horse for me, my son. I guess I'll go out with the herd and my daughter-in-law can cut up all the meat. She is quick on anything and you know I'm too slow on things like that so I just better go out with the herd." Then I told my wife she should cut up all the meat for him and let it dry so it wouldn't be so heavy for him to take along. Again the man said thanks to me. "I'm very glad that I've been eating nice fat mutton all this time. Since I came here I started to eat meat and I so enjoy it, and now you gave me this nice fat meat to take along with me. You all are so nice and kind to me. I've been to a whole lot of different places and I never saw any people that were so kind like you. You are the kindest people that I've met, so I'm so thankful about this nice fat meat. Thank you, father's brother."

Then before my mother went out with the herd we picked up the lambs and we put them away. There were about ten lambs. Then my mother went out with the herd

128

and I went over to where the horses were. When I got to the gate there were no new tracks around there. Not one of them came back to the gate. I rode way up in the canyon and there the horses were. They all looked fine and I knew they had enough feed and there was still plenty of snow on the ground up in that canyon. There wasn't any water in the canyon but they were using the snow for water. There was plenty of snow yet and I thought in about ten days the snow will be melted away. So I just let the horses stay there.

I fixed the gate up and I started back and then I thought, "I'll go over to my father's (Slim Man's) place." So I turned around and went to my father's place but only his wife was at home. I said to her, "Where is my father?" She said, "He's out with the herd. He's herding all the time. That's all he does." When my father came back with the herd he asked me, "When did you come, my son?" "I came here a little while ago. I was over to the other hogan with my mother for a while." He said, "I was out with the herd. I've been herding all the time because they are lambing. There are about forty lambs so that's all I tend to every day." Then he asked me if my sheep were starting to lamb too. I said "Yes, they are just starting, too. About ten of them had lambs. I guess by now there must be a little over ten. I left there this morning. I was up looking at my horses today and I thought I'll come over to visit you. I was going home but I turned around and I came here. I'm figuring to move back to where our other place is. I think there is a better place for lambing. I just fixed up the corral and I think we'll be moving over there soon." Then he said, "After you move how much work will you have?" I said, "I don't know but anyway it will be a lot of work for me because I have to put up another corral for the lambs. I got one up against the old corral but I'd like to have another one put up. What did you want to know for?" He said, "I'm thinking about moving over there, too. I thought if you haven't got much work you'll help us move over there." I said, "I don't think I'll have time because I am all alone now with only my mother and wife. You know my mother can't stand all the work and the man that stays with us is going home tomorrow. He was getting ready this morning and they

129

were getting his lunch ready for him so I don't know just how long he'll be gone. I'm figuring to separate all the sheep which had lambs. I'll cut them from the other bunch and I think I'll let my wife herd those and I'll start to herd the other bunch which are lambing. So now you see I won't have time to do any other kind of work, only what work I have to do. It's still too much for me, but anyhow I have to do it."

Then I started home. The man was still there. He had brought the herd back that evening. He had herded half of that day. Lunch was ready for us and while we were eating our supper I told about my trip that day. This man said to me, "Well that was nice, father's brother. I'd like to stay here till we move back to the other camp but you know we haven't got much grub now. I'd like to go back home, and I am thinking that I want to go to one of these stores around the river. I might get some grub for these skins from the old wethers and when I come back from there we will have some grub again." I asked him, "In about how many days will you come back?" He said, "Maybe in about eight or ten days. It all depends on getting grub. As soon as I get enough grub I will start back." He was getting ready, putting this dry meat in the sack. While he was packing up his things he gave us more thanks. Next morning early, as soon as he got dressed he said, "I will go after the horses." That was all he said and he went out. I said to my mother, "I wish that man would stay with us a little longer so that he can help us on moving." But my mother said, "Oh don't bother him. Let him go because he wants to go home. He would like to go back to his home quick so just let him go. I don't care."

I went out that morning and I went after the horses. After I brought them back everything was ready; all the things were packed, everything in bundles. Saddles and saddle-blankets were outside ready to put on the horses. While the two women were starting to saddle up the horses I went inside and started to eat my breakfast. After that I packed up the horses. This man had left already that morning. When we were through with the packing we started to move. We turned out the herd and we had quite a few little lambs. We

130

picked up the youngest ones which were not able to walk and carried them on horses. The others that were a little stronger we herded. On our way we picked up the little lambs that gave up while we were moving.

At a place called Where Little Arroyos Stop, at this little flat there was a big herd and that was Slim Man. He walked up to me, "You are moving now?" I said, "Yes, we are moving." He said, "I wish I was but it is kind of too heavy for me to move on account of these little lambs. These little lambs are not strong enough to walk yet but, anyway, I think we will move to that place some way. When we start to move will you come back to help us on moving?" I said to him, "Oh, no, I don't think so. I don't think I can because the sheep are just starting to lamb. We will have many lambs tonight and tomorrow so I've got to tend to my lambs also. But I will see when we get back to our camp. Maybe the folks will tend to the herds all right. I think they will so I will come back to your place tomorrow morning." He said, "That is good. Be sure and do that; I just can't do anything by myself. The herd hasn't had any water for two days. Now I'd like to cut those that haven't got lambs. I will do that early in the morning tomorrow. So when you come I'd like you to take them to the water for me." I said, "All right, I will do that," and then we went on.

We camped a little after noon and then as soon as we moved there I unpacked my horse and I went and got the baskets which the Paiutes make. I put the baskets over my saddle. As I started for the water I told them to just turn the sheep to the water after me but to keep the little ones here because they don't run fast. So I went on to the water. I filled the baskets up and I started back. On my way back there were the sheep coming and my wife was after the sheep. I met her and I let her have the horse that I was riding and I told her to take the water back. I got on the horse which she was riding and I took the sheep to the water. They were running as hard as they could to the water and they knew where the water was and they were at the water drinking and still running into the water. Those that hadn't got the lambs yet were slow. I waited around till they all came to the water.

131

When I knew they all had water I started back to the camp, to Gray Hills, where we wanted to move. On my way back there were some more little lambs. I just picked them up and carried them on my horse back home and I rounded up all the herds to one place.

There they had fixed the lunch already and, while we were eating, I said, "I want to go and take the horses back to where they were. When I take the horses back maybe I will just go to my father's place from there." Then I started driving the horses back. I took them back to where they were before. I looked all around and there wasn't much more snow, just a little around the shade. But I thought I would let them stay around there for a few days yet. There was some water there but the water was too salty so that the horses couldn't drink. They don't like the salt water. Then I went over to Slim Man's place.

When I got there we started to cut those which hadn't got lambs yet. They started to pack one horse and a burro and he said to me, "While you are here we might as well take that herd to the water first and then take them to where we want to move." There was a girl there, Who Went After The Enemies. This girl was Slim Man's niece (his real sister's daughter) and she got on this horse and we started to drive the herd to the water. Slim Man said to me, "Help her take the sheep to the water, and to where we want to move, and when you get there you can go back home." On our way to the water the herd tried to run. But I was in front of them waving my blankets, running my horse before them, riding back and forth in front of the herd trying to keep them back in order to go slow because there were many who would have lambs any minute. But not one of them had lambs. When we got to the water and all the herds had enough water we started to take them where they wanted to camp. While we were on our way a few of them had lambs and I just picked them up and got them on the burro. Some I carried on my horse. I took all the little lambs where they wanted to camp and the girl drove the herd after me. When she got the herd there we started to give the lambs to the mothers. When we were through I started back home.

132

It was around towards evening when I got home but the sun was still way up. I asked about the herd. "Have they had water again?" and they said "No," and I said, "I will take the herd to the water again." I told my wife to come after me and I took the herd to the water and while I was at the water my wife came after me and I told her to take the herd back. "I will go and meet the other folks. Maybe they have moved. Maybe they are on their way." Sure enough they were coming and I met them. They were having a hard time driving the herd with the little lambs and I said, "You have moved already?" and they said, "Yes, we thought we might as well move right now so we did, but we left a lot of our stuff where we were before." I said to them, "Are you going along all right?" and they said, "Yes." I said, "Well then I will go over to where my horses are. I'd like to get them down this evening; I think they are thirsty, too, because there isn't much snow up there." Then I went on and rounded up my horses. Some of them were way up on the cliffs so I had to walk up around the cliffs and drive them down. I got them out and took them to the water. They were all looking fine. While I was chasing them they were playing around, bucking, and kicking one another because they were feeling lively. I did this work all in one day. Then I turned around and I went up to where these other folks had moved. They had taken their herds to the water. It was around evening and they had a lot more lambs. I stopped there for just a little while and they said that they were coming along all right so I just started home. But way late in the evening their lambs were making an awful noise. I guess they had a hard time giving the little lambs to the mothers in the evening. All night they were carrying the lights around the sheep.

From there on we didn't do anything or go anywhere for I don't know how many days. We were just tending to the herd till all the sheep had lambs and till they were all good and strong. We had been counting the days that the man had set up for his return. He had said he would be back in eight or ten days but he didn't show up on that date. After ten days were up we didn't try to look for him anymore and this man never did show up again. From there on we sheared. When

133

we had just started a man came to our place. He was the brother of my wife (her real younger brother). I said, "I am very glad that you came. We have not got anybody to help us on shearing. I wish you would stay and help us." He said, "I will but I would like to go back today and come back tomorrow." "That will be fine," I said, "I want you to help us till we are through with the shearing," and he said, "I am willing to do that work." So this fellow left that day and the next day he didn't show up until the evening. From then on we sheared.

8

Slim Man talks about the good life . . .
The strange behavior of his property . . .
Packing and trading their wool . . . His wife
gets sick and he helps her . . . He visits
his stepfather.

One of these days my father Slim Man had come to our place. He asked for this man that had gone home. "Where is our man? I thought we had a good man to help us here but I don't see him around any place. Where is he? Did he leave you already?" he said to my mother. My mother said, "Yes, he left us; he put up a date but he never did show up on the day. So I don't look for him anymore and I don't care. I think he has another wife some place. And I don't think he is much of a worker. He knows we have lots of work to do. He knows that it is lambing time now and he knows the work was too much for him. That is why he left and I think he wants to get back to his other wife very badly. If he didn't have another wife he would have been back long ago so I don't think much of him anymore."

Slim Man started to talk to me, "Well that is all right, my son. You are a man anyway and so you must let that man go and tend to your own work. What work you have, do it right, don't be careless about it, keep everything in the right way, take care of every little thing that you have so later on you will have everything that you want. You will have sheep and horses and some properties. So just go and tend to your own business. Don't bother with others, let them go around suffering with starving and, if you just take good care of yourself and everything, you won't be suffering, you won't get hungry or anything because you've got what you want." Then he kind of repeated almost all of it again to me. "As I had said to you before you must take my advice. You must keep all my words, all my talks that I have said to you. You are still so young, if you remember all my words, all what I had said to you, you will have everything. You will, too. I know that because you are trying your best to get everything. You've got sheep, plenty of them now and you've got horses and cattle. Later on you will be just like your old father but I think you will have more sheep, more horses, more cattle and more properties than he because I know he had some sheep and horses and a few cattle but he didn't have much property. But I see now you've got sheep, horses, cattle and some properties already and by that you will enjoy this life."

Then he started to talk to my wife. "You joined us and you made up with this man. Since last fall you both were married and during the winter you have lived together and I am so thankful for that." He called my wife daughter-in-law. "These two were all alone and they'd been doing all the work by themselves. You know just how much work has to be done on the sheep and on the other things and that is what I am thanking you for. Maybe later on you will get tired of the work but you shouldn't. You must stay and help them as long as you live and take good care of all the things and take good care of your man. In that way you will live good too. Maybe sometime you will get lonesome and homesick. You will want to go and visit your folks every once in a while. I know you have not much to do at your own home so you just try and stay and help them along."

Then he started to talk to my mother, "My mother, you just take good care of yourself. I know you are getting too old now and I know you can't stand all of this work any more. You can hardly walk on foot all day long so you just take good care of yourself and stay right at home and watch the place. Don't try to overwork yourself because you are too old and can't stand the hard work, and take good care of your daughter-in-law. In that way you will have your daughter-in-law with you all the time. Don't get mad on any little thing to her, don't be mean to her. I hear sometimes about you that you are mean but don't be that way, my mother. Maybe sometimes you get excited about something and discouraged.

136

I know you get that way because you are old and that's the way with all the old people. All the old people get mad about anything but you watch yourself on that, my mother." My mother said, "No, my son, I am not that way. Maybe they talk about me that way but I am not." After that he and I just talked about things for a while. It was way late in the evening when he left.

This other fellow, my wife's brother, was there too. Then we went right to bed and the next day we sheared till noon and, in the afternoon, we started to shear again. We sheared about four or five days. Then I said to my wife's brother, "I would like you to help me take the wool to one of the stores." He asked me, "When shall we go?" I thought for a while. Then I said, "We will go in three days." And my wife said to me, "Why don't you go tomorrow or the next day? We can pack up pretty nearly all the wool today and tomorrow we will have all the wool packed up." But I said, "I have to go up on Black Mountain. Last fall I hid my things up on a tree. I want to go back and look at the things. If they are still there and if the things are all right I will leave them up there. If anything got into it I will just bring the things back down here with me, so I want to go up there tomorrow. The next day I have to get the horses and in around three days I will be all ready. You can go back home and try to get ready, too. Get a horse of your own and help me out with that. I think the best place to go is to Ganado so I think we will go over to that place." That's the way our plan was fixed and this man went back to his home.

The next day I started off towards the mountain. I went up as far as my horse could go. Then I just took the saddle off the horse and hobbled him and I started to climb on foot. I got way on top where I thought I had my stuff hidden. I went around to look for it. I had forgotten the place. I walked all around trying to find where it was. Soon I got to where I had hidden my stuff. There wasn't anything on the tree. I could see the cedar bark which I had put under my stuff. That was all I found on the tree and I just stood there and tried to look around. While I was standing there, there it was lying on the ground. It was about ten yards away from this tree. I was thinking and wondering what had happened to it and how it got down and what could have done it. Then I walked up to it. I walked around it. But there were not tracks of anything so I don't know just how it got down. But it was fixed just the same, like the way I had fixed it. Then I rolled it over and it had never been touched. I started to cut where I had sewed. I cut it open. I had three robes sewn over these things and I opened all these robes. Next to these robes I had a great big buckskin tied around the stuff. I untied that and I looked over all the things. Everything was there and everything was all right. Then I just fixed up all the things again and I started to pack it down. It was kind of heavy but I just put it on my back and started off with it.

I had a hard time to get to the edge of the mountain because there were too many woods and brushes. I started down with it. I had a hard time getting down. Sometimes it got caught on something and held me back for a while. I fell with it I don't know how many times. I got down to where my horse was and I was all sweaty. I threw the bundle down and I laid against it and rested there wiping the sweat off of my face. When I was good and rested I got my horse and saddled him up again and I put this bundle in back of the saddle. I fixed it so that it wouldn't slip on me, and I started back home but I still had a hard time going through the woods with this pack. Around towards evening I got home. I looked at the sun. The sun was still a little way up from the mountain.

There was nobody at home. I took the bundle off my horse and I found there was no water. I went for water and on my way I met them coming back with the herd from the water. I just passed them and went down to the water. I filled up my jugs, put them over the horse, and started back. After supper I began to tell about my trip. My mother said, "Somebody must have thrown the bundle down. I told you lots of times to go up and see if the bundle was still up on the tree but you never wanted to go up." Then I said, "Well, nothing happened to it. It just rolled down. Nobody had touched it. Everything was there and all right and I got it back down. All the things are there." She never did say anything more after that.

I went over to Slim Man's that evening and there he was at home. He told me about what he had been doing, about the work they had done, during all this lambing season and shearing. When he was through telling me about the work then he asked what I had been doing and I told him about my property. Then he said, "That's a serious thing that happened. I know about different things very well from lots of the old people. They say all the properties are alive. Some of them are men and women so they are alive. You shouldn't leave your property all alone that long. They must have got tired lying in the bundle and upon the tree where there wasn't anybody around, and maybe they couldn't stand it anymore. So they got down themselves. That's the way I'm thinking about it for you. Something will come up, something will happen any time maybe to you, maybe to some of your relatives. You don't know your relatives at all. You are just all by yourself here. You've been raised by your father's clanspeople, so that's why you don't know anything about your relatives." He meant my real mother and real father and brothers and sisters. "Maybe you or maybe one of your relatives will die. That's the way I am thinking about it. When the property gets that way without anybody moving it, if it moves by itself even just for a little ways, that means something bad will come up." And he said to me, "You ought to get someone that knows about it and have him do something for you but there isn't anyone who knows about anything around here. Your real father White Hair is the only one who knows about it but he is a long ways off from here." I said, "I don't think I could get anybody for that. I guess I will just let it pass. There is so much work to do around." He said to me, "All right. It's up to you." That was all he said and I started back home. There everybody was sleeping so I just went right to bed.

Next morning I said, "My mother, I guess you will go out with the herd today, and we two will start to pack up the

139

wool." She said, "All right. I will take the herd out." Then we started to cut the little lambs away from the mothers. I separated all the lambs away from their mothers and we left them at home. While she went out with the herd we packed up the wool. We were working on the wool till noon. Then we ate our lunch. Around that time my mother had come back with the herd. After that we continued packing up the wool and my mother took the herd out. But this time she herded right around the hogan. Towards evening we had almost finished packing up the wool. Around about that time my wife's brother came on horseback.

That evening after we stopped working and after our supper I thought I would go over to Slim Man's place again and I said, "I'd like to go over to my father's place." I went over to his place. I told him about what we were going to do tomorrow. I said, "We are going to take our wool to one of the stores. I am going with my wife and her brother, and my mother will be all alone. I don't know just how many days we will be gone but we will try to get back in about seven or eight days. I want you to help my mother for me while we are gone. We are leaving her alone with this work so I'd like you to help her." My father said, "We will help her and we will look after her and I will send one of my children over there to stay with her and she will be all right. One of my children will go over there to get water and wood for her and bring the horse back every morning for her." "That will be fine," I said, "I will be thankful if you do that." Then he said to me, "That's what we want to do. We want to help each other and that's why I always want to live close to you. We will help one another as long as we live so you can go and take your wool to some of the stores. Don't worry about her because we will be around there all the time."

Then I went back to my home. The next day right after dinner we started to pack up the horses and started off. We got to the store and there was Old Mexican. He ran out and he recognized me. He said to me, "I am very anxious to see you and glad that you came. You used to be my father or son-in-law by a woman that we used to call Little Lamb No Mother, Doggie Lamb Had Bow Legs." He said this to me

140

while he was laughing and I said to him, "No, no, I wasn't your son-in-law or father, Old Mexican, because I never saw this woman so I don't know what woman you mean." He said to me, "Yes, yes, you've been running around with this woman all the time." That was all we said to each other and after that I said to him, "I am very anxious to see you again and glad that I got here, but we are tired riding all the way here." He asked me when we started. I said, "We started two days ago." Then he said, "I know the distance. I know very well. It took you two days of travel from there to here and I know you are tired and your horses are tired, too, so you'd better unsaddle your horses and let them rest up and you take a rest, too, my partner, my friend." I said, "We are hungry. Since yesterday noon we had a little lunch. That was all we had. From there we didn't have anything so we are very hungry." Then he said, "It is only about noon now so you just unpack your horses and let your horses rest up and you rest up, too. I've got a whole lot to eat here and I will take care of your horses and you, too. Spend the rest of this day with me and tomorrow we will do the business till noon. It's up to you if you want to stay and spend another day with me. It is all right with me."

We unpacked our horses. I told my wife's brother to water the horses first. Then he took the horses up to the wash where there was good grass. I went into the store after Old Mexican and right away he called for my wife and she came in. He had a big dishpan full of flour. He put salt and baking powder in this flour and he gave it to my wife. He put out some coffee and some sugar with it and some bacon. He let us have some dishes, pots, and coffee pots. He told us to go out and build a fire and cook some lunch. "You've got enough there for this evening," he said to us. My wife went out and she built a fire and started cooking with her brother. When they had finished cooking they called me out. I went over where they were and we ate dinner. After that we started to trade with him. We took all our wool in the store.

He started asking me about the rest of his customers. He had known quite a few people all around the foot of Black Mountain and some lived up on Black Mountain. First he

141

asked me about Slim Man. I said, "Slim Man hasn't finished with his shearing. I don't know in how many days he will be through." He asked me if he was coming over here with his wool. I said, "I don't know. Maybe he will." He said to me, "Will you tell all of these friends of mine to bring all of their wool to me and tell them I will give them a good price for their wool and I will give them so much for their trip too, so will you tell them this for me?" I said, "Yes, I will."

After this he weighed up all the wool. He had a piece of paper and a pencil with it. Nobody knew what he was doing, only himself. None of us knew anything about the weight. When he weighed up all the wool he told us to come in the store. There he pulled out the drawer. Out of this drawer he grabbed up a handful of money and he started to count the money to me. He gave me twenty dollars for the first blanket of wool. That's the only one I still remember very well about the price. After he finished counting the money to me there was a pile of silver dollars and half dollars and quarters on the counter. I gave twenty dollars to my wife. Then I counted out some more money again and I gave ten dollars to my wife's brother. He was awful thankful for it. I just don't know how much the money was but I know it wasn't close to one hundred dollars.

We started to trade. I started in first. I got flour, one big sack of flour, and some coffee and sugar with it. I just don't know how much coffee it was that I bought. I bought all the grub that I wanted and then I said to my wife, "Now you go ahead with your trading." She bought a robe. Around at that time the blankets like this (grey army blankets) used to be only two dollars, some three, up to three and a half, and fancy robes used to be five and five and a half. She had bought one of the robes. This robe was just like the rainbow. It was striped with different colors. That was all she had bought and I had bought one just like it. There was a saddle hanging up on the ceiling that was handmade by a Navajo. It was a brand new one, a nice fancy one. He said to me, "Buy that saddle. It only costs fifteen dollars." He kept on saying this to me every once in a while but I didn't pay any attention to him. I just walked around the store. This other fellow to

142

whom I gave ten dollars didn't buy anything. He just put the money in his pocket. Pretty soon I made up my mind. I thought, "I will buy that saddle." So I told him to get that saddle down. He got it down for me and I looked at it and the saddle looked all right to me. Then I reached down in my pocket and counted out fifteen dollars and I gave it to him. This saddle wasn't his. There were a lot of Navajo in the store. The saddle belonged to one of these Navajo. He gave the fifteen dollars to one of these. Right away he started trading. We were in the store all day. When we went out I looked at the sun and the sun was pretty well down. So then I thought, "It's no use to try to go back today." So we two just went over where the horses were. We got the horses and we watered them and took them where there was good grass and there we hobbled the horses again. When we came back it was around sunset.

My wife said, "I am not feeling well. I've got an awful pain in my stomach." There were a lot of Indians around there, men and women. They told us to go in a hogan right close by the store where it was warm. We took all our stuff in this hogan. Just when we got in my wife started suffering from the pain that she had in her stomach. A lot of men and women came in. There was one woman who was kind of a medicine woman; we used to call her Woman With Gummy Mouth. She started to work and treat my wife, and a lot of us in this hogan just looked at her treating her. She worked on her till about midnight. Around about that time the pain was relieved and then we all went to bed.

Next morning my wife's brother went after the horses. Some women stayed there with us that night. They all started cooking and my wife was just lying there in bed. She was awful weak. After we ate I went out and the sun was pretty well up. Then I went over to the store and I told the trader about my wife. I said to him, "Maybe you've got some kind of medicine for that." He said, "No, I haven't got medicine of any kind and I don't know anything about medicine. Why don't you get some singer around here? Maybe they know something about that. If there was a hospital close someplace

143

I would take her there. I would help you on that and I wish there was a hospital close some place. I know very well the doctors will cure that pain in her stomach. There are lots of hospitals but they are too far away from here. I wish I could do something for her but I just don't know what to do about it so you ought to get one of the singers around here." I said, "I just don't know the Indians around here." Then he asked me again about her, "How is she now?" I said, "I think she is a little better this morning but she is weak." "Well, then, I will give you some more grub and I don't want you to go this morning. Wait and see till about noon. If she gets all right then you can go home this afternoon." So then I said, "All right." Then he asked me, "Is there anybody to cook for you?" I said, "Yes, there are some women in the hogan with her and they will cook for us." He gave me some more grub.

Around noon she was walking around outside and she wanted to go so we saddled up the horses and we packed all of our things and we started off. When we got on top of this mountain it was getting dark. We camped there that night. There was plenty of wood around there. I built a great big fire. She had a little pain again in her stomach and I broke some cedar leaves off and I put them over the fire and warmed them up and I put them on her stomach. Every once in a while I warmed the cedar leaves and put them on her stomach and soon the pain was over. Next morning we started on again.

We got to a place where there was a hogan. There we got off of our horses and we went inside and there was my mother, my father, and my younger brother.[1] They were all at home. Then I went up to my mother and she put her arms around me and I did, too. We started crying and then we all shook hands. There was a man there of the Red Clay clan. He was my stepfather. I went up to him and shook hands with him and he asked me, "From where did you start and how many days ago?" I told him. Then he said, "Go out and get a

1. The identity of these three is not clear. His real mother, according to the narrative in Volume I, is dead.

144

nice fat sheep. Kill it and butcher it for them. They must be hungry for meat by now. I know they are hungry for meat. And go out and unsaddle their horses for them and take their horses up to the water and take them where there is good grass. Up on top of this hill will be a nice place to put horses." Everybody started running. It was around early afternoon when we got to the place and this man had a son and a daughter. They were both grown up. They were my younger brother and younger sister, and there was another hogan close by them. A woman lived in this hogan. She had lots of children, boys and girls. They killed a sheep and butchered it and they unsaddled our horses and took our horses away and then I started telling about the trip. I told about what we were doing at home. Soon the sun was down. We didn't do anything, just told stories about our trip all day.

Then I told about my wife, that she wasn't feeling well now. Then my stepfather said to my mother, "You know about that. You know what medicine to use when you get that way. You go out and get some medicine for her and when she takes this medicine she will be all right." He named two kinds of plant medicines. Then she went out and got on the horse and went after these medicines. She brought the medicines back and she boiled these medicines. My wife took it and a little while after that she was all right. Next day she was well and they told us to stay for another day.

I don't quite remember just how many days we stayed there, maybe it was two or three days. On one of these days my younger brother said, "Let's go to my race track and I will run you a race." Right away I said, "All right let's go." I thought to myself that I will beat him easy. We went up to where the race track was. We took all our clothes off, nothing on us, just our g-string. We started off and when we got a little over half way he got a little ahead of me. I tried my best to beat him but I never caught up with him. He was right in front of me all the way to the line from halfway. That's where my younger brother beat me on the foot race. If I hadn't been riding on horseback all this time maybe I would have beaten him.

Then while we still were there at this place one day the

145

woman said to me, "Your younger brother says that you've got two saddles with you (that was my youngest brother, not the one I raced with) and he wants you to give him one of your saddles. He is old enough to ride on horseback but we can't get a saddle for him." I started to think about it. I wanted to have an extra saddle with me but I thought, "I will just give my old saddle to him." So I gave him my old saddle. He was so thankful for it.

I don't know just what we had been doing there for two or three days. We didn't have much to say to each other. This man (stepfather) was a quiet man. He didn't have much to say, only the first day and first night that we came he had told us about how they had been living. He told us all about his properties and all about himself and all about his children. That was the only time that he told us about all the things that they had been doing and he said, "We are all poor; we are not like you. We haven't got many stocks but you have. So we are not strong like you because you have been raised on everything and you've still got all the things and that's why you are stronger than us." He said to my wife and her brother, "I never knew you before. This is the first time we've seen each other. Now I know you and you both know me." And he said, "What is Giving Out Anger to you?" and my wife said, "He is our maternal grandfather." "Well that is right then. He is younger brother so you both are my maternal grandchildren." That's what he said to my wife. He said all this on the first day that we came. From there on he was quiet. He didn't say much.

In the afternoon, suddenly, I thought we'd better go. I said to them, "I guess we better get the horses and start on back to our home." They started to cook and this man said, "All right. I am very glad that you came to visit us and we were anxious to see you and glad to see you. That's the way to be. You must remember all the time. Come again sometime if you can. We always like to see you come around." About that time the horses were brought back and he said, "Your horses are looking fine. They are all big and stout. I wish I had horses like them. I've got some horses but they are just scrubby ones. I see you've got nice good-sized horses

146

and I know you'll get back without any trouble. I know your horses won't give up on you." This was the only time he spoke again. After we ate our dinner we packed up our horses. I thought we would get something from these people. We didn't get anything from them but I had given one of my saddles away. We just got some lunch from them. They had given us some mutton to take along with us. The mutton was all ready to be eaten because it was boiled. Before we started I asked them about the trail and this man told us how to go.

9

His mother quarrels with Slim Man
and leaves home . . . He finds her
and she scolds him . . . His wife is jealous . . .
More trouble with his mother.

When we got home there wasn't anybody around. I looked all around for the sheep but I couldn't see our sheep anyplace. I could only see one big herd and one little herd, too. That was all I could see. I looked all around while I was still on my horse. Then I got off. Before I went inside I looked all around the hogan. There were no fresh tracks around. Inside the things were all fixed way back in the hogan. It was getting dark when we ate our supper. After we finished I turned my horse loose and I said, "I will go over to my father's place. I will find out where my mother has moved." The other two started to fix their beds because they were tired from riding on horseback.

So I went over to this other place. When I got there everybody was home. As soon as I came in they spread out a sheep pelt for me and I shook hands with my father. "Well," he said, "You got back at last." "Yes," I said, "We just got back a while ago." "Yes, that's what they said. They saw you taking the horses to water." "Yes, I took the horses to the water and I brought back some water with me but there wasn't anybody at home when we got back." "Yes," he said, "nobody is home. Your mother was here three days after you left and she said to us, 'You are not taking good care of me.' And I said to her, 'Yes, we are taking good care of you. We help you on the water and on wood and we brought you back your horse every morning. What more help do you want anyway? Do you think we will carry you around?' When I said this to her right away she got mad at us and she just turned

148

around quick and went back home. When she had walked a little ways from us she turned around and she said to me, 'I didn't think you would speak that way to me. I know now you are an unkind man. That's the way you are and I know you are mean. I always think a lot of you but if you are mean to me I will be just the same way to you. I always think that you are my son and my baby but you are not that way to me and I will sure tell on you to my son when he comes back and I am sure that he won't like this and now I will go to some place. I don't want to be living close by you any more. I will just go and crawl around anywhere that I want to go. That's the way you want me to be. You want me to suffer.' I said to her, 'You can just go ahead; go wherever you please to go. I don't care if you suffer and it will be your own fault getting mad at a little thing.' While I was saying this to her she had said something to my wife, but my wife never said anything to her.

"So then she went back to her home. Afterwards we found out that she had gone down below Many Streams (Kayenta) to a place called Flowing Through The Pass where Woman Who Walks Alone lived, so she is down there now living with her daughter-in-law, and she has the herds, too." I said, "That's all right, my father. She gets that way sometimes and I know all the old folks get that way. They get disgusted over any little thing. I know it's her own fault. But you and I will be just the same to each other always. I don't want to be like her."

Then we let that go and he started to tell me about the wool that they were getting ready to take to the store. "We just got through shearing today. That was all we have been doing, shearing and herding, that's all of my story and I know your story is long so if you want to tell the story about your trip you can go ahead. We'd like to hear it," he said to me. Then I started to tell my story. When I had finished, everything was cooked and we ate. They had nice fat meat. I was so hungry for it. After we ate he asked me, "What do you want to do tomorrow? Do you think you will take all the stuff over where your mother has gone?" I said, "No, I don't think so because it's too hot out in the valley. I don't want to be out

149

in the hot weather but I will wait until tomorrow. Maybe I will know what to do tomorrow."

They cut me a front leg of mutton to take back with me. It was good and fat. When I got home my wife and her brother were fast asleep. I shook my wife up and told her, "Wake up and build a fire and cook yourself some mutton." When everything was done she woke her brother and we all ate again. We were sure hungry for meat.

After we ate next morning I went out and went to Slim Man's sweat-house. It was about ready. I just walked around there. Then I went over to the hogan and everything was ready to be eaten. They told me to eat and I said, "I just got through a while ago." "Even so, eat some more," they said to me. I sat down and ate some more. After we ate we went over to the sweat-house and we put all the rocks in the sweat-house and put a blanket over the door. We took all our clothes off and we went in. At noon we went back to the hogan and everything was ready again to be eaten. When we were through Slim Man said to me, "What do you want to do now, my son? Are you going to take all the stuff out where the herds are?" I said, "I don't think so. I will just take some grub over to my mother, and my wife will go back home with her brother. She has not visited her people for a long time now and I will let them take all the things over to their place." He said, "That's fine."

When I got home I just started right in and ate some more. Then we started to pack up the horses. We took all the things out and we got it all in bundles and we packed them on horses and I told them to take all the things to their home because if we left the things there somebody might get after it. I said, "I want to go after my mother." I put some grub in a sack. I took out some calico and a black robe which I wanted to take to my mother and I told the others, "When you get back to your home just turn the horses loose and they will come back over here. I just don't know when I will be back so you take good care of the things."

They started off and I got on my horse and started off, too. I went on and got to Many Streams, and below that place there was another place. I looked all around there, but there wasn't anybody around. I went down a little ways. There was a little point there and I went around this point and I saw a hogan. I went to this hogan where Woman Who Walks Alone lived. Right across from her place was where my mother was staying. I rode over there and she was just coming in with the herd. There was nothing there where she was staying. There was no fire, just a few ashes. She rode up to me and she got off of her horse and she came up to me and she just sat down. I asked her, "Where do you put your horse every evening?" She said, "I just turn my horse loose and the horse will go across here and my grandchild takes my horse up in the canyon for me every night and in the morning he always brings my horse back for me. He is a great helper, my grandchild is (she meant the husband of Woman Who Walks Alone), and sometimes in the morning, and sometimes the whole day, he herds for me. He will come here early in the morning and do a lot for me and he will sometimes turn out the herd and go out with the herd for me; so he is a great helper." Then she started to build a fire and I took the horses where there was good grass. When I came back from there she was done with the cooking. We ate our supper and then I started to tell her all about my trip. She said, "Where are the others?" and I said they both went back to their home this morning and I started to find where you were. I made a quick story. Then I said, "I'd like to go to my uncle's place." Then she said, "All right. I will be there, too."

So I went over to Woman Who Walks Alone's place. Her husband, Son Of Late Grey Hat (whom I called Uncle), was there. We shook hands and he asked me right away about my trip and I started to tell him. Then when everybody was through with their work they all came in. About that time the cooking was done. After we ate he said to me, "Now we are all ready for the story about your trip." Then I told all about my trip. When I finished with my story he said, "We ought to take our wool to that place. We just gave our wool away. We took every bit of our wool to Chinle and we didn't get much for it. We just got six dollars for a sack; some we got seven dollars for. I wanted to hold it back but they wanted to sell

151

their wool quickly, so that's why we took all our wool to Chinle. I wish I had taken the wool over to that place; I would have gotten more for it over there, but it's too late now." He was kind of sorry for his wool, but he had sold it already.

That evening my mother went back to the herd by herself and I stayed with these other folks. I said, "I want you folks to help me separate the bucks and billy goats from the herd, and I would like you folks to help me separate the little lambs from their mothers tomorrow morning. After we separate the bucks and billy goats I want to earmark them and I want to cut them. So I'd like you folks to help me on that. There are lots of them. I want to cut them and earmark them." They said, "All right we will. You just turn your bucks and billy goats in with our bunch." I had six bucks and three billy goats and I took them over with theirs, and those I never got back. They took them back a long ways from this place, way at the foot of Carágo Mountain. That's where they took my bucks and billy goats and I never got them back. That was a bad thing for me to do, to turn them in with theirs.

That morning the other folks came over and we separated the lambs from their mothers. When we did this I started in and made their earmarks. I just don't know how many lambs there were but I know there were a great many. The lambs which were mine were all white and those that belonged to my mother were all mixed. They were all different colors and a lot of them were spotted ones (or pinto). I made an earmark for my wife, too. I think it was eight or ten that I earmarked for her, and when I was through with this earmarking I started to cut the others. About noon I finished with the earmarking and cutting the lambs.

About that time my mother had come back with the herd and right away she started cooking. We both started to eat and after that I turned out the herd. I went out with the herd that afternoon. When I came back, just as soon as I came in, she put out the food and we both started to eat again. But she didn't have much to say and after we ate I said to her, "I want to go over to my uncle's place, Son Of Late Grey Hat." It was around evening when I got there. After a little while my mother came and there she started to tell about what my father Slim Man, had said to her. She said, "That man over there, I always thought that he was a son to me but he scolded me a few days ago. He was angry at me for nothing, but I just didn't pay any attention to him and I know that he is a mean man." She turned around and said to me, "And I think you are getting to be like him, too, because you always leave me all alone with all the work." This is what she said but I just let it go. She had stopped talking about that for a moment. Then she repeated it all over again.

This time I said to her, "How many more times do you want to tell about that. I am just tired listening to your talk. You ought to talk about how we should live and I don't like to hear about those things. I know what you said to each other and you ought to just keep quiet and let the people help you along. I want the people to help me along and I will help them along, too. I don't like to talk about the others like you do. Slim Man is my father and I am his son and I will help him along as long as I live and he will, too. I am so ashamed of you telling about people that way before my uncle and the others, and he has got his nephew and nieces here with him. That's why I am ashamed of your repeating the bad story over and over again. I know they don't want to listen to those kinds of stories. What they want to hear is a good story." About then she turned around to me again, "I told you you are getting to be just like him and I know that you are on his side and not on my side. You are getting to be mean more and more to me." This is what my mother said to me again but I just didn't pay any attention to her. I said to her, "You just go ahead and talk to yourself."

The others couldn't stand those kinds of talks any more. She used to run over there to them and she always told bad things about the people. So they couldn't stand it any longer. Later on they moved back to their country. When she was alone before she never had said anything but when the people started to help her along then she got that way, so I think the help is what spoiled her. Then my uncle said, "Let's drop all the bad talking. We ought to all talk about good things in life and the other things like our work that we've been doing on the stocks. We ought to talk about what should we do from tomorrow on, and the next day, and so on. I don't think we can get anything out of bad talks so we ought to talk about the good things. It's late now so you are tired and I think you ought to go home and go to bed and go to sleep."

Then she went and I stayed there overnight, and early the next morning we all got up. The others went ahead with their cooking and while they were cooking I said to my uncle, "I would like you to help me again this morning cutting some more little lambs. I didn't finish cutting them yesterday." Then he said, "All right, I will do that." When I came home with the horse I said to my mother, "I told my uncle to come over this morning to help me on cutting some more lambs again and he told me to kill a nice fat young lamb and I will do that, so I will go out and get a nice fat one." Then my mother said, "What do you want to do with the little lamb? Sure, they are nice and fat, all right, but there's not much to them. You go out and get a good sized sheep and kill that and be sure and get a nice fat one so that they will enjoy nice fat meat." Then I went outside and I roped a good sized sheep and I brought it over and tied the legs together. We cut the throat. Just about then they had come. Then my mother said, "You both butcher that sheep and I will do something else." Then they started butchering and she said, "You can just go ahead and cut up all the meat, fix it up nice, my daughter-in-law. I am glad you are here and can help me on the cooking." They had butchered in a hurry and then they started cooking. When the cooking was done we ate and after that we turned the herd out down to the wash where it was nice and cool.

Then we separated the little lambs, those which were not cut yet, and then when we separated all the little lambs which hadn't been cut my mother went out with the herd and Woman Who Walks Alone was working on the meat, cutting it up. I had the medicine fixed already, the medicine which I use on the little lambs after they have been cut so that they won't bleed much or swell much. Then I sharpened up the knives, and washed them with this medicine. Then we started to cut the little lambs. We finished with them just about noon. Just about then my mother came back with the herd. Then we returned the little lambs to their mothers and came home, and my mother started cooking with Woman Who Walks Alone. We spread out the sheep pelt in the shade and we were lying around there. We were both so tired cutting the little lambs. While they were cooking I went over to the herd to see how the little lambs were and they were all right. They didn't bleed much and when I came back from the herd my uncle had counted the little lambs and he said there were a little over a hundred. "It's just too many for you. You can't eat all of them by yourself. No wonder last spring lots of the old wethers died off. You ought to let us have some every once in a while." But I said, "That's not many. That's only just a few. I am wishing to have more than that."

Just about that time the cooking was done and in the afternoon I turned out the herds. I had been herding that afternoon and I kept on watching the little lambs that we had cut but they were all getting along fine. They weren't bleeding very much and in the evening I came back with the herd. Then we did what we always do. We ate and after we ate I went over to my uncle's place again. I always went to stay over night with him, and Woman Who Walks Alone was just like a real mother to me. She used to be very kind to me and I was just the same to her. When she talked to me she always said, "My son," first to me. When I got to their place they were so nice to me. Then my uncle told me about his life and lots of other different things. He told me all kinds of bad things that he had done. He was a gambler.

I started for my mother's early the next morning before breakfast. When I got there I got my breakfast and after I finished I herded all that day. I herded the sheep that day because I wanted to see how the little lambs were getting along. That was all I did for four or five days. In about five days the lambs that were cut were all right. Every evening I went over to my uncle's place and there I stayed over night every night. I didn't stay with my mother because she had only one sheep pelt and just enough blankets for herself. When all the lambs were well, I said to my mother, "I'd like to go over to my wife's relatives' place. It was quite a few days ago that she went back to her home. I'd like to go and see what she is doing."

On my way to where my wife was I found quite a few of my horses and I just drove them towards the water; I kept on doing that all the way. There were a lot of horses I didn't see but I thought they must be right around close to the woods where it was cool. Out in the valley it was just too hot for anything. I got over to a place called Woods Coming Out Into A Flat and that was where my wife's relatives' place was. They had a little farm where the water spreads out, and they had a nice crop of corn. She was in a hogan by herself but there was no fire there and she said, "I just came back from my mother's place. I went over there this morning because they are having Blessing Way. They are having this One Day Sing over my mother and I was just starting to go over there again. That's why I didn't build a fire here so let's go over there. You will get some food. There is plenty of food. We killed two sheep this morning. So come with me. You will eat nice meat there." I said, "All right; let's go there." I took out my robe that I had bought. This robe was striped with all different colors like the rainbow. I took this robe out of the sack and I put it over the saddle and I got on the horse and she sat behind me and we started off to her mother's place.

There was only one hogan there, quite a good-sized one, and there was a brush hogan beside it. That was where we stopped and got off our horse. She started the fire and she started cooking but she couldn't find any water—the bucket was empty. Then she said, "I can't do anything. There isn't any water. I told the boys to get some water this morning but they didn't. You can't make them do anything." Then she went over to the hogan and carried out some food. The coffee and the rest of the food were cold. I ate some of it; then I picked up the jugs and put them over the saddle. When I got to the water I started filling the jugs. I had them filled in a few minutes. I picked them up and put them back over the saddle and I started back. When I got the water back she said, "I will make better food for you. You ate some but it was cold and

156

now this time you will eat everything hot and fresh." When she cooked everything I started to eat.

Then I said, "I will take my horse over where there is good grass. Right up around those rocks I think there is a good place to hobble my horse." I got on my horse bareback and I hobbled it. There around those rocks, sure enough there was plenty of grass. When I came back I started to chop wood. I chopped the wood all up and I had a pile there. When I was through I came back in the brush hogan and my wife said to me, "They would like you to come in the hogan. There are some men in there who would like to hear some of your stories." I said, "That's the way with me. I like to hear some stories. I guess I will go in and hear their stories." Then my wife went over to the hogan and she told her mother to come out. My wife came back to me and she told me, "Go outside and go behind the tree; my mother is coming." So I did. I went out and went around behind the tree and I guess my wife's mother went in the brush hogan. Then I walked over to the other hogan.

Inside there was a man sitting. He was the one that wanted me to come in. Right away he said to me, "You are here. I'd like to hear about the trip that you made and tell me about some other things too." Then I said, "That's what I came in for. I'd like to hear some stories from you," but he said, "I haven't got anything to tell about. I want you to tell me about your trip." "I thought they had told you about it already." He said, "No, they don't want to tell me anything. I don't know why they don't want to tell me about things like that. Both of the grandchildren went with you but they don't want to tell about their trip. That grandchild is that way all the time. He doesn't talk. You can't get a word out of him so I want you to tell me all about it. I am all alone here and I am lonesome. But wait a while yet."

Then he told two boys, "Go and build a new corral for the horses. When you bring them back this evening just put them in the corral and tonight we will start with our singing. When we finish with twelve songs which are called 'house its songs,' then I will tell you to go out and I will give you corn pollen and you will put the corn pollen in the horses' mouths, over their heads, and along the neck and back, and down to the end of their tails. When you are through doing this then you turn them out and let them go back."

Then he said to me, "Go ahead with your story." I started with my story and I just made a quick story about my trip. Then I said, "I will go out of here. I'd better because the old woman might not like me to stay in here." I was just getting up to go out when they said, "Sit down first. Everything is cooked outside and they are bringing in some food to us so you stay and eat with us first." So I sat down again. Right away they brought in some food and we all started eating. Then I went back to the brush hogan. My wife had spread out a sheep pelt for me and she told me, "Lie here and I will go inside the hogan. When they finish singing the hogan's songs, I will be out again." So I lay there on the sheep pelt and I covered myself and everybody had gone inside.

The Singer was ready to start. Pretty soon they started with the singing. I just heard them sing six songs. Right then I went to sleep so I didn't hear the other six of the hogan songs. They had finished all those songs, and some more songs besides, while I was fast asleep. My wife had come out. I never heard her and I never noticed that she was lying right alongside me. There was a woman who had come to their place. That was Horse's Ass's wife. She had come out of the hogan too. While my wife and I were sleeping she threw a great big piece of charcoal on us, on my new robe. My robe was burned through. It made a big hole in about the middle of my robe. We both felt the heat and smelled that something was burning, and we got up and our robe was burning. She must have stood there by the door looking at us and my wife saw her run away from the doorway. My wife was awful mad and she started cussing. "That ghost woman, that big old asshole, that big peanut, that old whore there did it. I saw her. She just ran away from the door." She repeated that I don't know how many times. Then she said, "I will go after her. I will just beat her to death." Then I said to her, "Be careful, go easy on that. Don't make trouble. You mustn't say bad things when you are having Blessing Way at your place."

158

Next morning I brought my horse back. After we ate we both started back to the other hogan where my wife had been staying. She looked as if she were thinking about something and she looked like she was mad. But I didn't pay any attention to her and we started back. I was on horseback. It was quite a ways from this place to where she had been staying. On our way I asked her to get on the horse but she didn't say anything. She just looked down and walked along and we got back to where the other hogan was.

When we got there I didn't have anything to do. Then all at once I said, "Since I've got nothing to do I will go round up the cattle. I want the two boys to help me on that but they must have been up all night so they may want to sleep." She said, "No, I don't think they could go. That man that did Blessing Way for them last night said they shouldn't do anything for four days so I don't think they could go." "Well then," I said, "I will go and round up the cattle by myself." Then I went and I went over to Flowing Out Of The Canyon. There were lots of tracks around there of the cattle and I went up to the foot of the mountain. I found some around there and I went halfway up the mountain and rounded all of them up and started them down. They were kind of wild. They all ran down to the foot of the mountain and from there on out to Flowing Out Of The Canyon. There was a corral there and I got them in the corral. I fixed up the gate, and walked all around the corral and it was good and strong. Then I started back home but I turned around and I started roping the calves. I earmarked all that I had found. Three of them were bulls, I roped them and cut them. There were four bulls but one I couldn't get near because the mother of that calf was trying to get after me. I was afraid to go near so I just let that one go.

When I got home my wife was still looking the same as she was this morning. Then I said, "I got just a few of the cattle. I didn't get all of them. Lots of them had run into the woods. If there was somebody to help me I could get them all. So that's why I didn't finish work on the cattle." Then she said, "You didn't get through with the cattle because I know you have been over at that hogan all this afternoon." I told her, "Don't talk to me like that because I don't know what you are saying, because I am not like you. So don't talk to me like that." Then she said again, "That's true. I know you have been there all afternoon and that's why you didn't finish with the cattle. I know you are still running after that woman and she is still running after you. I know it because I found out last night she is jealous of me. That's why she burned the robe last night." I tried to stop her talking that way but she just kept on with it. From there on the jealousy was growing bigger and bigger and she kept on talking that way to me. I knew she wouldn't stop if I talked too so I just went after my horse.

Next day I started to where my mother was. I went down a little below Many Streams. She was there and there were two other persons sitting down. The herds were turned out and were moving along towards the north. I got off of my horse and tied him up and my mother was sitting with two visitors, a man and a woman. They were from the foot of Carriso Mountain. The woman was my older sister. I walked up to her. I sat down by her and she put her arm around me and I did the same and she cried because she was anxious to see me. Then my mother said, "There is a fellow herding for me so that I can stay with my daughter. She has come for me. She wants me to go back to her home with her. That's what she came for. She is going to take me back to her home." When she said this I said, "So you want to go back over where you don't know about the country. I know you want to go over there very bad but you don't know the country and the herd can't go across the flat like this. They won't get there because it's just too hot to travel on the desert. And they don't know the country. If you try to drive the herd across the desert you won't have any more sheep. As soon as you get them out on the flat they'll all die of thirst. There is no water across this big desert. You might just as well kill them right here. But I don't believe you will take the sheep across the desert. You might as well just stay right here and go close to the foot of the mountain where it's cool. You don't know

160

what you are talking about because you are getting too old. You were stingy for all the herds but you aren't now. You just want to herd them away, give them to all the animals. As soon as you get them out of here you won't have any more sheep."

When I said this to her she said, "That's the way you talk to me. You always hold me back on anything that I want to do." I said, "Yes, I am holding you back because I don't want you to be without anything. You just want to go after that old man. That's what you have on your mind." Then she told the others, "Every time I want to do something he stops me. He always holds me back and he always starts to talk to me like that. He is getting so unkind to me. He is just holding me here all alone and he makes me suffer. When I am all alone I won't have anybody to get me water, and I will run out of food and will have nobody to get me some food. One of these days I will thirst to death or starve to death and then he will like it and he will be thankful when I am gone."

When she said this both of the women started to cry. While they were both crying my older sister started to talk to me. She said, "Well my son, I didn't think you were that way to your mother. I didn't think you would treat your mother that way but I see you are treating her that way. No wonder she says she is suffering all the time. You mustn't treat your mother that way, my younger brother. I found out today that you are treating your mother that way. Have you got another mother any place like her? I don't think so. That's the only mother you've got. She raised you; she picked you up when you were a tiny baby and she raised you. She did a whole lot for you and you've grown to be a man now so you ought to help her along and take good care of her and do a lot for her like what she did for you. We've known her for a long time and we think a whole lot of her; even though we are a long ways from her we always think and talk about her. When we think about her we call her name, we call her Abaa, and everybody knows her and knows her name. And we think a lot of you, too, because she had raised you and we call you Son of Abaa and everybody knows your name by her." From

161

there on she talked a whole lot to me but I never did say any more words. I was afraid of them, because they were two together talking to me, while they were crying.

Then I told them, "If you both want to move away from here you ought to stop talking and crying. Crying and talking won't take you anyplace. I'd like to know just when are you going to move, today or tomorrow?" Then my mother said, "We wanted to move just as soon as you came. We thought if you came today we would start moving around this evening so that we will move across the flat while it's cool. Or if you came tomorrow we would go right away as soon as you came. But you are here now. We wanted to know what you thought about it." I said, "Yes I am here but I don't like for you to go today. I'd like for you to stay here for another day with me because you, my sister, are from a long ways. And my mother too because you want to take her far away from me. I didn't want her to go away from me that far but you want to take her back to your country and I see that she wants to go." When I said this my mother said, "Yes my son, I'd like to go back with them to their country but I am not leaving you forever. They just want to take me up where it's nice and cool. They want to take me out of this hot country. They don't want me to roast to death. They're afraid that I might thirst to death some of these days so that's why I made up my mind to go back with them. They say there is plenty of grazing for the sheep so that's why I'd like to go back with them where it's nice and cool. So you know now I am not leaving you forever, my son," she said to me again.

Round about that time it was noon and this old man who was with my older sister had come back with the herd, the man that we used to call Deer Spring[1] and we also called him Husband of Crazy. He had another name but I forgot that name. That name was given to him by Friend Of Old Hat. When he came back with the herd he said, "Come on with the water. I am about thirsting to death. I'd just like to know how you live out here in this hot place. I just can't stand the heat. Come on with the water." He was walking in while he

1. Later referred to as Nephew Of Who Has Land. The "older sister" was his wife. She was a member of the Bitahni clan.

162

was saying this and he was wiping the sweat on his face. "I wanted to go to where the water is but I just chased the two horses towards the water. I wish I had brought them back with me now. I can't go after them because it's just too hot for me." This is what he said when he came back with the herd and when he drank the water. When he shook hands with me he called me younger brother because his father was Many Goats and my father was, too, so they were clan brothers. That's why he called me younger brother. Then he said, "I don't see how you stand this hot weather way out here on this flat. You'd better get out of this place and go to where it's cool. You might roast to death or thirst to death if you stay around here any longer."

Then he asked me, "When did you come, my younger brother?" "I came here this morning when you were going out with the herd." "I didn't see you come," he said. Then I said, "Yes I had come here this morning." He asked again, "Which way are you going from here?" Then I said, "This is as far as I am going but I want to take my horse to the water and take my horse over where there is good grass. I will hobble my horse there." Then he said "I am glad that you are going over to the water. I just chased my horses over to the water this noon. I don't know if they got to the water. Maybe they roasted to death and thirsted to death before they got to the water. But if you see my horses any place take them to the water for me too, my younger brother. And see if they've got water and take them for me over where that black rock is standing. I had them over there last night. There is lots of good grass there." Then I said, "Yes I will, I will take your horses to the water but I don't think I will take them over where that black rock is because there are too many rocks. I think it is too hard for their feet so I will take them along with me where I want to put my horse." He said, "That's very nice." Then I said "When I come back from there we will sit around and tell each other some stories about things." "Yes, that will be nice," he said. Then I got on my horse and went down to the water. On the way there were the horses standing out in the flat and I went up to them and I took them down to the water. From there I took them where there was

163

good feed. I just turned them loose there and hobbled mine and I came back home.

They had some more food cooked and after we ate I said, "I came here this morning and these two women were talking about moving across the big flat to where it is nice and cool." And I told him what they had said and what I had said to them. "I think I will just let them go but I will be staying around here tending to my own work on other stocks of mine and other things besides." Then he said, "Yes, my younger brother, just as soon as we came here they started to talk about that and I just listened to them making all kinds of different plans. They were saying 'We will do this and that' and I didn't bother with them. I thought it's just too hot for the herds and I see they've all got lambs so I don't think the lambs could stand the travelling. But I didn't say anything about it. Don't think that I had made out plans that way for them." Then I said, "No, I am not thinking that way. It is their own plans and I know you can't turn them down." He said, "I know that when a woman starts on something you can't do anything with her so that's why I let them go ahead and talk about that."

Then he said, "When do you want them to leave here?"

"Well, we will stay around here today and tomorrow. I'd like for you to stay around here with me till it gets nice and cool. Then I guess I will just let them take the herd, let them go across the desert and they will find out how hard it is crossing the desert. Let them have a hard time." Then I just let this go and I asked him about their home. "From where did you start and about where do you live?" and he said, "We live up on Carriso Mountain, that's where we started from. We moved up there quite a few days ago. There are a lot of people living up there; a lot moved up there." "Is there lots of grazing up there?" I asked. "Yes, there is lots of grazing, all kinds of grass up there for all the animals and there is plenty of water. Even though the people are up there with their herds still there is plenty of food for the stock." Then I said, "How is it across the flat?" "Well, there is plenty of grazing all the way up here. When we were coming I looked all around and I saw there is plenty of grazing all the way up

164

to here." "Well, then," I said, "I guess the herd will cross the flat all right. If you don't start till it gets cool then I think they will be all right. But I don't know about the lambs. Maybe they will stand the trip all right maybe not, but anyway try to go slow with the little lambs and try to stop when you see the little lambs giving up." "Yes," he said, "I will watch close for them and I think we will get across this flat with the herds all right." Then we just let that go again and we were just lying around the shade.

After a while he asked me about the trip that I made to Ganado, and around the other places. I made a quick story about that because I had told that story I don't know how many times. Every time a fellow saw me he always asked me about that trip I made because they wanted to know the price of the wool and other things and they wanted to know just how many relatives there were over there and they wanted to know what my relatives thought of me. So I was tired of telling that story over and over again. So I just made a quick story about that and then I told him about how the people lived over in that country. I said, "All the people over there are living good." Then he said, "That is the way with us too over at our country. All the people live good. They haven't got any trouble. I said, "I guess it's that way all over. That's all I've got to tell about," I said to him.

Then he said, "I wish there was a sweat-house close by some place. Have you got a sweat-house close around here, my younger brother?" Then I said to him, "Do you want to have a sweat-house, older brother?" "Yes, my younger brother, I'd like to go in a sweat-house, I never had a sweat-house for a long time." Then I said to him, "Well if you want to have a sweat-house there is a sweat-house right across over there where those rock hills are but there's no wood close by that sweat-house. You have to go into the woods and get some wood." Then he said, "I guess I will go over and build a fire over there with the rocks. Have you got an ax around here?" "No," I said, "there isn't an ax around." "It will be all right just to pick up the wood so I will go over now and make up the sweat-house," he said. I said, "All right. I will go after the horse that we use for the herd. I will bring

165

the horse back home and one of these women will go out with the herd."

I went after the horses; he went to get the wood. I got the horses back and I told the two women," I got the horses back for you. One of you take the herd out. I want to go over to the sweat-house." I heard him breaking the wood up. Soon I saw the smoke rising up from where the sweat-house was. I picked up some blankets and I got some water and took them over to the sweat-house because when you go in a sweat-house you get thirsty pretty quick. When I got there he was about ready to take the rocks inside. We put the blankets over the door; we took all our clothes off and went inside.

He said, "I see that a man is living over here now (he meant Son Of Late Grey Hat). He used to live over where we live. Now I see that he lives here and I see that he lives with another woman. When he was living over where we live he had a family. I wonder what he did with his family and I wonder where they are now." I said, "Yes, he lives here with us now. Last fall he was moving across here. He just let his family go and he stayed around here. Pretty soon he asked my mother to get him a woman so my mother got him that woman with whom he is staying now. She used to be moving around here all by herself and now she is living with him and I think they are living together all right. I don't know just when he went across there to that country and brought back his nephew and his niece so they are both herding now." "Well then," he said, "that is nice. They are both herding now. They were doing nothing. They were both just going around to different hogans and they used to just go around where there was singing going on and I think this is a nice place for them to stay. I see there are lots of sheep and I think they have got plenty to eat, too, and just the same with the old man (he called him the old man even though he was not old), I guess he likes to stay here because he eats plenty of good meat." That's what we were talking about in the sweat-house.

Then I asked about that man. I said "When he first came here to our place he said 'I have some stock. I've got some horses and cattle and some property.' That's what he said

when he first came here. But I don't see that he brought anything back with him from there. Has he got anything over
there where he used to live?" Then he gave a little laugh and
he said, "No, no, he hasn't got anything. He hasn't got any
horses or cattle or sheep or property. He hasn't got any. I
know him very well. He has got a family all right, but he
always leaves his family alone and he goes out and gambles
and drinks whiskey and goes around with a lot of women
and he does a lot of bad things besides. That's the way he
was when he lived over there with us and now I see him
staying with that woman and I see she has got a big herd and
I guess he is getting plenty of eats." Then I said, "Yes he is
getting plenty of eats and that woman has got a lot of herds.
She has some horses and she has a lot of cattle and she has
got property. She has all that she wants and she was all alone
and now he joined this woman." Then he said, "Well, then
it's up to him; if he does good he will live good. If he tries to
do what he was doing before he won't get very far. I don't
think he will live long with that woman. If he starts to gamble
and drink again he will be poor all the time. If he puts all
those things aside and just goes ahead with his work, soon
he will be a man. He is a man now but I mean soon he will be
a rich man."

When we got out of the sweat-house the sun was pretty
well down. I went over to Woman Who Walks Alone's place.
She asked me about these two visitors. "I didn't see them but
my brother saw them but he hasn't met them yet. He just saw
that they are there at your place." I said, "Yes they are all
there. I was over at a sweat-house with that man. We just got
through with the sweat-house a little while ago. He went
back home and I started from there. I wanted to come around
here just to see what is going on." She said, "There is nothing going on, just the work we always have, that's all." Then
she asked me about that man, "Who is that man, is he Deer
Spring?" I said, "Yes, it is him. I think they are going back
tomorrow and they came to take the herd back with them. I
think they are going to move tomorrow." Then she said,
"What do they want to move for, it's just too hot to move."

I started back home and just when I got home the herd

was in and this man was coming back from where his horses were. The cooking was all done and when we ate it was night and we all went to bed. Next morning I said to my mother again, "I'd like to keep some sheep here with me, those that are not strong, those that I know couldn't stand the travelling. There are quite a few lambs that are too small. I know they can't stand the trip. I want to separate them and I want to keep them here. And I'd like to have some wethers, so I'll have some meat when I want to have some. I don't want to lose them and I'd like to have some with me all the time because you know very well I couldn't go without meat."

Then she said to me, "What are you talking about anyway? There are lots of sheep over where you are staying. You can get meat from them, can't you?" Then I said, "No, those sheep over there do not belong to me. They belong to those people." Then she said to me, "But you can always get some meat, can't you?" "No, I can't get meat from them, that's why I want to keep some for my own so whenever I get hungry for meat I will have some." This is what we said to each other in the morning. Then I said, "What I said, I mean it." I talked about that for a while again but she was just sitting there while I was talking and, when I got through I said, "We will start to separate them before noon but we will take the herds out this morning and let them have a little feed just around here close and we will start in before noon to separate those that are not strong and all the little lambs that couldn't stand the travelling." Then Deer Spring said, "Well, my younger brother, that is a good idea. I know some of them couldn't stand the travelling. If we start with them we will have lots of trouble. But I see that you want to separate them and keep them here. That's good, so we won't have trouble with them or lose them and I think we will get the rest across all right and I guess it will take us two nights to travel across. We will travel at night, not in the day time because it will be nice and cool at night." Then I said, "We will take the herd down to the wash where it is cool." Then she said, "I guess it will be all right. If you want to separate them you can separate them. But take good care of them. Don't lose any of them and you

168

said you want to separate some wethers and you can separate them too."

After we talked about this I said, "I will go down to the wash and see if I can find a good place." There was a little wash there. The wash had a bank on both sides. Then I got some greasewood and I made a little brush fence on both sides of this wash. When I got through with this I came back home, and when I came back they had killed a sheep and they had the herds out close around there and this other man had gone after the horses. After a while he brought the horses back and hobbled them nearby. I said, "I have the corral all fixed already. We will take the herds down there and separate those that are not strong." This man said, "That's nice, my younger brother. I was afraid that we might have trouble with them."

About that time the cooking was all done. They had some meat roasted and boiled and we had lots to eat. Then my mother said to me, "I laid this meat aside for you to take back with you so that you will have some meat when you get back home and we will take the rest with us." After we ate it was noon and we took the herd down to where I made this little corral and I started to separate those which I knew were not strong, the old ewes with lambs, and I separated some old wethers and I separated four ewes with the lambs which I earmarked for my wife. When I had separated all I knew were not strong there were close to forty altogether. When we came back from there they all started packing up the horses. The sheep that I separated I left in the corral. I said about the bucks and billy goats, "We will leave them all here because they are taking good care of them for us" (but I never got them back). "Now," I said, "You won't have any trouble with the herd. You will get across with the herd all right but be sure not to drive them in the daytime because it's just too hot for them, even though they are strong. So drive them at night. I think it will take you only two nights to drive them across. As soon as you get close to the mountain then you will be all right." And I said to this man, "Be sure and take good care of the herd for me and you know what to do so that

169

I won't be worried about it so much. I will take good care of these which I separated. I will take them up on the mountain where it is nice and cool in the woods and where there is lots of green grazing for them." About that time they were all ready to go. We all shook hands with each other and they left.

I got on my horse and I rode over to where Woman Who Walks Alone lived. She was all alone again and I asked her, "Where is the man (Son Of Late Grey Hat)?" And she said, "The old man just went out again. He drove the cattle over to the water and he wants you to go over and look at them again. Some of the cattle have calves and the calves are so small he is afraid that the herders might let the dogs go after the calves and they might kill the calves. He is going to watch them till they get away with their herds." Then she asked me about the dust. "What was that dust? What makes so much dust out in the flat?" I told her, "I got left all alone. They just left with the herd and I guess the herd is making all that dust." Then she said, "Well, then, you are all alone now." I said, "Yes, I am all alone but I think I will be all right staying around here. I came over here to tell you to take good care of my bucks and billy goats. I want to leave them here with you all this summer till fall." She said, "All right. We will take good care of them for you. Nothing will happen to them so don't worry about it. Have you got anything to eat or did you have something? If you are hungry I will make you some coffee before you go." "No," I said to her, "I just had lunch a while ago." "Well," she said, "Any way even if you had lunch I will make you some more lunch my son." I said, "No, my mother I've got to go back and turn out the sheep which I separated from the herd." She said, "Well then you will have some sheep with you and you will have some meat all the time."

Then I went out and I got on my horse and I rode back where I had the sheep. I turned them out and started off with them. Soon I got back to a place called Trail Along The Edge Of The Woods and there is where we had a little barn. I got back there with the sheep. When I got home to my wife there with the small herd they asked me, "Where did you get that herd?" and I told them where my mother had gone. Then my

170

wife said, "Oh why did she move away from here? Why did she move that far away from us? I think it's too hard for her moving across the flat in these hot days." "Well," I said, "I guess she could stand it. She wanted to go over to that country so bad so that's why I just let her go, but I told them not to travel in the daytime. I think they will make it all right if they travel at night." Then I told her, "Get on this horse (that was the horse I had been riding) and take these sheep over to your herd. Maybe they won't like it but anyway you take the sheep over and just turn them in with your herd. If they don't like to have these sheep then I will take them back and I will take care of them." She got on the horse and she took them to her herd and I said to her, "They are old ewes. They had lambs lately. I thought they couldn't stand the long distance. That's why I separated them and I thought when they get fat we will use them, and there are some old wethers in the bunch that we will use for the meat." When she left I went out and got some wood. When I thought I had enough I started to chop it up. She came back just when it got dark and I unsaddled the horse and took the horse a little ways and hobbled it. Then I told her what we had said to each other and about how the two women cried. Then she was glad about those sheep because I told her that we will have some meat all the time, whenever we want to have some.

10

He gets his gift horse . . . He
gambles . . . Jealousy and quarrels
with his wife . . . He helps hoe the corn . . .
His wife is mad again but they are reconciled.

next morning I got on my horse and I started from
there. I had heard that someone had driven the
horses down from the Black Mountain for the salt weed.
These horses belonged to Choclays Kinsman—I had heard
that the horses were still at a place called Canyon Wash.
When I got there they were in the corral where I cut the
calves. There were two boys driving these horses, Choclay
and another boy with him. I went there because a horse had
been given to me by Choclays Kinsman's wife. She was my
older sister and I asked these two boys about that horse. I
said, "A horse was given to me by my older sister. Is that
horse in this bunch? Do you know anything about it?" "Yes,"
they said, "That horse is in this bunch. When we started to
drive them down they had pointed it out for us and they told
us if you happened to come or if we happened to see you,
they wanted us to let you know about it. So now you are here
and the horse is here in this bunch." I said, "Help me on
that. We will rope him and we will put a saddle on him. Help
me to put the saddle on him and I'll ride him around here for
a while till he kind of plays out and then I'll start to chase him
down to where mine are."

It was a good-looking horse, a stallion three years old.
We tangled him up with the rope. When we got him down on
the ground we put hobbles on him. Then we put a bridle on
him and we put the saddle on him. We got him down on the
ground again once more so that we could untie the hobble.
As soon as he got up I grabbed hold of his ears and I got on

him while the boys were holding onto the rope. They chased the horse out with me on him and he started running off towards the flat. The boys got on their horses and they started after me. They were chasing me around all over the flat. Soon the stallion was out of wind. He was all sweated, all soaked up. The sweat was running down to his feet. Then they chased the horse back to the corral and I took the saddle off and put it back on the horse that I was riding. I put a halter on this bronco, and got the rope tied to the halter, and then I started to chase him down to where my horses were. They had turned out the horses and they started back to the mountain. Then I started off with that horse and I chased him down straight to the hogan where we had that Blessing Way. There were some boys around there. I took the saddle off of the horse which I was riding and turned him loose. The boys helped me put the saddle on this other horse and one of the boys got on this horse. He rode him around till he kind of gave up again. Then he turned the horse over to me and I got on him again and I started back over to my place. There was some food all ready to be eaten. From there on, I don't know for how many days, I just stayed around there at this one place. There was nothing for me to do, just to get food every once in a while when we ran out. Every day I saddled up my horse and rode him around. The n he got kind of gentle. I put the saddle on him again and I started off where the horses were. When I got there I got another one and I turned my gift horse in with the bunch. I had all the horses rounded up and drove them down to the water. There I just let the horses go.

I started to ride over to where some people had moved to the water around Anything Falls In. There was a hogan. I got there and there was a man named Who Has A Hat and there was a woman there too. She used to live up on the Black Mountain, but had moved there. She was lame. We used to call her Moves Her Hands Behind Her Back and there was another man there. We used to call him Turkey. There were a lot of men around there. They were all gambling. Some old men were gambling on one side and there were some boys gambling on another side. I stayed around there because I

173

kind of liked to watch their gambling. There was a lot of money piling up. There were saddle blankets and silver buttons and bracelets and rings piled around there. That was what they gambled for and I said, "I wish I had all the money and all the rest of the stuff. This is a nice place to be because there are lots of people around here and it looks to me that you won't be lonesome. I see everybody enjoys playing cards." Then Who Has A Hat said to me, "If you'd like to have all these things, money and the rest of the stuff, you just sit down and we will give you the cards and, if you are lucky, soon you will have all the money and the rest of the stuff. If you haven't got anything maybe you have some matches in your pocket. Start to play for the matches. Even if you have only one match start with that and soon you will have lots of matches and you will have something besides. So come on and start in." Then I made up my mind to try it. I never played before but I had been around where the fellows were gambling and that was how I knew all the names of the cards from ace up to king. I knew all the names of the cards but I didn't know how to play them.

When I made up my mind I sat down with the boys (the old men were playing together in one group, the boys together in another). One fellow asked me, "Do you want to play?" I said, "Yes I will try even though I don't know anything about it." Then he said "Get a hand. I will help you." So then they dealt out five cards to me. I reached down in my pocket for some matches. I got the matches out and I started to play. I had just a few matches and soon all of my matches were gone. Then one fellow helped me out with some more matches and I started in playing again. Soon all the matches were gone again and another fellow gave me a handful and I started playing again. The fellow who helped me play was trying his best for me to win some matches. Pretty soon I had just a few matches left again but at last we won some and I had a big pile of matches under me. I just grabbed a handful and gave it back to the fellow that helped me with the matches and the other fellow. Right away we started in playing again. When I had just a few more matches then I won again and I had a big pile of matches under me. Then I said,

174

"I will stop now. I don't want to lose all these matches again." The fellows wanted me to stay and play with them but I just didn't listen to them. I put all the matches in my pocket, I had two pockets full. I got up and walked over to where my horse was standing. As I was walking over to my horse I looked at the sun and the sun was pretty well down so I thought I'd better be going back home.

As soon as I got home I said to my wife, "I am so hungry." She asked me where I had been all this day. I said, "I was down to the valley and I got to a place where some fellows were gambling. I was watching them. Pretty soon they wanted me to gamble too. They wanted me to join them so I did. But I didn't gamble for big things. I just played for matches." When I said this to her she said, "You started that. Once you've started you will want to do that again. So now you are in the habit. Soon you won't have anything with you." She just let that go. Then she turned around to me and she said, "I know what you went down there for. That old thing is down there." (She meant this woman Horse's Ass's Wife.) "I hate that old thing because she burned the robe and the robe isn't worth anything now because she spoiled it. I wanted to beat her. If I had done that I would be satisfied, but not now. I just hate her. I know you've been around with her." When she said this to me I told her not to speak to me like that. "I hate that kind of talk because I don't know anything about it. I am not like you. I don't know anything about that bad talking so don't talk to me like that." This is what we said to each other and then, while she was saying this, she was running around there in the hogan and she was doing the cooking. She was doing the cooking while she was talking to me about that woman. But I just didn't pay any attention to her. I just started to help her cook. When we were done she put the things right in front of me and I started eating. She went to the other side of the hogan and started to work on the wool, sitting there with her back to me. I just went ahead with my eating. When I got through I picked up the dishes and put them away. She was working on the wool.

I went out and I took my horse up to the foot of Black

Mountain. When I came back from there it was dark. She was still working on the wool. I looked at her. I knew she was mad. I just didn't bother with her. I picked up the sheep pelt and spread it down. I made me a pillow. Then I lay down and covered myself with a blanket and, after quite a long while when I was about to go to sleep, she pulled the cover off of me. She said, "Get up. I want to fix up the bed." So I got up. I thought she was all right again. I went outside and walked around for a while. I came back inside. She had made up the bed and I just lay right down again and she lay down beside me too. As soon as she lay down she started to talk to me about that woman again. She was talking to me about that for a long time. Then I said to her, "I am just tired of your talking to me like that and I am tired. I want to go to sleep. Don't keep me awake." But she kept talking to me for a long while and then I said to her again, "I told you not to talk to me like that. Didn't you hear me? You ought to be ashamed talking to me like that. You must not talk about your relatives like that. She is your relative. She is your companion so you mustn't talk about her like that." But she just kept talking about her more and more so then I just kept quiet and soon I went to sleep. She was still talking and I don't know how long she talked.

Next morning when I woke up she had started the fire and was sweeping around it. I just rolled to one side again. I didn't get up. While I was still lying in the bed I heard the dogs barking. Then soon my younger brother came in. He said to me, "Haven't you got up, my older brother?" "No," I said, "I am still lying in bed." Then I got up and started putting my clothes on. I said to him, "You got up early this morning." "Yes," he said, "I got up this morning because I wanted to come over here to see you before you got away to some place. There are lots of weeds to be hoed over at our cornfield and I thought we would start hoeing the weeds today. If we don't they will ruin the corn, and I want you to help me on that, my older brother." I said, "All right, I am willing to do anything. I guess we will have nice fat meat, too." Then he said, "I haven't any meat but we will have

176

some. My older sister will go over and kill one before the herd goes out." Then I said, "That's nice. We will have some meat and I'll go over there. I want to go after my horse. I had him hobbled last night up on Black Mountain Strip. When I bring him back home I want to go down where I turned loose the one I got lately. I will saddle him up and ride him back and I'd like to cut him, too. I thought maybe when I cut him he won't go away from here. After I go to these two places I will be there." Then he said, "All right."

When I picked up my rope my wife turned around to me, "When you bring this other horse back you ride up to where the herds are and bring the sheep down here on horseback." Then I said, "All right. I will go and get the horse down and I will saddle him up and I will ride up there to get the sheep." Then I said to this other fellow, "You can go back now and I will be there as soon as I get my horse down." He went back and from there on my wife was all right again. She started running around there getting things ready, talking and smiling. Then I went out to where the horse was and I brought him back and I rode up there and right away they caught the sheep for me and I brought it back. She started butchering and she had the food cooked already. I just ate a little; I was in a hurry to go after this other horse. Then I said to her, "I am in a hurry. I'd like to go after this other horse before it gets too hot." She said, "All right. I will be all right by myself on this butchering." Then I got on my horse and started off down to the flat where the horses were. There was the horse that I was after and I started to round up the horses. I rounded them all up and started them down to the water. When I got down to the water with the horses there was a corral there close by this water. I drove the horses over to this corral and I got them in and I took the rope off of my horse and I roped this other horse. He was wild again so I started fighting with him for a long while. I put the saddle on him; then I got on him but he didn't buck with me, he just started to run around with me. I ran him around for a while. Then when he got all right I went back to the corral and turned the horses out. I just let them out and I started back home.

When I got there she had everything ready there for me

to take over to the cornfield. She had gone. I picked up the things which she had put in the sacks and I put them on this bronco. I had a little trouble with the bronco for a while putting the things on him. Then I got on him and started off to the cornfield. When I got there, quite a few fellows were hoeing. I took the things off my horse and I took the horse down to where there were a lot of salt weeds. I had him hobbled there. Then I went to the cornfield and started in with the hoeing. We were hoeing the weeds till noon. When we all went back to where the rest were cooking, everything was ready to be eaten. We had nice fresh fat meat.

After we were through eating some more people came and they said they wanted to help us too. That was Lost His Moccasins with his family and right away they cooked some more food for them. When they got through eating we all started out to the cornfield again. While we were going down another man came. He was a Bitahni clansman and there were ten of us hoeing again. We were all talking to each other about the funny things we had done during our life and we had lots of fun. There were seven of us men and three women hoeing the weeds. The weeds were good and thick. Every once in a while we sharpened the hoes so we had them sharp all the time. We just kept on hoeing the weeds and every once in a while another man would come and as soon as he came he would start to help us hoe. We just kept on doing that. Pretty soon we had hoed up the weeds on half of the cornfield. About that time the sun was pretty well down and one of the fellows said, "I've got to go home because it's quite distant and I've got to get back home before it gets dark since I've got something else to do at home." So then they started to leave. When they stopped hoeing we told them to go to the hogan to get something to eat before they left. They did and pretty soon just two of us were hoeing. We hoed till it was dark and we could hardly see what we were doing. We did a good job that day. We almost finished hoeing up the weeds. I said, "It won't take us long to hoe the rest of the weeds tomorrow. I am glad those people helped us in hoeing." "So am I, my older brother," he said to me. Then we started home and we got back after it was dark. The food was all ready to be eaten. We ate and after that I just went right to bed. I was so tired working all that day in the hot sun, that as soon as I lay down I went right to sleep.

When I woke up my wife was just starting to take the ashes out. She took the ashes out and she started the fire. Then she started sweeping and I got up, put my clothes on and put my moccasins on. It was still a little dark. Then I thought, "I will go down to the cornfield and start hoeing while it's nice and cool." When I was hoeing another fellow came and two more came and there were four of us hoeing early in the morning. When the sun was pretty well up they called us to come and eat. So we stopped hoeing and we went back home. Just as soon as we were through eating we went out and started hoeing again. We kept on till noon when they called us to eat again. There were only four of us hoeing all that morning and just as soon as we were through eating we went down and started in again till the sun was pretty well down. We were thankful and glad that we had finished and then we went back home. It had taken us two days to finish with the hoeing and we were tired from working in the hot sun.

Next morning as soon as I got up I thought about my robe that was burned. I thought, "I will fix that robe today." My wife was cooking that morning. When I dressed myself I went outside and walked around for a while. After I ate I started to work on the robe. There was quite a big hole through it. Before I started to weave I told my wife to get me some red twine. She turned around to me and she said, "I won't. Why don't you go and get that old thing Horse's Ass's Wife to get you what you want? I won't try and get you something." She was mad at me again that morning because I had started to work on this robe. When she said this to me I said to her, "I told you not to talk to me like that. You always think about something that I don't like and you always want to start trouble with me. I thought you had forgotten all those things. Maybe you would like to have trouble but I won't start trouble. If you want to start it you just go ahead and start it but I won't start trouble with you because I said before

179

I didn't like any trouble. And I said to you I didn't want to start the trouble with you." When I was talking this way to her she was talking to me, too, so I didn't quite understand what she said to me and perhaps she didn't hear what I said to her.

I just stopped talking and just kept working on this robe for which I got some white twine and some red twine. She kept talking. Then I said to her, "Aren't you going to stop talking to me like that? You've got no business to talk about her." When I said this to her she got mad at me again. Then she said, "I mean it. I hate that old thing. As soon as I see her I will sure beat her to death and then I will be satisfied with her. I sure mean it. I will go after her, that old Ghost. She is daughter of a Ghost. She is born by a Ghost. The Ghost had fucked for her so she is daughter of a Ghost." I said, "What are you? You said *that* because she has no mother and no father. They are both dead and you, your father and mother are still living, and my father and mother are still living. When your father and mother die then you will be Ghost's daughter. You had a husband before me. He didn't have any father or mother so he was Ghost's son and so we will all be Ghost's son and Ghost's daughter when our fathers and mothers die."

She quieted down for a minute but then she got up. She grabbed hold of the poker and she started after me with it. She tried to hit me with the poker but she didn't hit me. I guess she just made believe that she was going to hit me. I was just sitting there working on this robe. I never did dodge or move and she sure was angry that I just kept working on this robe. She just laid the poker down. She didn't say any more words and I didn't say any more words. When she put the poker down she sat on one side of the hogan and I just went ahead with my work. About noon I was getting hungry but she was just sitting there quiet. I just looked at her once in a while. She was sitting there with her back to me. She was just hanging her head looking down. I didn't know what she was doing and I just kept working on the robe trying to fix it like it was before. First I started to weave with some twine but that didn't look good to me so I had to take all that

180

out. Then I got some wool. There was nice white wool that I found I had. I started to work on that wool. I had it carded up and I had it nice and soft and I started to spin the wool. I spun it nice and thin. When I was through I wrapped it up and I got some soap weed and washed the white wool with it. I had the wool good and clean. There was a piece of red flannel which we had used on the decorated stick (used in a ceremonial). I took the thread out of it and I had that for red warp and when the white warp was dry I started to weave that in the robe. When I wove about half an inch it looked all right to me. Around about that time it was a little after noon and she was just sitting there quiet, looking down. I was getting more and more hungry. Then I thought, "I will weave some more. After a while I will cook something for myself."

Late in the afternoon I turned around and looked at her again. About that time she got up. I guess she was hungry then too. She went outside and she brought in some wood. Then she started up the fire and she started cooking. I was just about ready to cook but when she started I just let her go ahead with the cooking. When she finished she put out the things for me and she just walked back to where she was sitting before. I turned around and I started eating. After a little while I said to her, "Why don't you eat? Come on and eat with me. Aren't you hungry? If you don't eat you will starve to death. Come on and eat with me and forget everything." After a while she got up and she sat down and she started to eat. When I got through I started to weave on the robe again and when she got through eating she put the things away. Then she walked up to me and she sat down by my side. I said to her, "Help me weave on this robe." But she didn't say a word. She just sat there for a while. Then she said, "Let me help you." I said, "All right." She started to weave on the robe. We wove about an inch and a half. About that time the sun was down. We didn't get far on the weaving so we just laid it aside. I said, "We will finish it tomorrow so we will just let it go now." Then when we put the robe away I went out and brought some wood in and I built a fire and she started to cook. When she was through we started to eat but we didn't say much to each other.

Then I began to be sorry for what I had said to her. I kind of felt bad about her but I didn't say anything while we were eating. After we ate she started fixing up the bed. I went outside and walked around for a while. When I came back she had the bed fixed up. I took my clothes off and went right to bed and she did, too. Then I rolled over to her and I said, "I feel very bad about what we had said to each other and I am very sorry that I said something to you which I shouldn't say." When I said this I put my arm around her and she put her arm around my neck. Then I said to her, "Now let's forget about what we said to each other today and you mustn't try to talk that way any more and I won't either. I didn't want to talk to you that way but it's you that made me talk that way and I am so very sorry that I said what I shouldn't say to you. So now let's forget about that. We will both put it away and drop it. In that way we will live good. Let both of us try to live good; let's both of us try to be good to each other and if we do that we will live good and we will be happy. All the times like yesterday we've been happy. All day we had a good time and we had lots of fun out in the cornfield hoeing up the weeds. Let's be that way all the time and in that way we will live good all the rest of our lives." Then she said to me "I don't know just why I get that way. As soon as I start to think about her (Horse's Ass's wife) then all at once my mind will be off and maybe I start to talk but I just don't know what I say because my mind is off. I tried lots of times not to get that way. Now I am just the same too. I am very sorry for what I had said to you, too. Maybe I said something that you didn't like but I just don't know what I said to you because I was just like I was unconscious. But now I will try my best not to get that way any more." I said, "Yes, if you mean it then we will live good and we will be happy all the time." This is what we said to each other that night while we were in bed. Then I said to her again, "When you were very mad today you got up and grabbed the poker. As soon as you picked it up you ran at me with it. You were going to hit me with it but you didn't hit me. If you had hit me with that poker you would have given me a pain. I would be suffering from pain now or maybe you would have killed me if you

182

had hit me on my head with it. It wouldn't have been a good thing for you to do. You would have done a serious thing. If you had killed me you would have been taken off to some place far away from here or maybe you would have been killed too. So now try your best not to get that way. As soon as you think you are that way try to think about something else or do something so in that way it will get out of your mind. Maybe you can't but you just try. I guess you learned all that from your mother and from your mother's husband. They were fighting all the time when you were a girl. From the time they were married they started fighting and one of them would get licked. That's the way they were doing all their lives and I think you learned from them but you don't want to be that way." This is what we were saying to each other while we were lying in the bed. Then we were both tired talking. I guess we were both sleepy. Then I said, "Let's go to sleep now."

Next morning after we ate we started to weave again. We worked on that robe till noon and it was half finished. After we ate we started to weave again. We got through with it just when the sun was down. It took us a day and a half to fix up this little place. It was hard to do and we were both tired. That evening she had cooked some more food and after we ate we went right to bed again. She was all right all that day and the next morning after we ate we fixed up the robe. We cut all the threads off and all the yarns and we carded a little where we had woven and it looked like it wasn't burned. Then we had a new robe.

11

He has a visitor . . . Rounding
up and earmarking the cattle . . .
The chant . . . He patches up
a misunderstanding with Slim Man.

an old man we used to call Lots Of Boys came to our
place. He was a Bitahni clansman and he was my
maternal grandfather. He was with a boy. The boy was his
grandchild. They came inside and I spread out a sheep pelt
for them by my side. Then I shook hands with him. I said to
him, "Grandfather, I am glad to see you again." "So am I,
grandchild," he said to me. I said to him, "Where do you
keep yourself? Where is your home now?" He said "We
started from the top of the mountain from a place called Lake
In The Woods. I was lying down. All at once I thought about
you so right away I thought I will come down here to visit
you. I was wondering where you were. I know there are two
places where you always move, Anything Falls In and up
here at Where The Gray Hill Comes Out. I didn't know you
were here. We just came down from the mountain. We didn't
know where we were going but all at once while we were riding along my grandchild saw the hogan. So we went over to
that hogan. There I asked about you and they pointed across
here. So now we are here and I am glad that we are here."

He asked me about the good grass. Then I took the boy
out and showed him where the grass was and he took the
horses up there. "Well then," Lots Of Boys said, "We are
here and I am very glad to see you and glad that I am here,
and I would like to see your mother, too. I wonder where she
is living? From here I'd like to spend a few days with her. I
know I will have nice fat meat all the time every time I visit
her. So that's where we are going." Then I told him about her

leaving, and about separating the old wethers and lambs and some ewes which I thought couldn't stand the long journey. Then he said, "That's the way she was when she was young. When she was young she used to run around all over the place, all over the country to different places, back and forth. You can't stop her from anything like that. But later Old Man Hat warned her. Before she married this man she didn't have anything at all. When she married him she stopped running around because Old Man Hat held her back. From there on she became a woman. Old Man Hat had a lot of stock, sheep, horses, cattle, and some properties and that's how she got some stock, too. When the old man died she got some more stock and that you know all about. So that's the way she was. I guess she thinks that she is still young. That is why she wants to run around again. I know very well you can't hold her back."

Then he said, "The womenfolks are different from us menfolks. They think different from us and they talk different from us. We menfolks all have different minds, thoughts, and talks from the womenfolks so we can't tell who is right. Sometimes we menfolks do something right and sometimes the womenfolks do something right, and sometimes we menfolks do something wrong and sometimes the womenfolks do something wrong. That's why we can't tell who does the wrong thing or who does the right thing. But I know one thing about womenfolks. When they want to do something they will start it. You try to hold her back from it but you just can't. As soon as she begins to cry you can't do anything with her. You might as well let her go. So I think you did right and she did wrong. I know you did right because you separated the sheep that you knew were not healthy. She didn't know anything about it. You separated these sheep and you've got them here with you right now. You said soon you will have them all good and fat and I know you will." After he talked about all the things way back then he said again, "She must not think about you. She knows very well that she had only one baby and that's you. Now it seems like she doesn't care about you because she left you here all alone. She took all the herd across this big desert in

185

this hot weather. She ought to know better than that. She knows very well that it is too hot for the herd to drive across this desert and she knows very well there is not water across this desert, but she just went ahead and took the herd across. But even though she went through all this hot weather I don't think that she noticed it. If she wanted to go across to that place she ought to have gone in the right way and she ought to have left the herds with you and ridden across to that place and visited her relatives for a few days. But, instead of doing that, she took everything across and took everything away from you. I don't think it is right for her to do that, taking everything away from you and leaving you here all alone." This is what he said again.

Around about that time the cooking was all done. While we were talking my wife had fixed up all the things to eat. We had some meat left over from when we were over hoeing the weeds at the cornfield, and this meat was nice and fat but it was kind of dry. But my wife had the meat all softened. She had pounded the meat with two rocks and she had fried the meat with the fat and she had tortillas fried with fat. She had made everything soft and she laid out the things in front of us. Then we sat around and started to eat. He was very thankful about the food: "I so appreciate that I have some nice soft meat. This is the only way I could eat the meat. I can't chew much anymore, my grandchild, because you know I haven't got any more teeth. I was so hungry and I got enough to eat now. Tonight I will sleep well and I will have a good rest."

Then I said to him "Well, grandfather, we will fix up a bed for you and I want you to lie down and go right to sleep and get a good rest. I know you are tired because you rode a long ways. I know just how you feel so you can just lie down and go to sleep and take a good rest." Then my wife started fixing up a bed for him. He said, "We will sit around, my grandchild, for a while." Then I told him about what I had been doing. First I said, "When Old Man Hat was still living he used to talk a whole lot to us, me and my mother. She used to try to go to some places but the old man used to hold her back. Sometimes they quarreled over that and now she is all alone. I guess she thinks that she can go any place she wants to go. I tried to hold her back but she doesn't pay any attention to me. I was just working a lot on the herds. In the lambing and shearing season I always have lots of work and I tend to the horses and cattle. Besides that I tend to the corn-field. Besides that I travel around but I don't travel around for nothing. I travel around to get some food and that's what I did lately. I took all my wool over to Wide Reeds (Ganado). From there I went to Keams Canyon. I came around here from there and I brought some food and we had enough food but she took it all with her." Then I said, "I've got my plans all made out, grandfather. Some time ago I went up to where the cattle were and I got just a few of them. They all have calves and I earmarked the calves but I cut only three of them be-cause I couldn't do much all by myself. Today I got my wife's brothers to help me and they are going to help me tomorrow. I got me a horse for that and that's that horse standing out-side. I had him tied out there so that I can start out tomorrow early. That's what we are going to do tomorrow, grandfather. Now you just lie down and go to sleep and take a good rest. I don't want to keep you awake so long." Then he said "All right. Tomorrow I guess we will know what to do." Then he lay down and I covered him up. I got out another robe for him and I put that robe on him. He was so pleased about that.

Next morning while it was still dark I got up and I woke my wife and told her to make up the food and cook a lot so that we would all get enough. "Make enough so that we will have enough for our lunch." While she was starting the fire I started off where the horses were. Pretty soon I got them all rounded up and I got them down to the water just when the sun was coming up. When they all got water I drove them over to the other hogan. There were two corrals which the boys had put up, one for the sheep and the other for the horses. I got the horses in the corral and I hollered to the boys, "Come on with your rope." They came out with their ropes, and I told them to rope the horses which I wanted to use on the cattle. I asked them, "Is anybody else going?" They said my wife's sister and her two brothers wanted to go too, so they got another horse for my wife's sister. Then I went in the corral and roped one for my wife. Then we turned the horses out and led the horse for my wife and my horse back and the boys led their horses to their home. When I got home with the horses I tied them outside to the tree. While I was walking in I looked at the sun and the sun was pretty well up. I went inside. Everything was ready to be eaten. Then we sat around and ate, we two and the boy that was with my grandfather. But grandfather was lying down and I said to him, "Get up, grandfather, come on and eat." Then he raised up his head "No, no, grandchild, I have eaten already this morning. I don't know why I don't eat much in the morning. It's not that I don't like the food. I like the food all right but I just can't eat much in the morning and I am always that way, so you can just go right ahead and eat," he said to me. Then I said to him "Come on, my grandfather, eat some more, anyway." Then he said, "All right. I will just take a little again." And I said to him "Eat a lot, grandfather. Right after we eat we are all going up to where the cattle are. Do you want to stay here and just lie around and take a good rest today while we are up there working on the cattle?" Then he said "I will be lonesome all alone here. I'd better go with you. I like to see you working with the cattle and from there we will go back. I wanted to visit your mother but she isn't here so I guess we'd better go with you. We will start back from there to our home. Then I said to him "All right, grandfather."

Then I got out the robe I had let him use and I gave him this robe. It was a brand new one and I said to him "I give this robe to you, grandfather, because it won't be long till it starts to get cold again." He was so surprised, holding it up, turning it around, smiling, and he said, "This is great, my grandchild. I will keep this robe with me. This time I will keep it till it is all worn." He was so pleased with it. "I mean it. I will keep this robe till it's worn out. Every time I go someplace I get a robe from somebody. When I get home, when my grandchildren see that I've got a robe, they want it and they always take it away from me, but this time I won't

188

let them have it. I thank you very much, my grandchild. You are kind."

Then we all started to put the saddles on the horses, and started to get ready to go. We all got on our horses. About that time the boys were coming riding and dashing across to us. When they came up to us their sister was riding behind them, and when we all got together, we started. All the horses were lively. They all wanted to go like they were race horses and the old man was looking at the horses. He said to me, "You've got nice horses. They are all looking good and they are all lively. Are they all race horses?" he asked. "No, grandfather," I said to him. "They are not race horses. I just use them on the cattle." "Well, that's nice. That's the way to be." We went on. We went by Where Lots Of Rocks Were Washed Out, we passed that place, and we got to Flowing Out Of The Canyon. There we stopped and I told the boys, "We will scatter out from here." I pointed out a place for each of them to go and I told them "Don't go farther than Water Under The Rocks. But if you see some tracks on the other side you can go way around on the other side of Water Under The Rocks." Then I told the boy who was with the old man, "You ride straight up on that trail," and I told him where to stop and wait for the cattle. "Every time you see them coming just drive them down." So all the boys went off and I told the old man, "You can ride over to that corral and wait for us there, grandfather." I told him to gather up a little wood and have some water there, and we gave him a jug. We told him where the water was from the corral. Then he said, "All right. I will go over." And he went over to the corral and I started with the two women, my wife and her sister.

We rode way up to the foot of the mountain where I knew most of the cattle stopped. While we were riding along we looked around but we never saw any cattle. There were lots of tracks around but we couldn't see any of them. Then I told the two women to stay around there. I started off by myself and rode around all through the thick woods but I couldn't see any cattle. Soon I got way up on the cliff where I told the boy to be and the boy was there where I told him to wait. I asked him, "Did you see any of them?" He said, "I didn't see any of them while I was coming up here but a while ago a bunch of them came out of the wood and I just drove them down. That's all." And I said "I didn't see any of them. I've been all around in those thick woods and around the foot of the cliff. I've been all around in those gulches and around those gaps and passes. None of them are around there but there are lots of tracks. Then I climbed all around those thick places but I didn't see any of them."

While we were talking we heard a sound. Then somebody said, "Uh, uh." Soon a bunch of them came out of the woods and we drove them down the trail. Then I told the boy to wait there for the other boys and I went down after these two bunches. I got down to where the two women were. I told them to go after those two bunches that came down and drive them down toward the corral. When they went down I went back up again to where the boy was. A little while after I got up there we heard another noise. This time a big noise was coming towards us. We heard the sticks breaking and soon another bunch came out of the woods. They were tearing down towards us and the boys were right behind them and we got them down to the trail. There we all got together again. Then I asked the boys "How far did you have to go?" and they said "We went pretty far from here. We saw a lot of tracks but that's all we could find. We rode around all over but that's all we could find." Then I said "I guess we got them all." We started down after them. The two women had driven the cattle into the corral. We drove the others in and fixed the gate so that they wouldn't get out. I looked at the sun. It was just about noon when we put the cattle in the corral.

Then we built a big fire. I said "We haven't got enough meat with us so I guess we'd better kill one of these calves so that we will have some meat and we will be good and strong. But what will we kill it with? We haven't got anything with us." Then the old man said "Get a piece of rock. That's the way I used to kill cattle." So I sent one boy after a rock. He brought back a good sized one. It was kind of narrow and it

190

had points on both sides. Then I got on my horse. The boys opened the gate for me and I rode in. Then I thought, "The calves are too small to feed all of us. I'd better rope one of the yearlings so that grandfather can have some meat to take home with him and we will all have enough to take home with us." I roped one and then all the boys came in and roped the yearling and they dragged it out and got it down on the ground. They tied the yearling's legs. Then they got the rock and killed the yearling by hitting it on the head with the rock. Then we all sharpened our knives and started to butcher while the two women were making the coffee and the other food. It didn't take us long and we got the meat all cut up and they roasted some on the charcoal. Soon everything was ready to be eaten. The yearling was nice and fat and it was so tender. All of them were pleased and they enjoyed having nice fat meat. After we ate everybody was so thankful. I got up and walked around for a while.

Then I turned around and walked up to the old man and I said, "Would you like to have some meat to take back home with you, grandfather? Do you think you could carry some meat on your horse or maybe it's too heavy or maybe you don't care for meat? How about it, grandfather, would you like to have some?" Then he looked up to me. He was trying to talk but he could hardly talk. He just worked his mouth all around. It looked like he was chewing something and he was almost on his knees and he was kind of shivering all over when I said this to him. He was so tickled about it. He didn't know what to say for a while. At last he said, "Do you mean that, my grandchild, my baby?" I said "Yes," and he said, "Sure enough I would like to have a piece. That was what I wished for all these days. The cattle meat is the best meat. Yes, yes, grandchild, if you want to give me a piece I sure would like to have it." Then I walked over to where the meat was. I picked up the hindquarter and I laid it aside and I picked up the frontquarter and I laid it aside and I picked up one whole side of the rib and I said, "Here you are, grandfather." When he came up to me I said, "There, grandfather, there is a little piece of meat for you." I pointed to the meat for him. He almost fell over. He kind of danced a little be-

191

cause he was so pleased with it and he started saying "Thank you, my grandchild, my baby." I don't know how many times he said that. He kept on saying that for a long while. "You are so nice and you are a kind man, the kindest man that I ever saw. When we get home with it all of my grandchildren will be pleased about it and I know they will be so thankful because we haven't had any meat like this for a long time. I have got some cattle but they are a long ways off from here so we can't get any meat like this. But now we've got plenty and it will last us for a long time." He kept on saying thanks all the time.

Then I asked him "Do you still make saddles?" He said "That was all I had been doing but when I ran out of the raw skin then I couldn't make any more saddles." "Well, then," I said "Take that hide there." More and more he was almost running around. More and more he kept on saying thanks. He grabbed a hold of the hide and he started dragging the hide over to where the meat was but he could hardly drag it. Even if he couldn't drag it he just kept on and pulled on it. Then I helped him drag it over to where his horse was standing and fixed up the meat for him and we put it on the two horses. Then he said to the boy that was with him, "We will go home now, my grandchild, while we have meat." And he turned around to me and gave me many thanks again. "You are so good and so kind. This morning you gave me a robe and it was a brand new robe and now you gave me nice fat meat and the hide with it, and I just don't know what to do and what to say to you, my grandchild, and I just don't know how I will make it up to you." Then I said to him, "That's all right, grandfather, you don't have to make it up to me. I just wanted to give that to you because you are grandfather to me." Again he said thanks many times. "Now I can make some more saddles for my grandchildren because I got a whole rawhide."

Then he said "I guess we better be moving along. It's quite away from the foot of the mountain up to the top but we will get to the top before the sun goes down." Then I said, "All right" and I went up to him and shook hands with him

192

and I told him, "Watch your load. Don't let it fall because it is very heavy." He said "We will be all right, my grandchild." They got on their horses and left. I said to the boys "I guess we'd better get at the cattle. We will start in right now and we will be finished with them before the sun goes down." Then they all started to pick up the ropes and we got on our horses and opened the gate, and we rode right into the corral. I just stopped my horse right at the corral. Then I told the boys "You boys can just go ahead and rope the calves and earmark them just like their mother and be sure and make an earmark right. We will earmark them first. Then we will start to cut the others so you can just go ahead. I'd like to go after grandfather. I didn't ask him about one thing. I'd like to ask him about it before he goes too far." Then the boys said, "All right. You can just go ahead and we will do the earmarking."

I started after them and I caught up with them where they had stopped their horses. I said "Grandfather, I forgot to ask you about one thing." Then he said 'We'll wait. Let's get off of our horses." So we got off of our horses and sat down. Then he said "We will smoke while we talk." He reached down in his pocket and he pulled out his tobacco. While he was making a cigarette I said "It's just a little thing that I want to ask you about, grandfather. Where is my younger sister? Is she living up there with you or is she over at Carriso? I just want to know where sister is. I haven't seen her for a long time. She used to come and visit us and I used to go up there to visit her but I just can't now. I've got so much to do every day." Then he said "She is up on the mountain living with us. She wanted to come with us but I told her 'It's just too hot for you and it's a long ways for you to ride on horseback so you'd better stay.' She just cried after me like a little girl. I felt sorry for her but I know it was too far for her to ride on horseback in hot weather like this. If we had brought her down with us it would have been nice but anyway you will get to see her sometime." Then he asked me about the stock. First he asked about the cattle. "About how many is it that you have all together?" "I counted them when we got them in the corral. With the calves all together there

193

are forty-three but I missed four of them. Maybe these four have calves too. With these four that I missed that makes forty-seven. If they all got calves it will be fifty-one."

"Well then," he said, "That's quite a lot for only one man. I didn't think you had that many. And how about the horses, how many horses have you got all together? Do you think there are sixty-three all together? That's a lot too and I know about the sheep. You have a big herd. That's the way to be. I didn't get that far, grandson. We used to have one hundred and fifty horses all together but each of us had only a little over twenty and I see you've got a lot of cattle and a lot of horses and a big herd of sheep all by yourself. Maybe some of them belong to your mother but she won't live long because I know she is getting too old, so everything will be all yours." Then he asked me about my wife. "I know you have been married about a year. I guess by this time you have found out something about her. Are you getting along all right with her or not? How does she treat you? Have you any trouble with her?" I kind of laughed a little. I said "Sometimes we have a little trouble. We had trouble about two or three days ago and before that we had trouble so I don't know how we will get along later." Then he said "The reason that I ask you about that, my grandson, is because I know them very well. They are all raised that way. I know they always want to make trouble but you just don't bother with them. When they want to make trouble you just hold yourself back because I don't want you to be spoiled, because I know you are a good man." That was all we talked about. Then we left each other. They had gone and I went back to the corral.

When I got back they were about finished with the calves. They roped only three more and we earmarked them. Then I told them to rope the bull calves, and we started to cut them. There were quite a few of them that we cut. The last one we had a great time with. As soon as the boys roped this calf, the mother started to go after us, started to go back and forth, chasing us around in the corral. I told the boys to take the calf out. Before that I had told the two women to climb up the trees. They were fixing up the meat but they let everything go and they started running and both climbed up the

194

trees. "Now," I said, "Take the calf out and, when the mother goes out after it, we will take the calf back in and we will let the mother stay out. They took the calf out and the mother ran out, too. Then they took the calf back in. As soon as they got it in I was waving the robe right by the gate in front of this cow. But it just dashed right in. Then I told the boys "Take the calf out again. When you take the calf out this time we'll let her stay inside. They took the calf out and the mother was right behind the calf. We couldn't do anything. Then I put two poles right across the gate and I told the boys to drag the calf in. About that time this cow smelled the meat and ran over where the meat was. While she was over there hollering and making dust we took the calf in and then I started to cut the calf. I did a quick job on it. I cut it and earmarked it. Then we turned the calf loose.

The two women were sitting up on the trees saying, "That old cow got the meat all dirty. Take her away. Take her away. Chase that old cow away." When we were through working on the cattle we opened the gate for them and we turned them out and they started to run. As soon as they got out of the corral they ran back to where we had driven them. After that the two women climbed down off of the tree. When they came back one of her brothers said to my wife, "Are you afraid of that cow?" "Yes, sure, I am afraid of the cow." Then her brother said to her again, "Some time ago I heard that you were trying to go after and fight Horse's Ass's Wife. Aren't you afraid of her?" When he said this to my wife right away she got mad. All the three boys were laughing at her. They got her so mad. They just kept on laughing at her and she said, "Don't talk to me about that old thing. I just hate her. I don't want you to make fun of me about her. I don't like to hear of her." I was laughing too and she said to me, "You laugh! You don't know what you will get." Then I said to her, "Why shouldn't I laugh? Should I be mad while the rest are laughing." When I said this she said to me "You just shut up. Don't talk to me. I mean it. You will get something that you don't like." She was awful mad but her brothers were all laughing at her saying "I guess we have to climb up a tree because she might go after us." They just kept making fun of her. She didn't say any more; she just walked around there picking up her things. Then I said to her "Don't get mad about a little thing like that. They just want to have a little joke that's all. I know they want to have fun all the time so you just give every one of them some meat and let them take it back to their home. We will all get ready now. We will start back to our home."

The boys started to get ready and the sun was pretty well down. She picked up a hindquarter and rib. She laid it aside. Then she said, "There is some meat you all can have." Then I told the boys, "Cut up the meat in a chunk and all of you get a piece." So they all ran up to the meat and started cutting it up. They all had meat. Then they fixed their things and we were ready to go home. Late in the evening we got back to where the boys' and the girls' home was. I told the boys, "You boys can just turn the horses loose and let them go. They know where to go." Then we started on across to our place and when we got back home we took everything off of the horses and I just turned them loose, too. I took the things inside. While she was starting the fire I went out and gathered up some wood. I gathered enough wood to use that evening and enough for the next morning. Then she cooked a little and after we ate then we went right to bed.

Next morning I didn't have anything to do. We got up and made the fire and she started to cook. That night we had slept all right. We didn't start any more trouble. I was afraid that she was going to but we didn't have any. That day she cut up the meat; she cut it in thin pieces. She was working on the meat all that day. When she had it all cut up she put the pieces outside on the trees to dry so that they wouldn't spoil on us. I just went out and got some wood and I just lay around there for two or three days doing nothing. I only tended to the wood and to the water.

I think it was after three days I said, "I would like to go and see the horse I cut. I want to see how that horse is getting along. Maybe it got away and went back up on the mountain." I picked up a rope and a bridle and a small saddle blanket, tied them together, and threw them over my shoulder. I started off and I went up to where the horses were. The horse was still in the bunch and I was glad. Then I got one which I knew was tame. I thought I would go over where the fellows were gambling. I started and I rode up to Anything Falls In where Who Has A Hat had lived. I went down there because playing cards was on my mind. I knew they were still gambling because they always gambled at this place and there would always be lots of people there. When I got there I saw just a few fellows. Just the older men were gambling, some old, some not very old. I thought the boys were still playing but they were all gone so I just stood around there for a while. I was afraid to start playing with the older people. I thought they might skin me all to pieces.

Then I thought, "I'd better go." I got on my horse and rode over to where my mother's older sister Little Woman was living. I got there and she was all alone with her youngest daughter. Right away she said, "We are all alone. Where are you coming from, my son? I thought you were coming from a chant." Then I asked her, "Where is the chant?" "Don't you know where the ceremony is?" she said. "No," I said, "I don't know." "They are having the chant over at Where The Gray Hill Comes Out at Slim Man's place. I thought you were coming from there." "No," I said, "I don't know anything about that chant." She said, "They are having the chant over at that place. My son said he was going over to the chant and he was gone for a day. He said he was coming back in the evening but he hasn't showed up yet. And we are all alone now. There is a hogan across over there and Horse's Ass's Wife lives over there and they don't come around so I just don't know what to do." Then I said to her, "What do you think you want to do?" "I don't know what to do. We haven't got any food. We had a little corn but it is all gone now so I just don't know what to do about food." "Well why don't you come around to my place once in a while. Maybe those people over there will help you on the food. I think they still have some corn. If you come over there they might give you some and there is another relative who lives over that hill. It is not very far from there. You just try and go around among your relatives. That's the only way to get food,

197

if you tell about yourself just how you are fixed now. If you just stay here in one place you will starve, so you just start to go around, or come over to my place. Even if I haven't got much I will try to find something for you." Then I asked her about the chant again. "When is the last day of that ceremony?" "Tomorrow is the last day, my son," she said. "Well then," I said, "I guess I will start back to my home and from there maybe I will go over to that chant. I will see when I get back."

While I was on my way I was kind of sorry that I didn't help Slim Man. I didn't help him on that chant because I didn't know he had it. I was kind of afraid of him, that he might say something to me when I got there. But I didn't go over there to help him because he didn't let me know about it. If he had come and let me know about it I would have helped him a whole lot. This was the way I was thinking when I was coming home. When I got home I told my wife where I had been and that Little Woman didn't have any food. My wife said, "Why didn't you bring them back here with you? We've got some corn and we still have some meat. You ought to have brought them with you." I said "I thought about that. But I thought if I did that, if I brought them back with me, you wouldn't like it." "No," she said, "I know just how you feel when you run out of food so you ought to have brought them back with you." Then I said "She told me there is a chant, and she said tomorrow is the last day so I think I will go over to it."

Next day I started off to the Chant. I was kind of afraid that Slim Man might say something to me bacause I didn't help him. But I just went ahead. All at once, I thought I would go over to my uncle's place, that was Son Of Late Grey Hat, and to my mother's place, that's Woman Who Walks Alone. I hadn't been there for quite a long time now.

I started off that way. When I got to their place I went inside the hogan and my mother, Woman Who Walks Alone, was all alone. She spread out a sheep pelt for me right by her side. I shook hands with her. She started to cry, and she cried for a long time while she was holding my hand. "Every time when you come in it looks like somebody else is right behind you." (She meant her son who had drowned.) She talked about that for a while, how he used to be, how he used to talk, and how I used to be around with him. Then she said, I wonder why your mother doesn't think of you like I used to think about my son. She left you here all alone. I think she just doesn't care about you. But I was thinking about you all the time. I was wondering where you were and how you were getting along and I don't think she is thinking about you like I am and now she is way off upon Carriso. Maybe she is having a good time over there but I don't think she is having a good time without you." Then I said "I have kind of forgotten her by now and I am all right, my mother. I am doing all right. I am not even lonesome for her."

Then I asked about my uncle (Son Of Late Grey Hat). "Where is uncle?" She said, "He went out to see about the cattle; he is always around taking care of the cattle and he is always working on something. This morning he went to where the cattle are." I said "That's what I am doing, too." Then she asked me about the chant. "Have you been there my son?" "No, I haven't been there. I just passed there a while ago and I am kind of afraid to go because I thought if I get there the last day my father won't like it. He might say something to me." Then she said, "That's the way we are. We didn't go over to the place even though we knew that he had a chant, because we have so much to do." Then I said "Anyway I will go over." Then she said to me, "If he starts to talk to you, just keep quiet. Don't try to talk to him. I know he will say something to you so you just don't bother with him, my son. Get me a little wood, my son, we haven't got any. I guess the herders are coming in with the herd by now." Then I went out. There was a big stump there sitting up. I got that out, brought it back and I started to chop it. About that time my uncle had come in. He tied up his horse and walked right inside and I chopped up all the wood. I went inside and my mother was cooking. I walked up to my uncle and shook hands with him, "You haven't been here for a long while. Where have you been, my nephew?" "Oh," I said, "I was over among the Red Clay." And he said "I was wondering where you were." Then he asked me about the chant. I said "Yesterday I heard that they are having a chant and I just passed that place this morning. I started from home this morning. I was heading for that place but I turned around and I thought I would come over here first. I was kind of afraid to go over because Slim Man might not like it if I went there on the last day." He said, "That's the way with us, too. We knew that they were having a chant, but we haven't had a chance to go over because we have plenty to do around here."

Then my mother said, "The two of you go over now and take some meat with you. So that he won't say anything to you, put it right close to his mouth." When she said this we all laughed about it. Then my uncle said, "I think they've got all the meat they want. I know they killed some this morning so we will let the meat go and we will take some coffee and calico over to him." When the cooking was done she put it out ready to be eaten.

Son Of Late Grey Hat started telling about himself. "What you told me was right. When I came here you told me all about the works, different kinds of works. All these works are hard to do, you said to me. You were right. I found that out. You had said to me, 'Take good care of my mother for me, look after all of her things for her.' " I said, "I told you to help me out on that. I used to help her a whole lot. I used to go back and forth tending to the work, tending to my own and hers, too, and when you came here you started in and helped me on all the work. I guess you found it out now." "Yes," he said, "At first everything was too hard for me because I wasn't used to doing all kinds of work. I never worked like this all my life, and as I said before it was too hard for me to do all the work. I got used to it, but around the lambing and shearing season I was all in. So then I got on my horse and I rode back to where my nieces and nephews were and I brought them back to help me with the herding. From there on the work was less for me. They herd and I go around among the cattle. I have to go around every day because they are all getting calves, and besides that I work on wood and water and I help with the herd. But I think now I am used to it. At first it looked like I was fat. I used to be kind of lazy but

200

I found that I am not lazy and I am lively now. I am always glad and enjoy my work and I get enough eats of all kinds. I don't starve; I don't go hungry for meat. I don't go raggy. I am always about the same every day so I am thankful about that. I think it's very nice of you and you are the kindest people that I ever joined and I am so glad that I am here with you now."

"That's right," I said. "I know you have found out about everything and I am glad and thankful to you, too, because you helped me a whole lot, because if you didn't join us I would have had to do all the work by myself. So I am glad that you are helping me along, my uncle." Then he said, "That is all right. Before I joined you I used to be hard up all the time. I used to go around half starved. I used to go around ragged sometimes. I used to go around barefooted. All I did was run around on foot to different places to see if I could eat there. What I was running around for was gambling, drinking whiskey. That was all I had been doing, going around to the Sings and Enemy Way,[1] around to wherever they were having something. But when I came here I was built up again. You know when I got here I used to be skinny but now I am fat and this was all your mother's kindness. Now I never go around to different places. I have forgotten all about it. I am just tending to all the work. Now I like to do all the works and I think I've gotten used to it all and my wife says to me every once in a while, 'If you mean it, if you stay with me and live with me till one of us dies we will enjoy our lives. If I die before you then everything will be yours because you worked hard for it.' " Then she said, "Yes, that's right. I said that to him all right." When she stopped talking my uncle said, "I guess we will go over to the ceremony now. We will take a little coffee and a little calico with us."

He started to dress himself. He took out new pants, new shirt, new coat. He took off his old moccasins and he took brand new moccasins out of a rack. He put those on and he

1. This ceremonial is popularly designated by non-Indians as Squaw Dance. It is directed against the ill effects of enemy and alien ghosts.

201

got out a bunch of red beads. There were about five turquoise pendants on those red beads. He was holding them up. Then he said, "I don't think I will take these beads because the women might get after me for them; they might take them away from me." He put them down and he got out a bunch of white beads that had only one turquoise pendant on them. He put those on himself. When he was dressed up they both started to fix some food to take over to the Sing. They took out some coffee and some calico and, when he was all ready, we went out. When we got down to Anything Falls In we watered the horses and I said, "There is a little hollow right on top of this hill. I will hobble my horse up there. There is a lot of good grass down in this hollow." He said "I guess I will too, my nephew." When we got up there with the horses he said, "What a nice place it is up here. I am getting to know all the places now. I've never been up on this hill before." We took the saddles off our horses, hid the saddles away and hobbled our horses. While we were walking down we made cigarettes and when we got to the foot of this hill we threw the cigarettes away.

Then we started across to Where The Gray Hill Comes Out. We took our time walking across and we got there just when the sun was down. We walked right in and sure enough it was Hosteen Wind Chant Singer who was giving this ceremony. There were just a few men sitting around in the hogan. It wasn't a big crowd and Slim Man was sitting right by the Singer. They were giving the Wind Way chant for his wife. Slim Man said to us, "They were talking about you. When you talk about a man he always shows up. They came the last night because they knew the work was all done so they wouldn't have to do anything." I didn't say anything. Slim Man and my uncle were calling each other cross-cousin and partner. "Yes, we know all about that. We know there is not anything to do by now so that's why we came. So we don't have to do anything." This is what my uncle said. Then Slim Man got up and walked up to us and he shook hands with my uncle." "My cross-cousin," he said, and my uncle said, "Yes, cross-cousin." Then he shook hands with me and he sat down by us and said "I don't know where the boys have

202

gone. They haven't come in yet. There isn't enough wood chopped up for tonight. Both boys who do the work around here haven't come back yet and it's getting dark. I want them to chop some more wood when they come back."

When he said this I got up and went outside; I picked up the ax and started to chop wood and, when I got enough, I quit chopping and I went over to the other hogan where they were cooking. I came inside. There were several women in there and they said to me, "I wish you'd get us some water, my younger brother. The boys haven't come back yet. We've been waiting for them to get us some water. They both went after a horse which we gave to the Singer. They went to get that horse for him today so they don't have to go after the horse tomorrow. So I wish you would get us some water. There is a horse hobbled down here close over that hill." Then I went outside, took the rope and went to where the horse was hobbled. I got the horse, put the saddle on, and I put a goat skin sack over the saddle. I rode to Anything Falls In and I filled this sack and brought the water back. So there were two things I did that evening. Then I went over to the chant. I went in and sat down on one side of the hogan.

Then Slim Man started to tell about what he had done. He said "I started to think about this ceremony because my wife wasn't feeling good. I had a 'hand shaker' and he said it was Wind Way that was bothering her. The rest told me to get a medicine man called Big Hand, but I thought I will get this Singer that we have now because this other man had learned this ceremony not very long ago. I thought maybe he hasn't learned all of it yet. That's why I got this man here. I went after him and I brought him back and he started the chant. There wasn't anybody to help me for two days, just the children and I. Then the people started coming. They had heard that I was having a chant and they started to help me on it. Now we are through with it. Only this one more night and when the Chanter starts to sing you should help him sing all night. I will be glad when you all help me on that."

Then he said to me, "Where have you been keeping yourself? We didn't see you around for over a month now.

203

Before that you used to always come around. I'd like to know just why you never come around any more. Some time ago you left your mother with us and she got mad at us for nothing and she moved away from us, and she must have told you all kinds of bad things about me, things which I never did or said. I know she told you something bad about me and I think you believed her and I think that is why you never come around any more. You shouldn't believe what she said and you shouldn't believe what all the women tell you. All of the women are trouble-makers. They always want to make trouble between two persons and that's the way with your mother, so I think you believed what she said about me. She must have told you what I had said about you, and what I *never* had said about you. But I know she told you what I had said about you. If she did you believed her. That's the way I am thinking about you and I think that's why you never come around any more. If you believed her you are just like an old woman because old women believe one another. Even though they are telling lies to each other they will believe. If you believed what your mother told you, you are just like them." I was just listening to him. I sat there and I thought, "I will just let him go ahead with his talk." So I was sitting there keeping quiet and there was a crowd in this hogan. I was ashamed to talk back to him. I thought "If I talk back to him the people that are there might talk about me when they go back home. So I won't say anything to him tonight. I will wait till tomorrow when the crowd goes away." So I just let him go ahead with his talk. Then I guess what we had brought had been taken over to where they were cooking, coffee, sugar, and other stuff. About that time they brought in a lot of food. They set it all around.

Then Son Of Late Grey Hat said to Slim Man, "Even anything that is tough breaks, so that thing you are talking about is broken. Now the food has broken that thing. You ought to talk about something else instead of that. Stop the talking so that everybody will eat. Some of us don't like that kind of talk." Then Slim Man stopped talking right away; he got up and went across the hogan and sat down. He didn't say any more. He just sat down at one side of the hogan and everybody started to eat. While everybody was eating Slim Man said, "Just go right ahead and eat and eat a lot. I want you all to get enough and don't hurry. Just take your time eating. That way you will get enough. So you all just go ahead and eat and right after you're through we will start to sing. I want you all to help sing and when we start taking a rest once in a while, stop the singing and smoke. In that way we won't get tired of singing and we will get some more food right around midnight. So you all help me on the singing."

After we were through the fellows that brought the food came in again. They took all the things back to where they were cooking. Right after that they said, "Wet the basket, have it good and damp." So one fellow got up and wet the basket. They put that down on the ground. Then everybody sat around this basket and they started to beat the basket. One started off with the rattle. Then we all started to sing. We kept on singing till a little after midnight. Then more food was brought in. We stopped singing and started eating again. After we all ate and they took all the things out again we went on with the singing again till morning. Then the singing was over and Slim Man said, "Get the horses for the Chanter so he can go back to his home while it's still cool." He said to his boys, "Bring back all the horses that you see for these other men so they can go home before it gets too hot." Then one of the boys said "We got the other horse for the Chanter last evening and we've got that horse tied over there to the corral." "Well, then," he said. "Just go and get the horses for these other men." So they went. Then he said again, "Everything is about ready. I want you all to eat first before you go. They are about through with the cooking so everybody stay till after you eat, then you can go home."

Then Son Of Late Grey Hat said, "I will go now, my uncle." When he said this to Slim Man he turned around to me. "How about you, nephew?" We had hobbled our horses together. I said, "I will wait here. I will go after a while so just leave my horse there." And he said "All right, I will go right now and I don't think I will starve before I get home." So then he went and walked right out and I stayed there. After a little while they brought in food to us again. Before we started eating the Chanter took all his things outside. When he came back in we all started eating. Right after we were through they all left; only I stayed there. I just lay down in the hogan and Slim Man lay down, too. I guess everybody slept. We were sleeping all morning.

When I woke up it was almost noon. Just when I woke up he was awake, too, and he said, "We slept all morning. About where is the sun?" "It's about to the middle," I said. "I didn't think we had slept that long. You make up the fire there," he said to me. "Cook something, build up a fire and go over to the other hogan. Maybe there is something left over. Get some flour and some meat from over there and cook there. We haven't got anybody to cook for us so you just go ahead and cook something. We are hungry." I went out, brought in some wood, and I built up a fire. Then I walked over to where they were cooking and there was only one woman walking around outside around the shade. That was the woman they had the chant over. I went inside. There they were cooking.

I said, "I was going to cook but I see you are cooking." "Yes," they said "We are cooking." And they asked me, "Where is your father? Is he still sleeping?" I said "No, he is awake. He wanted me to cook but I guess now I won't cook because you are cooking." "Yes, you don't have to bother with it." Then I went back to the other hogan. When I got back inside he was sitting up smoking and I told him, "I didn't cook. They were cooking for us so I think soon we will have something to eat." Then I went over again to where they were cooking. They were through and they told me, "Take it over yourself." So I picked up the food and took it over to the other place. Then I went out again and went back and I picked up the coffee and I brought it in to him. Then we laid out the things and it was a little after noon when we were eating. Slim Man's wife came in. She had stayed in the hogan all night until morning. Then she went out, walked around until noon, then came in again. They had told her not to come back until after noon. We started to eat with her. When we got through Slim Man reached down in his pocket and took his tobacco out. He made a cigarette. While he was smoking I started to tell him about myself, about my mother and what I had been doing since I made my trip around to the stores. "I didn't know anything about the chant until yesterday. So then I thought I would come. If I had heard before you started I would have been here with you, helping you on the chant till it was over." This is what I said that afternoon.

Then I said to him again, "You talked to me some last night. What you said to me I can't locate because I didn't know what you were talking about. You talked about what I didn't know anything about. You said that I must believe what my mother had told me about you. But I never believed her on anything. She had been trying to tell me what you had said to her. I told her not to tell me about it so she never told me anything about you. I am not on her side, my father. Don't think that I am on her side. I want to be with you all the time. I want to help you on anything and I want you to help me on anything, too. I don't want to turn my back to you. Maybe you think I will do that or maybe you want me to do that. That's the way I feel about it. I guess she told all the things about you to the others but I just don't care about the bad talks. That's the way I am, my father," I said to him. Then he said to me "That's the way to be. I said something to you. Maybe it hurt you but now I am kind of feeling bad about it. You know me very well. When I get to talking about something I won't stop talking so don't feel bad about it, my son, my father." Then I said "I never feel bad about anything. Even if a big trouble comes up before me I never pay any attention to the thing so I am not feeling bad about anything. I always want to help somebody and I always do too." This was all I said to him. When I had finished my story about myself then he said "That's what I like to know. I am glad that you told me all that you have been doing. Now I know that you have been working yourself hard and I am glad that you told me all about it." He let that go.

Then he told me about two men who came from over the mountain. "They were both from Water Coming Out. They were here some time ago and they spent three days with us. While they were here with us they asked for you. Before they started back one of them said to me, 'Come over to our place as soon as you can. I see you are having a hard time carrying wood on a burro and I see you carrying wood on your back. I see it is a long ways to get wood so I think it's just too hard for you. So come around to my place. There I've got a wagon. I just got that wagon lately. It hasn't been worn yet. When you come to my place I will give you that wagon. When you bring that wagon back with you you can haul wood with it so you won't have a hard time carrying wood on your back.' The other one spoke to me again, 'I see you are having a hard time with all of your work. You both have so much to do and I think it is just too hard for you to do all by yourself (he meant my wife and I). When you come over to my place I will tell you some more about things we talked about some time ago. We said you used to have another wife and some time ago you both came over to our place. At that time you said the two women that were Red Clay had left you so we were kind of sorry about that. So then after you both went away from our place we started to talk about you. I've got a sister that you can have. This is the way we fixed it up among our-selves and I came here to tell you about it to see if you'd like it. We all want you to take my sister so then you will have another wife and she will help you a lot. So come around, come to my place will you?' he said to me. Then I said 'We will see when we get over to your place.' Then I gave both of them thanks. I was looking for you all this time to let you know about this but now you know all about it," he said to me.

Then I said "I am very glad to hear that and glad to know that you are going to have a wagon and I am glad to know about the other thing. I am so thankful about everything that you had told me and I am glad that we will have a wagon, my father." Then I asked him "About when do you plan to go over for that wagon?" He said, "I am planning to go about six days from now. You know—and he pointed to his wife—she has been treated; in four days from now she will wash her-self. From there on she can go any place she wants to go. You come around again in five days and I want you to help us on gathering up the horses. I know you've got your horses all at

208

one place and I want you to help me out with some of your horses and we will start from here with the horses." I asked him about the horses, "How many horses do you want to take?" Then he said "Well, I guess we will take twelve of them with us." (At that time they used to give twelve horses when they got married.) Then I said, "All right I will help you on the horses. I will help you with two horses, one will be tame and the other one will be a bronco. They are both good-sized horses." Then he gave me many thanks for the horses. "That's good, that's nice of you my son, my father. I knew you would help me with the horses and you did. Now I am glad of it and I guess I will have nine horses and one mule with it, so please come around in five days and help us on gathering up the horses so we will have them here ready to start in six days. I wish you could go with us but you told me that you have so much to do and I guess you want to go where your herd went to." That was all about that. I said, "I guess I'd better be going." So then I went out and walked across to where I had hobbled my horse. There was my horse standing about thirsting to death and I looked at the sun. The sun was pretty well down. I got on my horse and I rode down and watered him. I thought to myself, "I should have eaten before I left," but then I thought, "Oh, well, I'll eat when I get home."

12

His wife accuses him of deceiving
her and they fight . . . Slim Man
goes over the mountain for a wife . . .
Left Handed visits Woman Who Walks Alone . . .
He and his wife quarrel and almost kill each other.

I got home when the sun was down. There was no fire, only the cold ashes at the fireplace, and my wife was weaving. I said, "Why don't you have a fire? The fire is out." She didn't say a thing; she just kept on weaving. Then I went out and chopped some wood and brought it in and started the fire. While I was building it she said, "Can't you leave that old thing? I know you have been down to her place. I know you have been with her. You forget everything on account of her. I know you were there with her. You are only pretending that you have been over at the Sing, but you can't make me believe that." I said, "What are you talking about? You are always trying to make trouble. Every time I come back from some place you always act that way. You always start talking about something that I haven't got on my mind, something I never thought about. I have told you before, I don't know how many times, that you must not be that way. You must not talk to me like that." "I mean what I say. You are trying to make believe you never think of that old thing, but I know you have been there. I hate her. As soon as I see her I will take a stick and beat her to death." "Don't just talk that way. If you mean it, go ahead and do it. Don't just say you are going to." Then she threw down the weaving-tools and got up and said, "I mean it. I will do it right now, too." She grabbed a stick of wood, piled by the fire, and started out. At first I thought she was going to beat me with it. "I'm going right now and beat that old thing to death." "Go ahead

210

and do it," I said to her. I just looked at her running out toward that place. I put some more wood on the fire. I was thinking, "I'll just let her go ahead and do it." She kept right on going.

When she was about five hundred yards from the hogan, I thought, "It will be just too bad for me if I let her go ahead and start trouble with that other woman." I was afraid she might kill her, or get killed herself. So then I got on my horse and started after her. I rode up in front of her and got off my horse and grabbed her and took the stick away and said, "What are you trying to do? What is the matter with you? Are you crazy?" "Yes, sure, I am crazy. You make me crazy." "You act that way, and you look that way, but I won't let you go, because they might kill you." "I don't care. Let them kill me," she said, "that's what you want me to do. If I kill her, I'll kill her. If she kills me, let her kill me." She was twisting around, trying to go over to that place, and I kept holding on to her. We were there, jerking each other around for quite a while. Then she gave up, and I started back with her. When we got back we made up again. In a little while we were talking and laughing as though we hadn't had any trouble. We fixed up the fire, and she started cooking as though nothing had happened.

Two mornings after that I said to her, "I guess this morning I'll go down to see about the horses. From there I would like to go to my father's place. He wanted me to come over in five days. That's two days ago that he asked me, but I would like to go over to his place today, while I have nothing to do here. We were out of wood, but I got some yesterday, and we have plenty now. So this morning I want to go down where the horses are. I'll drive them down toward the water, and from there I'll go to my father's place." Then she said, "What did I tell you the other day? I told you not to go down to the valley any more. I don't like to hear about the valley. Every time you talk about the valley it hurts me, so I don't want you to ride toward that place, and I don't want you to walk toward that place."

"Well, how do you want me to go there? You don't want me to ride, and you don't want me to walk. Should I start

211

crawling? Even though you don't want me to go, I have got to go, and I want to go right now. My horses are around there, and I always water them there. I don't want to let my horses go without water. If I don't take them to the water they will die of thirst. I don't want my horses to go without water, so I'm going." "I told you not to go," she said. "I won't let you start for that place. I mean it. I even hate to look down to the valley. When you talk about the valley it hurts me so badly. I mean it. So you just stay right here." Then I thought to myself, "I had better shut my mouth," so I didn't say anymore. I picked up my bridle, and I got a horse, the one that used to be around the hogan. After I had saddled him up I went back inside. She was sitting there close by the fire. I passed her and walked over to where my robe was; I picked it up and started for the door. When I passed her she got up and grabbed the robe, without saying anything. She was pretty well mad by then.

I said, "What are you trying to do again? You just let me go. You are always trying to make trouble, but I don't want any trouble. I don't care to have it. So you just let go of my robe." "I told you not to go. Why don't you take my word? Do what I told you to do. I want you to mind me. Take the robe back where it was and stay here. You don't mind me at all. I want you to stay. I mean it." While she was saying this she kept pulling on the robe. Then I said, "Well, take the robe back where it was." As I said this I let it go and started out for the horse. And there she was, running after me. She grabbed me again, saying, "Where are you going? Can't you hear me? I told you to stay. So you just go back inside," she said, while she was jerking me around. But I didn't say a word. At last I pulled myself loose from her, and about that time the horse started walking away. She began chasing me around, trying to catch me again. I thought, "I'll just let her chase me, until she has chased me quite a way from the horse. Then I'll run over and get on my horse and get away from her." I thought she would soon give up. I started for Where Little Arroyos Stop. I was running toward that place, and she kept coming right on after. Soon she had chased me up to the foot of the mountain. I started climbing up a steep

212

place, I was climbing right straight up. Every once in a while I looked back, and she was climbing right up after me. We were both soaked with sweat. The sweat was running down my face, and hers too. When I got on top I went a little way, and there I stopped and gave myself up. I thought, "I'll let her go ahead and do something to me."

While I was standing there, waiting for her, she came up. She was almost out of breath. She grabbed me and started jerking me around again. Then she let me go. "I am going to kill myself. I am going to jump off this cliff," she said, as she started for the edge of the cliff. I didn't say a word, I just sat down there. She had gone. Then, while I was sitting there, I heard a sound. It was a footstep. I looked up, and there she was, coming back. I said, "I thought you wanted to jump off the cliff? I thought you had. Why didn't you? Was someone there, holding you back? If you had done that, you would be suffering by now. But you didn't do it. You only wanted me to come after you again. But I won't. From here on, whenever you start something like that, I won't go after you anymore. I did it once. I went after you when you wanted to start up trouble, but from here on you can go ahead. I don't care what you do." She was crying and holding on to my shirt as tight as she could for a long time. When she stopped she said, "Take me home. Take me home. I am about dead. I would like to have some water. I am about dying of thirst. Take me home." I didn't say a word. I just kept quiet and sat there with my head down. Then she put her arm around my neck and said again, "Take me home. Please take me home. I am about dying of thirst." Then I got up and started down with her, but I didn't say a word. In the wash out in the flat we drank some water and washed ourselves, and then went on home.

As soon as we got inside I picked up the robe again, without saying anything. But as I passed by her she grabbed it again. I said "What is the matter with you, anyway? I thought everything was out of you. You just let me go." She said, "I won't let you go, not unless we apologize first. I don't want to let you go while you are still mad. I don't want to let you go as we are now." I said, "What is wrong with me?

213

Nothing is wrong with me. I didn't do or say anything to you. I didn't do any wrong, so there is nothing the matter with me. You just leave me alone and let me go. I would like to go over to my father's place, so turn me loose." "I won't let you go until we have apologized to each other. After we have apologized to each other we will cook something to eat, and, after we eat, then you can go, but not before. I mean it. I won't start up trouble with you any more. I won't act like this to you any more. I mean it. So, please, go and get your horse, and when you come back we will have something to eat. So, now, give me the robe, and you go and bring back the horse. I mean it. I won't try to start any more trouble. I don't want to hurt you any more from here on. So, please give me the robe, and you go and get the horse." I said, "Do you really mean you won't start any more trouble?" "Yes, I really mean it," she said. Then I let go of the robe and she put it back where it was before. "Well, then," I said, "you start the fire and begin the cooking. I'll go and get the horse."

I walked over to the horse and led him back to where there was good grass. I took the bridle off, so he could eat, and hobbled him there and went back. She had started the fire and was cooking. I sat down for a while. Then I lay up against the hogan and started thinking. I thought, "I will leave her. There is not one on her side able to tell her not to behave like that. She has a mother and a grandmother and brothers and sisters, but I know they can't stop her. And there is her clansman, Lost His Moccasins, but I know he can't do anything with her either. I know very well nobody can stop her." I was tired of it, tired of her trouble. I had to stop her many times, but I couldn't. I thought, "If I stay and live with her it will be too hard for me, because I just can't get along with her."

After everything was cooked and we had eaten, just as she was putting everything aside, her younger brother came in. As soon as he stepped in he said, "I thought you were waiting for me. I see you have eaten already. I wanted to get something to eat here." While he was eating he asked us, "Where have you been? They say they saw you coming back from up above here. Where did you go? What did you go up

214

there for?" I said, "Ask your older sister. She knows about it. She will tell you about it." He asked her, "Where have you been, my older sister?" But she sat around, she turned her back to him and didn't say a word. "What did you go up there for? Was it for something you can't tell about? That's the way it looks to me." But she didn't say a word. He asked me again, "What did you go up there for, my older brother?" I said, "Don't ask me. Ask your older sister there about it. She knows." But he didn't ask her again. Then he let that go and said, "I came to ask you to help us clean the hogan, the one sitting by the cornfield. The womenfolk want to move over close to the cornfield because the rabbits are beginning to eat the corn. We will clean out that hogan, and clean all around it, and put fresh dirt on it. And we will make a little shade there too." I said, "All right, I'll do that. I am willing to help you. That's right, I suppose the rabbits are getting after the corn now."

When he left I picked up the shovel and hoe and walked over to where the hogan was. It was getting cool by then. I worked there, taking the dirt out of the hogan, until the sun was down. Nobody came that afternoon. I worked there all the next day, cleaning up the dirt around the hogan and gathering limbs in the woods for the shade. They didn't show up until noontime. I helped them with that the rest of the afternoon and all next day.

That evening, after supper, we went right to bed. While we were lying in bed I said, "We were both asked a question yesterday, but neither of us answered that fellow's question. And that was your brother. He asked you a question in a nice way. When he asked you he addressed you as 'my older sister' but you never said a thing to him. And when he asked me he said 'my older brother' to me. That was a nice way to ask a question, but we didn't answer him. We didn't tell him where we had been. I could have told him, when he asked me, but I was so ashamed about it, I just turned it all over to you, because I thought you weren't a bit ashamed about it. But you didn't tell your younger brother what we had been doing, and where we had been. I suppose you were ashamed about it after all, and perhaps that's why you didn't tell him.

215

You ought to be ashamed from now on. What I am thinking about now is that you had better put a stop to this trouble, all at once, right now. Maybe your mother told you to stir up all this trouble; maybe your grandmother wanted you to, but I don't believe your brothers have been telling you to make trouble. Tomorrow I would like to go to my father's place."

Here is where I told a lie. I said, "My father wanted me to go with him over the mountain, so I promised him that I would, and I would like to go. I haven't been across the valley for a long time. I would like to see the country across the valley and up to the foot of that mountain and I would like to see what it looks like up on top over on the other side. I have never been around on the other side, so I would like to go with him, because I want to see the country." When I said this she said, "No! I won't let you go, even though you promised him. Maybe you think you are going, but you are not. You just stay right here with me." I said, "Why? Even though you hold me back, I want to go, because I promised him I would. I don't want to back out. I don't want to hurt my father. If I don't go with him I will hurt him. He won't like it, and he might get mad at me about it. I see what you are trying to do. I see you are trying to make trouble between my father and me, but I won't have it. I don't want you to make trouble between us. That's why I want to go with him." She said, "I told you no and I mean it. I won't let you go. If I let you go, you won't come back. I know very well you are trying to get away from me. That's what you are trying to do with me. Perhaps your father told you he would get you another woman over the mountain. Or if you don't get another woman over there you might go from there to where your mother has moved, and you will never come back. And there you will get another woman. So I don't want you to go away from me." I said, "Maybe you are thinking that way about me. You are thinking of all kinds of things that I never think about, so you'd better stop talking to me about them." "I won't talk about them, if you stay here with me. I mean it. I don't want you to go away from me. I will only let you go as far as your father's place, and you can help him there until he leaves. Don't you dare try to go with him. If you do I will

216

start after you on foot. I mean it. I will. So you come right back from his place. I won't let you have that new saddle. I won't let you take that, and I won't let you take your clothes or your moccasins, or anything you have here. You can only take that old saddle, which you have been using all the time."

I couldn't do anything then. I was trying my best to get away from her, but she wouldn't let me. I tried to think of different ways of getting away, but I didn't know what to do. I had that new saddle and new saddle blanket and new bridle there, and, besides that, I had a lot of stuff, and some sheep, and that was holding me back. I didn't know what to do about all those things. So I just gave it up. I said, "Well, then, I will only go over to my father's place. I would like to go to-morrow and stay at his place tomorrow night, and the next day. I suppose we will start rounding up the horses. I know it will take us a whole day to round them up, so I will stay there another night. The next day, after he has left, I will come back. I wanted to go with him very badly, but you don't want me to go, so, now, I promise you I won't."

The next day I didn't go over to my father's place until late in the afternoon. When I got there I said, "I came here because I thought you wanted to go to where the horses were, perhaps sometime this evening, and stay there over night, and start early in the morning from there to round them up." He said, "I wish we could do that. It would be a good thing to do, but we haven't any horses on hand. If we had some horses here, we could start right now. So, I guess, we will stay here at home over night." That night he was talking about the trip he was going to make. I was sitting there, with my head down, thinking and wishing that I could go with him. I thought, "I will tell him about the trouble I have almost every day." But I couldn't make up my mind to tell him because I was so ashamed about it. So there I was just wishing, "I would like to go with my father. I would like to get on top of that mountain and see how it looks, and over on the other side, and I would like to see the people who live on the other side. But I just can't go."

The next morning, while it was still dark, I started up

toward Where Little Arroyos Stop, where my horses were. I rounded them all up at the water and then chased them over to where my corral was. The boys had the other horses in there already. The horses that were hobbled I untied and drove to the hogan. When I got back to the hogan everything was ready to be eaten, and after we ate they started getting ready, Slim Man and his wife and one of the boys, the one we later called Smith's Son-In-Law. My father put a new saddle blanket on his horse; on top of that he put a big buffalo skin and a new saddle. Then he put a new silver bridle on the horse and a bucksin rope. After that he got his new robe and tied that to his saddle. Then he began to dress himself. He put on his moccasins, brand-new ones, nice and red, with silver buttons on them. He put on his new trousers, new shirt and new hat. He got out a big bunch of beads, with several strands of turquoise pendants on them, and he put on a silver belt. That was the way he dressed. His wife did just the same. Her horse was decorated in the same way, and she put on her moccasins with buckskin leggings and a woven skirt. She wrapped a red belt around her waist, and on top of that she put her silver belt. Then she got out a big bunch of beads with lots of turquoise pendants, and put that on herself. The boy was dressed up in the same way. They were all dressed about alike, and their horses were decorated in the same way. And there I was, walking around, wishing that I could go with them. I was so sorry that I couldn't go. It kind of weakened me, thinking and wishing about it. I was walking around there as if I was suffering from pain. But I couldn't do anything, because my stuff was all at home, and I couldn't get it. That's what made me feel so bad.

Before they were ready to go he said to me, "I don't know when we will be back, but when we get there, after we have stayed two days, I will send my son back, because there are lots of things to do around here, tending to the wood and the water, tending to the sheep and horses. One can't do all those things alone, so I want him to get back here soon. When he returns, when you think he is back, you come over and help them once in a while. All of you go down to the flat and try and gather up the horses at one place. Don't let them scatter all around if you can help it. I want you to do that, my son," he said to me. "I don't know when we will come back, but we will start back as soon as we can." I said, "All right, I will be around all the time and help my younger brother." "That's nice, my son. Be sure and do that. Then I won't be worried, because I know you will be around all the time. And you know all about things."

Then, when they were ready, we all started off down to the corral where we had the horses. While we were going along he said to me, "I want you to help us drive the horses up as far as Caving Bank because they might scatter out and some of them might get away from us. From there on, I know, we won't have any trouble with them." I said, "All right, I will."

I had been wishing the same thing. I had been thinking, "I wish I could go with them all the way to that place." And I was sorry that I had married that woman, but I was married to her and couldn't do anything. When we got to the corral he looked at my horses and said, "What nice horses you have. They are all nice and fat. They all look like race horses. What nice horses you have. That's the way to be. I have talked to you about all the things, and I know now you have kept all my words. Keep your horses that way all the time. Take good care of them, and soon you will have a lot. That's the way I want you to be, my son, my father, my baby," he said to me. And there I was, sitting on my horse like a poor man. Everybody else was sitting on the best horses they had, and were all dressed up, and I was wishing that I was dressed that way too. Then he said to me, "You get in the corral and chase out the two horses you are helping me with." I rode in and chased out a three-year-old, and another one that was tame. Then they went in and chased out his horses one by one, nine horses and a mule, that he was going to take along, and one extra one for himself. He said, "When I get over there I will use that horse to ride around among my relatives."

Then we started off, driving the horses along. They kept going on the trail, and we were riding together after them. When we got to the top of Caving Bank it was almost noon. We stopped there, and he said, "I guess we will eat a little

219

lunch here. After that we will go on, and you can go back. I don't want you to go back without anything to eat. I want you to eat with us here first, so you won't be hungry." He said, "There isn't a good place to stop around here, so we will move on to White Rock Hill. On the other side is a place called Winds Cover the Water; we will stop there for lunch, where there is plenty of water for the horses." So we went on to that place, and there we unsaddled our horses and hobbled them. We built a fire, and his wife made some coffee. The rest of the food was already prepared. After lunch we lay around for a while, and then he said, "I guess we will saddle up our horses and go now. I don't know where we will stop tonight." When we had saddled up our horses he said to me, "I suppose you are going back now, my son, and we will be going too." It was in the afternoon that we parted there. When I got on top of White Rock Hill, I looked back, and there they were, going way out in the flat, and it made me kind of lonesome.

At Caving Bank I thought, "I will go over to Between The Rocks where my mother, Woman Who Walks Alone, lives. It was getting late when I arrived there. I tied up my horse and went inside, and there was my mother and her husband, Son Of Late Grey Hat. As soon as I got inside they spread a sheep pelt for me, and we shook hands. She asked me, "Where are you coming from, my son? Are you coming from up above here?" I said, "No, I am coming from down below, from One Black Rock Standing." "What were you after down there?" "I just went over to that place," I said. "This morning I went with the people along over there." Then the old man said, "Why did you go up there with those people? Who are those people? And what did you have to do for them?"

Then I started telling them about it. "What are they going over there for?" he asked. I said, "They are going over there, I think, to get another woman. That's what they are taking the horses over there for." He asked me, "Who are the ones who went?" I said, "The old man and his wife and his son. So, I guess, he will get another woman there." Then he said, "Oh my, oh my. Oh my, oh my." He kept saying this over and over. "Why didn't he let us know about it? He should have let us know. He knows very well we are still living here. Oh my, oh my. We should have gone with him. He ought to have let us know, and the other people who live around here. Maybe he thinks he is the only man still living. Maybe he thinks we are all dead. He should have let us know. I think he has forgotten us all." "Well," Woman Who Walks Alone said, "I think he has forgotten me. I always thought of him as my younger brother, and I call him 'younger brother,' but he doesn't say 'my older sister' to me. I wonder why he never let us know about it. How many horses did he take with him?" I said, "They took twelve." "How many of my horses did he take?" she asked. I said, "I don't know, my mother, I don't know which is which, because they are all alike. So I can't tell, because I don't know the horses very well."

Then her husband said, "I guess he took all of your horses. The ones he took must have been all yours. I don't believe to took one of his own. That's why he never let us know about it. How many horses did you put up for him?" he asked me. I said, "I let him have two of my horses." "Well," he said, "I guess he has left the country. Left us all for good. I don't think he will ever come back to this country. Let him go. We don't care if he never comes back. If he comes back, that will be all right too." Then my mother said to me, "You are worse than he is. You should have let us know about it. Why didn't you, my son?" "Well," I said, "I didn't get a chance to tell you, my mother. I have known about it ever since they had that Sing over there, but I just didn't have a chance to come here to tell you." "Well, then," he said to his wife, "You start cooking. Your son must be hungry. It's a long way where he turned around. It took him almost a whole day to come back. So you start cooking." While she was busy cooking, he said, "What a long way he went for a thing like that. He must have wanted that woman very badly. That's the way I look at it. I myself got married here, and I always think it's a long way to my home, even though it is not very far from here. And he went way over the mountain, way on the other side. You can't even see the country from here. He must have wanted to go over there very badly." Then he lay down, back against the wall of the hogan, and that was all. My mother was cooking; I lay there too, until the cooking was done.

After we had eaten he said, "Are you going back home now, my nephew?" I looked up through the smoke-hole; I thought, "It's getting too late." "That's right," he said, "You just take the saddle off your horse and hobble him and stay with us tonight." I said, "All right, I'll stay. I'll just take the horse to where there is good grass." While I was taking the saddle off the horse, my mother came out and said, "Take the ax with you, my son, and bring back some wood. We haven't any wood to start a fire with tomorrow."

That evening we sat around and my uncle, Son Of Late Grey Hat started talking again. "That's the way with some people. We are not all alike. Some of us are poor, some of us have only a few things, and some are rich. They have everything. And that's the way with the Many Goats, they are all rich. They have everything, and they don't care about the others. They won't bother with the poor. I suppose that's why he never let us know about it. He knows me very well. When I arrived here I didn't have anything. Perhaps he thinks I am still the same. Perhaps he thought it was no use letting me know. Perhaps he thinks I have got nothing. Nevertheless he ought to have come over here just to let me know about it. He should have come and said to me, 'My father, I came to let you know about something,' and he should have told me about it. However, he never thought of me. He never thought of either of us. But that's the way with all those outfits. They think they are the only people who possess anything. That's why I think he doesn't care for us. You have been around with them ever since you were a boy. They raised you, and, I guess, you know all about them, how they are, and what they are saying. No doubt you have learned a lot from them, but I don't want you to be like them, the way they are now. They don't care about the others. I don't want you to be that way. Keep all the good words with which they have been talking to you. I know you have learned everything from them. But, besides that, I want you to be a good

222

man. Care for the others. Help them along. Don't think you are the only one who has anything. Help the people, especially the poor. In that way you will have more helpers. If you try to help everybody, they will try to help you on something, even on little things."

I said to him, "You may be thinking that way about those people, but it's not that way. They are all good people. I know them very well. I have been raised there; they raised me, so I know exactly what they are. They are all good people. They are all trying to help the others. I know that whenever people from far off come to their place they always try to help them. They treat people nicely. When people come to their place, or it may be that only one person comes to their place, when he wants to return to his home, they will give him a horse, or one head of cattle, or a sheep; sometimes more. Or they will give him some of their property, and they will put up a big lunch for him. That's the way they are. So, what you said about them, is all just talk. I told you about it when you first came here. The only thing they don't like is a fellow who drinks, or who gambles too much, or a fellow who hasn't anything going around from hogan to hogan begging or maybe stealing something. That's the only thing they don't like around their place. They don't like drunkards, gamblers, and thieves. If a fellow like that comes to their place, they will begin talking to him about the good life. They even help a person with that, with their talks about life. That's the way they are. I know them very well."

When I said this to him, he didn't say any more. Perhaps he thought I was on their side. He looked as though he didn't like what I had told him about them. I thought to myself, "My mother has told them all kinds of bad things about these people, and they must have believed her. That is why they are saying that." Then he said, "We had better go to bed." After we ate the next morning he said to me, "You are going back home this morning, aren't you?" "Yes," I said, "I am going over to where my horses are and get me another horse. From there I will go back home."

When I said this Woman Who Walks Alone said, "Will you come back again sometime when you think it's going to

223

be a good day? I think soon it will start to rain. When it gets cloudy, and nice and cool, if a day comes like that, come around. I want you to help us on the cattle. Lots of the calves need cutting. So come, will you, please, my son?" "All right, I will," I said. "Yes, that's right," said the man, "I wish you would do that. I will be glad if you help me on that. You know the calves are all of a good size now; I don't think I am able to do the cutting all by myself. So come when you think it's a good day." I said again, "All right, I'll come. I'll look up in the sky for the clouds. As soon as its gets cloudy I will be here." Then I went out and got my horse and started off. I rode over to Where Little Arroyos Stop and Woods Coming Out Into A Flat. My horses were around there in bunches. At the water I got me another horse, one which I used to call Pumpkin-Belly, because he had a big round belly. He was small, about the size of a burro, and as tame as he could be. I saddled him up and got on. I thought, "I guess I will go over to where another woman (whom we called Little Woman) lives. I haven't been there for quite a long time now. I will go there and visit her." But when I changed my mind, I thought, "If I go around to that place I will sure get in trouble again." So I let that go. I walked my horse in a little trot all the way, thinking about the people who had gone over the mountain. "If I had gone along I would be with them now, travelling on a journey."

My wife's younger brother was there when I got home. We went inside together and he began asking me, "Where have you been? When was it that you left here? Was it two days ago?" "It was three days ago." "You must have gone a long way off someplace." "No," I said, "I was just around here." "You hobble your horse first," he said to me, "then I would like to know about the trip you have been making all these three days." I asked him, "Could you let me have some cornstalks? I would like to give some to my horse." He said immediately, "All right, you can get some yourself. Help yourself. Any time you want some for your horse just go over to the cornfield and get it." I said, "I'll wait. I'll get some after a while." Then I began telling him what I had been doing

224

these three days. I just made a quick story about it. When we got back to our hogan, my wife was sitting there; I knew very well she was going to start more trouble. I could tell it by her looks and her behavior. She never put out a sheep pelt for me. I was just lying on the ground. The boy said to her, "Why don't you make something? Build up a fire and cook something. What's the matter? You look as though you were sad about something." But she didn't say a word; she was just sitting there quiet. Her brother didn't say any more to her; he just got up and went home.

About that time the sun was nearly down. Then she got up and started the fire and began cooking. I was afraid to say something, so I just kept quiet. In a little while she laid out the food in front of me, and I began eating, but she didn't eat with me, she just sat there. After I had eaten I sat around for a while without any talk. Then I went over to the cornfield and brought back some cornstalks and chopped them up in small pieces for my horse. I was working on this a long while. The sun was down by the time I went back inside. She had fixed up a bed, but not in the right way. The sheep pelts were thrown one on top of another any old way. I walked up to the bed and lay down there without saying anything, and she wasn't talking either. I was sorry that I had married her. It was too hard for me to live with her any longer. I just couldn't get along with her. I thought, "Every time I come home from someplace she always gets mad at me." I was thinking about the seasons and the length of the year. I thought, "The summer is too long, and right after that comes winter, and winter is too long. It's that way. It's that way always. It's too hard for me to live with her all summer and from fall on all winter through. I just can't stand the trouble. I wish I hadn't married her."

I began thinking I would leave her. She was a pretty girl, but I just couldn't get along with her. I didn't like the thought of leaving her, because she was pretty, but then I couldn't stand her trouble. While I was thinking this way, she had been sitting up. Then she lay down, but not very close to me. She was lying there without a word for quite a while, for a long time. Then she said, "Where have you been? Why don't

225

you talk? What's the matter with you? Tell me about where you have been." "I thought if I began telling you about my trip you wouldn't like it. I know you won't, because whenever I tell you about my trip you always get mad about it. That's why I kept quiet." "I know why you won't tell me, because you have been down in the valley. I know very well where you have been. You have been down where some Salt clanspeople live." I said, "You are beginning to be jealous of everybody. I don't care to have you talk to me like that. I am tired of it. I can't stand your talking any more. I just can't stand it. Maybe you don't believe me, but I mean it. How will we get along, do you think, if you are always talking to me like that? I don't think we will live together long. So you had better stop. If you keep on talking like that, it will be just too bad for you." As soon as I said this to her she was mad. Then, when she started talking, I rolled over and put the robe all around me and covered up my head. I knew she wouldn't stop. And I was so tired, going around for those three days. She was talking, but I didn't know what she had said to me. Right away I went to sleep, while she was still talking.

Around towards morning I awoke. She was sound asleep. I went back to sleep, and when I woke up again it was morning. I was awake, but I was just lying in bed with my eyes shut. Soon she woke up, and I heard her go out. She brought in some wood and started up the fire, but I just stayed in bed with all my clothes on. I hadn't even taken off my moccasins that night. Then, while she was cooking, I got up and walked outside. I went over to where I had tied my horse, and he had eaten all the cornstalks. I brought back some more for him from the cornfield and chopped them up, and after that I went back inside. She laid out the food, and I started eating by myself. After a while she began eating, and she was the same as she had been the night before. We were eating there without a sound.

After I got through eating I went out and saddled up my horse. Then I went back inside and said, "I guess I'll be going. I want to go down to where Woman Who Walks Alone, my mother, lives. She wanted me to come down today and help them on cutting the calves, so I'm going down to

226

their place now." Right away she got awfully mad at me. As I was walking up to my horse, she ran out after me and took the bridle off. She threw the bridle away. Then she took the saddle off. She threw the saddle in another direction. Then she took off the saddle blankets. She threw them in still another direction. While she was doing this I just stood there and looked at her. Then I said, "Take them and keep them. Put the bridle on yourself, and put the saddle and blankets on your back and carry them around." While I was saying this I started coiling up the rope. I thought, "I'll get on my horse and ride down bareback." But as I started to put the rope around the horse's nose she grabbed it. I got on my horse, thinking, "I'll just twist the rope away from her," but she grabbed the horse around the neck. She put both arms around the horse's neck and grabbed his mane between her teeth. Then I couldn't do anything. I was very angry, but I didn't know what to do with her. I just sat on my horse there for quite a while. Then I walked over to where she had thrown the saddle, bridle, and blankets.

I gathered them all together at one place and then went inside and started packing up my things. I already had one big bundle fixed up and pulled outside, and was starting to get down my new saddle; then she let the horse go and started after me. She ran up to me and grabbed my left arm. She grabbed my wrist with one hand and my sleeve with the other. I was so angry, but I didn't want to do anything to her. I twisted my arm away from her; she was awfully angry too when I did this to her. She grabbed my beads and tore them off me and threw them away. Then she grabbed my shirt by the neck and tore it off my back, then the sleeves on one side and then the other. She tore off my whole shirt. I had on a pair of white muslin pants. She tore off first one side, then the other. She tore them off and threw them away. Then she grabbed my moccasins and tore those off around the seams, and she tore off both my leggings. I was standing without anything on, only my g-string. She started after my g-string, but this time I wouldn't let her grab hold of it. I let her go ahead with all the other things, but I didn't let her get at my g-string. She was trying her best to tear that off, but she just couldn't get hold of it. She grabbed hold of it two or three times, but when she grabbed it I twisted and jerked her around. When I did this she let it go.

She gave that up. Then she grabbed hold of my hair. It was tied up; at that time I wore it long. She unwrapped it and then wrapped it around her hands. It began suffering then. She was trying to twist my neck, but she couldn't do it. She was tearing my hair out in bunches, jerking me around by my hair. It gave me a frightful pain. I tried to get away from her, when I would twist one arm she would let loose with one hand, but it was too hard, because my hair was wrapped around her hands and was all tangled up. My whole head and neck were sore. I could hardly move.

About that time one of her younger brothers came. He must have been between fifteen and sixteen years of age. But he didn't say anything or do anything. He just let us alone. Maybe he wanted to see who would get licked. However, he began cleaning around us, taking away sticks and even pieces of rock. Maybe he didn't want us to hurt each other with that. He had cleaned everything away from around us, and there he was, walking around, looking at us fighting. While he was walking around us, I guess, he saw the beads lying on the ground, and he started picking them up. After he had them all picked up he took them back to his home.

I just couldn't stand any more, so I began unwrapping my hair off her hands. It was wrapped around her wrists, and I began to unwrap it roughly, even though it hurt me so much. But I couldn't get it off her hands. I started twisting her fingers, I twisted them hard, I twisted every one of them. Then she let go, she couldn't hold on any more. Her fingers must have been all sore. But then, when she let go with her fingers, she grabbed it between her teeth, and that was worse. I started with her towards the horse, and when I got close to the horse with her I picked up the rope and doubled it up and whipped her twice across the back with it. Just then the boy came again and chased the horse away. I looked all around, but I couldn't see anything, the boy had taken every-thing away. I looked for the whip where my saddle was lying, but the whip wasn't on the saddle. Then I looked over

228

to where my new saddle was, and there was my new whip on that saddle. I tried to go over there with her, but I couldn't drag her. The only thing lying close at hand was a thorn brush, tied up in a bundle, which she used to sweep with. This brush, is covered with little thorns. I started jerking her toward this broom. She had no moccasins on or stockings and, when I picked up the brush, I whipped her with it on the lower part of her legs. When I hit her the second time she cried out. When she cried out I got loose, but she grabbed my hair again with her fingers.Then I started in and kept on whipping with this brush. She sat down, but I jerked her right up again, and kept on whipping her around the legs. She was crying as hard as she could, but I just kept at it. Soon the blood was running down her legs. I guess then she couldn't stand it any longer, and she was so weak she could hardly stand up any more. Then she let my hair go. I said to her, "What is in you anyway? Ghost, ghost must be in you! You must be a ghost! You must be a coyote! You must be, because you grab and scratch and bite at me." I said this after she let me loose, but I kept on whipping her and jerking her around, even though I knew she was weak. Then she must have thought that I never would stop whipping her.

While she was crying as hard as she could she raised her arm up to me, "Please, please stop now, my husband. You are killing me. Please stop. Please forgive me. I won't do anything like this to you anymore. Please stop now." She had her arm around my waist, begging me to stop. So then I stopped. She raised herself up and put her arm around my shoulder, and was crying and talking to me for a long time. But I didn't pay any attention to her. After that we both started to the middle of the hogan and there we sat down. She was sitting there, crying, and there was I, with my head all swollen and my neck so sore, and sore all over my back where she had been scratching me. I was sitting, thinking what I had done to her. What I had done didn't satisfy me. It wasn't enough. I wasn't quite even with her. I looked around and there were my clothes all scattered out in pieces. I looked for my beads, but I couldn't see them anywhere, nor my moccasins either. I thought, "The boy must have taken them." I just sat there the way I was without anything on me, because, I thought, that was the way she wanted me to be. She was sitting there too, still crying, with her legs stretched out, covered with blood. She tried to talk, but she couldn't, because she was crying so much. But I didn't care. I thought I hadn't got even with her, and I was suffering with pain more than she was. At last, when she stopped crying, I got up. I thought I would go out and take a leak. When I was getting up she said, "Where are you going? What are you going to do?" "Don't bother me."

That was all I said; then I went out and walked around. I looked at the sun, and it was late in the afternoon, and we had started this trouble in the morning. I went inside and sat down again for a while. I made up my mind, "I will go right now. I will leave her right now." I got up and walked over to where my new saddle was. I got that down and the bridle, and I started to drag out my things that I had in a big bundle. While I was going to the middle of the hogan she got up and walked in front of me, and then she started crying again. She put her arm around my neck and said, "What are you trying to do? Are you going to leave me? Please don't go, my husband." I said to her, "Don't bother me. Let me loose. I am going right now. I don't want to stay here anymore, because we have done a very bad thing to each other, so how do you think we will get along? I mean it. I want to go right now. I don't want to stay with you any more, because I can't stand your trouble and your meanness. You are unkind and mean, so I want to leave you right now for good. I mean it. What you have been after for a long time, we have done at last. So I thought you were satisfied. So let me loose, let me go."

But she kept holding me tightly to herself, crying more and more, begging me not to go. "Forgive me, forgive me, please, my husband. Don't go. Drop your things, and stay here with me. I am sorry for what I have done to you. I won't do anything like that any more to you." She repeated these things many times, while she was crying. Then I let go of the saddle and bridle; I was tired of holding them up, and I was sore all over, so I just let the things drop, and there we were standing in the middle of the hogan. We stood there a long time, and I was tired, standing there with all my soreness. I told her to let loose. She let me loose, I picked up my old saddle, the one I used every day, and threw the stirrups and the cinch over it, and laid it down on the side of the hogan. On top I put the saddle blanket, and there I sat, with my head down, suffering from pain. While I was sitting on the saddle she got up and put the new saddle back where it was before, and she dragged back the bundle. She got down two sheep pelts and laid them on the ground, one on top of the other. Then she took down a robe and put it on the sheep pelts for a pillow. Then she walked up to me and took hold of my wrist and put one arm around my shoulder and said, "Come on. Get up. Come with me over to where I have laid the pelts." She started raising me up, holding me under the arms, begging and pleading with me. I walked over with her to where she had laid the sheep pelts and sat down. I picked up the robe and wrapped it around myself, and there I was sitting with all kinds of sadness and full of sorrow about myself, because I never had been like that before in my life.

I began thinking about my father, Slim Man, thinking, "If I had gone with him, I wouldn't be suffering as I am now. I would be enjoying the trip by now, if I had gone with him." I began thinking about all the others, my fathers and mothers, "They raised me, and I was raised by them, and they never even gave me a little scratch. They never talked to me in the very meanest way. They all took good care of me. They were all good to me. I never had to suffer from them. They never wanted me to suffer from anything. But today I am suffering from pain." This was the way I was thinking, while I was sitting there with not a thing on, with only the robe wrapped around me. While I was thinking about all this I was about to cry. I was sitting there almost crying, having all kinds of thoughts, but I didn't know which way to go, or what to do. There was no fire, only a little cold ash at the fireplace, nor any water. There wasn't a stick of wood outside. I may have been starving, I may have been almost dying of thirst, but I never noticed it. I just sat there thinking.

Every now and then the boy came over, but he never said anything. All the others were home, her mother, grandmother, sister, and two other brothers, but they didn't come around, only this younger boy. He came and watered my horse, and got some cornstalks from the field and fed him, and there we two were sitting without a sound, hearing only our breath. I was tired sitting up, so I lay down on my side, and the boy, after feeding my horse, went back home. From there he came back with some food, boiled meat, fried tortillas, and coffee. The meat was nice and fat, and everything was hot. He laid it between us and then walked out and went home again.

After he left she got up and put down some cups and sugar and said, "Come on. Get up and let us eat." She said this five times. As I was getting cool the pain was getting worse. I could hardly move. She put an arm under me and raised me up, saying, "Get up. Let us eat while everything is still warm." I sat up with the robe wrapped around me, while she kept saying, "Come on, and let us eat." But I thought, "I won't eat." I suppose I was hungry, but I didn't feel it. I just sat there with my head down. Then she stopped talking. I guess she thought she couldn't do anything with me, and let me alone. She started crying. She was sitting with the tears running down her cheeks. She laid the food aside, covered it up; everything was cold.

After a while I got up and went out to take a leak. She started right after me; I guess she was afraid I might run away from her. I walked quite a way from the hogan, and she was right behind me. When I got back inside I noticed that I was thirsty. I drank the little water that was there, and then walked over to my bed. Before I sat down she laid one more pelt on top of the others and one at my feet, and she made me a pillow. I could hardly lie down. I laid my head on the pillow as gently as I could, but I couldn't sleep. I began wishing and thinking. I had all kinds of thoughts on my mind. That and the pain kept me awake. She was sitting on a pelt close beside me, I suppose she was watching me closely.

I was lying there, waiting for her to go to sleep, thinking, "As soon as she sleeps I'll take out my new saddle and other things and put them on the horse and get away from her tonight." I was lying there, making believe that I was sound asleep, but I guess she was thinking the same thing, and so she was watching me closely. After a time she got up and put another robe over me. Then she moved the pelt she was lying on close beside me and covered me with her own robe as well. As soon as she lay down she raised up the robe and covered herself with it and moved right close to me and put her arm around me. I pretended that I had been awakened and began to push her arm away, but she held me tighter. I said, "Don't bother me. I am sensitive. Don't you know I have got a pain all over me? Don't move me around. Take your arm away from me." But she said, "If I let you go, if I take away my arm, you might get away from me." "What are you talking about? How could I get away? You know it is night, and you know I haven't got anything on me. And you know I am suffering from pain." However she kept holding me to herself, and from there on every time I moved a little she held me tight against herself. It was that way all night. Neither of us got a wink of sleep. When the morning came, when it was almost daylight, then she let me go.

She got up and was sitting there. There was no wood to start a fire with. Soon the sun was up, but I just lay in bed, thinking how I would get away. I had thought I would get away that night. I was going to take out all my stuff, put it on the horse, and go to my mother's place, Woman Who Walks Alone, to my clansman, Son Of Late Grey Hat. I was going to go the way I was, without anything on. But I didn't; I didn't get a chance. If my father had been home, I could have gone to his place without my things, but he was gone. Only the womenfolk were home. I thought, "It would be no use for me to go over there; those womenfolk couldn't do anything." So I didn't get a chance to get away that night.

When the sun was pretty well up the boy came over again. He walked around for a while; then he went down to the cornfield and brought back some cornstalks for my horse. Quite a while after he had gone home he came again with some food. This time he brought nice, fresh meat and a bowl of corn mush. The meat was nice and fat. It was roasted. He laid the food on the ground and walked right out again. Then she said, "Come. Get up, and let's eat." But I just lay

233

there. Then she got up and walked over to me; she put her arm under me and raised me up, saying again, "Come on. Let's eat." I said, "I told you not to touch me. Don't lay your hand on me. I am sore all over, and I don't care about eating. If you want to eat, go ahead. If you care for it, just go ahead and eat, but leave me alone, and don't touch me, and don't talk to me." "Why don't you eat? I want you to eat with me. If you don't eat, I won't either. If you begin eating, I will too. If you won't, I won't either." I said, "I don't care for it. And how will I eat? I can't eat with all this soreness on me."

When I said this she started crying. I said, "What are you crying for? You are just crying for nothing." She said, "I am crying for you. I am crying for what I have done to you." "What are you crying for me for? You said you were crying about yourself. I am not dead yet. I am still alive, and so are you. You may be crying for me, but I don't care. You are crying for nothing." "I am crying because you don't eat." When she said this she began to cry more. "I have been begging you to eat since yesterday, promising you that I will never do anything like that to you again. And I am still saying the same to you this morning, but you can't forgive me. That's why I am crying. I guess I have done a very bad thing to you, but I didn't know what I was doing. I was as if unconscious. I knew it was morning, yesterday, but from there on I must have been unconscious. I didn't know what I was doing, not until you had beaten me with a rope. I was aware that you whipped me twice with a rope. As soon as you whipped me I noticed it, and I saw the rope. By that you had awakened me. Before that I may have been sleeping. As soon as you whipped me with the rope I was awake. And I knew you had picked up that brush broom. I saw that, and you started whipping me with it on my legs. You kept whipping me with that brush for a long time. Then I was wide awake, and I became aware of the pain. It was hurting, and soon I saw the blood running down my legs. That awakened me still more. From there on my mind and thoughts all came back to me, and from there on I began to grieve for you; seeing you, I knew you were suffering from pain. I began begging you to eat with me, but you wouldn't take my word. That's why I'm

234

crying. I have pain myself on my legs, but I don't care. It pains me so much, but it's my own fault. If I had behaved, I wouldn't be suffering and have this soreness on my legs."

I said, "No doubt you are thinking that way now. I guess you have found out yourself that you did wrong. And no doubt you are aware of everything. From whom did you learn all those things? Who taught you? Was it your grandmother or your mother or your uncle or your grandfather? Who was it that taught you? Where did you learn it? You must have learned it from someone. How do you think we will get along, if we treat each other like this? You ought to know better than that. Lots of people, men and women, live together. Some of them have been married for a long time. Some of them have been married since they were young, and they are still living together, even though they are old. They live so long together because they have been good to each other, kind to each other. They keep each other's words. They mind each other. They obey each other. They take good care of each other and help each other right along. People who live that way live long. I mean a husband and wife, who live together that way, live a good life. They enjoy life. They are happy all the time. That is what I know about them. Don't you know a thing about people who live that way? I don't think you do. I know, now, you don't know what life is. If you treat me the way you have treated me now, how do you think we will get along?" After that I said, "If you have found out everything, you just start up the fire. Build a fire and warm up that coffee. Then we will eat."

She didn't say a word more. She got up and went outside and brought in a little wood, which, I guess, she had gathered up around outside, and started up the fire. After the fire was going she went out after some water. She sat the coffee pot by the fire, and the meat that was boiled, which they had given to us the day before, she put in a pot beside the fire. When she had everything warmed up she laid it right in front of me, and we both started eating. I knew then that I was about starved to death, and she must have been too. We had lots of meat, some boiled, some roasted, a bowl full of corn mush, a lot of fried tortillas, and a big pot of coffee. We ate until we had eaten everything. I was all perspiration. It was running down all over my face after I had finished eating. We were both through, because there was nothing more to eat. I wiped my face with the robe I had wrapped around me, and then I said, "Give me some water to drink." She got up immediately and made a little run to the water and gave it to me.

After I drank I took a deep breath. The pain was still with me but I was feeling well, and my eyes were wide open. I looked out, and everything was clear. I was lively, even though I had so much pain. I sat up, looking all around, and stretched myself a little. I couldn't stretch the way I wanted to on account of the pain. Then I said to her, "Now, what you wanted me to do I have done. You have been begging me to eat since yesterday, and now I have eaten. I am sitting here now in good health, and, I guess, you are too. However, I am ashamed; I am full of shame about myself and you. But I don't think you are. Maybe you are. You have made me think of a lot of things, from yesterday morning until a while ago. I was thinking about the things that I have around here, and the stocks that I have, the country which I am accustomed to travel around on, the mountains, and other places, and about all my relatives, and all about the trails that I am used to going on. You made me think of all these things. It almost killed me. You were going to kill me, but I am glad you left me alive. I am glad I am living right now. I didn't think I would live any longer, but you spared me; so I am glad now, this morning, that I am still alive. I have eaten, and I am glad to have drunk some water. I thought this was my last day, but now I know I am alive. Perhaps, from now on, I will live for some time yet. What do you think about me now? What do you think you have done to me? Do you believe you have done me good? Take the way I am sitting now. I am sitting here full of shame, because I have nothing on, only my g-string. Even my hair you have pulled all out. You have left only a little on my head. You should have torn off every bit of it. I want to be like this all the time from now on. I want to go around among the people as I am now, because that is the way you want me to be. So I will go around the way I am. No

236

doubt it looks good to you. Who was it that told you to do what you have done to me? Was it your grandmother or your mother? Who was it? Somebody told you to do it." "No," she said, "nobody told me to do it. It's my own self. I know now I have done a very bad thing to you. I am sorry for it. I will never do that again. I promise you. I mean it. From here on through the rest of my life I won't ever do that to you again. I am so sorry about you, husband." As she said this she put her arm around my neck and started crying.

I pushed her arm away, telling her not to touch me around the neck, because it was painful. She put her arm around my shoulder then, under the arms, and was holding me tight against her breast. "Honestly," she said, "I mean it, and I have promised you that I won't ever do that again to you." I said, "Even though you talk like that, I don't believe you, because you have said that to me many times. How can I believe you?" After every time that you have said that you have started up trouble again and have been treating me worse. It's bad now. Soon you will get that way again. Something will happen then, but neither of us knows what, because when you start it again it will be worse than what we have had, for you are getting worse and worse all the time."

We talked to each other a long time, saying the same thing over and over again. Then she let me go and went to her mother's home. A little later the boy had come again. I thought to myself, "I guess I am being watched." When the boy came he looked at me, and then he walked over to my horse, and got on him and rode him down in the wash. After he had watered the horse he tied him up again and brought up some cornstalks for him from the field.

About then my wife returned from her mother's place. It was noon. She had been gone for quite a long while. She started cooking. She cooked some fresh food, and we ate, but we didn't say much. After lunch she put the things away. About then the boy came again. This time he brought me some clothes. He laid them right in front of her, but he didn't say anything.

After he dropped the things he went right out. She picked them up and laid them on my lap. "There, put them

237

on. There are some clothes for you, so put them on." There were a pair of calico pants, a shirt, leggings, garters for leggings, garters which the Hopi make, and a pair of moccasins, and the beads, the beads she had torn off of me. They had strung them together the way they were. I was sitting there, looking at the things, and I was kind of sorry about them. They belonged to somebody and he had given up all these things for me. If she hadn't torn up all my things the man to whom all these things belonged would have them for himself. He had given them up on account of her. She was the one who had taken them away. I was sorry for the fellow who gave up these things. That is the way I was thinking about it. I just sat and looked at them. I looked at these things, thinking about them for quite a while. Then I picked them up. The shirt and calico pants were brand new. So were the leggings and moccasins. Everything was new. The leggings had strips down one side. The moccasin soles were from the Utes. I put on the shirt; it fitted me nicely; so did the calico pants. They were just right for me. Then the leggings, then the moccasins, everything was just right. Then I picked up the beads. I looked them over. The turquoise was all there. I didn't miss one. So I put the beads around my neck.

When the sun was pretty well down she got up and started the fire. She had brought back a little wood from her mother's place. She asked me, "Are you hungry?" "No," I said, "I am not hungry." "Anyway I will make some coffee." She went ahead with the cooking and, while she was doing that, I went out to where my horse was tied. I led him down to the water, and, after I brought him back, I got some corn stalks and chopped them up in pieces. When I got back inside she was done cooking. She had cooked a little and we started eating. After supper the sun was almost down. She put the things away and covered them up and started making up the bed. She laid out the pelts and made a pillow, then I walked over and lay right down. I guess I went right to sleep. I was so tired and sore all over.

I woke up all at once, and it was morning. I got up and walked around outside and gathered up some wood. She had started the fire, and I put on more wood. When the cooking was done she put the things right in front of me, and we both started eating. That morning, after we ate, we just sat around. Everything was all right, though the soreness on my head was still the same, and all over my body, where she had scratched me. But we had apologized to each other. That morning her grandmother came. She was there, sitting down, without a word for a while. Then she said, "What were you doing the day before yesterday? I heard you had been working all day. What kind of work were you doing, my children?" I said, "I don't know, so I can't tell." I pointed to her and said, "Ask her. She knows all about it." She asked again, "What were you doing? I heard that you had been working on each other. So I know what you both have been doing. I know you were beating each other all that day. How did the trouble start? Who started the trouble?" I pointed to my wife again, "She knows all about it. She knows who started the trouble, and she will tell you about it. But not I, because I don't know anything about it."

I thought then she would ask her a question, but she turned to me instead and started talking to me, "I know you are an unkind man. I thought you were a kind man, but I have found out now that you are not. You were whipping her and throwing her around all that day. I heard she was crying all day. I didn't want her to be treated that way. When she was still in her mother's womb I watched closely and took good care of her, while she was still inside her mother. Then she was born, and I took good care of her, and still more care of her. She never was hurt or suffered from anything, because I had been watching her closely and took good care of her. And when she grew up we never hurt her by any means. She never has suffered like this before. The day before yesterday is the first time she ever got into any suffering, because you were cruel and rough with her. And so I know now you are a mean man, treating her like that." After she had said this she went back and repeated it again. "I took good care of her because I wanted her to grow up to be a woman. I have never said anything to her that would hurt her. When she was a little girl she used to be with me all the time, because she knew I was taking good care of her and treating her nicely. I

239

never hurt her by anything. I never took a stick to her. I never talked to her in a cruel manner. I was always good to her. When she was a little girl she used to ask me for milk, and I always went out and got some for her, or any kind of food that she asked for. And when she would ask for clothing, if I had some calico, I always made a dress and a waist. That is the way I raised her. And here, now, the other day, I heard that she was crying all day. I didn't raise her for that. When you married her I was so glad, because I thought you would take good care of her for me. I let you have her, because I thought you were a good man. I thought you were a kind man. But I know now, you are not."

While she was talking I sat there with my head down, listening to what she was saying to me. Then she said, "That's that. You have done a great wrong. So now it is up to you. You have whipped her. You have hurt her. I heard you had whipped her with a rope, one that was tied to a horse. When you whip her with a rope or whip you have got to pay for that. When you use a rope or whip on a person you have got to put up a nice horse. So you have got to put up a nice good-looking horse and pay her that. If you had used a stick or your fist or your feet you would have had to put up some of your property. Or if you had some nice beads or turquoise pendants, and turquoise should be tied on to a bunch of beads, red or white, you should put them up, and pay her that for whipping her. So now you think about this. And I mean it. You have got to pay us. If you pay us something that is worth a lot we will be satisfied. If you give us something that we aren't satisfied with you have to put up something else, until we are satisfied. If you give us a horse, if it's not a good-looking one, you will have to put up a saddle and a bridle with it. You think about this now. We want you to pay us as soon as you can. If you have to put up something you don't want to lose, it is your own fault." I was sitting there, thinking over what she had said. "In a different circumstance," she said, "you would have to put up many horses, or a big herd of sheep, or you would have to put up a lot of property. You would have to do this if you had killed her. However you didn't kill her, you have only hurt her terribly.

240

You made her suffer with pain. I know she is suffering so badly. So now you think about what I have said to you."

She had stopped talking, and then I said, "I know all about what you have said to me, and I am glad to hear you talking to me about her. I was the same. While my father and mother were still at Ft. Sumner they married, and there I was made. They found out I was inside of my mother, and both of them began to take care of me, especially my mother. When she knew I was inside of her she began taking good care of me. She moved carefully, because she wanted me to be seen. When I was born they began carrying me around carefully, because they didn't want me to be hurt by anything. My mother, and another mother of mine, that is Asdza Abaa, both took good care of me. They were going around among the women who had babies and would bring the women back for me. I got my milk that way. They both paid for the milk. They did this for me, because they didn't want me to starve, because they wanted me to be raised. They were doing this for me until I grew old enough. They lost all that they had on me. They gave away all their beads, bracelets, rings, and some other stuff besides. That is the way I have been raised too. She wasn't the only one who was born. She wasn't the only one to be taken good care of. She wasn't the only one to be raised. My father and mother were married, and I was born of them. I was raised by them. They took good care of me. They handled me carefully for a long time. Even though I was old enough to take care of myself, they took good care of me. They got all kinds of things for me. So I am raised that way too, without any suffering, without any pain on my body, as I have now. This is the first time that I am in suffering from pain. That is the way with me. They didn't raise me for any purpose like this. When I grew up to be a man they used to say, "We will have a daughter-in-law by you." They wanted me to get a nice, kind woman. They wanted me to marry, so I married her. I thought she was a kind woman, but I have found out now that she is not. Quite a long time ago she wanted to start trouble with me, but I never knew a thing about it. She began to get mad at me about little things, because she was jealous of the others. The people by whom I have been raised never wanted me to suffer like this. They didn't want me to marry a mean woman. When I married her I thought she was kind, but I have made a mistake. Here, the other day, she got mad at me for nothing. She began dragging me around; soon she had my clothes all torn off of me. She tore all my clothes off in pieces. She started dragging me by the hair; she tore lots of it out of my head. I have never suffered from pain like this before. Today my whole body is aching with pain. I ought to get paid for that too.

"So, now, you know how I have been raised. Before I married, the people by whom I have been raised all talked to me about the good life, about how to live with a woman, about the stocks and properties, how to take care of all the things. They used to tell me about all these different things, and how to take care of myself, how to take care of all my clothes. They used to tell me that I shouldn't throw my clothes away, not until they had become ragged. My clothing was still new when she tore it all in pieces. If she hadn't torn all my clothes they would have lasted a long time.

"You have talked to her about a different kind of life. You must have been talking to her about the bad things. You must have taught her all about it. I know she has learned from you. You must have been teaching her how to be mean, how to be cruel to a man. I know she has learned all of these things from you. I don't think that is a good way to teach anybody. There are lots of places that I have gone where the men have talked to their sons and daughters, teaching them just the way that I was taught. Lots of places are that way. They don't want a man's son to marry a woman like her. Everybody wants to marry a good woman. Nobody wants to marry a woman like her. Nobody wants his clothes to be torn off his back. And here I have married her through my mistake. I married her because I thought she was a good, kind woman. I thought she was going to help me, and I was going to help her. I thought I was going to live well with her, but she started trouble from the time I married her. And now I just can't get along with her. I can't stand her trouble any more. I don't want to suffer from her any more.

242

"I am sitting here just like her. I have got a body just like hers. I have got everything inside of me just like her, and I am breathing just like her. My blood is just like hers, that she lives by. I am living by that also. And here I am sitting down in suffering and pain. I can hardly move my head. As you know my whole head is swollen. I am thinking about that too. I don't want to suffer for nothing. If I have to suffer I want to suffer for something. I have got to have something also, for my suffering. And if I get something for my suffering, something that is worthwhile, it must be something I am satisfied with. So, now, you think about it too. You know very well how I am feeling. You have been here long enough now. You know that I can hardly move, and that my head is still swollen. So I can't let it go. I want something for that too. So you think about that." While I was talking she was sitting there, smoking, making one cigarette after another. Then I said, "So you want to be paid? It's all right with me. I whipped her with a rope, if you want me to pay for that I am willing to do it, and I will be very glad about it. There is my horse outside; take that horse and have it. What property I have here is all mine. All the little things I have here are all mine. The sheep that I have here in your bunch are all mine, horses and saddles are all mine. So take that horse. I give you that horse for whipping her with a rope. And don't bother me from here on. I will take all my things, take them with me to wherever I want to go. So I am going now. I am going to leave today. I don't want to stay here any longer, because I wouldn't be able to eat or sleep if I stayed here. I might starve to death. If I stayed here I would be forever suffering. I would be unhappy all the time. So now don't bother me; I am leaving for good."

She said, "You said to me to take that horse that is standing outside. Do you mean that?" "Yes, I mean it. I told you that I gave you that horse." "Is that all? Just one horse?" "Yes. I told you that was all I was giving you. Not a thing beside. I told you everything else was mine. What I have here is all mine. I am leaving today. I mean it. I don't want to stay here any longer. I want to go right now. So take that horse and don't bother me any more from here on." "I won't be sat-

243

isfied with one horse. I am not satisfied with it, so I won't take it." When she said this she got up, walked out and went home. That was all about that. We had been talking to each other pretty near all day.

After she left I sat there and started thinking about the different things and I recalled my grandfather, Lots Of Boys. He used to speak to me about that. He used to say to me, when I was a boy, "When you grow up, when you become a man, you will get a woman. You will marry a woman. Maybe you will marry a good woman. Maybe you will marry a bad one. If you marry a bad woman you must not give her anything. If you begin by giving her anything, she will want you to give her more and more, until you have given her all you possess. When she knows you have given her everything, then, from there on, she won't care for you any more. She won't want you to live with her any longer. She will chase you away, or she will run away from you. And she will have all your things, and you won't have anything. You will be without a thing from there on. Nobody will care for you, because they will know you haven't anything." This was the way my grandfather used to talk to me.

The sun was pretty well down. The horse was still standing outside. Nobody had watered the horse or fed him. Then she said to me, "We haven't any water. Go and get some. We haven't had anything to eat all day. So you get some water, and I will cook." Right away I said, "All right." I brought back some water, and she started cooking. When I smelled the food cooking, I became hungry.

After we ate I said to her, "Since this morning your grandmother has been here talking to me. You know all about that, I guess. You listened to her closely, and know what she said to me. After she got through with her speech I started talking to her, and I guess you listened closely to me, and know all that I said to her. Now, what do you think about it?" She sat there for a while, then she said, "I was so ashamed about what she had said to you. I was ashamed about that. It is her own fault. She and the others were making me start trouble with you, because they knew you had

244

horses, cattle, sheep, and property. They knew you had everything, and they wanted to have all of it. That is why they wanted me to get after you. They are all urging me to start trouble with you. They have been saying to me, 'If you start trouble with him you will get him mad. When he gets mad at you you must try to fight with him. Get him real angry at you. Make him whip you. Let him beat you. By those means we will get some of his stock or property. We will make him pay, every time he beats you with anything.' Every two or three days they were telling me and urging me to go after you. 'By such means,' they said, 'we will get all of his things from him.' That is why I started trouble with you. And now I am so ashamed about it. I am very sorry. I am feeling very bad about you. I was sitting here, and you were sitting there, and I was looking at you all day. I knew you were suffering with pain, and that made my heart ache. So I am now very sorry for you."

I said, "That is what I have been thinking about them. I thought they had been working on me that way. I discovered that through you. This is why I never paid any attention to you. Whenever you started trouble I always kept quiet. You know I never tried to hurt you with anything. You were trying to get me mad; at last you did, and then I did what you have been after for a long time. You wanted me to hurt; so I hurt you. And now, since this morning, we have been talking to each other about that. You said you were ashamed about it now, and you told me that they have been urging you to start trouble with me, but what I said a while ago, I mean that. I said I wanted to go. I still have that on my mind. So I want to go."

When I said this she started begging me not to go. She was begging me for a long time. At last I gave myself up to her again. But I said, "It will be just once more. If you start it again, I won't say anything to you, because I don't want to suffer any more. I don't want to lose all my things. I don't want to give all my things away. So, if you really mean not to start any more trouble with me, then I will stay with you all the time. You have made me a promise like that lots of times.

245

Now, from here on, you watch yourself closely, try to get all of it out of your mind. In that way we will live long together."

She didn't say anything. She sat around for a while, then she went over to the other hogan, where her mother lived. I lay around there while she was gone. She was gone a long time. When she returned she didn't say anything. She looked sad. While she was starting up the fire I went out and took my horse to the water. Then I went down to the cornfield and got some cornstalks. After I fed my horse I went back inside. I asked her, "What are they saying about me? You have been gone quite a while, are they talking about me again? Your grandmother was here today, and you know what she said to me. I told her to take the horse, but she didn't take it. So I wonder what she thinks about it. Is she talking about that?" "Yes," she said, "she was talking when I came in. She was telling the others about you. She was almost through with her story when I arrived." I said, "Are all of your brothers and sisters at home?" "Two of my brothers were home. All my sisters were at home. She was telling them about you. She said she didn't want just that one horse. She wanted more. She said she thought she would get a lot of things besides the horse, but, she said, you were a stingy man. You don't want your things to go. When she said this she turned around to me and started scolding me. She didn't want me to live with you, because, she said, you were a stingy man. So she wanted me to let you go. But I won't let you go, even though they want me to. I mean it. I won't let you go. My grandmother said again, 'I don't want just that one horse. He wanted me to take the horse, but I didn't even look at it, because I wanted more.' She told all of us, 'Don't get that one horse, unless he puts up something else besides, unless he puts up another horse, or a head of cattle. Then we'll have it. But I don't believe he will put up anything else. This is the way he spoke today. He said he didn't want to let his property go. He wanted to take all of his property with him, and all the sheep, horses and cattle. "They are all mine," he said. So I don't believe he will put up something else beside that one horse. However, don't try to take that one horse.' This is what she said to us."

It was getting dark around that time, while my wife was telling me about this. She made up the beds, and after that she sat down and began spinning the wool. My wife said, "While they were talking to me I didn't say anything. And only my younger brother started talking. He said, 'I am ashamed about all these things, about what you have been doing, and what you have said. I have been lying here, listening to your talk, and I know what you have wanted. You wanted to take a lot of things from that man. But I don't think so. I will tell him not to do it, because he is my older brother and my brother-in-law, and he calls me younger brother. I like him so very well. When he says something to me, or if he wants me to do something, I always do it for him. And if I want him to do something for me, he will do it right away. So I like him. I don't want to work on him like that. I was so sorry for him, and I still am, and I am so ashamed at what you have been doing to him. But I don't mean you, my older sister,' he said to me. 'You did it, but those two there wanted you to do it. They made you do that bad thing to the man.' He pointed to my grandmother and my mother while he was saying this. 'It was you two who tore his shirt and moccasins off him. When I heard that he was sitting around without anything on I made him a pair of moccasins, and I gave him my leggings and garters and clothes. I am so ashamed about that. I am ashamed to go over and vist him again.' I said, 'That is right, my younger brother.' When I said this they both got mad at us. We all got mad at one another." Then I said, "What your brother said is right. I realize now he has more sense than any of you. The rest of you haven't got a bit of sense. You have hurt me, and you have made a story for me. If I live long enough, if I get old, I will tell all about this to the others. And as soon as my father returns I will tell him all about it. And I will tell it to my mother, and I will tell it to my grandfather, and perhaps the others and see what they will say. As soon as I see them again I will tell them all about it, and I know they won't like it. I mean it; I will tell all about this to them."

When I said this she threw down the spinning and grabbed me around the neck, "Please, don't. Please, don't tell them. If you tell them they will sure get after me about it, and if you start telling the others they will make fun of me. I am ashamed about it. So please don't tell on me." We both lay down in bed. While we were lying there, she said to me again, "Please, don't tell on me. I am afraid they might get after me. I won't ever do anything like that to you any more. If they try to make me do something to you again, I won't take their word. I mean it. I won't try to do that any more, and I won't let you go. I want you to stay with me all the time. I will take all your word from here on. I will take good care of you from here on. So, please, don't tell on me."

I said, "If you mean that it will be nice. When I first came I thought we would live a good life. When I was a boy my father, Slim Man, used to talk to me about this, and my grandfather, Lots Of Boys, used to talk to me, and Old Man Hat used to talk to me about different things. They all spoke of life, and how to live with a woman. They all said to me, 'If you marry, try to live well with a woman. Try to help her. In that way you will live long with her.' I took their word; I wanted to be that way. But you don't want me to. I have been trying to help you with everything. I have been going around trying to get something for you. I wanted to make you a good woman. I wanted you to have some stock and other things, but you just can't see it. You said you didn't want to let me go, you said you would behave from now on. Try to be that way, and we will live a good life and I will take your word and stay right here with you. I will let this pass. I won't tell about it."

Then I said, "I want you not to be jealous. Get that out of your mind too. Every time when I want to go out to some place you always hold me back. Perhaps you think that I am going around after the women, but I am not. I always go out to look after my horses, because I don't want to lose any of them, and the same with the other stock. And when we are out of grub I always go out and try to find something. That is all I have on my mind. You haven't anything like this on your mind, only jealousy. Every time I come back from some place you think that I have been around with the women. You always say to me that I have been around with Red Clay or

248

Salt. I don't like to hear that kind of talk, and my father, Slim Man, doesn't like it either. He doesn't care to have a woman who is jealous. He used to say to me, 'You must not be jealous, and you must not marry a woman who is jealous.' And I know of nobody who wants to be that way. So get that out of your mind. If you get that out of your mind we will live well. But don't try to hold me back on anything, because I will always go out to see about my horses. If you hold me back, pretty soon I won't have anything, or we might starve to death. So just let me go around in order to get something. In that way we might get somewhere."

She put her arm around my neck then, and started kissing me, but I wouldn't let her. She said, "You probably don't like me any more." "Yes," I said, "I like you, but I don't want to be kissed. What is kissing for? I don't see anything in kissing, so I don't want to be kissed. I don't care to be kissed all my life so I don't want you to kiss me." Even though I said this she wanted to kiss me. She tried her best, but I wouldn't let her. She was saying, 'I know you don't like me any more." I said, "Yes, I like you, but I don't want to be kissed. My father doesn't want to be kissed by a woman like you. And my grandfather who died used to say the same to me. They used to say, 'If you are kissed by a woman like that, she will take all your mind and thoughts out of you. She will kiss all your memories out of you. She will weaken your heart, and you will begin to be jealous of her. Therefore you must not be kissed by a bad woman.' That is why I don't want to be kissed, I won't be kissed by a woman in all my life. So don't try to kiss me. It won't get me anywhere." She tried her best to kiss me, but I didn't let her.

The next morning we both woke up at the same time. As soon as she awoke she got up and went out and brought in some wood and started the fire. After she had started the fire she swept around and took out the dirt and ashes. About then the herd was moving along close by us, back of the hogan. They must have gotten out of the corral. I said to her, "Stop them there, and kill one of the old ewes or old wethers. I guess they are fat by now, so catch one and butcher it." "I don't think I can catch them," she said. Then I ran over and roped one that was good and fat, and we took it over to the hogan. She tied the legs together and cut the throat. Just as we were starting to butcher, her younger sister came. She helped us, and when we were through she gave half the meat to her.

After breakfast she brought in some water and warmed it and made me some soap and told me to wash my hair. My head was still sore, but not very. I washed my hair, and she washed hers. After my hair was dry she tied it up. That day I lay around the hogan all day, and she was working on the meat.

13

Encounter with the wife of
Hosteen Black . . . He meets a man who
trades . . . The story of Slim Man's
trip . . . Gifts to his wife.

the next day after we had eaten I said to my wife, "I
guess I will go down to my mother's place. She
wanted me to help them on the cattle. So, I guess, I will go
down this morning while it is cool." It was cloudy that morning, and all around on the mountain, and in places out in the
flat, it was raining. She said, "All right." Then I saddled up
my horse and started down to Where Little Arroyos Stop.
There I got me a good-sized horse. It was good on cattle.
When I got down to Many Streams, where they had been living, nobody was around. They had moved away. I started
tracking them down along in the wash; they had taken sheep,
horses, and cattle. I was wondering where they had moved
to. I followed them down to Flowing Through Rocks; from
there they had moved right straight across to Baby Rock. It
was a long way from where I was. I thought, "It's no use
going after them."

There was a hill close by. I rode up this hill, and on top I
got off my horse and sat down. I sat there looking around;
then I thought, "I will go up to Hosteen Black's place to visit
him." I got on my horse and started down towards the wash.
There were a lot of trails coming down to the wash, and there
were fresh tracks, where some herders had been watering the
herds. I went up out of the wash, and as I was going along,
all at once, a big herd was coming down off the hill. A girl
was riding ahead of the herd towards the water. I rode behind a tree, she hadn't seen me; she passed by, and then I
went on top of the hill. There another woman was riding

251

behind the herd. I went behind another tree and waited. She was coming closer. And that was the wife of Hosteen Black. When I knew it was she I rode up and stopped my horse right in front of her. As soon as I stopped my horse I grabbed her bridle. "You are the one I have been wishing for for a long time. Now I have got you." When I said this she grabbed my bridle too. "I have been thinking about you for a long time, too. I have been wanting to meet you somewhere all alone. And now today I have got you." I said, "I was just joking." "I am not," she said, "I am holding you now for good. I won't let you go." I begged her to let me go. "No," she said, "I won't let you go unless you pay me. We used to get together lots of times. Whenever we met you always gave me a dollar or a half dollar, but now this time I want you to pay me more. Then I will let you go. If you don't pay me I will take you home with me." I said, "I would go home with you if you hadn't a husband. However I know you have a husband, so let me loose before somebody sees us." "No, I won't let you go. I will hold you here until you pay me." Then I said, "Well, let us go and hide away someplace. There I will pay you." Immediately she said, "All right, let's go."

We went to a little cliff at the foot of a hill, where there were lots of trees. There we got off our horses and sat down in the shade, where it was nice and cool. There she said, "I mean what I said to you. I want you to pay me. A while back I used to go around with you lots of times, and I never asked you for any pay, but this time I want you to pay me. I want something that is worth a lot." "Take that horse, then," I said to her, "Take it the way it stands, with all the things on it. I will go home on foot. I have got nothing besides." She said, "No, I don't want to take that horse. If I take that horse I won't have any place to put it. I want you to give me something that no one can see. If you have any money give it to me. I can spend that without anybody knowing it." "Well, then," I said, "I can't do anything for you. I wanted you to take that horse. That was all I had."

She said, "I have been around with you many times, and as I said, I never asked you for any pay, because I thought you were mine all the time. I wanted to give you my daughter, the girl who went ahead of the herd. Perhaps you saw

252

her. But you didn't wait. I know you couldn't wait, because you had seen the woman you have now. You knew very well she was just a whore. You got her, and you have her now. Maybe you think she is the only woman there is. I have heard lots of times that she was jealous of me. I feel the same toward her. I am jealous of her, and I hate her, because she has taken you away from me. So, as long as you stay with that woman, I want you to pay me. I mean it. I was intending to give you my daughter, but then I heard you had married that woman. I know her very well. She is just like a dog. Wherever she went there used to be a crowd of men around her. And there you picked her up. You were a good man. I know that very well. When I heard that you had married her I said you would be spoiled by her. I guess you are now."

I said, "You only said that. If I were still single you wouldn't be talking that way to me. You wouldn't care to have me come close to you, and I don't believe you would let me have your daughter. You only said that, because I am married now." She said, "If you were single I would let you have her right now, if you hadn't married that old thing. I hate her. So I want you to pay me. If you don't pay me I won't let you go." I said, "I have given you a horse with everything on it, but you don't want to take it. So can't you wait till something comes up, some kind of doings? When at some time Enemy Way comes up you should be there, and there I will pay you." She asked me, "What would you give me?" "I will give you a big buckskin." "That will be fine. I will say I got it from the store. Nobody would know anything about it. They will all think I bought it at the store. I will be looking for something coming up. As soon as they start something I will be there, and I will look for you. Be sure and be there too, and be sure you bring that buckskin." I said, "I will." Right after this we got up and went to a little space between two split rocks. It was a real hot day.

A little after noon, as we walked back to where our horses were standing, I asked her, "About where is your home? How far is it from here?" "Why?" "I am hungry. I haven't eaten since early this morning. I wasn't so hungry a while ago, but now I am, because you put me to work." "It is your own fault. If you hadn't grabbed my bridle I wouldn't

253

have dared to touch you. If you would like something to eat come over to my place. It's only a little way from here. I guess the herd is at home now. I am going right back from here. You go way around and get on the trail that comes out from Lots Of Wool. Come on that trail." I said, "All right. I will do that. I will be there as soon as I can." She got on her horse and went home, and I went back down to the water. There I took all my clothes off and took a bath. It was awfully hot that day.

When I got to her home everything was ready. They were just starting to eat. While we were eating she told her daughter to sit beside me. "We will eat with Red Clay's husband," she said, while they were laughing. "She can come after us now. She was going to come after us even though we were never close to you," she said to me. "As soon as you get back to her you tell her you were here with us, and if she wants to come over let her. I would just like to see her. There was another group of Salt who wanted you very badly also. They were looking for you. They were going to hold you but that old thing got you, and now she is holding you, and I guess you think she is the best woman of all. Don't let him go, my daughter. Hold him. Don't let him get away from you."

After lunch we were sitting around there. Only she and her daughter were at home. The husband was away. Two womenfolk were living in a hogan close by, but they didn't come over. She asked me, "Where did you start from?" I said, "I started from way up above. I was going to Woman Who Walks Alone's place, but they had moved. So, then, I decided to ride up around here to see where my father's horses were. I have been way out towards Lots Of Wool." When I said this she smiled; she knew I just said this. I didn't want her daughter to know that I had been around with her. I said, "While I was out there on the flat it got too hot, and I began to get hungry. So I thought I would go back home, but I came to this hogan. I didn't realize you were living here. And now I have eaten; I am thankful for that."

Then I went out and got on my horse and rode over the hill. On the other side I turned around towards Many

Streams, where Woman Who Walks Alone had lived. From there I took the trail that goes by The Lake and on to Anything Falls In. Smoke was coming out of there when I got to that place. There was a man, a woman, and a boy. I asked them, "Where are you coming from? I don't know any of you. You are strangers to me." The man said, "I guess we are all strangers to one another. We are coming from Green In Canyon." "Where are you going to?" He said, "We are just going around here. My children here wanted to visit their relatives." "What are they? What clan do they belong to?" "They are Red Clay. They said they wanted to visit the man we used to call Giving Out Anger. They say he is living around here somewhere. So that is where we are going. We are going to his place, because we know him very well. From there we will visit around and get to know some of the Red Clay people around here. I myself am Mud clan."

"Well, then," I said, "I guess you are my younger brother, or older brother, or my nephew or uncle. I am Bitahni." "Well," he said, as he came up and shook hands with me, "then we are younger and older brothers to each other." They were on horseback. Their horses were turned loose; there was lots of feed around there for the horses, and they each had a big bundle of stuff. I asked them, "What have you got in those bundles? Are you going to trade?" "Yes," he said, "If anybody wants to have some clothing, or something else, we will trade. That is why we have got some little things with us." I asked him then about a man I had known for a long time. "This man's name is Mister Wounded Kneecap. He is Bitahni. He is my uncle." "Yes," he said, "I know who you mean. He is my uncle, too. You are my younger brother." He came up and shook hands with me again. I said, "What have you got, my older brother? I would like to see some of your things." "All right. It's nothing. Just some rags," he said. He spread out a canvas and put a bundle there, the biggest one they had. He untied the bundle and got the things all out onto the canvas. There were two women's skirts which were both new and nice. And several blankets and robes of different colors, some plain, some with designs. He laid them out one by one. They were all brand

255

new. The skirts were nice. They were both woven thin. I asked him, "How much are these two things worth?" The woman said, "I want twenty head of sheep for one." I picked up a blanket. "How much is this blanket worth?" She said, "I want ten head of sheep for that blanket. That's what it's worth. Where we live they are buying them from one another at that price."

I looked at everything they had. I was there talking with them for quite a while. Finally I said, "If you want to come over to my place, I will be glad to have you there, and the others will be glad too, the people with whom I live. They are Red Clay." The woman said, "That will be fine. We will go there and become acquainted with your relatives." I said, "You can stay for a day or two, or as long as you want to." Right away the man said to his son, "Go get the horses, my son. We will go over there right now." Their horses were quite a ways off, and he told him, "Get on your father's horse." The boy got on my horse and brought their horses back. While they were starting to pack I got on my horse and started off. Before I left I told them just where my home was. I said, "Go straight to that point. There you will see a little patch of corn and two hogans and one brush hogan. That is where my home is."

As I was riding along I changed my mind about going over to where my horses were. I turned around and rode to where Slim Man's sister's daughter lived. She was home, and I said, "Where is my younger brother (Slim Man's son)?" "He just went out with the herd a while ago," she said. "Where is the one who went with my father? Is he home yet?" She said, "Yes, he got home last night." I said, "I guess I will go over and see him. I would like to know about the trip he made over the mountain." I was all ready to go when she said, "What are you so in a hurry about? Don't be in such a hurry. Can't you stay away from the women for a while? You always want to go back to the women." That was just a joke, because she was my niece. I said, "I am not in a hurry. I would like to go to my younger brother. I would like to hear his story about his trip."

256

Then she asked me, "Where are you coming from?" and I said, "I was down to Woman Who Walks Alone's place, but she has moved away. On the way back I met some people. I think they want to trade something for sheep. I told them to go to my place. I guess they will be staying at my place tonight." "What are they trading? What have they got?" I mentioned some things that they had. "Have they got any calico with them too?" she asked me. I said, "Yes, they have some calico." "Tell them to come over. We would like to have some." I said, "I don't know, maybe they will. They said they were going to Giving Out Anger's place. But I'll see when I get home." Then she said, "I am sorry I didn't visit my mother, but the burro I use got away from me. I don't know where she went. If I had had my burro on hand I would have gone down to see her before she moved away." "Yes," I said, "She has moved. I guess she has gone back to her country." "I am sorry I didn't get to see her. Now, I suppose, I won't see her any more." "Well," I said, "I guess I'll go over to my younger brother. I want him to tell me about his trip." I went out then and over to where my younger brother was. I shook hands with him and said, "I would like to hear about your trip, my younger brother." He said, "I got back last night. I don't know how to describe the country, but I'll try. It seems to me as though I have been dreaming, because I don't know the country and the places, so I will only tell you what I know." I said, "That is all right. Just tell me what you know. That's all."

"When you turned around and went back we started off from there. That night we camped at Cottonwood Pass. The next morning we started off again. We travelled along all day. When the sun was down, we went right along until we got to the foot of the mountain. There we stopped with some people who were living there, but I didn't know any of them. The next morning we started climbing the mountain. When we got on top we went quite a long way to a place called Hollow, then to another place called Lake Along Foot Of Cliff. At noon we got to where a lot of people were living at one place. While we were passing a hogan they told us where the people we wanted to visit were living. We went over to that hogan and stopped right under the oak trees. We unsaddled the horses we had been driving. We hobbled them, and while I started the fire my mother went over to the hogan to visit her relatives. When she returned she said, 'The womenfolk all say it's up to the old man. When he comes we will know what to do.'

"While she was gone the old man came to us. He shook hands with us and called my father younger brother. 'Well, my younger brother,' he said, 'I guess you folks had better stay here today. I have sent word around and some boys will be here tomorrow to put up a hogan for us. By tomorrow evening everything will be fixed. As soon as the hogan is up you folks just go in and take all your things inside.' My father said, 'All right,' and the old man went back home. Before sundown they drove the horses we had brought along into a corral and started roping them. There three fellows got mad at each other about the mule. Lots of people came around that evening and shook hands with us, but I didn't know any of them. The next day they started chopping down trees and putting up the hogan. A little after noon some more people arrived. They had kept back some of the horses, and whenever one of the woman's relatives arrived they gave him a horse.

"Toward evening they had finished the hogan. Everything was done. They had cleaned it out inside and cleaned around it, and hung blankets across the doorway and built a fire. They had built a very nice hogan for us. It smelled good inside, and I wished I had a hogan like that out here. In the evening more people came. They were having races that evening, horse races and foot races. It was a big crowd, just like Enemy Way. But I didn't know any of them. I was kind of bashful and never went among them. The hogan was packed with people. We ate twice that evening. There was lots of meat. They had killed lots of sheep. People were still coming in that evening. There were bunches all around us having a good time.

"Late in the evening they came, the old man and his daughter. The old man was carrying the water and his daughter was carrying the mush, and right behind them came more

258

women, boys and girls, bringing in all kinds of food. They set it all around, but I didn't get to see what they did with the basket, because I was way in back behind the people. After they had done something there with the basket they told everybody to eat. My mother had a big sack full of meat and fried tortillas. It was a nice girl that they gave to my father. She was a stout girl around sixteen. And there my mother was sitting as though her son were being married. She had gotten the sack full of food for a present. She was thankful about it. After everybody was through eating they took out all the dishes.

"My father took the basket and laid it back against the wall of the hogan. He said, 'I will use this basket until it is all worn out, because no one came after us for the basket.' He meant that none of his relatives had come along with him. If any had they would have gotten the basket. I said, 'Why didn't you take the basket for me? You should have taken it for me. I suppose the basket was brand new.' 'Yes,' he said, 'It was brand new. It had never been used. If you had told me to get the basket for you I would have done it, but you didn't say anything about it.'

"While everyone was sitting up and keeping quiet an old man started talking. He talked a long while. When he was through another started talking. He was a young man, a tall man. He called my father, 'father.' But I didn't know any of them. I didn't even so much as ask my father about them, so I didn't get to know any of them. This young man talked a long while about the life my father had lived. Then everybody left, except a few old men who stayed talking with my father. While they were talking I went to sleep. In the morning, when I woke up, they were just beginning to lie down; they had been up all night. When I brought back the horses they were sleeping. About the time the cooking was done they all got up. After we ate my mother said, 'I guess you had better be going back.' My father said the same. My mother had made some lunch for me, and I started back. I rode all day the day before yesterday and yesterday all day. I just walked my horse along, taking my time, and got back last evening. I brought back the lunch my mother had made for me and gave it to my grandmother. I guess she still has some of it. She was so thankful for it. This is all the story I have."

I said, "I am glad to have heard your story. Some people are coming over to my place. I suppose they are looking for me now, so I guess I had better go. They were from a long way. I want to hear some of their stories, too. I am very glad to know all about your trip, my younger brother. I had better go now. I have got to get back home to see if those people got to my place. They had some things they wanted to trade." "Where are those people from?" he asked me. I said, "They are from Green In Canyon. The woman is Red Clay. The man is Mud Clan. They said they were going over to Giving Out Anger's place. They may start for his place tomorrow, but tonight they are staying at my place." "What have they got with them?" "They have a lot of things, two or three bundles of stuff. They opened one for me. There were two skirts in this bundle and all kinds of blankets. They have probably got some buckskins too."

Then I went out. The sun was down. Before I left I went in again. I said, "I have never been around where the horses are. Now that you are back we will go and ride around there. We will start from here in two days, and it will take us two or three days to round them up. So I'll be back here again tomorrow. Tomorrow we will talk about that. You must make enough lunch to last us three days." "All right," he said. "I was down in the valley today where Woman Who Walks Alone had been living, but she has moved across the flat. I suppose she is back at Carriso now." Slim Man's mother-in-law said, "I knew she would do that, because that man who married her lives over at that place. I guess he wanted her to move back to his country. I know she wanted to go there, too. So they have gone." "Yes," I said, "They have moved across."

When I got home that evening, I looked all around, but there was no horse standing anywhere. I took the saddle off my horse and took him over to where I always tied him, and there the cornstalks were already chopped up. That was my wife who had fixed it up for me. When I got inside, there they were, sitting around. I said, "I didn't see any horses standing outside. Where did you put your horses?" The man said, "A boy came from the other hogan. He wanted to take them to where there is some good grass so I told my son to go with him." My wife said, "That was my younger brother. He took the horses up on the cliff." "That is fine," I said, "I know where they have taken them. There is plenty of grass for the horses up there. Here there is nothing but salt-weed." We sat around for a while. Then he started telling me about his trip.

The next morning after we ate I spread a robe on the ground and told him to unwrap that bundle. I took one skirt and one blanket. That was all I took. Two of the boys from the other hogan each took a robe, and the girl took all the calico they had. My wife took a red belt. He wanted me to take the buckskin also, but I told him I had plenty of buckskins. "This is all I wanted," I said, "only this skirt and blanket." Then I went out to the herd and gave him thirty head of sheep for these two things. My wife gave him two for the belt. The girl gave him two for the calico, and the boys each gave him three for their robes. The man tied up these sheep with soap-weed. He had them lying around waiting for our herd to go away.

After he had tied up all the sheep he walked up to me, reached down in his pocket and pulled out two strands of white beads with a turquoise pendant tied on to them. He gave me the beads, saying, "Here, my younger brother, here is another thing. I would like to have some more sheep for these beads." I said, "I haven't any more sheep, my older brother. That was all I had in these people's herd. There are only four or five left. That wouldn't be enough." I handed them back to him, telling him to keep the beads. "I haven't enough to pay for them. If you want some cattle, I have some cattle up on the mountain; if you want cattle I will go up and get them down." But he said, "No, I don't believe I could handle the cattle. I would like to have them, but it would be too much work for me, tending to the herd and to the cattle, and my son isn't used to it." "That is right, my older brother," I said. "It is too much work for you. The cattle would want to get away. Keep the beads. Take them along with you. Somebody might want them."

About then the herd was off, and we began cutting the soap-weeds with which they had tied the legs of the sheep. Then he went on with the sheep, and I went back inside. I had bought two things, and my wife had only one, just the belt. Then I gave the two things to her. I put them right on her lap, telling her, "Put those on. I have given them to you." When I said this she grabbed me and put her arm around me, saying, "Thankyou very much, husband. I have been wishing for these things. I had one of these skirts, but my mother took it away from me. I won't let these go. I will have them until they are worn. Thankyou very much, husband." "This is what I call helping each other, buying things for each other, getting something that is worthwile for each other. Those two things will last you all your life. That is the way to help each other, but not the way you have been trying to help me. You may have been trying to help me, but I can't see how you help me with your trouble. I don't call that helping each other. That is just ruining each other, trying to kill each other. But this way means great help." She grabbed me again, held me tight against her breast. "Don't talk about those things any more, husband. I don't wish to hear about that shameful thing that I have done. I don't care to hear about it any more. I am so ashamed of it." While she was saying this she was holding me tight to her breast. After that I said, "I will go and get me another horse. I would like to go over to my younger brother's place. Yesterday he wanted me to go round up the horses. I'll ask him about that, so I'll go over to his place now."

I saddled up my horse and rode over to his place. Only Slim Man's mother-in-law and her daughter were home. I said, "Where is my younger brother?" She said, "He went out this morning. He has gone after the horses. He got the burro and rode it down after the horses. He said he wanted to get one for himself to use around here. What did you want him for?" "You know I was here yesterday, and he wanted me to go round up the horses with him. I think I will go with him in three days, so you make up enough lunch for us, enough for two or three days, so we won't starve." Then she

262

asked me about the people who stayed at my place. "Where did they go to?" I said, "They started off this morning. They wanted to go to Giving Out Anger's place." "You must have bought a lot of things from them?" "No," I said, "I didn't get anything. Only the other people picked up something for themselves. I didn't get anything. Only one thing that was handed to me. That was a necklace of beads, but I didn't take them, because I didn't have anything to pay for them." Then Slim Man's mother-in-law said, "Why didn't you bring them over to us? Perhaps we would have taken something from them." Her daughter said, "Why didn't you get those beads for me? You ought to have gotten the beads for me." "Well," I said, "They wanted to go right ahead. That's why I didn't want to hold them back. So they left. They are on their way to that place." Then I said, "I guess I will go back home. When my younger brother returns tell him I want to go in three days from now, so that he will be getting ready. I will be back here again in three days." "All right," she said, "We will tell him when he comes back. And he will be ready to go then."

The next day I began softening up some sole leather. I wanted to make a pair of moccasins for my wife. I worked on it all day, softened the sheep hide, shaved off the wool and put it on the ground. The next day I began making the moccasins and a pair of leggings out of buckskin. She had some moccasins, but she didn't have any buckskin leggings. She was awful thankful about it. When they were done I told her to put them on. She put on the moccasins and the leggings and the skirt that I had bought her. She put the red belt around her. Over that she put her silver belt, and she put on her beads. She was all dressed up, walking around inside the hogan, thanking me for all the things. She walked around for a while; then she took them all off again. Everything fit her nicely. She said, "I wish I had some silver buttons to put on my moccasins and leggings. My younger sister had some silver buttons. I'll go over and ask her to give them to me." When she returned she brought the buttons back with her. She said, "I gave two goats for those buttons." That was all I had been doing that day, making moccasins and leggings and decorating them with silver buttons.

14

Rounding up the horses . . .
Gambling . . . Tales of Slim Man's
trip . . . Hunting for cattle . . . He
arranges a deal and he gambles . . . Women
are fickle . . . The power of songs . . .
Cutting the horses.

The next morning, after I ate, I saddled up my horse and rode over to Slim Man's mother-in-law's place. The two boys were all ready to go. They had their lunch tied onto their saddles, and the three of us started off. We were rounding up horses all that day. Late in the evening we got to Moon Water, but it was so dark by the time we got to that place we couldn't see anything. I had wanted to stay at G-string's son's place. When we got to the water I was hollering, but there was no sound, so we went a little way from the water on top of a sand drift, and there we unsaddled our horses and hobbled them and went to sleep. The next morning we saddled our horses and followed the trail up a little canyon to where T'estsozi's son lived. He said to us, "Where have you come from? You must have stayed over night last night close by." "Yes," I said, "we stayed down here close to the water." "Why didn't you come here and stay with me last night, my son?" he asked me. I said, "We didn't know where your home was. Yesterday morning we started from Anything Falls In. We were all over the flat yesterday, rounding up the horses. I was hollering, listening for a sound, but we didn"t hear anything." He said, "We didn't hear anything either. The dogs were barking; perhaps they heard you; but you didn't hear the dogs barking?" "No," I said, "we didn't hear anything. That's why we went up on the sand drift and stayed there all night. This morning we went down to the water and started following the canyon, and here we are."

264

Then he said to his children, "Well, my children, hurry with the cooking. All of these boys are your brothers. They are my children." While they were cooking he asked us about Slim Man. "Where is he? Is he at home?" "No," I said, "he went over the mountain with his wife quite a few days ago. My younger brother went over with them, but he was the only one to come back from there four or five days ago." He asked, "What did he go over the mountain for?" I said, "He got another woman over there. They wanted him to come. So, that's what he went for." "Where is the place? What place did they go to?" I said, "I don't know, because I don't know the names of places over in that part of the country, but my younger brother here said it was right on top of the mountain. Only this younger brother went over the mountain with him." He said, "He must have forgotten about us. He could have let us know about it before he went. However, I guess he forgot us. How about you? Did you go with them, too?" I said, "No, I didn't go. I wanted to, but I didn't get a chance." "Well, then," he said, "he has gone far away for another woman. I suppose he will be gone for a long time. I don't believe he will come back soon. But, anyway, I am glad to know that he has another woman."

Then he asked about Woman Who Walks Alone and I told him. "Well," he said, "everybody is moving away from us. I guess they are tired of living at one place. I wanted to go and visit my mother (Woman Who Walks Alone) sometime, but I know now that I won't be able to see her. She is far away from here. I heard that a fellow joined her. I heard she was married to a fellow named Son Of Late Grey Hat. Is that right?" I said, "Yes, they were married. He was the one, I think, who wanted to move back to his country." "I don't know him so very well. I only saw him two or three times. So he was the one who married her?" I said, "Yes, they married."

We were talking about this for a while, then he said to us, "I don't want you to go right away. Take the saddles off your horses and tie them up under the shade. It is too hot to ride around out in the flat, my children. Let the horses cool off. You can go after you have eaten something again, when it gets cool this afternoon. I want you to stay with me for a while." I told the boys, "Go out and take the saddles off the horses, my younger brothers, and tie them up where there is shade." They went out and I stayed there with him. He said, "They will be down at the water about the time it gets cool. They are just starting to go. That is the only good place to get them. A great many of them will be gathered around the water. So go straight for the water. You don't need to ride all over the flat for them. So all of you wait here until it gets cool.

What a lot of horses Slim Man has now. He is about the only one who has horses in this part of the country. First they were around Lots Of Wool. They are close to the river now. He is the only man who has many horses here in this country. I know why—because he knows all about them. He knows how to get them, and he knows how to raise them. Another man who has many horses in this country is Giving Out Anger." He said again, "I know why, because, I think, they know the names of the horses." (He meant the secret names for stud, female, and young; the names which they keep to themselves; which they don't even mention in their songs.) He said, "They know the names of the male and the female, and they know the names of the colts, according to male and female. That is what Giving Out Anger said; he said, 'I know the names of all of them. A man who knows the names of the horse can raise them, even though he doesn't care to. If he doesn't know their names he won't be able to raise them even though he tries his best.' That is the way it is with these two men, Slim Man and Giving Out Anger. But I don't know about the others. I don't know about Choclays Kinsman and Who Has Mules. However, I think they know the horses' names. I know they all have lots of stock, though not as many as these two fellows.

"How many horses have you got, my son?" he asked me. "I haven't any horses at all, my father," I said to him, but he didn't believe me. "You must have some." I said, "Yes, I just have a few of them." "How many have you got? Is it around one hundred or over?" "No," I said, "I have got only a little over sixty." He said, "That is a whole lot for one man. Some of us around here and over the country have only twenty horses. In places some people have only ten. That is all some of us have, and we think we have a good many. I know now you have quite a bunch of horses all by yourself. How many horses does Slim Man have all together?" I said, "I don't know how many all together, but once when we had them rounded up I counted to a little over five hundred. I lost count after that. It must have been close to six hundred that we had rounded up, and there were many that we didn't get." "That is quite a lot. However, I think Giving Out Anger has more than that. His son, whom we call Has Done It, said 'My father has three thousand horses all together.' But I didn't believe him. I don't think he has that many. I didn't believe him, because he said, 'Before my father moved his horses out of this country they used to be scattered all around Anything Falls In and around White Rock Hill, and all around Lots Of Wool and Chasing Down Place, and all around Cow's Water, and all around Iron Mine.' That is why I didn't believe him, because I didn't see any of his horses around here. I know he has many horses all right, but I don't think he has that many. He may have as many as a thousand now. I don't believe any person around here has three thousand horses."

In the afternoon the herders returned with the herd. They killed a sheep for us and started cooking. We had nice fresh meat that afternoon. After we ate we saddled up our horses. He came up to us and said, "Don't attempt to ride around. You don't need to ride all over the flat. I know no horses are out in the flat this time of day. They are all gathered at the water now. So you all go right straight to the water." When we got to the water at Narrow Canyon sure enough there was a big bunch of horses. After they all had water we started them down across the flat right straight to Lots Of Wool, and all over the flat there were small bunches just going to the water. By sundown we had them all rounded up in a little canyon. We fixed the gate across the mouth of this little canyon and that evening we went back to the hogan.

In the morning we told Slim Man's mother-in-law, "Take out the herd, so that we can take the boy who is herding down to where the horses are. He'll help us there, and he can make us some coffee this noon." She said, "I can't handle the

267

herd. I am not very good on foot." Then we said, "Put the saddle on the burro, and get on him and herd with that." But she said, "I have never yet ridden a burro. I am afraid of burros. I don't like to ride them." Then her daughter said, "I'll take out the herd, and you can go with the boy." We had our horses tied up all night, and as soon as they made some more lunch for us that morning we started off. When we got down to the horses, there they were against the gate. I said, "We'll take them out to another little canyon. It's too rough in this canyon. In the other one it's nice and smooth. It's a good sandy place." So we took them across the wash and put them in the other little canyon.

Then we started working on them. We put them down and I began to cut them. We did a quick job on five, but from there on it was getting to be too hard for us. They were getting stronger all the time, because we were getting tired. And it got so hot, and our hands were sore from burns by the rope. We had race-medicine with us, and every time I cut a horse I put this medicine on him so he would be lively and quick, so he would be strong and long-winded. We cut ten of them, and then it was noon. The boy had lunch ready for us. We stopped working and took a long rest. After lunch we lay around in the shade. Our hands were sore and hurting us more and more every minute. In places the skin had peeled off.

The oldest boy said, "I just can't hold the rope any more. I don't think I am able to hold it any longer." I said, "Well, if we can't do much more we will quit now. But we will rope two of the wild ones and break them." He said, "All right." There were a whole lot of them that had to be cut, but we couldn't handle them all by ourselves. So we roped two and got on them. The other two boys were right behind us, chasing us around out in the valley. Late in the afternoon they started chasing us up towards Where The Gray Hill Comes Out. I stayed at their place until around towards evening, and then started home. But I couldn't let the horse go, so one of my younger brothers chased him home with me. There after we had hobbled him he got on his horse again and went back, and I went inside the hogan.

My wife had about finished cooking, and she was looking happy. After we ate I began telling her about the trip we had made out in the valley. When I said, "out in the valley," I looked at her, but she was all right. Whenever I talked about the valley she always got mad about it, but this time she seemed not to mind; she didn't get mad about my trip.

I went out and got the horse the next morning and tied him to the pole. After breakfast I said, "Put the bridle and the saddle on the horse for me while I hold him." She said, "All right," so we went out and I held his ears while she put the bridle and saddle on him. She made a quick job of it. Then I let him loose, but he didn't do anything, so I said to her, "I'll ride around and try to break him. I'd like to ride down to where the people always gamble. I'd just like to see them." She said, "What do you want to go there for." I said, "Well, I don't know, maybe I'll start gambling with those fellows." "You don't know anything about cards, so why do you want to start gambling." I said, "It won't take me long to learn." She didn't say any more about it, and I got on my horse and started down to the wash that comes out from Hay Footed. I crossed that wash, and soon I got to where they had gambled.

Who Has A Hat and his friend from Shiprock always had many people at their place. When I got there a crowd of people were there. White Horse and Who Has Children were there, and Has Done It, and some other men that I knew. They were all gambling. I walked around watching them gamble for quite a while. I watched them play. There was plenty of money, half dollars and dollars. That was Has Done It's money. He had brought all that with him. They said to me, "Don't just watch. Come on. Get in and play some." I said, "I have got nothing to play with. I haven't got a nickel." "Pawn something to us," they said. "And we will give you some money." But I said, "I haven't got anything to pawn." "Yes," they said, "we all know you have lots of things. Pawn one of your horses. We know all your horses. They are all good-looking horses, so pawn one to us." I began thinking about it, and after a while I made up my mind. I said, "I will pawn one of my horses for a dollar." One fellow said, "Pawn it to me for two dollars." I said, "No, I just want a dollar." Then Who Has A Hat said, "Go ahead. Take the two dollars."

Sometimes I almost lost all of it. Sometimes I won again. But at last I had lost the two dollars. Then he gave me two more. I lost those, and he gave me another two. As he gave them to me he said, "What kind of a horse is it that you pawned to me? It's not a scrubby horse, is it?" Before I could say anything about it a fellow sitting behind me said, "Scrubby horse. What are you talking about? I know what kind of a horse he pawned to you. He pawned a horse which he has been riding around all the time. Didn't you?" he said to me. I said, "Yes." "Well," he said, "that's a very good-looking horse. I know that horse very well. It's worth about thirty dollars, so you haven't put up any money yet." But this fellow had only said that. He didn't know any of my horses.

Pretty soon I began giving a dollar back to him, every once in a while when I won some. Late in the afternoon I had paid him all back, and I had won only three dollars and a half. Then I quit. I got up and walked over to my horse. They were all looking at me; they all said, "Where are you going?" I said, "I'm going to take my horse to the water. I have had him standing here all day, and he's about dead of thirst." "Come back again when you have watered the horse." "Well, yes," I said, "I will." Then I got on my horse and rode down to the water. There, after I had watered him, I started home.

I took my time going back. The sun was almost down when I got home. I gathered up some wood and went inside; she had the cooking all done. After supper she said, "This morning after you left one of my younger brothers was here. He said they were going after the horses but they haven't come back yet. I think they are going to the store. They finished weaving a rug this morning. I guess they are going to take that to the store." That was what she told me that evening, but I didn't say anything about my trip. While she was fixing the beds one of the dogs began to bark, then another, then all of them began barking. After she had fixed the bed she went over to the other hogan. She wasn't gone very long. She came back and said, "The boys are back with the horses."

270

The next morning, after we ate, the boys were all ready to go. Then I reached down in my pocket, got out three dollars and a half, and gave that to her. I said, "Take that to the boys and tell them to get you some grub, flour, coffee, and sugar. Where are they going?" "They are going to Blue Canyon," she said. She was very thankful about the money. She took it and some hides that were lying around over to the boys. The next two or three days I didn't do anything, just rode the horse around trying to get him gentle. When the boys returned from the store she went over to the hogan and brought back some flour, coffee, and sugar, and some little things for the skins she had taken over. We had eaten early that morning, but she started cooking again, and we ate some more, I said, "I would like to go over to where the horses are and get me another horse. After that I would like to go to where the cattle are. The time we gathered them up I missed some. I want to go up and see if I can find any of them." She said, "All right."

That morning I started off to Slim Man's mother-in-law's place. As I was riding to the hogan where she lived I looked over to the other one, and there was my father Slim Man. He came out and went over to the wood pile and started chopping wood. I turned around and rode over to his place and tied up my horse. He had chopped a little wood and taken it inside. I went inside after him, and there he was, sitting down, and his wife, too. He had a sheep pelt already spread out for me. We shook hands and he said, "We got home last night a little after midnight. I never did count the days. When was it that we left here?" "Oh," I said, "it must have been about fifteen days ago." "Well," he said, "I didn't think we were gone that long. Where are you going?" I said, "I want to go where my horses are. I'd like to get another horse. I only wanted to stop here for a while. I didn't know you were home." He said, "Yes, we got back home last night. You had better let the horses go. As long as you have come here you and your younger brother go over to the sweat-house, build a good fire with some rocks, clean out the sweat-house, and put new cedar-bark inside. I am tired from riding. I need a good rest. We will all get a good rest, my children." One of my younger brothers and I went over and fixed the sweat-house. After we had been in and out of the sweat-house a few times he started telling about his trip, about his marriage to the young girl whom he left on the mountain and how he brought the wagon as far as Dark Water.

Then he asked about Woman Who Walks Alone. "I heard that she has left and moved to Carriso. Is that true too?" I said, "Yes, they moved to that place quite a few days ago." He asked, "Did they take everything across with them?" I said, "Yes." He said, "I had a yearling in with their cattle, I guess they have taken that yearling too." "Yes, I guess they did. They have taken my bucks and billy-goats. I don't know how I will get them back," I said. "About how many horses did they take with them?" "They took quite a bunch of them, but I know they all belonged to them. They took all the tame horses and some wild ones, and they took the mules with them too." He said, "I thought they would do that, because that man of hers is just like a dog. He goes everywhere. He goes all around like a starving dog. But it's all right with me. I didn't like him so well, so I am glad he has moved out of this country. However I would like to get my yearling back. And you must go after your bucks and billy-goats and bring them back too. Don't let them have them." I said, "I'll see about it. Maybe I'll get them back; but I will see about it later on." "Yes, be sure and get them back. Don't just let them go." Then he said, "I guess we had better quit now. I guess we are all good and rested, so we'll quit now and go home."

When we got to his home the food was ready. After we ate he asked me, "Which way are you going now, my son?" I said, "I wanted to go to where my horses are to get me another one, because I would like to go over where the cattle are." He asked, "What do you intend to do with that horse you are riding now, my son?" I said, "I guess I'll turn him loose when I get down to the water." "You better not," he said, "When you get another horse bring that one back up here for us. My son will use that horse around here, and when he becomes gentle we will use him for herding. I am glad that you have broken him. I thank you for that." I said,

"I'll do that. I'll bring him back up here." Then I went out. I looked at the sun, and it was a little after noon. I started off, and as I was going along, whenever I saw some horses, I started them down towards the water. My younger brother was there waiting for me, so I didn't have to take the horses all the way back to their place.

I got home when the sun was almost down. That evening I said, "Tomorrow I'll go up to where the cattle are. I would like to start early, so that I can be up on the mountain while it's cool, so I wanted you to make me some lunch now." My wife cooked some food and boiled some meat. After the meat was cold she put the lunch in a sack for me and hung it up. The next morning when I woke up she was almost done with the cooking. After we ate I went out and got the horse ready; then I went back inside and she handed me the lunch. She said, "You ought to have brought a horse or two back with you. If you had done that the boys could have helped you. They are all at home, and they haven't got a thing to do." "Well," I said, "It's too late now."

I started off while it was still real dark that morning. It didn't take me long to get to the foot of the mountain. It was still dark when I started climbing up. When I got to where the cattle were it was daylight. I started looking for the cattle; I was riding all over. There were some here and there, but I was only looking for the ones that I had missed the other time. I didn't see any of them. Late in the afternoon I started some of them down towards the water. I was thirsty, and there was no water up on the mountain. At the foot of the mountain, where there was water, I let them go.

I drank some water and watered my horse; then I thought, "I'll go over to Lost His Moccasins' place. Maybe they have seen them somewhere." When I got there I tied up my horse and went inside. There he was, and his wife was home also, and one of his daughters and one of his sons. I guess the others were out some place. Some of his children were herding. I shook hands with them, and he asked me, "Where are you coming from?" I said, "I'm from down below. You know where my home always is. I started from

273

there early this morning. I was up on the mountain, and that's where I am coming back from." "Was that you driving the cattle down to the water?" he asked. I said, "Yes, I got a few of them down from off the mountain. I have missed four of them. I rounded them up some time ago, and I missed four. I thought they might be back in the bunch, but they are still missing. I saw all the others, that we rounded up here once, but these four are still missing. I have been all around, but I didn't see one of these four. Perhaps you or your children have seen them someplace on the mountain or down at the water." He said, "I don't know about your cattle. I never pay any attention to them. There is always a bunch of cattle at the water every evening, but I don't know whom they all belong to. I don't think any of my children know anything about your cattle. They have been way up on top of the mountain twice, where our cattle are. Both times they killed one, and brought the meat down, but those were our own cattle that they killed up on the mountain. So I don't know, I may have seen them, or maybe my children have seen them, but we don't know anything about your cattle." I said, "I guess I had better be going. Where is my uncle living?" I meant Walk Up In Anger. He was Bitahni. He was Lost His Moccasins' son-in-law. He was married to his daughter. He said, "He lives down below here. It's just a little way from here. Down at the place called The Lake. He lives there. He has a little cornfield there and some peaches. He lives there all the time." "Well," I said, "I'll go over to his place."

I went down, following the wash. Sure enough there was a cornfield, and his hogan was sitting up on a rock hill. I tied up my horse and went inside. It was a good-sized brush hogan that he was living in. He spread out a sheep pelt for me. Before I sat down I shook hands with them, my uncle and his wife and his mother and his children. There was quite a bunch of them living in this same hogan. After I shook hands with all of them I sat down. "From where are you coming, my nephew?" he asked me. I said, "From down below. I started early this morning from my place, and I have been up on the mountain all day. I got tired of climbing, so I just started back." "You must have been after your cattle."

"Yes," I said, "I have missed some. I thought I would find them this time, but I didn't so I just gave up hunting for them. I was up there where the other people live. I only stopped there a while, then I thought I would come to your place." "Well, then, did you get something to eat?" "No," I said, "I was only there for a while." "Well, then, you must be hungry. Cook something for your son," he said to his wife. "Hurry up. He is hungry."

They all started to get at the cooking. "Are you going home after you eat?" he asked me. I said, "No, I would like to stay here with you tonight, my uncle." "Well, that's fine, my nephew. Then take your saddle off your horse, and both of us will go down to the cornfield and bring up some cornstalks for him." So we did that, and when we got through we went back inside and there the food was all ready to be eaten. After I ate—I did all the eating by myself, they had already eaten—I started telling him about the cattle. It was evening then. When I had finished my story he said, "Yes, I know they killed two head. They said they had killed them up on the mountain, but I don't believe so. They had given us some meat the first time they brought some out, and by the taste of it I don't believe they killed that on top of the mountain. I could tell it by the taste. Those cattle on top of the mountain are wild. If they had chased them I would have been able to tell it. But what they had brought out hadn't been chased at all. And they started from their place in the morning and brought the meat back the same day. So, I think it is one of yours that they killed. That was a female that they brought out the first time. The other was a steer. I know very well it was yours, because they had your cattle driven out to their place. While they were trying to kill this steer the steer got mad and ran his horns into a horse's shoulder. I know it was yours. They gave us some more meat. It must have been three or four years old. I could tell by the hind quarter. They had given us a hind quarter. I didn't see the head, but I really do believe it was yours. I have never been up on that mountain, because I haven't got anything to go up there for. But those people up there I know always go up on the mountain, and every once in a while they will have some cattle meat. I don't

275

know where they are getting the meat from. I have only six head, but I have them right around here close all the time. This spring all of them almost died on me. They were covered with bugs. Their hair was all peeling off. I put all kinds of weeds on them. I gathered up all kinds of weeds and boiled them, and then washed the cattle with these boiled weeds. I had a hard time killing off the bugs. They are just beginning to pick up now. Their hair is only now beginning to grow. So I keep these six head around close to me all the time, and also because I thought someone might get after them. How can you stand all the work that you have? You ought to have someone to take care of the cattle for you. I don't see how you handle all the work by yourself. I know you are tending to the sheep, to the horses, and to the cattle, besides a lot of little works. So you ought to get someone to take care of your cattle for you, and you ought to take your cattle off the mountain. If you leave them up on the mountain, soon you will lose them all. They are beginning to kill them off on you now. So you had better do something about it."

Then we dropped that and he started asking me about the people, about my mother and Woman Who Walks Alone and my father, Slim Man. He said, "Well, everybody is moving away from you. How will you get along all by yourself? Your father will be moving over the mountain where his new wife lives. When he moves over the mountain you will be all alone. What can you do then?" "Oh," I said, "I will be all right, even though I am all by myself." "Well, you are among Red Clay. I guess you will be all right with them, nephew." Then I got up and walked outside for a while, stretching myself. When I went back in they had fixed my bed for me. He said, "I guess we had better go to bed now, my nephew. I know you are tired riding all day on the mountain, so just go to sleep and take a good rest." I said, "Yes, I am tired, and I am tired all the time. I never get enough rest. I am tired always." When I said this I took off my moccasins and lay down. He said, "Our corn is getting ripe, and the peaches are beginning to get ripe too. How about your corn?" "I guess it's about the same," I said. "In a couple of more days it will be ripe too." Then I said, "I heard that they are going to have

276

the Night Chant over at Along Red Rock. I think they will have it soon." "Well," he said, "I guess we will all be going to that place. It is not so very far from here." I was telling him about this while we were lying in bed, and then I went to sleep.

The next morning after we ate I said, "I guess I had better be going home." "What are you going to do about your cattle?" he asked me. "Are you going to ask those people about where they got that meat?" I said, "I don't know how to ask them. I don't know how to get at it, for nobody saw them, and I don't know whether they killed mine. So I don't think I will try to ask them about it." "That's right. If you ask them about it, they won't tell you. If you ask them, they will only get mad at you about it, because they are that way. I know. Even though they were yours they won't tell you." I said, "That's what I am afraid of. They will certainly get mad at me about it. So I'll just let it go, because I didn't see it, and nobody saw them killing my cattle."

When I got home my wife was making green corn bread. She said, "The corn is almost ripe. That's why I'm making green corn bread. But I haven't got any wood." I started riding up to the wood then. From there I dragged a good-sized log back home. After I had it all chopped up I built a big fire for her to get the ground good and hot. She said, "Half of the cornfield is ours now. They let us have half of the corn. So you can get corn stalks for your horse whenever you want to." I was glad about that. That evening while we were lying in bed I told her about my trip. She said, "Sure they killed your cattle. They are always killing cattle, even though they don't belong to them. I know that uncle of mine, Lost His Moccasins, he is a big thief."

After we ate in the morning I said, "I'll go and take my horse back to the bunch and get me another one. This one doesn't eat cornstalks very well, so I'll turn him loose and get one that eats cornstalks." I saddled up my horse and started off. I passed my father's place and got up to where the horses were and started them down towards the water. While I was at the water at Many Streams somebody came riding towards me. It was a woman. When she rode up I recognized her. It was Hosteen Black's wife. I shook hands with her, saying, "Where are you going, my spouse?" She said, "I am going over where the people are gambling. My man went over yesterday. I told him I would catch up with him today." "What is it that you are going after him for?" I asked her. She said, "We are going over to a place called Cátohi. Some of our relatives live there. They gave us some cattle some time ago. That's what we want to go over there for. I think we'll start for that place today, or maybe tomorrow. It's up to my man."

I said, "Help me drive the horses into the corral." She said, "All right." We drove them into the corral and there I roped one and put the saddle on it. I said, "I wanted to go over to that place too, where they are gambling, but I haven't any money. Would you put up some money for me?" She said, "I haven't any myself. I never thought to take some. I haven't any with me now. I have some at home. I'm sorry. I haven't got a cent right now. Perhaps my man still has some. Yesterday, when he started from home, he took thirty dollars with him. Maybe he has lost them; maybe not." Then she said, "Give me one of your cattle. How much do you want for one head, a good-sized one?" I said, "You belong to me, so to you I'll let one good-sized one go for twenty dollars." "If you give me a good-sized one I'll give you ten dollars for it. You said you would let me have it for twenty dollars, but I'll just give you ten, and the other ten will be the buckskin that you promised me. In that way we'll be straightened out. When you come up to where they are gambling you ask my man for ten dollars. Tell him you will pawn one good-sized head of cattle, and make a date, put up so many days, and when the date is up he will know it is 'dead.' He'll know the cattle belongs to him then. When we arrange it this way I do really believe we won't get caught. Then we will be settled." I said, "All right," and the plan was fixed. I was glad she had planned for me that way. I told her, "Go on ahead. I'll be there." She rode on. I stayed around the water quite a long while, then I started off for that place too.

Lots of horses were tied up under the trees there. They had a big brush hogan. There was a big crowd; fellows from different places gathered there. Everybody had a pile of money. I walked around them to different places, looking at them gambling quite a long while. Then I said, "Someone put up some money for me. Anyone who puts up ten dollars for me I'll pawn one head of cattle to him." They said to one another, "Come on, you put up some money for him," but no one put up any for me. Then Hosteen Black got up and walked away over the hill. I guess he went to take a leak. When he returned he walked over to where his wife was sitting out in the shade with some women who were there. When he walked up to his wife I walked over there to him and said, "Put up ten dollars for me. I'll pawn one of my cattle to you for ten dollars." He said, "I don't think I've got that much money. I may have only five." Then his wife said, "Five! What did you do with all the money? You took thirty dollars with you yesterday. What did you do with all that? Put that five dollars up for him, and I'll give him the other five sometime." He was standing there, looking down to his feet. Then he pulled his pouch around in front, opened his pouch, got out ten dollars and gave them to me. She asked him, "Have you got any money left yet?" "Yes, there are only two dollars left." She asked him again, "What did you do with all the money? You always lose. You never win. Every time you come to this place you always lose. So I want you to go now. Stop gambling now. We'll go to the place where we are going." He said, "Wait a while. I have two dollars left. I want to gamble for that." Then he walked to where they were gambling and sat down again, and I walked over too. But I only looked at them. I thought, "I'll wait," so I just stood there, and watched them.

Then I started gambling with the boys, but I didn't win. I kept on playing until a little after noon, but I didn't win anything. Then all the fellows said, "We are getting hungry." Just about that time the herders were home with the herd. There were two big herds at this place. The fellows put up a quarter a piece and took it over to the womenfolk. It amounted to two dollars, and there they were, coming back with a good-sized sheep. They killed and butchered it, and while they were cutting up the meat the rest of us built a big fire. When the fire had burned down they started roasting the meat on charcoal. There we all ate that afternoon, but I didn't eat much. Right after everybody had eaten they started gambling again. Late in the afternoon Hosteen Black had won some money. I don't know how much. He put it in his pouch, got up and walked over to his wife. Then they started off for where they said they were going. I stayed there. I quit playing with the boys and started gambling with the older fellows. When the sun was about down I was so hungry I began wishing for food. I was a dollar and a half to the good. That was all I had won. I tried my best to win some that day. And then I started home.

When I got home I took the saddle off my horse and tied him up and got some corn stalks for him. I was so hungry. My wife was sitting in the hogan; she had the food all ready to be eaten. She had made a lot of green corn bread, besides that some white bread, and there was a lot of meat. She had killed a sheep that day. After I had eaten I felt fine, and I thanked her for the food. I said, "I have been down where the people were gambling. I have been gambling also. I pawned one of my cattle to Hosteen Black." I didn't say anything about his wife. She didn't like to hear about her. She asked, "How much money did you pawn the cattle for?" I said, "I pawned one for ten dollars." "How big a one did you pawn?" "I told him I would pawn a good-sized one." She said, "It's not worth it. We will get the cattle back. Did you lose all that ten dollars?" "No," I said, "I didn't lose any." I had on a vest; I had the money in my vest pocket. She grabbed hold of my vest and took out the money. She counted it out, and it was eleven and a half. "That's all I won, only that dollar and a half," I said. She put the money away somewhere, and we went to bed.

The next three days I stayed at home. I didn't do anything, or go any place. But the morning after I said to her, "I would like to go down to where they are gambling. I would like to gamble again. Maybe this time I'll win something." She said, "All right, but I won't let you have all the money, because you'll lose it all." She only let me have the dollar and a half and kept the ten dollars with her. I didn't say anything.

280

I picked up the dollar and a half and put it in my pocket and started off.

But there wasn't anybody there except Turkey. Everyone had gone home. I stayed around for a while, then I said, "I came here thinking the crowd was here still. I was going to gamble." Then Turkey said, "We'll gamble, my younger brother." I said, "I haven't got any money to gamble for." He said, "I thought you came here to gamble. What did you come to gamble for?" "Oh," I said, "I was going to pawn something." "Come on," he said, "sit down. We'll gamble. Pawn something to me. Whatever you wish I'll take it. I've got some money left yet, so pawn something to me, even if it's only for a quarter. Start off with a quarter." But I didn't say anything. I sat down in front of him and told him, "Take out your cards." Then I reached down in my pocket and got out a half dollar.

Late in the afternoon one fellow arrived on horseback. His name was Yellow Thief. He walked up to us after he had tied up his horse and said to me, "Well, my son-in-law is gambling." "Yes, I'm gambling," I said. "I didn't think you gambled." "Oh, I'm just learning," I said. He sat down, and the three of us played until the sun was almost down. Then Turkey said, "We will stop for awhile. You two go and gather up some wood, so we'll have a light tonight. After you gather some wood, and after we eat we will start gambling again." We two went out, but I said, "I don't think I'll stay tonight, because I don't think I'll win anything, and I'm afraid I might lose when I get sleepy, and besides I don't know much about playing cards. So I had better be going home."

While I was riding along towards home I counted my money. I had won only five dollars. I said to her the next morning, "I would like to go over to my father's place." She said, "What are you going over there for?" I said, "Oh, I just want to go and visit him. I haven't been to his place for quite a few days now. I want to go and see what they are doing. They may want me to help them with something." She asked me, "Are you coming back from there, or are you going somewhere else?" "I can't say. If they want me to help them, or to go off somewhere for them, then perhaps I'll have to

281

stay away. If they don't need me for anything I'll come back today." Then she grabbed my vest. "What did you do yesterday? Have you won some money again?" she said, while she was searching my pocket. When she found the five dollars and a half she took a dollar and a half and handed four dollars back to me. "If I let you have all the money to carry around with you you might lose it all. So I want to keep this eleven fifty here at home for you, so you can get your cattle out of hock with it." There she had pushed me into a corner, and it was my own fault. I should have hidden some of the money away.

I put the four dollars in my pocket and started off to my father's place. They were all at home. My father said, "We have just finished eating, but there's a little left over. If you want some go ahead and eat." I ate a little. Then he asked me, "Where are you going my son?" "I'm only riding around here, just to see what you folks are doing." "We are not doing anything, but it's a good thing you came, my son. We are almost out of grub. I wanted the boys to go and get the horses, but they were kind of lazy this morning. They didn't go. So I'm glad you came, my son. Could you let us have one of your horses to go to the store at Round Rock?" "Yes, I'm willing to do that. When do you want to go?" "Today, just as soon as you get us a horse." I said, "How much stuff do you want to take to that place? How much grub do you want to bring back from there?" He said, "There are quite a few skins and hides and a little wool." I said, "I don't think one horse could carry all those things, so I'll get you two." "All right, that is fine," he said, "you go and get the horses, and about the time you come back we'll have the sweat-house ready here." I made a quick trip to my horses and back.

Before the boy left I gave him the four dollars I had and told him to get me some grub too, flour, coffee, and sugar. When he started off three of us went over to the sweat-house. We put the rocks inside and the blankets over the door; then we took off our clothes and went in. We had been going in, back and forth, three or four times. Then my younger brother quit and went home. My father and I stayed there. I said, "I was down where the fellows have been gambling. I stayed

282

there all day until sundown. That's where I got those four dollars. I didn't have a cent." He asked me, "How did you start to gamble?" "I pawned one head of cattle to Hosteen Black's wife." "Was Hosteen Black there too?" "Yes," I said, "he was there." "Did he know you had pawned a herd of cattle to his wife?" I said, "Yes." "How much did you pawn it for?" "I pawned it to her for ten dollars." He said, "Is that all?" Then I told him about what I had done. I said, "I had promised her a buckskin some time ago, but I had no way to take the buckskin out of my hogan. That's why I let one head of cattle go for ten dollars. She wanted me to do that, so I wouldn't have to give her a buckskin. She told me I should keep the money." He asked me, "How did Hosteen Black act toward you? I heard some time ago that he was suspicious of you, that he was suspecting you were after his wife. That's why I asked how he acted toward you." I said, "I never noticed. He may have been thinking of me that way, but he was the one to put up ten dollars for me. If I hadn't done this I was going to come up here and tell you about it. I was going to ask you for a buckskin to give to his wife, but now it is all arranged with her." "If you had told me about it I would have been willing to help you out on that, my son."

Then my father asked me about the people with whom I had traded. "I heard some people stopped at your place. I heard you had traded with them. Where were they from?" I said, "They were from Fort Defiance." "About where did they say they were living?" I said, "They said they were living this side of Fort Defiance." "What was their clan? Perhaps I know them." "The man said he was Mud clan. The woman said she was Red Clay. She is Greasewood Woman. There were three of them, a man, a woman, and a boy." "Oh, yes, I know them very well. I know the man is Mud clan, and I know Thorny Woman very well, too. The man's father's name is Black Goat. What did you get from them?" I told him. "So you got two things. Are those two things for yourself, or for someone else?" he asked me. I said, "I got them for my wife." "That's nice. That's the way to treat one's wife. How do you get along with her? You ought to know by this time.

283

How is she? Is she treating you right? A while back I heard that she and her mother had a scrap, and that her mother had taken all the things away from her. Did she ever get them back?" "No," I said, "she never got anything back. Some things were given to us by my mother, and we have some things now which we have been getting ourselves. We haven't anything that doesn't belong to us. What we have now is all ours. I'm getting along all right with her." He said, "I'm glad to hear that. When I was among the Red Clay they didn't treat me right. I had a hard time with them. Those Red Clay are hard to get along with. That is why I left them. Since I left them I have never seen my children. I had two children; I don't know how they are getting along. Tell me the truth about her. How is it? How is she acting toward you, and how is she treating you? I know exactly how they are. Don't be afraid to tell. I know exactly how they treat a man. I know her mother and her grandmother; neither of them ever did treat a man right. They'll live with a man for a few days, then they'll begin to treat him cruelly, until the man isn't able to stay any longer with them. They have had pretty near all the men around here and some from way on top of Black Mountain. Those two women's children all have different fathers. So tell me about her. How is she to you?"

Then I said, "I really don't know. Sometimes she acts funny to me." "How?" he asked. "Oh, sometimes she gets mad at me over a little thing. And she gets jealous of some women." That was all I told him. I didn't tell him what she had done to me, that she had torn off all my clothes, because I was afraid about that. He said, "Once a woman begins treating you like that she will get worse all the time. But don't let her start working on you that way. When she begins to treat you badly, if you think you can't stand any more, just come over and see me about it, and I'll know what to do for you. I wish we had gone over the mountain together. If you had gone with me I would have gotten a woman for you there. There were two women at this one place. They were of one mother, and they both looked exactly alike, like twins. They both had nice grey eyes, and one of those I got. Neither one had ever yet received a man. If you had been with us I would

284

have gotten the other one for you. But as you are being treated right where you are you had better stay there. But whenever hard trouble comes up you just come over and tell me about it. Then I will see what I can do for you, my son. I guess we had better quit now. It's cooling down on us" (the sweat-house).

It was afternoon when we got home. The food was ready, so we started right in eating. After we ate Slim Man said, "Where do you think you will go from here, my son? Are you going back home?" I said, "I guess I'll go over to where my horses are. I didn't get to see all of them, and I want to take them down to the water." He said, "All right. Could you let me have one or two of your horses again? I would like to go to where my horses are too. I haven't seen my horses for a long time, so I am kind of eager to see them. And I want you to go with me, my son." He said to me, "If you let us have two horses then all three of us will go." I said, "Yes, sure I'll let you have the two horses." "That will be fine," he said.

The next morning, when I awoke, it was almost daylight. Slim Man was still sleeping. My younger brother had already gone after the horses. He was back about the time the food was cooked. After breakfast we saddled up our horses and started down to Many Streams, down to Anything Falls In, and down to Lots Of Wool and Rock Cliff Ridge Coming To An End, and started rounding up the horses. There were bunches of them all over the flat. We rounded them up and drove them into a canyon, and there we roped three of them. It was a little after noon. He said, "We'll take the horses out of this canyon and drive them out in the flat towards Lots Of Wool, and then we'll come back here, and from there we'll go down to Moonlight Spring. We'll stay with G-string's Son tonight. From there tomorrow morning we'll go around by Narrow Canyon and round up the horses in that part of the country."

The sun was pretty well down when we got to Moonlight Spring. We watered the horses, and after we had some water and washed ourselves we started up to where G-string's Son lived. The sun was almost down when we got there. We tied up our horses and went inside. The people there had eaten a while before so they started to cook some more for us. The old man said, "Hurry with the cooking. We haven't any meat. We just ran out of it. I didn't know you fellows were coming. However we'll get some more in a little while. Go out and kill one," he said to his children, "so we'll have nice fresh meat." Then the boys and girls went out, taking knives and rope with them, and his wife started cooking. When she had finished he poured us some coffee. "Drink some coffee first," he said. About then his children had brought in the meat, and they started roasting some and boiling some. We drank coffee and ate some corn bread. Slim Man said, "We didn't have any lunch with us, because we expected to be back home the same day. But by afternoon these two boys were hungry. They didn't say so, but I could tell it by their looks, so I thought we would come over here to your place, and here we are. Now we are saved. I guess the boys are glad now; they have had a cup of coffee, and I know it has warmed up their stomachs. I know they are feeling good now." By then the meat was roasted and some was boiled. They had given us some roast meat and we started eating again. We all had enough.

After we ate they started talking. First they talked about where we had been riding all day. After that Slim Man told about his trip on top of the mountain, and how he got another woman, and the wagon he was given. G-string's Son said, "That's fine. You have got a wagon and another woman. I'm glad to hear about that. Perhaps, sometime, we will use your wagon. That's a big gift for you, my uncle. There isn't anyone around here who has anything like that. You are the only one, and the first one to have a wagon out in this country. So that's very nice. I am glad about it and thankful, even though it's not mine, my uncle." "Yes, that's the way with me," Slim Man said. "Soon I will have something new." G-string's Son said, "You got two things, you got a wagon and a woman, but the wagon is the main thing. I know it will last you for many years, but about the woman, you can't tell anything about them. Perhaps she is all right, perhaps not. And it's too far to that place. Even though we are here with our women in the same hogan someone always comes around

286

and gets after our women. Even though we watch them closely we will find them running around with other men. That's the way with women. So we can't tell anything about them, whether she is a good woman or a bad one. However, it's up to the woman's father and mother. If they think enough of you they will watch her for you. If they don't, then she will be running around with men, because you won't be with her all the time. She knows about a man now. She tasted you. She knows the taste of a man now, so if you are gone from her for many days, she will be wishing for a man, and the first thing you know she will be running around with another man. That's the way with all the women. That's the way with a lot of them around here now. Therefore that's the only thing we can't tell about. But the wagon—when you bring it back no one will get away with it. However it's all right. If they think enough of you then you may have that woman for your lifetime. If not she will run away from you. But stay with her as long as you want to, my uncle." Slim Man said, "I'm not so crazy about the woman, so maybe I will only go over to her place once more. Perhaps I will make two trips; because it's too far for me to go back and forth. However, I'll see about it later on, my nephew," he said. About then I went to sleep.

I awoke. It may have been after midnight. They were still sitting up. I heard them singing; G-string's Son was learning some songs about the horses. When I woke up again it was morning. They said, "We had better get a little sleep," so they lay down and went to sleep early that morning. When everything was cooked the women told the two old men to get up. The men were kind of mad about it. They were saying, "What do you want to wake us up for? Why don't you leave us alone? Let us sleep! You shouldn't bother a man when he is sleeping." They poured some water for them, and they washed themselves. Then we started eating.

After breakfast they were talking again. G-string's Son said, "Last night I was learning some songs about horses, but I didn't quite learn them. However, sometime I'll go over to your place to learn these songs, my uncle, because I want to

287

learn them. I want to learn the songs about the horses, about the sheep, about the property and about different kinds of beads. I want to learn all about this, my uncle. So I'll be over at your place sometime around in the fall, or perhaps early in the winter. However, it depends on my work. Whenever I haven't anything to do I'll go over to your place for these songs, my uncle." Slim Man said, "Yes, if you want to learn you had better come over and ask about the different things. It will be fine when you learn some songs. It is good to know them. If you don't know anything about the different things then you are not strong at all. If you know some songs about the stocks or properties or life then you will be strong. You will have power. You won't starve. You won't go ragged. So you had better learn some songs about these different things, my nephew." "Yes, I want to learn. I didn't know anything about the songs. I had a father, G-string. He was a man, but he didn't know anything, no songs of any kind. He was good for nothing. He didn't have anything. That's the way he was, starving poor all the time. That's the way it was with my father. I really do believe that these songs are holy. I know your thoughts and mind and your talk are holy. The whole body of yours is holy. Whatever you wish for you will have. That's why you have so many stocks and property; but I haven't got anything. I have got a few herds, a few horses, and a little property that doesn't amount to anything. Sometimes I go hungry and poor, because I am not strong. I haven't got the power to take things. So I do really believe that all the songs are holy. There are only two of you who have horses now, you and Giving Out Anger. Only you two have so many horses now, not only horses, but other stocks as well. I am so very thankful about the songs that you are teaching me, my uncle, my mother," he said. "I sure will come over to your place. When I get there, please teach me all the songs, all that you know. Don't hold any of them back on me, my uncle, my grandmother," he said again. That was all they said to each other; they just gave thanks to each other, and after that we got up and went out.

I got home just as the sun went down. I took the things inside and said, "When I left here two days ago, when I got

288

down to where Slim Man lives, they wanted me to let them have some of my horses to go to the store. I let them have two horses and one of the boys went to the store. He got back last night. He brought me those things, for the four dollars I took with me." She thanked me for the food, and I said, "We have been rounding up horses for two days. We have got the horses in the corral now. Tomorrow we'll start working on them. I would like one of the boys from here to help me. Go over and tell them about it." She went over and one of her brothers came back. I told him about it, and right away he said, "I'm willing to help. I always like to work on the horses." "We need a cook too," I said, "because we will be down there with the horses all day." He said, "We will go with my older sister. I have got three horses, I'll bring the three horses back and we will go with her, and my younger brother too." I said, "That will be fine."

In the morning he came over with his younger brother, leading one horse. We saddled it up, and the four of us, my wife and I and her two younger brothers, started off. When we got down to Slim Man's place they were all ready to go. There were horses and burros standing with saddles on them; the whole outfit was going. The boy who herded all the time was going, too. One of the girls, that was my sister's daughter, had gone out with the herd. The rest were all going, except the old woman. She stayed at home. Everybody was ready. There were six of them from there, and we four made ten. Slim Man said, "We are all going. Everybody wants to go down to see the horses. I don't see what they want to see the horses for. There is nothing to see; still they would all like to see the horses, so they are all going down."

When we got down where the horses were there were so many of them, all moving around, we didn't know which to look at. Slim Man said to the womenfolk and the small boy, "You all gather up some wood. Start the fire. Build a good fire, and some of you get water and start cooking." To us he said, "All you boys start in. Rope some of those two- to three-year-old stallions. Let's see how many we'll cut." We started in, working on the horses, starting to cut them, and the rest started cooking. The boys had lots of fun, roping the horses, getting them down on the ground and tying them up

289

for us. My father and I did the cutting. We had cut a little over ten by noon. Then they hollered at us to eat, so we all went over where they were cooking. Right after we finished eating we started working on them again. In the afternoon, we had cut a few more. He said to the boys, "Better stop roping them for a while. We'll only cut these two, so you had better stop for a while." When we had finished cutting they untied them, and they both got up.

Then Slim Man said to the boys, "Rope one that you think is good and fat. We'll kill one and take the meat back with us." The boys went in the corral, carrying around the rope way in the middle. They said, "We don't know which to rope. They are all alike." He went in, saying, "What's the matter with you fellows?" He pointed out one and they roped that. It was a roan. They got that horse out and killed it with a hatchet. Then he said, "Let the women-folk butcher it. Butcher that horse," he told them. They all started butchering while we started working on the horses again. When the sun was pretty well down he said, "I guess we had better stop now. It's getting late, my children. We have quite a way to go to our home, and we all have a little load. We all have some horse meat to take to our home." We had cut a little over thirty. We didn't do much again that day.

There were lots of them still to be cut. We had cut all the young ones. He had wanted to cut some of the old ones, but we never touched any of them. We were tired and our hands were all sore. After we had turned the horses out to the wash to get water, we went back to where they were cooking, and we all ate again. After our lunch my father said, "Do you ever eat horse meat? Do you like horse meat, or not?" My wife said, "Yes, we do like horse meat. That's the only meat I like. We have all been raised on horse meat, so we all like it." Then he said to his wife, "Give them some meat. Get what you want and give the rest to them." She said, "I have got a hindquarter all ready. My daughter has a frontquarter and one side of the rib. That's all we want. You can take all that's left there." Then one boy picked up the whole back bone, and the other picked up a front quarter and the other side of the rib. We picked up a hind quarter. Then we started back to our home with nice fat meat. We all had a big load. We were thankful for the meat. And the horses were out in the flat, scattered about. It looked as though you had torn up an ant hill; they were moving around out there so thick, neighing to one another, the females running around back and forth for their little ones, and the colts running around looking for their mothers. It looked just like an ant heap. Before we started he said, "The Night Chant will be over in four more days, so get ready. We will all start from here in two days and take our wives with us. We will all go with our wives. And take a lot of food with you, so you won't go hungry while we are at the ceremony." I had never thought of going with my wife, but when he said we would go with our women, she was glad. I had never gone around with her. I always thought it was shameful to go around with one's woman to any place. So then she wanted to go right away. She was awful happy about it.

15

The Night Chant[1] . . . Tales of
his mother and her strength.

my wife was happy the next morning. She got up
early, started the fire, swept out the hogan. She
was running around there doing her work. I knew she
wanted to go. After she got through with her work she
started to fix up her clothing, started to fix up the things she
had. I was ashamed to go with her. That day when the boys
brought back my horse for me I just tied him up and got him
some cornstalks. I stayed at the hogan that day. I didn't go
anywhere or do anything, just sat and lay around. Every once
in a while I got up and ate some horse meat. My wife was
cutting up the meat in thin slices. When she had it all cut up
she put it out on the trees to dry. There was a whole lot of
meat around all over on the trees. She had boiled and roasted
some for our lunch along the way. She had everything fixed
up that day.

In the evening she said, "I want to go with you, so tomorrow you get me a horse." I said, "I'm not going after the
horses. I have got my horse standing out there, and I am
going to use that. Tomorrow morning I will go over where
the other people live; from there I'll go with them. So I am
not going after the horses." She said, "I won't let you go by
yourself. You may think you are going alone, but I don't
think so. I won't let you go alone. I want to go with you.
That's why I have fixed up some lunch. I have everything
ready, so you go and get a horse for me tomorrow." I didn't

1. One of the more spectacular Navajo ceremonies. Included in the Chant is an initiation ceremony popularly known as Yeibichai from the principal figures represent-
ing Yei divinities.

say any more. I thought if I said something again she would get mad at me.

So the next morning I said, "I'll go over and get some horses." She hung around me close that morning. She probably thought I might take something, like my new clothes or robe. When I led the horse close to the door she handed me the bridle that I always use, saddle-blankets and saddle. She got those out for me and said, "Be sure and bring the horses back as soon as you can, so we'll get an early start." I didn't say a word. I just got on my horse and went. I got all the horses down to the water and caught one and led it back home. The others I left in the corral at the water. As I was leading the horse home, there were Lost His Moccasins and his wife riding along. They said, "We are going to the Night Way." That was all they said, and they passed by. When I got home my wife had everything outside, ready to be put on the horses.

She started saddling up the horse, and when we were ready to go I said, "We'll go down where the horses are. From there we'll get another horse." When we got to the corral where the horses were I roped a mule and I told her, "Go and catch that blue horse." She got the horse out and I told her, "Put the saddle and things on it." I was kind of mad, but she was happy. She was already in a hurry, but she didn't have the saddle blankets fixed right. Then I said to her, "If you are going among the big crowd you'd better fix your horse up well, and you had better fix yourself better." "I'm fixed up all right," she said while she was laughing. "I don't call that fixed right. You've got your saddle blankets all crooked. They are not even, and the cinches are twisted." So then I loosened the cinches, took off the saddle, fixed the saddle blankets, put the saddle back on, and tightened the cinches. "You better have everything fixed the way it should be," I said, "I don't want to have to work with you all the time. You've got to have things fixed up nicely yourself." "I'm fixed up all right. You don't have to bother about me all the time. And you shouldn't worry about me, because I am all right." Then I got on my mule and started off. I didn't wait for her. It was about noon already when we started from this

293

water. When I had ridden quite a way I looked back and there she was coming, beating the horse as hard as she could and kicking him on the belly.

Close to where the others lived we met the boy herding sheep. He said, "They went early this morning. They waited for you for a while. They thought you weren't coming, so they left." Just beyond Looks For Antelope we caught up with them. There were Lost His Moccasins and his wife, and Slim Man and his wife, and I with a woman, too. We went along out in the flat, trotting our horses. Soon we got to the edge of the red mesa and started down to Many Streams. When we got to the foot of the red rocks we stopped our horses and my father said, "We'll get off our horses and take the saddles off. And get your new saddle blankets out and put them on top of the others, and take out your buffalo skins and buckskins and lion skins." Everybody dressed up there. They all put on new moccasins and new leggings and silver belts and beads, and silver bridles on the horses. The women put on their moccasins and leggings and their skirts, and right on top they put a red belt and on top of that a silver belt around them. Then they got out their blankets. Lost His Moccasins was the only one to wear a straw hat. When everybody was ready we started off again. The sun was getting to be pretty well down. As we were riding along I looked at my wife; she looked like a swell woman when she was dressed up with all her things. Everything was new, and from there on I was kind of proud about it. I wasn't feeling ashamed, because she had on everything new. Everything that she had on had never been used before. That was the first day that she had put them on. The two older women had had their things for a long time, I guess, because they looked as though they had been worn a long time.

We started crossing the valley, and as we crossed the wash my mule was beginning to give up. He was out of wind. He was just too fat to ride that far. I let the others go and went along behind them. When we got to the crowd everybody was looking at us. There was a big crowd all around the hogan, and people were scattered out all over. The sun was almost down. All at once it started to blow. The storm

294

struck the ground all at once. Everybody was there with their robes over their heads. People and horses were frightened. The wind was whirling around; we couldn't see anything for a little while. I don't know what kind of wind it was. It struck the ground all at once, and in a little while it stopped. When the storm was over, right after that, it was as nice as it could be. Close by us was a man on horseback. This old man said, after the wind was over, when everyone was quiet, "I thought this was the last day for us. But it was just a little torture. It was just a tease." Everybody started talking, and pretty soon they were laughing. It was kind of funny, when he said that, right after the wind, when everyone was quiet. He looked as though he was mad, but he was always that way. He was looking around, moving his head, looking over all the people. Across from us two buckskin horses were standing together. They were both alike, very nice looking horses. There were two young men sitting on them, and they both looked almost alike. That was a Red House clansman and his younger brother, whom we now call Mister Weapon.

A little while after that the sun was down. We started taking our saddles off the horses, and when we had taken off all our things, Slim Man changed his mind. He said, "We had better saddle up our horses again. We haven't any place to put them. So we had better go around and look for some of our relatives." We saddled up again and started around among the people. There was a man sitting on horseback; he had a good-sized horse. My father knew this man. He was called Hosteen Moqui. We rode up to him and he shook hands with Slim Man. They were holding each other's hand for a long time, saying older brother and younger brother to each other.

Then Slim Man turned around to me and said, "Shake hands with your father. That's your father. He is my older brother." I shook hands with this old man; he held my hand for a long time, saying, "My son, my little one, my baby." Slim Man said, "Old Man White Hair is his father." The old man said, "*Who* is his father? You say the man whom we call G-string's In-Law is his father? Whom do you mean? Thin Mexican's son, White Hair?" Slim Man said, "Yes." "Oh, that's the man. I knew him very well. So that is his father. Well," he said again, "My son, my little one, my baby."

Then Slim Man asked him about Many Goats and Red House. "Are there any of these clans living around here?" The old man said, "Yes, but there are no Many Goats, only Red House, living over at the foot of the rocks." "How about Bitahni?" "There are lots of them living around here too." "How about Red Clay?" "Some of them are living down below also." "Well, then," he said, "I guess we two will go where there are some Red House." He meant he and his wife. They went, and my wife and I went to where some Bitahni were living, while Lost His Moccasins and his wife went down to where some Red Clay were living. We all went among our relatives.

We got to one hogan where a man was walking around by the door. His name was Gray Hair, and his children were Bitahni. That's where we stopped that evening. We went inside and shook hands with him and his children. He said to them, "I guess you know him or perhaps not. But I know him. He is a Bitahni clan." Then his wife said, "Oh, yes, we know him. I know him very well, but I don't know about the children. But I guess they still remember him. While we were living up at a place called Muddy Water he visited there. From there on I got to know him. I know him very well." Gray Hair said, "Oh, yes, I remember now. He visited us there all right, the time we were still living at Muddy Water." His wife said, "I am very glad to see you, my son. My, you are getting to be an old man now." I said, "Maybe, sometime, I will be an old man." They began fixing a place for us.

While they were fixing a place Gray Hair said, "This is a poor place. There is no feed for the horses, nothing but greasewood. Only way on top of the rocks is there lots of feed for the horses. However, it's too late now. The trail goes up quite a way from here. But I don't want you to climb up the cliffs at night. We haven't anything to tie your horses to. There are some poles lying around right back of the hogan, take one of those and set it up someplace, so that you can tie your horses to it. Then you can go to the cornfield and get some cornstalks." There were a lot of people there at his

296

place, but they all had their horses up on the rocks. After I set up the pole I got some cornstalks for the horses and the mule; then I went back inside. My wife was sitting way back in the hogan. Everybody was cooking.

I sat down by Gray Hair, and he asked me about my wife. "What is your wife? What outfit does she belong to? What clan does she belong to?" I said, "She is Red Clay. She belongs to Giving Out Anger's outfit. Giving Out Anger is her grandfather." "Well, so then she is my granddaughter. Giving Out Anger is my older brother. Even though he is Red Clay and I am Start-Of-The-Red-Street People, nevertheless Red Clay are all our relatives. So Giving Out Anger is my older brother, and One Who Understands is my older brother, too; and so is Tall Man. So then you are my grand-daughter." Everything was cooked and they gave us some food and some cantaloupe and watermelon. He said, "That's all we've got. We haven't any meat. We have had a big crowd for nine days now, for nine nights, and this afternoon we ran out of meat."

Then I said to my wife, "Where is our lunch?" She got it out; we had some horse meat and some mutton, which we had fixed up for our lunch. I pushed it over to him and said, "Here is some antelope meat and deer meat and some jackrabbit and some cottontail. They are all mixed together. So if you want to taste wild animal meat here you are." He tasted some of it and said, "This is what I want. I have been wishing for this kind of meat for a long time. This is the best meat of all." He began eating the horse meat; he didn't bother with the other. When we were all through eating he was so very thankful for it. It was dark then. He said, "I guess we had better get ready and fix up our things. And those of us who would like to go to the doings tonight will all go together. We will see the dance tonight. Maybe we will stay all night, or if we get tired then we will be back tonight," he said to the others who wanted to stay at home.

We two started getting ready, and he was running around getting ready, too. We were just about to go out when his wife said to us, "What do you want to hurry for? The doings won't start for quite a while yet. So you had better wait a while, my son," she said to me. "I would like you to be with me for a while. I don't want you to just run away from me. We won't have a chance to see each other again while you are here. You better stay with me for a while." I said, "All right." Her husband had come back in and she said the same to him. Then she said, "We used to live up at Muddy Water. You know we used to live up there. While we were still living there you visited us, and that's quite a long time ago. And now this is another time that you have visited us. I am very glad you have visited us again." Her husband said, "Yes, we are all glad to see each other again. I guess we are all glad. We used to live up at Muddy Water, but the water washed away our cornfield. That's why we moved down here. We moved here because my son-in-law got the water out from the wash up here. He was the first man to put up a cornfield here at this place. When the people knew he had got the water out of the wash up here to this place, they all started moving down here, and we moved down, too. All the people who live here now used to live up at Muddy Water. But there is nobody living up there any more. So my son-in-law is great. He is the first man to make an irrigation ditch, and the first one to start a cornfield here."

We talked about other things for a while, then he asked about my mother. "Where is your mother? Is she living up that way? Why didn't you bring her too? Maybe she didn't want to come." I said, "She is not living up there. My mother moved across over to another part of the country. She moved to Carriso. So, I guess, she is living over in that part of the country." "Well, then, you must be all alone over there at the foot of the mountain." "Yes," I said, "I am all alone, but I don't think I'm alone. There are lots of people living all around, so I am among the people all the time." He said, "She used to be just like a man. When she was young she used to be a tall stout woman. She used to do all kinds of things, just like a man. A while back, a little while after the people returned from Fort Sumner, the men used to gamble with a particular game. I don't know how they got mad at each other, but they started fighting. They were all big and tall. They were all husky men. There were three brothers on one side. One was Who Killed The Moqui (that was the man, Old Man Moqui, whom we had just met) and Bad Eyes, his younger brother, and the next youngest, Burned His Goats. They were brothers. They were all tall and big. Those three started fighting with another man. His name was Rabbit Hat, and he was Gray Hair's wife's full brother. (My mother used to call him younger brother.) They had been fighting for a while; then I guess she knew they wouldn't stop so she walked over to where they were fighting and started fighting them. When they grabbed her she just gave one swing and the men were twisted around and fell to the ground. Pretty soon she grabbed one of them who had a stick. She twisted the stick away from him and started to beat him with it. Soon he gave up and fled. Then the other two came up and started fighting her. She just gave a crack over one fellow, and he was down on the ground. The other was almost beaten to death by her. The one who got the crack on the head was unconscious for a while. After he regained consciousness he started crying. That was Bad Eyes. She had whipped these three men, and everybody was standing around her. She gave them a good talking to. That's the way she used to be. She was not afraid of anything.

"That's what she did once, and I still remember her by that, and I don't think any woman could do that today. I guess now she is pretty old. Is she?" "Yes," I said, "she is pretty old now. I don't believe she could lick anybody now." He said, "Oh, I wish she were here now. I would like to see her again. I wonder why she didn't come. But perhaps she has got to stay with her herd, or perhaps she didn't have any way of coming. Or maybe she is too old to come this far. Still I wish she were here now." After that he said, "I guess we had better go now to see the dance."

Then my wife and I went over to where they were having this doing. But they hadn't started the dance yet. After a while they started dancing. They danced until after midnight, then they stopped because there were no more dancers. In those early days they used to stop dancing around midnight or a little after, so everybody would get a little sleep for the next day and last night. When we got back we fixed up our bed and went right to sleep.

In the morning we all got up, and the women started cooking. I went out and walked around outside, then I went to the cornfield and got some more cornstalks for the horses. When I came back from there I asked about the water. "Is there any water around here close by? I would like to water my horses." Gray Hair's wife said, "There is no water close around here, my son. There is water quite a way above here, and there is water at Water In Reeds, and another over on the other side of this rock, at a place called Water Under The Rocks. There is also water right in that little cliff, but I don't think you will get the horses up there. That water we call Water Fucks A Woman." I said, "Why is it called that?" "Well," she said, "whenever a woman goes up there for water some men will be there in that cliff, and there they will get after the women. Even somebody's wife they will get after. That's why we call that water Water Fucks A Woman. So you must not let your woman go to that water alone. Someone will get after her." She was laughing as she said this. "I guess I won't send her over there alone," I said, and she laughed some more.

After breakfast I asked about Son Of Dead Questioner. They said, "He is living right across there, a little above the cornfield." I said, "I guess I'll go over to his place. He is my grandfather. I would like to visit him for a while." We saddled up our horses and rode up to his place. He was at home, and we shook hands with him, but he didn't quite recognize me. He began asking me what man I was. I told him, "Asdza Abaa is my mother." Then he said, "Oh, yes, I remember you now, my grandson. Asdza Abaa is my mother's sister, but I always call her my mother, so in that way you are my grandson. Well, then, I know you now." I asked him about the water again. He said the same thing. "There is no water around here close by. There is water way above, and there is water at Water In Reeds. However at Water In Reeds there is plenty of water. That water is damned up, so there is lots of water over there. If you want to water your horses you had better take them there." I unsaddled them and got on the horse bareback and started leading the mule. While I was going along there were lots of fellows going ahead of me and some coming behind, and some returning from the water and passing me. It was that way all the way to the water and back. But I didn't know any of them. They were all strangers to me, and I suppose I was a stranger to them. When I returned from the water only the womenfolk were there at that place. My grandfather wasn't around. I asked them, "Where did my grandfather go?" They said, "He saddled up his horse and said he was going down to the crowd. So I guess he is down there." They had the cooking all done, and after we ate we saddled up the horses.

As we were going back down to where the crowd was, there was Son Of Late Grey Hat riding toward us. We met him there and shook hands with him and he said, "Well, you got here my baby, my nephew." "Yes," I said, "we got here yesterday." "Whom did you come with? Who else came there?" I said, "Six of us came together yesterday, we two and my father and his wife, and Lost His Moccasins and his wife." "Where did they go to? They are not around." I said, "We separated yesterday evening. Two of them went to the foot of that rock, and the other two went down below. We have been up here a little way." He said, "I just came over this morning. I started from the foot of the mountain yesterday, and I got to Water In Reeds last night. I stayed there last night, where some of my relatives were living." Then he said, "We didn't let you know when we left. We left all at once, because we couldn't stand the hot weather any more. So, then, we started to move to the mountain. We didn't stop until we got on top to a place called Old Men Lie. We have been up there. The day before yesterday we came down off the mountain to Water Flowing Out; from there I started yesterday."

Then he said, "The bucks and billy goats of yours are still up on the mountain. I have some folks there taking care of them for me. I always go there to see them every once in a while. I know they are taking good care of them. They are all getting fat, so you don't need to worry about it." But I didn't say anything, I asked him then about my mother. "Where is

301

my mother living? Do you know?" "Yes, she lives up on the mountain still. The people living up on the mountain had Enemy Way some time ago when I was there. She was there. That's the only time I saw her. I haven't seen her again, but I know she is still up on the mountain. He went down to the cornfield and we rode up to the crowd. There was nothing doing.

People were here and there, scattered around. Some were making a brush hogan of greasewood. That was the only kind of wood there was. There was nothing for us to do, and so we rode up to the top of a big sand hill. From there we looked all around, there were people scattered all over, scattered out in the greasewood and all around the cornfields. After a while I said to my wife, "Well, we haven't anything to do, and there is nothing doing until noon. So we'll go back to where we stayed last night. When we get back there you make up some lunch for tonight." She said, "All right," so we started back.

While we were going to that place some fellows came riding straight toward us; that was Nephew Of Who Has Land and some of his friends. "When did you come?" he said, while we were shaking hands with him. "We came yesterday too," he said. "We have been living up on the mountain all summer. Two days ago we moved down. Three children were herding for us, a girl and her two younger brothers. We had our herds together while we were still on the mountain, but we separated them now. So the girl and one younger brother are herding one herd, and the other boy is herding the other. The womenfolk are at the cornfield now. The corn is all ripe, ready to be worked on." I said, "We are going back to where we stayed last night." Then I said, "Do those womenfolk still remember me?" "Yes, they are always talking about you. They are always bothering about you. So I don't think they have forgotten you." "That's nice." I said, "I'm glad to hear that. Tell them I'll be there soon. I'll go over sometime after this chant is over. We two will go back to our home, and then from there I'll get a horse and ride across. So tell them to look for me any time." He said, "All right, I'll tell them that you are coming. So you are going back where you had stayed last night? Whereabouts is it? Whose place is it?" I said, "It's only a little way up here, where Gray Hair lives." He said, "Cook us something. We haven't eaten since last evening. We'll be there at noon." I said, "All right, we'll have something for you."

Then they went on and we went back to our place. Then Gray Hair's wife said to us, "I saw you two passing by here a while ago, my son." I said, "Yes, we passed by here this morning. We have been down to the crowd, but there was nothing doing." "Well, so that's why you didn't stay long." I said, "Yes, we didn't stay long because there was nothing going on, so we just turned around and started back. I wanted my wife to make up some lunch for tonight." She said, "That's fine. You two just help yourselves. There is plenty of corn, some still green, some dry, so just go ahead and make yourselves lunch." Then I picked up a robe and walked down to the cornfield. I broke off some ears, some still green and some dry and I brought back quite a load. Then she started working on the corn. While I was down in the cornfield I saw lots of ripe cantaloupe and watermelon, so I went down again and brought back a load of each. I had a big pile of melons, waiting for those fellows to come. Then I went down to the cornfield again and brought up two loads of cornstalks. I chopped them up in pieces and gave them to my horses. Close to noon some boys returned from where they had the herds, and brought some meat back with them, one sheep and a goat.

Just about when the cooking was done those fellows came. There was a crowd of them. There wasn't room for them all inside, and some stayed outside. Everybody was eating. While they were eating some more people came, but the cooks were cooking right along. They started taking the saddles off their horses, and Gray Hair was running around among the people, shaking hands. They said to him, "Our horses are hungry, and we are hungry too." He said, "There is lots to eat here for you. Just go ahead and eat all you want. I have plenty of food, and there are lots of melons, of two kinds. So you just go ahead and help yourselves. Don't starve yourselves. And about your horses, there is lots of feed too, lots of cornstalks that you can give to your horses." Then they

303

were all thankful about that. "That's very nice of you, my relative-in-law," they all said to him. It's a good thing you came to be our in-law. We are all glad and thankful for your kindness." Some of them went down to the cornfield and brought back cornstalks for the horses. After they had fed them, when everybody was together again they all started eating. There was plenty of food for everybody, and the cooks were cooking right on. They had a great day that day. When everybody had had enough to eat they were all thankful. They were sitting and lying around there talking, and Gray Hair said to all, "When you are hungry, just eat. Don't be afraid. Or if you want some feed for your horses, just say so too. There is lots of food here. I have plenty of food and plenty of cornstalks. If you want some more cornstalks for your horses, just help yourselves on that. And some of you have women with you. Tell them to make some lunch for to-night. Make lunch for yourselves, so you won't go hungry to-night. Get some cornstalks and chop them in pieces for your horses, so they will eat tonight. Don't starve yourselves and don't starve your horses." They all started getting at the corn-stalks, and some of the women started making lunch to use that night. A lot of them had a big load of cornstalks on their horses, while others stayed there chopping the cornstalks in pieces. We two had everything ready. I had saved a lot of melons. Then when everybody had gone, all the people who had been there had all gone down to the doings. We two stayed there.

Gray Hair's wife said to us, "Well, my son, my daughter-in-law, make some more lunch for yourselves, I don't think you have enough, because you have given some to the crowd, so make yourselves some more, my children." I said, "I guess we'll do that. We have plenty, nevertheless we'll make some more. We will use it tonight, and we will have some to take along on our way back." So I said to my wife, "Go ahead and make some more. Are you tired?" "No, I am not tired," she said. She got up and started making some more lunch, and I said, "I'll take the horses to the water again." When I came back, my mother, Gray Hair's wife, said, "Cut up some more meat, my son, and boil it, and I will

304

cook some other food here. We will eat again. We will eat right now. I don't think we have all had enough yet, because we had a big crowd all day. So now we'll eat lots for tonight." Then I got up and started cutting up some meat. I put the meat in a pot and set it on the fire.

Then the old man said, "What do you think you will want to do with your horses, my children? Do you want them taken down to the ceremony? Or do you want them to stay right here? There is nothing to tie them to down there. You had better leave them here." I said, "I'll leave them here. Here is a good place. It's quite a way down there. It will be hard for me to carry the corn stalks down there, so, I guess, I'll let them stand here tonight." "You better leave them there," he said, "they will be all right." The cooking was going on, and I asked about a big pile of greasewood that was there. "Where did you get all that wood?" I said. The old woman said, "There is a whole lot of it behind that point, my son. It is just like a forest, and that's where I got it." "How did you bring it all that way?" I asked. "By burro," she said, "I started working on the wood all by myself, from the time they started up for the ceremony. I did that all by myself, my son. I had been driving the burro back and forth for wood, and soon I had a big pile. None of the boys helped me. They were all afraid to touch it, because it has stickers. That's why they don't want to bother with it. So I did it all by myself. They did the same down at the flats but they had burros and horses. They have been going back and forth for wood too."

Then, after we ate, I got some more feed for the horses and I tied them up well and we got ready to go to the Night Way. We left our stuff there. We took only our robes and lunch. The doings were going on. Three of the "Yei" (Masked Deities) were treating the patient that evening. After they had treated the patient they treated the hogan also. Then they went away and that was all over. Then the people started fixing up their places, building fires on each side, south and north. They had built the fires in a row. There was quite a space between for the dancers, and behind the fires all their things were piled. Everybody was sitting down, having their lunch. Soon there were lots of people on both sides, and there was my father, Slim Man. We found each other there that evening. "Have you a place already?" he asked me. "Yes," I said, "We have a place." "Where?" "Right across. Straight across over there," I said. "Well, I guess I will take my wife over there, too. We will leave the womenfolk together there." So he went and got his wife, and we went back to where my wife was sitting. He asked me, "Did you get some meat?" I said, "Yes, we have some." "We didn't get any meat," he said, "but as long as you have meat we are saved."

Then when everybody had sat down, when everybody was quiet, they started the dancing. They had a lot of fire on both sides, but even at that it didn't give enough light. One party would dance for a while and then quit, and then another party would come and dance. They danced right along. About midnight everybody started getting their lunch. They said to me, "Go to the hogan and get a pot to boil some meat in, and get some coffee pots, too." When I got to the hogan I looked at the horses; they were standing there; they were all right. Then I took the pots back and they started cooking. Everybody was eating while some of them were dancing. We ate, too, but I didn't see anything different. The dances were all the same. So it meant nothing to me. That was all that we had been looking at that night. I had thought the dances would be different, and that the parties would be dressed differently, but they were all the same.

After midnight there was nothing doing any more. Everybody had eaten his lunch. The dance was all over. They said, "There are no more dancers." So everyone just went to sleep, I guess. The womenfolk who were with us went to sleep, but the old men, Lost His Moccasins and Slim Man, were up all night, talking with a lot of other old men, while I was walking all around. Way out behind the people I found lots of the men drinking whiskey, but I never got a taste of it. Soon after I got back to where the old men were sitting, morning came. Then the last dancers came out and started dancing, and that was the end, and everybody started moving.

Slim Man said to me, "Where are you staying?" I said,

"We are staying at Gray Hair's place. We have our things and our horses there." "Well, we will start back early. Try to get ready as soon as you can," he said to us. I said, "I don't think we will start back this morning. I would like to stay. I would like to go around to visit some of my relatives. I haven't gone among them yet, so I don't think we'll go this morning. Perhaps this evening when it gets cool." "Well, that's all right," he said, "but we will go right now, while it's still cool."

When we got back to the hogan they started cooking. I had been helping them cook and watching the fire for them that morning. I didn't go to the water. The boys had taken the horses there for me. A few fellows came, and when they had cooked, we all started eating. Everybody had enough to eat again that morning. We began getting ready, started fixing our things. I had gotten some more cornstalks for the horses, and they were still eating. I said to my wife, "If you want to make a little lunch again just go ahead. The lunch you made is all gone now. The people ate it all up last night." She said, "I'll make some more." Then I lay down and went to sleep. All at once they woke me up. "Wake up. Your horses are tangled up in the rope. Your horses entangled themselves." I woke up and untied the horses and tied them up again and then went back inside and lay down and went to sleep again. When they woke me again it was noon.

After we ate, the old man, Gray Hair, said, "Get some more cornstalks for your horses, or chop up some corn for them. Do they eat corn?" "No," I said, "they don't know what corn is." "Well, then, hobble them and turn them loose in the cornfield. As long as they don't eat corn it's all right. Have you got enough lunch to take along? If you haven't you had better make enough for yourselves. Have it already cooked. When do you want to start back home?" I said, "I guess we'll start back when it gets cool." "Well, make yourselves enough lunch, and find something to take water in. There isn't any water on the trail, except here at Many Streams. That's the only place you can get water. From there on there isn't any. So you had better find something to carry water in, so you'll have some on your way." "Oh, we'll see about that ourselves," I said. Then I took the horses down to the cornfield and hobbled them, and I brought back more cantaloupes and one watermelon.

In the afternoon I said, "I guess we had better get ready. We will go from here. I wanted to visit around, but I don't think I will." The old man, Gray Hair, said, "I'm very glad you two came to visit me and I am thankful to you because you helped me a whole lot. You two were the only ones to stay around here and help. The rest of the people who came here were just seen around. They just stopped for a while, and none of them thought of helping. They all knew we had lots to do. You two were the only ones who realized what things had to be done, so I am very thankful to you," he said. He pointed to my wife, "It's a good thing she came with you. She has been cooking and helping around since she came. Others came, but they never thought of helping. So I am glad," he said. I said, "We are too. We are thankful to you, too, because you took care of us. A good thing we came here to your place. We didn't get hungry, and our horses didn't get hungry. We are just about getting fat. We are very thankful about the food. It's a good thing you planted some corn and different kinds of melons. So I am very thankful," I said to him. We put everything in the sack, our lunch and some green corn and some melons.

Then we got the horses and saddled and packed them up and got on them. While we were on the horses everybody came up to us and shook hands. Then we started off. We passed by where they had had the doings. There was nobody around, just piles of ashes in a row on both sides. We passed the hogan and went on to the wash. There were two persons, a man and boy, riding ahead of us. This man's name was Chatterer. I shook hands with him, and he asked me, "Where are you from?" I said, "From the foot of the mountain. We are going back there. Where are you from?" He said, "We are from a little below Slow Running Water." "Well, then," I said, "We will go together. That's where we came from." He said, "All right," and we went on, crossing the valley towards Many Streams. I said, "We came on the trail from Slow Running Water, and on to Where Antelopes Are Looked For, and down here to Many Streams." "That's where we came too," he said, "Then we will go together until we get to Where Antelopes Are Looked For. A little below there a trail branches off to our home." "Is there water down where you live?" I asked him. "No, there is no water around there. We get water from quite a way off from where we live."

Then, while we were riding along he was telling me some things; he was talking about the crowd. "What a big crowd it was. What nice horses the people had, and how dressed up the people were." Then he said, "I was in the hogan there. Some old men stayed there in the hogan, and they were talking about one fellow." I said, "What had the fellow done that they had talked about?" He said, "Last night one young man put on a mask, and he had a swollen neck. Around under his chin was all swollen. Even though he was like that he had put on a mask and danced. They were talking about that. They said it was a serious thing to do. He had done that dangerous thing for some kind of reason. Some kind of sickness will strike us one of these days. These old men said that once a dancer coughed into a mask while they were dancing; not long after he did that a big whooping cough epidemic came up and a lot of people died. And another time, they said, while a dancer had a mask on, during the dancing, he had farted, and not long after that some kind of stomach trouble came up and a lot of people died of that. I don't know what kind of sickness this young man called for. He didn't do that for nothing. He knew very well he shouldn't put on a mask while he had a swollen neck. This is the way the old fellows had been talking about it. They were all scared of that." I said, "Oh, they just want to talk. That's all. They like to talk all the time. I don't believe anything will happen." "Well," this man said, "I don't know. Perhaps nothing will happen. Perhaps something bad will come up." When we got to Many Streams we watered the horses and got some water for ourselves and then started off again, climbing the rocks up to the top of the red mesa. When we had gone a little way on top I heard something, and that was the cantaloupes that had gotten real soft on us. We stopped and took them off the horses, and, sure enough, they were soft. They

309

were about to break. We sorted out all the soft ones and ate them up. There were some others that I knew would get soft on us in time so I gave them to this man. I said, "Here, you take them. You live closer, so you take them." He was thankful for it. He said, "We never got a taste of any, even though we were down at those big cornfields. Thanks. I will take them back to my children, and they will all get a taste of melon."

When we got to Where Antelopes Are Looked For the sun was down, and it was dark by the time we got out into the valley where the trail branched off. The man said, "From here we branch off. Right here is where the trail branches off, so I guess we will take this trail now, my younger brother." I said, "All right, we will just go ahead too." Then we went on. We got to Slow Running Water late that night. On top there we took the saddles off our horses, and I took them quite a · way back and hobbled them. I guess it was a little after midnight when the horses were about to pass us. My wife heard their footsteps and woke me up, saying, "The horses are passing us." I got up and chased them far back, and then came back and went to sleep again.

Early in the morning they were about to pass us again, so then we got them there and saddled them up and started off again that morning. We didn't go very far that morning before the melons got soft on us again. We sorted them out and ate some of them and some we put in a sheepskin sack that we had. The real soft ones I put in the robe on my mule. We had a long ride from Slow Running Water to Where Little Arroyos Stop. I said, "We will go around that place and start all the horses down to the water." There we got us two other horses. It was late in the afternoon. We passed by Slim Man's hogan and got home when the sun was pretty well down.

The melons I had were all soft, but my wife had the softest ones that had about turned to water. She dumped them on the sheep pelts. About then her three brothers came in and started eating these soft ones. They knew we were bringing melons with us. That's why they came as soon as we got back. When they had had enough they took some back to their home. We had started the fire and we had some water.

310

We had brought back plenty of food, but everything seemed to be dry, and we didn't have any fresh meat. We had some out on the trees that had been there for four days, but she said, "I don't think we will be able to chew on this meat. It's as hard as a rock." Then she went over to the other hogan and came back with nice fresh meat, one whole side of mutton. She said, "There is nothing left of the melons. They have even eaten the seeds and skins. They must have been hungry for it," she said, laughing about it.

16

Talks with Slim Man and his uncle
about his "affair" . . . He makes love
to Hosteen Black's wife and she gives him
money for the calf . . . He tells Slim Man
his story and makes up a story to tell
his wife.

The next morning, after we ate, I said, "I'm going
down to my father's place. I want to know what they
are doing now, and I would like to know what kind of plan
they have. Maybe they are planning to do something, and
perhaps he needs me on something. When we were down to
The Night Way he said to me, 'As soon as I get back I will
go over the mountain.' I would like to know about that, too. I
would like to know how soon he is going over the mountain.
Besides I have got something on my mind too. Down where
they had the chant there were some fellows from the foot of
the mountain, and they told me that they have been looking
for me every day, expecting me there any day. So I would like
to go there too. That's what I have on my mind." Then she
said, "If you are going to that country you are not going
alone. When you go across I will go also. So you are not going
alone. I would like to get to know the people there also. So I'll
go with you." Then I thought about the money, and when I
had my horse ready I said, "Where is that money? I would
like to take my cow out. I don't want it to go dead on me. The
date is up now, so give me the money. I will take it back to
the man. I will pay him back and get my cow back." She
reached over to a sack and gave me the money. She didn't say
anything.

I put the money in my pocket and rode down to my father's place. He said, "Well, when did you get back?" "We

got back yesterday," I said, "And this morning I thought I would come over. I would like to know what you are doing, and I would like to know when you are going over the mountain." He said, "I don't know when I will go, but I am going soon. My son is out someplace. I don't know where he went to. As soon as he comes back I will send him down to Lots Of Wool after the mules. If he brings the mules back tomorrow I will go the next day. I don't know just when I'll be back with the wagon." I said, "I want to go across to Carriso where my mother went. I am anxious to see the herd. Down where they had this Night Way the fellows from that part of the country were telling me that they have been looking for me every day, so I would like to go there too." He said, "That's very nice, that you are going after your mother and the herd. You must be lonesome for your herd by now. I know a man can't stay away long from his herd, or horses and cattle. I guess you would sure like to see your herd."

After we had talked about that I said, "There is one more thing I want to mention to you. I told you about it the other day. I told you I had pawned a cow to Hosteen Black. I have miscounted the days, maybe it was yesterday, maybe today, that I promised I would pay him back on the date. If it was yesterday the cow is his. If it is today it is still his. I don't know what to do about it. The eleven dollars were taken away from me by my wife. She kept this money because she didn't want to let the cattle go, and she just gave it back to me. I told her I would take the cow out of hock, and now I don't know how to get out of it." "Are you afraid of that woman (your wife)?" he asked me. I said, "Yes, I am afraid of her." "You mustn't be afraid. You leave the money here with me, and you go and ride up to where the cattle are and take that cow down to them. Let them do whatever they want to do with it." I said, "This cow has a calf." "Well," he said, "take the calf down also, and tell them to give you some money for it. Or kill the calf and take it down to Green Slope Up and get some corn. The people who live down there would like to have some meat. So you go after the cattle now. You just go ahead. Do what I tell you to do. Maybe you are afraid of her. I know you are, but what has she got? She

313

hasn't any nails. She hasn't any teeth like an animal. She hasn't any horns. So you don't want to be afraid of her. And we didn't want her from the beginning. We wanted to get a woman for you, and you know that, but she spoiled our plan. We would have had a nice wedding, if she hadn't broken it up for us. When we were about ready she went in and got you. And you know that. That's why I have it in for her. If she gets after you, she will get after me, and I will talk to her. So you just go and get the cattle down and take them to those people, and if she ever gets after you about it, you just come over. Don't be afraid to tell me, and don't be afraid of her."

I said, "Which way shall I go?" He said, "You just cut across right below their place and go around and come back to the trail way on the other side, and take your time going up the mountain. Maybe you will find some cattle there at the water. If there are none at the water you ride up and try and get them down before sundown. Get them down to the water where the corral is and put them in the corral and separate those two and drive them down here. If you find them today drive them down tonight to the water here and put them in the corral." Then I gave him the money. I said, "I guess I'll go now. I don't know if I will find some today. If I find any I will bring them back here tonight. If I don't see any of them I will stay up there someplace over night. So I don't know whether I will get back today or tomorrow." Then they gave me some food and I started eating.

While I was eating he said, "You look as though you were scared. But there is nothing to be scared about. You don't need to be scared, because I am always with you. Even though something bad comes up, I will be right there with you all the time. So you don't need to be afraid. You don't want to be staying at one place all the time. You don't want to stay with one woman for the rest of your life. While you are young you had better go around among them. So you had better let her go now, and get another one, and stay with her for awhile again, and let her go, and get yourself another one. That's what you want to do while you are still young. Don't you know when you are staying at one place you get tired? You will be tired staying at one place. The same with food.

314

When you are eating the same food all the time you get tired of it. After a while you won't care to eat any more. The same with your clothing. If you wear one suit all the time you get tired of it. You will want to throw it away and get a new one. The same way with your bedding. When you sleep at one place, when you have a bed at one place, you get tired of that too. When you sleep at one place, pretty soon you can't sleep. You will be rolling all around, instead of resting up. You will get tired. Then you won't like to sleep there any more. When you get a new place to sleep, then you will be sleeping well. It is the same with everything." He was talking like this to me, while I was eating. I just kept quiet and listened to him. Then when I was through eating, just as he was through talking too, his wife came back in, and he asked her, "Where have you been?" She said, "I was over the hill gathering up some wood." He asked, "Are the herders coming back with the herd?" She said, "I didn't see them. I was up on the hill but I didn't see them."

Then I went out and got on my horse and started down towards Anything Falls In. I went down to Anything Falls In, instead of going around the other way. There I watered my horse and started off again, following the wash to the point we call The Middle Point. I went up following the point to a place called Big Trees Standing Up. From there I went across to Flowing Out Of The Canyon to where Walk Up lived. The corn was pretty well ripe. They had nice cornbread there, and everything was ripe. They gave me some food, and after I ate I said, "I guess I had better go now." Just about then his wife went out and I said to him, "I would like you to help me on the cattle, my uncle." He said, "Are you going after some cattle?" I said, "Yes, that's what I'm going up the mountain for. I would like to get down some cattle, so I would like you to help me on that." He said, "All right. I haven't got anything to do, so I'll go with you. I am willing to help you on that, my nephew." I said, "On our way to the mountain I will tell you something else, my uncle." and he said, "All right, let's go."

We crossed the wash and rode straight to the mountain. We walked our horses, and I started telling him about it. He

315

used to be a good friend of mine, that uncle, that's why I told him about it. I said, "I have been running around with a woman." "What woman is that?" he asked me. I said, "Hosteen Black's wife." He said, "Oh, yes, I heard about that. I heard that Hosteen Black says you have been getting after his wife. Is that true that you have been around with her, my nephew?" he asked me. "Yes," I said. "The other day I was going to where the fellows were gambling." And when I had told him everything he laughed about it for a while. "That's a good scheme, and it is a good idea. If you don't pay her, sometime she may get after you. That's the way with all the women. She might get after you, and the first thing you know she will get you in trouble. However, now, I think, you are safe." We were laughing about it; about that time we got to the foot of the mountain. There were fresh tracks going up. Quite a few cattle had gone up the mountain. He said, "These cattle must have gone up the mountain this morning. I think this is one bunch that always comes out to the water every evening. That's all I ever see every evening, just one bunch. I know them very well." I said, "We'll track them. I suppose they are close by someplace, so we'll track them, and when we catch up with them we will bring them down."

We tracked them way up on the mountain; we tracked them all around the woods, around the cliffs, around the steep places and around the canyons. Finally we got on them way in a little gulch. Quite a few of them were lying around there, and this was the only bunch that was tame. We looked at them there; we rode around them; but we didn't see any more. There were more tracks all around, but they were old. We went riding up around the steep places, where there was thick wood. We thought we might find some there, but we didn't see any, only their tracks. I said, "I guess we will go back to that other bunch. I don't think we can do anything, because the wood is too thick." Then we went back to where the cattle were lying and drove them down to the foot of the mountain.

When we got out on the flat, there was a bull coming right ahead of us. This bull was mine, too. He was coming back from the water. When we met the bull he stopped the cattle. We tried to drive them ahead, but he wouldn't let us. We had a great time there with the bull. We picked up some rocks and started after him, hitting him on the horns; then he would raise up his head and wiggle it around. But we couldn't chase him away. We could make him run all right, but he would dodge around and go back to the bunch. Then we cut some out and drove just a few of them ahead, and let the others go with the bull. When we got to the corral with this little bunch, there was the bull, coming again, and the other cattle right behind him. We just opened the gate for them, and the bull ran right straight in. Then we took out one cow with her calf and chased her quite a long way from the corral. Walk Up said, "You will be all right from here on. I will go back to the corral and turn the others out for you, my nephew." I said, "All right," so he went back.

It was almost sundown then. I went ahead, took my time from there on. Finally I got to Anything Falls In. When I got them in the corral there it was late in the evening. I fixed up the gate so they wouldn't get out and started back to my father's place. I got back there late that night. I took the saddle off my horse and tied him up and went inside. It was dark. Everybody was sleeping. I started the fire, and when I had made a little light, my father awakened. He raised up his head, saying, "Is that you?" I said, "Yes." Then he woke up his wife, and told her to warm up something for me. After I ate I went right to bed.

When I went out the next morning and looked over where I had tied my horse, my horse was gone. He had gotten on the trail and gone all the way back to Where Little Arroyos Stop. I caught him there in the bunch and got on him and started the horses down towards the water. There I got another horse and started back. I got back to the hogan when the sun was pretty well up. After I had eaten Slim Man said, "I think today I'll send the two boys after the mules. These mules, I think, are around close to Lots Of Wool. I know they are always around there. When they bring the mules back up here tonight, then I will start tomorrow early in the morning to where I was planning to go. So it is up to you. Whatever you want to do just go ahead. You said you wanted to go across to Carriso. When do you think you are going?" "I don't know just when, but I'll go whenever I want to. However, I'll know after tomorrow."

He said, "I don't know when I will be back, but I know I will be gone for many days. I have to go over the mountain to visit around again and around on the top. Then I will go to where they said they were going to have my wagon for me. From there I will start back. So I don't know how many days I will be gone. Remember about your younger brother. Come over sometime again, before or after you come back from the other country, and help them on the horses, just to look at them. Round them up a little, and if you want to break some of them you can go right ahead and break them, so that we can use them around here."

I went outside. The two boys had saddled up their horses. They were ready to go after the mules down to the valley, to Lots Of Wool. I thought I would ask them to help me drive down the cattle. While I was getting my horse ready my father came out. He said, "Did you get the cattle?" I said, "Yes, I have them in the corral." "How many are there, that you have got in the corral?" "Only two. The calf and the mother." He said, "What do you want to do with the calf? Do you want to let the calf go, too?" "No," I said, "The calf is mine." "When you get down there with them I think they will take the calf away from you too." I said, "I don't think so, my father, because that woman knows what she is doing. She is watching herself closely. She doesn't want to get caught, so I don't think she will take the calf away from me." He said, "If they want the calf tell them you want the money for it. Don't just give it to them."

Then I told him about the time I met this woman, the time I promised her the buckskin. I said, "After she took the herd back home I got to her place, and there she said to me, 'I was going to give you my daughter, but you had grabbed that woman, and now you are hanging on to her, you can't let her go. I heard she was jealous of me. She isn't the first one that got you. I was the first. I received you before she did, and I always think you are still mine. It is this way, my

318

daughter,' she said to the girl, 'So you hold him there. Don't let him get away from you.' "

Then he said, "No doubt she said that to you all right, but don't take her up. You must not grab at it, because I know her very well. She goes around with men all the time, even though she has a man. And she is raising her daughter in just the same way. She knows all that her mother has been doing. So I don't want you to take her words. If you do, if you become Hosteen Black's son-in-law, even though you become his son-in-law, he will be jealous of you, and his wife will get after you all the time. And whenever he catches you with her, that will be the end of you. There will be a lot of trouble for you if you join him. So I don't want you to go there. I am telling you this because I don't want you to get in bad. I have said to you that if this man ever catches you with his wife that will be the last of you. When he catches you he will grab anything, a stick, or perhaps a rock, or he may have some kind of gun or bow and arrows, or if he has a knife, he will sure kill you with that. And, if he only hurts you, you will be suffering for a long while. Or you might kill him. So that's why I don't care to have you join them, my baby," he said to me. "I am telling you this because I think a great deal of you. You are the only one that is close to me," he said.

Then I got on my horse and started off. The two boys had already gone after the mules. I went to where I had the cattle and started them down, following the wash. I got way out in the flat and started along the foot of the red mesa. Far up on this big flat I saw the boys chasing the horses. When I got on to a hill out in the middle of the flat I saw a herd going down to water. It was quite a distance away, and there was a person riding a horse behind the herd.

I started chasing the cattle down to where the herd had passed; they had gone over a hill to the water, and the herder had stopped his horse right on top of the hill. Then I just let the cattle go there out in the flat and rode up to this herder, and it was the woman to whom the cattle were overdue. She said, "We were coming with the herd. All at once, we saw a

319

little black spot way above. My daughter saw this black spot first. She has gone to the water with the herd. When you came close then I knew it was you. When I recognized you I followed slowly after the herd. When I knew it was you I stopped my horse here. Does that cow belong to me now?" I said, "Yes." "The calf too?" "No," I said, "not the calf. The calf is mine." "What do you want with the calf? They are both of them mine now, because you have chased them down here, and you have done your pleasure lots of times. So one head is not enough. Therefore those two are mine now." I said, "No, I don't want to let the calf go. I brought the calf along because I thought if I just chased the mother she won't go. That's why I started driving them together, and sure enough I didn't have any trouble all the way."

She said, "You have let the cattle know the way. When that cow there wants to go back she will know the way to go, because you let her know the way. You ought to have taken them across to Many Streams and from there chased them down to Black Rock Standing, and from there you ought to have chased them between the two rock points. If you had done this it would have been all right, because, as you know, we have got a fence across these two points, and we have got a good gate there. If you had taken them around that way, then, if she ever wanted to go back, if she ever tried to, she would have no way to get out. But now I don't think we can do anything with her, because you let her know the way. You did this because you haven't a bit of sense, just like all of your father's clan, and just like all those of your own. They all haven't any sense at all." When she said this I got off my horse and walked up to her, and I lifted her dress and touched her. "Now," I said, "You can tell me that I haven't any sense. You can say that as many times as you want to." Then she said, "Now, both of the cattle are mine." But I said, "No, I don't want to let the calf go, because it isn't the first time that I have touched you. I have been touching you for a long time. If this were the first time, then I might let the calf go too." "You ought to have chased them around the other way. Once she starts back there is nothing to stop her," she said. But I said, "I didn't know where to go. I didn't know the crossing. I intended to go way around, but then I thought I would cut right straight across, so that's what I did."

She said, "I wonder what we will do with them. Where shall we take them? I mean it, that calf is mine, too, because," she said, "you have been with my real sister. That's why the calf is mine too. I will tell her that you have paid her, and that calf will be hers." "No," I said, "I have never yet touched her. I stayed with her one night, but I never touched her. I went right to sleep. I didn't wake up until morning, so I never did touch her at all. If I had touched her at that time I might let the calf go, but I don't want to let the calf go." Then she said, "We'll go down to the cattle. I want to look at them." It was a nice young cow, and the calf was like a yearling, even though it was a spring calf. There she said, "I am very glad you have given me a very nice looking cow, and it's a good-sized one. That's why I am very thankful to you about it. We will chase them down for quite a ways. There is lots of feed for the cattle. We will take them down there." Quite a ways below there we let them go. "Will they get away, do you think?" she asked me. "No, I don't think so," I said, "I had them in the corral last night, and they are pretty hungry, so they'll stay. When they get enough feed they will just lie down. I don't think they will go." She said, "We have our cattle way down below. You can see them from here. We got some from way off, those I said had been given to us over at Catohi. We turned them in with our bunch every night so that they would get to know each other. Around towards evening we will chase these down to the bunch and put them in the corral with the others, and soon she will get to know the other cattle and I don't think she will get away."

So then we started back. While we were riding along she rode up close along side of me, and put her arm around my neck and turned my head around and kissed me. She was the only one that kissed me; I didn't let anyone else. I said, "You always want to kiss me, and you are the only one who does. What's the kissing for? Why is it that you always want to kiss me? What is it good for? Is it good for anything?" She said, "Sure. I always like to kiss you, because I think of you a lot, and I love you so well. Kissing means love. When you think a

321

lot of a person, if you like a person so well and love him so well, then you kiss a person. So kissing means love. You are the one I love most, and you are the only one who is so sweet to me. That is why I always kiss you. I think more of you than all the others." I said, "How is that, that you think more of me?" She said, "I always wish for you. I always wish that I were living with you." "Why?" I asked her again. "Well," she said, "because you are so good to me. You are so nice to me, and you are so sweet to me, and because you have got all kinds of things. You have got stocks and properties. That's why I always wish that I were living with you. I wish now we lived together," she said, while we were riding along.

I said, "What you said to me a while ago I haven't forgiven you for." "What did I say to you?" "You know. You know very well what you said to me, and I haven't forgiven you yet." Again she asked, "What was it?" I said, "Don't you know? Have you forgotten already?" "I guess I have," she said, "but tell me. What did I say to you?" "You said that I didn't have a bit of sense. You said to me, 'You have no sense. You are just like all of your father's clan and your own clan.' That's what I mean. So I haven't forgiven you for that." She laughed and said, "That's right. Don't you know you are just like them? You haven't got a bit of sense, just like them." Then I said to her, "We will go in that creek there." "What for?" she asked. "I will forgive you there," I said. We rode to a little creek at the foot of the red mesa, and there I forgave her again.

She said, "We will go back home now, and I want you to stay with us today and tonight, tomorrow you can go home." I said, "What will I stay here for? I have got nothing to do here." "Don't say that. I mean it. I want you to say with us today and tonight. Sometime ago, when she was a small girl, I promised you my daughter. Later I said the same thing to you again. So I mean that; I have given you my daughter. You will stay with her today and tonight, because I have given her to you." Then I said, "No, no. Don't try to get me in trouble. You think you are doing good for me, but I don't think so. It sounds very good, but I don't want to do that. It's not because I don't like you, my wife, my spouse," I said to her, "I can do whatever you want me to do. I can help you out on anything. I can obey you, but not on that. So don't talk to me about it. As I said, it's not that I don't like you. I like you, and I love you, and you said the same to me. If you like me as well as all that, why do you want to put me in bad? So don't talk to me about that. If I stay here, if I take her and start to live with her, you will be after me all the time, and there you will make trouble for her. So I just don't care to do that." "I didn't think you were hard-hearted. But I find now you are unkind to me, Son Of Abaa," she said. She named me there. "Now I don't know what to do about myself." As she said this she dropped her head and was about to cry. We didn't say anything to each other for quite a ways. I put my arm around her and said, "I didn't mean to hurt you by that, my wife. Maybe I did hurt you, but I am sorry. You know very well if I joined you, you would be thinking of me all the time, because we would be close by each other. Even though we are not close to each other now we always get together, so that's what I am afraid of. And the man will see us. When he finds us I will be killed by him or he will be killed by me, or you will be killed by him. That's what I am afraid of. I don't want you to get killed, and I know you don't want me to get killed. We might get killed by a stick, or a rock, or an ax, or by a gun. We don't want to be killed. We both want to live long. So don't be feeling bad about it." She said, "I wasn't thinking about all that, but you are right. I didn't think of all that. That is why I felt very bad. But now we will put all that away."

Then, in that short while, we made up again, and so we kept going, riding along together. "We will go to your home now," I said, "You have been trying to hold me here; I wish I could stay. I wish I were single. Then I would stay. You want me to stay very badly, but somebody is hanging on to me. And you too. If we both were single, then it would be all right, but, in this way, we can't do anything. If I were single, and even though you were married, I would have taken your word, but, as it is, I am afraid to stay long at your place. If I stay tonight, tomorrow will be my last day. And you won't like that, because you always want to see me every once in a

323

while. If I got killed tomorrow, then how will I come to see you again? So you had better let me be alive. And you likewise. If we are both alive, we will see each other as long as we live. You don't want to live for just a short while. You want to live long, and I feel the same way too. So, now, I will go home with you, and after I eat there I will be going back home."

Her husband, Hosteen Black, wasn't home. When I asked for him she said, "He left here some time ago. He said he was going down to Upper Green Spot. So I suppose he is down there. He won't be back, and I don't expect him soon. He may be gone for a month, he said, because there is gambling going on there all the time. So I don't expect him soon." We arrived at her home then. Her daughter was back with her herd. Before we went inside I said, "I want you to help me with ten dollars again, my wife. If you do that I will let you buy that calf. The ten dollars that you gave me, I didn't lose any of it gambling. I used that on grub, so I want to get some more grub if you will let me have ten more." But she didn't say anything. She went inside and I went in also. Her daughter had come back and was sitting there. There was no fire. She said to the girl, "Why is it that you haven't got a fire?" Then the girl got up and went out.

While the girl was out gathering up wood she said to me, "I will help you out. I will give you five, and my daughter will give you five. I will tell her about it, and the calf will belong to her. When her father comes back I will tell him she bought the calf, and I will tell her to tell her father that she bought it. But I don't want to let her see the five dollars I intend to give you. I will ask her for five dollars, and I will give that five to you right there before her, and I will tell her, 'You have bought that calf for five dollars.'" I said, "It will be fine." And I thanked her for that. "I am very thankful to you." She gave me the five which were hers, saying, "Here are the five dollars I am helping you out with. The calf is worth six or seven dollars, but I'll give you ten dollars for it." I thanked her.

After the girl brought in some wood she started up the fire and cooked a little food. After we ate she asked her daughter for the other five dollars. The girl got it out, and they handed it to me. I thanked them, and they thanked me too. Then she said to the girl, "Get ready. As soon as you get ready, take the herd out. After you take out the herd I'll come after it, and you will go down where the two cattle were chased. Maybe they have started back already. So you go down and see if they are still there. If they are, just stay right there with them. I want you to help us on the cattle before you go." She said to me, "Go and ride down where our cattle are and bring them up to where you chased the other two. We will get those two in the bunch. I want you two to tend to the cattle, and I'll tend to the herd." While they were getting ready to go out I said, "I'll go down to the water first. I haven't watered my horse yet. I want to water my horse, and after that I'll come back here again. About that time it will be cool."

Then I got on my horse and started off towards the water. There I watered my horse, and I took off all my clothes and took a bath. After that I put my clothes back on and started back again. They were just taking out the herd. It was cool. The girl had the horse saddled and was ready to go. Her mother said to me, "You go right straight to Black Rock Standing. The cattle may be around there. There are three cows and three calves and one little bull. That's seven. They are always together there at Black Rock Standing. Take them up to where you chased the other two. You help us on that, even though you don't like us," she said to me. The girl started off and I went right after her. When we got to the edge of the red mesa I looked all over the flat; there were not cattle anywhere. I pointed off a place for her, I said, "Way out in the flat where those thick greasewoods are, that's where I chased the other two. Maybe they have gone off. If they are not there then they will have started back. You'll see the tracks. But I think they are lying in those greasewoods. You go down and ride straight to that place." Then she started off, and I started off too, down to Black Rock Standing. From there I drove the cattle up to where she was with the other two. They were all lively. The calves were playing, bucking and kicking one another. They had a great time, I suppose,

325

because it was nice and cool. One of the cows had horns hanging straight down to the jaw. I said, "What's the matter with that cow? Somebody must have twisted the horns. He must have twisted them down, he must have thought it would be a good-looking cow." She laughed and said, "What are you talking about? No person would bother a cow's horns. You are just like our paternal uncle," she said to me, as she laughed again. Then I started tickling her. I grabbed her tits and tickled them. Her little tits were just coming out. Even though she was a small girl she liked being touched. I tickled her for a while, then I let her go. I said, "I think the cattle will be all right. I want to go back to my home. I have been away from my home so long now. If I stay any longer I will be in trouble."

As I started off there was that woman coming down from the mesa with the herd. I went right straight towards Many Streams. Soon I got to a place called Flowing Over Solid Rocks. Then I went on to where Woman Who Walks Alone used to live and on to where my mother used to live. I passed there and got down to Many Streams. There I watered my horse and had some water and washed myself again. From there I went along The Lake, and I began thinking about the girl. I was kind of lonesome for her. I started thinking about her; I tried to get her out of my mind, but I just couldn't, and pretty soon I got to Where The Gray Hill Comes Out. I was thinking what my father would say to me. "Or," I thought, "he might be gone over the mountain. If he is still at home I wonder what he will say to me." I was thinking, as I was riding along.

When I got to his place the mules were standing there. Some horses were standing around too. I tied my horse up to the trees and went inside. Everybody was home, and the cooking was about done. After we ate my father said to me, "Are you going back to your home now?" "Yes," I said, "I am going now." When I went out there was a horse standing a little way from the hogan. I said, "Are you going to use that horse that's standing over there?" My father said, "No, we are not going to use him. Why do you ask?" I said, "I want to

326

ride him up to my home. I have been riding this horse for two days now, and he hasn't had a bite of grass yet, so I think he is hungry." Then my father said, "All right, we are not going to use that horse, so you can go ahead and saddle him up." I brought the horse back and saddled him up and turned the other loose. I was just going to get on the horse when my father came out. He walked up to me and said, "You didn't tell me about your trip. About how you came out." I started telling him about it, but I said, "We ought to go inside and tell about that." I said this, because my sister's daughter was always laughing over little things. I wanted her to laugh, because I always liked her laughter. She had a nice laugh. But he said, "No, we don't want to let them know." If we had gone inside and started telling about this she would have laughed herself to death over it. That's why he didn't want me to go inside.

He used to like to listen and hear about the women. He told me, "Sit down and tell me about it." Then he sat down, and I sat down, too. At first I wasn't going to tell him about it, but then I started in and told him my story. And I told him a lot, but I didn't tell him what I had done to her daughter. I let that go. Then he started laughing; he laughed for a while, then he said, "Well, then, you are safe. That's right. What you said to her is right, and I told you exactly the same when you started from here. I said that to you because I didn't want you to get into trouble, my son, my baby. I am just like her (Hosteen Black's wife), I think of you the most, as much as of my own children. I think more of you. That's why I didn't want you to get into trouble, my son, my baby," he said to me again. "I didn't want you to join Hosteen Black, because I know he is a bad man. If you ever go close to him you sure will have a hard time with him. So you just remember my words, not only mine, remember the words of Choclays Kinsman and His Horse Is Slow and Who Has Mules. Remember our words, so you will be safe all the time." Then he said, "You must never join Hosteen Black. Don't go close to him any more."

Then he asked me about the money. "Have you got the money with you now, my son?" And I said, "Yes." Then he said, "I'd like to borrow some money from you, my son. I have run out of money. I haven't any money on hand. Only one of my sons still has some money. I was going to ask him to lend me some, but since you are here again I want you to lend me some of your money. If you hadn't gotten back today I was going to take the money you left with me. So think about it. If you wish to lend me some I will be glad, my baby. You know I am going far away, and I can't do anything without money. There are stores at certain places; that's why I want you to lend me some of your money. Soon the lambs will have wool. When I get the money for it, I will give your money back then, my son." I said, "All right, I am willing to help you out with that. I know how it is when you travel around, when you haven't any money." As I said this I reached down in my pocket and gave him the ten dollars which I had gotten from that woman. He said, "You have skinned those women down there. You got more money than your calf was worth. If I tried to scheme like that I wouldn't get that much money for a small calf," he said, as I gave him the money. He was glad about it, holding it in his hand, moving it around and sort of smiling. Then he said, "I guess you had better be going back now."

When I got home my wife had just a little fire going. I said, "I wanted to get some cornstalks for my horse but it's too dark." "Why don't you gather up some cedar bark and light it and take it down to the cornfield with you?" she said. So I did; I lit some cedar bark and looked for a hoe and went down to the cornfield. When I came back from there she had built a fire and had some food all ready for me. She put it out in front of me and I started eating. After I ate she put the things away. Then she asked me, "Where have you been all this time?" I said, "You know I started from here yesterday morning. I got down to my father's place, and when I got there he was very glad that I had come. That's what he said. And he told us to go and get the horses and bring some horses back for him, because he was going over the mountain again. He wanted to take some horses with him over the mountain. So after we had eaten there the two boys and I started off together down as far as Many Streams. From there

328

the boys went out the other way, out towards the other flat, and I started down towards the flat, down toward Hosteen Black's flat. But there were no horses on that flat, so then I thought I would go over to his home because he might know something about the horses. Hosteen Black was the only one around, so there is where I gave him back the money. So I am square with him now.

Then on the other side of Lots Of Wool we three got together again. We had been looking for the horses all day. We found a lot of them but they weren't the ones he wanted us to get. It was the mules that he wanted, but we didn't see the mules yesterday all day. We had been hunting these mules yesterday all day. We had been hunting these mules until it got too dark on us, so we had to stay out in the flat all night last night without anything to eat. Then early this morning we started hunting the mules again until late this afternoon. We were about to give up, because we were about starved. We were just about to give up looking for them, when finally we got on to them. They had been hiding themselves in a little hollow. Then we started chasing them right straight for the water. There we put them in the corral and caught them, and we got them back this evening. So that's where I have been with the two boys," I said.

She seemed to believe me. Every time I gave a look into her eyes she seemed to believe me, but then again she seemed as though she didn't. When I finished my story she said, "Who was it that chased two cattle down on the other side of the hill? My older brother was over on the other side of the hill, and there he happened to see the tracks. He said somebody had chased the cattle down towards the valley. Did you see the tracks while you were down in the valley?" she asked me. "No," I said, "I was down there going back and forth, but I didn't notice them, because I wasn't looking for the cattle, so I didn't see any tracks down there." She said, "I was over at the other hogan today, and there is where I heard that. My older brother said, 'I mean it. Someone chased two cattle down towards the valley, and I know who the man was, because I know the horse's tracks. It was my brother-in-law's horse's tracks behind these cattle. I know his horse's tracks

329

very well. So it's he who chased the two cattle down.' This is what my older brother said. When he said this the women-folk started talking about it. As they were all starting to talk about it my younger brother told them to shut up. 'Every time you hear of some little thing you always start to talk about it. You all just want to make trouble.' he said. But they kept on talking about it. Again my older brother said, 'My younger sister there, her man is just making fun of her. Your man is just making fun of you,' he said to me. Then again my younger brother told them to stop talking like that about little things, but my older brother said, 'I know the horse's tracks very well.' So I wonder who that was,'' she said.

Then I was pushed into a corner, but I said, ''Maybe he thought that was my horse's tracks, but it wasn't mine at all. And he knows very well there are lots of horses' tracks alike. I know he just wants to make trouble for us. And I told you that I have been out in the flat, looking for the horses with the boys for our father. The horse that I rode from here to his place I turned loose when I got there, and they let me have this horse, which is standing outside now. I have been riding this horse all day yesterday and all day today, and when we got back with the horses there wasn't an extra horse there so I had to ride the same horse home. And that's this horse stand-ing outside. So I don't know what he is talking about. Maybe you believe him, but you shouldn't believe every word that has been said. If you believe every word you hear it will make you crazy. So you mustn't believe everything the peo-ple say.'' When I said this she quieted down. Then I said, ''Tomorrow I want to go to my father's place again. I would like to be there when he leaves. When he starts from there I will go with him for quite a ways.'' When I said this she said, ''You are just saying that. I know what you are going to do. You are going along with him.'' I said, ''No, I am not going along with him. I just want to go a little way with him. And I'll come back.''

330

17

Slim Man gives him advice . . .
He gambles and wins and wins
against G-string.

When I awoke she was still sleeping. I woke her up and told her to start the fire and cook something. "I would like to go down to my father's place early this morning, before he leaves. I want to see him go." Then she got up, and I put on my clothes and moccasins and went outside. I walked down to the cornfield and cut some cornstalks with a hoe, and when I had enough I brought them home and chopped them in pieces for my horse. Then I went inside, and she had the cooking done. She laid out the food and we started eating. After we ate I went out and saddled up my horse and started off. I got down to the water first and watered my horse and then went on to my father's place. I got there just as the sun was coming up. They hadn't brought the mules back yet; there were no horses standing around, and there was no one outside. I thought he had gone already. When I went inside they were just starting to eat. About then the boy was back with the mules. He said, "The mules were quite a way down below. I caught up with them way on the other side of Dead Water." My father said, "I thought those mules would do that. They are Tcindi (ghosts)! They always want to get away from you. I am afraid they might get away from me, but I've got to take them. I may have trouble with them, but I guess I'll take them with me." After we had all eaten he said to his boys, "Put the saddle on that one mule for me."

They went out and decorated the mule with all his outfit, and he began to dress himself up. He put on all his good clothes, then he put on his beads and belt. When he was all dressed up he looked like a real young man. Then he said to all, "You know what I have said to you. You remember that. You know what to do around here. You know what to do about the herds and horses and other things. Be sure and take good care of the things, and take good care of each other. Take good care of your mother. She knows what to do about everything, so take good care of her. I don't know just how long I will be gone, but, anyhow, I will try to come back soon. So I will go now." I said, "I will go with you perhaps as far as where my horses are. Maybe a little way on the other side. So I want to go quite a ways with you, my father," I said. He said, "Fine. Let's go. I will be glad to have you go with me, my son."

Then he walked out and I went after him. He got on the mule and started leading the other one. I got on my horse and we started off. When we got to the trail I started riding close beside him and he asked me what I had done when I got home. He was kind of laughing. When I told him my story he laughed some more about it. I said, "I almost got in trouble again, but I tried my best to get out of it. I think I am out of it, but maybe not. I am kind of worried about myself, because I have made up too many lies, and because I have stolen my own cattle away from myself. That's what is worrying me, my father."

He said, "That's all right, you mustn't worry so much, and you mustn't think about it. If you think about it then it worries you. Even though you have lost your cattle you made good out of it. You have teased a woman for it, and you got money for it. You have money on hand, and I am using some too. What you still have on hand we will use too. When we go hunting we will use that money; we will get some grub for it. So don't worry so much about it, my son. I know how your wife is. She knows all about men. I know she used to be going around with lots of men. She knows all about it. I know just how she is. So don't bother so much about her. However, it's all up to her. If she ever gets you in trouble I will see about that. It will be all up to me, my son. So don't be afraid to tell me about her. You must look out for yourself closely. When you know she is starting to put something over

332

on you you mustn't let her. When you know she is starting something, some kind of trouble, you mustn't bother with her. Try to make her stop. If you think you can't stop her, don't bother with her. Keep away from her, as you did last night. I am glad now that you are safe. It is hard to tell about women. However, I know you know nothing about it, because you haven't found the different ways of women, for you are just beginning to go around with women. I know all about them, for I have found out lots about them. You don't know what she is doing. She may be running around with men, but you won't know it. Even though people know she has been running around with men they won't let you know and she won't tell you. And you are the only one being watched closely. I know she is watching you, trying to find you with a woman. So now I want you to watch her too, because I know she is running around with men. You are always away from home. When she knows you will be gone for two or three days, as soon as you go away she starts off to look for men. I know she is doing that, even though I haven't seen her going around with men since you married her. However, I know she always ran around with men before you married her, so I know very well she is doing it still, because she has been raised that way. She always wants to do that, but you don't know it. Now, from here on, you make believe you are going off someplace. Tell her you will be gone two or three days, and then you hide yourself someplace nearby, and see what she will do when she is all alone. I know very well you will find her the first day. So you start to work on her like that. If you do that you will find out for yourself. So start this on her, just to find out what she will do, because she is working on you that way; so you must do something for yourself, too. What I am telling you is all for your own good, because I don't want you to be spoiled. As I said to you the other day, you are the one that I think about the most. That is why I don't want you to be fooled. Don't fool yourself about her. She is trying to fool you, but don't let her. She is holding you tight now, just because you are the only young man around here who has different kinds of stock. You have quite a big herd of sheep, horses and cattle, too, and you

333

have some property. She is trying to get all that away from you. So you mustn't let her boss you, and you mustn't tell her 'The herd is all yours, horses and cattle too.' And what little property you have, you mustn't let her get hold of that. You mustn't give her anything that is worth a lot. If you do that she will want more; she will want you to give her more. If you give her what she wants, if you just go ahead and start giving her something, soon you will be out of things; you will be out of stocks. That's what I mean by don't let her fool you. You back out all the time, because if you start giving her things or stocks, when she knows you haven't any more she will just kick the dust over you, and, when she kicks the dust over you, then she will run away. And there you will be, sitting or standing, without anything. But you hold everything for yourself, and she runs away from you, you will have something to start on again. You will be ready to get another woman. So you just hold yourself on all these things, my son, my baby," he said, while we were walking our horses.

We had gone quite a way, I didn't realize we were so far from home. "Now you remember all that I have said to you. I told you to look out for yourself. If you do that, then you won't suffer. Try not to be forever thinking of her. You know very well now she is not a good woman. You have already found that she isn't. Therefore you don't want to think mostly about her. If you start thinking just about her, you will get excited. You won't know what you are doing. Soon she might make you crazy. So you mustn't think only of her. Just get her out of your mind if you can. What I want you to think most about is your stocks and what little things you have besides, and of your own self. Go around and work on your stocks. Try to raise them. Try to improve them, and try to get more things. In that way you will enjoy your life. So don't put yourself in sorrow. Don't put yourself in sadness. Think of all your things. Don't think of any other thing, only what you have. If you do that, if you take all my words, you will soon have more stocks and more of other things, and soon you will be the only rich man around here. If you take the women's words, you won't get anywhere. So you just stay with your stocks and things. Have your mind on them all the time, day and night have your mind on them."

This was what he was telling me all the way from home while we were riding along close together. He always talked to me like that every once in a while. He wanted me to be a good man all the time. He wanted me to live good, and he wanted me to enjoy life. That's the way he always talked to me. He said, "There is one more thing that I don't want you to do. I don't want you to start beating your woman. Once you start then you will want to do it again. You will be in the habit of doing that. So you mustn't beat up your woman, even though she wants you to do it. You must keep yourself away from that. And you mustn't start to get jealous about her. If you start to get jealous of her, then you will be jealous of her all the time. I don't want you to be jealous about your woman. If you are jealous of her, if you beat her, they will discover you, and soon all the people will know it. They will all know you are jealous, and they will all know that you beat a woman, and, if sometime you want to marry again, nobody will want you. All the women, and everybody, will be afraid of you, and they will all talk about you, and they will all make fun of you. Soon you will be just like a fool. They will begin making fun of you right to your face, calling you a jealous man, calling you woman-beater. They will have some kind of nasty name for you, and you will be ashamed about it. So you mustn't start these things. That's what I mean. I told you to watch yourself closely; be careful of yourself; be careful of all that you do. You must not try to make yourself a bad name. You must not try to make yourself a fool. Try to be a good man all the time, and then everybody will think well of you, and everybody will look up to you. If you are careful and try to live well everybody will know you are a good man. If you live in this way no one will make fun of you. Everybody will be afraid of you. They will all be under you, and you will be above them, if you live well. You will find all that I have said to you later on. If you live long, if you take my word, you will remember me by that, as long as you live." Then that was all.

We were way on the other side of Where The Little Arroyos Stop. We got up on the hill, at the place called Tree Holding Up A Load; when we got on this hill he stopped his mule. "Let's get off, and we'll have a smoke," he said. We got off and sat down there and he pulled out his tobacco. He used to smoke chewing tobacco. He got that out, and he got out his knife and started shaving some off. After he got through with it he gave it to me, and I shaved some off too. We made a cigarette and started smoking. While we were smoking he said, "I guess you are going back from here. When do you think you will want to go across to your herd, my son?" I said, "I don't know just when, but I will try to go as soon as I can. Perhaps in two or three days. I am anxious to see them." He said, "Yes, I think you are right, for it has been quite a long time now since you have looked at your herd. I guess you sure would like to see your herd again. It's like that with all the stocks. If you have stocks you always want to see them, every once in a while, and it has been quite a long time since you have seen them. What do you think you will want to do with the herd? Do you want to bring the herd back over here? Or do you want to leave them there?" I said, "I don't know what I will do. However, I will know when I get there. I will see how they are getting along. If they don't look good to me, then I'll get them back over here. If they are all right, if nothing is bothering them, then I guess I will leave them there. So I will know what to do about it when I get there. And I will see about the bucks and billy goats too." He said, "I don't know when I will be back, but I will try to come back as soon as I can. After you come back from there try to have your horses ready, and when I return, right after that, we will go hunting. So you be ready. I told the boys to have the horses ready for me, too. So have that on your mind. As soon as you come back from that place you get ready. I don't know who else will go with us, but we will see when I come back."

Then after we had finished talking and had finished our smoke we got up, and he said, "I guess you had better go back, and I will be going ahead too." I said, "I hope you will have a good trip. However, I have no doubt you will." I went up and shook hands with him. Then he got on his mule and started off, leading the other one.

I got on my horse and started back down to Where The Little Arroyos Stop. There I got another horse for myself and started chasing the one I had been riding to my father's place.

That horse belonged to them; they had been using it to herd with. When I got to their place I went inside. Slim Man's clan niece was sitting in the hogan; she was a niece of mine and a cousin; and his wife was there too. She told his niece to make a little coffee and lunch for me. After I ate his wife asked me, "About how far from here did you turn around and start back, my younger brother?" "I went as far as Tree Holding Up A Load with him, my older sister, from there I came around to where my horses were. I drove them down to the water and there I got me another horse." She said, "I suppose he is about to reach the top of the mountain by now. Which way are you going from here? Are you going back to your home?" I said, "No, my older sister, I think I'll go down to where the people were gambling. I only want to go down to see if they are still gambling. Maybe the people who lived there have moved. So I think I will go and take a ride down to that place. I gave eleven dollars and fifty cents to my father. I told him to keep it for me here, so I would like to have a dollar and a half out of it. I want to leave the ten dollars here." She didn't know anything about that money. "Well, I don't know about the money at all. When did you leave the money with him?" she asked. "I left that money with him just lately. He put it in a leather bag, my older sister." She said, "I wonder why he didn't let me know about it? He never said a thing to me about the money, so I don't know where he has put it." I said again, "He put the money in a leather bag. I know he put the money in that bag." Then she reached over behind a stack of sheep pelts and got out the bag and started searching in it. Finally she got the money out. Then she untied it and gave me a dollar and a half. I said, "This is all I want. I am going down to where they are gambling and gamble for it." Then the other woman said to me, "What do you want to carry money around for? I know what you want it for. You want to give that money to the woman." She said this because she was my cousin. She was laughing as she said it.

I went straight down to Anything Falls In. There I watered my horse again, and then headed right straight for that place. There was nobody around, not a horse standing out anywhere. I tied my horse to a tree and went inside. There was Hosteen Who Has A Hat. I shook hands with him. "From where are you coming, my younger brother?" he asked. "I'm coming from home," I said, "I came to gamble, but I don't see anybody around, so there is nobody to gamble with." "Where have you been all this time? There has been a crowd of people. There was lots of money. I lost all of mine," he said. "Only my older brother still has some left. The crowd left here three days ago. However, they are coming back again today, because they know my older brother has lots of money left. They are all after him. You ought to have been here when the crowd was still here. Maybe you would have won some money. But, I guess, you'll win some when they come again. They are coming today, I know. There has been quite crowd here for three days and three nights from different places. When they left they all said, 'We will be back again in three days.' That's today. Some of them wanted to go to Round Rock. They were going to take something there in order to get some money. I had fifty dollars. They had been trying to take it away from me for three days, until the last night I lost all of it. And this other man over there, my older brother, Turkey, I think he has about thirty dollars left. They are coming after that today. I guess a lot of them will come from different places, because they were saying they would let all the gamblers know that we had put up a date. So I think we will see some new gamblers." "Well, then," I said, "before the crowd comes I'll lie down and go to sleep."

When I was about to sleep the dogs began barking. He pushed me, saying, "Get up. Some gamblers are coming on horseback." I raised my head and saw them getting down off their horses, but I just lay there still. One of the fellows walked up to me and kicked my feet around, saying, "Wake up. Get up. What do you want to sleep for? Do you think there is nothing to do? We are here to open up a work." That was White Horse. There were two of them. They were both younger brothers of mine. I shook hands with them. They spread a robe on the ground, and then they all sat down and got out their cards. Has Done It got his cards out. Badger For His Pet had a deck. He got that out. But he said, "I

338

haven't got any money. One of you put up five dollars for me. I will pawn a revolver to one of you." Has Done It picked up the revolver and gave him five dollars.

When they were about to start gambling Turkey came over from the other hogan. He said, "Come on, you fellows. Start up. Why don't you start? Are you waiting for me? As soon as I start gambling I won't wait for anything." They said, "We will start playing for a nickel first, then for dimes. We'll come out easy first." They started playing a new game, ni'idjahi.[1] I sat looking at them for awhile, then I got my money out. However, I never made a choice for myself. When the fellows put their money on one of the cards I put my money there too, if I was sure they were going to win. If I was sure they had missed I put my money with the dealer. So I just kind of jumped different ways. Soon I had a little money in my hands.

Then the dealer and the others stopped me, because they realized I was picking up all their money. They told me to get my cards out. I said, "Where are the cards? I haven't any cards." They said, "Borrow a deck from someone." I said, "I don't want to borrow cards from anyone. I'll deal all right if I have the cards." "Buy a deck from that man. He has got some new cards," they said, pointing to Who Has A Hat. He said, "I bought a deck of cards for fifty cents, but I want to make a dime on it; so I'll let it go for sixty." I said, "All right. Give up the cards." I gave him sixty cents, and he gave me the cards. They were brand new, hadn't yet been opened. One fellow was dealing, and they told me to bet. I was afraid to bet, so I only put up a quarter. He turned up the cards one at a time, and there I won. I won a quarter. Then Has Done It dealt again. I didn't bet against him. When he was through Badger For His Pet dealt. I bet him fifty cents, and I won again. Then it was my turn. First I dealt out an ace and a king. Badger For His pet picked up the king and slapped it

1. A dealer deals out two cards face up. A player places his money on the one he expects to be duplicated first (e.g., the suit is irrelevant. If a 10 and an 8 are up, the first card duplicated wins.) One card belongs to the dealer; the second belongs to the other players. A player may bet on either card but the dealer has the disadvantage that he must cover all the winning bets. The deal passes around, everyone dealing once.

down on my money pile. "I don't know how much you have there, but I'll bet all of it." I turned over the cards one by one; I started searching; I had turned over quite a few cards and there came my ace. He said, "Count your money." I counted my money. "Six dollars," I said. He counted out six dollars and gave them to me.

From there we started going after one another. They said, "We will bet against one another, even though we are friends or brothers. We will gamble like this until sundown." So everybody bet against everybody else. My money was going up and down, rising and falling, but I felt that I wouldn't lose. I had a feeling that way all that day. At first, when I started, I was kind of shivery all over, but I got the feeling not to lose. Then I wasn't afraid at all, so I just stayed with it. Sometimes I won, sometimes I lost, but I stayed right with it, and I never noticed that the sun was down. When I happened to look up, we were gambling in a brush hogan, the sun was down over the mountain. I began fixing my cards. I said, "The sun is down. This is as far as I want to play." They all said, "Come on and play. You haven't won anything yet. Come on and play, and win all the money. You are the only one who's lucky." But I fixed up my cards, put them back in the package and put it in my pocket and started counting my money. I had won twenty-three dollars. I had a dollar in my pocket, so that made twenty-four that I had. I got out my red handkerchief and put the money on it and tied it up. They all wanted me to stay. They all wanted to pawn something to me. One fellow gave me a new robe, "Put up four dollars for me," he said. I gave him four dollars, and I had twenty left. That was all I took. Then I got up and went out. As I was walking up to my horse they were all hollering at me to come back in, naming the things they wanted to pawn to me, but I didn't pay any attention to them. I got on my horse and started off.

I got home that evening before it was too dark. There was a horse standing where I always tied my own. I led my horse over there and tied him up there, too. There were plenty of cornstalks piled up; so I walked inside. There was an old man sitting in the hogan. That was G-string. My wife said, "My grandfather came today, and I have been with him all day." I walked up to him and shook hands and said, "When did you drop in, *cadane?* [2] You are quite a stranger around here, *cadane.*" "Yes, I guess I am a stranger all right, *cadane,*" he said to me, "because I haven't been around here for a long time. I came this afternoon. I wanted to come to your place to eat some wild animal meat, which you have killed around here, *cadane,*" he said to me again. We were both calling each other *cadane,* because he was Red Clay, and he was married to my father's clan. He said, "That's what I came for, to eat some wild animal meat, but my granddaughter there says you haven't killed one yet. Is that true?" I said, "I have killed all the animals around here. There are no more animals around here now, only the dogs. However, I am going hunting soon. When I return from hunting then I will have plenty of meat. Then you will have some meat." "Oh, that's fine," he said, "I am glad to hear that." I asked him, "From where did you start, *cadane?* And where do you think you are going?" He said, "I started from my old place, from Narrow Canyon. I started from there a little before noon. I came right straight on and got to Giving Out Anger's place, but he wasn't home. They had the herds up on the mountain some place, and he had gone up to his herds, so there were only the womenfolk at home. I didn't want to stay with them, so I started off again. I kept coming, thinking I would stop some place when the sun went down when I got to a hogan. And here all at once I got to one, so I stopped and there was my granddaughter at home. I didn't know you all lived here. So then I thought I would stay for the rest of the day and tonight. I'm just traveling around, just visiting around. Now tell me about the trip that you made today."

I started telling him about it, and when I got to where we had been gambling I said, "I watched them gamble for a while, then I thought I would pawn something, so I pawned what little I had." I didn't mention what. "They put up some money for me and I started gambling with them until sundown, when I took out what I had pawned. Then a fellow

2. My son-in-law. Used reciprocally. Here they are joking with each other.

pawned that robe to me," I said. "So I started back after sun-down. I didn't have any cards. Never carried a deck of cards in my life, but I bought a deck and gambled with that." "Let's see the cards. What kind of cards are they?" he asked. I took the pack out and handed it to him. When he opened it up he said, "Ai······! These are dandy cards you got, *cadane*. It's a nice deck. Don't lose it, not until it gets all worn, but not before, because cards are scarce around here. No place to get them, except far off." He was turning them around, looking at them while he was saying this to me, and holding them in his hands and dealing them out. Then he started playing with them.

While he was playing I lay down by my wife. I reached down in my pocket and got the money out and handed it to her. She grabbed it with both hands. She grabbed the money and my hands with it, and she was so surprised about it too. She untied it and counted the money. After she had counted it I said, "Give me back just one." She shook her head and said, "No." She tied it up again and hid it away someplace. Then she said, "We haven't eaten yet." She had the cooking done in a little while, and, when she had put out the food, I said to the old man, "Eat, *cadane*." After we ate she put the things away.

Then the old man said, "When I was young, when I was still a boy, I started to gamble with different kinds of games, many different games which we had made ourselves, and then these cards appeared. When we first saw them we started gambling with them, and everybody wanted to have a deck. Everybody liked it and liked to gamble with it, because it was something new. Everybody liked it and we are still gambling with it, and we put the other games off. We put all that away, on account of these cards. And now I guess every-body has forgotten all about the other games, because we don't make them any more. When you first start gambling with any of these other games, if you win the first time, then you always win. You are always lucky. If you lose the first time, then you always lose. You will always be out of luck. And whenever you win something you mustn't fuck for it. You mustn't give what you have won away for fucking. If you

342

do that, you will be out of luck, because you have given away what you have won for fucking, and the fucking wins away from you. So you mustn't do that. You must always keep what you have won. It's that way with all the games. The same with this deck. And every time you win you must pray, say that you will win some more. Then you sure will. That's the way it goes." He talked to me like this after we ate; then after he was through talking I said, "I guess we had better go to sleep. I don't want to keep you awake, because I know you are tired, and I am too. I have been riding all day in this hot weather, so I am tired riding too." Then we made up his bed and we all went to sleep.

After breakfast this old man said to me, "Let's play cards, *cadane*, but I don't mean we will just play. I mean we will gamble." This man used to be a big gambler, and I was kind of scared to play with him, but I said, "Whatever you say is all right with me." He said, "Yes, we will play. We will gamble. Even though you are *cadane*, and even though I am *cadane*, though we speak that way to each other, we won't give each other anything. We will gamble for what we have. In that way, if one of us wins, then we will give something to each other. So let's gamble." I put up the robe that had been pawned to me for four dollars. I said, "What shall we gamble for? Something like this, or shall we gamble for money?" He said, "I haven't got any money. I have a robe, so we will gamble for that. Yours is worth four dollars, and mine is worth only three, so I'll let it go for three dollars." Then we started gambling; pretty soon I had won a dollar from him. About that time the sun was up close to noon. I said, "The horses must be thirsty, and I think they are out of feed too, so I'll take them to the water and feed them some more." He said, "Oh, yes, that's right. We have forgotten our horses. They must be thirsty by now all right."

When I came back from doing that I went inside and we started gambling again. About noon I had won the robe from him. Then we ate lunch; after lunch he put up his bridle. The bit was a hand-made bit, which the smiths used to make, and the reins were bought at the store. "The bit itself is worth two dollars," he said, "and the reins and line, all the leather

343

part is worth a dollar. So the whole thing is worth three dollars." I said, "All right." It went back and forth, one way and then the other, all afternoon until sundown. There wasn't any wood, and it was getting dark. We stopped a while and ate some lunch that evening, but I didn't get any wood. After we ate I took two poles off the brush hogan and put them in the fire. Late in the evening I had won the bridle. Then he put up a double saddle blanket. It was brand new, with a red ground and all kinds of designs in it. It was a nice fancy saddle blanket. He said, "I'll let this go for four dollars, *cadane*." I said, "I guess maybe you think it's worth that much, but it isn't. Saddle blankets like that are worth two and a half. So make it worth two and a half, *cadane*. Four dollars is too much." He said, "No. Even though you say it's only worth two and a half I won't let it go for less than four." So then I just told him to come on. He put that up for four dollars and we started in again.

We had been sitting up all that night; it had been going one way and the other. Early in the morning, just as the sun was coming up, I won the saddle blanket. So that made three things that I had won from him. Then I said, "It's been a long time since we started gambling. We have been sitting up all day and all night, so we had better stop. We are tired. We have had enough gambling." I picked up the cards; then I got up and grabbed the saddle blanket. This saddle blanket was spread on the ground. We had been gambling on it, and he was sitting on it. I was going to pick it up when he grabbed it. He said, "I don't want to let this go, *cadane*." We were both holding on to the saddle blanket; I said, "Why? I have been sitting up for these things all day yesterday and all night last night. I didn't want you to put them up. I didn't tell you to gamble with them. You wanted me to gamble with you. I didn't want to gamble with you at first, because I was afraid, because I knew you had been gambling all your life, and I knew you knew all about it, and I just started. I don't know much about gambling. I don't know much about a deck of cards. That's why I was afraid to gamble with you at first. So that's why I don't want to sit up for nothing." He said, "Even though it's that way you have won two things from me, so

344

just take the two things and let me have the saddle blanket." Then I thought, "He is poor," I didn't want to hurt him by anything, so I let him have the saddle blanket and picked up the robe and the bridle. After we ate that morning he went out and put his saddle on his horse, and he put a rope around the horse's nose. Then he got on the horse and went. I guess he had gone back to his home. My wife started laughing about it. She said, "What do you want to win all of his things away for? Poor old man. He has no bridle and no robe." "Well," I said, "It's he, himself, who wanted to lose his things. I'll get a little sleep. Maybe I'll sleep until noon. I won't bother with the horse. Help me on that." She said, "All right, I will tend to the horse. You can go ahead and go to sleep."

Then I lay down and went to sleep. I must never have moved at all. All at once she was pushing me, saying, "Get up and eat." I woke up and it was noon. I walked outside and washed myself and we started eating. She said, "I have been working on the corn, taking the ears off the stalks. I have finished with that. I have them piled all around in the cornfield." So after I ate I picked up a robe and walked down to the cornfield and started packing the corn back to the hogan. I was going back and forth for the corn all afternoon until sundown. After I had brought in all the corn we started husking it. We almost finished with that. While we were working on that that evening she was telling me what the old women had been saying about the old man. She said, "The womenfolk were all laughing about the old man, because he was riding without a bridle and without his robe. They were saying, 'It's his own fault. He thought he would win all the things that he saw around there, but he was mistaken. So now he has gone home without a robe and without his bridle.' This is the way they were talking about him," she said.

When it got real dark we quit husking and went back inside. We only had a little lunch that evening and went right to bed. The next morning after we had finished husking the rest of the corn I took it up on top of the brush shade. There I scattered it all out to let it dry. That afternoon the boys were still hauling corn back to their home, so I walked over and helped them pack it in. We had it all brought in when the sun was pretty well down. About that time the womenfolk had finished with the cooking. They told me, "Go behind the hogan. Everything is about ready to be eaten inside, so you go behind the hogan and our mother will go out."[3] I walked behind the hogan. I was behind the hogan for a while, and then they hollered, "Now, come in quick." I started—at first I didn't know which way she had gone—they hadn't told me which way to come in, but I just decided myself. I thought, "Maybe she went out towards north." So I made a quick start towards the south side, and there I almost bumped into her. I scared her so very much she was almost out of breath. She screamed out and almost fell down. I just passed her and went inside. Just as I got inside I heard her crying. The boys all started laughing about it, while the womenfolk inside were kind of mad at each other about it, saying, "Why didn't you tell her to go out the other way? Why didn't you go out with her? Why didn't you do it." The boys were all laughing. By the time we were through eating she had stopped crying. I was kind of scared about it, so I walked out and started home. While I was going home I felt sorry for her, that I had scared her so very much.

While my wife was cooking the next morning I said, "I'll go and get a horse for myself and have it ready for tomorrow. I'll start tomorrow morning across to Carriso. I think I'll go over to that place." She said, "How about me? Aren't you going to take me too? Don't you know what I said to you— that I was going with you? And here you are, saying you are going alone." I said, "Yes, I'm going alone, because I want to make a quick trip. I don't want to wait for anything, so I'm thinking that I will go alone." She said, "Don't think you are going alone. I guess you are thinking that way, but I am going, too. So tomorrow you get two horses." I didn't want to bother with her any more; I didn't want to talk to her any more, so I said, "All right, if you want to go it's all right with me." I didn't do anything that morning. In the afternoon after

3. The mother-in-law taboo in action. A son-in-law is not supposed to see his mother-in-law.

346

a little lunch I saddled up my horse and rode up to Where The Little Arroyos Stop, where my horses were. I started them down to the water and there I got the blue horse and the mule, which we used when we went to the Night Chant.

18

He and his wife visit his mother . . .
Sickness in the valley . . . He
treats a young girl . . . They are all
in sadness . . . Trading trip . . . They claim
a witch caused the sickness.

the next morning we dressed ourselves in our good
clothes and started off. We left our home just as the
sun came up. As we were passing Where The Gray Hill
Comes Out I said, "I'll go over to those hogans. You go
straight ahead to Many Streams, just keep on this trail to
Many Streams and we will go on to The Lake. From there we
will take the trail that branches off to Place Of Many Lakes.
So stay on this trail and go ahead and I will catch up with
you, maybe before you get to Many Streams.

She went on and I turned around and went to my father's
place. They were just about through eating. They told me to
eat, so I ate some more. I said, "We are going across the
valley to Carriso. Two of us are going." "Well, where's the
other one? Why didn't she come in?" asked Slim Man's Wife.
I said, "She went on down, so I came up here by myself."
"Why didn't you bring her here too? We are always eager to
see her, but, I don't know, somehow or other she doesn't
come around. We are always glad to see her, but she never
visits us. So you are going over to that country?" I said, "Yes,
we are going across." "When do you think you are coming
back?" I said, "I don't know exactly when we will get there."
She said, "You can't make it. It's too far. You can't make it in
a day." "Well," I said, "That's all right. If we get there tomorrow it will be all right." She said, "I don't know about our
man. We don't know where he is by now. Maybe he is over
the mountain; maybe he is on top. I am kind of worried

348

about him, because," she said, "a man came here yesterday, from Upper Green Spot. He said, 'Some kind of sickness, some kind of disease, is spreading all along the valley, all the way down and all the way up. It's going so fast, too. The people have swollen throats, all swollen around the neck, and some of them are choking to death.'[1] That's why I am worried about the old man, and you, too. Why do you want to go into the place of danger? You ought to wait until it settles down." I said, "Oh, I guess it won't bother us. I think we will be all right, and we have started already, so I guess we will just go on ahead to the other side of the valley. I guess we will be all right. I don't think that sickness will bother us."

Then Slim Man's Wife said to me, "You had better take some white and yellow corn flour. I suppose you have your corn pollen with you?" "Yes, I have my corn pollen with me, but I have no corn flour of any kind." "We have got some, which we always use. I suppose you know how to use it," she said. "Use the white corn meal early in the morning, make a sacrifice to the morning, and at noon, sacrifice to the sun, when it gets to the middle of the sky, and in the evening you sacrifice to the evening. You use the white corn meal in the morning, and at midday you use your corn pollen, and in the evening you use the yellow corn meal. Then the danger won't bother you. You can't get into a dangerous place. Even if you do get into a dangerous place, nothing will hurt you." They tore off a piece of white muslin for me about six inches wide and put the two kinds of corn meal on it for me. They said, "Now you use that every day and every evening. Don't forget about it."

Then I started off again. I went out in the flat; there was my wife way on the other side of Many Streams, close to The Lake. I caught up with her on the other side of The Lake by the blue clay hills. When I told her about the sickness she was scared, she was afraid to go on. I said, "I believe the man whom we caught up with the time we were coming back from the Night Chant, the man whose name I told you was Chatterer. You know what he said to us, and sure enough

1. There was an epidemic of mumps at this time.

349

sickness of some kind has started, and so I believe him." She was awful scared about it then. I said, "You don't want to be afraid of a little thing. And you mustn't be afraid of a sickness like that. If you are scared of it you sure will get it. If you don't care, if you are not afraid of it, then the sickness won't bother you. So you mustn't be afraid of it. It's a serious thing that is spreading around, so you must pray for yourself, that's all. In that way nothing will hurt us, if we both say prayers for ourselves." We rode through many nice places and finally got to Nephew Of Who Has Land's home. Nobody saw us until we got to the hogan, and there a woman came out. She recognized me right away. "Oh, here is your younger brother out here," she said. That was Nephew Of Who Has Land's wife. Then we started to unsaddle the horses. The sun was still up, but it was almost down when we got to that place. So we had made it in a day. We took the saddles off the horses; then I took them down to the cornfield and hobbled them there and came back inside the hogan. People were sitting all around; my mother was there with her sister's daughter. All the womenfolk started crying. They were sitting all around me, holding me and crying. Then they shook hands with my wife. Only my mother cried over her daughter-in-law. There were three old women, three sisters, besides my mother, living there together. Nephew Of Who Has Land's wife, who came for my mother that spring, was the oldest. The other two were mother's sisters.

After we had all shaken hands and while they were cooking I asked for an old wool carder. They gave me one and I walked over to the horses. I thought they must be all dry by now. I went up to them, and they were dry. They were white with dried sweat. I combed them with this wool carder, I carded all the sweat off of them and they were looking fresh again. About then Nephew Of Who Has Land came back. He said, "I have been up on the mountain." We shook hands there outside. He was eager to see me, and I was eager to see him, too. "When did you start?" he asked me. "You must have started yesterday." "No," I said, "we started early this morning, but not so very early. We started this morning just as the sun arose, and we just got here a while ago." He said,

"I didn't think a man could ride over here in a day. I didn't think one could make it." He was walking around the mule. "I didn't think a mule could make a trip like that. What a nice mule you have! It's got a nice build to it." While he was saying this he was walking around and looking at the mule.

About that time the sun was just starting to go down. "Did you come with the woman?" he asked me. "Yes," I said, "we both came." "That's nice," he said, "I am very glad you have come to visit us." "We feel just the same. We are glad we got here." Then he unsaddled his horse and turned him loose and went inside. When I got through I let my horses go and also went in. They laid out the food and we started eating. Then he said, "He told me something outside. He told me you had started this morning, but I hardly believed him. Is that true?" he asked my wife. She said, "Yes, we started this morning when the sun had just arisen." "I didn't believe it at first, but now, I guess you did make it in a day across this whole valley. I didn't think a horse could make it. But what strong horses you have. I don't think any of our horses around here could make it. However, if we tried, maybe we could, but I don't really think so. I know the distance." He was talking about that and about our horses, what strong horses they were, while we were eating.

His wife said, "Come and eat. What are you talking about? You ought to have horses like that. Every time you go to Round Rock or over here to the river, your horses always give up, and you'll be walking behind your horses and chasing them back. That's because you don't give them any exercise. You ought to have your horses like that. I know all your horses. They are all lazy. None of them can stand a trip, because you never go on them for a long journey. When you use them you only use them around here close by, and whenever you go a little distance they give up on you every time. So you ought to have horses like that—and stop talking about it, and come on and eat." Then he started eating and I started telling them what I had heard.

"We started from our home this morning, and while we were coming along by Where The Gray Hill Comes Out I

351

thought I would go over to the people who live there, so I went over by myself. I told my wife to go ahead. There those people said that a man had come to their place and this man had said that the people had some kind of sickness, some kind of disease, spreading among them; that the people had sore throats, swelling around the neck under the chin, and it was spreading awful fast, all up and down in the valley. That's what I heard from them this morning. While we were coming along we didn't see anybody, coming or going. We met nobody, and nobody met us, and we didn't stop any place around the hogans. So we don't know if that is true or not." They said, "That's what we heard too. They say all the people who live down in the valley have that swollen throat, around Upper Green Spot and all along that valley and over here Among The Black and down below here at a place called Rough Worthless Canyon. They all have the same disease. We don't know what kind of disease is spreading."

The man said, "When we were down to the Night Chant we didn't see or hear anything, but as we came back they said, 'A man had a sore throat and a swollen neck. Even though he was like that he put on a mask, and everybody was so scared of it. They all said that man shouldn't do that. Perhaps he knew he shouldn't do that, but he did it, so I think he is the one who is the cause of this sickness. That's the way some of us talked about it, for in the early years they said a man shouldn't put on a mask if he has a cold, or if he has a little sore on him, or if he has eye trouble or stomach trouble, or if he has some kind of sickness, he shouldn't put on a mask. And that's what this man did. Therefore we all think he is the one who caused it." Then he said, "We will put that off. We shouldn't talk about it, so we will let that go. I was up on the mountain, but I only wanted to go up for a ride. Only three camps are still up there. I didn't hear any news any place, so I have nothing to tell about it."

We talked for a while that evening, then I thought about the cornmeal. I reached over and got it out and said, "I got this cornmeal this morning. They told me to take it along, so I did. This is from Slim Man's wife. She told me, 'Early in the morning, while it's still dark, when morning is just rising, you go out and sacrifice to the morning. At morning you should use the white corn meal, and at midday use your corn pollen to sacrifice to the sun. And around in the evening, before it gets too dark, sacrifice to the sunset, while the sky is still nice and yellow.' That's what she said to me." My mother said, "That's right. You should have those things with you all the time. We should all have it, but none of us has anything like that now. One of you go out and get some corn and grind it up," she said. Then Having A Wife went out and brought in two white and two yellow ears. They started grinding it, and they told him that wasn't enough, so he went out again and brought in some more. They ground that and then mixed it with mine and tied them up separately, the white and the yellow, in a white cloth.

My mother said, "You should pray for yourself and sing for yourself. We should all do that. That's the way they used to do when I was young. When at any time a sickness started, like a cold, or sometimes some kind of sores that come on the whole body, or sore throats, everybody used to have corn-meal, and they all used to sing and pray for themselves, so that the sickness wouldn't spread, so the sickness wouldn't bother them, and so the sickness would go away soon." When they had it prepared we all went outside and began to sacrifice to the sunset. We picked the white meal up in our hands and sprinkled it around from the northeast towards the south, towards the west and towards the north, because we believe that anything bad goes on to the north. While we were sprinkling the meal we said, "The sickness won't bother us. It will never seize us. It will just pass us by. It won't bother us; it won't catch us and we won't catch it, and it will disappear right now. It will not spread. There will be no sickness among us. We will live well. We won't suffer from it. We will live well and be healthy." When we were through with that we all went back inside. Everybody fixed up his place, and we went to bed.

But while the rest were lying in bed we sat up. Nephew Of Who Has Land said to me, "Well, what is your plan? I would like to know about your plans. You must be planning to do something about your herd." I said, "Well, I don't know. I didn't make out any plans. I just happened to think that I would come over. That's what I would like to know too. I would like to know about the plan that you have. But I just came over to see how the herds are getting along, and I would like to see the bucks and billy goats. I wonder where they are. I am anxious to see them." He said, "We haven't any plans that we have made out. When we came across we got here with the herd and we went straight up the mountain with it. The herds are looking fine. We never lost any of them. And when we were driving them across not one of them gave up. So we have been upon the mountain all summer. We moved down not long ago. They are all looking nice, but I don't know about the bucks and billy goats. I heard that they still had them up on the mountain at the place called Where Old Men Die Off, so I don't know what they look like. However I believe they are taking good care of them. When Son Of Late Grey Hat moved across, when he moved back up here, at White Rock Sitting Around, he drove all the people away from that place. He has got his herd up there at a place called Sheep Butte, and he has his horses and cattle there, too. So that's what he did. When he moved back there he drove all the people who were living around there way on the other side. A lot of them used to live around the water at Black Rock Ridge; there was a man named Hosteen Rabbit, who used to live there with his whole outfit, and there were a lot of Red Clay who used to live there too; they all got chased out by him. He doesn't allow anyone to come around close to him. He has picked up a big place for his herd, horses and cattle. So he is living up there by himself now."

Then my mother got up and said, "They are all of them tired of herding now. At first, when we moved across, they put the herds together for two or three days. Then they separated them again, because, they said, it was too hard herding them that way. That's why they separated them again. One boy has been herding for me, that is one of my grandsons, but he is tired of herding now. I know he is, so I just herd myself on horseback. They all got tired herding for me. I don't know why they don't like to herd. I thought they were going to take care of my herd, and I thought they would take

354

care of me, but I don't know why they don't care about my herd, and they all don't care for me any more. I am suffering now, because I have to herd myself, and I don't even have any grub. They won't give me any grub. I was wishing for you all summer. I haven't got any grub now, not even a little coffee. When I think of you, when I look across to where you are, I start to cry. The crying doesn't do me any good, but I cry anyway. When I was with you I never suffered like this. I was never without grub, and here now I am suffering from starvation. Sometimes when I come in with the herd there will be nothing done, there will be no food saved for me. Then I just start crying. That's the way I am. I was wishing for you to come all summer. I was thinking, as soon as you come, before it gets too cold, while it's still warm, I wanted you to take the herds back. This is the way I was thinking about it."

Nephew Of Who Has Land said, "There isn't much feed for the stocks around here. I don't know how the stocks will make out this winter. We had no rain all summer. That's why everything is dry. The stocks live on sagebrush, and some other brushes besides, and the leaves of trees. That's all they live on. But those are the stocks that have been raised here. I don't know about your stock. I doubt if your herd would stand the weather, if you kept them here. That's the way it is. There is no feed around here, not enough grazing for the herds. So you think about it my younger brother. How about down where you are living? Is there much grazing there?" I said, "Yes, there is lots of grazing all around out in the flat up towards the foot of the mountain, and especially up on top of the mountain. We have rain every once in a while, and there is plenty of water around the washes and springs. So there is good grazing up there, and the stocks around there are all looking fine. They are all good and fat. It's that way all around out in the flat and along the foot of the mountain."

Early the next morning, while it was still dark, everybody got up. They built a fire and swept out some dirt, then they all started cooking. Nephew Of Who Has Land said, "How about meat? We haven't got any meat. Think about that." Then my mother said, "Don't just talk about it. One or two of you get the herds and kill one." The two boys went out to the herds up on the hill and drove them down close to the hogan. It was still dark. My mother said to me, "You go out and rope one. Hurry up, so we will have some meat." I picked up my rope and went out. There was a big herd. The two herds were together. These people used to have a herd bigger than ours. Most of theirs were all black. Ours were white. I roped a two-year-old wether and brought him up to the hogan and we killed that. The man said, "One isn't enough for all of us. Get another one." Then the boys roped another, so we killed two sheep that morning. They were all helping to butcher the sheep. My mother and her daughter-in-law were butchering one and the others were butchering the other. They had built a big fire, and they all started cooking, roasting meat outside. There was a whole lot of smoke all around, the smoke that comes from roasting meat.

Before we started eating we three went inside, the woman who was my wife and my mother and I. I said to my wife, "Get out ten dollars. I will give some to those whom I love the most." She took out a small buckskin sack and gave me ten dollars. I gave four dollars to the boy, my nephew, who had been herding for my mother. I gave one to my older sister, and two to Nephew Of Who Has Land, my older brother. The three dollars that were left I gave to my mother. Everybody was thankful about it. They all gave me thanks for the money. And there I was sitting without a cent in my hand.

After we ate we sat around and talked. I said to Nephew Of Who Has Land, "I would like to go to one of the stores. There is a store over at Round Rock and another over on the river. I would like to go to one of them. Could you lend me one of your horses? If you haven't any on hand perhaps I could borrow one from someone I know around here." He said, "I have got one which I was riding yesterday. That's the only one I have on hand. I think that will be all right. I think that horse can stand the trip to one of these places. You ought to go to the river. I think things are cheaper over there. When do you think you are going? Do you want to go

356

today?" I said, "That's what I was thinking. I think I will go this afternoon, and if I get there this evening sometime I will stay there tonight, and tomorrow I will get back sometime in the afternoon. Or perhaps I won't go until tomorrow. I would like to visit some of my relatives around here, too. There is my grandfather whom I would like to visit, Old Man Quiver, and there are others I would like to visit. Maybe I'll visit them first." When I said this my mother said, "You had better do that first, my son. They will be eager to see you, so you had better go around among them and visit them. Do that today, and tomorrow you can go to the store." I said, "I guess I'll do that, I'll go around and visit them today, and tomorrow I'll go to the river."

Nephew Of Who Has Land's sister-in-law said to me, "If you are going over there take a dollar, which you gave me, for some coffee." Then Nephew Of Who Has Land said to me also, "Take the two dollars which you gave me and get me some coffee and flour too." His wife said to him, "Why don't you go yourself? He will probably have a load of his own. We don't want to make too much of a load for him, so why don't you go yourself? One horse can't haul much of a load." "Where can I get a horse? I have loaned him mine. If I had a horse I would go," he said. "Borrow a horse from Beautiful's Mother. She has a horse. Ask her to lend it to you. I don't think she is going to use it today or tomorrow. So go over and ask her." He said, "Well, you go out and ask your younger sister if she would be willing to lend me her horse." "Why don't you go out yourself? Are you afraid to talk to her? You go out yourself and ask her. She won't say anything. If you ask her she will lend it to you." He said, "I don't like to ask her myself. Go out and ask her for me. If I ask her she might say she is going to use it, and she might not lend it to me. That's what I am afraid of." "Oh, you don't want to get up. That's all," she said. She shouted to her, "Beautiful's Mother, come in for a moment." She came in and said, "What do you want with me?" Her older sister said, "We would like to use your horse to go to the river, if you are not using it. I told him to go out and ask you, but here he is sitting like a mutt. He doesn't want to get up. That's all. So we

357

would like to use your horse to go to the store with." She said, "All right, you can have the horse. I'm not using it."

"Well, now we are going together, my younger brother," he said to me, "I'm glad I'm going with my younger brother. We will have a nice trip. I am glad we are going. We will go right now, while we have a horse." His wife said, "Don't talk that way. You are not going today, because your younger brother wants to go around and visit. I want him to go and visit today, and go tomorrow." My mother said, "We would like to get some grub as soon as we can, because my daughter-in-law says she has come for the herd. She wants to take the herd back to her country. And my daughter-in-law says this place isn't much good for our herd. There isn't any grazing around here; so that's why she says she wants to take the herd back. So I am glad about it." I said, "I guess we had better start tomorrow. We can start anytime tomorrow and take our time and we can stay at that place over night." "It's all right with me. You had better go around and visit first, my younger brother," he said to me. "Yes," I said, "I think I will do that. I will go around today."

Then Nephew Of Who Has Land said, "I was going to ask you something. While I am thinking about it now I think it's a good chance to ask you. That's about the woman there." He meant my wife. "I know the clan she belongs to, but I don't know her father's clan. What is her father's clan? And who is her father?" I said, "Her father is Bitter Water, and we call him Mr. Tooth. So she is Mr. Tooth's daughter." He said, "Oh, is that right? I know him very well. So that's her father? So she is a daughter to me?" And he got up and walked over to her and shook hands with her, saying, "My daughter, my baby, I didn't know you were my daughter. But now I know you are, my daughter, my baby." She said, "I didn't know you either, but I know you now, my father." They hadn't shaken hands till that day. So that's where they got to know each other. Then he walked back to his place and sat down again. His wife said, "So she's your daughter. If she is your daughter what do you want to hate her for? You said you hated her very much, because she was married to the same outfit that you are married to, because you and she are married to one clan. Didn't you say that?" she asked him. Then she turned around to my wife, "He was saying that about you. He said he hated you because you are married to the same clan that he is married to. That's why he said he hated you very much." They laughed, and he said, "No, no, my daughter, don't believe them. They are just trying to make trouble for us. Don't believe them. I never said anything about you, my daughter." They had their little joke there. Then he said, "I am really Bitter Water. Years ago, the story is, that there used to be just one outfit of Bitter Water. Somehow or other some branched off. They travelled around, and soon they got to a place called Deer Spring. There was water there, and it was a nice place, and there they located. They became so well acquainted with this place that they didn't want to leave; and that's where a lot of them were raised. Pretty soon there were a lot of people who had been raised there, so they were called Deer Spring People. Then some others branched off from Bitter Water. They located at a place called Clumped Trees, so they happened to be called Clumped Tree People. However we really belong to Bitter Water. So I am Bitter Water."

I said, "I guess I'll start to go around and visit. I will go up to my mother's sister's place first. I guess the horses will be all right." He said, "Yes, you just go ahead and visit. The horses will be all right. They have enough to eat. There are a whole lot of cornstalks there, and there is water right there too, right in the middle of the cornfield, so you don't need to worry about them."

When I got home from visiting my mother's sister's place there was a crowd of people there, most of them old women. A lot of them were from down below. Some were Bigatxa's children, and some of them were Old Wagon's children. He was my older brother. His two wives and children were there. The two women were sisters. There was a crowd outside under the shade, and the same inside the hogan. I went around among them and shook hands. I shook hands with all who were outside; then I went inside and shook hands with all of them. A little while after I returned my mother's sister came in. As soon as she came in she said, "I came here to see my son's wife." She walked up to her and they shooks hands with each other. My mother said, "That's what they are saying, every one of them. When they came here they all said the same." Then some more came. That was Nephew Of Who Has Land's outfit. Some of his relatives came. So there was a big crowd there all that day. They were all eating; everybody had a good time all day. I said, "I started from here and went straight to my mother's place. That mother of mine there," I said, pointing to my mother's sister. "Then I started from there again; I went to another hogan. There were only womenfolk at home. From there I went down to Stout Man's place. He was all alone. I sat around with him for a while, then I went to Bitahni Clansman's Younger Brother's place, and there he and his wife were home, and his daughter was sick. She had a swollen throat. Little Deer Spring was treating her all night last night. He went home this morning. I looked at the girl and she was awful sick. I don't think she will live." Nephew Of Who Has Land said, "I was there the other day, and she was suffering from it, but there was no one there treating her." When he said this his wife said to him, "Well, why didn't you let us know about it? You never let us know."

Another woman said, "Yesterday one of my daughters got a swollen throat, and last night she had a pain from it, and this morning one side of her throat was swollen. She said, 'I would like to see my father. Tell my father to come and see me. Tell him I would like to see him.' That's what she said this morning." She meant me. I said, "It's quite a distance down to that place." "Don't talk about the distance," my mother said, "You go down and see your daughter. I thought you came to visit around. So you better go down and see her." I said, "I will go over after I eat something. I haven't eaten anything yet, since this morning." Then while the rest were eating my woman started cooking something for me. After I ate I said, "I guess I'll go down to that place. I may be gone all day." The womenfolk from down below were starting back and I said, "I guess I'll go back to their place with them." My wife said, "What are you trying to do? You are trying to go around among the sickness. Perhaps it's some-

360

thing dangerous. You had better stay here." I said, "You must not talk that way about the sickness. You must not be afraid."

That morning we had all said our prayers, but we didn't say any prayers at midday, because there was a big crowd at our place. I went out and started after the womenfolk. When I caught up with them another woman said, "One of my daughters said she had a sore throat this morning, too." When we got back to where the girl was sick, she was lying in bed. As soon as I got inside she sat up. I walked up and sat down by her and she put her arm around my neck and started to cry for a moment. Then she let me go and said, "I heard that you had come, my father. That's why I wanted you to come and see me. I like seeing you so much. I got an awful pain in my throat yesterday morning. When I got up I had a sore throat. It wasn't swollen. It just hurt me when I swallowed my spit, or whenever I swallow anything it hurts me. And last evening it started swelling, and it grew big this morning, so I don't know what to do about it." The right side of her throat was swollen. I felt around with my fingers and it was kind of soft, but hard in the middle, and the other side was just coming up. "I don't know what to do about it either, my daughter," I said. She said, "I have an awful pain from it, and that's why I wanted you to come over and see me, my father. Just to see me, that's all. I don't know where my father went to, but he's not good for anything. He just goes around all the time, and he doesn't know anything. He knows nothing at all." I said, "I am just the same too, my daughter, my baby. I don't know what to do for you. I haven't got anything with me."

Then I said to the others, "Have you got a piece of shell?" They said, "Yes, we have got a piece." I said, "Give me that." They searched and got it out and I told them to warm some water in a cup. They warmed a little water and I rubbed this shell on a stone. The powder that I made from it I put in the water. Then I had the gall of a wild animal and the gall of birds, all mixed up, I had this tied up in a little buckskin sack. I got that out and put some in this warm water and mixed it with the shell and I gave that to her. I told her to

361

swallow some. "Don't drink it down so fast. Just swallow it as slowly as you can and keep some in your mouth. Hold it in your mouth and kind of work it around in your mouth and throat, and rub some on the swelling. I think it will cure you." She did as I told her to do. And they brought in the other girl, who had contracted a sore throat that morning. They wanted some for her, so I gave her some, too. She was a small girl, about three or four years of age. The other was about fifteen or sixteen. I hadn't expected anything, but there I got a single saddle blanket from my daughter. I got a ring from the others. That's what I got for my treatment there. The saddle blanket had been used quite a bit, and the ring was just a plain one, with no settings in it, only the silver. After I did this little treating I started back.

There was a little arroyo close by. Just as I got to this, just as I was starting down, I heard a footstep behind me. I looked back; there was the girl's mother coming after me. Just as I looked back she grabbed me. I was scared. As soon as she grabbed me she put her arm around my neck. "What kind of medicine have you got? I would like to know. Please, my man, I would like to know. What kind of medicine did you use on her?" I said, "What is it? Has the medicine done anything to her? Is she unconscious? Or what?" "No," she said. "She says the medicine worked on her so quickly, and she says she is feeling well all over. This medicine has set on the swollen place and she said, 'It's feeling good, and the pain has settled down.' So that's why I would like to know what medicine you have." I got scared of two things. I thought the medicine had made her worse, and when she put her arm around me I was sacred of her husband.

I started down the arroyo with her, and she kept holding me around the neck. When I got to the foot of the bank I sat down. She sat down too, by my side, close to me. I said, "Why are you holding me against yourself so tightly? And what are you calling me "my man" for? You shouldn't call me that. That's one way to call a fellow, but neither of us has ever touched the other. Why do you happen to call me that?" She said, "Once you came across from your country to here, and you stopped at Tall Man's place. From here Tall Man loaned

362

you a horse, and you went over the mountain. While you were coming back from that place, you came back by Sheep Butte, and there is where we met. But we never touched each other. Even at that my man claims that we had touched each other. That is the way he talks to me, every once in a while. That's why I am calling you "my man," even though we have never touched each other. That's what he wants us to do. If he didn't want us to do that he wouldn't talk to me like that."

I said, "Oh, yes, I remember that we did meet each other there, but I never thought anything of the kind. I know we had been talking to each other for quite a long while. But that was no silly talk. We never did act silly toward each other. I know I asked you about where the people lived, I know we had been there quite a while, but I never did see anybody around at that time." "Neither did I," she said, "I never saw anybody around, but perhaps someone had seen us far off while we were talking to each other. Way back, a few years ago, the first time you moved across here, not long after the old man, Old Man Hat, had died, maybe you remember that too?" she asked me. "Yes," I said, "I remember." "That's the first time, he claims, that we had been around. And one of his sons doesn't call him father at all, because he thinks that my son is your son, so he doesn't call him son. He calls his son Abaa's grandson. That's what he calls his son, even though it's really his son. And this younger daughter of mine, she is now five years of age, he doesn't call her my daughter. He claims she is your daughter, too. So that's twice that he thinks we have been together. That's why I am acting foolish toward you."

I said, "What you are asking me for is not a medicine at all. Maybe you thought it was some kind of weed, but it's not. What I have is gall, gall that comes from different kinds of birds, from eagles and so forth, and different kinds of animals, from bear and so forth. The gall of these birds and animals. So that's no medicine. So what do you want with that thing? You don't want to have anything like that." "Even at that," she said, "I wanted to know what it is, I want you to give me some. I mean it, please, let me have a little." She kept on calling me "my man." I said, "Have you got anything to put it on?" "No," she said, "I haven't got anything." "This thing has got to be put on a buckskin, and it shouldn't be just given away, so I don't want to give you some for nothing, even though you call me that." She said, "If we go back to the hogan I think I can find a piece of buckskin, and maybe I will find something else besides to give to you." She kept on calling me the same thing. I said, "What do you think about me, when my older brother talks to you like that? How do you think about me?" "I always think that if at any time I get to see you again we will do what he claims we have been doing. When he talks to me like that I always want to do it. That's the way I am thinking about you." "Do you mean it?" "Yes," she said, "I mean it." "Well, then, if I were to tell you we will hide away someplace would you do it?" I asked her. "Sure," she said, "That's what I would like to do." I said, "Well, we will see later on, but not now. We will go back to the hogan, and there I will give you a little of what I have got." When she got up she said, "I mean it, that you are mine now. Even though we haven't't done anything yet, you are mine and I am yours."

I laughed about it, and then we went back to the hogan. Before we got back I put my arm around her and turned her head towards me and said, "Have you ever been kissed?" "Sure," she said, "I have been kissed lots of times." I said, "Do you like to be kissed?" "Sure that's what I think of most." Then we kissed each other back and forth for a while, and went on. As soon as we got back inside the hogan I said to my daughter, "Your mother has done something to me, and she wanted me to come back home with her. She wanted me to stay here. What do you think about that, my daughter?" She laughed; she didn't say anything. Her mother said, "It's he himself who did something to me. He has worked on me, so that's why I brought him back, and I am going to hold him here now." My daughter was lying down there and laughing about it. Then I said, "You better not talk that way before my daughter. She might tell her father." The woman said, "No, she won't tell. She doesn't care to tell anything to her father, and she knows all about what he always says to me about you."

Then she reached over a pile of things and got out half a buckskin. I told her to cut out a piece where it was thin. She cut out a piece and stretched it and gave it to me. I said, "This thing shouldn't be given out with one's fingers. It's got to be taken out with an arrowhead." "I have got some of those too," she said. She got one out; it was a nice long arrowhead. She gave that to me, and I dipped out this stuff with it four times on the buckskin. Then I gave it to her. She lifted it close to her mouth and inhaled the gall, saying, "Thanks. I haven't got anything to give you for this. How about that arrowhead?" I said, "This is what I have been wishing for." She gave it to me; she told me to keep it. "I give you that for this," she said. I did the same; I inhaled the arrowhead because it now belonged to me; I would live long by means of it, and I would have it all my life. Then I put it in my pocket. She was thankful about what I had given her. Again she said, "Thanks," and inhaled the gall again. We were there, talking to each other, silly, for a while, and it got hard. It kind of moved me around it got so hard, and I didn't know what to do about it. I could easily have worked on her, but I just couldn't make up my mind to do it. I knew she was just the same way too. I knew it by the way she was sitting. She was moving around too, working her legs, squeezing them together, but I didn't want to do it, even though I was all aching from that, because I had just treated the girl a while ago. If I had not treated the girl I could have worked on her. So I started out. When I crossed the arroyo where she caught me, from there on I started walking kind of weak. I think that hardness caused it.

When I got home the crowd that had been there was gone. Nobody was there. None of the womenfolk were at home, only my older brother. The sun was almost down. I asked, "Where have all the rest gone to?" He said, "A little while after you left they all went over to Bitahni Clansman's Younger Brother's place, and they haven't come back yet. How about down there?" I said, "The oldest girl had a swollen throat on one side, the right side. However on the other side the swelling is just beginning. Another girl, a small girl, has a sore throat too, but it hasn't started swelling yet. They told me to do something for them, so I did." He asked me. "What did you use? What did you put on, my younger brother?" "Oh," I said, "I just got different kinds of weeds that grow around the cornfield." "What kind of weeds? What do they look like?" "Oh, I just went over to the cornfield and pulled up all the weeds that were around there, so I don't know what they look like." "Tell me what kind of weeds and what the name of the weeds are that you used, my younger brother. Tell me, please, so I will know." "No," I said, "You mustn't talk about it. You must not ask for a thing like that, while there is no sickness around here at your place. If someone were sick, or if you were sick, then I would give you some and tell you what it is, but not when you are well. So you must not ask for it or talk about it," I said to him. I said it because he was trying to get after me about it; he was pressing me close about it. When I said this, I guess he was kind of scared and he quit asking me about it.

We were sitting there when two of the womenfolk came back. That was Red's Mother and her youngest sister. My wife, my mother, and Beautiful's Mother were still up there. When they returned they said, "That poor baby is going to be a goner. There is just no hope for her. She lay there just breathing a little. It's a shame they didn't do anything for her. They have lost her now. If they had done something for her right away they might have saved her, but now I don't think anybody could do anything for her, because she is too far gone. But, anyway, they have gone for a medicine man. But I don't think he can do anything. Perhaps he will do something, but it won't do her any good. When we got there, only his relative was there and his wife, and Red's Mother's wife. They were just frightened. They don't know what to do about it, so they were just holding their little baby." I thought, "I'll go over." But I just couldn't make up my mind to go because I knew she was too far gone. "Even if I did something for her it wouldn't do her any good," I thought. When the sun was over the rocky hill my wife and my mother and Beautiful's Mother came back. They said the same. "There's no hope for the poor little one. The poor little thing

366

is dying. They haven't brought Son Of Angry Talker yet, but I don't think he could do anything. I don't think she will live long," my mother said. "I felt it with my hands, around all over the swelling, and it was hard. The poor thing is about to choke. I don't think she will pull through the night." They were talking about it like that, while they were beginning to cook, but when they had put out the food none of us could eat, for we were all in sadness. After we had eaten a little, I know none of us ate much, they put the things away and we sat around for a while. Evening had come. It was a nice evening, a nice sunset. We had all said our prayers outside, then we came back in and sat around in sorrow. When it got real dark they said, "Two of you had better go over again to see how they are coming along." But none of us went. We stayed up late that night. I said, "We shouldn't go to bed early when an illness or some kind of disease is going around like this. We shouldn't go to sleep early. You must go to sleep late in the evening. The same in the morning, you shouldn't sleep late. As soon as you get up go outside, and if you have some white corn meal, sprinkle that to the morning and sacrifice to the morning, and at midday use your corn pollen, and around in the evening use the yellow corn meal. If you haven't got any kind of corn meal, if you only have corn pollen, use that in the morning, at midday, and in the evening. And you must say your prayers three times a day. In that way illness of any kind won't bother you. It will be far away from you. This is what I heard from some of the older people," I said. Then they all said, "We didn't know anything about that. We don't even know how to say our prayers." I told them what to say for themselves. "Just beg that you will never get any kind of sickness, or any kind of disease, and believe me you won't get it, because I have done it and I know. So you must pray for yourselves."

Early in the morning, while it was still dark, when the sun was just rising, we got up and went outside and sacrificed to the morning and said our prayers. When we were through we went back inside, and the womenfolk were crying. I thought, "I'll go over," and I said, "I'll go over and see what they are doing." Nephew Of Who Has Land said, "We will go." I said, "All right, let's go." We got there while it was still dark. The girl had died and Bitahni Clansman's Younger Brother was holding his daughter, he was holding his daughter on his lap, crying as hard as he could, crying like a woman and his wife was there too, shedding tears. We both sat down beside him and talked for a long time. Then he quieted down. He let go of his daughter and said, "I will fix her myself, the way I want to, so that I won't be worrying about her so much. That's why I want to fix her up myself." He told us, "You two had better go on home." When we returned from there we told the womenfolk what had happened. They asked us about Son Of Angry Talker, but I said, "We don't know anything about him. We didn't ask about him. Maybe he came, maybe he didn't, because some of the Singers are afraid. When a patient is about to die, if they know that a patient is about to die, they are afraid to come, so maybe, he knew about it and didn't come. We didn't see him there this morning, so I don't think he came." Then all the womenfolk started crying. Some of them were related to the girl, and my mother was her grandmother, so they all started crying. When they were through crying they started cooking. They cooked some food and laid it out, but we didn't eat much again, on account of that. We couldn't eat at all. We just couldn't swallow the food. When we tried to swallow it it stuck in our throats.

After we ate Nephew Of Who Has Land said, "I guess we had better go to the store this morning, my younger brother, because, I think, you are in a hurry to go back, and I think you had better. You know there is a serious thing spreading around. We don't know what will happen, so we will go to the store today, and we will try to come back as soon as we can. I would like you to stay with us for a while yet. If it weren't like this I would have kept you here with me for a few days, but when there is sickness going around, there is no happiness. We can't stay together in joy. We don't want to gather together in sorrow, so I think it will be a good thing if you return to your country as soon as you can." I said, "All right, we will go to the store today, and when we

368

come back from there I will think about moving back." While he was after the horses I said to my wife, "Take good care of our horses. Let them go without a hobble in the daytime. Just turn them loose, and around toward evening hobble the horse so he won't run away from us. But don't bother with the mule. Leave the mule alone. I know the mule won't get away, because he is only following the horse. But don't forget to hobble the horse at evening." And I said, "You go ahead and work on the meat. Have it good and dry. We'll use that on the way back." She said, "All right, I'll do that, and I'll remember all."

About then he had brought the horses back and we put the saddles on them and started off. We went right along; we never stopped until we got to the river at a place called Cut Off Mountain. There in the cottonwoods along by the river were some hogans. He said, "Let's go over to those hogans. Some Standing House people live there. Maybe we will get something to eat. We have some lunch, but it's all dry." So we turned around and went over. There were only three women at home. He said, "Where is the man?" One of them said, "I think they have gone to where some fellows are gambling. There's gambling going on above here where Tsisko lives. I think they have gone up there." Nephew Of Who Has Land said, "We would like to stop here for a while. Can you feed our horses for us, and feed us, too?" Immediately they all said, "Sure, just take the saddles off your horses and let them cool off, and then turn them loose in the cornfield. We have all the corn off the stalks." We were so glad about it. They all started to get at the cooking. One started fixing up the fire; one started setting out the dishes, and one went for water. They cooked some food for us, but they didn't have any meat. When they put out the food we got out the meat which we had along for our lunch; it was already boiled. We laid it out and pushed some towards them and we all started eating.

They were so thankful for the meat. "We were so hungry for meat," they said. "We are glad to have tasted some of your meat." We said, "We are also so thankful about the good food. We were so hungry too. We haven't eaten much

369

since yesterday, because we were put in sadness. A girl took sick. She had a swollen throat, and early this morning she died right close by us and the womenfolk were all crying, so that's why we didn't eat much. We were so hungry, but now we have had enough and we are so thankful to you all." We lay around there for a while after we ate. Then Nephew Of Who Has Land said, "I guess we had better start again. I guess our horses have had enough, so we had better go now." We went over to the cornfield and got our horses and saddled them up again.

Then he said to them, "On our way back we will stop here again. Could you give us some more food if we stop?" Again they all said, "Sure, just stop here again. We are only too glad to give you some more." Then they asked about me. "We know you well," they said to him, "But who is that man? We don't know him." He said, "He is from far away, from Black Mountain, from a place called Anything Falls In. There is where he is from. He came to our place two days ago from there. Don't you know him?" "No, we don't know him," said the oldest one. "Don't you know they used to move all around here among us. The woman whom we call Abaa is his mother." Then the older woman said, "Oh, yes, I remember now. At that time he was young, but now he is getting old." She said this even though I was just a young man. Then he asked about the trail and the crossing, and they told us which trail to take and about the crossing. "When you start across you will get into a deep place for a little way; then from there on it's not so very deep," they said. While we were going along toward the river he said, "That younger one used to be married to 'you.' She married a Bitahni, but it looks as though she is not married now. When we come back to their place again we will see about it. If she hasn't got a man we will stay there tonight. Those other two are holding on to one man. They both have the same husband." I said, "I don't want to stay there over night. They might take all our things away from us. We can stop for lunch; that's all." He said, "All right," and we went on. We went across and down, following the river. It was quite a way from there to the store (Aneth). This store was run by a man called Round.

While we were tying up our horses he came out and shook hands with us, calling us "my friends." He said, "Come in. Take your things inside. Untie your things and get them down off your horses." We took the things off our horses, and the trader picked up the skins and hides Nephew Of Who Has Land had brought along, and we went inside after him. He weighed the skins and hides, then he threw them back into the other room. At that time skins and hides used to be worth a little more than they are now. Then he started trading. He got two sacks of flour, some coffee and sugar, baking powder and salt, some calico and little things. When he finished I started in. I got two sacks of flour and baking powder with it, coffee and sugar. I only bought a little grub for myself, about five dollars worth. Then I bought some calico for my mother with the three dollars I gave her, and a pair of overalls, shirt, and red scarf for the boy. That was for the four dollars that I gave him. After we got our things fixed up we took them outside where our horses were standing. Then I thought about the .44 cartridges, but I didn't have anything to buy them with, only the single saddle blanket that I got for the little treating I did. I took that off from under the saddle and took it inside and said to him, "I forgot all about the cartridges." While I was saying this I laid the saddle blanket on the counter. He picked it up and put it on the scales. He weighed it, after he weighed it he threw it back in the other room, and gave me a dollar for it. I asked him, "How much is a box of cartridges?" "A dollar a box. There are fifty cartridges in a box," he said. So he gave me a box and I went out, put my things on the horse, tied them to the saddle, and we started back.

When we got back to where we had stopped before we unsaddled our horses, we turned them loose in the cornfield. Then we sat down against our stuff outside under the shade where they had the fire. He said, "Make us some coffee and a little lunch." They said, "Well put out your coffee and flour." He took out a package of coffee and said, "Take half of it, and give me back the other half," but they took the whole package away from him. Then I told them to give me a pan. They gave me one and I put some flour in it. I gave it to them and said, "You probably have some baking powder yourself." One said, "Yes," and one said, "No." But the one who said, "Yes," said yes first. So I said, "Well, then, I won't put in any baking powder, as long as you have some yourself." Then the one who had said "No," said to the other one, "Why didn't you say no, too? You ought to say no, so that he can give us some." I only gave them a little flour. I didn't want to let them have a whole sack, and I didn't want to let them take the flour out themselves, because I was afraid they might take it away from me. I gave them a pan full, then I lay against my things again. They all started cooking. "There was nobody at the store," he said. They said, "Maybe they are all up at Tsisko's place, where they are gambling."

I started whispering to Nephew Of Who Has Land. I said, "As soon as we eat lunch we'll go on again. I don't want to stay around here long, because I am afraid they might get after us for our things. That's the way they talk, and that's the way they look, and that's the way they are acting toward us, so we had better go right after we eat lunch. I don't want to stay here all day and all night." He said, "All right, we'll go right after we eat." I was glad when he said that. So right after we ate we got our horses and saddled them up again. While he was still putting some things in a sack he called for his package of coffee, and the one to whom he gave the coffee said, "The coffee is mine now, because you gave it to me, so it's mine." He didn't say any more about it, and they said, to me, "You haven't given us anything yet. You must be stingy. You didn't give us a little coffee or anything." I said, "I wish I could. If the things belonged to me I could have given you something, but the things I have got are not mine. I only came to the store for some people. So they are not mine." One of them said, "Oh, you are just saying that out of devil-try. I know very well the things all belong to him." I said, "No, I mean it. The things are not mine. If they were mine I sure would give you some."

By then we had the things all tied to our saddles, and we started coiling up our ropes. While we were tying our ropes to the saddles they said, "What are you hurrying for? You ought to stay for the night. Soon the sun will be down, and it won't be long then before morning comes again, so you ought to stay with us tonight." Then he whispered to me, "Let's go. Let them talk. I know what they want to do with us, so let's go." We got on our horses and started off. The sun was pretty well down. We went on, but we didn't get home that night. We went as far as a place called White Cliff On Mesa. Then it got too dark on us, so we stopped. We laid our saddle blankets on the ground and went to sleep. In the morning we started on again, until a little after noon.

As soon as we got to the hogan all the womenfolk came out. They were all happy, because we had brought back plenty of food. They were all glad and thankful about it. They started cooking, some of them making coffee, some roasting, some boiling meat, some frying tortillas, and, after all was done, we started eating. That day I said, "I think we will start back tomorrow morning, while we have some grub." My mother said, "Yes, that's what I was thinking too, while it's nice and cool." She said to my wife, "You start in now to have the things ready, and have the lunch ready, so you won't be bothered with it tomorrow. Boil some of the dried meat. After you boil it take it out and pound it with rocks. Have it good and soft and put it in a sack. Then all you need to do is open the sack and eat it every time you stop for lunch. Have all your things ready. Have everything ready to be put on the horses." She said, "I will, but I think I won't boil the meat. I will let it go the way it is because I like it when it's dry." My mother said, "All right, take it the way you want to."

I asked about the two girls that I had treated. "How about the two girls who had sore throats? How are they getting along? One had a swollen throat; the other was just starting." They said, "They are all right. The one that had the swollen throat, the swelling on her is down, so we think she is well now. There are two children and an older one who have the same thing up here. That's what we heard. We don't know how they are getting along." We sat around waiting for the good nice evening. Then, at the time when it gets to be so nice toward evening, we went out, took the yellow corn meal and sacrificed to the sunset and said our prayers. The next morning we took out the white corn meal and made our morning offering, and, after we had said our prayers, we went back inside and they started cooking.

After we ate they all went over to separate the herds. Even the small children went, and only the two of us, my wife and I, stayed at the hogan. While she was getting the things ready I went after the horses and brought them back and put the saddles on them. When we were about through packing—my wife had left some food there for my mother, flour, coffee, sugar and things like that—they all came back. "We got the herds separated," they said. "We separated them and your mother has taken the herd down." Then we got on our horses and started off. We went down and started following the wash, and when we got to where the wash comes out into the open there she was just crossing to Flowing Out To One Place. There we caught up with her. We shook hands with her. "Take good care of the herd, and take good care of yourselves, my children," she said to us. "I hope you get across without any trouble. Don't attempt to stop any place for two or three days. Just keep on going till you get back to our country. And when you get back with the herds take very good care of them. And I will be back there too, perhaps late in the fall; but before it gets too cold. I wanted to go back with you right now, but my children want me to stay with them for a while yet. So that's why I want to stay."

But I found out later that the reason she wanted to stay was because she had a man there. This man's name was Son Of Dead Belcher. He was Red Clay. He visited her every once in a while, but she never told us about it, and none of the people there had said anything about it. I don't know why they didn't let us know. Perhaps they thought I might not like it. I said, "Well, I guess, my wife will take good care of the herd. That's what she says, so I think she will take good care of them. I don't know about myself. I think I'm going hunting with my father. My father has gone over the mountain; as soon as he returns he wants me to go hunting with him. I don't know when he will be back. Maybe he'll be back before we are; maybe not." She said, "I am very glad you both came, and I'm very glad you wanted to take the herd

374

back with you, because they all got tired of my herd. I thought they were going to take good care of the herd for me. They were taking good care at first, but then, all at once, they got tired of it. They just let the boy herd alone, but he doesn't take care of them well. Pretty soon he got tired of it, too, and began to run away from the herd. So I had to herd myself most of the time, and you know very well that I can't stand herding. So it was too much for me. But now I am very glad you are taking them back with you. I don't know why they all want me to stay with them for a while yet; so I thought I would."

I said, "That's the way it is everywhere. Nobody will try to take as good care as you want them to. Nobody will take good care of things which don't belong to them. You always talk about your relatives, saying they will take good care of your herd and yourself. You have found out now how they are. The time you wanted to move I tried to back you off, I tried to turn you down, but you just didn't mind me. You went, and now you are saying that none of them are taking care of you. That's the way it is all around. No matter where you go nobody will take care of your things and yourself. Everybody tends to his own things, to his own work. Nobody will try to work for you. Now, I guess, you have found out all about it." Then I told my wife to go ahead with the herd. She went after the herd, and I said, "And she is just the same. You don't know anything about her, and I don't know anything about her, even though I am staying with her. She gets kind of funny towards me every once in a while, so I don't know what she will do with the herd. Maybe she really means what she said to you. Maybe she will take good care of the herd, or maybe not. Neither of us knows anything about her. And as soon as my father returns I will go hunting with him, and I will be away from the herd for I don't know how many days, and she will be all alone. But I'll see about it when we get back. Maybe I'll take the herd someplace; maybe I'll let her take care of it. However, I'll know what to do about it when we get back."

Then I started off, and my mother went back too. When I had almost caught up with my wife I thought about the bucks and billy goats. I had forgotten all about them. When I caught up with her I said, "I have forgotten all about the bucks and billy goats." She said, "I was thinking about it yesterday but I forgot about it again. From there on I never thought of it any more." "Well," I said, "You go ahead with the herd. You know how we came and I'll go back." I started back and caught up with my mother before she got to the hogan. I told her, "I have forgotten all about the bucks and billy goats." She said, "I was thinking about it, but I thought it would be too hard for you. There are only two of you, and it would be hard, driving them with the herd. I thought you would have a lot of trouble with them, so that's why I didn't say anything about it. But they will be all right. We can get them and take them across some time. It's too late now to go after them. They are way up on the mountain. It's a long way to that place. If you go after them now you won't get them down before tomorrow evening. So you had better just let them go." I asked her, "When you start back from there can you take them along with you?" "No," she said, "I don't think I can handle them. They will all run away from me. However, we'll get them across sometime. We'll let them herd them for us for a time yet." So I let them go and turned around and started back after the herd again. I was so sorry for the bucks and billy goats.

I caught up with my wife way out in the flat, and there I noticed the herd wasn't as big as it was the time they started them across. I said, "The herd seems to be small to me." She said so too. "It was a little over one thousand," I said, "They are now close to nine hundred." My mother hadn't said anything to me about the herd, so I don't know what had happened to the rest of them. I was sorry for that too, that the herd was so small. But we said, "I guess she has used them for something for herself, or maybe she has given some away around where there were doings. That's what she always does," we said. That night we stopped at the place called Water At The Edge Of The Cliff. We took the herd into the little cave there, and we camped out in the open in front of the cave. The next morning early we started off again without anything to eat. We took the herd down to the foot of the cliff, then across the valley straight toward Big Oak. We drove the herd into the little canyon there. It was quite a little canyon with caves all around.

In these caves the water was dripping down. We took the things and saddles off the horses and made a fire and boiled some coffee and ate our lunch. After that we sat around waiting for it to get cool. A little after noon it got cloudy. A breeze came up and it got cool. Then we started on again. When we got to the top of this little canyon a man came riding right straight towards us. He rode up to us, and that was Slim Grey Hat. He was a member of the Tangle People Clan. I shook hands with him and he called me younger brother. He said, "This morning my children saw the herd come down from the rocks and go across the valley, and they saw it go into this little canyon. Then they saw smoke arise, and I thought I would come over to see who it was, and that was you, my younger brother. Can you give me a sheep? I am hungry for one. Our herd is not here. It's far away, so we are without the herd down in that cornfield," he said, as he pointed way out across the valley. "That's where my place is," he said. Then he reached down in his pocket and got out two dollars and gave that to me. Then I rounded up the herd and gave him one of the ewes. "Thank you very much, my younger brother. I will have good meat." He tied the sheep's legs together and carried it back alive.

Then we started off again. We kept on going straight to Bank Always Caves Onto The Water. When the sun was pretty well down we got to this place. There the sheep had water, and we watered our horses and had some water ourselves. It was a nice cool place around this water. From there on it was nice and cool, because it was cloudy, and there was a little breeze. We kept on going, crossing a little valley, until it got dark. The next morning we started off. We didn't have anything to eat again that morning. At noon we got to Baby Rock wash. There was a lot of water. The herd had enough water there. We made a fire and took the saddles and things off the horses, and the herd lay down on the ground. There was no grass of any kind, only greasewood, so I tied the horses the the greasewood, and we made some coffee and ate

377

lunch. Then I thought of going to the cornfields. There were some cornfields up towards Baby Rock. It was quite a long way to where they were. After we ate I said, "I'll go to those cornfields and see what people live there. Perhaps I know some of them. I might get some cornstalks from them for the horses." I tied up the mule good and tight and started over on horseback. Two hogans were sitting up quite a ways apart. A horse was standing by the lower hogan, so I started for that one.

Some people I didn't know were sitting around. I got off my horse and walked up to where they were sitting. Sure enough, I didn't know them. Only the women were home, four or five of them sitting around. I said, "Where's the man?" Then the woman who was rather old said, "The man went down below with his son. They went down to the lower part here this morning. Some kind of sickness is going around all over, up the valley and down the valley and all around, all over down at Upper Green Spot, and all over around Cottonwood Rows. A lot of children, some small and some grownup, and some adults, a lot of them have died off on account of this sickness. That's what we are hearing about every day and every night. It is something awful that is happening all around. And so the old man and his son went down below where a lot of people live. A man was tied up down there. This man we call Hanging From His Neck.[1] The people who live down there claim he caused this sickness. They all claim that he is the one who called this sickness down upon the people. They got to thinking this way about him, because they said, 'He is a witch.' So that's why they caught him. He is tied up in a bundle, they say. They tied up his legs and his arms behind him, and they have him tied there to something. That's the way we heard about it. That's why the man went down there to see about it."

I said, "Who is the man? I don't know him. What clan does he belong to, and what is his name?" She said, "He is Red House, and everybody calls him Hosteen Fast Runner." I

1. According to Left Handed (when questioned) two men were killed as witches, Hanging From His Neck and Hairy Beads.

said, "Oh, yes, I don't know of him, but I have heard of him lots of times." She asked, "How about around where you are from?" "I don't know. We passed here the other day and went across to Water Flowing Out; around that place it was just starting. Only one girl has died from it. I think it is just beginning around the foot of the mountain. It's the same around Rough Worthless Canyon, and all down in the valley to Hogans Sitting Up and all over, they say. I don't know about our place. We have been across to Water Flowing Out, where we started from two days ago, but we didn't see or meet anybody all day the day before yesterday, not until yesterday noon when a man came to us. We gave him a sheep. He wanted one so we gave him one, but we didn't talk much with him, so we didn't hear anything from each other. And yesterday, from there on, we didn't see anybody, until now. We stopped down here at the water. The horses didn't have anything to eat; there was nothing to eat for the horses, so I came to see if you would give me some corn stalks." She said, "Yes, you can have some. There are some piled around in back of the brush hogan. Take as much as you want." "That's what I came for," I said. I tied some up in a bundle with my rope; then I gave all the women thanks and started back with a big bundle of corn stalks.

We gave them to the horses and while we were waiting for them to get enough feed I told her what I had heard from that woman. She said, "Maybe the sickness is all over the country. I wonder how it is over at our country." But I didn't say anything about it; I just said, "We had better go again. I guess the horses have had enough eating now." We left and crossed the valley. When we got to a place called Flat Sloping Up the sun was almost down, but I said, "We will stop and camp here again for tonight." We were glad that we were getting close to our place. The next day we went along all day and got to Many Lakes that evening. There we camped again that night, close to our place. We didn't bother to eat the next morning. We started off with the herds from there, crossing a big flat. Finally we got to Many Streams. It was almost noon time. There wasn't much water there. Even though many streams were flowing down from the rocks it wasn't enough

379

for the herd, but they got a little and we watered the horses. As soon as we had had lunch we started off again. We went on to The Lake, and finally we got to Anything Falls In. The sun was almost down. There the herd had all the water it wanted. I watered the horses, and we were glad when we got to that place. I said, "I guess we had better stop and camp here again for tonight." So we did. I told her to let the herd down in the wash to eat some greasewood. She said, all right, and I told her, "Take the things off the horses, wherever you think it's a good place to camp." She said all right. I said "I'll go after the horses." There were some going far away. I said, "I'll go after them. Maybe some tame ones are in that bunch."

Just as I said this, there was my younger brother (Slim Man's Son) coming for water. I shook hands with him. He said, "I am after some water." I said, "Has your father come back yet?" "No," he said, "he hasn't come back yet. Are you just coming back?" "Yes," I said, "We are just coming back, but we are back to our place now, and we are glad we are. Did you see those horses?" I asked him then. "No," he said, "I didn't see them." "I'm going after those horses," I said. He said, "All right." He went down to the water, and I started off after the horses. When I caught up with them there were two tame ones in the bunch. So I started driving them back down to the water and there I roped one. I tied him up and turned the rest of them out. In the morning, while it was still dark, I saddled up that horse and started off towards Where Little Arroyos Stop. I rode all around there. When I was way on the other side the sun was up. Then I started all the horses down towards the water. After they had had water I drove them into the corral and roped two of the tame ones, and took them back to camp. The two that we had been using I turned loose into the bunch.

My wife had lunch ready and we ate. After we ate we started off once more. There was one place where we used to camp with the herd, and I asked her, "What do you think? Shall we take the herd over where we always camp, or do you want to take the herd back to our place?" She said, "We will take the herd over to our place, to where there is another camp across from us. It's close to our place. We'll take the herd up there." I said, "All right, you go ahead with the herd. Go slow and take your time. I want to go around to Where The Gray Hill Comes Out." While she went along with the herd I started off towards my father's place.

19

Working on the corn and herding . . .
Slim Man returns from over the mountain
without his new wife but with his wagon . . .
They move and prepare for hunting . . .
And they hunt.

I got to the hogan where my father's children lived, and
tied up my horse and went inside. Slim Man's wife,
my older sister, shook hands and asked me, "Did you get
back, my younger brother?" "Yes," I said, "we are just getting in. Where is my father? Hasn't he come back yet?" "No,"
she said, "he hasn't come back yet. How long ago was it that
you two (Left Handed and his wife) went across? It must be
close to ten days ago." "Yes, I think it's around about that
time," I said. "Well," she asked, "how does that country
look? How are the people living? How are they getting along?
Some time ago a man came here. He said some kind of
sickness was going all around and a lot of people had died
from it. He said the people had sore throats and when it got
worse a lot of them choked to death. That's what we heard
from him. Is that true? Have you heard anything about it?"
"Yes," I said, "that's what I heard." She said, "When I heard
about these sicknesses I began to worry about him. He has
been gone for about ten days now, so I'm worrying about
him. I wonder if the sickness is going around the whole
country. I wonder if the sickness is around over on the other
side of that mountain. Have you heard anything about it?" I
said, "I didn't hear anything from on the other side of the
mountain. Perhaps it's just around the valley." "I wish he
would be back soon. However, I'm sure he will start back as
soon as he can when he hears about the sickness. If he heard
that the sickness was going around down in the valley and

382

spreading out he certainly would start back quickly. I don't think he will stay away when he hears about it."

She was worrying herself about my father, but I said, "You mustn't worry so much. And that's the way with us all, we mustn't worry about one another so much. Don't think that the sickness will be all over. Think only that it won't spread, and that it will disappear. They say when you are afraid of the sickness you sure will get it, so don't think about it so much." That was all we said and I started home. My wife had the sheep across from where we were living. There was no corral; she had them out in the open, but the herd knew the place, because we always camped there too. The two of us went to the hogan and cooked some food, and after we ate we picked up our sheep pelts and blankets and took them across to where the herd was.

The next morning we went back to our hogan and started up the fire. While she started cooking I went after the horses. After we ate I said, "You take the herd out, and I will go after the horses. I would like to bring one back. I would like to keep one around here all the time. You put the saddle on the horse and take the herd out." She said, "I am so very tired. I would like to take a rest today. I'm sore all over, so I'll go and tell my younger sister to take the herd out for me. I'll tell her to help me out on the herd." I said, "All right, tell her to do that for you today. Just stay at home and take a rest." When she came back from the other hogan she said, "My younger sister is going to take the herd out. She is willing and glad to do it." I said, "That's nice. That's the way I want you to be all the time, help one another herding, so keep that up."

Then I got on my horse and started off. I went a little above Where The Gray Hill Comes Out and then up to Woods Coming Out Into A Flat Far Out Into The Valley, then to Where The Little Arroyos Stop. There were the horses. I got one there, one that was real tame. It always stayed close around the hogan and never tried to get back to the bunch, and it used to be so gentle. I got him and turned loose the one I had been riding. I got back home a little after noon. Everything was ready to be eaten. While I was eating she said, "The corn is good and dry. It needs to be shelled. And the dogs are taking it away." After I ate I went around, and sure enough the dogs had made a trail up onto the hogan. When I got on top the dogs had taken away lots of corn, and it was good and dry.

I got down and went over to a hole where they had kept their corn all winter long, and started cleaning it out. It was kind of damp down at the bottom. When I had it all cleaned out, about then the sun was down, I built a fire in the hole to dry it out. That evening we went over to the herd again, and there we stayed over night. In the morning after we ate I said to her, "I guess you'll take the herd out now, and I'll work on the corn." She said, "I'll go over and ask her to take the herd out again for us. If she takes the herd out again we will both work on the corn." When she came back she said, "She is taking the herd out again." So then we both started working on the corn. We were hauling it down off the hogan to where the hole was all morning. After lunch we started putting it in the hole. First I went down and took out all the ashes. It was good and dry at the bottom, and the walls were nice and dry, and it had got hard. We put all the corn down in the hole, then I put poles across, and over the poles I put a lot of cedar bark. Then I covered it all up with dirt. I fixed the hole up nicely. I had been working on this all day.

The next morning I said, "We'll take the herd over to your herd and I'll separate mine." We took the herd over to where the other herd was and separated the sheep that belonged to me. There were only five of them left. She said, "I would like to separate some of mine too." So she separated some of hers and put them into my herd. She separated twenty goats and one billy goat, twenty-one in all. I started the herd out towards the edge of the woods, and then we walked back to the hogan where I saddled up the horse and then went after the herd. I was herding all that day and the next day. For two or three days I did nothing but herd. Then I said to her, "I'll go over to my father's place this morning, and you take out the herd. Yesterday I was herding down toward the valley and it looked as though something was standing outside close to the door of the hogan at my father's place. So I would like to go over. Perhaps he is back with the wagon. If he's back, I don't think I'll be back today." She started out with the herd, and I started walking down to my father's place. It was quite a distance. We had only one horse at home, and she was using that on herding, so I walked over on foot.

There was a wagon standing by the hogan. It looked funny to me as I walked around it. It had no box on top. I thought it was supposed to be that way. I didn't know it had a box. Then I walked inside and there my father was, lying down. As soon as I walked in he got up and put out a sheep pelt for me by his side. Just as I sat down he put his arm around me and I put my arm around him. We were both holding each other for a long time. Then he said, "I came back yesterday noon. The boys have gone out to the sweat-house. I guess they are about ready with it." I said, "I thought I saw something yesterday by the door of the hogan when I was herding down in the valley. When I looked from there I thought I saw something, and that was the wagon that's standing there now." He said, "I had a very hard time coming back. I suffered a whole lot. I started from Water Coming Out six days ago, and there is where I threw the top of the wagon away. There was a box on the wagon. I threw that box down, because it was too heavy, so heavy the mules couldn't pull it. When I got to White Rock Hill the mules wouldn't pull any more, because both of them had big sores on the shoulders. That's the way I came back, my son. I sure did have a hard time coming across, making roads, filling little washes, cutting down trees, taking out rocks, smoothing the little hills out. Some places I got stuck and had to push the wagon out; where the mules couldn't pull it out I had to kind of carry the wagon around. So I am all in. I could hardly move this morning. That's why I sent the boys over to the sweat-house."

About then the boys returned from the sweat-house and said, "We got the fire started. It's about time to put the rocks inside." He said, "We two will go over. We will take the blankets over and put the rocks inside. One of you go around where the horses are, and one of you take out the herd. And one of you go and get some water and bring it to us, because we will be thirsty. So bring us some water. Don't forget,'' he said to the boys. Then he picked up some blankets and gave them to me and we started for the sweat-house. The rocks were ready, so I put them inside, and I put the blankets over the door. We took all our clothes off and went in. It was nice and hot. The rocks were all red hot. As soon as we got inside he said, ''You tell me about your trip first.''

When I told him about the fellow they had tied up, he said, ''I have heard lots about people like that. A lot of them have said that they were witches, but I don't believe them. I don't think any of them are witches. A lot of them have spoken that way about themselves, and they have been killed on account of it, and they have been killed for nothing. I don't know how they get to say and claim that they are witches. Maybe they want to be killed. Perhaps they go crazy. Perhaps they get tired of living. I don't believe any of them. I believe only how the sickness started. When they had the Night Chant one of the men there had some kind of sickness. Even though he knew he had some kind of sickness, he didn't care, he put on the mask, and after he took it off another man put the same mask on himself, so he caught it from that. They kept on passing the same mask among themselves, and that's how many of them caught it from one man. And when they got home their whole family caught the sickness from them. I don't believe any person called the sickness down upon the people. It spread from one man, that's all. So they ought to let that man go. They have him tied up for nothing. I am sure they will kill him some time, and it will be his own fault, because he claims he is a witch. But I don't think he is.''

I said, ''That's the way I heard about it there, down in the valley, and from there on we didn't hear anything about it. It took us five days to get across here with the herd.''

''Well,'' he said, ''You did well. Even though you were driving the herd it took you only five days to get across. You did very well. But I, even though I was coming with two mules, it took me six days to come across and get back home. The day after we separated at Tree Holding Up A Load I finally got to Water Coming Out, to Yellow Man's hogan. I stopped that evening at his place, and there was the wagon standing there. They had brought the wagon there for me. I gave him many thanks for that, and he gave me many thanks also, 'because,' he said, 'after the boys brought the wagon back here we used it a whole lot. We had been dragging poles around our corn field for a fence, but when we got the wagon we started hauling poles on the wagon, and that is your big help. You helped us with the wagon.' I said, 'It's all right, you helped a whole lot more than you think I did, because you dragged that a long way through the mountain. Therefore I am thanking you a whole lot.' After I had given him thanks for bringing the wagon over to their place he started telling me about where they had got the wagon. He said, 'They got the wagon from Fort Defiance. The agent there gave out wagons to many places on the reservation. There are wagons all over the reservation, in far away places. The next day I borrowed a horse from him and left my mules there at his place. I told him, 'Tie the mules onto the wagon and let them drag it around, so they will learn how to drag it. They only know how to drag poles of wood, so let them drag the wagon around, and they will learn.' When I got on top of the mountain to Lake Along The Woods nobody was living around that place. A whole lot of people had lived there, but they had all moved down to the foot of the mountain.

"Finally I got to the foot of the mountain to Scratch Out Water, where the people whose daughter I had married lived. When I got there the old man wasn't home, only the boys and womenfolk. His wife came out to me; I thought, 'I'm still being remembered.' I stayed with the people that night, and that night the old man came home, that is Grey Eyes. In the morning he came in where I was staying and started telling me about his daughter. He said, 'A few days after you left here a fellow got after her. She said, ''The man tried his best to do something to me, but I didn't let him, so he just gave it up and let me go.'' This is the way my daughter was telling us about herself,' the old man said. I stayed there again that day, and the next day, the night after he told me about his daughter, I thought, 'I will find it out tonight.' In the begin-

387

ning they had told me she had never received a man, and the first time, when we took the horses up to them, I had stayed with them for a few days, but I never had bothered with the girl. So, then, when he told me about her, that night I worked on her, and she had been fucked many times. She was as though she had had a baby many times. That's what I found out that night, after I got through with her. Then I said to her, 'I thought you had never yet received a man. I see you have been worked on lots of times.' When I said this to her she felt very ashamed about it. She never said anything, and that morning she went back to the other hogan. And that morning the old man came in again. As soon as he came in I told him about it, and he felt very bad about it, too. He said, 'I'll see about it now. The womenfolk will find it out, so I had better go back home. They will find it out pretty soon.' So the old man went out.

"While he was gone I was sitting there all alone thinking about what had happened. I was sorry then about the horses that I had given away for nothing. I had given my horses away for another man. That's the way I was thinking about it while I was sitting there all alone. Then the old man came in again. He said, 'We have found it out. The womenfolk got after one another about it, and they found it out in a little while. The girl said the man had fucked her. She said, "I fought with the man. When he got after me I fought him for a long time, until I gave myself up. I couldn't do anything more, so I just gave myself up to him." So you are right, that you found out she had been around with another man. That's what she says, my younger brother, so don't be so sad about it. We will go around among some of the elders, some of the head ones, and we will get that man who got after her, and we will let the elders talk about it, and see what they will say. We will see how they will fix it for you, my younger brother. None of the womenfolk want you to go without fixing it up for you. They all want you to stay; so I am thinking about you just the same too. We will go among the people now, to tell them, and we will get the man here too. We will have a meeting about that for you my younger brother.' I said, 'I have got nothing to do or say about it. It wasn't my idea to come over

388

here to this country. You sent for me yourself. You got me here, and you've got me in sorrow now. Not about her. I am not a bit sorry for her. I am sorry for my horses. That's all.'

"Then the old man went out. I guess he went around among the people. That evening a big crowd arrived. A bunch of people came from different places and started talking about it. There was one man, his name was Supernatural Power (he used to be a headman), he came and started talking about it. He questioned the man who got after the girl. The man said, 'Yes, I did it, but I had never thought of doing that to her. She herself started coming around close to me. Pretty soon she got too close to me. Then I thought she must like me. So, pretty soon, I asked her about it. I said to her, "Do you like me?" and she said, "Yes," and that's how we made up. We did wrong. So it was she, herself, started thinking about me, and pretty soon she got herself under me. It's up to you now. You can do whatever you want to do with me, because I know I have done wrong. I have done it, and I can't get out of it, I know. I am sorry about it, but the sorrow I have won't help me out a bit, so you can go ahead and do anything you want to do with me. I never realized she belonged to my clansman.'

"Then Supernatural Power said to me, 'Well, I can say nothing about the two young folks, but I can say something about you. These two young people didn't do anything wrong but you have done wrong. I know you have a wife and children, and you are a long way from here, and you married this girl. That's a very wrong thing for you to do. You ought to know better than that. I see you are kind of an old man now; you ought to have better sense than that. If you want to say something bad about it, or if you want to do something bad about it, I will see what can be done. I will take all of you to Fort Defiance, and there I will turn you over to the Headman, and he will see about it. However, I know he won't like it. He will keep you there in jail, and he will let these two young ones get married. I know that's what he will do. He will let them go, and he will let them live together, and you will be staying in jail, suffering. So it's up to you. If you want to say something about it, just go ahead,' he said to me, and he was calling me 'my son.' When he was through talking I said, 'I have got nothing to say or to do about it. I didn't want to come over to this country, but all the people from here wanted me to come. That's why I came to this country from far away, and now I see they have got me in bad. So I'll just let them go and live together, because they like each other, and they are both young, and I am old now. I know I can't do anything with her, so I'll let them go and live together.' When I said this all the people who knew me, and all who lived around there, started saying, 'no.' They all didn't want me to go. They all wanted me to stay with the girl, but I never said anything. I just sat there quiet, for a long time.

"They all came up to me and begged me to stay. They didn't like this man, because his father was of the same clan as the girl. They didn't want to let them live together because he was the girl's cross-cousin and the girl was the boy's cross-cousin. So they didn't like to let them go ahead and live together. They begged me for a long time to stay with the girl. Then, when it seemed as though they wouldn't stop begging me for that, I said, 'All right, I'll stay.' After they were through talking about it they all left; only she and I, just the two of us were left there. I asked her about it myself. She said, 'I did it and I am sorry I have broken your heart, but from here on I won't ever do that. I have harmed you very badly, but I won't try to think about that kind of bad thing any more. From here on I won't hurt you by anything like that.' I said, 'All right, but I know very well you never did it once. You have been fucked lots of times. I know that very well. So don't make believe you have been worked on only once. Don't try to think that you will make me believe that, because I know all about it, because I have found out about women, and I know just how it is, so I know you have been fucked lots of times.' But she begged me a lot, saying she would never do that again. I stayed there with those people for a few days, then I started back to where the wagon was. Before I left the old man came to me and said, 'Are you going home?' I said, 'Yes, I am going.' He asked me, 'Are you leaving us for good? Are you?' I said, 'I don't know. I can't say. It is up to life. If I live tomorrow, or the next day, or if I live for another month, perhaps then I'll come again. If my life is short then it may be I am leaving you for good.' He said, 'Be sure and come again as soon as you can, and remember us all the time. That's the way we thought and spoke about it a while ago, we, the two old folks. We won't let you go. We won't forget you. We will remember you always. Whenever you come we will have everything ready for you.' I told him, 'Maybe I will. It depends on life.' Then I went back over the mountain to where the wagon was standing. They had the mules broken in to the wagon. They had made a team out of the mules in a little while. They were just as tame and gentle as could be hitched to the wagon.

"I stayed at Water Coming Out overnight and the next day I started back. I went through woods where I had to chop down I don't know how many trees, climbing over hills and going down, taking rocks apart. Finally I got out to the valley. When I started following the valley I didn't have to do much work, until I got to Bush Standing Up. There I had a hard time climbing up the sand hills again. When I got on top from there on I didn't work as much. That is the way I came back. It took me six days to get across with the wagon." However he hadn't mentioned the places where he had stayed at night. He only said, "It took me six days to get home from Water Coming Out."

We had been going in and out of the sweat-house all that morning; in the afternoon we quit and dressed up and went home. His wife said, "You must be all roasted. You went to the sweat-house early this morning, and you have been there all morning and this afternoon. Why do you want to roast yourself?" He said, "The sweat-house is good for a person, good for all your body, getting the bad sweat out of you. If you don't get the bad sweat out of your system you will get sick from it. That's why we have been at the sweat-house almost all day. It's a good place to rest up. It's a good place to talk about different things. So we are all rested up now." She said, "Why don't you stay at home and lie down and take a rest at home where it's nice and cool? How could you get a rest in a hot place like that? And why don't you stay at home and tell all your stories to us? We want to hear stories about

391

things too. We are just like you, we all like to hear about something. You two went far away from home, and there is where you tell all kinds of stories to each other."

Then he said to me, "We will start hunting as soon as we can, before it gets too cold. If it gets too cold, it won't be much fun. If we start hunting while it's still warm, we will have lots of fun, so I think we will start in about seven days. We will try to get some good meat and skins for ourselves. However, we have got to move out from here towards the foot of the mountain first, to where there is plenty of wood, to where we always camp. After we move to the foot of the mountain, when we get all straightened up, then we will go. So it will be in around seven days. You try to get ready before that. What do you think you want to do about your herd?" I said, "I think I'll take the herd up to the foot of the mountain too, because this is not a good place where I have the herd now. And there's no wood around there close either, and there's no good place for the horses. When I want to hobble the horses I have to go a long way up on the mountain. So I think I'll move my herd too, close to the same place you move to." "Well, then," he said, "that will be good, if you move close to me. Since we have a wagon now, the wagon will take all the things at once, so we won't be going back and forth for them. Be sure and get ready in about seven days." I said, "Yes, I will try to get ready. I'll see what I can do about my herd, see if I can get anybody to herd for me." After we ate some lunch that afternoon I said, "I'll go back home now, and when I get home I'll tell what you have said. I'll know what to do then. When I know what to do, I'll come again, in two days, and let you know."

While we were lying in bed that night I started telling my wife all about what I had heard from my father. I told her "He and I are going hunting in seven days, and he is going to move up to the foot of the mountain, so we ought to move up there, too. If you want to move get your younger sister to herd for us, or one of your younger brothers. Get one of them to help with the herding, and he or she will stay with you while I'm gone, and there we'll have wood close at hand all

392

the time. And maybe I'll borrow the wagon and haul some wood in it. If I borrow it, then I'll bring two or three loads, and that will last a long while." Then she asked me about the wagon, "How does it look?" she asked. I said, "The wagon is not very new. It has been used a lot. The paint is worn off in spots. Some places you can see the wood, some places you can't. So it's not very new." She said, "That will be all right with me. It's all right with me, but I don't know about the others. I'll have to go and see them first. If they are willing to herd for us then it will be fine. If they don't care to herd then it will be all right too, I'll herd myself. So I'll see them about it tomorrow. Even if they don't care to go with me I'll take the herd up there by myself, close to the other people." I said, "That will be all right too. It's all up to you. If you want to get one of them you can. If they don't want to come, then you can go ahead and tend to the herd by yourself. That's what you wanted to do."

Then I said, "My father suffered a lot. When he started from Water Coming Out he had to work hard coming across. He was all tired out, so we have been in the sweat-house all day. I'm glad I'm going out hunting with him. I would like to get some deer meat. I have gotten kind of hungry for deer meat. I am tired of eating sheep. I would like to get a taste of deer, and I would like to get some skins. I'm out of buckskins. Even though I still have one, I would like to get some more. Then when I come back from there we will all have some deer meat, all the womenfolk will have some. So I'm not going away for nothing. I'm going away for something to eat and for some more property."

The next day I took out the herd. I was herding all that day. In the evening she started telling me what her people had said, "I was over to the hogan, and I told them all that you had told me," she said, "I told them that you were going away for a few days, that you were going hunting, 'So I would like to have one of you stay with me while he is gone. We will take the herd up to the foot of the mountain!' They didn't want to go at first. They wanted the herd to stay right here, but I told them, 'There is no feed for the herd around here close by, and there is no feed for the horses close around here, and there's no wood. That's why we would like to take the herd up to the foot of the mountain.' At last they said, 'One will go with you.' So we have a herder."

The next morning while she was putting the saddle on the horse to take out the herd I went down to my father's place. Nobody was at home; they had moved, so I started to where they had said they were going. When I got to that place they were shearing the lambs. I helped them and we got through shearing that afternoon. Then they turned them out and took them back to the herd. They had sheared quite a few. They had quite a stack of wool. After that I told him, "We are going to move up here too." "When do you think you are going to move?" he asked me. I said, "We will move up here tomorrow. We got a herder, so I know I'm going along for hunting." "That's fine," he said, "I went down to Red Sheep's place yesterday, while these folks were starting to move, and told him we were going hunting, and he said he wanted to go with us. He was very glad to hear about that. He had been thinking about hunting, but he had nobody to go with. So we are going with him."

We ate there that afternoon, then he said, "I would like to shear some more tomorrow and the next day. We'll take the wool along with us, and when we get down to the river I'll sell it and buy some cartridges and some grub too, and maybe I'll have a few cents left over. I have used all the money that you loaned me, my son, but I may give you back five dollars when I sell the wool. That's why I would like to shear some more, because I want to give that money back to you. What do you intend to do? Do you want to shear also?" I said, "I don't think so. I won't have time to bother with shearing, because tomorrow I'll start to move up here, and by the next day I'll have all my things up here. And it's only five more days before we go hunting. After I move all my things, then the next day I'll have to tend to the wood. I may be working on the wood for two days, so I have got no time to monkey with shearing." "Well, that's all right, you don't need to worry about yourself," he said, "for we have some money on hand."

While she was beginning to cook the next morning I

394

said, "Go ahead with the cooking, but don't wait for me. I'm going down to get the horses, and I'll go around where the people have moved, and I'll eat there, so you don't have to wait for me." Then I put the saddle on the horse and started off. There the food was about ready. After we ate he said, "What are you going to do now? Are you going after the horses?" "Yes, I thought I would go after the horses and get two of them, but now I have changed my mind. I would like to borrow the burros from you." He said, "Go ahead, put them on the wagon and take the wagon back with you. In that way you will make one trip. The wagon can haul many things." But I said, "No, I don't know how to use the wagon." When I got home with the burros my wife was just taking out the herd. Then we started packing up the burros; we put a lot of things on them and moved where I had built the corrals in the springtime. As soon as we moved there I began working on the wood. I had some dragged in by burro, and then I turned them loose.

The next morning I said, "I'll try the wagon this time." So after we ate she took the herd out and I went over to the other hogan. I said, "I would like to use the wagon." Then they helped me put the harness on the burros. I didn't know anything about it. Then I started on foot to chase the burros hitched to the wagon back to where we had moved. I passed by our place and went into the woods. There was lots of wood close by there, a lot of it lying around. I began picking it up and putting it on the wagon. When I had a little load on it I thought that was enough. I didn't know how much a wagon could carry. I thought perhaps I had too much on it. I was afraid it might break down. I walked along the side and got the wood back. I took it off the wagon and went up into the woods again. I walked alongside of it; I was afraid to get on. When I got into the woods I put a little more on it. I thought it had carried the wood all right. I started, and the burros, it seemed, were not working so hard. It wasn't so very hard on them. They were going along easily, and it wasn't very hard for them to pull. I was wondering why the big thing wasn't heavy. When I dragged one big log by burro, even though I had both of them on one piece of wood, they had a hard time dragging it back to our camp, and here I don't know how much wood I had on top of the wagon. I was sure surprised. In the afternoon I ate some lunch and after I ate I went up in the woods again. This time I put on more, and it was just the same. The burros both were going right along easily. Once more I went up in the woods. This time I had a big pile on it, but still they didn't pull hard on it. In some places the wagon started going by itself. It kind of pushed the burros ahead.

I got four loads in that day, but I never tried to ride on the wagon. When the sun was almost down, while the herd was coming in, I took the wagon back to where it had been standing before, and there they took the things off the burros. Slim Man began to talk about hunting. He said, "We must have a sweat-house before we go. We should clean ourselves, so we'll have a sweat-house, and we'll wash all our clothes, so we'll be all clean. That's the way to hunt. After we have been in the sweat-house and cleaned ourselves we don't want to go near the women. We want to remain separate from them. We will be doing this for one whole day, and the next day we will go. In that way we will get some deer. If we don't clean ourselves, then we can't get anything. So that's what we'll do before we go. We don't know how long we will be gone. It all depends on how the deer will be. If we can't get anything then we'll just turn around and come back. If we kill some, and if we keep on killing some, then we will stay until we think we can't get any more. So we don't know just when we will be back. You must tell your woman to behave. Tell her not to monkey around with another man. I know they are sure to do that. If one of our women starts to monkeying with another man we won't get anything. Even with just the touch of a man, we won't get anything, and we will find it out too by the deer or by the crows. So tell your woman not to bother with the men. When she behaves here at home we will get all the deer we want. So tell this to your woman when you get home." Then I started home. I got back late in the evening.

The next morning after breakfast we killed a sheep. I told her, "Cut the meat in thick pieces. Have it outside and let it dry, and I'll take some along for my lunch, and you can have the rest here at home." Then I turned out the herd. I was herding all that day. In the evening when I returned with the herd there was a horse standing at home. That was her younger brother, the youngest boy, who had brought us some lunch. They had made me some lunch, two different kinds of corn bread. He said, "I brought you over some lunch to take along with you." "That's very good," I said to him. Then he said, "I'm going to stay here too. They told me to just turn the horse loose." I turned the horse loose for him; then I said, "I ought to have asked one of the boys to go with me. Maybe one would have gone. But I didn't, and now it's too late. Tomorrow we have lots to do, so I haven't time to go and ask him."

While the two were starting up the fire in the morning I said, "Go ahead with the fire and cook yourselves some food, and just go ahead and eat, and don't wait for me. I'm going over to my father's home to see what he will say. I'll get something to eat over there." They were cooking over there. I said, "I came to get the sweat-house ready." He said, "You had better wait until this noon. This other man won't come until then, so we will wait for him. Come around again about noon. Then you can get the sweat-house started." I went home again after we had eaten. There they were just turning out the herd. I lay around till noon. Then we had a little lunch. After lunch I said, "I'll go over again. Maybe the man has come. I have got to start up the sweat-house."

But this man hadn't shown up yet. They had sheared some more sheep; they had quite a pile of wool. One of my younger brothers was packing it up. After he had packed up the wool we went over to the sweat-house and built a fire on the rocks. Then we went back. Lunch was all ready, and they had started eating. I ate some more there too. After lunch I took the blankets to the sweat-house, and after I had put the rocks inside and put the blankets over the door Slim Man came, so we took off our clothes and went inside. It was awful hot. We couldn't stay in long. Every little while we went out. As we came out for the fourth time someone was riding and leading a pack horse to the hogan. That was Red

397

Sheep. We recognized him when he got off his horse there at the hogan. We went in again; while we were inside we heard him coming by the door. He said, "How is the sweat-house? Is it warm?" "Yes, it's awful warm," said my father. Then he stepped back and took off his clothes and came in. After a while he went out again; we were lying around outside for a while until we were cooled off, then we went back inside once more. Red Sheep said, "Ever since you came over to our place I have been working, trying to get ready to go hunting. I made a corral first. It took me two days. Right after that I began cutting poles for a hogan. I was cutting poles all that day. The next day I started putting up a hogan; it took me a whole day again to put it up. And the day after, Hosteen No Eyes and I got some cedar bark; we put that all over the hogan, and then we put on the dirt. After we had cleaned it out and cleaned all around it I began working on the water. I fixed up the water; then right after that I moved over to where I had put up the hogan. Finally I got everything moved up to that place, so I am all in. It's a good thing you had a sweat-house. I was just wishing for it. I wanted to have a sweat-house myself, but I just didn't have time to do it. So this morning I got the horses and packed them up and started leading one up here. I just got here a while ago."

About that time we were good and hot again; then we went out and lay around outside for a while. After we went back inside we started singing. We sang some hunting songs; we sang for a while, and then when we got all good and hot we went out. Then we went in once more and sang some more hunting songs and then we quit. It was late in the afternoon. They said, "We will quit now, and we have got to wash all our clothes." After we got all dried off we carried our clothes home. There we washed our hair with soapweed, and after that our clothes. After we had eaten some lunch I carried my clothes back home and spread them out to dry.

About then the herd was coming in. That evening, after we ate, when my wife and her brother were there together I said, "You both know all about the herd. You know how to herd. You know how to take care of the herd. You know everything about the sheep, and you know how to take care of

398

the hogan and other things. And you know how to take care of yourselves. Still I don't know how you will be when you are all alone." I said to the woman, "I know you will be all alone at home, so I don't know how you will behave. Maybe you will behave, or maybe not." She said, "Don't think that I'll go crazy. I know what to do. Don't be worrying so much. I'll be all right. We both will be all right with the herd and other things. So don't think I'll go crazy." I said, "Well, then, I won't worry about you. I'll be glad if what you say is true."

The next morning I saddled up the horse we used for herding and started off along the edge of the woods right straight to Where The Little Arroyos Stop. I got the tamest bunch of horses and started them home and put them in the corral. They had the food ready when I got home. After we ate one of the others took out the herd. I said, "I'll go over to the other hogan. I want to find out when they are going to start. If they say they want to start this noon or this afternoon, I'll take the horses to water. I'll find out." I got on my horse and rode over to their place, and there they had their horses all packed up. They were ready to go. I said, "Are you ready to go?" Slim Man said, "Yes, we are all ready, just little things to get yet. All the rest of the stuff is packed." I said, "I'm not ready yet. I just got the horses back. I thought you wanted to start this noon, or this afternoon sometime. I have to water the horses first. I haven't watered them yet." They said, "We will water the horses on our way. We haven't watered our horses yet either, so you go back and get ready now." Then I turned around and started back. At home I got out the two horses I wanted to use, saddled them up, packed up one, and started over leading that packhorse.

They were tying up their bundles, tying up their packs. When they had it all fixed up they put out some more food for us. Slim Man said, "Come on. Let's eat. All of you come on and eat, and eat lots, because we are going a long way. We will be travelling all day today, so we'll eat lots now." We all sat around and started eating; we ate a lot. One of his boys was going so there were four of us and each of us had a pack horse. He started talking to the others. He said, "Take good care of the herds and other stocks and take good care of one another. We don't know how long we will be gone. It all depends on how we make out. If we kill a lot of them in a little while, then we'll be back soon."

Then I asked for my money, the money they were keeping for me. They gave it to me and I said, "I'll use this for my food and for cartridges, whenever we get to the store." They said, "There are stores all along the river." Then we started off. When we got out in the flat he started singing. We sang some songs, and then went on out to The Lake and on to Many Streams. That first night we camped at a spring below White With Reeds. After we had sung a few songs that evening we sat around for a while until late in the evening, and then we went to bed.

The next day we crossed the river. Finally we got to White Rock Point when the sun was pretty well down. We stopped at the store, and there they sold their wool and bought some food and cartridges. I don't know how much they got for the wool, but there I got five dollars back from him. "Since you have some money I'll just give you back five dollars," he said to me. I said, "All right." "I'll give you the other five in the spring, when I sell my wool." I said, "All right." We all got some food and cartridges. It was night then, late in the evening, when we started on from that store. We had a little light by the moon. It was two or three days after the first quarter, so the moon gave just a little light. We went on that night for quite a ways, until the moon was about down. Then we stopped and unpacked our stuff and hobbled our horses. There was a whole lot of feed for them. We built a fire and had some lunch. After we ate we sat around for a time, and then we started singing again. We sang some songs and then went right to bed. Early in the morning we started off again. From there on I didn't know the places. We went along through the sagebrush and through the woods. There was nothing but sagebrush and thick woods in places. Finally we got in a little canyon. In this little canyon there was a road. It had been worked on not long before. There were fresh tracks of men, horses, and wagons. We followed the road up in the canyon; when we got almost to the top there was a wagon and some white men

400

working on the road; two of them going ahead of the wagon, making a road, and one driving. They said, "bueno," to us. When they said "bueno" to us, we said the same to them. We said "bueno," and they nodded their heads. We passed them and went on into the woods, around to where the canyon begins.

Slim Man pointed to a big point on the mountain, and said, "There is water right at the foot of that point. We'll camp there, and from there we'll hunt. So we want to hurry, so that we'll get there before sundown." We went right straight for this point and got there before sunset.

We hunted for nine days. I killed six deer and the others killed ten. When we killed a deer we butchered it, laid the meat on branches and carried it back to the hogan. Then we took the meat on the branches inside, cut it up and laid it on trees. Every night after we ate we laid our guns on the ground in a row and sang the hogan-song, the fire-song, the day-song, the bow-and-arrow-song, and the sleeping-songs, and then went to bed.

On one of these days as I was tracking a deer I got onto a bunch of them in a little valley. They were all females. When I got near to them two crows came along close above me. They were playing around; then they sat on the limb of a tree. They were kind of talking to each other for a while and then they started kissing. Pretty soon two small kids who were standing there started playing. They did the same thing the crows had done. Then they separated and were grazing and I shot the biggest deer. So then I knew that kissing was being done at home. If I had noticed water or anything dripping out of the deer's vagina I would have known that something else had been done.

On the last day we hunted, Slim Man's son and I were alone at camp. Two white fellows rode up. They got off their horses and looked all round outside and into the hogan. The trees were red with meat and there was a pile of meat inside the hogan. They stood there a while, talking and laughing. But we couldn't understand them. They rode away to the east.

Next morning we discovered that all our horses were gone. We found tracks of six white men and they had chased

401

our horses with the hobbles on. Slim Man, Red Sheep and I tracked them and found an empty house with dishes lying around where they had eaten. They had driven the horses into a corral and unhobbled them, all except mine who was kind of wild. From there we tracked them north.

Then Slim Man and Red Sheep went on to track them further and to get Ruins, who was in that country with a bunch of fellows. I went back to guard our camp with Slim Man's son. We slept in a cave on a cliff and went back to camp only to eat. We stayed that way for three nights and then Red Sheep returned with Slim Man, Ruins, and some of his party (Hosteen Standing House, his wife, Ruins' son, and Many Goats). Slim Man said that when they were coming back from Ruins' camp they saw that some cowpunchers had horses and cattle in three places. Slim Man wanted to go back and start a fight with the cowpunchers and he was planning to do so. But as they went along they met two groups of friends, Bursting Foot and some of his partners, and another bunch of men. They begged Slim Man not to start trouble and spoil their hunting. So Slim Man said, "They spoiled my plans and I told them to go ahead."

Next morning Slim Man, Ruins, and I started off to track the horses and the others stayed at our camp. We got to where there were some houses close together. We went into one and there was a crowd of white fellows just starting to eat. There was no sound. They just looked at us with their eyes wide open and some had their mouths wide open. We stood there and then we rode away.

We got on to the tracks of the two groups of fellows Slim Man had met and, when we found where they were camping, stayed there overnight. Next morning five of these fellows joined with us to track our horses. As we started off Bursting Foot said, "Even though you want to shoot or kill someone you mustn't attempt to shoot unless they start. If they want to start trouble then you can go ahead."

We found our horses' tracks and went pretty far tracking them but then we missed them. Then we came on to a house with a tent beside it down in a canyon. There was only a young girl at home. I guess she was scared. She was all red and after a while she turned white. One fellow knew a little English. He said she told him she didn't know anything about the horses nor where the men were. So we went on.

Slim Man tried hand-shaking to find out where the horses were but after his hand rose it dropped and he said, "It quit on me." Then Dacahi's Paternal Grandparent tried. He took his corn pollen and put it on his hand. His hand started shaking. He made three circular motions. Right on the third circle he said, "Your horses are up there." After he made these motions he patted me on the lap and started pushing me. He did this to me twice and motioned and pointed off to a point telling me the white fellows were up there. That is what he did and sure enough when we got to the foot of the point there were two white fellows running and jumping down off the cliff. Three of us stopped at the bottom at the one little place where they could get down. The other five fellows were waiting near by. The two white men got down to where we were, passed us and started for where the house was in the canyon. One of them had his hand on a revolver. One of the young fellows called Hunter wanted us to jump off our horses and capture them but Ruins said, "Go easy you fellows." So we backed out and sat still on our horses. The two white fellows went back to their house and the one who didn't have a revolver went in and got one. Then they stood in front of their house aiming their guns toward us. One of the old fellows said, "Lets go before they shoot" and we rode off.

We rode over three round hills and there, at the foot of the third hill, were our horses. We drove them through sage brush and woods and, way late in the night, we got back to where Bursting Foot and the other fellows were waiting for us. There we had our horses without any trouble. We were so thankful and I believed in that man who shook his hand. I believe him by the motions he made, by the three circles that were the three round hills. And Slim Man said, "If we didn't have our guardians we would have been killed when we were asleep that first night when the white men captured our horses. The white men too, have guardians and their guardians told them not to harm us and not to shoot us."

Next morning the two groups of fellows left us to go on with their hunting and Slim Man, Ruins, and I went back to our camp where Red Sheep, Hosteen Standing House, and the others had stayed. They said they had been hunting but, though the deer were close, they never did kill any. Slim Man said, "That's the way it is. If some kind of trouble comes up then you can't kill a deer or anything." Then Hosteen Standing House said, "Maybe they (the white men) think we are stealing their horses and cattle and killing their sheep. But all we are thinking about is the deer meat and skins. We don't think of any other thing. I guess they are thinking and talking about us like that." And it was like that but we didn't know it. A rule had been made that there wouldn't be any more hunting around their mountain. That's what we found out afterward.

Then we decided to go back to our country without hunting any more. So next day, after we had made a sweat-house and had been in it we divided the meat among ourselves and before we left the camp we made all those offerings that we knew. On the way home we camped overnight and stopped at a store where some of the fellows sold kid skins and then camped overnight again. Then Slim Man, his son and I went on together and Red Sheep joined Ruins and his partners and went on with him. We camped again and next day got home when the sun was pretty well down.

20

He is jealous of his wife . . .
The One Day Sing . . . His wife is
unfaithful to him and they quarrel . . .
They move and visit his wife's relatives . . .
Talk about property and marriage . . . Ceremony
for a new hogan.

When we got back from our days on the hunt every-body was still living there. Slim Man and his son went back to their hogan and I went on and got back to mine too. We were living about 300 yards apart. The herd was in. The boy who was herding for us was just getting off the burro. As soon as I rode up to the hogan my wife came out, and when I got off my horse she ran up and grabbed me. She put her arms around my neck and hugged me, holding me against her breast for a long time. Then I started taking the things off, and she carried them inside. I hobbled the horses, and because they had drunk a while before I didn't take them to water or any place. The boy was out gathering up wood, and after we had taken everything inside she called him over and he came in and she told him, "Go and get the horse, my younger brother. We haven't any water. We have only enough to make coffee, so you go and get the horse and get some water." Right away he said, "All right." He picked up a rope and went after the horse and put the saddle on it and got the jug and went after some water. When he brought the water back she started cooking. I had made a place on the tree for the meat and the skins too. We had only a little meat in-side and she boiled some of that.

After we ate I began telling her about my trip. When I had told her what had happened, about the white men taking our horses and about how Ruins and the others helped us get them back without anyone getting killed, she said, "No wonder I had bad dreams every night. I started dreaming that way ever since you left here." I said, "That's what happened to us, and so we had to leave that country. We had killed only sixteen deer. If the white men hadn't taken our horses away from us perhaps we would have gotten thirty, or maybe more. So we got only sixteen." She said, "Yes, I had bad dreams every night after you left here. I was wondering why I dreamed that way every night." That was all, and we went to bed. I slept separate from her, because my father had told me not to go close to the woman, "not until you have cleaned yourself up. You should get in the sweat-house and wash all your clothes. Wash yourself all over. Take all the blood off of you. You shouldn't have any blood on you; so you must do that," he had said to me, "You shouldn't bother with the women with deer blood on you, because it's dangerous." But then she had run up to me already and hugged me. She wanted to kiss me but I didn't let her, and I told her why; so she didn't kiss me. I told her about that before we went to bed. She was going to fix a bed for me right close to her, but I told her about that; so we slept separate that night.

Then next morning I said, "I'll go to the sweat-house, and you two can go ahead and cook and eat. I'll get something over at the other hogan." Then I picked up an ax and walked over to the sweat-house and chopped up some wood. Just when I had the wood ready two boys came up and started gathering up some rocks, piling the wood and rocks together. When we had the fire going good we went back to the hogan. "Did you get started on the sweat-house already, my children?" Slim Man asked us, "Have you built a fire with the rocks?" "Yes," I said, "We have the fire going already." "That's fine. We will go to the sweat-house and stop whenever we want to." The food was all laid out in front of us and we all started eating. After we ate he said to two of his boys, "One of you take out the herd, and the other hitch on to the wagon and get some water, so that the herder can rest up." The boy who had been hunting with us stayed at home. Then my father and I went to the sweat-house, and went in, back

406

and forth, until noon; then we quit. He went home, taking the blankets with him, and I went back to my home.

While I was going back my wife passed me with a jug. She was after some water that they had hauled up to the other hogan. When she brought the water back she made me some soap and I washed my hair and then my clothes. After I had washed them I washed myself all over with soapweed. That afternoon the boy who was herding for us said, "I want to go home." I said, "Well, go and get your horse." My wife said, "What are you hurrying back home for? You ought to still herd for us, my younger brother." I said, "I have told him already to get his horse. I guess he can go back on one of mine." So I told him to get one of the horses. "You can ride one of my horses back to your home, and bring the horse back tomorrow. Be sure and water the horse before you start back up here with it." He got the horse and put the saddle on it. I told her to give him half of the meat, so she did, then two of the hearts and some fat with it, and I gave him one skin. He put it on the horse and went late in the afternoon. So the two of us were left alone again, and my mother wasn't back yet.

I was around with the herd the rest of that day, and the next morning I took the herd out again. When I got back in the evening I asked about the horse. "Did he bring the horse back?" "No," she said, "he didn't bring the horse." That evening I went down to my father's place. He said, "I am thinking about one of the Singers, but there is no Singer around close anywhere. I have been thinking about this all day. There was only Curly Haired, but he is way over at Timber Mountain, hunting. There is Hosteen Liar. I wonder how he is? I wonder where he is living? I wonder if we could get him in order to take some of his corn pollen?" I said, "I don't know exactly where he lives now; he used to live down at a place called Hill Across. Perhaps he is still living there. Perhaps if we ask someone about him they may know where he lives. But I think he is living around close to Hill Across. Sometimes he moves down to Thief Rock. They are the only two places that he moves to." He said, "I wanted you to go

407

and look for him, but I don't think you can, because there is nobody to herd for you." I said, "Yes, if I had someone to herd for me I would go. I'm willing to go, but there is no one to herd for me. The boy went back home. He hasn't brought the horse back yet. I guess he doesn't want to bring the horse back, because maybe he thinks we will make him herd again. So I have to herd." He said, "Yes, I know you have to herd yourself, and I know nobody from their place will herd for you. The boy won't, because he has found the herding too much for him. I know they won't herd sheep that don't belong to them. But it's all right. Perhaps we'll get that man some way."

I was out with the herd again the next day. When I returned home in the evening the horse was hobbled there. I said, "Did he bring the horse back?" She said, "Yes, he brought the horse back this noon. I told him to get some wood, so he got me some wood, and I told him, 'I will cook something for you before you go back.' After he brought in some wood he went out, and when I had the cooking done I went to look for him and he had gone home." The next morning I said, "You take out the herd today, I want to go and look at my horses." She said, "All right," so I saddled up my horse, and when she had taken out the herd I started off to where the horses were. I rode over to Woods Coming Out Into A Flat, then up to Where Little Arroyos Stop. I rode all around there and gathered up the horses, and I had missed one. I looked all around there, but I didn't find it, so I started them down to the water. There was the horse I had missed. Somebody had been riding this horse. It had been ridden a long way. That's the way it looked to me. It was sweaty and white with lather. There the horse got back into the bunch, but I didn't know who it was that rode my horse around. I got another horse and led it home. When I got back there was no water, so I picked up a jug and tied it on to the saddle and started down to the water again. As I was on my way back home I met her with the herd. "Get on this horse and go back home and cook something. I'll stay around here with the herd."

That evening I asked her a question, but first I told her

what had happened close before me about the crows kissing and about the deer. Then I said "What did you do while you were alone at home? You must tell the truth about yourself, because I know very well you have been doing something. If you try to say you never did anything, I won't believe it, because I have found out already."

When I said this to her she felt very ashamed about it. She dropped her head almost to the ground for a while. Then she said, "I don't know how many days ago you left here—I don't know just how many days after you left two boys came here one evening and Who Went After The Enemies was with these two boys. They came here; they wanted to play the moccasin game. So we started playing. The two boys went on the north side, and my younger brother joined them, and I and Who Went After The Enemies were partners. While we were playing Who Went After The Enemies had forgotten where she had put the rock which we had been hiding in the moccasins, and they got after us about that. She had the rock in her hand, and they got after her. They started taking the rock away from her; they started fighting (in play) about it, and when she was about to give up she handed it to me, and I took the rock, and they got after me about it. So I fought with them over the rock, but they didn't take it away from me. Then we told them to play right; so then we started playing again." That was my oldest younger brother, and another boy. He was living around close by. It was those two boys who came around one evening. "That was all we did that night," she said, "Nothing more." When she said this I said, "No, it wasn't all. How about the kissing?" "No," she said, "I'm telling you the truth. You wanted me to tell you the truth, so I am."

I said, "You are not telling the truth, because I know very well you have been kissing with one of these boys. That's the way I found it out, by the two crows, and they were telling me the truth. Even though they were birds they told me the truth. Maybe you don't believe that they can tell the truth. When you are hunting, if the crow sees a deer close by to you, the crow will come down close above the deer and talk as if he were saying, now, Kat! When he sees a deer he will say it, just like that, and when you sneak up under where he is flying around, sure enough, you will see a deer, and you'll kill a deer right there. So the crows are true about the things." But she kept on saying no, so I thought it was no use asking her, so I just let her go. Then I just began to watch her close. I started to sneak around her close from there on to find one of these boys. From there on I started to get jealous. I couldn't get it out of me. I tried lots of times not to be jealous but I always thought about it (what had happened before) so I was that way from there on.

Two or three days after this I went down to my father's place, but he wasn't home. I asked, "Where's my father?" My older sister, Slim Man's wife, said, "He went after the Singer yesterday." "What Singer did he go after?" She said, "I don't know, but he said he wanted to go and look for Hosteen Liar. If he finds this man, perhaps he'll bring him back. If not, maybe he'll bring back someone else with him; so I don't know. He went yesterday, and I guess he is coming back today." That was all she said, and I went back home. The next morning I got up and put on my clothes and went out and started chopping up some wood. I was thinking I would go over again as soon as I got enough chopped up. But while I was still chopping my younger brother came over. He came up to me and said, "I came for you. They want you to help this morning. They want you to get some soapweed." "Is there a Singer there?" I asked. "Yes," he said, "They got back last evening." "What Singer did he get?" "He came back with Hosteen Liar, so they want to have One Day Sing today." I said, "I was thinking of going over again this morning for a while. After I came back from there I was going to take out the herd; so how about the herd?" He said, "Who Went After The Enemies will take the herd out for you." So I said, "All right, you go and get the horse and bring it back here for her, so that when she comes she can use the horse for herding." When he went after the horse I chopped a little more wood and then I walked down to their place and there they were having One Day Sing. Right away they said, "Go and get

410

some soapweed. We will use it this morning. We are going to have One Day Sing today." I said, "All right."

Then I walked up to the old man and shook hands with him. This Hosteen Liar was my grandfather. He was Red House clan. When I shook hands with him he said to me, "My grandson, my baby." Slim Man said, "I sent for you to get us some soapweed, and I want you to help us today." I said, "All right, I'll go and get some soapweed right now." "Wait a while, until they kill some sheep. After that you can go," he said. I said, "All right," and sat down again. And then after they had killed some sheep they told me, "Now you can get some soapweed." When I returned with it I gave it to Hosteen Liar and he told me to fix it up. They gave me a basket to put it in and I poured some water in it and made up the soap for him. When I had finished the suds were level with the top of the basket. Then Hosteen Liar got up and started treating Slim Man with some of this soap. After that my father washed his hair and then he took a bath in it. When he was through Hosteen Liar dried him off with white corn flour, and right after that said a prayer for him.

After the prayers he sat back in his place, "Now we are having One Day Sing, my grandson," he said to me. "Yes, I see that," I said. From there on we were having One Day Sing. My woman came and helped cook. We were both there all day, but nobody came around. Late in the evening Hosteen Liar started singing. I was the only one that helped him sing. He sang the hogan song first, then from there on he sang a great many songs. I didn't know what kind of songs they were. Toward morning he started singing songs of some god. He sang that until morning, and then we stopped.[1] So that's where I stayed awake all night.

Then Hosteen Liar said, "I'll go right now, my grandson, because I have got to go and do lots of things. I want to hurry back." I said, "What is it, my grandfather? Where do you have to go? And what do you have to do? You don't want to be hurrying back. You ought to stay with us yet awhile."

1. Slim Man was the only one treated because he was the leader of the hunt, but the prayers had been said for everybody there at the hogan.

"No, my grandson, I have to go right now, because my grandchildren have killed each other." And that was Hanging From His Neck who had been killed. One of his brothers killed him; his clan was Red House. "So," he said, "that's why I have to get back in a hurry."

I had come to Slim Man's in the morning, and they had never told me anything all day and all that night. They were telling stories to each other, but not about that. Slim Man was telling about the trip that we had made, and that was all that he had been talking about all day. He had known about this killing, but they didn't tell me about it until that morning. "I will tell you just that little piece of it," Hosteen Liar said to me, "since we want to have everything straight. That's what we were begging for all day yesterday and last night all night; so we don't want to talk about those things right now. But I have told you a little bit about it, and you know it now. Perhaps later on you will know more about it, my grandson." I said, "I didn't know anything about it till now. I guess we will know more about it after awhile." "Yes," he said. "We mustn't talk about it right now. I will tell you a little about the people who have died. A lot of Red House people died with this—some kind of fever—down in the valley. Some places only one or two are left at home. They all have died of this disease. Most of these people were Red House, so that's why they murdered him. That's all I want to say about it, but no more. Is there anyone getting my horse?" Someone outside said, "Yes, a fellow went after your horse." Not long after that they brought his horse back for him. He saddled it up, tied everything to his saddle and left. I didn't know what he got for that singing.

Then my wife and I went back to our hogan. I went right on and got a horse we used for herding. I was about to drop. I said to her, "I would like to sleep some this morning. If I take the herd out I might fall asleep and lose the sheep, so could you take the herd out?" She said, "All right, I'll take it out." I put the saddle on the horse for her and while she went out with the herd I went inside and lay down and went to sleep. I was sleeping until a little after noon; then I got up

412

and started walking after her. I got up on the hill; I looked for her, and there I saw the sheep coming along out of the woods, but there was nobody with the herd. It was going along by itself. I looked all around but I didn't see anyone anyplace. And then, when I didn't see anybody behind the herd, I got off this hill and started across to another hill. That was quite a big hill. I walked about half way up this hill and then sat down. The herd was passing me. Pretty soon the herd had passed me and passed over my tracks. When it had gone down quite a ways from me I looked around. There was a little cluster of trees out a little in the flat away from the woods; she rode out of that little wood, coming after the herd, tracking it right along across the flat and she passed me and into the woods. I looked to where she had ridden out, and there I saw another rider. He went out toward the east. Immediately I noticed the horse. I knew just what horse it was, I knew the horse very well, but I didn't recognize the man. I got off the hill, walked out to where she had ridden and started to track her back. I wanted to know what had happened in that little cluster of trees. I tracked her horse back into the wood, and there in the middle of this little bunch of trees was a little place where the ground was smooth and hard, just like a rock. There was a little place like that, but I couldn't tell what had happened, because the ground was hard. The horse she had been riding had been tied on the south side of this hard ground, and the other horse had been standing on the east side. She had walked up to her horse twice, and the man had walked up to his horse once. I knew very well that a robe had been spread on this hard ground, but I couldn't tell what they had done, but I guessed they had fucked. I thought, "They wouldn't be getting together for nothing."

I recognized the man's tracks. I knew his tracks very well. That was Son Of Who Has Mules, whom Slim Man had raised. It was he. I started walking back. It was quite a ways to our home. She had gone back to the hogan with the herd, and I just followed her all the way back. She had unsaddled the horse when I got there. I took the herd inside the corral and fixed the gate. The sun was about down. Then I picked

413

up a rope and brought some wood back to the hogan. I made two trips and about that time she had cooked some food. I started eating, but I could hardly swallow anything. Every time I tried to swallow something it stopped and almost choked me, and it was hurting me so badly that I thought I had better stop eating. By the looks of her I could tell that she knew very well that I had found out something about her. I knew very well she had done wrong, by her looks and acts. It was night then. She made the beds and we lay down, but I wasn't saying anything. I just lay there in bed. Then she said, "Where have you been? You were coming back the way I came back with the herd." I said, "I was there, where you were with a man. That's where I have been." Then, I guess, I had almost killed her with that. She choked her breath, for I don't know how many times. I said, "Yes, I was up there. I know just what you did with that fellow. I know you have been doing that with him, but you said you never have been doing anything, but I know you have been doing that right along."

She said, "I never have done anything. I tell you the truth. I was sitting there in the shade and he came and rode up to me. He got off his horse; he sat down a little ways away from me and asked me about the horses that they use for herding, but I said, 'I didn't see any horses around here.' That was all he asked me about. When I told him that I didn't see any horses around there he got up and got on his horse and went on again, and I got up and got on the horse and started after the herd. So he wasn't there long." I said, "Don't try to tell me all those things, because I know very well what you both were doing. I know all about it, so you don't have to tell me anything. "What are you saying? Maybe you think I did something wrong with him but I didn't, and he didn't even touch me. He didn't come close to me. He had been sitting a ways from me, but he didn't sit long, just for a while. Then he got on his horse and rode away."

Then I just quit talking about it. I thought, "I can't do anything about it. And I can't say much about it." This fellow was my younger brother, and we had been raised by this one father (Slim Man). So that's why I stopped talking about it; I

414

just let it go, but I thought, "I will ask the man about it. Even though I know he won't tell, I'll ask him anyway." "I won't try to talk about it anymore," I said, "Because I know you won't tell, even though you did it. I know very well you have done it; nevertheless you have denied it. But don't think I have believed you. I don't believe you a bit, and you have made trouble among us, between us all. That's what you have done," I said to her. "No," she said, "I never did anything." She said this many times, but I told her I couldn't believe what she had said. Nevertheless she kept on saying, no, and begged me, putting her arm around me, saying, "Don't talk that way to me, because I never did it." But I told her to stop talking about it, "We will both just let it pass, even though it happened." She kept on saying no, saying she had never done anything. That was all, and we went to sleep. The next morning she cooked some more food, some deer meat, and I ate a lot. I thought to myself, "It's no use for me to starve myself."

After I ate I got the horse and saddled him up and turned out the herd. I was herding all that day. In the evening, when I returned with the herd, she said, "There isn't any water," so I got the jug and went down to the water. I got some water and watered my horse and came back. From there on I began thinking about it. I thought, "I will just put this thing away, until another time, until I find her doing that a second time, then I'll take her back to her home."

Then next morning I went out with the herd again, and was herding all day around in those woods, until evening. In the evening I returned with the herd, took the saddle off the horse and hobbled him, and then took the herd inside the corral and fixed the gate. After that I picked up an ax and walked up in the woods. While I was cutting up some wood, I heard somebody chopping close by me. I laid down the ax and walked over where I had heard the chopping. That was my younger brother Son Of Who Has Mules. I said to him, "Lay the ax down first and come up to me." When I said this I sat down. He laid the ax on the ground and walked up to me, and I told him to sit down. He sat down close to me.

I could tell right away that he had done something. I

415

said, "You have done wrong, my younger brother, so tell me the truth about it. You have been with the woman close by that little cluster of trees. That's what I want to ask you about. Therefore you tell me the truth." He felt very ashamed about that. After a while he said, "What did she say?" I said, "You needn't ask me about her, because I know what she has said, but I want you to tell the truth to me also. You don't need to ask about her, because she has told me already." He just sat there for a good while; then he said, "Yes, my older brother, she herself made me work on her. She had been trying to make me do that for a long time, and there she rode up to me and told me to get off the horse. So I did. Then she grabbed me and jerked me up to herself. You know very well I have never been around with a woman, so I didn't know anything about it, so she had worked herself on me. She showed me everything and told me how it should be done. So I just went ahead the way she wanted me to do. So I have done that, my older brother. I am telling you the truth." There I found out that they had fucked each other. I said, "Well, what do you think about it? Shall I tell our father about it? Should I tell him? Or what do you think about it?"

Then he became so frightened. After a long silence he said, "I am afraid of my father, so, please, my older brother, could you let that go? Can you let me get by with that? I told you the truth right out. I never tried to tell you a lie, so please don't tell on me, because I am afraid of him. He will give me a good scolding for that, and he will say the same to her. So, please, don't tell. I won't ever do that any more to you. I won't hurt you with that any more. This will be the first time and the last time. So, please, don't, my older brother. It's she that made me do that." He begged me not to tell, "Because I hadn't been thinking of a thing like that before. She was the one that put me in trouble. She knew all about it, I didn't know anything, but she got after me. I have done wrong. I know I have hurt you, but from here on I won't do that any more." I said, "If you are truthful about it, it will be all right with me. If you stop right now, if you quit at once, then you won't get into big trouble. If you are only lying about it, if you go ahead and do it again, then it will be just too bad for you. You have done it now. You have learned it. You know how to work on a woman, and I know you are wishing for it all the time. So, if you stop bothering me like that right now, you will be safe."

When I said this he was about to cry, and I felt very sorry for him. I knew then he hadn't done it. I knew that she was the one who had gotten after the boy. Then he got up and walked up to me and held my hand, and he put his arm around me and I put my arm around him. "I have hurt you, my older brother, but don't think about it now, and I won't think about it any more. I am sorry that I obeyed her. I am sorry that I did what she wanted me to do, but I won't do that on you any more, my older brother." "Well," I said, "that's all right. I know it's not your fault. I am not going to do anything to you. I only wanted you to tell me the truth about it. That was all, and we will be brothers always, until the rest of our lives. That's the way I am thinking about you, my younger brother. You will always be my younger brother," I said to him, and that was all.

Then I walked back to where I had laid the ax, bundled up the wood, and hauled it back to the hogan. I dropped the wood, took off the rope and went inside. She seemed sorrowful. She was around there, quiet, and I guess she had seen us. I didn't say anything. She cooked some food, and we both ate. It was dark then, so she fixed the place where we were going to sleep. While I was lying there I said, "You tried your best, you tried hard to get away with what you did. I know very well what you have been doing. I found out a little while ago. He told me about it just now. He has told me everything, and he told on you. He said you made him do that. He said he didn't know anything about it, and I know that very well. I know very well you got after him yourself. You have put my younger brother and me way apart. You have separated us. You have made a great big canyon between us. You know there was nothing between us. We were close and connected to each other, but you have torn up everything."

When I said this she didn't say anything, she just started crying. I said, "What are you crying for?" "I am crying, because you made me cry. What you have said to me made me cry." I said, "What do you want to cry for? You shouldn't cry. You didn't cry when you were doing this. You made yourself cry. I never did anything to you, and I won't do anything. I am not thinking of doing anything to you. I am not going to hurt you for that. You have hurt yourself. Nobody told you to do that. It's your own fault. You put yourself in that thing. I didn't force you into it. You hurt yourself. No one else hurt you. Therefore you don't need to cry. From the time I married you you started treating me cruelly. You were trying to put me in trouble all the time. Once you put me in great sorrow and sadness. You did a very mean thing to me once before this, but I just let that ride. Even though I suffered so much I never told on you, and now you have hurt me still more, but I let it pass again. I have made up my mind not to tell on you, even though you have hurt me so badly. However from now on whenever I catch you doing anything like that or if you hurt me again with something, I won't forgive you. I am telling you this, and I mean it. The next time I won't forgive you. I have forgiven you twice now, and that's all. Don't think I'll forgive you again. So you had better be careful, from now on. You were born in it. You were raised in it. Ever since you got to know things you have seen your female relatives doing those things, and you have learned from them. From the first time you saw them doing that you have had it on your mind, and when you grew up you wanted to do it, and once you did it, from there on you wanted to do it again, and you have been doing it right along. That is all you have been thinking about. You had been around with many men when I got you. Even though I have been with you all the time you have been thinking about the others, and I know you have been doing that with them. I know very well you are around with men as soon as I go off someplace. And I can't tell you to stop it, because I know you won't, and nobody will stop you. So you don't need to be crying about that. But I mean it, the next time I won't forgive you. This time I have put it away already."

When I said this she almost lay on top of me. She put her arm around my neck and held me against herself so hard and said, "Do you mean that? That you won't tell on me?" I said,

418

"Yes, I mean it. For now you know this is the second time you have hurt me. I mean it, the next time I won't forgive you. This time I have forgiven you once more, and that's all," I said to her. But she never said that she had done it. She never admitted it. I thought she was going to say that she had done it, but she never said it. So that was all, and then, after I had said that to her, I covered up my head and went right to sleep. She never said any more to me. I don't know how long she lay awake.

The next morning when I got up she got up too and started the fire and began sweeping. After she had swept up she took out the dirt and ashes and started cooking. From there on I felt as though I were very sick. She had gotten me that way, by what she had done, by how she had treated me. I was kind of sick from that, thinking about it, but I just kept on going with what little work I had. I had never thought of anything like that before, because I had never been put in that kind of situation, and it sure hurt to be treated like that. Before that I hadn't known anything about it. And I had been doing that myself. I had been around with women; I had had lots of fun with them, and I realized I must have been hurting her very much by that. But after she had done this, then from there on I was thinking that way. I was thinking she was right; but before that I never thought that I was hurting her. However, after she treated me like that then I knew it hurt.

For several days I did nothing but herd. It was around when the water begins to freeze, when a little crust of ice forms on the water that I said to her, "I would like to take the herd up on the mountain before it gets too cold, because I know up on the mountain the feed is still green. But around here everything is dry; so that's why I would like to take the herd up on the mountain, and we'll take two or three horses up there with us. I don't want to take all the horses up there, because they will easily get away. That's the way I am thinking about it. What do you think? Do you want to go up or not? Say so, then I'll know." She said, "Why should I say no? For I am with you all the time. How do you think about me? You know very well I am with you all the time." "Well then I

419

will get the horses and we will move up to your home first. From there we will take the herd out this morning and tomorrow we will start to move. So today you get the things ready." She said, "All right." I was herding all that day on foot. About sundown I brought the herd back, put it in the corral and fixed the gate. She had brought in some wood, so that I wouldn't have to do it, and when I went inside there was plenty of water; and the food was ready to be eaten. After we ate I said, "I'll go down to my father's place. I just want to see where he is."

I walked down to his place, and they were just putting out the food. They had sat around and were beginning to eat. They told me to eat, but I said, "I have just eaten a while ago." "Even at that," he said, "eat some more." So I went ahead and ate some more. He said to me, "Even though you have just quit eating, you should take a little again. So eat a lot." My younger brother was there, but he ate only a little. He poured a little coffee into a cup, took a few swallows of food and then went out. I guess he went to the other hogan where his grandmother and sister and the little boy who herded lived. The four of them were living together in one hogan. I said, "We are going to move tomorrow up on the mountain, but I guess we'll move up to her place first. I don't know how many days we will be there. Then from there we will move up to the mountain. I would like the herd to get some greasewood up there, and other feed." He said, "That's all right. You can just go ahead and move, my son. I don't think I'll go over the mountain again, because I am afraid of the snow. It may have snowed deep upon the mountain. We know it snowed when we were hunting, and I see it snowed upon the mountain here. I am afraid of that, and so I am not going over again. (He meant to Water Coming Out, where he had his other wife.) I don't think I'll try to go, because I am afraid of the cold. Even though it's not real cold yet, still I'm afraid to get out in it, because every time I go out I get a chill. Even though it's not real cold yet, still sometimes it gets real cold around evening and at night and in the morning, so I think it's getting too cold up on the mountain. So I won't try

420

to go again. I guess I'll stay around here. Are you going to take the horses up there too?"

"No," I said, "I'll leave them down here where they are now. If I get them up there they'll get away from me, and pretty soon I won't have any horses. I'll only take three or four up with me, just those that I want to use, the ones that I know won't get away from the hogan. I'll leave the rest down here. You said you were going to move up there; when you move up to that place, or even before, help me by watching my horses for me, so that I won't be worrying so much about them." "Yes," he said. "We will take good care of them, and if I want to use one or more of them I'll use them. I want to let you know about that now, so you will know I am using your horses." I said, "All right, any time you want to use them go ahead. If you want to use some of the horses you can use the mule." He said, "No, no, not that! None of us will go near the mule, because we are all afraid of it." I said, "What's the matter with the mule? Nothing is wrong with it. The mule won't hurt you. The mule is gentle. I just used him a few days ago. I rode him across the country and herded back on him, so there is nothing wrong with him." He shook his head and said, "Even at that, I'll never go near him. No one will go near him." I said, "Well, then use the white horse, and if you want to use another get the black one. If you want to use three at once, use the grey horse." "That's all right. We are not afraid of the horses, because we know they are all gentle. I don't think we will use all of them at once. That's very nice of you, my son. You know we have horses, but we can't get them quickly enough. They are far away from here, you know, way down in the middle of the flat, and you know it's getting colder every day; so we will use the horses that you mentioned, which are close."

The next morning, as soon as I got up, I went after the horse which we had been using the herd with. I saddled him up and started off to where the horses were. I rode up to Where The Little Arroyos Stop and started rounding them up. When I got them all rounded up I drove them back the way I had come and put them in the corral. Then I got four horses

421

and tied them up to the trees and let the others out and started them down to the water. Then I went inside and started eating. She had eaten already and began saddling up the horses outside.

After I ate I fixed up the things I wanted to leave there. I put them on an old robe, tied the robe together and carried it into the woods. There I found a good place upon a tree and hid them away. We had two horses packed up and a few things on the other two. Then I turned out the herd and we started off, both leading a packhorse, to Trail Along The Edge Of The Wood, where her home was. We intended to camp across from her home, but we changed our minds and took the herd close to their corral, around in back, and there we unpacked all our things. I took the saddles off the horses and hobbled them and she went over to the hogan. In the meantime I made a brush hogan back of the corral and built a fire. About that time the herd started off again. I was going to go after them, but a woman was walking after our herd. That was her younger sister. She herded for us that afternoon. After a while my wife brought some food to where I had made the brush hogan. She had made some tortillas and coffee and roasted some meat. After we ate I said, "Did you tell them that we were going up on the mountain?" "Yes," she said, "but they don't want us to move up there. They want us to move with them down to Navajo Mountain. They said they were going to move to that place, because there was plenty of feed for the stocks. They said there were all kinds of grass, different kinds of feed, greasewood and other feed, down in that country; so they want us to move down to that place with them." I said, "They can move down to that place if they want to, but I'm not going down there. I won't act like a dog. A dog, you know, will go any old place where people are moving. Even though he doesn't know a person he will start after him. So I won't act like that. Let them move down to that place. I'm moving up on the mountain."

The next morning after I brought the horses back she said, "When do you want to start moving? Are you going to move this morning?" "No," I said, "we will stay here for two more days, and then we'll move to the mountain, but not today." "They wanted to know if we were willing to start moving this morning. That's why I asked." "No," I said, "we will stay around here for two days more. Can anybody herd for us again today? Go and see if they will help us on herding again today, because I want you to go with me down to where we buried the corn." She went over to the hogan and came back and said, "Yes, they are going to take the herd out for us." While they were taking out the herd we saddled up the horses and rode down to where I had buried the corn. We opened the hole and took some out; it looked nice. When we had enough we covered the hole again. I fixed it up the way I had had it before and we started back. It took us all that day to shell the corn. When we were done we had a seamless sack almost full. Around evening when the herd was in again I got them up close against the corral. When we were moving around, whenever we stayed out someplace with the herd at night, it wouldn't move at all. It would stay at one place all night. That evening while she was cooking, one of her younger brothers came. He asked me, "When are you going to move again, my older brother? Are you going to move to-morrow?" "Yes," I said, "I guess we'll go tomorrow; but I'm not sure yet; maybe the next day." About that time the cooking was done. The boy who had been herding for us that day was still there and we all ate together.

The boy said, "How about it? We wanted to play the moccasin game tonight. We played the game once, and we would like to play again with you tonight." I said, "All right." So after we ate they went back to their home, and there they came, four boys with their sister, five of them. One of the boys, the one who herded for us, got on our side. He wanted to be our partner. Then I bet against the oldest boy. He said, "I'll bet against you with one kid." I said, "All right, I have a goat too." And my wife bet her younger sister with a goat too, and the boy who herded for us bet against one of his older brothers. I have forgotten what he bet with. So we all bet one another. They had a hundred and two sticks made up already, tied together in a bunch, and they had a round ball that we were going to use to hide. That was already made, and a little stick that we were going to use on the moccasins. They laid these things in the middle of the hogan; then they cut out a piece of corn-husk. They blackened one side and threw this thing up, and we were calling for the black side, and they were calling for the grey. We were all saying, "Black! Black!" and they were all saying "Grey! Grey!" When this thing dropped to the ground, the black side was up, so we got the little round bundle. We hid it, behind a robe, in one of the moccasins. Then the boy took the robe away. One fellow picked up the stick; he pointed to one moccasin, saying, "This hasn't got anything in it." He got the dirt out of it, and nothing was in it, except the dirt. Then he pounded on another, "This hasn't got anything in it," he said. He took all the dirt out of it; there was nothing in it but the dirt. So there were two moccasins left, filled with dirt. Then he went back across to his partners, "Two moccasins left," he said, "so you go and get the ball out, wherever you think it is." He gave the stick to one of his partners, and he walked across towards us. He beat once on one of the moccasins, "The ball is in this moccasin," he said, as he beat once on the moccasin. He started taking out the dirt, and he got the ball out. He carried it back across with him and they hid it. We started going back and forth with this ball for three or four times, guessing it right; then from there on one side or the other would be missing a few times. It went that way for a long time until, all at once, they started missing. They were trying to guess where the ball was, but they just kept missing it. Soon we got all the sticks, and we had won. So we won the two goats.

Then we played once more. "I'll bet against you with one wether goat, my older brother," he said to me, "a five-year-old wether goat." "What color is it?" I asked. "A red goat," he said, "and he has got grey ears." I said, "All right, I have got a five-year-old wether too. Mine is black, and has grey ears also." The two women bet against each other with kids again. I don't remember what the boy did. We started playing again. We were playing right along. Their side would start missing for a while, and then when the ball would go to the other side we on our side would start missing. It went like that for a long time, and then we started getting all the sticks again. I was all in. I was tired and sleepy, but we were getting all the sticks. They kept on missing. Finally we almost got all. We had a hundred. "This is all that's left," they said. They all came across with the two sticks; they dropped them down before us, "Well, here we go. This will be the last, and we will have lost again." While he was saying this he pounded on one moccasin, "Nothing in this," he said. He took all the dirt out. Nothing was in it. He gave the stick to one of his partners; as soon as he got the stick he pounded on one. "Nothing in this moccasin," he said. He started taking the dirt out of the moccasin, and nothing was in it, except the dirt. Then he gave the stick to the third boy. As soon as he got the stick he pounded on one. "Nothing in this moccasin," he said. "No use guessing," he said while he was pounding on one again. He started taking out the dirt, and there was nothing in this moccasin. So they got the ball out. They knew where it was, because there was only one moccasin left. They got out the ball and picked up the two sticks and went back across. Right away I thought we had lost, even though we had a hundred sticks. I walked across with the stick, pounded on one moccasin and said, "Nothing in this moccasin." But the ball was in it, and that counts ten. So we gave them ten sticks and we started to go back and forth. We never got the ball out. Every time we went across we missed, until in the end, like them, we had only two sticks left.

It was way after midnight. It may have been almost morning. It seemed that way. All three of us went across, took the two sticks with us and I said, "Here we go. This is the last. If I miss, I miss, and I'll lose. If I take the bundle out, then that will be the end, and I won't lose. We will all just quit. What we have bet will be ours again. If I miss then I have got to lose. If I get it out I won't attempt to hide it, because I'm so sleepy and so tired, we'll just stop altogether, and what belongs to us will be ours. How is that?" I asked them. "That's all right," they said, "whatever you say is all right with us. So just go ahead; do whatever you want to do."

I laid the two sticks on the ground before them and pounded on one moccasin. "Nothing in this," I said. Sure enough there was nothing in it, except the dirt. I skipped one, pounded on another and said, "This moccasin hasn't got anything in it." There was nothing in it, only the dirt. So there were only two left. We started guessing which moccasin had the ball. It took us a long time, thinking and deciding. I said, "That ball is in this moccasin." I was holding one and my wife was holding the other, saying, "The ball is in this moccasin." I thought, "Perhaps I have missed." I wasn't so sure myself, so I told her, "Go ahead with yours, and get the ball out, and I'll let mine go." And those three boys were all singing and hollering, having all kinds of fun. She started talking out the dirt, and while she was doing that she said, "The ball is in this moccasin." Then the boys got worse. They all got up, dancing around, beating on a stick or bucket or anything they wanted to pound on. They sure did have lots of fun with us. So we missed. It was in the moccasin that I was holding. That was the last. We had lost. If we had taken out the ball, we wouldn't have lost, even though we had only two sticks left.

That's the way it goes. When you get tired, if you have two or one left over, if you want to quit, then you can quit on one or two sticks, and then you won't lose. So then we had lost. We took the moccasins out of the hole; the boys had gone back home, and we just dropped over and went right to sleep. We only slept a while. When I got up she was still sleeping so I woke her. She got right up and I started the fire and she started to warm some water. After we had washed ourselves—we had been in the dirt almost all night—I said, "You hurry with the cooking. I would like to get an early start for the mountain, and you can go and get the kid that I won last night. That little kid is still mine, so bring it back over here and butcher it. I'm going after the horses." So while she started on the cooking I went after the horses. I tracked them pretty far before I caught up with them. I put a rope on one and hobbled the others and then chased them back to the hogan. She had butchered the little kid and was there with her younger brother, the boy who had been herding for us. When I got back with the horses she had laid out the food for me but I told them to eat some more. They had already eaten, but I said, "Eat some more, because we won't get anything to

426

eat until we get on top of the mountain." She said, pointing to her younger brother, "He is going to herd for us again. They told him to go with us, so he is going with us up on the mountain." I was very glad about it. "Well, well, that's very nice that you are going to help us on herding again, my younger brother," I said to him.

I got up; I was chewing on the food; I didn't have it chewed well, but I swallowed it that way, because I was so glad about the boy. I hollered to the old women, I said, "Thank you. I am very glad you have let us have the boy. I am very glad he is going to herd for us again. Thank you very much, my mother," I said to the two old women. They were in the hogan close by. The one who was my mother-in-law was a paternal cousin. Her father was Mexican People, and so was my father's father. The other, the older woman, I just called her my mother. I was sure glad about the boy. Then I sat down again and started eating. I said to the boy, "It's very nice that you are going to help us again, so, as soon as you eat, you can take out the herd and just go ahead with them slowly toward the foot of the mountain. Just let them feed, don't try to drive them fast. We two will start to get ready. As soon as we have everything ready we'll start after you. Have you got a saddle?" "No," he said, "I haven't got a saddle. I only have an old saddle." "Well, get your bridle and whatever you have, blanket, robe, and you can ride one of those horses that are extra." So he went and got his bridle and bridled up a horse. We had fixed up the horse for him.

Then he got on and started off with the sheep. We took our time with our things. When we had everything packed we had a lot of junk, and enough food to last us a long time. We loaded the pack horse and put some things on the horses we were riding and started after the boy. He had gone straight over toward Where Lots Of Rocks Were Washed Out, and when we got to that place, there he was. We caught up with him and went right along. I had turned the packhorse loose into the herd, and he went right along among the sheep. We got into a thick wood and started going uphill. It was a real rocky place, so many rocks, small and large. We went along through such a rough place until we got to the foot of the mountain; then we started going up. It was pretty steep. The trail would wind a lot. About the middle of the mountain I saw the cattle tracks. I was sorry. I knew I wouldn't see them again, because I couldn't do much all by myself. So I started sorrowing for my cattle, but I couldn't do anything about it. Finally we got to the top, to a place called White Valley Coming To The Edge. The sun was down.

We had been climbing up the mountain all day and didn't have a bite to eat. We stopped the herd there where there was lots of feed of all kinds. There was a little snow on the mountain, and the herd was feeding around in the evening. I said, "We'll stop and camp here for tonight. Hurry with the cooking. Cook plenty, so we will all have enough. I know we will eat a lot, because we didn't have anything all day." The two went on with the cooking, while I hobbled the horses and started walking around the herd, until it got dark. Then I rounded them up to where we were camping. As soon as you would round them up to one place at night they wouldn't move again. They would be right at one place, all night. Everything was cooked, and we started eating. We ate a lot.

After we ate we had a big fire and sat around it. I said, "I am so sorry about my cattle, because I didn't get to see them again, not since the middle of summer. That's the last time I saw them. From there on I never got to see them again. I wonder how they are by now. Perhaps they are all alive yet. Maybe some have been killed again. I wish I had a helper. I wish I had a real brother or nephew or clansman so that he or they could help me on herding the sheep and taking care of the cattle and horses, but here I am all alone, and I can't handle all these things by myself."

She said, "Well, it's your own greed. That's the way I am thinking about you. I know, you are just by yourself, but you want to have more sheep, more horses, and more cattle, even though, I know, you can't handle them all by yourself. Nobody wanted you to do that; but it's you, yourself, always wanting more of something. That's what I have heard lots of times. Almost all the people who come to our place talk about you like that. Even though you are alone, even though you

428

have nobody to help you, you always want to have more herds, more horses, and more of everything. And the people can't understand how you are keeping them all. They say they all know there is lots of work with only the sheep. Even a small herd, there is lots of work to it. So they were wondering how you can stand all these stocks and other work. They can't imagine how you do it. So I am thinking that way, too. Why do you want a lot of stock?" I said, "It's not I who wanted to raise a lot. I don't want them. But it's they themselves raising themselves. Every spring they will renew themselves, improve themselves, even though I don't want them around. In the springtime there will be a whole lot of lambs and kids; there will be a lot of colts, and the same with the cattle, they will have calves. And exactly the same thing happens with property. Even though I don't want it a fellow will hand something to me, begging me to take it, and they make me take it. So you see now, it's they themselves raising themselves."

Then I said, "I know they are talking of me like that, but the things themselves, once started, go on. That's the way with all the stocks. But when you haven't got anything, even though you try your best to get something, you won't get it. You will be without things all the time. You will just be wishing for things, and I don't call that a life. You will be going around begging for things. You will just have your spit in your stomach, that's all. But like the way we are now, then anything that you wish for you will have. As soon as you wish for something you will have it. That's the way it is. So let them talk. Don't pay any attention to that kind of talk. Just think about the things we have. If you do that then you will enjoy your life. When you are without things then you won't enjoy yourself. That's the way with myself. That's the way I was taught by my old grandfathers, mother and father and clansmen. I listened to their talks and picked them up and kept them to myself, and that is what I am going by. You know I was raised in the midst of things, so that's all I'm thinking about. You mustn't listen to the people. You must keep at your work all the time. That's what I want you to do. I want you to tend to your own work. I picked you up, because

429

I didn't want you to starve for different kinds of food and for meat, and I don't want you to go in rags. I don't want you to go poor. I picked you up because I wanted you to have everything, and you will have everything that you want. I have got you now, and you are with me in the midst of all kinds of things, and you know that. Even though you know it you don't pay any attention to it. You ought to think about these things. You ought only to think about the herd, horses and cattle, besides what little property we have. But I know you don't think about them. I know you are always thinking about troubling me in some way. All you think about is men, and you know very well you can't get anything out of that. If you go and do a lot of bad things with the men soon you will be a poor woman. You will be a fool. Everybody will make fun of you. You don't want to get that way. You don't want everybody to make fun of you. So you ought not to think about the bad things. If you just stick to your work you will be the same as you are now all the time. Nobody will make fun of you. Later on everybody will look up to you for help of some kind, because they will know that you have everything, and nobody will make fun of you. So be like that all the time," I said to her. "Now what do you think about it? Which way do you think is the best? Without things? Or would you like to have things?"

She said, "I would like to have things. I don't want to be without them. I want to be as I am now all the time. I know now I have enough to eat and enough of everything. I want to be like that all the time, and I won't listen to the other's talks. I want to be with you all the time, and I won't leave you. I am very glad that I married you. If I had married another man I wouldn't be the way I am now. That's the way I am thinking about myself. From the time I married you you started taking care of me so very nicely, and you have been feeding me a lot. Since that time I have gotten all I wanted from you. You bought me some clothing the time we went to the Night Chant. I dressed up in these clothes, and you decorated a horse for me, and we went to the chant, and I wasn't a bit ashamed of myself, because I had good clothes and a nice decorated horse. And we went across to Carriso the same way. When you took me across to that place I never was ashamed of myself, because I was dressed up in good clothing. I am very glad about that, and I want to be like that all the time, and that's why I want to be with you all the time."

But I didn't believe her. I knew very well she only said it, because she always had a man on her mind. So, even though she said that, I didn't believe her. I never thought she meant it. I said to her, "If you are truthful about that I will be very glad about it. If you are not truthful about it then you will be without things. If you hold on to your work then you will be the same always, and you will be healthy and strong and lively all the time. So, if you mean what you say, then I will be very glad about it, and I will be thinking about you all the time. I will try and help you always. Whatever you ask for I will think about it and if I am able to get something that you want I will surely get it for you. But if you forget everything and run off from me, or if you get yourself in trouble again, then it will be your own fault. It will be just too bad for you. So you want to be careful on everything." "That's the way I want to be. I want to be the way I am now, and I have said that to you already, and I have promised not to hurt you by anything more, and I mean it. So, please, don't think of me that way. Don't think I will hurt you again. I am listening to your talk, and I know you want me to have everything, and now I'm thinking that I will be as I am right now all the time."

Then I said to the boy, "And you are just the same too. You don't know where you will be, and you don't know how you will be. Now, I know, you are only running around to different places. If you do that, only run around to different places, you won't get anywhere. You will be without things all the time. You'll only be running around. Perhaps you'll soon start begging for things, and the people will start hating you, and you will sure get in trouble of some kind. Maybe you'll take something that doesn't belong to you, and that's stealing. If you get caught at that you'll get in trouble, and lots of other things that you don't know about will get you in trouble. So you ought to be in one place all the time. You have a herd at your home; you ought to tend only to your

431

herd. By doing that you will get something out of it. And if you stay with us and herd for us all winter, around in shearing time you can get some wool. Or perhaps you will want the money. If you want the money I will give you some when I sell my wool." She said, "I guess he will be with us all winter, because I know he hasn't got anything to do at home, and I know he will be glad when he gets some money or some wool. It will be a good thing for him when he gets some money. Then he will have new clothes. If he goes back to his home he won't get any money there. Even if he were to herd all winter nobody would give him any money or any clothes." I said, "It's up to him. If he wants to stay he can stay. If he wants to go back home, he can go back home. So it's up to him."

That was all the talk we had that night. Then we fixed up our bedding. The boy didn't have any blanket or robe, so I told her to get out a robe for him. "I see he hasn't got anything to wrap himself up with." She got out a robe, the one that was striped with all different colors like the rainbow; she got that out and gave it to her younger brother. "Thank you, thank you, my older sister," he said. Again he said, "Thank you very much, you have given me a robe." She said, "Don't thank me for that. I didn't give you that robe. The robe wasn't mine. It belonged to your brother-in-law. Thank him for the robe." The boy said, "He didn't give it to me. Maybe it belonged to him, but you got it out of the sack, and you handed it to me. I got the robe out of your hand. That's why I am thanking you." I just laughed about the boy. He was so tickled about it. He spread it out and said, "Thanks to you both. What a pretty robe you have given me."

The next morning we all got up. The herd had scattered out and started eating. I said, "Let them graze around." I looked and there the horses were close by. "The horses are around close to us. They didn't go very far." There was all kinds of feed for the horses, all kinds of grazing for the herd. We had a big fire going and cooked some food and started eating. While we were eating I said, "We will move again. We will move on this morning, down to where White Rocks Are Standing. We will camp there. I think there's more feed

432

for the herd and horses and there's water there, too. We'll move down to that place today. So, as soon as you eat, you can start off with the herd," I said to the boy. "And we will start packing up here."

After we ate I got the horses and he started off with the herd, and we started saddling up, putting the things on the horses. We got everything on the packhorse and then started after the boy. We caught up with him at Cattails Standing Up and went on with the herd following the sage brush valley. The valley comes out from a place called Another Canyon. A little way below that place we turned around toward White Rocks Are Standing. We went around the rocks and camped on the other side, the southeast side, where we thought it would be nice and warm from the sun. The sun was almost down when we got to that place. It was quite a ways from there to White Valley Coming To The Edge.

As soon as we had everything off the horses I hobbled them and started to make a brush hogan. The sun was down when I got through with it. Then I started gathering up some wood, enough for the night, and I rounded the herd up against a little cliff there. It was sure a nice place, all kinds of feed for the animals. This was where we used to live a long time ago; when I was a little kid we used to live there. The hogan was still up, just the poles, the dirt and cedar bark were off, and the corral we had had there was all down to the ground. Everything looked real old to me. That was where Who Has Mules had learned some songs. This was the second time we moved there and I sure did like that place. I liked it because there was lots of feed for the herd and horses.

Next morning we got up early. Right after we ate I told the boy, "Take the herd out. As soon as they get enough bring them back. They will have enough around by noon. When they have had enough grazing they will be wanting to lie down, so if they start to lie down bring them back." He took out the herd and I picked up an ax and started cutting some new poles for the hogan. The old ones were full of cracks. At noon I ate a little lunch and right after that went into the woods again. The boy didn't get back with the herd

433

at noon. I was working on the poles all that day. Around evening I came back and right after we ate I went to bed. The next morning the boy took the herd out again and I cut more poles until noon. After lunch I started gathering up the ones I had cut and when I got them all together I cut some more until evening. After breakfast the next morning while the herd was out I gathered up the rest of the poles I had cut. I decided I had had enough and started building the hogan. My wife was gathering up cedar bark to cover it with. When the sun was almost down I had finished putting up the poles and started putting on the cedar bark and I put on a little dirt, just around the top. I had to take the dirt up with a robe. We didn't have a shovel. After I put the dirt on top we built a fire inside, hung a robe at the doorway, and then made a white spot on the east side with white corn meal, then on the south side, then the west, and finally on the north, inside the hogan. I marked the hogan with spots in four places, and sprinkled some around inside, and then we carried in our things. After that I got out my corn pollen and we all took some and sprinkled out some for ourselves, saying, "We will live well in the hogan. We will live a long life. We will have enough to eat all the time, and we will have more of everything. And we will be on the good path, all the time, and we will be full of joy. We will live in joy. We will have a joyous life all the time." This was what we said as we sprinkled the corn pollen.

The boy went out with the herd again the next day, and I started making a corral. About noon I was about half finished with the corral and a fellow rode up to us. That was my younger brother, one of Who Has Mules' boys, whose older brother had gotten after my wife. He got off his horse and shook hands with me. "When did you move here, my older brother?" he asked me. "We moved here about four days ago," I said. "Are you going to live here for some time?" "Yes," I said. "That's why I put up a hogan, and now I'm making a corral; so I don't know when we'll move again. Maybe we'll live here all winter. It all depends on how the feed is. Where are you from?" He said, "I'm from Water In Reeds." "Is that where you home is?" "Yes, that's where we live." "Is your father at home?" "Yes, he is home," he said. "Whereabouts are you going?" I asked again. "I'm going around all the places looking for cattle." Then I asked, "Whereabouts is Choclays Kinsman living?" "He lives up here at Willows Coming Out. I just passed by his place a while ago, and I passed his herd, so he is living up there."

I said, "Yes, we have moved here, and I don't know how long we will stay here. There's very nice grazing all around. Well, then, my younger brother, help a little on this corral. I think soon we will have some food to eat." He said, "All right." He tied up his horse to the tree and started dragging in some branches to where I was making a corral. While he was working on it I went over to the hogan, and there my wife was cooking some food. I said, "Cook enough. There's my younger brother helping me. He is looking for cattle, but I told him to help me a little, so he is." She said, "I think I have enough food cooked for all of us, and soon I'll have everything ready." Then I went back and began dragging in more branches.

When she called us we went back to the hogan, and there I asked him about the cattle. "Are the cattle all around here?" "Yes," he said. "Some of them are way up on top of the mountain, and some are around here. I will go around Green Around The Canyon. I think a lot of them are down in there. They always gather around there, so I guess I'll ride down to that place." "Why are you looking for them? Are you going to kill one? Or are you just wanting to look them over?" "Yes, I just want to ride around among them. I just want to know how far they get out here. I don't see any tracks here. Sometimes they get way out here, around about this time, but I guess they haven't started to come out this way yet. We killed one a few days ago, so I'm not killing one right now."

Then, after we had eaten with him, I said, "When you get back tell our father that I would like to have some of his cattle meat. I don't want to kill a good-sized one. I would like to have a yearling. So when you get home tell him that I want to kill one of his cattle. I wonder what he will say, if I kill one." He said, "I don't think he'll say anything. I guess it will be all right, but I'll tell him what you have said." I asked him,

435

"Is his earmark different from yours?" "No," he said, "The earmark is all the same, and there are no other cattle around here, only ours." "Well, then," I said, "I will kill one, and you just tell him what I said. I'm kind of hungry for cattle meat. Even though I have got some cattle, they are way down almost to the foot of the mountain, and it's hard to get them, and hard to get them up here. If I kill one down there it will be too much of a load for me. That's why I said I would kill one of his. So you tell him that for me, my younger brother." He said, "All right, I will." "So you don't think he will say anything about it?" I asked. "No," he said, "I don't think so." "Well, then, I will kill one any time I want to." That was all. He said, "I guess I had better go and look around and see where they are."

He got on his horse and rode away, and I walked over where I was making the corral and started working again. I was working on the corral all afternoon, until sundown. I had it well fixed, and I had cut some poles for the gate. When the herd came in we drove them all in the corral and I fixed up the gate. In the morning I asked the boy about the horses. "Did you see the horses anyplace?" "Yes, they are quite a ways in the woods. I saw them there." "Is there any snow up in the woods?" "Yes, there is some snow all around in the woods." After we ate I said, "I'll go over to where the horses are." I picked up a rope and walked up in the woods, and there I saw only two. I started looking for the other two; pretty soon I had tracked them back the way we had come. I caught up with them in White Valley Coming To The Edge where the trail branched off toward Another Canyon. They had gone that far. I guess they wanted to get down to the foot of the mountain. I got home with them in the afternoon. I said, "They had gone pretty far. The other two are still close by, up here in the woods. There is lots of feed for them; but I don't know why these two were going away from us. I was thinking I would go over to my old father's (Choclays Kinsman's) place today. I am eager to see him and my older sister, but it's getting too late now." She said, "Why don't you go now and stay up there over night?" I said, "I guess I'll do

436

that." After we two had eaten I put the saddle on one horse and started off leading the other up into the woods where the two other horses were. After I had hobbled the one I was leading I went on.

21

He visits his old father . . .
Rounding up the horses . . . How
to live . . . He learns songs about
stocks and properties.

The sun was down when I got to Willows Coming Out. A little way from that place, on the south side, was where they were living (Choclays Kinsman and his wife). The herd was just coming in. I rode up to the hogan and tied my horse to a tree and walked in. There was my older sister sitting in the hogan. My old father wasn't home. I walked up to her and sat down by her, and she put her arm around me, and I put my arm around her. Right away she started crying, and while she was crying she started talking. "My younger brother," she said, "I have missed you all this time. You left us here alone, and we were suffering. When you were up here with us we weren't suffering like this. You used to be around all the time, helping us on everything, water and wood, and helping us on the herd, and on everything that we have. When you left us here, from there on we started doing all the work ourselves, and it is just too much for us. I was wondering why you left us, and why you never came and visited us. I was thinking you must have heard something awful about me, or about your father. Someone must have told you something about us that hurt you. That's the way I am thinking about you. And I always thought, 'I wonder what I have done and said to him?' But there was nothing that I had done or said to you. I never hurt you with anything. So why is it that you have pushed us away, my younger brother? I always think of you, and I am always glad to see you. I am glad to see you now again. I am glad you have come."

438

Then she said, "I heard that you had married, and I sometimes think about that. I start thinking, 'Maybe his wife doesn't want him to go around among us. Maybe his wife is holding him back on everything.' I think that way sometimes, because I know lots of women are that way. They don't want their husbands to go around. They will hold their husbands back on anything. When a woman is jealous about her husband she will do that. She won't let her husband go any place. So sometimes I get to thinking that way, since I heard that you had married. Because when you were single you used to be going all around among us, and I always used to talk nice about you, because you used to help us a lot on all things, and you used to go to the stores, even though the stores are a long distance off. In the summertime, even though it was hot, and in the winter, even though it was real cold, you used to go around for us lots of times. Even though it was hot or cold you didn't care. So maybe it's your wife who doesn't want you to go around any more, my younger brother."

I said, "I never heard anything bad from you. I guess maybe you have thought that way of me, my older sister, but I never heard anything from you that hurt me, and I know you have never said or done anything to me that would hurt me. I know very well you never have hurt me by anything. And no one kept me away from you. You said maybe the woman had kept me away from you, but it's not that way. It's myself that has kept me away from you, because I am way down in the flat. It's quite a distance from there up to here, and you know that I am only by myself. Even though I haven't got many herds I have got to tend to them. Nobody is helping on that. And I have got a few horses; I have got to tend to them, and nobody is helping me on that. And I have got a few head of cattle, and I have got to tend to them, and nobody is helping me on that. Besides that I have got some little work, like a field of corn; I have got to tend to that by myself; and around the hogan I have got to look after things, water and wood and food, and I have to do all this by myself; so there is no chance for me to go around among you people. And even though I do all these things by myself I go to Slim

439

Man's place and help him. I am helping him right along. Even though he has got lots of help I have got to be there when he wants me to help him. That's the way it is with me, my older sister. We moved down here to where the White Rocks Are Standing Up—the two of us were coming up alone, but they loaned us a boy, the woman's younger brother, so we have got help. He is helping us on herding. That's why I had a chance to come up. So I started, and I have gotten here now, my older sister. I guess that's the way with us all. We are thinking the same, and I know everybody needs help and wants to have help. When I was up here I used to help you all the time. I used to go wherever you wanted me to go, but ever since I moved down I haven't had a chance to come and to visit you. But I always thought you were getting along all right. And now I am glad that I have visited you, and we have seen each other again. We know we are still living, and I am glad of that, my older sister."

Then she got up and took down some sheep pelts and laid them down close by where my old father's bed was, on the north side of the hogan. She said, "I didn't want to cook any more food. I had some cooked already for the herders, but it is all cold, and some of it is left over from this morning and this noon, so I guess I'll cook some fresh food." While she went on with her cooking I asked about my old father. "Where has my old father gone to? Is he out someplace?" "Yes," she said. "He went out this morning. He goes out every morning. He goes up to the top of the mountain to round up the horses. When he gets some of them rounded up he brings them down here and then drives them to the water. That's what he's been doing now for a few days. I guess he is coming back. He'll be back in a little while." "Where are all the others, the helpers," I asked her. "They are all out there in the corral." "What are they doing?" I asked, "Are there some sheep or goats having little ones? It sounds that way to me." "No," she said, "There are some lambs that haven't got any mothers, a lot of them that we raised, and those are the ones we are still feeding with milk. That's what they are doing. They are feeding the little lambs. If we don't feed them they will be making a noise all night. As soon as they

440

get a little drop of milk they will keep quiet. So, I guess, that's what they are doing."

Just then the boy came in. He shook hands with me, and then the other boy, that was Choclays Kinsman's slave, came in. He shook hands with me. Then the girl came in. She was a helper of my old father. She stood to the fire for quite a while. I guess she had decided to shake hands with me, she walked up and shook my hand; we just shook hands; we didn't say anything to each other. (That was another woman that I used to go around with. I had been around with her where she was herding.) My older sister said, "Why didn't you say something to each other while you were shaking hands. You only shook hands, without a sound. Why is that?" she asked. I laughed about it and the girl was smiling. I said, "I thought that was all right. I was eager to see her and glad that she shook hands with me. That's the way I thought about her as she shook my hand, and I guess she had thought the same about me." My older sister started laughing, "How could you tell that you were both thinking about each other that way?" she asked me. She was laughing about it for a long time.

Then I went out, took the saddle off the horse and hobbled him, and took the saddle inside and laid it against the hogan and used it for my pillow. A little while after that the dogs began to bark. Then I heard a sound outside. I heard the step of a horse, and I heard someone take off the saddle and I guess he had hobbled the horse there. Choclays Kinsman came in and sat down beside me; he put his arm around me and I put my arm around him and we both wept. My old father was looking so very poorly. That's why I wept for him. We held each other for a long time. Then, I was kind of observing this girl. She had grown up to be a woman. She used to be thin, and there she was looking healthy and stout. She had a big butt, and that made me wish for her. So I was looking and wondering how I would get a chance again. And I was wondering if she was the wife of my old father. She was a good-looking woman. The cooking was about done and my old father said, "Why don't you cook some more meat? Even though the meat is dry you ought to cook some more." They

441

brought in some dry meat and put it on the charcoal to roast, and then my older sister started pounding it with a rock. When she had it good and soft she put it in the grease and fried it a little. When it was done they laid the food out for us two. The others began eating also, separate from us.

My old father said, "I was up on the mountain. I have been going up there every day, bringing the horses down. It gets cloudy every once in a while. I thought it might snow any time, so I'm afraid of that. That's why I'm trying to get all the horses down here. He was helping me," he said, pointing to his slave. "I thought he was coming up after me, but he never showed up. I don't know what he had been doing all day. That's what I am doing for a few days now my son, bringing the horses down. I haven't brought them all down yet. I didn't get any of them down today, because I was up there all by myself. I found some, but I couldn't do anything with them, because they were kind of wild, and the woods were too thick. I got on to one bunch which used to belong to my older brother (Old Man Hat)—there is a grey stud with this one bunch of horses—I started them down; I got them down as far as where the trail goes down; then they turned around and they all ran away from me. I just let them go. I thought it is no use for me to bother with them. I knew I couldn't do anything with them alone. If he had come up we would have them driven down, but he didn't come up again today. There are quite a few more of mine still up on the mountain. Maybe I won't get them all down, but I'll try.

"That's all I have to tell. I have got nothing more to tell, so I want you to tell me what you know about the country down at the foot of the mountain and out in the flat and about yourself. What have you been doing all this time, and where have you kept yourself? We haven't see each other for a long time, but I guess we are all alike; we have got so much to do." I said, "I haven't got anything to tell. I have got nothing to tell about." "Don't say you have got nothing to tell about. Don't try to make me believe you. I know very well that you have lots to tell, because I know you people down there married way over on the other side of another mountain. I heard that you people had driven some horses over

442

there, so there is lots to tell about that. And not long after that the people had a Night Chant at Along Red Rock, and I heard that you people were there, and not long after that I heard that you went across the country for hunting and that has got a lot of story to it. So come on with your story," he said to me. My older sister was laughing about it. "Oh my," she said, "I know now there are lots of things to tell about. I think you won't get through telling about all those things tonight. I know it will take you all night to tell about those things," she said to me while she was laughing. "I don't think we will get any sleep."

He said, "First tell about where you started from yesterday or today. Where are you living?" he asked me. I said, "I started from a little below here, on the south side of Water In Reeds. You know where the White Rocks Are Standing Up?" He said, "Yes." "Right at the foot of those rocks, that's where I started from this morning." "Oh, have you moved up here? It sounds like it." "Yes, I have moved up to that place." "Well, then," he said, "we will let that go first. Go ahead with the other story."

Then I started in and told him about that last summer, about how Slim Man had gone over the mountain. I just made a quick story about that; not very closely, I told him only the main things. Then I made another quick story about the Night Chant. When I was through with that, I started telling him about how my father had gone over the mountain again for the wagon, and how I had gone across to Carriso for the herd. I said, "My wife and I brought the herd back with us, and my mother stayed over at that country, and she is still over there. She hasn't come back yet." He said, "I guess she is still hunting." When he said this, my older sister started laughing. "Hunting!" she said. "She must be eager to hunt. She has been hunting all summer. How much longer does she want to hunt?" she said while she was laughing.

Then I told him about the trip that we had made across the country to hunt. I made a quick story again about that. I said we had been camping at one place and our horses had been taken away from us. We had been left on foot. Some people helped us and we went after our horses and we got

443

the horses back from the white men and no one was hurt. He said, "A while back when any tribe treated you that way the people used to go after the enemies. If they didn't catch up with them then they just gave it up, but if they did catch up with them one side had to be killed. There used to be a fight to it. There used to be lots of shooting to it. There used to be killing in it. But now nobody is doing that any more. I am glad you got the horses back, and I am glad all of you, my children, got back. Not one of you got hurt. That's the way to do. You don't want to be dead right now. I'm glad you didn't start trouble. I am glad that all of you came back. That's the way we are hearing from our headmen. They all don't want us to start any trouble, not any more with any tribe. We know we would all have been gone long ago if the Americano had not picked us up. We would all have been gone long ago, but he picked us up and hid us away and took good care of us.[1] Then he brought us back to our country, and we were all glad that we had come back. When he brought us back he told us not to steal, not to kill any more. He told us to behave. He told us to take good care of one another, not only among ourselves, of everybody. He didn't want us to be enemies of any tribe. I guess those fellows had known all about this, and I guess that's why they didn't try to start up trouble. I am very glad about that. But all of these things that we had been told by them (the headmen) we have kept to ourselves. Some of us still remember his word, and you don't know anything about it, my son, my baby," he said to me. "But I am glad about you all, that everyone of you had come back to your country without any trouble. I am glad about that." I told him all that had been done and that had passed that summer. We kept awake pretty near all night.

We all got up early the next morning and the girl who helped there started the fire, and all the helpers were helping around. She started cooking and when she was done we all started eating. After we ate my old father said, "Go and get the horses. Those that we use around here every day and

1. A reference to the captivity at Fort Sumner, in 1864–1868.

444

some others that we hobbled. Bring all of them back here. And I guess your older brother's horse is hobbled too. His horse is probably around here close, so get his horse for him also. Which way are you wanting to go this morning, my baby? Or what did you want here? Did you want anything here?" he asked. "Yes, I put up a hogan, and I haven't got a shovel to use on it, so that's what I came here for, to borrow a shovel from you. If you have one I would like to borrow it." "Well," he said, "we have two shovels. One of you get the shovel that we have hidden in a cave." Then he said, "I want you to help me today. Oh, wait, have you got a herder?" I said, "Yes, I have got a boy herding for me." "Well, then, it will be all right. I want you to help me on the horses today. I would like to get some horses down. I would like to get my older brother's horses down, too" (he meant my father, Old Man Hat). "All three of us will go up."

Meanwhile the boy had brought the horses back and we started saddling up. While we were tying our robes on to the saddles my older sister said, "You had better take some lunch along with you. I will fix you some lunch right now, so you had better wait." The old man said, "No, we don't want to carry any lunch around with us, too much trouble carrying lunch around. We don't want to lose time eating lunch, so we don't want to take it," he said, and we got on our horses and started off to a little canyon where they kept the horses they had been using. We changed horses there and started off again, down toward the west, quite a way down in the canyon to where the trail went out. We went up out of the canyon on the trail to the top and then started running our horses way up along in the woods. He said, "We want to hurry. We want to get to the edge of the mountain. When we get to the edge of the mountain we will turn around and scatter out." He told his slave to hurry on. He was leading us, going ahead of us running his horse, and we were going right after him. The old man said, "There are two horses always together, the two tame ones. Be sure and look well for those two, when we turn around. And there is another one also, who used to be by itself all the time. Maybe they have gotten together somehow, maybe not. This one never joins

445

up with any horse. He is always alone. So we'll look for those three when we start back."

Finally we got to the edge of the mountain and there he said to us, "Now we will turn around from here, and we'll search for the horses. We'll all meet one another down where we got out of the canyon, where the trail goes down in the canyon. We two will go way out and make a big circle, and you," he said to me, "can just turn around from here and start straight back down, but zigzag back and forth in the woods. Look closely for the horses. Every horse you see start down to the trail. Once you get them started on the trail they will keep on going. This grey stud's bunch will be down in these woods someplace. I know you will get on to it. It's a big bunch. When you get on to them, kind of scare them, ride up to them as hard as you can go and start them toward the trail. As soon as they get on the trail they will go." Then we branched off from one another and started down.

I went through the thick woods winding around, going back and forth. While I was going along I got to some horses' tracks. That was the big bunch they had talked about. Choclays Kinsman's slave, who had gone out towards the south had driven them towards the trail. Every once in a while I got on to the trail and the tracks of this big bunch. While I was going along I heard the old man holler. I answered him and he hollered again, so I turned around and started riding up to where he was hollering. He kept on hollering and I was hollering too. Soon we met and he had the three horses that he wanted to find. "These were the main ones that I wanted to get, and I got them. They were in the third point from this one here," he said, as he pointed to one that was close to us. "These were the main ones that I wanted to get, and I got them now. And that big bunch too, so I guess we'd better just go straight on down after this big bunch."

When we got to the trail he started hollering for his slave, "Choclay, Choclay," he yelled, "I have got the horses, so come, we are going home." But there was no sound. "He hears me, but he won't answer. He never hollers. Even though you holler to him he won't say anything." We went

446

on down that trail, driving those three horses. Every once in a while, as we were driving the horses down the trail after this big bunch, he hollered to the boy, but we didn't hear a sound from him. All at once we got on to the bunch. They had stopped at a little bare spot. As soon as we got on to them they beat it on to the trail, and we started after them as hard as we could go, but we didn't see them any more. We could hear their steps and see the dust; we could hear the noise they were making under the trees, and breaking up the branches. They tore down to the edge of the canyon, and the old man just kept hollering. The boy hadn't shown up yet, but I guess he was coming close. We couldn't see him, the dust was so thick.

When we got close to the edge of the canyon I went down toward the west to a little point and there at the edge of the cliff some of them were coming. I met them there and started them back and hollered, "There they go. They have gone back toward you." When I got close to the trail he hollered, "Down they went. We got all of them down." While he was still saying this I rode up to where he was, and there was his slave, too. We got out to the foot of the cliff and up into the canyon where the fence was. All of these horses had gone to the canyon. There was my horse close to the fence. I got him and saddled him up again and turned the other one loose. Then he thanked me a whole lot for helping him, even though I hadn't done anything. Those two were the ones who found the horses, but he was thanking me for the help I gave them. He said, "We got all the horses down, and now I won't worry about them. If we hadn't got them all down I would have been worrying about them all winter, but now I won't be, because I know we have got them all down. Now we'll let it snow. Let the snow come down. We don't care now," and he repeated all he had said to me, thanking me for helping.

We got back to camp just as the sun was going down, and the herd was just coming in. They had a big bunch of sheep. They had a little over two thousand. While they were coming toward the corral I looked at the herd. It looked like a big flood to me. They got them in the corral and the herders were all there with them. We took the saddles off our horses and I tied mine up and we went inside.

There my older sister was sitting by the fire. She had everything ready. As soon as the old man came in he said, "Put out the food. We are all hungry. We want to eat something right away." She started putting out the food, and after we ate he began talking about things, about the stocks, about life, about the different relatives, and about the land, about the feed and water, and about food of different kinds, and about the different kinds of meat, and about clothing and property. He talked about things like that, saying how to get a herd, how to get all of the stocks, and how to get them feed all the time, how to get fat meat, how to get different kinds of food for yourself. He said, "When you have all the stocks, property and land and different kinds of food for yourself you will live a good life. You won't go hungry. You won't go ragged. You won't go poor. You won't get to be a beggar. You won't beg for things. If you are lazy about all the things then you won't be a man. You won't enjoy life. You will be begging for things all the time, and nobody will like you. That's the way it is," he said. "You have been raised on talks of this kind. Your father raised you with all his talks. You have been raised by him, and so I guess you know about the different things. I know you do, because I know you are trying to get different kinds of stocks. I know you are trying to get ahead, because you have heard lots of things from the old man. He is dead now, but you remember his words. After he died we started talking to you, and we have all helped you by our talks, and I guess you have picked up a lot of them. And that's what you are going by now, my son, my baby," he said to me.

And the old woman was sitting there spinning the wool into yarn. There was lots of it piled beside her. She was sitting there spinning the wool while the old man was talking. "That's the way it is," he said. "I know you are having a hard time by yourself. We know even at that you are trying to get something more. Even though you can't handle it all, nevertheless you are trying to get more all the time. But that's the

448

way to do, my son, my baby. Even though you have real brothers and sisters, we don't know them. You know them. You have seen them, but they are far away from you, and I know they won't come and help you. And there are some of your close 'brothers' around here, but not one of them will help you. So you must go ahead and try to do what you can, and keep yourself well all the time. Don't drop anything, even though it's too hard for you. Hold on to it, and later on you will see everything. That's the way the old man was. He had seen all kinds of things, and he died, and we two now are getting real old, I and the fellow who lives over at Water In Reeds, whom we call Who Has Mules. We are both getting too old now, and you know that. But I am very glad that you have come and visited me. That's the way to do. You must remember us all, because we had picked you up, and we have raised you. We helped you a lot, so now this is your chance. You are still young, you are just a boy still, so this is your chance now. Try to help us, with whatever you want to help us with; or we will call for help; we will look up to you from now on, for you had been that way, and we had helped you a lot. That's the way it is."

And again he said, "So it's that way. Now you can go right along with your work. Try to get somewhere, even though you are all alone. Perhaps later on you will have a helper. That's the way my older brother used to be. He had everything, and he told you more than what I am telling you now. You heard a lot from him. He had raised you with that. And all of us are talking exactly the same. You know I am talking to you just as he used to talk to you, and if you go down to Long Mustache he will talk to you exactly the same, and if you go to Ruins he will talk to you exactly the same, and if you go down to His Horse Is Slow he will talk to you exactly the same, and you know very well that Slim Man is talking to you exactly the same. So every one of us talks exactly the same. However the talks that we have we didn't make up ourselves, we learned them. We got them from the old man (Old Man Hat). He used to talk to us like this all the time, and we still have his word. We still remember all, and that's what I am using all the time, and I guess you know that," he said to me. Then he started naming a lot of other men, "There are lots of old fellows who have lots of stuff. They all have lots of stock. They are living well. They have a big herd, a big herd of cattle, a big flock of horses and a big place for them, and a lot of property. They are living well because they aren't lazy. They still all have these things, and they are getting more and more of everything. So you try to be that way. And they all talk exactly like us. They are all talking to one another, all talking to the others about how to get stocks and property, and how to live a good life, and how to enjoy life. And that's all we are talking about, and I know you know all of these different kinds of talks, because you have been raised with them. That's the way with all the people, that is, some of them. Not all get that way. Some have only a few things. Some have a lot of things, and some have got nothing, and we know all about just how they have things or haven't. So I guess we will stop talking. We don't want to talk all night. We want to have some sleep. I know we are all tired, so we had better go to sleep."

Then I said, "I am thinking about something." "What is it? Say it right out." "I would like to hear some of your songs about the herd, the horses, and the property. I would like to hear some from you, my old father. I learned some, but I have forgotten them all, and I have got no one to ask about them any more. So help me on that, straighten some of the songs out for me, and what I don't know I would like to learn from you. That's what I mean, my father," I said. "What do you want to do with the songs?" he said. "What do you want to learn more songs for? You know enough songs. I know you know a whole lot of songs. I think you know too much. Why do you want to get more things? You have enough now, and you can't handle what you have got. I asked you about the cattle, and you said they were down at the foot of the mountain. The last time you saw them was last summer, so it's just like driving them away. And I asked you about the horses, and you said you left them down there too. You may be holding on to both, but it's just like driving them away, like as if you don't care about them any more. You said you had a herder, and I know the people are herding for you, so what do you want with the songs? Where are you going to use them? You have got enough songs. You have got enough of everything. You can't handle them by yourself. The cattle and the horses, you just drove them away, and here you are saying you want a song about the stocks, about the horses. You can't handle what you have got."

I said, "I thought you wanted me to get things. I thought you wanted me to get more things, and here now you are saying to me, 'Quit, right now,' saying to me that I have got enough things. So I would like to know which way you want me to go?" He said, "The songs won't do you any good, so you don't have to ask me about the songs. The songs won't help you at all. The songs are just 'songs.' That's all. Nothing to them. If you want to get more things you don't want to be lazy. You want to work for things. Get up early in the morning and work for the things until night and work at night. In that way you will get things. When you get things if you start to take good care of them soon you will have a lot of things that you want. But like the way you are, you can't get things. You have got your cattle and horses way out in another country, and who is taking care of them for you? No one. Those cattle and horses belong to anyone who comes along, anyone that gets on to it. If he wants to use it he will use it, and pretty soon you won't have anything. If you want to get things you don't want to be lazy. You want to tend to your things all the time. Take good care of your things. Try to raise them. Try to improve your stocks. Don't let them run all over the country the way you are now. You can't get anywhere if you remain like that."

I said, "Even though you talk to me like that I don't pay any attention to it. What I am begging you for is all I am thinking about. I really mean it. I would like to learn some, my old mother, my old father. I would like to learn some of the songs from you, even though I can't handle them all. I don't know what will happen to my stocks. Maybe they will be all gone. Maybe it's just for nothing. Maybe it will be just a waste. Even at that I would like to know the songs. And I don't know about the woman (his wife). She is real new. She

451

is real young. She doesn't know enough yet, so I don't know anything about her. If she gets to know about things, then I will have a great deal of help. If she doesn't know anything, or doesn't care about things, there will be no use getting things. So I just can't tell about her. Even at that I would like to learn some songs." "That's right," he said, "you don't know anything about the woman, and nobody knows. As soon as you get a woman you don't know what will happen to you, but you know very well that something will happen to you. That's the way you get to feeling. So nobody in the world will know about women. But with some, when you join them, you will feel right away that you will live a good life with them. Just a few of them are that way. That's the way it is, and you are right," he said to me.

Then the old woman, my older sister, said, "What are you both talking about? Stop with your talking. You don't know when to stop, unless somebody stops you. That's the way with you," she said to the old man, "So stop your talking and go ahead on the songs. He would have learned a lot by now, and here you have been talking a long time for nothing; you didn't get anywhere with it, and you didn't get anything out of it. If you had started as soon as he asked you about it he would have learned a lot by now. So go ahead and let him learn some of the songs. You are getting too old anyway. Some day you will have dropped with all the songs and nobody will know what songs you knew. So you had better let him learn some from you, while you have still got a memory."

He said, "I'm just saying that, and he knows I'm just saying that to him. All that I said was just joshing. And I am not stingy with the songs. I am willing to teach someone the songs, but no one has asked about them. You are the first one that has asked about them, and I am very glad you have. I never thought about the songs. I never sang any songs. I never did use them, so maybe I have forgotten all of them, but we'll try. We'll start with the lamb songs. That's what you want to start on first. There is where it starts, because when the little lamb is born it will crawl around in the dirt. Soon he will get up and soon he will be running around and begin

452

growing. Soon it will be a great big sheep and begin to grow lambs all the time. If it's a buck it will make a lot of lambs and grow lots of sheep. If the lamb is a ewe she will begin lambing and grow a lot of sheep, so there's where you start from, because you want to grow something, so we'll start from there. That's what we'll start on first. We'll start with the lamb song."

He started singing; he sang one song; then he started on another. He sang that, and then another, and after he sang that he sang one more. He sang four songs. "Now I guess you have picked them up already. You repeat them now by yourself." I started singing, went back and forth with it, and I got them almost straight. I thought I could remember them so I put that off. Then he started on another set. He sang a few more songs for me, but that was hard. But anyway I just kept repeating them, going back and forth on them for a long time. Then I got them almost straight. "These songs are to prevent the lambs from suffering and to prevent anything from bothering them. If you use these songs on them they won't get into a sand creek; they won't get into a little arroyo; they won't get caught on the trees; they won't catch cold; they won't get any kind of fever. So you had better learn them," he said to me. Then, even though it was too hard for me, I just kept at it. The first four I had learned well, but these next four, I just couldn't get straight. Then he told me, "Just learn the words first, without the tune. Begin and learn the words." I started on it, but it was just the same, and so I started singing again. "If we get through with these four songs there are another four right after this, so you'd better hurry and straighten them up." I tried my best, but I couldn't get them straight.

All at once they said, "It's morning." They opened the door and pushed the blanket aside and we looked out and it was morning. He said, "We will lie down for a while, while the cooking is going on. I think we will get enough sleep all right." We stopped singing and lay down and went to sleep immediately. When they had the food ready they woke us up. We washed ourselves and all of us sat around the food and started eating. Afterwards we told his boys to get the

453

horses. "Get all the horses that we hobbled, and get your older brother's horse, too. And after you get the horses go over to the sweat-house and gather up some rocks and some wood and build a fire on the rocks. Have it good and hot for us. I don't think he is going home today, because he wants to learn some songs. He just started last night, and we will get a little rest too; we didn't sleep all night, so you boys do that for us." But then he turned around to me and said, "I guess you know better than these boys about the sweat-house, so you and Choclay go over. Let the horses go first and start up the sweat-house." So Choclays Kinsman's slave and I went over; we took the ax and gathered up some wood and rocks and built a fire. And we took the rocks out which were inside, and the cedar bark, and put new cedar bark in. Then we went back to the hogan and I said, "I guess the fire is about burnt down." "Well, then, pick up some blankets and take them over, and I guess the rocks are about ready to be put inside." I picked up some blankets and took them to the sweat-house. The rocks were a nice red hot, so I put them inside and hung the blankets over the doorway. Just about then he came, and we took off our clothes and went in. We stayed a little while until it got too hot and then went out. We stayed outside a long while and then went in again, but it was awful hot. We couldn't stay in there long. We got out again and I threw the blankets up over the top of the sweat-house. I had it open for a long time. After I had let a lot of the heat come out we went in again and it was just right.

He said, "I guess you still remember the songs you heard last night. I guess you had better start on them again. It's nice to know them. You already have some stocks, and when you learn these songs you will hold them with it. Your stocks won't get away from you. You will be holding on to them for a long time." I was working on the songs almost the whole day. The first four songs I had learned pretty quickly. The next four were long. I started on that set, but I still didn't get them straight. I almost got it. I thought, "There will be another chance sometime." I let those four go and started on another four. They were short ones. I kept repeating them until I got that set all right. Then I said, "I guess that will be

454

all for now, my father, I'll come again sometime, and then I may learn some more." "Yes, that's the way it goes. All right, we will quit then." It's getting too late, so you take the blankets off the door, my baby," he said to me.

When we got back to the hogan he said, "Hurry with the food. We are pretty hungry, teaching one another songs. However we haven't learned anything." The food was already cooked. They were around the fire and had it nice and warm. While we were eating my older sister said, "You both must have been wishing for the sweat-house so badly. You went to the sweat-house this morning and you have been in all day. I thought you would quit long ago. I had the things all cooked and started waiting for you two. I have had everything ready; maybe it's cold; maybe it's still warm yet. However I kept it warm for you." He said, "Yes, that's all I have been thinking about, the sweat-house. You know I haven't been in the sweat-house for a long time. I have only been thinking about it and wishing for it. The boys don't seem to know how to start it. I was going to show them sometime, but I just can't get a chance to. However we are back from it. We have been in the sweat-house and we are now at home. That's all."

After we ate he said to me, "Now you go outside and pick up an ax and go and get some wood. Bring enough wood for tonight, so that we will be able to keep the fire going all night tonight again. We will be sitting by the fire all night again tonight, learning the songs, and tomorrow we will have the sweat-house again, and there you will learn some more, and the next night you will learn some more; we will stay up all night again, and the next day there will be a sweat-house again, and then you will learn some more. I don't know how long before we will be through with it. That's what you want. You called for the songs, which I didn't want to let out, which I didn't want to let anybody know, which I wanted to keep to myself. I didn't want anybody to learn my songs, but here you called for it, you begged for it, so you have to learn all of it, not just a piece of it."

Then my older sister started laughing, "Well, my, how long do you want to hold him here? It looks as if you are going to hold him here for a long time. He was in a hurry. He had put up a hogan, and he came here for a shovel. He wanted to put some dirt on the hogan, and they are looking for him every minute, so he's in a hurry. He has got lots to do at home. What do you want to stay up all night for? And you said, 'Tomorrow there will be a sweat-house again, and the next night,' you said, 'we will be up all night again, and the next day the sweat-house again.' Well, my goodness, what are you trying to do with him? You better let him go now. I know he has got a lot to do." He said, "What are you talking about? What did you say last night? I thought you wanted me to let him learn some songs. And he himself asked me for them; so he has got to learn. He will go home after he learns all the songs. He has to stay up all night for it, and he has to be in the sweat-house all day for that, until he learns, and then he can go."

I walked outside and picked up an ax and went in the woods and chopped up a lot of wood. I brought three big loads on my back. About that time it was evening. As soon as I got inside he told me, "Repeat again. I'll listen to you so that you will repeat them all. Start in from where we started the first time." I began to repeat them; I repeated every one of them. He said, "That's fine. You went over them all right, and it's correct. I want you to learn some more. Maybe all, because it's good to know them and good to remember, so I want you to learn more. I am not stingy with you, my baby, so you must keep at it. And I don't want you to let anybody know them. I don't want you to use them for anybody. I want you to keep them to yourself. This is for your own good. Use them only for yourself." After I repeated all of them he said, "Everything is all right. It's correct. Only two or three places you are not saying in the right way." So he told me about it. "Here's where you are saying it like this, but it's not that way. You just listen to me. And the sound, when you mention the word, you should say it like this, so that the sound will go just like this. And here's another place, it's just the same again. You have got to have the sound in the right way, and you should say the words right and plainly. So it's like this." Then he started singing and I just listened to him right along. After he was through with it I started singing alone. When I got through he said, "Almost. You almost got it." But he told me to let that go. "We'll let that go now. Let's see you try the property songs, start on them. The properties have little ones too. There is a baby in the property, and these little ones have songs, so start on that. Everything has got young ones. Everything has got a baby, sheep, property, beads, horses, and all other things have young, and they have all got songs."

He sang one song, then another. After he sang that he sang another and then another. He had sung four songs again. When he was through with it, "Now," he said, "you can go ahead on it. They are all pretty easy." But it was just too hard for me. I just sat there for a long time. I was thinking that I couldn't learn it. I was thinking to myself that I would never learn those songs. He said to me, "What's the matter with you? Aren't you going to repeat them?" "I didn't quite catch them," I said, "if you repeat them again, maybe I'll get it then." He started to sing again; he sang the whole four songs again, but still I didn't quite get it. It was too much for me. I tried and kept on repeating these four again and again, but I never got them straight. Then I went outside. It was way over midnight. When I went back inside he asked me, "What is it? Is it getting to be morning?" "About," I said. "What do you think? Do you think you could stand it all night again? Or are you getting too sleepy now? If you want to sleep, say so. I don't want to keep you awake all night again." He wasn't a bit sleepy, and I was almost dropping over. Right away I said, "I guess we'll go to sleep now." "All right, I know you want to sleep, so go to sleep, my baby," he said to me, "and tomorrow we will start on it again; so you go to sleep now." Then I lay down, and he did too, and right away, I guess, I went to sleep.

They woke us again in the morning, after they had the food all laid out. We got up and washed and started eating. "We are big sleepers," he said, "that's all we want. We don't want anything besides. Here we are; we have been sleeping all night and pretty near all day. Look where the sun is. It's almost noon time." He just said this. The sun was only a little way up from the mountain. My older sister said, "That's the way I'm thinking about you. You two don't do anything but sleep and eat. You ought to work, and here you both don't do anything but sleep all night and all day," she said, laughing.

She laughed about us for a long while. When we were through eating he said to me, "What do you think? Do you think you want to go back home? Do you want to go back now?" I said, "I'll go back anytime today." "Well, then, my little one, we will have a sweat-house again. After we come back from the sweat-house, then you can go. You are on horseback. You can get back in a little while. So we'll have a sweat-house this morning. Where's the shovel? Did you bring the shovel back for him?" he asked. My older sister said, "Yes, the boy brought the shovel back. It's lying outside." "Well," he said, "that's fine; so you won't have to go after it. And you can have it. I give that shovel to you. I don't want you to come back and forth for it, borrowing it every once in a while. You should have one with you all the time."

I went out to see where it was, and it was lying there. I picked it up and laid it against the tree. Then I went back inside and thanked them both. Choclays Kinsman's slave and I went down to the sweat-house and gathered up wood and rocks and built a big fire. After that I went to the hogan and came back again with the blankets. While I was putting the rocks inside he came, and we took off our clothes and went in. It was awful hot again. We went in and out three times, and then from there on it was all right. It was nice and warm. I started on the songs again. I was at it until noon. I had them about fixed in my mind. I knew them; I could remember them all right, but in some little places I couldn't say it in the right way. However he told me to let it go that way. "You will catch on to it yourself sometime," he said. "I guess we had better quit. Take the blankets off the door."

I went out and took the blankets off the door, and it was afternoon. After we dressed we went home. The food was all ready and we washed ourselves and then started eating. After lunch we sat around for a while. The boy had brought my horse back that morning. He said, "I suppose you are going home now, my son, my baby?" "Yes," I said, "I guess I had better be going back. They must think something has happened to me. They are about to worry for me. They don't know where I am. They are about to run around for me, so I guess I'll go home now," I said. "And when I get home, I don't know just when, perhaps I'll go over to my father's (Who Has Mules') place. The other day his son arrived while I was working on the corral. He helped me a little on that. He said he was looking for the cattle. Before he left I told him I would kill one of the calves, whenever I wanted to, and I told him to tell his father, so he would know about it. He said he would.

I asked him, "If I do that what will he say to me? Will he get mad about it?" and he said, "No, I don't think so. I don't think he will say anything about it." And then my old father said, "Oh, I guess he doesn't care. I know he won't say anything about it. He is thinking about them as though they were little kids. Even though you killed a good-sized one he won't say anything, now that he knows it already. And he doesn't care, with us. But with the others, if he catches someone killing his cattle he sure will go after them, until he gets paid. But about us he won't say anything. I wonder when you'll kill one? If I knew when you were going to kill one I would like to go down and eat a piece of it. I am hungry for cattle meat. I have got tired of eating sheep meat. So I wonder when you'll kill that calf?" Again he said, "About how many days before you'll kill that calf, my baby? I mean it. I want to be there for a piece. If you intend to kill one don't kill a spring or summer calf, kill a good-sized yearling. That has got a good taste to it. These summer calves haven't any taste to them. They have nice soft meat all right, but there is nothing to it. But the yearlings have a good taste to them. So kill one of the yearlings. He has got so many he doesn't know what to do with them. They are just running away from him anyway." I said, "I guess I'll kill one of the yearlings in two days." "Well, then, I'll be there, and I'll stay there with you, maybe one night, maybe more." I said, "I guess I'll be going now." "All right, go ahead, my baby," he said. "I am glad you were with me for a long time, for two days and two nights and another day again. We stayed together quite a long while." Then I walked out, picked up my saddle and carried it over to where the horse was standing. I saddled him up, picked up the shovel and started off. It was getting pretty late. As soon as I went over the hill I beat it on to home. The sun was almost down when I got home, and the herd was back.

22

His mother returns . . . Exchange
of beads for bucks . . . His old
father visits him . . . They move to where
it is nice and green . . . He angers his
wife with his criticism . . . His mother
lectures her daughter-in-law.

When I got close to the hogan it looked as if there were something new there. I got a feeling like that when I rode up close to the door. The boy ran out, and I looked right over his shoulder to a tree, standing close by the hogan. There I saw the saddle sitting up on the tree. I recognized it. That was my mother's. I asked the boy, "Where are the horses?" "Back of the hill," he said. "They were all there in the valley just a while ago. They were there when I was bringing the herd across." "Well, then, get on this horse and ride him over there and hobble him with the bunch." He got on the horse and went. I walked inside; there was my mother sitting in the hogan on the north side. I walked up to her and shook hands with her. She pulled me down to the ground to herself and started crying, "I had a hard time coming across," she said. Then I walked to the other side and she said, "I came up here yesterday. It took me three days to get across the valley. I got to her home," she said, meaning my wife's home, "and her relatives were going to move the next day. That's what they said when I got there. 'We are going to move tomorrow. We have got everything all fixed up.' Your wife's relatives said you had moved up here, but they didn't know to what place, or just where, so I stayed there with them the night before last, and yesterday morning they started moving, early in the morning. I went along until we got to White Rocks Canyon. From there I branched off from

461

them and came up to the top. I didn't know just where you were, but I kept on coming, tracking you. Some places I lost the tracks, but every once in a while I got on to them. That's the way I caught up with you. I came here yesterday afternoon."

I told her about my visit to my father's place and about getting the shovel. I didn't tell them about all we had been doing. I didn't say that I had been learning the songs, because they didn't know anything about it anyway, so I just let that go. "We left some of our things down at the foot of the mountain," I said. "Some of our old pots and dishes and old sheep pelts and all the little things, and we have some corn buried down there. I don't know how they are; maybe they are getting after our things, or maybe not. I am kind of worried about them. Did you stop at the other people's (Slim Man's) place? They were saying that they were going to move to another place. I wonder if they have moved yet or not." She said, "No, I didn't know where they were, so I didn't get to their place. I didn't know anything about them until I got to my daughter-in-law's place. They told me where they were, but I didn't get over, because I didn't have anything to go for, and I wanted to catch up with you, because I was so eager to see you. That's why I didn't go to their place." But I knew why she hadn't gone over. It was on account of what she had said to Slim Man before she left. Then I said to my wife, "Fix up a bed for me. I want to lie down. I'm so sleepy."

While she was putting down the sheep pelts my mother said, "I wonder what they have been doing? They must have been doing something all night. If they didn't do anything at night why is he so sleepy?" My wife said, "They must have been out every night with the wolf (kidding, alluding to the witches). I think that's what they have been doing. They have been out every night in the wolf's skin." But I didn't say anything about it. I just went to bed and went to sleep right away.

We all got up the next morning, started the fire, and while they were starting to cook I picked up the rope and walked over to where the horses were. They were right there

462

in the valley. I got them back, and, after we ate, I said to my mother, "Some time ago, I forget when it was, Who Has Mules' son came here, and I told him I would kill one of the calves that belong to his father. I guess I'll go and get it today. If I don't get it today I'll stay out over night and have it here tomorrow; so I'm going now.

Then my wife said, "Some people have come here. They have moved down here below us." My mother said, "Those are the people I tracked all the way up. I got to their place, and they are down below here." "Who are those people?" I asked. My wife said, "It's Lost His Moccasins, my uncle. His wife came up here. She wanted to know where you were, and I told her you had gone up to your old father's place. She wanted you to help them on the hogan. They say they are cutting poles for the hogan. And the next day a boy came. He asked for you and I told him you hadn't come back yet, so he went home again. They wanted you to help them on putting up a hogan. I don't know how many they want to have put up. They use our ax every day to cut the poles with."

I said, "I wanted to go tomorrow. That's the date I had put up for my old father, but here there's no meat. I didn't eat any meat last evening and this morning either. I was going to put some dirt on the hogan today, but I guess I won't. I'll get the cattle back here first. After I kill one I'll start to work on the hogan. I'll be good and strong then, after I eat some cattle meat. So who wants to go with me? Do you want to go with me?" I asked the boy. He dropped his head and his older sister said, "He is afraid of the cattle. He is scared of them." "Well, then, you saddle up a horse, and we'll take a ride up to where the cattle are."

She got up right away and put the saddle on one of the horses and we started off, over a big hill and down to the valley and up. When we got to the valley that comes from Green Around The Canyon I told her, "Go in that valley there," the valley we used to call Fire Stone Burning. I said, "Lots of them are in that valley. Ride way around them and start them out this way. I'll go up in Green Around The Canyon, up in these canyons, and those I see I'll get out here, so you go ahead." I got only a few of them out, even though I saw a lot of them in all these canyons. I got on to one, a very nice fat yearling. It was a good-sized one. When I got these few out to where the other valley was she was there with a big bunch, but they were all alike.

All the yearlings were good-sized and nice and fat. We started driving just a few of them down in the valley. We had them trotting along, but when we got a little way with them they were almost out of breath, with their mouths wide open. So we walked them until they got rested and cooled off and then we started trotting them again. We didn't get very far with them before their mouths were wide open again. I said, "It's no use driving them fast. We'll just let them walk all the way. We'll get home with them anyway." So we took our time driving them down in the valley. Finally we got them back to the hogan. The sun was pretty well down, and we had started with them in the morning. It had taken us all day to get them back to our home, even though it hadn't been a long way.

When we got the cattle back there was Lost His Moccasins' wife sitting there with my mother. We killed one of the calves close by the hogan and butchered it and cut up all the meat. I gave Lost His Moccasins' wife one front quarter, and she took the head and the feet and all the insides back with her. She was awful thankful. When we were through with everything I started putting dirt on the hogan. I got just half the hogan covered with dirt when the sun was down. The next day as soon as I had eaten I started in again. That was all that I was doing that day. I finished around sundown.

The other people who had moved up, that is, Lost His Moccasins and his children, had put up a hogan too. They wanted to use the shovel that day, but I told them to come around in the evening for it. Just as I was through with it one fellow came. "Are you through with the shovel now?" he asked me. "Yes," I said, "There it is. I'm through with it, so you can take it and use it. As soon as you get through with it bring it back."

The next morning I said, "I wonder if I could use some of their bucks? I wonder if my mother would let me have a few of them? I would like to use them. We haven't got a single one in the herd. One of you go over today and see if they can lend us some, and I'll take the herd out this morning. I'll let the boy take a rest. He has been herding right along, so I'll let him stay at home today." My wife said, "The things are all alike. I don't think you get tired herding, but I think you get tired when you stay at home. I know you will, because at home there is always lots to do, getting water and wood and other things, cleaning around the hogan, so I don't think he will get any rest." "Well," I said, "Even at that I think he would like to stay at home." So I took out the herd that morning. I was out all day, until sunset.

My mother had been down to those people (Lost His Moccasins). She started telling me about it; she said, "I went down to those people this morning, and there I said what you had said this morning. I said to that woman, 'I came here for help. Could you help me?' I said to her, 'This morning my son said, "I will borrow some bucks from my mother." He spoke of you, and that's what I came here for, so could you lend us some? But she never paid any attention to me. I said exactly the same thing again; I thought perhaps she hadn't understood me well enough, but again she didn't say anything about it. Then I thought, 'If I just sit here and talk like this I won't get anything,' so I took off my beads, and I gave my beads to her. I said, 'Here, my father's sister, I'll give you these beads. Why is it you don't answer me? I would like you to help us with the bucks, father's sister,' I said to her when I laid the beads on her lap. She picked up the beads, and after quite a long while, said, 'Well, come around then tomorrow morning, and I'll see about it. I may have one in the herd, so come around in the morning.' "

The next morning we all went down with the sheep. While the boy was rounding up the herd we three went over to the corral, and there they gave us a black buck. They handed it to us over the corral, and I just turned it loose into our herd, and then they gave us another. That one was black too. They gave us four. Every one of them was black, and that was rare. We sure appreciated those four black bucks. Then they started handing us sheep, and when they were through

465

with the sheep they started on the goats. They gave us ten goats and twenty-six sheep. Including the bucks they gave us forty head for the beads. We gave many thanks to them. While the others were still there I started out with the herd. I went over a hill and there the boy caught up with me. He said, "I want to herd with you." I said, "All right." We were herding all that day. When the sun was almost down we came back.

When we were putting the herd in the corral there was my old father (Choclays Kinsman) riding up to the hogan. After we fixed the gate we went in, and there he was, sitting down. "Fix my horse for me, my children. Is there any feed around here?" "Yes," I said, "Plenty of feed around here," and I told the boy to take the horse to where the others were. When the boy came back we all started eating. After we ate we sat around. He said, "I was going to come yesterday, but I had to go around looking for the sheep. They had taken the herd down to the salt-weeds; while they were down there they had lost some, and they had brought back the herd without those they had lost, and last night they were coming in all night long; so I had to go down this morning. The coyotes killed a lot of them. And that's what I have been doing all day. What weren't killed I brought back home, and then this afternoon I thought I would come down here. So I started. I just took my time and it took me all afternoon to come here."

I said, "When I came back there was no meat, so the next day I went up and got the cattle down and killed one. That was two days ago." "Well, that's nice. You have killed one, and I see it was nice and fat, and I have eaten some now, and I sure did like the meat." Then he began to talk about the place there. "I wonder how many years ago you lived here? How many years ago was it?" he asked my mother. She said, "Oh, I just don't remember. It was quite a while ago. Around that time I was good and strong yet. That hogan there, I made that hogan. I cut the poles and gathered them up, and after I had gathered all the poles I started building up the hogan and I put that hogan up. I was good and strong at that time. I

466

used to carry big logs around. I think I was stronger than a man. I know what a man could lift I used to lift; so around about that time I was still a strong woman." But they didn't say how many years ago it was that we lived there.

After that I said, "I don't remember any of the songs. They are all gone away from me. I can't think of one. Perhaps the songs don't want me. However I'll try it again tonight my father," I said. Then he started singing the first four songs. He sang them, and then I started singing them. When I was through with those four he told me to repeat them again; so I repeated all of them. He said, "The first four are all right; you've got it nicely." Then he sang the next four. When he had sung all of them, I started singing again. I had sung all of them, but I knew I didn't have it right yet, and that's what he said to me. Those four were the hardest ones. I repeated them two or three times, but I just couldn't get them straight. Everything was all right, except two places, where I couldn't say it right. He told me, "Let it go. You've got everything all right." Then he started singing another four. When he was through I started singing again. That was a little easier. From there on he just kept going along. It was a little easier, and I went along right after him. After he had sung a few of the songs I would sing right after him, and he was telling me, "That's nice and correct." I learned quite a few songs that night. The next morning after we ate he said, "I want to go back this morning. I have got so much to do. That's why I want to go back as soon as I can. I don't want to stay away from my home very long, because there are lots of things to do."

Then he asked, "Are the bucks still with the herd? It sounds like it." "Yes," I said, "We just got them yesterday. The people who live below there gave us the bucks. I guess those are making the noise." "Who is it?" he asked. "Oh, it's Lost His Moccasins. They moved up here after us." "Well, then," he said, "I guess I'll go and visit them before I go. What's the matter with your bucks?" I said, "They are not here. A fellow (Son of Late Grey Hat) took them away from me. He took them across the country last summer. I went across to that country, but I didn't get them back, because he

467

said they were up on the mountain. But he may have had them down at White Rocks Sitting Around. He lives there. Maybe he had them there. Perhaps he lied to me. So that's why we had to buy them yesterday."

He said, "Well, then, I don't think you will get them back, even if you tried, because I know that fellow very well. I know him, know just how he is. He hides things away. He is a great cheater and liar, and he's a great thief. He is a story-teller. He will make you believe him, because he is a great gambler, and so your bucks are gone forever. And that old woman, (Woman Who Walks Alone), big and round and fat, I know very well. When she was around here with us she used to be a very good woman. After she lost her son, from there on we started to take care of her real closely. We all took good care of her, and you know that yourself. But ever since she married that man she never thinks about us any more. She doesn't care about us. She doesn't care about the others, and she is worse than he is. So I don't think you will get the bucks back. I mean it. You never will get them back, even though you tried your best. He has hidden them someplace, and he will gamble for them. He had nothing to gamble with, but now he has, and I'll bet you he had those bucks right there with him. He only told you that they were up on the mountain. He knew very well you wouldn't go there after them. That's the way with that man. He is a big liar, and you had believed him. I know he will make a fellow believe him."

Then he said, about the songs, "You will get them straight sometime, and this isn't the only time to learn. Maybe I'll come here again, or you can come up any time you want to. I want you to learn all the songs, because it's good to know. You can use them any time you want to, and everything is true about it. I know that, and everybody knows it. There are lots of things in these songs. I know it very well, and she knows it very well too," he said, as he pointed to my mother. "And that's the way my father used to say, and my older brother, Old Man Hat. So you had better learn all of it, and try and keep at it until you learn all, because it's good for you."

Then, while he was still there they had the food cooked

up again, and I said to him, "I want you to eat some more, my father, so you won't go starving." He said, "All right." "When you go," I said, "I want you to take some meat along with you." Then he was very thankful about it. "That's very nice," he said, "I have been wishing for meat like this for a long time, and here I started eating the meat as soon as I came, and I am still eating. It will be very nice if you give me some." I said to the woman, that is, my wife, "You go out and give him one whole side of the rib." She went out and got him one; she said, "I laid the meat on the tree for you." "Thank you very much, my grandchild, my baby." (Her father was brother's son to him; that's why he called her "my grandchild.") Then, after we had eaten, he went out, cut the rib in two, tied it together over the back of the saddle, and started off.

From there on I just tended to the sheep. I don't know how many days later it snowed at night, about six inches deep. I know that morning I went out with the herd; I got the herd back about sundown, and that evening I went down to the other people's place, to where Lost His Moccasins lived. He said to me, "I see you were bringing the herd back this evening. How far did you go with the herd?" I said, "I went up toward the mountain." "How is the snow up there?" I said, "It's a little bit deeper than around here." "I have been herding all day too. Around in the woods the snow is pretty deep, but I like our having snow." "That's the way with me too," I said. He asked, "Are you going to move again sometime to any place?" "Yes," I said, "As soon as the snow goes down I want to move to Rock Standing Up. That's where I used to camp also, and there is a hogan and corral there, so I guess we'll move down to that place." "That's what I'm thinking, too. I would like to move down to White Rock Point. That's where we camp too. There is a corral and hogan already setting up; so I want to move down there too, maybe around the time when you move."

We lived there for many days, and when the snow was almost gone I got a horse and started riding down to where I wanted to move. I wanted to see what the country looked like down there. I got out to the place called Lower Water. I got some water there and watered my horse. Then I started down and got to where we had killed a cow once. I just took a look at that place. I went down and got to where I was almost killed by a horse. I just gave a look at that place and went on out to Rock Standing Up, where we used to camp. The corral was rotted to the ground but the hogan was still sitting up. It was real old. I just gave a look at that place and went on, crossed the wash, then went over and got to where we had another camp. Everything looked nice to me, when I got out to that place. One could see a long way out all over. It was a nice level place; no tracks of any kind, and the feed, none of it was bitten off. There was nice grazing all over. Then I rode quite a way down out in the flat and turned around and started back. I thought, "I wil move to this place."

When I started back I thought I would go around by White Rock Point flat. I only wanted to know how the place looked. When I got out in that flat that was the richest place of all, more feed, more grazing, and not a thing bitten off, no tracks of any kind. Everything looked nice and fresh, and everything was green. The tall grass was ripe and dry, but underneath it was nice and green. Then I thought to myself, "I ought to take this place." But I had already taken the other, and Lost His Moccasins had already taken this; so I was sorry for it. I got back home late in the evening. After I unsaddled my horse the boy took it up to where the others were and hobbled it for me. Everything was waiting for me, ready to be eaten. After I ate I said, "I have been riding all around. I started from here and went through lots of places. I got to Lower Water and out in the flat. I passed on and crossed White Rock Wash. Everything is looking nice all over. I got to where we used to camp, and then to another camp of ours, and that was the best place. I looked all around, and there was plenty of feed for the stocks. So then I turned around and started from there out to White Rock Point flat, and that was the best place of all, better than the others. I ought to have gotten that place, but these other people had already wanted to move there. That was a nice place."

Then they said, "Why didn't you get that place? You told

them that you were going to move down that way. If you
hadn't told them, I don't think they would have thought of
moving to that place. But we'll move there anyway." I
said, "Let them move to that place. It's not a very big place
anyway. Soon they won't have much feed. Out where I want
to move is a great big place, so let them move there. I guess
we'll start moving in two days. Tomorrow I want you to get
everything ready. I wonder how much of a load we have got
now?" "There is less of everything now," my wife said, "We
brought a lot of food with us, but that has pretty well gone
down. We have only some meat left, but that's not much. I
don't think we have much of a load." "Well, then, tomorrow
get everything fixed. Have it ready for the next day."

The next day the boy took the herd out, and we started
putting things in sacks. Some we bundled up. We had finished with it about noon. After lunch I went down to Lost
His Moccasins' place, and there they were, all in the hogan,
sitting around. His wife asked me, "Where were you all day
yesterday, my son?" I used to call her mother and she called
me son. She said, "Your younger sister saw you riding down
toward the flat. How far did you go?" I said, "I have been
riding all around out in the flat, around White Rock Point,
around where you want to move, and that was the best place
that you picked up. That's where I have been riding around. I
only rode around out there to see what the country looked
like. Everything looks all right. Everything is nice and green
yet." "When are you going to move down to that place?" she
asked. "I'm thinking of moving down there tomorrow," I
said. She said, "I think we had better move." That was all we
were talking about for a while. I asked them, "When are you
going to move?" She said, "We would like to move right
away, too, but we haven't got the horses on hand. We had
just turned them loose, and they said the horses were up at
Valley Coming To The Edge; so I don't know where they are
now. But I guess tomorrow, perhaps the next day we will be
moving too." "Well, then," I said, "I guess I'll go home."

I went out. The sun was almost down. When I got home
the herd was in. I asked the boy about the horses. He said,
"They are at the same place all the time." "That's nice," I

said. "We are going to move tomorrow." "Where to?" he asked. "Way out in the flat. It's a very nice place where we are going to move to. Here you have to herd in the thick woods, and it's too hard for you. Out in the flat there you won't have any trouble with the herd."

In the evening Lost His Moccasins and his wife came. They said, "We never yet have had a real good visit together. We heard that you were going to move tomorrow, so that's why we came." "Yes," I said, "We are going to move tomorrow." Then Lost His Moccasins said, "I thought you were going to live here all winter, and I thought you would move back up from here. There is lots of feed all over on the mountain. I don't know what Who Has Mules will say to us if we move down to the flat. We are afraid of him, because I know he doesn't like anybody to get on his place and he will say that where we are moving is his place. I think soon his cattle will all be out there. His cattle get out there around about this time. Maybe they are just starting to get down there now."

I said, "I guess he won't say anything to us, because he knows we are moving around for feed. I don't think he will say anything, so we will move down there anyway, tomorrow." They were there for quite a while that evening, and she was thanking me again for the meat. "Thank you very much, my son, that we all had nice, fat meat. We all like to get a taste of meat like that, and we all did, and I thank you for that." I said to her, "You don't have to thank me for that, and don't thank me for it, because it wasn't mine." "Even at that," she said, "he himself won't give us a piece. I know very well Who Has Mules wouldn't give us a piece; and here you had killed one and we all got a taste of it."

Then she said, "I would like to know if you believe my son-in-law. I heard that he told you that we had been killing your cattle, and maybe you had believed him. When I heard that I felt very ashamed about it. We never bother with anybody's property. We got some meat down from the top of the mountain twice, and that was ours, so he is lying about us to you, my son. I don't know what he wants to do with us. He is trying to do something with us. So you mustn't believe him." I said, "Yes, that's what he told me, and I think he is

472

right on that, because he said he knows it very well. He knows all about you, and he saw it, so, on what he knows and says, I think he is right. He told me all about it, all about the times you brought the meat. He told me that he had some from you twice. He said he got some meat from you, and he is pretty sure of it, that you had killed some of mine, and he knows very well just where you had killed them. So I don't think he is just wanting to lie about you; so I believed him. He was telling what he had known about you himself. You said here you never saw any of my cattle, but I won't let it go. Sometime I want you to get together with him; in that way we will know everything. This way we can't find out anything." But she kept on saying no. She said, "I never have killed any of your cattle," and Lost His Moccasins said exactly the same. But I told them, "It's no use talking about it, because we haven't got anybody to talk with, we are talking here about that for nothing. We will stop talking about that until we get him some time, and then we'll talk about it." That was all and they went back to their home. It was way late in the night.

As soon as they went we crawled in bed and went to sleep. The next morning after we ate I told the boy to get the horses, and I told the others to fix up the things and have them ready. When the boy brought the horses back we saddled and packed them up and then started off with the herd down toward where the other people lived. We passed them and went down through the woods, going over hills, crossing the arroyos, and late in the afternoon we got out to the place called White Rock Point. I said, "We will camp here for tonight, because it is quite a way yet to where we want to move."

So we stopped there late in the afternoon, where the other people wanted to move, at White Rock Point. We spent the rest of the day there and toward evening we rounded up the herd, and after supper we all went to bed. The next morning I told the boy, "Bring the horses up here." They were around close. He got them up to where we were camped. After we ate I told the boy to take the herd along. "Just go ahead over the hill and then down." When we had packed up everything we started on after him. We caught up with him way on the other side of the hill. We kept on going, going over some plain hills, going through some rocky places, rocky hills, until we got to where we wanted to camp. The hogan was all right, and the corral was all right too. Both were sitting up well, not much to do on them. They only needed to be renewed. We got there late in the afternoon. It was quite a big place. One could see far away from where we camped, all over to every direction.

After we had eaten I told the boy, "Take the horses way up on the rocky hill. It's a big place on top. Take them up there and let them go loose. Don't hobble them. They have been hobbled for a long time now. They need a good rest; so let them rest." It was quite a ways, way on the other side, where I wanted him to take the horses. When he went off I started out with the herd. That evening I came back, and the boy was back, too. "It's a very nice place for the horses," he said. He had gathered some wood; he had a big pile. That evening, after we ate, I lay right down, because I was so tired.

From there on, I don't remember the days, I was just tending to the herd. I had renewed the hogan and the corral, and had been working on the wood, water, and things like that. No one was around. Nothing happened. I didn't go any place. One evening, as soon as I came back with the herd my wife said to me, "We are about out of food. I haven't been paying any attention to it. After you left here with the herd I began to look over the things, and there was not very much food left. What we use most is about gone, that is, corn." "Well, then," I said, "I guess I'll have to go down and get some. I wanted to go anyway, so I guess I'll go and see how the things are. Maybe I'll go down tomorrow by myself, or perhaps I'll go with the boy." She said, "The boy is herding. Let him herd. We two will go." I said, "All right, we will go tomorrow." I walked over where the boy had taken the horses the next morning; there were no horses around. I went all over on the place; then I tracked them down, way on the other side. They were out in the valley on the other side of the hill. It was quite a long ways before I had caught up with them. They were nice and fat. I started driving them home and got back just about at sunset. I had been out all that day after the horses. I hobbled them right there at the hogan, and after we ate that evening we all went to bed.

The next morning I got the horses and put the saddles on two of them and we started off. We went on, crossing the flat, over the hills and valleys and across White Rock Point wash. We saw the other people's tracks there. They had moved up in the wash. Then we started going through the woods and soon we passed where we had lived before. We went on up to Cattails Standing Up, and up on that trail to Valley Coming To The Edge. There the snow was pretty deep; about a foot deep, I guess. Then we started down.

Somebody had ridden back and forth on that trail. When we got to the edge of the mountain to Valley Coming To The Edge there was a big drift at the edge of this cliff. The trail came up between two split rocks, a kind of narrow place. There it was filled with snow. There were no tracks there. This rider had gone back and forth through this drift, but it had all filled again. It was as though nobody had ever been through it. It must have been about six feet deep. I started pounding it up with a big stick, moving down. I was working on that almost all day. Finally I had made a space throuh which we could lead the horses. After we had led them down quite a ways I walked back up there and started gathering up some wood and throwing it down in this narrow place. I threw a big pile of wood down in there and then I started a fire. When I had the fire going good I went down to where my wife was waiting with the horses. We led them a ways further and then got on and rode down to the foot of the mountain, to the place called Rain Water Always Brings The Rocks Out. When we got there the sun was setting over the mountain. I said, "We'll camp around here any place, because out where we used to live there isn't any feed for the horses, and around here there is a little feed for them." We rode back up the mountain on to a little cliff and there we stayed that night.

Then next morning we started off without anything to

eat. We almost froze that night, and it was real cold in the morning. We went down to the foot of the mountain and then out to where we had lived, to our summer camp. No snow was there. We took the things off the horses, built a fire, got some wood and water and started cooking. First we hobbled the horses, even though they had had nothing to eat. They were chewing on the old corn stalks that were lying around. After we ate we went down to where we had buried the corn. We got it all out and took it back and started pounding on it. We shelled it there. It was almost two sacks full. We finished with it around late in the afternoon. After we had eaten a little lunch again we started back. When we got about half way up the mountain the sun was down, but we kept on going and got to where I had built a fire on the trail. The fire had done a pretty good job. The snow was melted away. We went on up and stopped where we had camped the night when we were moving. There was the brush hogan that we had put up that night. We cleaned out the snow, and then I built a big fire. There was plenty of feed for the horses.

The next morning after we ate we started saddling up the horses. When I had put the saddle on mine and put the corn over the saddle I wound up the rope. After I had tied it to the saddle I turned around to her, and she had the saddle on the horse's shoulder. I walked over to her and said, "What are you trying to do? Don't you know how to saddled up a horse yet? This isn't the way to saddle up a horse. You know very well we are going down hill. You ought to know better than that." I loosened the cinches and slipped the saddle back where it should be and then tightened the cinches again. It was cold that morning. She had walked back to the fire; I had made her mad. After I had tightened the cinches I put the corn over the saddle and the blanket right on top for her. I said, "Now I have got the things ready. Get on the horse and let's go."

She stood there for a long while without any sound. At last she walked up to the horse and got on. I started off and she started after me. I trotted my horse right along easily, and pretty soon I was quite a ways ahead of her. She was coming along after me, just walking her horse, even though the horse wanted to trot she held it back. I got quite a ways away from her, about a mile, I guess, then I couldn't see her any more. When I got around a point, on to the sunny side, I stopped my horse and got off. Then I got out my tobacco; I shaved some off—at that time I used to smoke chewing tobacco—and made a cigarette, lit it and started smoking. When I was about through, she came up walking her horse. She just passed by me; she never gave me a look. Then I went after her. I stayed behind her and said, "We had better hurry, because we have got to go a long way yet. We don't want to stay out tonight. We want to get back today, so hurry on." But she didn't pay any attention to me. Then I whipped the horse she was riding, but she held it back. I said, "What's the matter with you? You are getting stubborn about little things. What can you get out of it? You are always wanting to start something. There's nothing to be mad about, and you have got to learn something. You must pick up things. Anything you don't know about you must ask how it's to be done. In that way you will learn something. I showed you how to saddle up the horse because I want you to learn how to put on a saddle, and you are mad about it."

I was talking like this to her, when she backed up the horse, stopped it and jumped off, saying, "Here, take the horse. You don't want me to ride it, so you take it along." Then she started walking toward the hill, and there the horse was standing. Pretty soon she had walked to the foot of the hill; then she got on top and was going over. And there was no place for her to go; nobody lived close by. But she just kept on going. Her people had moved to Navajo Mountain, and her clansman had moved way down to where we had moved, and there was nobody living around there. There she was, and she didn't know where she was going. When she went over the hill I got off my horse. I tied the two horses together with the bridle and started after her with a whip. I got on top of the hill and there she was, sitting, and the tears were running down.

I said, "What are you sitting there for? Why didn't you keep on going? What stopped you? Where did you think you were going? What kind of a plan have you made out? Get up

477

and let's go. We want to get back before sundown. Where do you think you are going anyway? You are always trying to put me in trouble. But I won't let you keep on doing that to me. What kind of food makes you that way? I would like to know what kind of food gets you that way? You must have swallowed something. Get up and let's go." I said this to her three times, but she just sat there.

Then I walked up to her; I grabbed hold of her hand and jerked her up. "If you don't want to move I'll make you move around. I'll whip you with this whip. Maybe that's what you want me to do." When I said this I gave a swing with the whip, and then she started running away from me. "I mean it," I said, "I'm going to whip you hard with this whip. I have been easy with you right along. Even though you treated me badly I never have hurt you yet, but this time I'll give you a good whipping. That's what you need. Maybe that way you'll learn a lesson," I said to her while she was running along ahead of me. We got down off the hill and back to where the horses were standing. I told her, "Get on the horse and go." She got on the horse and started off ahead of me. I was sure going to whip her that time, but I didn't; so we went on again. She was crying, and I told her, "There's nothing to cry about. I wanted you to learn something, to learn how the things should be done. I showed you how to fix a saddle on a horse. You ought to be glad and thankful about that; so there is nothing to cry about." And there she was just walking her horse again, but I just went along after her.

From there on she started trotting the horse, and we started going along all right. Soon we got to Cattails Standing Up and then down through the small rocky hills. Soon we got out to White Rock Point wash. When we crossed that the sun was down. We went along across that valley and over a hill. Finally we got back home late that night. We would have been back before sundown if we hadn't had that trouble. I was going to hit her that day, but I didn't, so nothing happened to her.

When we got home I took the saddles off the horses and hobbled them and took the things inside. My mother had the food all ready to be eaten. I was very hungry, and I guess my wife was, too. We had eaten a little that morning, but we hadn't had anything to eat all the rest of the day, so we were pretty hungry. I didn't pay any attention to her. I just went ahead with my eating. When I had had enough I made a quick story about where we had gone, but I didn't tell what we had done on the trail. I let that go. That was three times that she had hurt me very badly. First she had torn my clothes off and pulled my hair, scratched me all up, and I had suffered from that three or four days, and next she had hurt me by a man, but I just let that go. She had hurt me very badly with that, and this was the third time that she hurt me but I let it go again.

Then next day I told the boy to take the horses back to the others. I had taken the herd out that day. I got back around in the evening. I took the herd in the corral and fixed the gate and went inside the hogan. There they had the food all ready for me, some cornbread and mush and some meat. After I ate I took out my tobacco and started cleaning a corn husk. After I had smoothed it out I shaved off some tobacco and made a cigarette and lit it and started smoking.

Then I started talking. I said, "Even though a man thinks he is getting along fine with what little he has he always has trouble through another person. Another person troubles him all the time. Even though he has a little stock of different kinds he gets to be treated that way. He gets to be treated very bad sometimes, and that's the way with me. I'm trying to get ahead, trying to get more stock and more property and more food, trying to be good all the time, and here you are, all the time bucking me, ever since I married you. If you keep doing that to me how will we get ahead? How will we get along? Whenever I try to help you on anything, when I sometimes begin to tell you about something for your own good, trying to teach you something, you never like me to talk to you about the good things. The good talks always hurt you badly. I never was like you. I have been raised in many hardships, which sometimes I thought were too hard for me, but I just kept at it. And I have been raised in lots of talks, and everybody is still talking to me, about how to get things, how to live, many things about life. However I always enjoy

479

hearing someone talk to me, and I always like to learn something from another fellow. I always want to be shown something. When a person wants to teach me something I always like it. I never get sore or mad about it. That's the way with me. When I first picked you up I thought you were that way too, because I knew you had a mother and a grandmother, and you have lots of clansmen. I thought they had been teaching you a lot of things, but I see you have not been taught anything."

When I said this to her my mother said, "What have you been doing? What have you done to each other? Your talking sounds as if you had been doing something to each other. What is it?" she asked. So I told her what had happened. "I thought you had done something to each other," my mother said. "What do you want to do that for, my grandchild, my daughter? You shouldn't act like that. When you live with a man you must obey him. You must let him teach you things. It's good to live with a man. When you live without a man you will be as though without arms and legs. I didn't think you were that way. When you live with a man you must do whatever he tells you. Let him show you, let him teach you. You will learn a great deal from him. That's the way I was. When first I got a man I didn't know what to do. I didn't know anything. He began to talk to me, to show me things, to teach me things, telling me many things about life. When a man is good to you you must be good to him. I don't care to have you spoil my son. I don't wish him to be spoiled by anyone," she said. "Now, what I have said to you, you must remember. I mean it, I don't want you to spoil him. I don't want him to be spoiled because I think of him as though he were a little infant still, because I picked him up when he was an infant and carried him around and raised him through many difficult things. He was almost taken away from me many times, but by taking good care of him I saved him from many bad and hard things that came around. I mean starving, going poor, going hungry for meat. He almost starved to death on me once for want of meat. I got some meat for him and saved him with that. And I saved him from many sicknesses that had come along. By taking good care of him he was saved, and he was raised. Not only I but all his fathers took good care of him. Every one of them still thinks of him as though he were still a small boy.

"That's the way we all think of him. I never thought that you would marry him. He was going to be married to one of his mother's father's clan. If he had married one of them he might have been treated well, and here you are treating him badly. I know you are treating him badly. I know you are hurting him very badly by different things." When she said this she began to cry.

Then my wife said, "Yes, I did that. I am very ashamed about it now, and I am very sorry for what I have done. From here on I won't do that any more, my grandmother, my old mother," she said. "I don't know how I got that way. I just can't think how I got that way. I must have gone unconscious or something. If I had been in my right mind I wouldn't have done it. However, I won't do that any more from here on, because I am so ashamed of myself. I am very sorry that I did it." "You better be," my mother said, "because if you keep on doing that you will both ruin each other. You won't live well. When you have trouble between yourselves you will be unhappy. So just put that away and forget all about those bad things and start to live well. In that way you will be happy all the time. You are both young, and the two of you will live a long life, so be good to each other all the time. Don't make fun of yourselves. If some of the people were to find out about you they would begin to talk about you among one another and begin making fun of you. You don't want anybody to make fun of you; so try and be good to each other," she said to us both.

23

His mother is ill and is treated . . .
Lost His Moccasins diagnoses the illness by
hand-trembling. . . And fetches Slow to
perform the curing rituals.

When we got up in the morning my mother said, "I
am aching all over, but through my breast is the
worst. It feels as if there were something running through
me. It gives me an awful pain from front to back." She was
sitting and holding her hand on her breast and moaning. "I
was starting to ache yesterday. I was that way all day and last
night, but early this morning the pain got worse. It hurts me
awfully bad now. But, I guess, it will be better after a while."

Then she said, "We had better move out of here, up to
where our other camp is." I said, "I thought you had an
awful pain? What do you want to move for?" "Well, even
though I have a pain we'll mome today," she said, "and I will
get over it, because when I get this way, if I go around with it
I will get out of it. If I just stay at one place and lie with it I
get worse. If I go and move around with it I will get over it
soon. So we better move today." "All right, we will move up
there to our next camp over by that hill," I said, as I pointed
to the hill. It was just a little way to that place. "The hogan
needs to be renewed, and the corral is all down to the
ground. I'll have to build that over again. The hogan I won't
have to tear down, that's sitting up all right," I said, "so if
you want to move right away I'll go and get the horses." She
said, "Yes, we'll move. Go and get the horses."

When I got back to the hogan I saddled up the horses
while they were starting to pack up some little things. When
we were all packed up we started off. The boy had gone on
with the herd. It was about three miles to that place. When

we got there we unpacked the horses and turned them loose. While they started on the cooking I started to work on the hogan. I covered it with cedar bark and dirt, but I didn't get finished with it that day. Before it got too dark I took some of the dirt out of the hogan and we cleaned a little in the inside and built a fire. Then they ground a little white corn and I made four white spots and sprinkled some around inside the hogan. After that we took all our things inside and the cooking started.

My mother was lying there; she said "The pain is just the same." After we ate and put away the things and fixed our beds, she said again, "Something must be wrong. The pain is getting worse. Come and look at my back for me. The pain on my breast isn't so bad, but through me, back to my back, is worse. See how it looks. Look at it for me."

My wife walked over to her and rolled up her waist and we both looked at her back. There were two sores close together. It looked as if she had been burned. I don't know what made it blister. She said, "It gives me an awful pain." But we couldn't do anything about it. We didn't know what to do. We only looked at it; that was all, and then we went to bed.

In the morning after we ate the boy took out the herd and I started working on the hogan again. When I got through with that I started working on the corral. Around in the evening when I got through with it, we took the herd in and I fixed the gate and walked back to the hogan. My mother was lying there, working herself around and moaning. After we ate my wife said, "I looked at her back again, and there were more sores all around the two places, and her breast is starting to develop sores too. She has a round red spot on her breast, and around this red spot are a whole lot of little ones, just like pimples. I think she is having an awful pain from that. The sores on her are getting worse, so we had better do something for her." My mother said, "I know what's bothering me. I think it's witchcraft. I don't think it's anything besides that." That was all, and then we went to bed.

After we ate in the morning I said to the boy, "Go and get the horses. I would like to ride one around." He started off immediately, and I said, "I guess I'll go down to Lost His Moccasins' place. I'll bring him back. He knows Evil Way, so I'll take a ride down to his place and bring him back and he will treat you with Evil Way." Then, while the boy went after the horses, I started gathering up some wood. Just as I quit working on the wood—I had quite a pile gathered up—the boy came back without the horses. I said, "Where are the horses? Didn't you see them?" "Yes, I saw them. They are down in the valley, close by here. I had forgotten all about the rope, so I only looked at them and started back." I said, "That's all right," so he walked over to the corral and turned out the herd.

A little while after that I went down to where the horses were and rode one back and put the saddle on it and started off to Lost His Moccasins' place. I went down to White Rock Point, and from there up to the top where his camp was. He was home and asked me about my place. "About where are you living?" "We were living over at Rocks Standing Up, but we began to run out of grazing, so we moved to our other camp, up towards the woods. We moved up there two days ago, and that's where I'm from," I said. "Is there much grazing up in there?" he asked. "Yes," I said. "There is more grazing up there than where we had been living. But," I said, "you have got the best place here in the valley. There is a whole lot of grazing. More than you want." "Yes," he said, "there is a lot of grazing, a lot of feed for the animals. This is the finest place we have been to." "Yes, it has been this way all the time," I said.

They started cooking some food, and he asked me, "Where are you thinking of going? Are you going to any place?" "No, I came here for you to help me out," I said to him. "My mother has a sore on her back and on her breast. There are sores on both sides, front and back, and she thinks that a witch is bothering her; so I want you to treat her with some of Evil Way. That's what I came here for, my uncle. I want you to treat your sister with Evil Way." "When did she start to get sick?" he asked. "Three days ago. All at once she said she had a pain on her breast and back, and now she is getting worse. I think she has got an awful pain from those

484

two sores, so I want you to treat her. And I would like to know what you use. If you want to use something, some kind of weeds, tell me what kind, so I can gather them up. I think you can get everything in this White Rock Point canyon."

He mentioned some weeds to me and said, "Everything is down in White Rock Point canyon, so you go down and gather them up and take them back with you." Then, while they were cooking, I started off to gather the weeds he mentioned. There were a lot of them around the foot of the rocks. It took me quite a while to gather them. When I had everything gathered up I went back to his place and we started eating. After we ate he said to me, "I haven't got any horses around here close by. The horses are way down in the valley, so I guess I will go back with you on foot. And what kind of Evil Way ritual do you want me to treat her with? There are two ways that I know. One is called the Rite For Dispelling Monsters and the other one is the Shooting Way Chant;[1] so which one do you want me to treat her with?" I said, "I don't know, but perhaps after you tell her about that she will decide it for herself. So we will let that go," I said.

Then he gave me his medicine bundle, and I tied it to my saddle, and he started walking ahead of me. When we got to the foot of the hill I got off the horse and told him to get on, so he did and I started to run ahead of him. We crossed one valley and went over a hill, then across another valley. Soon we passed where I had first kept my horses. We went up following the hill. Finally we got back to the hogan when the sun was down. Then he told me to go get a flat round rock. I went out and started looking for one; there were lots of rocks, but they were soft. Just when it got real dark I found one. When I brought it back to the hogan he said to me, "Now, you burn all the weeds that you gathered." So I started burning the weeds. And my mother wanted to be treated by the Shooting Way Chant. "Monsterway isn't very much to me," she said. "It has a short song, and not many songs to it; and the Shooting Way Chant has long songs and many songs, so I want to be treated by that." He said, "All right."

1. Evil Way (above) is a form of Shooting Way Chant.

I had burned all the weeds and had worked down the pile of black ashes until it was just like powder. When I had it ready he said, "Bring that black stuff over here close to her. I did that and he started singing and my wife started painting the black ashes on my mother. He went on with his singing, and I helped him, until my wife had my mother all blackened up with these ashes. When we got through with it he said, "You two go out"; so the two women went out and I took out the rock with the black stuff on it. When I took the rock out they went back inside. I came back in too, and that was all.

Then my wife warmed up the food, coffee, and other things, and we all ate. After we ate I said to him, "I want you to help me out again with your hand-shaking ritual. Perhaps you could find out some more about what she is being bothered by; so I want you to help me out on that, my uncle." He said, "I don't know, but we'll try it. I am not a good guesser. Sometimes I guess things right, sometimes not, so I am not a good guesser, and not a good hand-shaker, but I will help you with that." He got out his corn pollen and put some on his hand, and then started asking what kind of thing was bothering her. He asked about a lot of things. (In asking, in praying, they are begging to be told what is wrong with the patient. They ask these questions of Gila Monster, who, they say, shakes the hand. They name two kinds of lizard, black and spotted.) When he was through with that then he started singing and shaking his hand. He had been doing that for quite a while, then he quit. He sat back, he sat close by me and said, "A witch was bothering her all right, but that is off of her now. However, one thing is bothering her worse. She knows it herself. She bothered a thorn which had been used in Wind Way and put away. It had been hidden away and she found it, and she must have handled it. So that is what is bothering her very badly. And there is no one knows anything about it around here; only across the country, where she was. Way over at the foot of the other mountain, around that country are the elders who know about that. They are the only ones who will cure her, but no one around here knows about it."

I was sitting there looking at his hand every once in a while, not believing him at all. I thought he was just saying it, just making it up. I thought, "How can he find a thing like that and at that distance?" I was wondering what told him. While he had been shaking his hand I had looked all around him and on his hand, but there was nothing around him and nothing on his hand, only corn pollen. So I didn't believe him one bit. He was starting to make a cigarette, and while he was doing that his hand started shaking again. Pretty soon he laid the tobacco down and started patting me on the lap. Then he started up on my face; he got hold of my ear and began twisting it, and rubbed my nose around with his one finger. All at once his hand dropped down. He started working on his hand, cracking his fingers, and said, "You didn't believe what I said a while ago, that is why my hand started shaking again. If you had believed me, it wouldn't have done that, but you didn't believe what I said." I said, "No, I didn't believe it at all. I didn't believe what you said, because I was wondering how you could tell anything just by shaking your hand. There is nothing around you that could tell you. How could you find anything like that, and it's a long distance to that place, where she was. When I thought all about this, then I just didn't believe you at all." "That's what this hand-shaking said, that you don't believe. If you don't believe, it's all right with me."

Then he said, "Well, we will find it out right now. See who is right. She knows it very well. How is it? Where did you handle one of those thorns that had been used on a patient?" Then she got up, "Yes, that is true," she said. "When I was across the country I was herding around in sagebrush. The goats were running in all directions, and, as I was going around them, I picked up sticks and threw them at them, backing them up. I picked up another stick. I was going to throw it again, but when I picked it up and swung it, it felt kind of heavy. Then I looked at it, and there I was, holding a thorn. It was decorated with things, with feathers, so I got scared of it and threw it down. I don't know how it fell on the ground. So that's what I did. That thorn had been used by a medicine man. He had treated a patient possessed with evil

487

spirits, and that was the thorn he had used. That's what I found out afterwards," she said.

Then he said, "See, I guess now you believe. I don't think she is telling a story about it. You had better get one of the medicine men, and you had better be quick about it. If you don't she will get worse. As soon as she is treated by that she will be well. So, now, you had better think about it right away and get one of the elders." I said, "I don't know what elder to get. How about yourself, my uncle, you ought to know, because you have been around those lots of times, around where they had those rituals." "No," he said, "I don't know anything about it. I know just a little, but that won't do her any good. She has got to be treated with the whole thing. So you had better get her one of the elders that knows about it." I asked him, "How about it, could you help me on that? Could you get one of the elders for us, because I can't go myself. You know I have got lots to do around here." He said, "All right, I'm willing to help." "You can go and get the one you know best, the one who you think is the best on that." He said, "I think Slow is the best man to get, so I'll go and get him." I said, "Tell him I will give him a horse to come up here. I will give him a horse for his trip and treatment, and then when he gets here, there will be more that I would like to give him. Don't come back without any elder. Be sure and bring one back with you, my uncle," I said to him. "Yes," he said, "I will do that. I will bring one back with me. I don't like to go and ride around for nothing, so I don't want to come back without any of them." I said, "Be sure and get one for us. And now help me with what you know." He said, "All right. I have a little medicine for it, and a few songs, two pieces of a song, that's all I know."

Then he got out his medicine and his rattle, put some medicine in the water and started singing. After he sang a few songs he gave the medicine to her. When he was through with another piece of song he said, "I guess we will treat her a little with the Shooting Way Chant songs." After he had treated her with that it was way late in the night. He said, "We had better get a little sleep, so we will all go to bed." In the morning, after we ate, he started treating her with more

488

Shooting Way Chant songs. After we ate at noon he said, "As soon as I get home I'll get ready. I'll have my horse ready, and tomorrow early I'll go straight over White Rock Point hill. I may be gone for two or three days. I know it will take us two whole days to come back. If I get Slow, if I start back with him, I know we will get as far as Hill Across the first day. We will stay there at night, and the next day, around toward evening we will be back here; so perhaps I'll be back around in four days. But I can't tell; it all depends on them.

After he went back to his home I stayed around there, tending to the wood and other little things. The next morning it started snowing. It snowed all that day and all night. While the boy was herding I stayed at home tending to the wood for three days. On the fourth day I took the herd out in the morning. It had snowed quite a lot. The snow was deep and in some places the drifts were piled high. I was thinking about whether he had got one of the elders or not and wondering if he would come that day with one of them, or if he hadn't been able to get one on account of the snow. I was thinking in this way all the day while I was herding. Around toward sunset I brought the herd back. The food was ready to be eaten, but there was nobody around. I sat by the fire cleaning the snow off my feet. I had my feet wrapped up in old rags, and there was a lot of snow on them, and it was kind of icy around my ankles. I was sitting there by the fire beating on these circles of ice around my feet when all at once he came in with Slow. "Here we are," he said. "Better hurry up. We are cold. Fix a place for us."

We all got up and hurried around fixing a place for them. We never heard them coming. Nobody had been outside looking for them, because it was getting late. We didn't think they would come that day. Even the dogs hadn't seen or heard them. Then they took their moccasins off and took all the things off the blankets and sat down, close to the fire. I had told the boy to build a big fire. I was pretty cold too. My feet were almost frozen. When we were warmed up Lost His Moccasins said to the boy, "Go out and take the saddle off my horse and hobble him for me, my nephew."

489

I went out with the boy and took the saddle off the medicine man's horse and told him to take the horses up where the others were. When I came back inside I said, "I am very thankful that both of you will help, and thankful that you both came. I didn't think you would come on account of the snow. I know what the winter is like. I know just how it is when it gets this way, I have been in it lots of times. I have been in it when it was like this, and I have been in it when it was worse, and I know just how it is when you are riding on horseback. But you didn't care about the cold. You wanted to come; you wanted to help me, and I am very thankful. I want you to help me with what you know. That's why I sent for you."

Then Lost His Moccasins said, "I didn't speak long to him. As soon as I spoke one word to him immediately he said, 'All right, let's go.' However it wasn't snowing out there. We got in the snow around on the other side of Hill Across. So I don't know; perhaps he is sorry that he got here. Maybe he will have a hard time going back. But we don't care about him. We don't care how he gets back." That was only a little joke. I asked Slow, "Where are you living?" He said, "I'm living there at Tall Mountain."

Then Lost His Moccasins started telling about the time he started from his home. "I started in the morning. I rode down and stayed out over night, and the next day I got to his place. I stayed at his place for two nights, then we started, yesterday morning, and got as far as Hill Across. That's where we stayed last night. From there we started this morning. It took us a whole day to come up here." Then, after we ate, the medicine man started singing. He sang a few songs and gave some medicine to my mother, and as soon as he was through we all went to bed. While the others were building a fire in the morning I dressed up and said, "I am going to get some things that you want to use. I have got to go down in White Rock Point canyon for them, so I guess I'll go now."

Then he told me to get some sumac and I started out. When I was almost out of the hogan I said to them, "One of you get the thorn. It is close around here. There are a whole lot of them on that black rock hill. That hill is covered with

490

thorns. So one of you can go over and get some, and when I come back from this other place I'll get the soapweed, and that's close around here too." Then I went out and started off for the things they were going to use. When I brought the prayer stick materials back with me they had the thorn. There were only two things that hadn't been brought yet. That was the soapweed and the dirt. But the soapweed was close around the hogan, and they were working on the feathers and on the prayer sticks.

They said, "We have got the thorn all ready, and they had the four stones there, too, to put the different colors on. While they started working on the thorn I got the soapweed and the dirt. When they were through decorating the thorn they put that aside, and then the medicine man spread out the dirt. He fixed it nice and round and then put the basket right in the middle. Then he picked up the soapweed and put it in the basket and started pouring water in from four sides. He filled it half full, and then made the soap. He said to my mother, "Go around the fire and come around the basket and wash with the soapweed." She did that. She got up and went around the fire and around the basket. Then she took off her waist and untied her hair and started washing it. When she got through with her hair she started washing herself all over. After that they took the dirt and the soapweed out. Then they set out the four stones, which had different colors on them. He wet the different colors with water and started drawing on her. First on the front on her breast he drew what we call White Spirit Wind. He had this White Spirit Wind up right on top where it was sore and then on her back he drew what we call Yellow Spirit Wind right on the sore. The sore was right on the middle of the breast on both sides just about even. When he was through with this drawing then he gave her some more medicine we call za'nit and that's all kinds of pollen mixed up together.

After she took this medicine then he started treating her with what he had decorated, the thorn. When he stopped treating her he picked up his corn pollen, put some on her, and sprinkled some out for her, making a trail with it. Then she went out, and after they had taken out the four stones she

491

came back inside and put on her waist again. From there on we had the closing ceremony. At night, late in the evening, I spread out a blanket. On it I put a new robe, and right on top of the robe, which was folded, I put some calico. That was all. Then he put the basket on top; he had the thorn in the basket, and started singing. He kept on singing all night, until morning. Then he made a trail with some more corn pollen for her and she went out and inhaled the morning. Then she came back, and he took out the thorn, and, I guess, he had put it away someplace.

After he came back he said to me, "You go and get my horse back for me, my younger brother, and the horse that you gave me. I want to start right now. I don't know how the trail is; maybe it snowed pretty deep; so I will go this morning before the snow gets too hard. I don't know when I will get out to the other side" (of the country, his home). About that time the food was all ready. They put it out for us and we started eating. I told him to eat lots, "Because you are going a long way." Then, after we ate, I got the horses for him and he saddled up and put on his things and started off. Lost His Moccasins went back with him, but I suppose he stopped at his place.

After Slow went back my mother said, "The pain quit on me all at once, just as soon as he treated me with that thing (the thorn). And my whole breast seemed like it was nice and cool and I began to take whole deep breaths. Before that I couldn't get my breath. Now I am breathing just the way I always do."

After four days the drawing on her was off with the sore. In four days when she was taking a bath everything was dry and where it was sore there was just a white spot on both sides.

24

Moving again to get out of the snow . . .
His wife goes into the sweat-house with him . . .
He goes to the store and they move again.

From there on the boy and I took turns herding. We
didn't do anything, except sometimes gather up wood
and look at the horses. There was no place to go, nothing to
do besides herding, gathering up wood, and getting water.
There was nobody to visit. Nobody visited us, because there
wasn't anybody living close by. Everybody was living a long
way off. After many days, when the snow was beginning to
melt, I thought I would go down to another place to see what
it looked like, and I wanted to look around for the grazing. So
I said, "I would like to go down to Hill Across and see how
that place is. If it's a good place we will move down there."
They said, "All right, perhaps out there the people are living
close by one another. Up here there is no one living close to
us, and it's a lonesome place."

Then I started off down in the flat to the foot of the
mountain. I got on top and went along. There was quite a
little snow on top. When I got way on the other side, to the
edge of the mountain, I looked out over the country. Some
places were white with snow, some had little white spots on
the ground here and there, in some places there was no snow
at all. But there was a little snow around the hills. Right away
I thought, "Out there in the flat is a good place. There is no
snow out there, so I'll move down to that place. No use staying in the snow all the time." Then I turned around and
started back.

As soon as I got to the foot of the mountain I started to
run my horse. This mountain that I went over is part of Black
Mountain Strip. It goes down toward the west, way out in the

flat a little beyond Blue Around The Lake. I got home before the sun was down.

Next day I said, "I would like to go over to the other people's place. I want to visit them. I would like to see my mother again before we leave here." That was Lost His Moccasins' wife. "I'll tell them that we are going to move. Maybe they want to go too; so I'm going down on foot." Then my wife said, "I want to go too. I haven't been to anyplace for all this time, so I'll go with you." "Well," I said, "it's just too far for you on foot, so if you want to go I'll get the horses." But I didn't get back with the horses until way late in the afternoon. They had gone pretty far. I said, "It's very late now. I don't think we will go today. I'll just hobble the horses now and we will go tomorrow. I don't want to go down there and just turn around and come back; so we will go tomorrow."

In the morning while they were starting the fire I went out to where I had hobbled the horses. They were around there. They hadn't gone very far. I got them all back. There were only four of them again. Then, after we ate, the boy took out the herd and we started off. We chased the other two along until we got out to the valley where there was good feed. There we stopped and hobbled them and then went on into White Rock Point and down that trail to where their home was. The two boys had just taken the herd out; it was still early in the morning. They put out a sheep pelt for us, and after we shook hands we sat down.

They said, "We are out of grub. There is nothing to eat." "We haven't got anything for you," my mother (Lost His Moccasins' wife said). "But anyway I'll try and fix something for you. We ate all we had made this morning. We have some corn down at our summer camp. We hid some away in a hole. I wanted the boys to go down and get some, but they don't want to go. They are afraid of the snow. They are afraid it must be pretty deep. They don't think anyone could go through there at Valley Coming To The Edge." I said, "I don't think anyone could go through now, but why don't they go just to see about it? Maybe it's not so very deep. They ought to do that," I said. "I have told them to do that too," she said, "but they won't go, so now I have just let it go."

Then I said, "We are planning to move down to Hill Across. That's why we came to visit you, before we left, so that you would know that we had gone. I was up there on the mountain, and when I got to the edge I looked down and out over the country, and it looked very nice out in the flat. In some places there were little strips of white snow. In some places there was only a little spot here and there. In some places there was no snow on the ground at all. So we want to move down to that place."

She said, "Well, then, are you going to leave us all alone up here, my son? If you move we will be all alone, and we will be lonesome. Even though we have been living a long way from each other, still it seemed as if we were living in one hogan. That's the way we have felt about it. But you are going to move away from us. I guess we will move too. Sometime we will start to move back. If we move we will go up and follow the valley." I said, "There isn't much snow here now, and there was only a little on top of the mountain, and way on the other side there is no snow. When I looked out in the flat toward Cows Water there was no snow down there, only a whirling wind was running around. I could see it plainly from the top of the mountain." When I said that they began to talk as if they wanted to go out to that place right then and there. I said, "That's where we are going. I don't like to stay in the snow all the time. I would like to be out of it, so I guess we will start moving tomorrow."

Late in the afternoon I said, "We had better be going back. It's quite a way to our place, and we have got to find the horses on our way back." She said, "Well, then, I am glad you two came and visited us. We haven't seen anyone around. Nobody has visited us yet, since we got here, so I am glad that you both came. And we didn't notice the day at all." I said, "We had a visitor once. The other night a man stayed with us. I don't know how he happened to come to our place." "Who was it? What man was it?" she asked. "This man belongs to The Yucca-Fruit-Strung-Out-In-A-Line People. His name is Hosteen Sick." "Oh, yes," she said, "I know him. I wonder where he was from?" I said, "I think he is from down below. He said he was looking for some horses,

495

and that's the only man who has visited us." "We had no one around at our place," she said. Then I said, "Well, I guess we had better go now." "Go ahead then, my children," she said. "I am very thankful to you for visiting us."

Then we got on our horses and started off, back to where we had hobbled the others. We unhobbled those two and put our saddles on them and started off, driving the two we had been riding. We got back to our hogan before the sun set. The herd was just coming in. We took the saddles off the horses and I took them a little way from the hogan and hobbled them. Then the boy and I took the herd to the corral, and after that I gathered some wood. When it got dark I quit and went inside, and lay against the hogan. My wife was telling my mother about the trip we had made. She was about through. Then I said, "Yes, they didn't have much food. They didn't have any corn, nothing besides the meat. They only had meat; that's all, and some coffee with it. They are going to move back toward White Valley Coming To The Edge, so I guess we will move tomorrow as early as we can."

We all got up real early the next morning. When I brought the horses back the food was all cooked and we started eating. Right after we were through I said to the boy, "Saddle up a horse and take the herd out. Just keep going. Don't hold the herd back. Let them go right ahead. I don't know where we will catch up with you. It will take us quite a while to pack everything, so you go on with the herd." He saddled up a horse which we always used for herding. It was the tamest one. Then he turned the herd out and started off, and we started packing. We didn't have much of a load. We didn't have much food, just a few things like a little corn. I know we didn't have any coffee.

When we were packed we got on our horses and started up the valley. It was quite a distance up the valley. We followed the boy all the way up to where the valley starts, then through many woods over a hill. When we got out of the woods on the other side of the hill where there was another valley there was the boy going along with the herd. We kept on going across that valley, then through more woods. Soon we got to the foot of the mountain. Then I said, "It's getting pretty late. Soon it will get real cold, so we had better stop here and camp. If we go to the top we will get cold. We could make it all right, but it will be awful cold, so it's better for us to camp here." They said, "All right, we'll do that." So we unloaded our stuff and unsaddled our horses and hobbled them. There was lots of feed for the sheep and horses. Nothing was around, no animals. The grazing looked pretty good, nothing had been bitten off.

I said, "How will it be if we camp here for a few days?" "No," they said. "We are tired of living in the snow. We want to go right on. We want to get out of the snow, and we haven't got much grub." I said, "We don't care for grub. We can live on meat." "No, the meat by itself is not good for us, so we had better be going on tomorrow." That was all we said, and then toward sunset we rounded the herd up to one place. My wife and my mother said, "We haven't got much meat." "The meat isn't good for you—what do you want to talk about meat for?" I said. "Don't talk to us like that! Go and get one, so that we will have nice, fresh meat for our supper tonight." Then I caught one and carried it over to them and they killed it and butchered it, and we had a lot of meat again. After we ate we went right to bed. Toward the middle of the night I was cold, so I got up and built a big fire. Then I walked around the herd, but they were all right, and I came back and crawled in bed again and went to sleep. When I woke up I was a little cold again. It was morning.

We all got up and I built a big fire and we started cooking right away. The horses were around there close, and after we ate I brought them back and we saddled them up and packed. When we got everything on the horses we started with the herd over the mountain. We got to the edge of the mountain on the other side in the afternoon. The snow was pretty deep, but it was soft. First I drove down the goats. That made a trail, and then we started the sheep. As soon as they got through the deep snow they started running. They had made it so slippery that we had to lead the horses down. I led my mother's horse down, while she made a cane and walked down as carefully as she could so that she wouldn't fall. When we got down to where there was a little dirt we got on the horses again and went on down after the herd. They had gone on because they were hungry for saltweeds. We could hear them making a noise way down. When we got part way down the mountain, to that big flat that we call White Plain Space, there was the boy with the herd. There were all kinds of feed and lots of saltweeds. The herd was grazing there as if they were all lying down. Not a one was moving. I said, "We will camp here again."

It was real close to sunset when we got out to that place. We unloaded our stuff and took off the saddles and hobbled the horses. There was lots of feed for them. Then before the sun went down I thought about a hogan. It was pretty cold. I said, "There used to be a hogan and corral above here. I'll go over and see if they are up. I want to see if everything is still up. Maybe they have torn it down." It was quite a ways up to that place. When I got there the hogan was up and it was nice and clean. It was nice and clean outside, too, and there was some wood piled there. The corral was a little small for our herd, but some of it could be removed and it could be easily enlarged. It was a very nice place. I went on top of a little hill and there was a nice sweat-house sitting up, and the wood was piled by that too. I was very glad about that. So I thought, "We will camp here for a while, until it gets a little warmer."

When I got back I said, "The hogan is up, and the corral is up, but it's a little small for our herd. However it can be made bigger. The hogan is clean inside and out." Then my mother said, "Let's go. We will move up there right now. It's so very cold. We don't want to stay out in the cold." "It's quite a ways," I said. "You had better stay here tonight. We are about warmed up now. If we start to move we won't get there perhaps until around close on to midnight, because at night the sheep won't go as they will in the daytime, so we had better not move tonight." My mother was afraid of the cold, so I chopped off some branches and the boy and I built a little brush hogan and gathered a lot of wood. We had a big pile. Though it was real cold out, it was warm in this brush hogan, even though the top was all open. So we camped there that night. The next morning we got up and built a big fire and started cooking. After we ate the boy took the herd and I got the horses. We saddled them up, put all our things back on them and started after the boy, to where the hogan was. The people who had lived there must have left the place early in the fall. It looked that way. And there was lots of feed all around which never had been touched.

It was a nice little place there at this little spot. When we got there we unloaded our stuff and took the saddles off the horses, and I hobbled them while they ground some white corn for the hogan. While they were doing that I said, "I'll go up to the sweat-house. Go ahead with that. You know what to do about it. And when you get some water bring some to me at the sweat-house." I took the ax and shovel and blanket. The wood was there already. I chopped some in pieces and gathered some rocks and built a fire. Then I took the rocks out from the inside, and the cedar bark, too, and got some new bark and put it in. When the rocks were good and hot I put them in, put the blanket over the door and took off my clothes and went inside. It was so hot I didn't stay long. When I got out there my wife had the water. I walked over to her and drank some.

She said, "I want to go in with you. Can I?" I said, "If you want to, I guess it will be all right. It's up to you." She said, "I'll go in with you." When she started working on her clothes I got up and walked to the door and went inside. I was sitting way back in the sweat-house with my back to the door, and, I guess, when she had undressed herself, she came in. I only heard her; I didn't even look back to see. When she pulled the blanket down over the door it got real dark. We went in and out many times. She had one of her dresses by her so then when she went out she put that around her. That's the way we were in the sweathouse. My father, Slim Man, used to say, "You can go in the sweat-house with a woman if you behave. When you go in the sweat-house with a woman you mustn't bother her, because it's a serious thing to do. It will trouble you; so you mustn't bother a woman if you go in the sweat-house with her." That's what he used to say, so that's why I never even touched her. I was afraid that

499

something might happen to me. So I sat away from her, way back inside, and she was close to the door.

We lived there for quite a few days. Nothing happened and nobody came to our place. All that we were doing was herding and working on the water and wood. We were plumb out of grub. We had lots of meat all the time and a little corn, but that was all, nothing besides. But even though we had only two kinds of food, we didn't go hungry, because we had lots of meat and a little corn with it. Both were strong. We made cornbread in a few different ways, and then we made mush out of it in a few different ways also. That was all we lived on for many days until the snow was all gone, although there was still some on the mountain. It was kind of warm during the daytime, and it wasn't cold at all at night.

So then one day I said, "Tomorrow we will shear a few of the wethers. After we shear some I'll take the wool down to Blue Around The Lake for some grub. We have been out of food for many days now, so tomorrow we will shear some." Immediately they all said, "All right." Next morning I said the same thing again. "Go ahead with the shearing, my children. As soon as we have enough sheared, I'll go." The two of us, my wife and I, started shearing that morning, while the other two, my mother and the boy, were butchering one of the wethers. It was a nice, young one. All at once she hollered and started cussing herself, because she had cut open the guts and got the meat dirty. She was talking and working on the meat with the boy, but we didn't pay any attention to them.

When we were about through shearing I told the boy to go and get me a horse. This boy used to be quick on anything. Even though he was small, he was lively. He picked up a rope and ran over the hill after the horses, I had told him which one to bring. Quite a while after he left we had everything ready. The food was ready too. Just about then he came, riding the horse I wanted. After we ate I saddled up, put the wool over the saddle and tied on some goatskins and sheep pelts. It was a little after noon. The boy had taken out the herd. I went down to the foot of the mountain and started riding through the woods, then out and over to Hill Across. Just when I got to Where The Water Ends the sun was down, but I kept going until I got quite a way down on the other side. There I stopped and stayed that night. In the morning while it was still real dark I got the horse back over to where I had my things, saddled up, put the things back on and started off. There was nothing but sand for quite a distance. Finally I got to Blue Around The Lake, to the store there when the sun was pretty well up.

The white fellow came out to me. His name was Mister Gray. That's what we called him. His son we used to call Worn Out Hat. They were both there at the store. When I took my stuff inside the old man shook hands with me and called me grandfather. "Where are you from, my grandfather?" he asked. "I'm from Hill Across." I said. Then his son shook hands with me and asked me the same thing. "Where are you from, my grandfather?" he said. "I'm from Hill Across." Then he asked me where lots of the people were living. I said, "I don't know where the people are living. I just don't know," I said. Then he said, "You must be off someplace alone. How is it that you don't see anybody, or don't know where the people live? I thought you were living with the people." "No," I said, "I was living way up on the mountain close to a place called Willows Coming Out, and nobody was living up there. Then I moved down to the foot of the mountain. I moved to a place called Hill Across, but a little on the other side. That's where I'm living, and there are no people living close around there. So that's why I don't know anything about them."

"The reason I asked you about these men," he said, "is because I know them very well. I know they have a lot of wool. I wanted you to tell them that we will give more for wool, my grandfather. That's why I asked about them. How much wool have you got, my grandfather?" he asked me. "I can't say. I don't know just how much I have got." "Be sure and bring your wool over when you shear your sheep," he said. "We will give you what we think it's worth, and we will treat you right; so be sure and bring all your wool to us, my grandfather." I said, "I don't know. Maybe I will, maybe not.

501

It all depends on the horses. The horses that I have are poor. They are not able to carry wool this far. They are not strong, because they are not fat. If the horses were fat then I could take the wool as far as I wanted to. You know I have got poor horses. You saw the horse that I rode here was poor and skinny."

He said, "That's what I call a horse! You have got a nice horse, nice and fat. I don't call that a skinny horse. I call that a very nice horse, my grandfather." He walked over to where his father had dumped out the wool. They were talking to each other for a while; then the boy said, "My father says you have got very nice wool. This is the first time he has ever seen such nice clean wool. And he said that he knows you have very nice fat sheep. He said he could tell it by the wool. He said, 'I wish I could see his herd.' That's what my father said. So be sure and bring all your wool. We will give you more for it, and we will treat you right." The boy used to talk in Navajo just the way we talk, but his father didn't.

Then he said, "We will give you something to eat. How about it, my grandfather, are you hungry or not? Maybe you don't want anything to eat." "That's what I came here for, something to eat. I haven't eaten since yesterday morning. I didn't eat all day yesterday and last night and today. So come on with whatever you want me to eat." "All right, we will get you something to eat. We will fill you up in a little while." he said. "How have you been living without anything to eat? You said you haven't eaten since yesterday. How did you keep yourself alive? How about at your home? Have you got some food?" "No," I said. "Nothing, no coffee, no flour, no corn, nothing at all." Well, how did you keep yourself alive? What have you been living on, my grandfather?" "I lived on meat. That's all. Nothing besides." "What you say is true, my grandfather," he said, "I believe you, because I know it. I go out among the people; I have been to lots of places, and it's that way all around. Everywhere I go the people have meat and nothing besides. I know that is all they live on. I know that, my grandfather, and you are right on that." "What do you go around for, my grandfather?" I asked him. "I just go around and visit them, and besides visiting I hunt among the

502

old ruins." "That's what I am going around for, my grandfather. And that's how I found out that all the people live on meat, and nothing besides."

Then he gave me a little flour. He put baking powder and salt in it for me, and he gave me some coffee and sugar already mixed up. And he gave me a coffee pot and frying pan and a cup. "Go out now and get yourself some wood and build a fire and go ahead with your cooking. And eat a lot. If you want anything more just come and tell us, my grandfather. I suppose you have some meat with you, my grandfather?" "Yes," I said, "I have got some meat." "Well, then I will come over and eat some of the meat you have for lunch. I want to eat some meat, my grandfather." I said, "All right, I have got some with me." Then I went out, and he gave me a little wood and I started a fire. Then I made the dough and fried some tortillas.

Just as I began to eat he came over. I got the meat out. It was boiled. I had a whole quarter cut up, and started eating. He said, "I thought you had some meat, my grandfather. I like to eat meat. And I know you have got nice fat meat, because I could tell it by your wool." I gave him a piece of the meat where there was lots of fat on it, and he started eating. "This meat tastes very good to me, my grandfather. You must have all your meat nice and fat, my grandfather."

"Yes," I said, "I guess they are all just about the same. You said you hunted among the old ruins. What do you do with what you find? Do you use it for something, my grandfather?" "Yes, and that's what it's for, coffee, flour, and sugar, and all the other things which I have in the store. When I bring something back with me I sell it, and that's how I have got all the stuff that I have in the store." "How do you bring them back?" I asked him. "I ride around, and I take a horse and a mule with me for packing. When I find something I put it on the horse and mule and pack them back with me. Then I sell it." I said, "It must be worth a whole lot, my grandfather." "Yes," he said, "It's worth a little, but not so very much. But even at that I have gotten a good deal for it. Some of these ruins were rich. Some of those people knew a whole lot about different kinds of ceremonies." "How can

503

you tell that, my grandfather?" I asked him. "When I dig out the graves some have big jars of pottery all around them, with different kinds of beads in them, and some have a lot of different kinds of stones and arrowheads, like what the singers have now, and different colored clay, black, blue, white, and yellow, just the same as the singers have now; so that's how I can tell it. I can tell it by that. They knew a whole lot." He was sitting there, eating the meat, saying, "This meat tastes very good to me, because it's nice and fat. I like to taste meat from you people, because, I don't know why, you make it taste so very good."

After we were through eating he went back in the store, and I picked up the dishes that he loaned me and took them back inside to him. My horse was standing there, not eating anything. But at that time we never thought about feeding a horse hay or corn. And the horses used to stand long trips without hay or any kind of grain. That's the way the horses used to be at that time, but now you have to feed the horses every once in a while. So I let my horse stand outside, just taking a rest. When I got in the store I gave the dishes back to him over the counter, and he gave me six dollars for the wool. I have forgotten how much the skins were, but anyway the money that he gave me was a little over eight dollars. Then I started buying some grub; I bought three small sacks of flour, sugar, and some coffee and other food. I bought quite a bit of grub, and some calico and thread with it.

As soon as I took out all my stuff he started saddling up my horse. It was a pretty heavy load, but I got on anyway and started off. The horse started off on a trot and seemed to be going along as if without any load at all. I kept trotting him along, across quite a stretch of desert. When I got to the middle of the desert it was around noon. I thought, "I'll stop here and let the horse cool off and feed a little." There was a lot of grass, a lot of feed for the horse. As soon as I unpacked and turned him loose he dropped to the ground and rolled around, bathing himself in the sand. Then he got up and shook the sand off himself and started feeding. I just lay against my pack. I was feeling well and lively, because I had eaten a lot at the store. I wasn't hungry, so I just sat there against my load, looking at the horse eating grass. Late in the afternoon when I knew my horse had had enough I walked up to him and brought him back. After I saddled him up and put all my stuff back on again I got on and started off. When the sun was down, I kept on going, even though it got dark, until I got to a place where I knew there was a lot of feed for the horse, so I stopped there around the middle of the night. I took the saddle off the horse, and hobbled him, and lay down on the saddle blankets and went to sleep. In the morning, as soon as I got up, I looked for the horse, and there he was, right close by, so I put on my moccasins and walked over and led him back. Then I saddled him up, put all my stuff on again and started off. From Thief Rock I went on to Hill Across, through the woods and up to where we lived.

The herd was close to the hogan; I guess the boy was looking for me. As soon as I got back he came running from the herd. I took off the load, took the saddle off the horse, and everybody was around me. They were all glad. My wife said, "Thanks," many times to me, and the others said the same. They took all the things inside and built a fire and started cooking and frying tortillas. I had bought a pair of overalls for the boy. I gave that to him, and he put them on, and I had bought him a fancy handkerchief to put around his head. He was tickled to death about it. They said to him, "You have forgotten your herd. Go back to the herd. You only turned it away." "Let them go," I said. "They are around here close. They won't go away and get lost. Let them go." He was standing around, looking at his overalls, taking the handkerchief off his head every once in a while and looking at it and then putting it back; and he was tending to the fire while the others were cooking.

After everything was cooked we all started eating, and afterwards they all started thanking me for the food again. My wife was thanking me first, then my mother, then the boy. "Thanks for the good food. We had very nice food. All because you went a long way for it, and because you didn't think of the distance. Even though it's a long distance, you always go for food like this. You have brought us nice food, and we all enjoyed it, and we are thankful for that. Thank you

505

very much for bringing us food from a long way." My mother said this to me, and my wife said the same. After we ate the boy went back to the herd. We went on living there. Nothing more happened, and nobody came around. All that we did was herd, take care of the horses and look about for wood and water. We were using the snow for water, but it was beginning to melt on the mountain.

Perhaps it was four days after I returned from the store, in that fourth morning I said, "I want to walk over to Hill Across to see about the water and grazing. I think there is a lot of grazing, I know there is, but I don't know about the water, so I'll walk across and look around. I'll go to where we used to camp. Close to that there used to be water at two different places, so I'll take a walk over there." After we ate in the morning I started over to Hill Across. I walked all around up in there. There was lots of feed and lots of water upon Hill Across in the rocks. There were big hollows in the rocks, and every one of them was full of water. Then I walked down to where we used to camp, to where there used to be water, and there was lots of water at both places.

When I got home that evening, just at sundown, they had everything ready. The food that I had brought had been cooked, and we all started eating. After they had put the things away I told them about the walk that I had made. I said, "I walked across and the place looks all right, good grazing all around and lots of water all around up on top of Hill Across. When I got down to where we used to camp the hogan was still up and so was the corral, and Slim Man's hogan and corral were still up too. I walked all around there where my father used to camp, and down to where they used to get water. There was lots of water down in the arroyo, and there was lots where we used to get it too. So I think we will start moving across there tomorrow morning."

In the morning after we ate the boy got the horses and I told him to take the herd and go ahead. I pointed out a place where there was a little hill, and I told him, "Take the herd across to that hill. There is where we are going to move. When you get up there with the herd you will find the hogan and corral right at the foot of that hill." He said, "All right." I

506

said, "As soon as we get ready we will come after you." When he left with the herd we started packing. It took us quite a while to pack up all the things.

Then we started off across to the place that we wanted to move to, where my father, Slim Man used to live. The boy was there already with the herd. That hogan had been used by some people, and the corral was built up nicely. So we stopped there and unloaded and I took the horses down to White Plain Space, where there was lots of feed for them. I just turned them loose there and went back to where we had camped. They had cleaned the hogan out, and had cleaned around it, and had built a fire and made the four white spots inside with cornmeal, and they had taken everything inside and cooked the food. Just when I got back the herd was in too. When we got through eating the sun was down. They put everything away, and the boy and I started gathering up some wood for the night and the next day. So there we started living again.

25

He goes on foot to Slim Man's place . . .
Stories of the witch who was killed . . .
He helps his wife's relatives and refuses
to marry his wife's sister.

While we were sitting around that evening my wife said, "I felt lonesome all day today. I almost wept, when I got to the edge of that cliff." "What made you feel that way," I asked her. "What have you been thinking about?" "When we got to the edge of the cliff I looked all around out in the flat and I thought about my old mother and my younger sister and the two younger brothers of mine. When I thought about them I almost cried. So that made me so lonesome all day. I would like to see them," she said.

I said, "I didn't know you were that way. I wonder where they are living by now? When those two Mud People were at our place, at that time, they said they were living at a place called Once He Had A Son. I don't believe they have moved down the other way. If they have moved I think they have probably moved up this way, so I suspect they are living around close to Tall Mountain. Well, then," I continued, "you must get up early in the morning, as early as you can, and cook some food. After I eat I'll go over to where I left the horses last fall. I'll go up there on foot. So you must get up early and cook some food for me." "Are you surely going on foot?" she asked. "Yes," I said. "It's a long way to that place. Why don't you ride a horse up there?" she said. "I don't like to ride one of these horses that we use around here. They are poor, so I don't like to ride them that far. It's not so very far. I'll go down to White Plain Space and from there over to Another Canyon, and then from there on I will go right straight for Where Little Arroyos Stop. I think the others may be living around there yet." It was about thirty-three or thirty-four miles from where we were living.

She got up the next morning and I built a fire for her and she started cooking. The boy was sleeping and my mother was sleeping too. We cooked some food in a little while and then I started eating. When I was through I started to get ready. Just about then my mother got up. As soon as she got up she said, "What are you trying to do? Are you surely going on foot to Where Little Arroyos Stop?" "Yes," I said, "I am going to that place on foot." "Why don't you get a horse, and ride one of the horses that we have around here? It's just too far for you," she said. I said, "I don't want to use one of those horses, because they are all poor. I don't think they could stand that distance." "Then you think a whole lot about the horses, instead of yourself."

While she was talking I had stepped out. I didn't say another word. I went out and put the rope over my shoulder and started early that morning, while it was still dark. I got down to Space Plain and started following that flat that we call White Plain Space. I passed that whole place and got down, crossing the valley, to Water Under The Rocks and headed for Flowing Out Of The Canyon. Soon I crossed that wash, then on out to another valley to the trail that comes down from Valley Coming To The Edge. It was noon then, but I just kept on going, running right along. Way down this side of Flowing Out Of The Canyon there used to be water. I stopped there and got out a little lunch that I had with me; it was a piece of tortilla. I ate that and drank some water and then started off again. I crossed that valley and then on straight to Where Lots Of Rocks Were Washed Out and then to Trail Along The Edge Of The Woods. I started passing our summer camp, and soon I got to Where Water Bursts Forth From The Mountain.

When I got to that place I started giving out. All at once the sweat was around my eyes. As soon as that happened I got weak, but I just kept on going and kept wiping off the sweat around my eyes. When I got to the top of Where Little Arroyos Stop I saw the herd coming toward the hogans, and the people walking around the hogan. The sun was pretty

509

well down. As I was walking up to the hogan my father, Slim Man, was standing outside, looking at the herd and talking to the herder. "Be careful with the little kids. Drive every one of them in the corral. If you leave them out, they will go away, the mothers will go away with their little ones, so drive every one of them in the corral."

He was standing close to the hogan, talking to the herder. When he was about to turn around he saw me. "I didn't think you were coming. I was hollering so to the herder, maybe you thought I must be cussing or something," he said. I walked up to him, and I put my arm around him and he put his arm around me. "My baby, my little one, my father," he said to me, and I said the same to him. Then we went inside and he put out a sheep pelt for me and I sat down. "I'm so very tired," I said. When I said this he got some blankets and laid them in back of me, saying, "Lie against this and take a rest." "Yes," I said, "I need a rest." We were sitting there all alone. The rest were out tending to the herd. Their goats were all having kids, and they were working on that.

Around evening they all came in. As they came in they shook hands with me. At last my younger brother came in, my father's real son, and shook hands with me. Then his mother said, "Is that all? Just shaking hands? I thought you wanted to see your older brother so badly? Why don't you put your arm around him and say, 'My older brother, I am so glad to see you.' " Then he sat down by me and I put my arm around him, and we were holding each other for a while. I was so anxious to see every one of them.

Then my father said to me, "You must be from the top of the mountain, from One Black Rock Standing." "No," I said, "But I am from about the same distance as that place." He guessed it right away. "You must be from Hill Across." "Yes," I said, "I'm from there. You know where we used to live some time ago? That's where I started from this morning." Then my older sister, Slim Man's wife, said, "Well, why do you want to go on foot like that, when you have lots of horses to use? What do you want to do with all those horses? I thought they were for use. You have got lots of horses and here you are on foot from a long way off." My father said, "It's not that way. He wants to know just how far he could go on foot. That's what he wants to find out about himself, how great a distance runner he is. And he is exercising himself. Go ahead and start cooking. Cook some meat, make some coffee and fry some tortillas. Hurry on with it."

Then they started cooking, some tending to the fire, some tending to the coffee and some to the meat, and some started making dough. When they were through with the cooking they laid it out and we all started eating. I was so tired. I was kind of shivering all over, and I was sort of weak. When I started eating I was all sweaty, but I just kept on. All at once I looked up, I had been so hungry, but now I had had enough, and I felt lively again.

When we were through eating they put the things away and then I lay back against the pile of blankets and asked about my horses. "Where are my horses? Are they still around here?" He said, "No, they are not around here any more, but they have been around here all winter. As soon as the snow melted away they started toward Two Parallel Washes. They are around there by now. They just kept going after the snow toward the foot of the mountain. But every one of them looks fine. They are all good and fat. They are not poor. We used two, one in order to get some grub for ourselves, and the other one was for driving up some horses. We drove some horses up here and killed one for meat. Then we have also been using the mule." I said, "Well, I thought you were afraid of the mule." "Yes, we were afraid of him but once we used him we found out that he was all right; so then we were not afraid of him any more. So we have used some of your horses. I am very glad about that and thank you for it." I said, "That's all right. That's what they are for, to be used. I came up here for one or two of them." He said, "So the horses are all looking fine, and they are all still right together. Whenever we wanted to use one we rounded them all up, and the boys say not one of them is missing. They are all here, they say. I don't know all of them, but the boys do. So they are all together."

Then he said, "Since we moved here nobody has visited

511

us yet. There is Red Brown Sheep, living down off that way some place, but he never comes up, and we never go down to his place, so we haven't visited each other all winter long. And no people from the top of the mountain have come down, and we don't go up either. That is all. Now tell us where you have moved. Tell us about that." I told him and then I said, "I wasn't thinking about coming here but yesterday my wife said that she had become lonesome. She said, 'All at once I thought about my old mother, my mother, my younger sister and younger brothers. When I thought about them I got lonesome for them.' So that made me come up here. I thought I would come here for the horses and take them back, and then from there on I thought I would go with her down to where those people are living. This is the way I thought about it. So when I get back with the horses I guess I'll take her over to her people's place."

My older sister, Slim Man's wife, said, "I wonder why they always move down to that place, to Navajo Mountain. They always want to move down in that direction, and it's far away. They ought to live close by, or they ought to move up the mountain and live up on the mountain close to their son-in-law" (meaning me). My father said, "Don't you know what they are always moving down to that place for? That is the only place where they can get a good fucking. They always want to move down there because they know that is the only place where they can find a big cock. That is why they always move there." She said, "Oh, go on. You always start talking about those things. That's all you think about."

After they had had a little joke among themselves and we had all laughed about it, I said "I don't know what to do about the horses. I'm thinking of taking them halfway up the mountain." He said, "What do you want to take all of them up there for? Why don't you just take the tame ones, instead of taking them all? The others, the broncos, are good for nothing. They are not ready to be used. Why don't you leave them where they are, and just take all the tame ones up there; for they are of use anytime." I said, "I guess I will do that. However I'll see about it tomorrow. I'll see what to do about it then." "I guess you had better go to sleep. I had better stop talking to you. When I begin to talk I don't know when to stop, so I guess I had better quit right now, and you go to bed and take a good rest. I know you are tired. Tomorrow we will have a sweat-house, and your younger brother will go and round up the horses for you. We put up a corral against the sheep corral for the horses. He will bring them all. He knows where they are, so we will let him go after the horses, and we two will go to the sweat-house. After we come back from the sweat-house, then you can drive the horses up to where you want to take them, perhaps only the tame ones, or perhaps you want to take them all; but it's up to you."

Then they fixed a bed for me and as soon as I lay down I went to sleep. Before I knew it it was morning. It seemed to me the night was short. They started cooking and I got up and walked outside. I was sore all over. It was awfully sore around my shoulders, and my legs were sore and stiff. I could hardly walk. I walked around, working my legs up and down, stretching myself, and the soreness kind of settled down. After we ate he said to his son, "You go after your older brother's horses. Round them up for him and bring them all back and put them in the corral. He wants to look at them. I guess he is eager to see his horses. I know he is because he has been away from them a long time now, so be sure and bring all of them back with you. We two will have a sweat-house." Then I walked out and picked up the two axes and he picked up some blankets, and we both started for the sweat-house. We chopped some wood and gathered some rocks and built a fire on them and then sat around watching the fire burn down. After that I put the rocks inside and the blankets over the door, and then we took off our clothes and went inside.

While we were inside he said, "When we get out I want you to go back to the hogan, and tell them to have the food ready for us, because we didn't eat much this morning. We'll be hungry when we quit here. And I guess your younger brother will be back with the horses. If he is back, if he hasn't started yet, tell him when he gets to where the horses are to get one and turn his horse loose, because that horse of his is not so very good. I don't think that horse will stand the whole

513

day's trip. And be sure and bring some water back with you," he said to me. We didn't stay long inside, because it was too hot. When we got out I put my clothes on and went back to the hogan and told them what he wanted me to say. My younger brother was just starting to saddle his horse, so I told him what his father had said. Then I got some water and took it back with me. He was still sitting inside.

After we had been in and out a few times he started telling me what had happened through the winter. "Down in the valley there were lots of people who died off with some kind of disease. A whole lot of Red House clan people were down in the valley. Most of them died. And the sickness struck up here to the foot of the mountain, up on the east side. The people who lived there died from it. The whole outfit of Red Hair, whom we call Dead Sinew's Son, that whole outfit of his died off, and a whole lot of other people living at the foot of the mountain on the east side had died from this disease. And around toward spring, that's not very long ago, they killed a man down in the valley. They killed a man whom we used to call Hairy Beads. The man we called Mr. Pants killed him with a club, because they claimed he was a witch. They claimed that he had caused the deaths, so that's why they killed him.

"When I heard about that I didn't care to listen to it. I didn't care to ask about it, because I don't like to hear anything of the kind. I hate a story like that. That's the way with me; so I didn't ask how they killed him. That's all I know. And there is no grief for them. I am not a bit sorry for people like that, because they themselves want to be killed. Perhaps it's because they have got tired of living. It's their own fault. They, themselves, claim that they are witches, so they themselves want to become Tcindi (ghosts). That's why they talk as if they were ghosts already. They don't care about the people. When a man wants to be killed he begins to claim that he is the one bewitching the people, killing the people with his witchcraft, and that's why the people believe him and want him to be killed right away. They get killed, I think, because they are tired of living. Most of us want to live for some time,

514

and we care for all our people, and I don't see why they are not that way. However they just want to be killed, that's all. So we don't want to talk about that, because it's dirty, real dirty to me to talk about it. So we'll let that go."

I thought he was going to tell me a story about it, but he put that away; then he didn't say any more about it. He asked me, "What do you want to do with the horses? Are you going to take all your horses up to the mountain? Or are you just taking the ones that are tame?" "Yes," I said, "I guess I will just take the tame ones up there and leave the others down where they are now, and I would like you or my younger brother to look at them once in a while for me. As soon as the snow melts away take them down to where they were before. Take them straight down to the water, so then from there on they will know where to go. You won't have any trouble with them because they always go to one place. I want you to help me out on that. You know I can't come up here and take care of them because it's a long way for me to come. I would like to be where I am for some time yet, until the grazing gets scarce; perhaps it will be around shearing time. I only want to take two horses back with me. I don't know just when I will be up here again." He said, "I don't think the snow will be on the ground much longer from here on. I think the snow will be gone in about fifteen days on the mountain. But we will go after your horses for you, so don't worry so much about it. We know what to do. I think, though, we will move back to Where The Gray Hill Comes Out in two more days, because we have been using the snow and it's all gone now around here, so we'll move back to that place. It's not so hard to us to move, because we have got a wagon and we can put all our stuff in. It carries a whole lot. We use the burros. The mules that I used on the wagon, they must be down at Lots Of Wool. It's a long way to go for them, so that's why we have been using the burros all winter, hitching them onto the wagon. They are good pullers. They can pull a wagon, even though the wagon is loaded up with lots of things. So it's not so very hard for us to move around now."

Then he said, "I haven't been over the mountain yet,

515

since I came back from there the last time. It's been a long time now. The fall has passed, and the winter has passed since I came back from that place, so I guess they think that I have quit them. Perhaps they have got another man. That girl had a man already. I guess she is staying with him now, because he is young and I am old now. So I don't think I will go to that place anymore, because if I go over again they might not want me, or maybe they have got another man. I don't like to go and get in bad. Even though they wanted me to come every once in a while, it's been a long time since I was there, so I don't think I'll go to their place any more, my son," he said to me.

I said, "That's right. You can't tell, maybe they have got a man now. That's the way some of them do. Lots of them that I know have done that around here. Even though their man is not far off, they don't think about him, they just go and marry another. But even at that you ought to go around when the horses get fattened up, after the lambing and shearing, just to see if they still remember you. By that time there will be lots of feed everywhere for the horses. Why don't you take a trip to that place once more, just to see about it. If you find that they still remember you, then it will be all right. If you find that they have got another man, then that will be the end. Then you won't have to go over there any more. That's the way with the women. You can't tell anything about them, my father," I said to him, "but, anyway, you ought to go over again, just to see if they still care for you. If not, that's all right too." That was all that we had been talking about. Then we quit. We got out, took the blankets off the door, put our clothes back on, and went back to the hogan. It was just about noon. My horses were in the corral, and they had everything ready to be eaten.

As soon as we got inside we washed ourselves, and then all of us started eating. After lunch I said, "I would like to use one of your saddles." He said, "All right. The saddles are all outside." They used to have lots of saddles. He made them himself. Some belonged to the women, some to the men. "They are all outside," he said, "blankets and everything are out there. Take whichever one you would like to use." I took

516

the rope over to the corral and got two horses. I tied one up to the tree. Then I picked up his saddle, but the stirrups were too long for me. Then I picked up the one that belonged to my younger brother. That was all right. The stirrups were just right for me. I put that on my horse, and then went back to the corral and got all the horses that were tame and started driving them up toward the mountain, up one cliff, then between where two cliffs come together and up on top of the second. I let them go and took a ride all over up there, just to see about the feed. There was all kinds of feed, grasses of all different kinds and saltweeds of all different kinds. It was a very nice place. Then I started back. I got down off the second cliff, and down to the first, where the two cliffs came together. There was a gate there, but I left it open so they could come down out of this place when they ran out of water. When I got back to the hogan I tied up my horse and went inside.

"What are you going to do, my son? Are you going back today?" he asked me. "No," I said, "I don't think so. It's getting too late to start now. I could go right now, if there were any people living around Flowing Out Of The Canyon, but I didn't see anyone when I was coming. If I knew some people were living there I could start right now and get over to that place tonight, but I don't think I'll start until tomorrow." "Well, that will be better," he said. "You had better stay and take a good rest tonight." So then I went out and unsaddled my horse and led the two of them to where there was some grass and hobbled them there. When I got back to the hogan the sun was down. The herd was in, and all of them were working on it. There was no wood, and no one to get it, because they were all working on the herd, so I gathered up a big pile and went inside.

About then they were through working on the herd and came in and started cooking. After we ate he said, "I guess we had better go right to bed and take a good rest tonight." They fixed our places for us, and we went right to bed. I was feeling fine, because we had gone to the.sweat-house. There was only a little soreness on me, but I didn't feel it much. In the morning I went after the horses. They hadn't gone so very far. After we ate that morning he asked me, "Are you going to start now?" "Yes," I said, "I'm going back today." "When do you think you'll get back?" "I'll take my time going back. I guess I'll be back about sundown." Then he said, "You can use one of your younger brother's saddles. It's a long way to ride bareback, so take one of the saddles and use that." "That will be nice," I said.

Before I started I asked them, "Have you still got some corn? If you have I would like to have some. I ran out of corn." He said, "Yes, we have some left yet that we got from Upper Green Spot. A fellow brought us some from there. We still have some left." They gave me half a seamless sack full.

The sun was almost down when I got home. As soon as they saw the corn lying over the saddle they grabbed it and took it inside, saying "Thanks very much. This is what we have been wishing for." I took the horses up to where there was lots of feed, where the others were, and hobbled them there. I didn't want to turn them loose. I was afraid they might go back on me.

When I got back my mother was cooking some corn in a skillet. She cooked it a little and then ground it into meal and made corn mush. We were all so hungry for corn. After we ate my mother said, "I have been herding yesterday and today, and the boy was tending to the wood." I said, "That's nice. You helped the herder." Night had come and we all went to bed. While we were lying in bed I said, "I started from here. When I got down to Flowing Out Of The Canyon, a little on the other side, about noon, I got hungry. I went down to the water, and there I ate my lunch. Then I started from there again, on to Where The Water Had Washed Out The Rocks and then on to Trail Along The Edge Of The Woods; then up to where we had lived, then up to where you had a good time," I said to my wife. She didn't say anything, just dropped her head. She was quiet about that. "And on to where you fought with that woman," I said to my mother. She laughed. I guess she had thought about it. "When I was about to that hill a little way on the other side I got weak. All at once I gave out. But I just kept on moving myself along to Where Little Arroyos Stop and on to the top of the hill where we lived. I got there just as the sun went down. I was all played out. I was so tired when I got there." My mother said, "It's such a long distance to that place. It's a long way to go on foot. No wonder you were tired." I said, "I got there and they were working on the little kids. The goats were having little ones. After they finished with that they all came in. They made the food and we ate, and then we went right to bed. The next day my younger brother went after the horses for me and my father and I went to the sweat-house. We were there until noon.

"I thought he was going to tell me a lot of things, but he didn't. He only said that Hairy Beads had been killed, because he was a witch. That's all I heard from him." My mother said, "Did they kill him? Poor cousin. I never got to see him. I won't see him any more. It's too bad that they killed him, but it's his own fault. If he had kept quiet about himself I don't think he would have been killed, but, I guess, they had found that he was a witch." "Yes," I said, "That's all I heard. Down in the valley many people died. Most of them were Red House Clan. And the disease struck along the east side of the mountain, around Peak At The Foot Of The Mountains. A lot of the Dead Sinew's Sons outfit died. Many people along the foot of the mountain have died. That's all I heard from him," I said. In the morning we started the fire, and while they were cooking I walked over to where I had hobbled the horses and brought them back.

After we ate I said, "I guess we'll start this morning to find where her people live. You take good care of the herd, wood and everything," I said to the boy. And to my mother I said, "You can stay at home and watch the place and cook for the herder. That's all you have to do. We are going today. We don't know when we will come back, but we will try to come back soon." I saddled up the horses, put some blankets on them, and then we started off, down toward the flat and across the flat. Soon we got to where we had heard they were living, but we didn't see anything. While we were going along we got onto a herd's and some horses' tracks. I said, "This might be them. I guess they moved back to where they

519

were. I don't think they have moved way on down." We had stopped there for quite a while. Then I said, "We had better follow these tracks." So we started off, following the tracks until we got to Water Under The Rocks. A hogan was there. We knew some people were living in that hogan, so we rode up and stopped our horses and got off. And she recognized one of the dogs. She said, "They are living here. I know the dog." She walked over to the hogan while I stayed there with the horses. She was gone quite a while; I heard them crying for a long time. I guess they were anxious to see one another again.

After a while three of her brothers came out. One of them had an ax. They shook hands with me and said, "We came to build a hogan." The sun was almost down. They started cutting branches off the trees, and we built a small brush hogan. Then they gathered up some wood for us. About that time she brought over some roasted meat. "This is all they had," she said. "Just meat, no other kind of food. They have run out of food, and this is all they have been living on, just meat." We had a little corn with us, and some flour, coffee, and sugar; she took half of everything over to them. When she returned she said, "They are all very thankful about the food, and they are all happy and glad that we came and visited them. I told them where we had been all winter. I said, 'We have been up on the mountain all winter, and then we moved down to the foot of the mountain, and that is where we started from this morning.' And I said, 'There is lots of grazing up along the foot of the mountain, all different kinds of grass are coming up, and some are green, and I see the grass around here hasn't started yet. But up there it is getting to be a nice place. Soon there will be lots of grazing.' When I told them about this they all wanted to move back immediately. They said, 'Let's move back tonight.' They only said that, but I guess they will move back up there soon." We stayed there that night, and in the morning we started up the fire, and she took back the sheep pelts that they had lent us that night.

When she came back she said, "They want you to take the herd for them this morning. They want you to go ahead.

They want to move this morning, and they want to make some lunch for you, so you will have some this noon on your way. And they want to use the two horses of yours. They want to go and get their horses. So they want you to take the herd on foot, and they said you ought to get to Water In The Rock about noon. When you have lunch there then you can go on, and perhaps we will catch up with you when you get on top of Tall Mountain. They want you to wait for us there. They think they will start moving from here about noon. That's what they want you to do." I said, "All right. If they want me to help I am always glad to do anything they want me to do."

Then she started cooking. "They are butchering a sheep, so I guess we will have some fresh meat soon," she said. I asked her, "Where have they been all this winter? Where have they been living? Did they say?" "Yes," she said, "they said they had been living here, and when it snowed, they said, they had moved down to Navajo Mountain and lived on a point. There was a big point there, and that's where they had lived all winter. The boys said they saw a lot of bones lying all around there. They were wondering what had killed the sheep at that place." I said, "When I was a boy we lived there for one winter, and there we lost a lot of sheep. We lost over half of our herd there at that place. That must be it." "I guess that's what they saw," she said. "Where have they got the horses?" "They said the horses were down below, along those points, along in those woods, so they think they will have the horses gathered up around noon. They have got my uncle's horses out here too." She meant Lost His Moccasins. "They want to take them back for him." Then, after we ate, she went over to the hogan again and brought back one side of the rib. She roasted that for me and I ate once more. She said, "They are fixing your lunch for you." While I was eating she brought my lunch over for me. "They have the herd out for you," she said. I said, "All right."

Then I walked over to the herd and started herding them over a hill and across a big stretch of valley and along in the woods. Finally I got to the cliffs and went on top with the herd to where they said there was water. I rounded them up there. They had quite a big herd, mostly goats. Almost all of them were red. As soon as I rounded them up they lay down and I walked over to the water and opened my lunch—some roast meat and fried tortillas. After I ate I lay around for a while. It was afternoon. Then I started on again, going along uphill. When I had gone quite a ways from where I had stopped at noon I looked back out into the flat. There was nothing moving out there. Finally I got to the top of Tall Mountain.

Then I saw a small black streak coming way out in the flat. I stopped there on top, thinking I will wait for them here. They were coming closer all the time. I herded around there, and just as the sun went down the boys rode up to me. "I guess we will camp here. That's what the women folk said, my older brother." They took the herd over to a little bunch of woods where they had stopped. In the meantime my wife came up to me. She was riding a very nice horse. Right away the boys started chopping branches off the trees, and making a brush hogan for themselves. Then they came and put one up for us. I gathered wood and she went over to the other camp and brought back a little water and we had the fire going and she cooked.

The next morning as soon as she started the fire she went over to the other camp. When she came back she said, "The water is all gone, I only got enough to make coffee with, so I don't think we will have any tortillas or any kind of bread. We will only use meat. That's all. They want you to go on with the herd again this morning. They are going to make you some more lunch. They are short on saddles too, so my younger sister is using yours." I said, "All right, I will go." She made some coffee, cooked some meat, and that was all we ate that morning. After we ate she went over to the other hogan again and brought me back my lunch. It was nothing but meat. "That's all you have got to eat this noon on your way. They had no bread of any kind because there was no water." I said, "This is all right. This is a whole lot."

They had started the herd for me. I walked over and one of the boys, the one that always helped me, came and said, "You can go on with the herd, my older brother. On your

522

way stop at Many Springs Coming Out At One Place. You will get there about noon, perhaps before. But stop there and have lunch, and then you can go ahead again. When you get to Many Coyotes just stay there and wait for us. Perhaps we will stay there again tonight." I said, "There is lots of grazing around that place, so I guess it will be all right to stop there." He said, "I don't know when we will start again, maybe around noon. We have to round up all the horses. They got all scattered out last night. However, as soon as we get the horses back we will start after you."

I went on with the herd, crossing a little valley, going through woods, going over rocks, until I got to Many Springs Coming Out At One Place. I ate my lunch there at noon. Then I started off again, going along through woods, through little sage-brush flats, through rocky hills, and soon I got to Many Coyotes, close to the water, about when the sun was pretty well down. I stopped there and built a big fire. I wanted them to see the smoke coming out, so as to know where I was. The herd was grazing around me while I was sitting and lying around the fire waiting for them. About sundown they caught up with me. They brought the two horses of mine over and I hobbled them again that evening. I said, "I have been waiting here for a long time. I thought you were going to catch up with me way out in the valley." "No," she said, "We didn't start until afternoon. The boys didn't find the horses until then, so that's why we started late. But we just kept going along, and, even at that, we got here about sundown."

In the morning after we ate I said to her, "I guess we had better go back from here. I would like to go back. We have been away from our place for quite a while now. But go and see first. See what they will say." When she came back she said, "The womenfolk don't want us to leave them. They don't want us to go from here, 'not until we get to where we want to move,' they said. They want you to take the herd again for them, 'because,' they said, 'we are all too lazy to herd. We are not good on foot; so we want him to take the herd for us. From here on it should be herded on foot, it's too rough from here on to herd on horseback. It's got to be done

523

on foot, and there is no one to go on foot, only the women-folk. The boys are all tending to the horses.' So they want you to herd for them," she said to me. I said, "All right, I'll take the herd. If they want me to I'll take the herd for them again." "But they don't want you to take the herd right away," she said, "They said, 'We will all move together when the boys gather the horses. When they bring the horses back, then we will all start together.' That's what they said." I said, "Well, then, I guess I'll take the herd out and let them graze around here." I was herding until about noon. About that time the boys had brought the horses back.

After we ate and when we were ready we started moving again. While the others moved on ahead we three, my wife and her younger sister and I, started after them with the herd. We went on slowly, through the woods and through the rocks. There were lots of little cliffs all the way, small arroyos and big arroyos, and lots of water. When we got to the edge of where the two cliffs came together, the one from Another Canyon, the other from White Plain Space, we had a hard time with the herd, taking them down on that trail. Finally we got down to the foot of the cliff, down in the canyon, and across to one of the points on the other side. A hogan was sitting there, and a corral too, and there is where they wanted to move. They moved to that hogan at the foot of the cliff. We camped out in an open place. When the boys came down from the top of the canyon they gave us some wood, and we built a fire and started cooking.

After supper I said, "I guess we'll start climbing the cliff tomorrow morning. We have got to go back to where we came down; so that's what we are going to do tomorrow morning." I was lying there, and she was sitting by the fire, and I said, "I'm awfully tired going on foot for three days. I thought it was closer than that, but I know now it's a long way from where we started." That's all I said. Then she got up and went over to the hogan, and I went to sleep. All at once I woke up. She was starting up the fire. She had just come back from there. I looked around and it was late in the night. She had been over to that hogan for a long time.

After she started the fire, she put out the sheep pelts, laid

524

them out, and we went to bed. Then she said, "My mother wants you to have my younger sister, and my younger brother said the same. My old mother and my older brother didn't say anything about it. But my mother and my younger brother, the two of them, were saying that you could have her. They want you to make up with her, 'because,' they said, 'he is a big helper. We know that he can do anything.' That's what they said." Right away I said, "No. Perhaps you think of me that way. Perhaps you have talked about me that way, but no, I don't want to do that. And how about you? Where are you going? It's no good for me. They always go off in the country a long way from here. They always go moving down to where I don't like the country, and I move up on Black Mountain Strip where they don't like the country, so I don't want to do that. If I did that and then wanted them to go on top of the mountain they wouldn't do it. And if they wanted me to go down to where they always move, I wouldn't go to that country. So I don't want to do that. So don't talk to me like that." She said, "Why, you ought to." "No," I said, "I don't want to do that. It will be just too hard for me."

I thought to myself, "I know why she wants me to take her, and I don't believe her. I don't believe her people said it. I think it is she herself who started talking it over with her people. She is the one who started it, but I just don't want to do that. She just wants to get me in more trouble. Even though the women are far away from her, she always hates them, is jealous of them and always wanting to go and kill them, and I have lots of trouble with her.

"If I did that she might get after her younger sister. She just wants to quit me. She wants to go around among the men. That's all she wants. And if she left me with only her younger sister, sometime the whole outfit would move, and there I would be left all alone. I know that girl won't stay with me, because she always goes around with her mother."

We hadn't said any more about it for a while. Then she said, "Why don't you take her? Do you mean it, that you don't want her?" "Yes, I mean it. I don't want to take her, because I haven't got anything to give. That's all they want."

525

"You are not poor, and you are not alone. What's the matter with all your fathers? You have got all kinds of things, and there's Slim Man, His Horse Is Slow, Choclays Kinsman, and Who Has Mules. They all have stocks of all different kinds. Why don't they help you?" "Yes, they have got everything, but it doesn't belong to me, and I don't want to ask for it. That is what you all want, you are just trying to get something out of me, and then get me in trouble. That is all you want to do with me. Therefore I don't want to do that; so don't talk to me about it." That was all. Then I put the blanket around me and covered up my head and went to sleep. In the morning when I awoke she was still sleeping. I woke her up, told her to get up, "It's morning now." She moved around for a while and then got up. She had never done that before. And she was quiet. I knew then she was mad.

After we ate I said, "I guess we had better be going back this morning, up to my mother and the boy. I am kind of worrying about them now. I didn't think we would leave them alone for all this time, so I want to get back up there. I don't know what they are doing by now. One is so young, and one is so old. There are lots of ways in between them (what the boy doesn't know and the old woman can't do), so we will go back this morning. And when we get there we might move down this way a little. There is a whole lot of grazing right on top of this canyon, and I see there is lots of water all around, so we will move down from where we are now."

She didn't say anything about it for a while, for a long while, then she said, "They haven't got much of a load. Why don't you go up there alone." I said, "What do you mean? I am with you, so we will both go. There are lots of things to be carried around, and you know one is young and one is old. We have both got to take care of them, so we had better go. Why are you so quiet? You are looking so sad. What made you so sad? What are you sad about?" "No doubt you notice how I look. You made me look that way." "Why? With what?" "Because you don't want us. You don't like us. I know you don't care for us." "What do you mean, anyway? When you start talking like that that means you want trouble.

526

But don't start it, because there is nothing to start trouble about. If I didn't like you, or care for you, I wouldn't be with you. I wouldn't have herded for you for a long way on foot. I did that because I care for all of you, and I like and I want you all. That's why I am with you. If I didn't like you, or if I didn't care for you, I would have chased you away last fall, when you treated me so badly, but I didn't because I wanted you and liked you. But the thing that you talked to me about, I can't afford it. I haven't got enough things to keep two women. I can't even do much for you, so I don't think I can stand it."

She was mad at me about it. She was sitting there quietly. I knew she was mad. I said, "If you really think of me that way I won't say, 'all right,' by myself. I won't give myself up to you the way I did the first time. I didn't let anybody know then about my marrying you, and they didn't like me for that. So this time I will let my father know about it. He is the only one I can let know, no others. You know I haven't any elder clansmen. So we will let that go now until I let him know, and see what he will say about it. If he approves of that then we will talk about it again. However I think he will. I am sure he will." I only said that to her to make her get over her madness. I didn't really mean it. I only said it to her. I didn't want to do what she had wanted me to do, because I knew it would be too much trouble for me if I began to go around with the two of them. She looked better then. She thought perhaps I meant what I said, but I didn't, because I was afraid of them, afraid that they might start lots of trouble with me. Then, when she seemed to be all right, I got the horses and we left that place.

26

Moving again . . . He visits
his "wife" who holds him . . . The
dangers of women.

We got back to our hogan when the sun was almost
down. The herd was in. I unsaddled the horses
and told the boy to take them back to the others. "Where are
they?" I asked him. He said, "They are down here at one
place all the time. There is lots of grass all around there."
"Well, then, take them down there." So he got on one horse
and started leading the other and I went inside. I stood
around for a while, then I walked out again and gathered up
some wood. About that time the boy returned and we went
back inside. After we ate I started telling my mother about
our trip. We sat around for a while and then went to bed.

The next morning I said, "We will start moving this
morning toward the canyon. There is all kinds of feed down
in there, so we will move down today. So hurry with the
cooking." And I told the boy to go after the horses. He went
and brought them back right away. After we ate I told him,
"Saddle up a horse and go on with the herd, but don't drive
them fast. Take your time. Let the herd go slowly." When the
boy started out with the herd my wife said, "Don't you drive
the herd down fast without letting them get anything to eat.
Go slow and let them feed." He said, "I'll just drive them
down and let them go and I will ride down to where the
others moved." "Don't you do that," she said, "go slowly
with the herd, and take it down around evening."

Then he went on and we started packing. I saddled the
horses and packed them up for the other two, and tied everything tight onto the saddles because we were going down in
many little canyons. When we got everything on the horses
we started off after the boy. We went on riding through many
little canyons until finally we got to the foot of the canyon.

The boy was already there with the herd. As soon as he saw us coming he beat it on to the hogan. It wasn't so very far to where they lived. We stopped against the foot of the cliff across from where they were camped. There was no hogan or corral, but there were lots of good places for the herd.

We unloaded our stuff and I took an ax and rode up in the canyon and started chopping the branches off the trees. When I thought I had enough cut I dragged them to the edge of the cliff with the horse and then threw them down. After that I cut a lot of wood and dragged that to the edge of the cliff and threw it down. When I got back down in the canyon I turned the horses loose and drove them down in the flat. I knew they wouldn't get out of the canyon. There was lots of feed for them and the herd. Then I began making a brush hogan against the rocks. The two women had gone over to the herd. It was a very nice place down in this canyon. Everything was green, and I knew soon it would be lambing time. The herd looked that way, and it was a good place for lambing. I wanted to stay and have the herd lamb there. Toward evening the herd was back and we rounded them up against the foot of the cliff. I knew they wouldn't move until morning. There were only the three of us then. Our herder had gone back to his home. I knew he wouldn't come back, because he was eager to see his people.

Early in the morning the herd started moving. When they had all started out I went after them and herded them around until sunup, and then brought them back to the hogan. Right away they all lay down again. They had the food ready, and after we ate I said, "Shear some sheep, and I will go and look for the horses. I don't see the two that we have been riding. I only saw the others, so I'll go and look where they are." When I brought the others back I told them, "Use one of these for herding, and around noon you can bring the herd back and shear some more. I'll go after the two horses. Shear as many as you can, because I want to go to Blue Around The Lake again for some more food. If we don't do that soon we will be out of grub again."

Then I got on the horse and went out in the flat and around a point. There were their tracks. They had gotten on

529

the trail and gone on to White Plain Space. I tracked them on; soon I got out to Water Under The Rocks and on to Flowing Out Of The Canyon. From Water Had Washed Out The Rocks I began going slowly, because I knew they wouldn't stop until they got back to where they were before. As I was riding along to where we had moved that fall (the place where we played the moccasin game) I noticed some people were living there. They were shearing. I thought, "I'll turn around and go to that place to see who they are," so I turned my horse around and rode over; and that was Hosteen Black's outfit. There was Asdza No Teeth and the two daughters of hers and her granddaughter. Those four were shearing. The sun was way up, halfway to noon.

As soon as I rode up they said to me, "Come and help us. We are tired." I got off my horse and walked up to them and shook hands with the old woman first. She was the daughter of a clan grandfather of mine. I said, my aunt, my daughter, to her, and she said, my father, my son, to me. Then I shook hands with her younger daughter, then with the girl, and then with the girl's mother (Hosteen Black's wife) who was my 'wife.' As soon as she got hold of my hand she held it tight. "I mean it," she said, "You help us." Then she pulled me down close by her side. I said, "Let me go. I'm afraid." "What are you afraid of? There is nothing to be afraid of. Every time you come close around me you always say you are afraid. You always say you are afraid of your wife. You won't be with her all the time, so you don't have to be afraid. Come on with those shears," she said to her daughter.

The girl walked over and gave me the shears, and the mother said, "Take them. You didn't want her; I would like to see if you don't want her shears." The old woman, my aunt, said, "That's what they always say to me; 'We would like to have one of your Red House people.' They are always asking me for one, so you just go ahead and play around with one of them." The two women, her daughters, said, "Yes, we would like to have one for each of us, but I guess while we have one we'll start monkeying with him." They said this while they were all laughing. I was sitting there, with the shears in my hand, while she kept holding me tight.

I guess she was eager to see me again. I was eager to see her too, but I was kind of afraid. I told her to let me loose, but she kept holding tight on to my hand. I said, "I don't know if I can help you. I would like to, but I am after my horses. My horses ran away from me last night, and I'm tracking them. They may have gone back to where they were before so I'm going after them." "We saw those horses passing here this morning. They passed by just as the sun came up. They were passing here when the dogs went after them and one of them kicked one of our dogs. The dog was lying there for a long time, and those horses ran on down. After a long time the dog got up, and he is lying under that tree now. That was a good sheep dog of ours, and your horse killed him. We don't think that dog will live. So you must pay us for that," they said to me.

I said, "Neither I nor anybody else threw that dog under the horse. The dog himself got under by his own meanness, so it's his own fault that he has been hurt. So there is nothing to pay for. Well, then, I suppose the two horses have gone as far as Cowahi Mountain by now. I don't think I'll be able to catch up with them. They will be back to where they were before noon, so I guess I'll just take my time going after them. I wonder whether Slim Man, my father, has moved out to Where The Gray Hill Comes Out yet, to where their hogan is?" They said, "Yes, they are there now. When we were moving up from down there we passed their place, and they were living there then."

The old woman heard that I asked about my father. "Yes," she said, "that old fellow there, we heard that he was talking about us in a very bad way. We heard that he tells everybody about us in a very dirty way. I didn't think he was that way. I always thought of him as the only one who was good, but he is not. He used to come to our place last fall; he would stay over night or two nights, and when he went back to his home he would start telling about us, saying that as soon as the sun went down we all started working on him, that we all took our turn fucking him all night until morning, and in the morning he would have the tracks of our vaginas all over him. This is the way he tells the others about us. That old nasty thing."

531

"Stop talking about things like that. Aren't you ashamed, talking about dirty things?" her daugher, Hosteen Black's wife, said to her. "Go away and make some coffee. Don't talk like that among us." I started laughing, I said, "The tracks of the vaginas. I wonder what kind of tracks they make? I wonder if they have feet? I wonder if they have moccasins on or are barefooted? I wonder what kind of tracks they make?" I said, while I was laughing about it. Then I said, "I don't think he said that, for I know just how he is and how he talks. I have known him ever since I was a small boy, and I never heard him talk about anything like that. Someone has just made up that talk for him. Somebody is just making a remark about him. I don't believe he said that."

They said, "We all believe it. We all think he talks that way about us. And it's true that he used to come around to our place at night and during the daytime, around in the arroyos, and in the washes and little canyons, in the woods, around the cliffs, among the rocks, and on the rocks where no one would see his tracks. He came to us at our home and out around where we go. Sometimes he came when one of us went after wood or water, or out herding. He came around us lots of times, so that's why we all believe that he said that nasty thing about us. And you are just the same. You used to come around during the daytime, around where we were herding, around the same places, and at night too, and you have done just as your father has been doing to us. No difference to it. You are just like him. Perhaps the two of you are talking about us like that. But if we hear that you are talking about us we sure will get after you and take away something that you think a lot of. So don't you dare talk about us like that. Don't start it." That was Hosteen Black's wife. "I mean it," she said, "I believe he has been talking about us that way. When I heard that it sure hurt me. And you are just the same. No difference in the two of you. You both are just alike. When he comes to our place we know everything about him; we know his talk and his behavior, and all the other things about him, and you too. There is no difference between you. You talk and act exactly alike. So I don't think anybody is making remarks about him. I know very well he

532

talks about us that way, and I know you talk about us that way too. Don't say you never talk about us."

I said, "What are you saying? Don't say or think that I have talked about you in that way. That's something I don't like to hear. Yes, I have been around with you many times, but nobody knows anything about it, just I myself, that's all. I wouldn't dare say anything about you and myself, for I am afraid of everybody. I am afraid that if I said something about you and myself to someone he or she would go to your place with my talk and tell you what I said. I am always afraid to say something about other people, so don't think that I have been talking about you, my 'spouse,' my 'wife.' Please don't think of me like that. Please don't," I said to her. "I have been around with you lots of times, and I am thankful for that. I never said thanks to you before. This is the first time that I have thanked you, but I mean it. I am not just making fun of you."

"Even though you talk that way, I don't believe you. I know you have been talking about us lots of times, so now you have got to stay. That man of mine heard about you; he found out that you have been around with us, so he left us last fall. He went down to Navajo Mountain. So now you have a good chance to stay. I mean it. I want you to stay. I won't let you go. We will all hold you here. You have got to shear all the sheep. After you get through with the shearing you have got to take us down to the store."

When she said this to me she scared me. I didn't know what to make of it. I began begging her not to do anything to me, "Please, 'spouse,' my 'wife,' don't speak to me that way. I didn't think you would talk to me with that kind of talk. If I had known that I wouldn't have stopped here. I wanted to stop because I was eager to see you people. I was going to pass by, but I recognized all of you, so I thought I had better stop here for a while, because I was eager to see you all again. I thought, 'I will stop here just to shake hands with you all.' But here you start talking to me about something that I didn't have in my mind. I am afraid. I am afraid of your husband, and I am afraid of that woman of mine. And my father is just the same. He is afraid of his wife, and I am afraid of him too.

So, please, don't talk to me that way. We all don't like to get in trouble. I know you don't want to get in trouble, and I don't want to get in trouble either. So, please, forget all about it. Put everything away, and let's talk about something that is good for us. Let us talk about the good things, instead. We won't get anything out of that. If we talk like that to each other, you know very well we will spoil each other. So let's forget about it, my 'wife,' won't you please?"

She said, "Even at that I will hold you here all day today. I want you to help us shear all day. I won't let you go right now." Then she said to her daughter, "You get on his horse and go over to the hogan. Get the jugs and go and fetch some water on his horse. Bring some water back, and you and your old mother start cooking. When you come back from the water unsaddle his horse and take it away to where there's some grass and hobble it there. We will hold him here all day today and tonight."

They had quite a few sheep tied up. When we had sheared them all she said, "Let's go home. I guess they have got the food ready for us. After we eat I want you to put up a brush shelter for us right here at the gate, so we will have shade. We'll shear under that. After you put up the shelter we will start shearing again. If you don't do what I tell you to do I won't let you go. I mean it. I will hold you here. We have got your horse, saddle, and everything; we won't let you have it unless you do what I tell you to do for us. If you do what I want then I'll let you go." I said, "If you want me to help you, I guess I'll help you. I will do what you want me to do even though I am afraid. If someone comes around, they will see me working here, and then right away, he or she will start telling about me, and then I will be in trouble; or I might be killed for that. And I don't want to be killed. I want to live for some time yet, and so do you. But anyway I will help you just today."

At the hogan they had made some coffee, and the old woman had made tortillas, but she had made them hard, and she had burned them. There was nothing there but coffee and hard burned tortillas. "Why don't you cook better than that," my "wife" said. "Why didn't you roast or boil some meat? I

534

don't call this good food. You know better than that." The old lady said, "You know very well I can't cook. I can't cook any better than that. And besides, I didn't have any water to boil meat with. That's why everything is dry." Then my "wife" warmed up some water, took out some flour, put baking powder and salt in it and started making dough. Then she put the fat in the frying pan, got some grease out of it, and started frying some tortillas and boiled some meat. When she had the cooking done she laid out the food and we all started eating. She said to me, "Sit beside me." I sat down by her and she said, "I don't want any space between us. Sit closer to me." I moved up to her and put my thigh over her lap. "Now," she said, "That's the way I like it. We can eat a lot that way too."

Then she said to the old woman, "You told on your father, and you have got your father in trouble now. If you hadn't said anything about him we wouldn't have held him here. He would have gone after his horses long ago. You told on him and you got him in trouble, and here we are holding him for that." The old woman said, "Yes, I said something, and that's what they are saying about him." She meant Slim Man. "He didn't say it to me, but I heard about them (Slim Man and Left Handed), that they were talking about us that way." "Now you stop talking. You are starting in to talk again. You just stop and go ahead and eat. We don't want to hear anymore," her daughter said to her. The old woman stopped talking and ate what she had made, the hard tortillas. She was sitting a ways from us, eating all by herself. I felt all right, because she had said she would let me go after I had finished the brush shelter and after I had helped them shear.

While we were eating I began to think about what they had said, and that made me laugh. I couldn't hold my laughter back. Then she said to me, "Come on and eat. What are you thinking about? Don't laugh. Stop your laughing, and come on and eat." When she said this to me she got me started laughing again; I couldn't stop. She said, "You are just like your father, no difference. You laugh like him. You talk just like him, and all your acting is just like his. I never saw such a thing before. There is nobody else that way, only you two. When you start laughing you don't know when to stop." I laughed a long time. At last I kind of quieted down, and went on eating. I felt kind of ashamed about laughing so much, but I just couldn't help it. That's the way I used to be. Once I started laughing I couldn't stop, until I got tired of it. She said, "You have been laughing so hard you must be tired out because of it, so you eat lots. Don't be bashful. Nothing to be bashful about, so don't be bashful with us. We are all your women. You have done something to her," she said, meaning her daughter. I said, "Be careful about what you are saying. You are starting on something else again. I have never touched her." "Yes, you did. Don't say you never touched her. I know you did." "I don't know anything about it. Where was it? Where did I touch her?" "Yes, you know very well, and I know it too, down at Black Rock Standing. There at that place you touched her, the time you went down to the cattle with her. There, she said herself, you had said something to her and she had said to you that she was agreeable. She said, 'When I said this to him he started after me and chased me around,' and you caught her and tickled her, tickled her tits. That's the way she told me about it, so don't try to hide yourself. I know everything about you." I said, "Well, what are you talking about? You shouldn't talk to me like that. That's something I don't know anything about. You are just trying to put me someplace. I never bothered her in my life. You are just making that up for me."

After we ate we went back to where we had been shearing and she said, "We will put some sheep in the hogan. We can get one hundred in there. That's all we'll put in. After that you can start on the brush shelter, right here by the door, while we are shearing." We rounded up the sheep, they had a big herd, and started putting them in the hogan. It was quite a good-sized hogan. We kept putting them in; soon they said, "We have got fifty in the hogan," then they said sixty, then seventy, and after a while eighty. Then the hogan was full. They fixed the door, so they wouldn't get out, and after that we tied up twenty more outside. Then she said to the old woman, "You can take the herd down the valley, along that big arroyo. That arroyo will help you take care of the sheep. But don't let them go down too far. As we shear the others we will let them go down that way, and they will get into the herd themselves." After we had tied some up outside, while they were beginning to shear, I picked up an ax in order to cut some branches off the trees. When I thought I had enough, I got my horse and dragged them back. I made a good-sized brush shelter. When I was through with it I unsaddled my horse and hobbled him again, and then started cleaning up inside the shelter and all around outside. I had it nice and clean so that the wool wouldn't get dirty.

Then they gave me a pair of shears; they had a lot of them piled up, and all were sharp, and I started shearing. They were all quick. As soon as I had sheared two they would each be calling for another. (Apparently he sheared two to each woman's one.) We kept on working; we didn't have anything to eat from before noon. When there were only a few left inside the hogan one of the women went back to the hogan to cook. We got through around when the sun was pretty well down. Just about then she called us to supper. As soon as we turned the sheep loose they would get up and start running down in the valley. They wouldn't stop until they got back into the herd. It was nice that way; we didn't have any trouble driving them around. Then we piled up the wool and sharpened the shears.

They had the cooking all done, and, when we got back to the hogan, we started eating right away. After we ate I said, "I guess I had better go now." "You aren't through with your work yet. What do you want to go for?" she said to me. I said, "What shall I do next? It's too late for shearing now, and besides the herd is way down in the valley. By the time we get the herd up here the sun will be down." "I don't mean shearing. You haven't fixed the wool up yet. I want you to fix up the wool. There is some piled over there by the corral, and some there by the hogan. I want you to pack it over to the foot of the cliff, back of that big rock, in that cave," she said. "Take all the wool into that cave. If we leave it piled out here the goats and lambs will tear it all up, when they start playing on it. So get it out of the way." I said, "What are you trying to do with me? Are you trying to kill me with work? If I hadn't stopped here what would you have done?" "Well, that's what you came here for, to do the work for us, so you start taking that wool to the cave." I said, "All right, I'll do that," and I told them, "come on and help me take it over."

When we took over the first load we cleaned the cave out. It was a nice place, quite large, nothing in it but a little dirt. After we had swept out the dirt and put the wool in there she said to me, "I want you to build a wall on each side for us." I said, "Everything is just too much for me." "Don't talk that way," she said, "come and build the wall." So I started gathering up rocks and putting up a wall on both sides, while they were bringing in the wool. We got all the wool in the cave about sundown. The herd was still out in the valley. She said, "That old woman hasn't any sense at all, just like a 'clan relative.'" She meant me. I thought, right away, "I won't forgive her that. Before I go I'll do something to her."

It was getting to be evening. From there I walked over to where my saddle was, picked up a rope and went after my horse and brought my horse back and put the saddle on it. She was sitting by the fire. The herd was in the corral. When I had saddled up my horse I led him up close to her. She was making coffee and roasting meat. "Don't go. Wait until you eat some more. I am fixing this food for you." So, when she had cooked the meat, I started eating and she did too, while the others were working on the herd. After I had eaten I got up and she got up also. "I am very thankful to you for helping us all day. I have kept you here since morning and you have done all that I told you to do. You have been working all day, so I am very thankful to you for that." Then she walked up to me, put her arms around my neck and kissed me. "I said something to you that I didn't mean, so don't be thinking about it. What I said, I didn't mean it. But I do mean that I am thanking you for helping me," she said. I said, "I am not thankful yet. You haven't paid me back yet for my work, so you have got to. You told me to do things for you, and I have done everything. Now you have got to do what I tell you to do." "What do you want me to do for you?" she asked. Then I said it right out. "I want to fuck you. That's what I want, and then I'll be thankful. I will go after that." "All right. Get on your horse and ride up in those woods and then down and come back around that hill. I'll be there as soon as I fix my things here. I'll put everything away, so that the dogs won't get at it. Those others will be working on the herd. They won't be through until late in the evening."

I got on my horse and rode up in the woods and turned around and started down a little way, back to the hill where she wanted me to stop. Soon she came up to me and I went up to her and I fucked her. Later I asked her about the old man. "Where is he? I didn't believe you when you said he left last fall. I don't believe it. Where did he got to? Tell me the truth." She said, "Yes, I was only fooling you. He left five days ago. He said he wanted to gamble with the Paiutes. He said, 'I'll be gone around seven or eight days, or maybe a little more.' So that's where he went." "I knew he hadn't left you. I knew he was around here, and I knew he was still with you. That's why I said I was afraid to be around here." "Yes," she said, "He went to that place. He said to us when he left, 'Go ahead and shear. Maybe I'll be back about the time you have sheared all the sheep. As soon as I come we will take the wool to one of the stores. Perhaps to Blue Mesa Point, or perhaps we will take the wool down to Blue Around The Lake."

I said, "I was down to Blue Around The Lake the other day. I had sheared ten sheep and took the wool down and got six dollars for it. Those fellows there want a whole lot of wool. And he wanted me to tell all the people who have lots of sheep. He wants to give more for the wool, so I think I will take all my wool to him." "Maybe we will take our wool to that place too," she said. "Yes," I said, "I am going to that place, to Blue Around The Lake. That's the way I heard if from those storekeepers. They want to give more for the wool. They want to get all of it. That's why they told me to tell all the people who have sheep. I really don't know how they are. Maybe they will give more all right, maybe not. But I know when you get there they will treat you well. That's the one thing I like about them. So it's up to you. If you take your wool to that place it may be all right, or maybe some other place will give you more than they will." She said, "I don't know where we will take our wool. It will be up to him when he comes back. But I would like to go down to the place that you spoke of." I said, "But don't tell him that I told you, because he won't like it. I mean it, I am afraid of him. If you tell him that I was here and told you that, he won't like it. He might get after me about it, or he might get after you. Even though you say you are not afraid, I am for you because I don't wish you to be hurt by him, and I don't care to get hurt either. So don't tell him that I told you that." "He won't say anything. I'll tell him that you told us while we were all together, but I won't tell him about your help. If he asks about that brush shelter I'll tell him that some people came to visit me, and they put it up for us. I have got lots of ways to get around that, so you needn't be afraid."

"What will you say? How will you tell him about that?" I asked her. She said, "I told you there are lots of ways for me to tell him and he will take it right away. I'll tell him that you came through here. I'll say, 'Son of Abaa came here on horseback while we were all shearing together, and asked about his horses. His horses had run away from him, and he was after them. He stopped here for a while, just to ask about his horses, and as he was going to start off again I asked him where the wool was high. "Is there any place around where they give more for the wool," I asked him,' I will say to him. And I'll say, 'He said that he had been down to Blue Around The Lake, and had been sent around by the storekeeper among the people who have lots of wool.' When I tell him this I'll say, 'That was all he said and he left. He was in a hurry to go after his horses. So he didn't get off his horse, and he didn't stay long.' This is what I'll say to him."

I said, "Even though you don't tell him, one of the others, or his daughter, will start telling him about it, for all you know. One of those will tell him about me." She said, "No, I don't think so. I know they won't. I have got fixed what I want to say to them. I'll tell them something so they won't say you were here all day and helped us, and his daughter won't tell him anything. He has tried lots of times and she has never told a thing to him. He used to say to her when she was small, 'I will give you to son of Abaa when you grow up.' He had been saying that to her all the time, until you married his relative. Since then he hasn't said that anymore. I don't think she will tell him anything, even though he asks about it; so no one will say anything about you." "If it's that way I will be very thankful," I said. That was all, and I said, "I guess I had better go on down to the other place." It was very late in the evening. She said, "You don't want to go around the hogans during the night. You had better stay." I didn't say anything for a while. I was standing, leaning against my horse, and she was leaning against me, for quite a while.

Then I said, "I'm awfully scared. I don't know what to do. I can't make up my mind." "What do you want to make up your mind for? You don't have to make up your mind about that. Let's go back to the hogan. You can go tomorrow." "Do you mean it, that you want me to go back?" "Yes, sure I mean it, so let's go back. Stay tonight. Come on," she said to me. Then I said, "All right, let's go." When we got back everybody was asleep. I unsaddled my horse, and when I came back from where I had hobbled him she had fixed a place for me and herself right at one place. I took off my moccasins and lay down; we were awake for a while, but I was tired and soon went to sleep.

I didn't wake up until morning. As soon as I woke up she was awake too. I said, "I had better go now. It's about daylight." "You had better wait," she said, "until you get something to eat. Then you can go." I said, "Thanks, but I had better go right now. I will get something to eat down below, so let me go. Don't hold me here again all day." "No," she said, "I won't hold you. You helped me a whole lot yesterday, that's why I don't want to let you go without anything to eat." "Well, that's all right. I will get something to eat when I get down to the other place." Then she said, "All right," so I got up and put on my moccasins and walked over to where my saddle was. I bundled it up and put it on my back and started packing it away from that place. It was still real dark. I kept on going, looking for a black spot, but there was no black spot anywhere. At last I saw one quite a ways ahead of me. I started right straight for that spot. When I was close to it, it moved, and when I had walked up to it there was my horse. I put the rope and bridle on him, saddled him up and got on and beat it down to the other place. I got out of there as though I had been chased.

While I was riding along I began to think about my home, about myself and the others. I thought, "I must have lost my mind yesterday all day and all last night. Yesterday morning I started from home, told the others that I would be back soon, and told them to shear some sheep. I guess when they got through shearing they were looking for me all day and last night. They must be wondering what has happened to me." This was the way I was thinking while I was riding along.

When I got to my father's (Slim Man's) place I got off my horse and tied him up and walked inside. Everybody had just got up. My father was still lying in bed. As soon as I walked in he said to the others, "Put out a sheep pelt. Spread it here." They spread a sheep pelt for me beside him, and he said, "You must have stayed overnight close by." "Yes," I said, "Right here, close by our summer camp." "Well, then," he said, "Go and build a fire at the sweat-house." "Where is the ax?" I asked him. "The axes, I guess, are lying outside." I walked out, picked up an ax, and got on my horse and rode up to the sweat-house. Then I gathered some rocks and built a fire. After that I took the rocks out from the inside and then rode back to the hogan. They were about through cooking.

While we were eating he asked me, "Have you and your wife been to where you wanted to go? Have you moved to someplace yet?" "Yes," I said, "We have moved down below to Water Up High. We are living there now. That's where I started from. When I was here I took the horses back. I got back there in the evening, and the next day we started off down to the lower part of the country. Her people were living at Water Under The Rocks. We got there about sundown, and stayed there over night. The next morning they moved back this way. It took us three days to come to Water Up High, and that's where her people are living now." About that time we had finished eating.

542

As soon as we were through he said, "We had better go to the sweat-house. The rocks must be ready to put in, and there we can tell stories to each other." Before we left he said to his boy, "We are going to the sweat-house. You go and round up your older brother's horses for him, and put them in the corral. Get on his horse and ride up to where the horses are." Then he gave me the blankets and told me to go ahead. I took the blankets along and he carried the water. When we got there the rocks were ready to put in. After we put them in I put the blankets over the door and we undressed and went in. The rocks were red hot. It made the whole inside glow. It was so hot we couldn't stay any longer, so we got out and he told me to let the blankets up, so that some of the heat would get out. I had the blankets pulled up to let some of the heat out for a long time. Then I pulled them down again and we went inside, but it was still the same, just as hot as it was before. We didn't stay long. We pulled the blankets up for a while again and then went in. That time it wasn't so very hot.

Then he said, "Now you can go ahead with your story." And I told him what I had been doing. As I was telling him about Asdza No Teeth, her daughters, and her granddaughter, Slim Man said, "Don't hold anything back." I said, "Right here I won't tell about it, because it's a very bad thing. I heard a very nasty thing from them, so I won't tell about that. I am ashamed to tell about it." He said, "Come on with it. I told you not to hold back on anything, so come on with it. Tell me about it. There is nothing to be ashamed about. You know we have been in many bad things, and we know about many bad things, and we have done many bad things, which we ought to be ashamed of, but we had no shame about them, so you come on and tell about it. Some of the people have done real bad things, and even so they tell about it. Like when a man or woman starts jumping in the fire, the people will start asking him or her what they had been doing, and the man or woman will say, 'I have had relations with my younger brother, my older brother or my older sister or younger sister.' Even though it's something like that they will tell about it. And some go crazy, and when they ask about what they have done they will tell; they will say, 'I have fucked my niece, my cross-cousin, or my aunt and that's a very bad thing to do, but even at that they will tell about it. And there are some other people who learn about witchcraft. When they get caught by that, when they ask about that, they will say, 'We sure are witches. We are witches and that's why we can fuck our mothers, our older sisters, our younger sisters and young mothers and aunts, and all the others.' Even though there is great shame attached to it, nevertheless, they tell about it. Therefore there is nothing to be ashamed about, so come on and tell me about that thing." Then, when he talked to me like that I thought, "Oh, well, I guess I'll just tell him right out. It's about him anyway."

So then I told him what they had said about him and what I had heard from them. But I didn't tell him what I had done there, and I didn't tell him what they had said to me about Hosteen Black. I only told him what they had said about him. He enjoyed hearing about it. When I got through telling him about it he said, "What they said about us, that is their own fault, their own planning. They are all alike. They think and talk exactly alike. Not one of them is a good woman. One is just as bad as the others. Whenever a man comes to their place they will stop him even though he is going some place in a hurry. They will stop the man only for one thing, and that's fucking. And that's what they have done to us. We didn't know them at first, but once we saw them and knew them they started that on us. They themselves said to us, 'Come around at night. Come around where we are herding, around the water, around the woods, around the arroyos and cliffs and on the rocks.' They said to us what we had not been thinking about ourselves. So they don't need to be talking about that. They don't have to be sore about that. Maybe they are mad about it, but they themselves are making up all these things for themselves. Like you now, you were going along after your horses, and they held you all day yesterday and all night last night. They took your mind away from you. If they had been good people they would have let you go, and you would have taken your horses back to your place yesterday, and you would have started as soon as you got back and be on your way now. Maybe you would be going to Thief Rock, or way on the other side, to Blue Around The Lake; you would be close to that store now, and here they have been holding you all day yesterday and all last night. I don't call that good manners. They think they are good people, but they are not. Even though they may be sore about what they heard about us, they are making everything up themselves. They are very bad people. That's the way I am looking at them."

Perhaps he was sore about what I had told him. Then we got out of the sweat-house. We lay around for a while until we got dry, and then dressed and went back to the hogan. When we got there the horses were in the corral. My younger brother had brought them back for me. I didn't look at them; I just passed the corral and went inside. The food was ready and we started eating. The others had eaten already.

After we ate I walked over to the corral to look at the horses and I missed the ones that I wanted to use. My older sister, Slim Man's wife, said, "Your younger brother saw them as he was driving the horses back, but he just let them go, because he was on his way with these. They were quite a way off toward the foot of the mountain. He is sure about that," she said. "Why don't you go and ask him to ride up there again. Go ahead. Tell your younger brother to go and get the horses for you." He was outside, chopping wood, so I walked over to him and said, "I missed the horses that I want to use, my younger brother, would you go and get them for me? Your mother said you saw them someplace up toward the mountain." "Yes, sure, I will go after those horses for you, my older brother. They are up in Woods Coming Out Into A Flat Far Out Into The Valley."

I was going to go that day, but it was getting to be too late. I thought, "I had better stay here tonight again. Tomorrow I'll start back early." Before he started off, before he got on his horse, I said to him, "When you take a ride up there, if you find them, take them down to the water. After they get water bring them here." He got on his horse and went off and I went back inside and sat down beside my father. He took his tobacco out, shaved some off, made a cigarette and

545

started smoking. I started smoking too. Then his wife said, "You must like the sweat-house so very much. You must like to be in it all the time. Every time you two get together you always go to the sweat-house. You must both like it." He said, "Yes, that's above everything. The sweat-house is the one thing for everybody. And it's made to be that way, so that thing is above everything. When you go into one of those things you always get to hear something big. You always hear big news. You always hear a very nice story, when you get into one of those things. When you are out here, or even in the hogan, you can't hear about anything. That's how I just heard a very big story. I never heard a story like that before. This story that I heard today is above all. That's the kind you hear in the sweat-house."

When he said this he laughed. "What I heard started from Trail Along The Edge Of The Woods. He said that as he was coming by that place he got caught. Some people were living there whom we know. He got caught by them. He was there all day yesterday and last night. That is where he stayed overnight, drying himself up. He is all dried up, so you make a very nice soup for him. Make a good soup for your son," he said to his niece. She laughed and said, "I don't think he is dry, because he has been with salt. Salt won't make you dry. It will make your mouth water, so I think he is that way all over, so he doesn't need any soup." They all started laughing about that. Then my older sister said, "No wonder you both have been in the sweat-house all day. I know what you have been talking about. When a fellow begins to talk about something like that then he will open his eyes and ears and mouth. That's the way with him," she said, meaning her husband. They were laughing about it for quite a while.

Then he said, "Way back, a few years ago, they had hold of my wrist. I couldn't get away from them. I tried my best to get away by different ways, but they just kept holding on to my wrist, holding me tight to themselves. Finally I got away from them. That was two years ago. And then they grabbed you and they have been holding you by the wrist. And they began leading you around the cliffs, along the edge of the cliffs, so that you would fall off, and they have been leading

546

you around at the point of a gun, so that you would get shot, and they were leading you around under axes, so that you would get hurt by that. For two years now, and you never noticed. Maybe you notice it now, or maybe not. You don't know where you are. Like yesterday and last night. Yesterday you left home; you were in your right mind, and you knew where you were, until you came to their place. There you lost your mind, all your senses. You forgot everything, forgot all about yourself. You didn't know where you were all day yesterday and last night. And there she started leading you around, around the cliffs, along the edge of the cliffs. She started to seek the highest cliff for you to jump off of. She led you around looking for a gun, but she didn't find a gun any place yesterday and last night. She couldn't find anything that would kill you, so this morning she let you go, and now you are safe, you are alive, and I guess you have found out all about those things now, so you had better get away from here. Don't try to go near her anymore because if you keep going around with her soon you will be gone, and you don't want to be gone right now. You want to live for some time yet, so you had better quit going over to their place once and for all," he said to me.

He frightened me with that. He meant that I might get killed by her husband. "I am telling this to you for your own good," he said. "I want you to live a long life. I want you to be out of dangers like those. And that's the way I have been talking to you every once in a while. Whenever I thought you might have forgotten things I always started talking to you about things like that. I don't want you to forget all about yourself. I want you to remember, not forget about yourself. Women like those, when you start to go around with them, they will sure get you into a dangerous place. So whenever you get one you mustn't kiss. If she wants to kiss you, don't let her. If you let her kiss you, or if you kiss her, as soon as you do that, she will take and kiss all your mind out of you. She will kiss everything out of you, and you will kiss all her mind out of her, and you will have all her mind in you, and she will have all your mind in her, and you will be thinking about her all the time, and she will be thinking about you all the time too, and you won't have any sense, and she won't have any sense either, and you will go crazy for her, and she will go crazy for you, and you will be running after her all the time, and she will be running after you. Finally, your life will be ended and hers will be ended too. And when fucking you mustn't be where a draft is circling around you. You must be headed toward where the draft comes from, so that it will take everything away from you, so that you won't inhale her breath, or anything. If you do, your mind and senses, everything, will be lost. So you must be careful on all these things. And that's the way I have been talking to you, and you know it. I don't want any of you to get into any danger, my children," he said to us all.

We were there, sitting around while he was talking. "That's the way it is, so you must try to hold yourself back on those things. If you just keep on going at it, soon you will be out of things. Soon you won't have any herd, or horses, or cattle, or property; nothing. You will be poor. You will get yourself into a state of starvation. That's the way you will be if you stay with those things. If you stop at once, then you won't get that way. And you have got a nice woman. When a bad woman gets between you two she will split you away from each other, and from there on you will be unhappy all the time. When you have lost everything, lost your woman, when you are all alone you will be in grief and sadness, and you will be unhappy all the rest of your life. You will be spoilt forever. You don't want to get yourself in that state, so stop it right now, and then you will be happy all during your life. If you take all my words, you will have everything. You will live a good life, and you will live a long life. You will be the same all the time, having everything, and more of everything, and soon you will receive grey hair, soon you will be old and you will have children, perhaps one or two, perhaps more, and perhaps later on you will have grandchildren, and perhaps you will have more of them too, and you will know everything for them, and you will be talking to them just the way I am talking to you now, and that's the way I want you to be. I want you to talk just as I am talking. Not only among your children, but to everybody. So remember and keep all my words. If you take them and keep them to yourself, I mean it, you will receive grey hairs. I mean it, you will get old," he said to me.

"So what I have told you you must remember. And as I said before, this is for your own good, and I am right on that. I want you to take my trail. I want you right behind me all the time. I want you to keep all your stock, property, and all the other things. I want you to be on one trail with me all the time. Don't try to get off the trail, and you will enjoy everything. You will enjoy life. I want you to be like that. I don't want you to get off the trail, and I don't want you to get in trouble. If you get off the trail you will sure be in trouble sometime soon. I know as soon as her husband finds out he will surely get after you. When he gets mad he will lose his mind. If he once gets that way toward you, that's as far as you will live, so I don't want you to meet him. I don't want you to get in bad. That's why I am talking to you. I think more of you, that's why I am saying this to you, my son, my father. Now be sure and remember my words. You must keep my advice, as long as you live. This will be all," he said to me.

I said, "I have picked up everything, and I will keep everything in my mind. All that you have said I have put into me. I have got it all in me now. What you have said to me is all right, so that's why I picked up everything from you, and I won't let it go. I want to keep it with me as long as I live, my father, my son," I said. "I am very thankful about it. You have talked to me like that many times, and I am always glad about it, my father, you were right on everything. You said that I was out of my mind yesterday and last night, and I was too. I never thought of anything. I had only been thinking about one thing all day and all night, and this morning, when I left there, my mind all came back to me. As soon as I got all my mind back I shivered all over for a while. I was scared and frightened, and I still am, because I have done wrong, but as you don't want me to do that anymore, I will do as you say. I won't try to do it anymore."

About that time the boy had brought the horses back for me. I heard them neighing and walked out. There he was, just driving them in the corral. The sun was almost down. I thought, "It's no use for me to go right now. I had better stay again tonight." So I put a rope around one and turned the others loose and let them go. I thought, "I will get them again tomorrow." I led the one that I had roped over on to the other side of the sweat-house and hobbled him there. It was getting dark already. If he hadn't talked to me I was going to stop at that same place again that night. I had been thinking that way. I had been thinking, "I will stay overnight with her again," but when he talked that way to me, and I had promised him that I wouldn't do that again, that kept me back. So I thought, "I had better stay here with him."

That evening they started cooking, and that woman started poking fun at me. I used to call her my niece and cross-cousin. She began making soup, saying, "Even though I know you are not dry, nevertheless I will make you a soup. I know salt won't get you dry. It will make you water everyplace. I know you are not dry, but I will fix you some soup." I said to Slim Man, "What you have said to me is right, and I always like to hear you talk. I know you meant everything you said, and that's the way I was, I was in trouble and I was in danger. All the women are trying to get me in danger and in trouble. That's the way I am right now. I am in trouble right now, and I haven't told you that. I mean the trouble I have with my wife, and what they have said to me. They want me to take another woman. That's what I mean." He said, "If you are in trouble, you shouldn't hide yourself with it. You must tell it and let someone know it, and then, perhaps, someone will try to get you out of it."

Then I started telling him about myself. "When we, that is, the woman's people, moved down to the foot of the cliff, when we first moved down with them, that night she said to me, 'My mother and younger brother want you to take my younger sister. Those two want you to do that. My older brother and old mother didn't say anything about it. So you must do that.' When she said this I told her not to talk that way to me. I told her, 'I don't care to hear that. And how about you? Where are you going? I am with you, and I don't want to be with another one. I don't want to hold on to the

550

two of you. It would be lots of trouble for me, so I don't want to do it. And besides I haven't got anything to give for her.' She said, 'You have got everything, and your father has everything too. He will pay for you.' I said, 'What my father has is not mine. What he has all belongs to him. I don't like to go and beg him for things, so don't talk to me about it.' When I said this to her she got mad at me. She was mad all night. So that's the way it is. I just can't make up my mind to do it. I have been thinking about it ever since she said that to me."

"Well," he said, "I guess you have made up your mind as to what you are going to do. You said you had been thinking about it, and I suppose you know what to do now." "No," I said, "I don't. That is why, when she said this to me, I told her I would come up here sometime and tell you about it and see what you would say. That's why I am telling you about it now. So I would like to know what you think about it. I will leave all to you. Whatever you say I will do. But if I take her it will be just too hard for me, because they always move far away from here. They always move way up on the other side of Navajo Mountain, where I don't like the country, and I always move up on top of Black Mountain, and they don't like to go up there. They don't like that country. So, if I take her, when they want to move down to that country, I will be left right here, and it will be just too bad for me. So, that's why I said that I couldn't make up my mind on that thing. Therefore, it's up to you," I said to him.

When I said that to him he said right back, "It's up to you. Whatever you want to do, it's up to you. However, I think it will be just too bad for you if you do that. That's the way I am thinking about it. It is not that I don't want you to do it, but, as for myself, that's the way I think about it. I said it was up to you. If you want to do it, go ahead, but I will tell you just what I think about it. That woman that you have now just wants to go away from you. She is trying some way to get away from you, because she must have another man or two. She has got plans with men, and that's why she wants to get away from you. When you take the other girl, as soon as you take her, she will be gone and the first thing you know she will be with another man. That's what she wants to do.

There you will be with the young girl who doesn't know anything, and you will be sorry. It will be a great deal of trouble for you. Perhaps sometime her people will start moving way out into another part of the country, and that's all they have, just that one girl, and they don't want to leave her; when they move away with her you will be left there all alone. You will have all kinds of minds, all kinds of thoughts, all kinds of wishes. You will be in sorrow and sadness. You will be in bad. You will be in many troubles. You will have trouble with everything. That's the way you will be. It will be just too bad for you. This is the way I am thinking about it for you. That's the way I am thinking about it now. You may think about it differently. But, as I said, it's up to you. If you want to do it, go ahead. If you only want to work on her once, that will be all right too. But you'll find out. If you come out all right on it, so much to the good. Maybe she will be all right. But I don't believe you will have both of them. The one that you have, I am sure, has another man. She wants to get away from you and go to him. I think that's what she wants to do. So you just go ahead and do it. You will find it out yourself. They always try to put something over on a fellow. Perhaps they are trying to do that with you. Every one of them has a different father. The old women, her mother and her grandmother, have been worked on by many different men, and all of their children, all the boys and the others, no two of them have the same father. And they know how to work on a man. They know how to put something over on a man, and I think they are trying to do that to you.

That's the way I am thinking about it. But this is not that I don't want you to do it. It's all up to you. So if you want to try it, just go ahead. Maybe you will come out all right. I have heard a whole lot about them. Way back, their old people, who have been dead a long time, were like that. Not one of them married right. Not one of them lived well with a man. They don't know how to live with a man. They don't know anything about a good life. They only know how to trouble a man. They are trouble-makers. That's all they are. Those two women, the older one, the grandmother of hers, has been around with many men, and her mother is just the same. She never was married. I know it very well. The men have been around with her, one after another, and that's how she got all her children. And she has raised them in the same way. They all know about men. They know all about mens' cocks, the different sizes, different lengths, different tastes, different feelings that they get out of it. They know all about it. That woman of yours knows all about it, so she must have received one better than yours, and that's what she wants to put herself on. When a woman receives one that is just right she will want to leave you, even though you have everything. She won't think about it. She won't care about what you have. If she finds a man's cock that is just right for her she will go and get that man. Even though the man hasn't got anything, she will run away from you to that man, just for the cock, that's all. That's the way women are."

Then his wife said, "You have been talking about one thing since evening. That's all you have been talking about. You ought to change it around and start talking about something else." He said, "Yes, we both know that. I guess we all know that. And he is not talking about it. I am the only one who is talking about it. I talked about it because I want all of you to consider the many different ways. It is that way with everything, many different trails, many different things, many different tastes. We all know that, but every once in a while a fellow has to tell something like this about it, and that's the way with me. I am saying this before you all, I am talking to all of you. I want you all to think about it, to think about good ways and bad ways. I don't want any of you to get in bad. I want all of you to be good, to live well, to live long and to be happy all the time. And I want you to hold on to your stocks and to your properties. I don't want you to let your stocks and property go. I don't want you to go poor. That's why I am telling all this before all of you. But, I guess, now you have picked up everything, and now we will all go to bed. Fix up your places and we will go to bed. We should have lunch first but I guess we will let that go. It's late in the night. Soon it will be morning, and we will be all right. So let's all go to bed." Then they started fixing the places; they fixed a place for me and we all went to bed.

27

His wife and her mother quarrel . . .
His wife is unfaithful to him . . . They
separate and he leaves alone with his herd . . .
He tells a clanswoman about his wife . . . All
the sadness in him disappears.

One day I got in a quarrel with my mother-in-law. My wife and I wanted to go to our cornfield one morning. We had one horse packed with our things. This horse was in a bunch of sheep that we started to drive along. We were on our way to our farm when my mother-in-law caught up with us. She just passed by me and ran after her daughter. I wasn't looking at her when she passed by me, but after she passed and caught up with her daughter who was riding a horse she jumped up and reached for her. She held the bridle and started to take her off of the horse. She pulled her daughter off down onto the ground and there they began to fight. They were fighting, wrestling, and throwing each other around; soon her daughter was on top of her. She got up and she went under her daughter again. Then her daughter just sat on her mother. I was sitting on my horse riding around the edge of the herd watching them fight, and the sheep were all scattered out. My wife was still sitting on her mother, and the old one just couldn't do anything. It was hot in the morning, really warm, getting hotter and hotter all the time, and they were both sweating, and this old woman was about to give up.

When she couldn't do anything more to her daughter, because her daughter was stronger, she begged her, "Quick, stop fighting." She begged her daughter for a long time, but her daughter wouldn't let her go until she gave her some strands of beads. The old woman left and walked back home and my wife walked up to me and said, "I let her go because she gave me these beads, red beads and one strand of light beads with it. That's what she gave me." So that's how she let her mother go, because she got these beads from her. My mother-in-law always said, "I don't want my daughter to go away from me. I want my daughter to stay with me all the time. And he is trying to take my daughter away from me. That's what he is doing. All the Many Goats are taking the daughters away from their mothers." But I had a farm with a little patch of corn. I had to stay there so I could do my work on the field. And she started the quarrel because I was taking my wife to the cornfields.

Way back, years ago, that's the way they used to be, these old women. They used to talk about their sons-in-law all the time. Maybe some of them, a few of them, were good, those old-timers, those womenfolk. Some of them will be rough with you, like my mother-in-law, but a lot of them, I know, they won't talk about their sons-in-law. The woman that talks about her son-in-law is a no-good woman, the way I think about it. That kind of woman always makes trouble, always tells her daughter to get after her husband.

After the quarrel was over, we started with our herd. We started down to our farm after it was getting cool. The cornfield was quite a ways from where we were. When we got there we put our herd under a tree where there was shade, and we unloaded our pack horses and started the fire. After the fire was built my wife went into the herd and grabbed one lamb and butchered it. So we had mutton cooked under the shade. The corn was about a foot high. I started hoeing the weeds while she was herding the sheep around the cornfield. When it got cool, she put the herd under the tree where there was shade and she helped me hoe. At that time I had a lot of sheep, a big herd. Then there were the horses. I used to have a lot of horses there near the cornfield. I really wanted to get down near the cornfield because I had horses close by.

From there on she didn't love her mother at all. She didn't want to go back to her. I don't know what the mother was thinking about her daughter. Her daughter said, "I won't go back to her anymore. Never in my life," that's what she said. From then on we lived at the cornfield all that summer. We lived there and the corn and everything was ripe.

One day my father, Slim Man, told me to go with him to the San Juan river to visit. We left my wife alone. Before we left I talked to her and I said, "Be sure to take good care of the sheep. And the same way with all the horses. You know which horse we always use for herding; so you must hobble that horse all the time, so you can use him in the morning when you want to go out herding. So every morning you get this horse and get on the horse and herd with this horse." And I said, "Maybe we will be gone about seven days, maybe not; maybe we will come back before, or maybe after."

Then we started and went to a place called White Rock Point, where the store was. From there on we started again, up towards the mountains, way far off, to a place called Point Between The Two Streams. My father said, "Here we will meet the fellow who makes silver. This man is my friend, he is my good friend, so we will go to his place. Above there, a Paiute lives, close by. This Paiute is my friend too. When we get to these two places, we will stop there overnight." When we got there we stayed overnight where this Paiute was living. The next morning when we were about to start off, his friend, this Paiute, gave him a rifle and a buckskin. Then we got to another place where the silversmith was living. We stayed there overnight and they were just talking all night, talking about different things; I didn't pay any attention to them. I just wanted to sleep because I was tired from riding. Before we started off again, this man gave Slim Man two great big buckskins and two smaller buckskins, but I didn't get anything from that man.

Then we started back home. We had been gone about three days then and my wife was by herself. We stopped at the store and I sold the skins that I had brought along with me. I bought an umbrella for my wife because it was so hot at that time. I thought about her clothing too, so I bought some calico for her, a skirt and dresses. We started back from that place when the sun was already down, and it was nice and cool; we stayed outside overnight and the next morning we started again across the flat. We crossed the place called the Big Oak; we passed that place, and then we got down to a place where the stream comes in. We crossed that stream, and we headed up for a place where some people were. We lived close by there.

When we got back to our place it was four days since we had left. We got home when the sun was pretty well down. It was cool then. There was dust rising right across from where we lived; and I saw a lot of dust on the other side of the wash. When we crossed the washes, there was a lot of dust rising up, and we were wondering what it was. Around that time the sun was pretty well down, and it was over the Black Mesa. I saw a lot of dust rising, and I wondered what made that dust rise. Maybe the sheep were raising the dust.

The wife of my "father," this was Slim Man's brother so I called him "my father," said to me, "Well, something has happened. A bad thing has happened to you." She said, "You were not at home. That's why the herd of yours, the sheep that belong to you, got into another bunch, because your wife has been doing something bad." Then I asked her, "What has she done, what kind of a bad thing has she done?" She said, "She has done wrong, she has done a bad thing. That's why your herd, your sheep were alone without anybody to take care of them. That's why they got into another bunch. Yes, she met a "husband." Yes, she met a husband. That's why she didn't care for your sheep at all. So they have been trying to separate them for two days now—maybe by now they've got them all separated. They've been working on it for two days. She made a "husband" for herself. That's why she didn't care about your sheep any more."

The story that I heard was tough on me it seems like. I couldn't think or do anything when I heard about her; it felt like somebody had hit me in the head with something hard. At that time I was young and my heart wasn't tough enough for those kinds of things; that made me almost faint.

She had everything ready to eat, and she gave me some corn mush, then some of our dried peaches that were boiled; I started to eat these things. They were cold. They had been sitting for a while I guess; that's why they were cold. Just

557

when I started eating, that's when she told me about this woman. All that I remember was I started to eat; from there on I just didn't know anything. Maybe I ate, maybe not, maybe I had enough, maybe not. I didn't know what I did; I was out of my mind. Maybe I ate some, maybe I didn't eat; I just don't know. All I thought about was my sheep, my herd; that was all I thought about. I was wondering and worrying about my sheep; and the way I heard, they were into another bunch; maybe they had been into even another bunch too, maybe two or three bunches. That's the way I was thinking about my sheep, all that while. That was all I thought about. By thinking of that, I just didn't know whether I ate or not. I was feeling that way, sitting there, and by that time the sun was down and I looked up and looked over to where the sheep corral was, and I saw the dust rising up there where the sheep corral was. It was quite a ways from where I came back from the river; it was about a mile from there. That's where my sheep corral was, and I saw the dust rising up there after the sun was down. Right there, close by that corral of mine, these women were living, my wife's grandmother and her mother. In a while the dust was settled down. Then there was no sound at all.

I just sat there thinking, and I never did say anything more; I didn't say any word at all. All I felt was my heart, it seemed to be beating so fast. It felt as if my heart was getting bigger and bigger all the time. Then I got on my horse and started off for the corral. I got back to my sheep corral after the sun was down, and it was just getting dark when I got back there. There wasn't anybody around, just the sheep were in the corral. Then I got off my horse, took the saddle down, turned the horse loose, and stayed there overnight. I put the saddle there where I was going to sleep; I laid my head against the saddle and there I lay by myself; it was pretty dark then. I went to sleep there.

All at once I woke up. I felt something right at the tip of my toes; it looked like something rubbing on them. I looked over to my feet, and there she was, sitting right by my feet. No, she was standing right there at my feet. She was standing there, kicking me at the tip of my toes; that's what she was doing to me. When she thought I was awakened, she asked me, "When did you come back?" I said, "I came back when the sun was way up yet." "I was here just around that time," she said, "but there was nobody around." This is what she said when she was standing, she was standing, she didn't sit. She said, "The sheep went into another bunch. They were all mixed in another bunch, and we have been watching on them, trying to separate them for days. Now I think we've got them all separated, except for three. Only three of them we didn't get out of the other bunch."

Then I said, "Who did this other bunch belong to?" She said, "It belongs to a woman, Rough Woman. Her herd was mixed up with these sheep." This woman we called Rough Woman; it was her herd that was mixed up with mine. I said, "Well, maybe she might take good care of my sheep." Then I said again, "Why did you separate them? You ought to have left them with her bunch." That's what I said—I said this just for fun. As soon as I said this, she got so mad about it! She was mad at me, and she said to me, "Well, if you like Rough Woman, why don't you go over there right now." Then she said, "I don't want you anymore. From here on I just don't want you. You can just go over and live with that woman." But I didn't say anything more to her. After she said this she walked away. It was dark, and I thought she had gone home; her home lay a little way from there. I thought she had gone home but she had stopped about fifteen yards away from me, and that's where she stayed overnight. After she left, after she walked away from me, I just covered myself up and went back to sleep. When I woke up, it was early in the morning. As soon as I was wide awake, I got up and put on my clothing. I looked around, and there was my horse standing, right close, about one hundred yards away from me. I looked around, and there I saw her just getting up. I started walking over toward my horse. I started to put my saddle on the horse. I didn't have anything with me, just the saddle; that was all. I put the saddle on the horse, looked around again, and she had left. She was gone.

The sun was just coming up. I started off with my sheep, across to where she said the three sheep were. When I went a little way with my sheep I looked back, and there she was coming, running after me. There she was coming, and there was another one coming behind her—it was my mother-in-law, the one that was coming after her. I guess she wanted her to go after me. She didn't bother with me; she just ran right in front of my sheep, and she started the sheep back, without saying anything, and I had my horse there between them. And they started to separate the old goats—there were some goats in among the sheep. The goats were easy to separate because they were all black goats. She had put her goats in with my bunch; she had twenty head. In the few years' time that I lived with her, three years, she had a lot of goats. She started separating the goats; soon their goats were separated out of my herd, and my mother-in-law was taking care of the goats. When they were through separating the goats, they started off, and my herd started going ahead again.

I saw her running after me again, but she didn't bother with me at all. She went to the front of the herd and as soon as she got into the bunch, she grabbed one of my great big wethers. This one was four years old; its head was all brown. That's what she caught there; she threw it to the ground and stepped on it. When they were separating the goats, she didn't bother the other sheep. I had given her many of them, but she didn't bother with them. They just separated their own, just the goats. I went over there to her. When I rode up to her, I got my horse right close by her, and I said, "What do you need that wether for? You didn't want the wether or any of my sheep; you didn't want them; you didn't care for my herd." That's what I said to her. "So what do you want that one wether for? You don't want all the herd; and you don't want me anymore; you want me to be in dirt, ashes, and things like that, with my sheep; so what do you want that one wether for? What do you want with that one wether? Whenever you want one, maybe more, you could have it; whenever you want meat, you could have it; you could have all the meat you want. But you didn't want any of my herd at all; you have put me off with my herd, so what do you want with that one there? You have put me off. You have put me in the ashes with my herd. You don't want me anymore, and you don't like me anymore. But you can go; you can have that wether, and I won't do anything to you at all. I won't slap you, I won't hit you, I won't kick you; I won't do anything to you. You can just take that sheep with you. You can go now; do whatever you want to do. In hot weather, cold weather, thirsty, and starving, things like that you can put me in."

And I said to her, "You are an unkind woman, that's what you are." I said this to her when she was kicking on this wether. She started crying. She cried as loud as she could, and I didn't say anything more to her. She was crying as hard as she could. "So you can go and I can go too, all alone with my herd. I'll just take care of my herd, that's all. I've got horses and cattle. I don't know what to do about it, but maybe I'll just let them go. I'll just take care of my herd. That's all I'm going to do from here on. You can go and I can go all alone. You were willing to be around with all kinds of different men. They've got different bodies and different places to live. You'll get a lot of different tastes out of it and you'll make a living on it. Maybe that's what you want to do. So you can go and live on men." That's what I said to her.

Then I said to her, "I'll be along again to see how you're getting along. I'll be around in about two years from now. I'll see how you live by that time. Maybe you'll have a lot of sheep, horses, and cattle. Maybe you'll have a lot of other things. So I will know in two years' time when I get to see you again." She was crying, and I said to her, "Now you can go and I can go too, all alone." Then I started off with my horse, away from her. She took off her belt and tied the wether with it. She tied the belt around the neck of this wether, and she started to lead him toward her home. That was the last I saw of her.

When I went quite a ways from there with my herd, I looked forward and there I saw the dust rising. They were just kicking the sheep that belonged to Rough Woman out of the corral. The sheep were always getting out; almost all of them were black. So when I got there, I said, "Three of my sheep were in with your bunch, and I came for these sheep of mine." I asked her, "Do you know that I've got three sheep in your bunch?" And she said, "Yes, I know." Then I said to her, "What do you think, do you want them in with your herd, do you want my herd mixed up with your herd, and do you want me to go out and herd with you?" Again I said, "Can I put my herd in with yours, and then we'll herd together. What do you think about it?"[1] She didn't say anything. I said it again to her but she still didn't say anything. That was two times that I gave her a chance. After that I didn't say anything more; I just rode up to her herd and I started to look for my sheep. She came up, and I said to her, "You know my sheep, so would you catch them for me, and give them to me?" Then she caught one and she started over to me and she gave it to me while I was sitting on the horse. I carried it over to my herd and turned it loose over there and rode back and got another one. I went back and forth three times and got all three sheep of mine. When I got all three I started off with my herd. That was all I said to her, I didn't say how I had meant it; I just said that to her, and never did say anything more. That woman died two years ago in her old age. She was younger than me; I don't know why she died. I didn't have anything to eat all that morning; all that half day I never did get anything to eat.

About noon I came back with my herd, and when I got back with my herd I went over to my "father's" wife's place. She had everything done, ready to eat. She had mutton boiled and it looked good to me. At that time flour was scarce; you couldn't get flour any place. We were far away from where they had white flour, and all we had was corn flour. So she had some of that too. There I ate; I ate a lot, and all at once I had enough. But the day before, when I came back from the river, I didn't remember about eating. Maybe I ate, maybe not. But this time I know I ate and I know I got enough.

After I ate I just stayed around there for a long while. Around when the sun was going down toward the west, it got cool and I started out with my herd again. After the sun was down I came back with my herd again and I stayed there

1. If she had herded her sheep with his, he would have married her. She didn't want to. He offered to live with her even though they were related.

562

for two days. I started thinking about my mother. My mother had been gone for many days; she left us early in the spring to go across the flat area to Mountain That Turns Around. She had gone over to that place to visit her relatives. I thought about her and I thought I would leave the place and take my herd across the plain after her. I wanted to go after her. But I stayed there another day. A fellow whose name was Who Has Mules had come there to this woman's place. This man was Slim Man's brother, Old Man Hat's nephew. The brother of Old Man Hat was there too. So we were there sitting and all I thought about was that I was going to leave that place; I was going to start out with my sheep when it got cool. That was all I was thinking about.

Old Man Hat's brother then spoke to me. He said to me, "Do whatever you want to do. You can go. The woman that you were living with is still alive. You will get to see her again sometime. But when she is dead, you won't get to see her anymore. But now she is still living and sometime you will get to see her again. So you can go, my grandson," he said to me. The other fellow spoke to me, the fellow named Who Has Mules. "You are leaving, but I don't know why you want to leave. You've got a lot of things all scattered about. You've got horses and cattle, maybe you've got some mules or burros too. What are you going to do with them? Are you going to leave them here and go without them?" That's what he said to me. "Whenever you get to see her again, maybe sometime she'll make up her mind to go and live with you again. If she wants to do that with you, from then on you'll have all your mind back to you."

The other man who raised me, Slim Man, was lying down quietly, with his hand against his cheek, lying there quietly and not saying a word. Maybe he was thinking about what these men were saying, and maybe he was thinking of me too. Maybe he was thinking of a woman for me. At that time women were scarce; it was hard to find another one. That's the way he was thinking. I know he was thinking about a woman, thinking where he could get another woman for me. He couldn't think of one; that made him lie there still, thinking. By that time it was getting cool; the sun was down.

So I started with my packing. I packed up my stuff ready to go. I had a lot of stuff. I laid out two great big buckskins on the floor, and put my things on them. These things were buckskins, lion skins, rope, buffalo skins, saddle blankets, and other things. I had two great big bundles, and I was thinking of putting these two bundles on one horse. "I'll have a pack horse when I leave after the herd. When I go far away, I think I'll just turn the pack horse loose, just turn him into the herd. That way it will be easy for me." That's the way I thought about it. I got two horses and I saddled one and packed the other and after that I went back to where they had talked to me.

When I got back there, I said, "Well, I am moving now, my father." That's the way I spoke to him. "I am leaving now. I am ready to go." And he said to me, "Well, I know you've got a lot of things packed, two bundles. I don't think you can carry those bundles on the horse. You'd better fix it some other way. I think you can go on one horse. You can leave one horse. I think it's better leaving one. Let's put all the things back of the saddle on one horse; that way I think you'll be all right. If you want to take the other horse, that will be too much work for you." That's what he said to me. "Unpack all your stuff, and just put it over back of the saddle, and use one horse. You can carry all your stuff on one horse, so you have to leave one. Two horses are too much trouble for you." That's what he said to me, and right away I did that.

We went back to my place, and when I got back there I loosened up my bundle, and I just spread one of the big buckskins on the ground and started to lay things flat on the buckskin, and I just folded one fold of these things, buckskins, rope, saddle blankets, and other things. I made one bundle; it was a great big bundle that I made. I went to tie everything together and tried to lift it; it was kind of heavy. I lifted it back over the saddle and tied it to the saddle. I got a small jug for water. I thought I'd take it along, because there was no water in the flat. Then I got a long bucket; this bucket was a copper bucket, made out of copper, and a little dipper. Then I got some salt too. I had a lot of salt and I got some and tied it into a rag. I got these things in a sack and put that over

564

the saddle, where I could sit on it. I picked up a great big sheep pelt for my bedding; I put that over the saddle so I could sit softly on the horse. That was all I took from that place, just what I used all the time. There were a lot of things that I left there—pans, buckets, and a lot of other things.

So I started off with my herd. I left there while it was still hot yet. But it was getting a little cool. After I went quite away we reached a large hill. The sheep ran over this hill and made a lot of dust. The sheep were going over this hill, and when they were all over the hill, I was riding behind, and when I got on top of this hill, dust was rising up. This hill wasn't a great big hill; it was not high; it was a kind of low hill. My sheep had all gone over this hill. I got behind them, and then I got on top of this hill. Oh, how they made dust fly up in the air.

Around that time the women that I had left had started crying, all of them. That's the way I heard about them. When I was over the hill they all started crying. They said to my wife, "You go after him with your younger sister and you catch up to him and beg him not to go. You say to him you will give your sister to him. Maybe by that he will change his mind and come back." That's what they had said to her. That's the way I heard about them. At this time her sister was real young; she hadn't come to be a woman yet; she was close to it. That's the girl that they wanted to send with her after me, and get me to stay. That's the way I heard about them. But she didn't; she was just crying. She didn't know what to do. So when all the sheep went over this hill, I was on top of this hill.

They used to say when you leave a woman, when you leave your wife, you turn around when you get on top of the hill. That's what they used to say. All at once I thought about that; when I got on top, I thought maybe I'd look back. That's what they used to say, whenever you leave a wife, if you get on top of a hill, you always look back. So there I thought about that; I turned my horse around and looked back to where I left my wife. I could see her home. I could see the hogan, the hogan that they used for shade. I could see those two; it was quite a distance. I could see that far; at that time, I had good eyesight. I looked back, and I could see the outline and the brush hogan too. There were some people walking around it; I could see them walking around the hogan. Then I just turned my horse around and went over this hill. When I went over, I don't know what I was thinking. Maybe I was thinking, but I don't know. I was out of my mind, I guess. Looked like I couldn't even hear or see anything. It seemed to me that I wasn't going anyplace. It seemed to me like I was staying still at one place. That's the way I was. It looked like I wasn't going any place; but I knew I was going because I could see the herd going, and I knew I was behind them.

All that day I didn't have anything with me, that is, food. I just had a little jug for water and a little bucket and some salt. That was all I had with me when I was going along with my herd. When I was on this big flat, I could see my horses all scattered around. Then I started to go after them. I thought I would take them with me too. I rounded them up, and started with my herd. The horses were going along with the herd. They were all mixed up with the herd, and I just went along with them. I think it was a little over thirty horses that I had rounded up. I had that many horses, and there were many sheep. There must have been over one thousand head. I went down toward the northwest in this big flat, going along with my herd and my horses, and around about that time, the sun was pretty near down. And I got to a place where it was good for my herd to be that night. We were on a big hill, and I got my sheep on top of this hill, and the horses too. They couldn't get down because there was a high peak way on top. There was only one way that they could get out, one space where they could get out. But I wanted to watch them, I wanted to be up all night to watch them. When I got all my herd and horses on top of this hill, I took the saddle off of my horse, hobbled him, and chased him into the bunch. It was around dark then. There I was sitting, where I had laid my saddle. I sat there, watching them. Anytime when they wanted to get out I chased them back. That's what I did all night. It was a long night. Every time the horses went to get out, I just grabbed up my old blanket, and shook it toward

566

them and chased them back. That's the way I had been doing all night.

It was about morning, and all at once I went to sleep, and I don't know how long I slept. I heard the horses running, right under the rock. As soon as I heard them running I got up and started after them. I tried my best to turn them back but I couldn't. I worked hard, and ran back and forth, but they just were running as hard as they could. I couldn't turn them back at all. There was my horse that I was using, hobbled right against me too. But I stopped one horse. Then I put the rope on it and bridle, and I put my saddle on it, and I got on my horse and started after the rest of the horses. They were way down below, as far as they could go. I tried my best to get them back but I couldn't; they were going as hard as they could go. My horse wasn't fast enough to get them back so I just let them go. I turned around, and I looked up to where the sheep were. They were coming down off of this hill. I rode up there and I got back up on this hill where my things were. I put my things back on the saddle again, and went after the sheep. I started out with my herd again, down toward a place called Dry Spring, looking back every once in a while to see my horses going, making dust. Down I went to this place, the place called Dry Spring. I was just thinking about the horses and cattle; the cattle were up on the mountain, and I let them go too, because they were way up on the mountain. I just went ahead with my herd. All at once I came upon a lake, and I started toward that lake. I just kept going to this lake. I didn't know whether I was thinking or not. Maybe I was moving around, maybe not. I didn't know. I just couldn't tell what I was doing. All I knew was I was after my herd; that was all I knew. So I just kept on riding after my herd, down to this lake. Soon I got there and the herd was so thirsty they sure made a noise when they saw this lake. Running down, trying to get drink, they were just going as hard as they could go so they could get water. I got down there; I rode around them, saw them drinking, and looked around.

There was a hogan close by. This hogan was a little ways from this lake; it was just a brush hogan, I guess. On this hogan was nothing but rags, all over, so that must have been a brush hogan, with some people living there. Then I thought to myself, "I'll go over there to see who the people are." I rode over there, thinking I might get something to eat. I was without anything, so I was really hungry. After the sheep had drunk they stopped there at the lake. They lay around there in the shadows; it was pretty hot. When they were still there, I rode up to this hogan. There was a woman; her clan was Bitter Water, but her father was the same clan as my father. Her name was The War Split.

As soon as she saw me, she said to me, "Where are you from, my son?" I was thinking about her, why she said that to me, but then she said to me again, "Where are you coming from? I am glad to see you, my father." That's what she said to me again. Her father was my father's clan; that's why she said to me, "my father." At first she said, "my son," to me; but I was really her father. Then I said to her, "I . . . I don't know what I am doing; I don't know where I am going; but I am going off someplace. I had a wife and she did a wrong thing with me so I left her." Then she said to me, "Well, my father, I am so sorry about this. I know that sometimes you will be in bad luck. And that's what you're in now. And a lot of them, a lot of those people, say the same bad things. Because those people (Red Clay) are bad. They can do anything with you; that's what they've done with you now. I know those people, and everybody knows them too. Those people who live there can do anything they want to with a man. That's why any man who is married to those people doesn't stay there long, because they do things like that. Even those with husbands go around with other men. That's the way they are, that's the way those people are who live there and that's the way all of the Red Clay people are. They go after another man, for a husband to them." And she said, "I just don't know what to do about you. I am so sorry that you are all alone now, and that you're going off away some place. Maybe you know where you are going, but even at that, I am sorry for you, because you are all alone now, with all those hurts. I have nothing for you; I can't get a woman for you; I've got three girls living here, but they are real small, and

568

they are good for nothing, because they are small." That's what she said to me.

So she had some milk there, left over; she put that on the fire for me, and she added a little, just a little piece of mutton, dry mutton. She put that over on the charcoal and roasted it for me. That was all she had, but I got enough, and there wasn't any coffee at that time. There was coffee around but it was so scarce it was hard to get it. The stores were way off, far away. So that was all I had there, milk and a piece of meat, that was all. That's the way she spoke to me. Then she said, "You are the only one that has got things to live on. No other man lives the way you live. I know they can't find a man like you again. Maybe they will try their best to find a man like you, but they can't get him, because just a few men are like you. I know you've got a lot of things to live on. And this woman you left, I know she can't get another man just like you. But it's all right, my father, you can just go ahead with your sheep; I know you'll get another woman soon. That's the way I am thinking about you, my father."

Then I left that place. I went on with my herd, even though it was a really hot day. When I got to a place called Baby Rock, there was shade around the foot of these rocks, and the sheep were around these rocks where there was shade. I took the saddle off and hobbled my horse and went under the rock where there was shade and I lay there. I turned my horse loose there, hobbled and eating up the grass, and I was there in the shade lying down. I went to sleep, oh, quite a while, I guess. I don't know how long I slept. When I woke up it was getting cool. Then I got my horse back to where the saddle was. I saddled up the horse and got on him and started up with my herd again. Down I went with my herd, going lower and lower all the time, toward Where The Green Valley Enters. There was a point there, I was just going straight for that point, a little ways above Where The Green Valley Enters. I was just going ahead for that point.

When I got to this point, on top of this high hill, the sun was pretty well down. I saw two riders coming up to this lower point. I saw them going up there. They went up to the foot of the upper rock point. They got down off their horses and they hobbled them there; I saw them coming down. It was a woman and a boy. They just kept coming towards me, and I was just going ahead with my herd. Soon they got down and they got behind the herd and they stopped there; I went up to them. I knew this woman. She was one of the clan of Red Clay again, and I knew her very well. When the herd went down, I went after them with my horse, and I put my horse in front of her. She stopped there, and stood there. I grabbed a hold of her dress, and asked her, "Are you the two who hobbled the horse way up on the cliff?" and she said, "Yes." I asked them, "Where are you living?" and she said, "Way over there, across that wash, way over, some hogans across, above those hogans where there's a brush hogan, that's where we live." And I said to her, "I hold you for good, and I mean it. I grab hold of you for good." That's what I said to her. And she said to me, "What do you mean by that?" Then I said to her, "We stay right here tonight. Then tomorrow we go back to your home." She said, "No, no I won't, because I am afraid of your wife. I know you've got a wife." "No, I don't have a wife, none at all. I don't know where she went to. She went and left for good," that's what I said to her. "You're a liar. I know you're lying to me. I bet you she's coming right after you now." Again, I said, "I don't have any wife, none at all." And she said to me, "No, you've got a wife. I know it because you've got a sheep pelt with you. That means you've got a wife." That's what she said to me. "You've got a wife, because I know you've got a sheep pelt there with you. And a man who has a sheep pelt with him, that means he's got a wife, so I know you've got a wife."

So I just started to play with her there for a while and I had a good time there laughing and playing with her. I didn't do anything to her, so she didn't become my wife at all. And the boy was there standing by us, looking at us. I wanted him to go ahead, I told him to go home, but he just stayed there, standing there looking at us. He didn't go. Maybe if the boy had left, if the boy had gone home, maybe I could have done something to her, maybe we would have had a lot of fun. But the boy didn't go. We were there for quite a while. It was just about getting dark then, and I was thinking about her, and her clan; she was Red Clay again. Then I thought to myself, "I'd better not bother her, because she is Red Clay. If I married her, she might do just the same thing again to me." That's the way I thought about her. So then I just let her go, and she went home. Then everything that was in me, in my head, and in me, was out. All the sorrow and the sadness disappeared from me. From there on, I had my mind back and everything was back to me. I was all right from then on. That was because I spoke to this woman and played with her a little. That's what made me kind of happy again. I had all my mind back, and she was the one who brought everything back to me, because I had played with her there for a while, laughing and talking with her. So she chased everything away from me. While we were playing, the sheep were right there close to us. They lay there on the ground, and it was dark. After they left, then I started out with my sheep again, and I found that I was in good shape. I knew things then; I just went along from there in a happy way. Before that, I almost choked-like, my breast filled with something. And when I played with this woman, I don't know how but all at once it disappeared. Everything that was in me was gone.

index

573

Clan help: limits to, 46, 129-34 *passim*, 354-55, 375; Left Handed fearful about failure to help, 198; *see also* Blessing Way, Choclays Kinsman, Evil Way, His Horse Is Slow, Lost His Moccasins and his wife, Night Way, Shooting Way, Slim Man, Slim Man's brother's wife, Slim Man's Son, Walk Up, Who Has Mules, Who Has Mules' Son, Wind Way, Woman Who Walks Alone, Yellow Singer's Wife

Corn: hoeing, 2, 176-79; storage, 8, 9, 115, 384, 423; gift of, 126, 277, 518; preparation of, 345-46, 383, 384, 423, 476

Corn flour: use in illness prevention, 349; use in One Day Sing, 411

Cornmeal: consecrating hogan, 76, 92-93, 434, 507; use in Evil Way, 81; use in illness prevention, 353, 367

Corn pollen: use on hunt, 25-27, 38; use after death, 85, 110; use in illness prevention, 87, 349, 352-53; use in Blessing Way, 92, 99-100, 157-58; use in consecrating hogan, 93, 434, 483; use in illness, 93, 368, 370; use in hand-shaking, 104, 486; use in Wind Way, 491-92

Death: attitude toward, 79, 81-83; fear of, 105, 368; omen of, 105; death of girl with swollen throat, 368; *see also* Corn pollen, Folk belief, Old Man Hat's real sister, Yellow Singer's Wife

Deer, *see* Hunt

Evil Way, *see* Abaa, Cornmeal, Old Man Hat's real sister

Folk belief: success and failure on hunt, 28, 33; death, 81, 85, 101-2, 118; property, 139, 457; kissing, 249, 409-10, 547; illness, 309, 350, 366, 367, 383; gambling luck, 342-43; sex behavior, 401; guardians, 403; separation, 565; evidence of marriage, 570

Fort Defiance, 387, 389

Fort Sumner, 79, 444*n*1

Gambling: with gamblers, 173-75, 197, 269-70, 278-81, 338-40; Left Handed's

Wife's complaints about, 175; *see also* Folk belief, G-string

Gifts: from Left Handed to wife, 6-7, 64, 261, 262-63, 342, 505-6, 556; from Slim Man to Left Handed's Wife, 6; from Choclays Kinsman to Left Handed, 50, 59-60; from Choclays Kinsman's Wife to Left Handed, 50, 172-73; from Choclays Kinsman to Abaa, 59-60; from Choclays Kinsman to Woman Who Walks Alone, 60; from Abaa to Left Handed's Wife, 64; from Woman Who Walks Alone to Left Handed's Wife, 67-68; from Left Handed's Wife's relatives to Left Handed, 126, 277; from Left Handed to step brother, 146-47; from Slim Man to Left Handed, 150, 518; from Left Handed to Lots Of Boys, 188-92; from Left Handed to wife's relatives, 196, 356, 432; from the brother of Slim Man's wife over the mountain to Slim Man, 208; from Left Handed's Wife's brother to Left Handed, 237-38, 247; from Slim Man to Left Handed's Wife and brothers, 290-91; from Left Handed to Abaa, 356; from Left Handed to Nephew Of Who Has Land and his wife, 356; from Left Handed to his wife's brother, 432, 505; from Who Has Mules to Left Handed, 435-36, 459; from Left Handed to Lost His Moccasins' Wife, 464-72; from Left Handed to Choclays Kinsman, 469; *see also* Cattle, Corn, Horses, Who Has Mules

Giving Out Anger: horses owned, 267, 288

Gray Hair and his wife: where Left Handed and his wife stayed during Night Way, 296-308

G-string: characterized by son as without property, 288; visits Left Handed and Left Handed's Wife and gambles, 340-47

G-string's Son: visit from Slim Man and Left Handed, 285-88; learning songs about property, 287-88; *see also* G-string, Slim Man, Slim Man's Sons

Hand-shaking: diagnostic use in illness, 104-6, 203, 486-87; belief in, 403; in finding horses, 403; skepticism about, 487; *see also* Corn pollen, Slim Man

Headmen: function of, 389-90, 444

His Horse Is Slow: clan help with cattle, 5-6

Hogan: building of, 10-11, 68-69, 75-76, 433-34, 445; consecration of, 76, 92, 434, 483, 507; renewal of, 90-91, 464, 474, 483; cleaning out, 507; *see also* Cornmeal, Corn pollen

Horses: roundup, 2, 3, 50-53, 56-57, 264, 267, 285, 445-48; as marriage payment, 6, 7, 82, 209, 388; gift of, 50, 172-73; killing horse at burial of Yellow Singer's Wife, 108; cutting of, 268, 289-91; killed for meat and gift, 290-91; theft of, 401-3; *see also* Choclays Kinsman's Wife, Giving Out Anger, Hand-shaking

Horse's Ass's Wife: burns hole in robe, 158; Left Handed's Wife jealous of, 158, 175-83 *passim; see also* Marital quarrels

Hosteen Black: pawning cattle, 279-80; suspicious of wife's relation to Left Handed, 283; *see also* Hosteen Black's Wife

Hosteen Black's Daughter: visit from Left Handed, 251-53, 319-25 *passim*, 530-41 *passim*; sex play with Left Handed, 325-26, 535-36; *see also* Hosteen Black's Wife

Hosteen Black's Wife: affair and adultery with Left Handed, 251-54, 319-25, 530-42; offers daughter in marriage to Left Handed, 252-53, 322; payment for sex, 252-53, 278-80, 318-25 *passim;* pawns cattle, 278-80, 313-18 *passim;* characterized by Slim Man, 318, 327, 544-47; fear of husband, 322-23; Left Handed deceives wife about, 328-30

Hunt: purpose of, 8, 393; timing of, 8; behavior and taboos, 19-21, 23-4, 36, 40, 396-98, 406; preparation for, 19-20, 38, 394; function of leader, 23-24, 28, 35, 37-39; songs, 25-39, 398, 400-1; trade on, 25, 400-4; sacrifice, 27, 404; division of deer, 28-29, 36-37, 404; sweat-house, 36, 37, 40-41, 397-98, 404; purification rites, 397-98, 406-7; rituals about meat, 401; cause of failure, 404; *see also* Blessing Way, Corn pollen, Folk belief, Red

Sheep, Ruins, Slim Man, Tunes To His Voice, White men

Ideal behavior: in marriage, 65-66, 136, 235, 248-49, 334-35, 480; property, 65-66, 334; work, 65-66, 449-50; old age, 136-37; good talks, 153-54, 204; toward mother, 161; women, 248, 334

Illness: treatment by ceremony, 77-81, 104-6, 202-6, 485-92; treatment by medicine or weeds, 143-45, 361-62; protection against, 261, 349, 367, 373-74; cause of, 309, 352, 378, 386, 412, 487-88, 514; behavior approved during, 367-68; *see also* Abaa, Corn flour, Cornmeal, Corn pollen, Folk belief, Hand-shaking, Left Handed's Wife, Old Man Hat's real sister, Prayers, Shooting Way, Slim Man's Wife, Songs, Unnamed girl, Who Has Mules, Witches, Yellow Singer's Wife

Incest: consequences of, 543-44

Initiation ceremony, *see* Night Way

Left Handed's Wife, 1-17 *passim*, 44-6, 56-68 *passim*, 77, 81, 90-102 *passim*, 103, 113-40 *passim*, 146-50 *passim*, 170-71, 194-96, 251, 260-63, 269-71, 277, 281-82, 288-91, 312, 375-80, 383-85, 392-97, 405-9 *passim*, 461-81 *passim*, 493-500 *passim*, 506-9, 518-19, 528-29, 556-57; adultery, 1-4, 413-19, 557-58; visits to relatives, 11-14 *passim*, 121-26, 156-60, 419-37 *passim*, 519-27; quarrels with mother, 62-66, 554-55; clan characterized, 65, 194, 284, 512, 568, 571; trading trips, 140-44; illness, 143-46; at Night Way, 292-311; characterized, 313-15, 332-34, 418, 431, 451-52, 480-81, 552-53; sweat-house, 499-500; offer of sister as wife to Left Handed, 525-27, 550-52; separation and divorce, 565-66; *see also* Blessing Way, Gambling, Gifts, G-string, Lost His Moccasins and his Wife, Lots Of Boys, Marital quarrels, Nephew Of Who Has Land, Sons Of Who Has Mules

Left Handed's Wife's brother, 132-34, 137, 140-47, 150, 176-79, 187, 189-96, 214-15, 224-25, 228, 231-33, 237-38, 247, 271-72,